MAKING UKRAINE

Making Ukraine

Negotiating, Contesting, and Drawing the Borders in the Twentieth Century

Edited by

OLENA PALKO and
CONSTANTIN ARDELEANU

McGill-Queen's University Press
Montreal & Kingston • London • Chicago

© McGill-Queen's University Press 2022

ISBN 978-0-2280-1101-9 (cloth)
ISBN 978-0-2280-1333-4 (ePDF)
ISBN 978-0-2280-1334-1 (ePUB)

Legal deposit second quarter 2022
Bibliothèque nationale du Québec

Printed in Canada on acid-free paper that is 100% ancient forest free (100% post-consumer recycled), processed chlorine free

McGill-Queen's University Press gratefully acknowledges the financial contributions of the Ukrainian Canadian Civil Liberties Foundation (UCCLF) and the Canadian Foundation for Ukrainian Studies toward the publication of this volume.

Library and Archives Canada Cataloguing in Publication

Title: Making Ukraine: negotiating, contesting, and drawing the borders in the twentieth century / edited by Olena Palko and Constantin Ardeleanu.

Names: Palko, Olena, editor. | Ardeleanu, Constantin, editor.

Description: Includes bibliographical references and index.

Identifiers: Canadiana (print) 20210394781 | Canadiana (ebook) 20210394811 | ISBN 9780228011019 (cloth) | ISBN 9780228013334 (ePDF) | ISBN 9780228013341 (ePUB)

Subjects: LCSH: Ukraine—Boundaries—History—20th century. | LCSH: Ukraine—Historical geography.

Classification: LCC DK508.157 .M36 2022 | DDC 947.708/4—dc23

This book was typeset by Marquis Interscript in 10.5/13 Sabon.

Contents

Maps   vii

Foreword   xi
Ulrich Schmid

Acknowledgements   xix

Note on Transliteration and Translation   xxi

Introduction: Making the Borders of Contemporary Ukraine   3
Olena Palko and Constantin Ardeleanu

PART ONE   NEGOTIATING BORDERS: GREAT POWER DIPLOMACY AND UKRAINE'S BORDERS

1   Ukraine's Borders at the Brest-Litovsk Peace Conference, 1917–18   67
    Borislav Chernev

2   Poland's "Civilizing Mission" and Ukrainian Statehood at the Paris Peace Conference   86
    Elżbieta Kwiecińska

3   The Path to the Treaty of Riga: The Establishment of the Polish-Ukrainian Border, 1918–21   109
    Jan Jacek Bruski

4   From the Molotov-Ribbentrop Pact to the Territorial Agreement of "the Big Three": Redrawing the Polish-Ukrainian Border in 1939–52   138
    Damian Karol Markowski

PART TWO   ESTABLISHING THE BORDERS
OF THE SOVIET REPUBLICS

5   Emerging States and Border-Making in Times of War:
    Negotiating the Ukrainian-Belarusian Borders in 1918   163
    Dorota Michaluk

6   Contested Lines: The Russo-Ukrainian Border, 1917–29   189
    Stephan Rindlisbacher

7   Overlapping Spaces: Negotiating and Delineating
    the Ukrainian-Moldovan Border during the Interwar
    and Wartime Years   210
    Alexandr Voronovici

8   Crimea's 1954 Transfer to Ukraine: A Practical yet
    Contested Union   238
    Austin Charron

PART THREE   DELINEATING UKRAINE'S WESTERN BORDER

9   The Formation of the Polish-Ukrainian Border in Volhynia,
    1918–21   263
    Serhii Hladyshuk

10 To Reach beyond the Carpathians: The Integration
    of Transcarpathia into Soviet Ukraine, 1944–45   289
    Iaroslav Kovalchuk

11 The Making of the Romanian-Ukrainian-Moldovan Border
    at the Maritime Danube in the Nineteenth and Twentieth
    Centuries   307
    Constantin Ardeleanu

Conclusion: Making and Unmaking the Ukrainian-Russian
Border since 1991   329
Tatiana Zhurzhenko

Contributors   355

Index   359

Maps

0.1 Ukrainian lands as part of the Russian Empire, 1914. Prepared by Dmytro Vortman. 6
0.2 South Russian dialects and vernaculars. Prepared by Pavlo Chubynsky and Kostiantyn Mykhalchuk, 1871, and accessed through Wikimedia Commons. 16
0.3 Territories claimed by the Ukrainian People's Republic at the Paris Peace Conference. Excerpt from "Mémoire sur l'indépendance de l'Ukraine présenté à la Conférence de la paix par la delegation de la république ukrainienne" (Paris, 1919). Accessed through Wikimedia Commons. 19
0.4 "Map of Ukraine," by Stepan Rudnytsky (Vienna: G. Freytag & Berndt, 1918). Ukrainian Community Society of Ivan Franko, accessed through Wikimedia Commons. 21
0.5 Territories claimed by the Ukrainian People's Republic, December 1917. Prepared by Dmytro Vortman. 23
0.6 Territories claimed by the Ukrainian State, June 1918. Prepared by Dmytro Vortman. 24
0.7 Territories claimed by the Ukrainian People's Republic, December 1918. Prepared by Dmytro Vortman. 25
0.8 Soviet Ukraine, 1921. Prepared by Dmytro Vortman. 27
0.9 Soviet Ukraine, 1939. Prepared by Dmytro Vortman. 27
0.10 Soviet Ukraine, 1937. Prepared by Dmytro Vortman. 30
0.11 Soviet Ukraine, 1940. Prepared by Dmytro Vortman. 32
1.1 Northwestern boundary of Ukraine by the Treaty of Brest-Litovsk, 9 February 1918. Excerpt from *Texts of the Ukraine "Peace"* (Washington: Government printing office, 1918), 10. Accessed through Wikimedia Commons. 79

2.1 The Curzon Line between the Second Polish Republic and the Soviet Union, first proposed in 1919. Prepared by radek.s, January 2007, and accessed through Wikimedia Commons. 90

2.2 Territories claimed by the Second Polish Republic at the Paris Peace Conference. Prepared by Teofil Szumański and distributed by the Polish Delegation in Paris, 1919. Accessed through Wikimedia Commons. 95

2.3 Density of Poles in 1921. Prepared by Eugeniusz Romer in *Polski Atlas Kongresowy*. PAN Biblioteka Kórnicka, 1921. 102

4.1 The map from the secret appendix to the Molotov-Ribbentrop Pact showing the new German-Soviet border, 28 September 1939. The map is signed by Joseph Stalin and German Foreign Minister Joachim von Ribbentrop. Photograph of the document by the defence of Von Ribbentrop and Hermann Göring, Nuremberg Trials, 1946, and accessed through Wikimedia Commons. 141

4.2 Ukrainian lands during the Second World War, 1942. Prepared by Dmytro Vortman. 144

4.3 Soviet Ukraine, 1952. Prepared by Dmytro Vortman. 155

5.1 Ethnographical map of the Belarusian tribe, 1903. Prepared by Iefim Karski, and accessed through Wikimedia Commons. 166

5.2 Map of Polesia, 1935. Excerpt from Michał Marczak, *Przewodnik po Polesiu* (Brześć nad Bugiem, 1935). 171

5.3 Territories claimed by the Belarusian People's Republic, 1918. Author unknown. Accessed through Wikimedia Commons. 180

6.1 The formation of the Russo-Ukrainian border between 1919 and 1928. Excerpt from Stephan Rindlisbacher, "From Space to Territory: Negotiating the Russo-Ukrainian Border, 1919–1928," *Revolutionary Russia* 31, no. 1 (2018), 89. 191

7.1 Map of the Moldovan ASSR. Excerpt from I. Eftodiev, *Geografia Moldovei*, Editura de stat a Moldovei, Balta, 1929. Accessed through Wikimedia Commons. 223

8.1 Map of Crimea. Prepared by Maximilian Dörrbecker (Chumwa), 22 March 2014, and accessed through Wikimedia Commons. 241

8.2 Soviet Ukraine, 1954. Prepared by Dmytro Vortman. 249

10.1 Carpathian Rus', 1919–38. Reprinted with permission from Paul Robert Magocsi, *Carpathian Rus': A Historical Atlas* (University of Toronto Press, 2017), 49. 292

10.2 Soviet Ukraine, 1945. Prepared by Dmytro Vortman. 302

11.1 The Danube estuary, 1867. Prepared by Heinrich Kiepert in *Zeitschrift der Gesellschaft für Erdkunde zu Berlin*. Accessed through Wikimedia Commons.   310
12.1 Ukraine, 2018. Prepared by Dmytro Vortman.   333
12.2 Ukraine, 1993. Prepared by Dmytro Vortman.   339

Foreword

Ulrich Schmid

Ever since its incorporation as a modern state, Ukraine's wiggling borders have fluctuated with the changing politics of Eastern Europe. Territories were turned into states, smaller countries were integrated into bigger ones, border regions were added and lost. Famously, Transcarpathia changed its political status during the twentieth century no less than seventeen times. This disturbing historical experience has given rise to the following well-known anecdote:

> A visitor, encountering one of the oldest local inhabitants, asks about his life. The reply: "I was born in Austria-Hungary, I went to school in Czechoslovakia, I did my army service in Horthy's Hungary, followed by a spell in prison in the USSR. Now I am ending my days in independent Ukraine." The visitor expresses surprise at how much of the world the old man has seen. "But no!," he responds, "I've never left this village!"[1]

As this example shows, states moved their borders over places, and places suffered more often than not from these changes in statehood.[2] This process has still not come to an end. Notably, Ukraine recently suffered a military aggression that led to the annexation of Crimea by Russia and the loss of administrative control over much of the Donbas. The death toll so far has exceeded 13,000. This change of border has also affected the aggressor. After the dramatic events of 2014, Russia does not possess an internationally recognized border on its Black Sea coast. This has led to interesting solutions on Google and Apple maps: for Russian users, Crimea is shown as part of the Russian Federation; for Ukrainians, it is still a part of Ukraine. For users elsewhere in the world, there is a dotted line between the peninsula and the Ukrainian mainland.

And Crimea is not the only contested territory within the Russian orbit: the Kremlin is a military entrepreneur elsewhere in the former Soviet space. The *de facto* state of South Ossetia is able to exist only thanks to Moscow's ongoing military and financial efforts. Moreover, this isolated new polity implies a slow process of "borderization." What had been an "administrative fiction" on the ground is now a physical barrier that has created closed spaces for people and goods.[3] It seems likely that the Kremlin envisages a "reunification" of its own North Ossetian republic with South Ossetia and the eventual integration of this territory into the Russian Federation.

This notion of "borderization" may also be applied to the history of Ukrainian statehood. The contributions in this volume show how difficult the construction of state borders has been in the Ukrainian case. Many factors have influenced the end result, which has often been imposed rather than negotiated. Following Georg Jellinek's seminal definition of statehood, we can discern several factors that influence "borderization." Jellinek considered a state to be viable if it possessed a state territory, a state people, and state power. The state territory is mainly the result of wars, politics, and history or sometimes simply inertia, whereas a state people is the product of ethnic, linguistic, and religious discourses. State power relies on international recognition and the diplomatic decisions of more powerful states.

STATE TERRITORY: WAR, HISTORY, AND INERTIA

The principal factor in the painful border-defining process in and around Ukraine has been war, most prominently the First World War. The demise of the German *Kaiserreich* and the Habsburg, Russian, and Ottoman empires left a power vacuum that was eagerly exploited by national movements. Within this development, a key problem was the rivalry between simultaneous state projects. However, most of these proved to be short-lived: national republics in Armenia, Azerbaijan, Belarus, Georgia, Moldova, and Ukraine collapsed in the face of military intervention by the Red Army. Poland would have met the same fate had it not been for the "miracle on the Vistula" in August 1920 that saw Józef Piłsudski's forces, following his brief Kyiv expedition, repulse a Soviet counteroffensive. Had Marshal Mikhail Tukhachevsky succeeded in capturing Warsaw, Poland would have become a client state of the Bolsheviks during the interwar years.

Another important facilitator of "borderization" besides war is the politics of history. Most prominently, Vladimir Putin resorted to historical arguments for the annexation of Crimea, highlighting that Russia was baptized there and had heroically defended itself there, during both the Crimean War and the Second World War. Similar narrative approaches can be found in the establishment of the Ukrainian borders; throughout the Ukrainian nationalist historiography, Poland and Russia have been characterized as Ukraine's main enemies. In the traditional martyrological narrative, Ukrainian lands must be freed from the Polish and Russian yoke.

A final important source of "borderization" is inertia. Borders, having once been drawn and having existed for a certain amount of time, tend to persist. The most prominent instance of this phenomenon is the continuity of the borders of the former Soviet republics that emerged as independent states in 1991. Another example is the so-called Curzon Line, which was proposed after the First World War but did not come into effect until after 1945, when the Polish-Soviet border needed to be defined.[4]

STATE PEOPLE: ETHNICITY, LANGUAGE, RELIGION

When talking about state territories, Jellinek distinguishes between "dominium" and "imperium." "Dominium" refers to the state's possessions, whereas "imperium" refers to the state's rule over its people. For Jellinek, "imperium" clearly prevails, because only individuals can become subjects of state power.[5] In his analysis of the state people, Jellinek omits all cultural factors, convinced as he is that neither "tribal community" nor culture (he explicitly discusses language and religion) can define a nation.[6] From his perspective, all that matters is the legal status of the citizens. However, the definition of "nation" in the newly emerging states in Central and Eastern Europe often encompassed ethnic, linguistic, or religious criteria. Ideally, in the creation of a nation, these three elements coincided. In the Polish case this meant the unity of all people of Polish descent who spoke the Polish language and adhered to Roman Catholicism. Indeed, the stereotype of the "*Polak-katolik*" had already been coined by the nineteenth century.[7] In 1927 the Polish politician Roman Dmowski wrote in his influential publication *The Church, the Nation, and the State*: "Catholicism is not an appendage to Polishness, coloring it in some way. It is, rather, inherent to its being, being seen as constituting its very essence. To attempt to dissociate Catholicism from Polishness, and to separate the nation from its religion and the Church, is to destroy the very essence of the Polish nation."[8]

However, it was clear to the national leadership that such an exclusive definition of the Polish nation was not viable for the new state. The Polish constitution, implemented in March 1921, for example, referenced a "Polish people" without providing any detailed definition. Article 114 privileged the Roman Catholic Church as the "confession of the overwhelming majority of the people"; however, Article 113 guaranteed freedom of religion.

In Ukraine, a conservative position like that of Dmowski was hardly possible. Even a Ukrainian ethnicity was difficult to define. Under the last tsars, the Ukrainian language had been banned for forty years, until 1905, and several churches with an Orthodox rite competed for the position of "national religion." These difficulties were evident in the First Universal of the Central Rada, tabled in June 1917. That founding document of the Ukrainian People's Republic was addressed to the "Ukrainian People," defined ambiguously as a "people of farmers and workers." The author of that Universal, Volodymyr Vynnychenko, stated repeatedly that it was impossible "to consider the national question outside of the sphere of social questions."[9] Tragically for him and his country, Vynnychenko failed to account for Russian Bolsheviks' subsequent efforts to monopolize the ideology of nationalities.[10]

Even more problematic was the situation in the northwestern Belarusian borderlands, where ethnic categories could never have taken hold. Ethnographic research from around 1900 shows that individuals in this region variously identified themselves as "Russians," "Catholics," "Lithuanians," or – most prominently – simply as "locals" (*tutejszye*).[11] Given these vaguely defined criteria, it would have been extremely difficult to establish a border along ethnic lines.

Two ethnic arguments can be discerned as a basis for territorial claims. First, when a territory is disputed, the presence of a majority ethnic population living on it often serves as justification for its annexation. Second, when the population there constitutes only a minority – as was the case with the Polish aristocracy (*szlachta*) in Ukraine – territorial claims are typically cast as a "civilizing mission" to enlighten the rural population. However, this second argument is ultimately self-defeating: if the "civilizing mission" succeeds, those thereby civilized are then entitled to national self-determination and, eventually, their own nation-state at the expense of the "civilizing" power.

STATE POWER: INTERNATIONAL RECOGNITION AND DIPLOMACY

Jellinek's third constituent element of the state, the possession of state power, also has a direct effect on the creation of borders. In the Ukrainian case, state power depended on various sponsors. In the closing years and immediate aftermath of the First World War, Imperial Germany and later Soviet Russia promoted the cause of Ukrainian statehood – in both cases for quite self-interested reasons. The weakness of state power in Ukraine at this time can be inferred from the first Treaty of Brest-Litovsk, signed in February 1918, between the Central Powers and the Ukrainian People's Republic. In exchange for what was a mere semblance of independent statehood, Ukraine was obliged to supply Germany and Austria-Hungary with grain and other foodstuffs.

Poland fared better, at least in the interwar years, having been the only Central European nation explicitly mentioned in US President Woodrow Wilson's famous Fourteen Points. Indeed, the support of the United States would be crucial for the resuscitation of an independent Poland at the Paris Peace Conference, held at Versailles in 1919–20. Wilson's Point Thirteen stated: "An independent Polish state should be erected which should include the territories inhabited by indisputably Polish populations, which should be assured a free and secure access to the sea, and whose political and economic independence and territorial integrity should be guaranteed by international covenant."[12] The territorial definition of the new Polish state was, of course, highly ambiguous. What did "indisputably Polish populations" mean? Dmowski, who led the Polish delegation at Versailles, interpreted this notion broadly, proposing that the borders of the new Polish state be drawn up largely according to the 1772 delineation of the Polish-Lithuanian Commonwealth. Dmowski also proposed that Poland include parts of Silesia (Oppeln, Gleiwitz, and Těšín), as well as vast swathes of Lithuanian, Belarusian, and Ukrainian territory in the east. However, during the peace talks in Riga (1921), the Polish delegation found itself in a dilemma between the construction of a homogenous nation-state and extensive territorial claims that would create new national minorities.[13] The debates over the borders of the new Polish state demonstrate how difficult it was going to be to implement Wilson's guiding principle of self-determination, especially with regard to Point Ten, which called for political autonomy for the nations within the Habsburg monarchy: "The peoples of Austria-Hungary, whose place among the nations we wish to see safeguarded and assured, should be accorded the freest opportunity to autonomous development."[14] However, in June 1918 Wilson came to the conclusion that only the division of Austria-Hungary into sovereign nation-states could guarantee this goal. The Ukrainian question was especially problematic in light of Wilson's abstract provision. What should be the destiny of Galicia and its capital, Lviv? The Poles referred to this territory as "Eastern Galicia" and to its principal city as Lwów.

A similar problem arose with the Carpathian Rus, which according to the Hungarians had for centuries been part of "Upper Hungary" (*Felvidék*). This territory, which could have become either an autonomous Rusyn state or part of a united Ukraine, was eventually folded into the new nation of Czechoslovakia. The fledgling Czech government in Prague was eager to establish its rule in the provincial town of Ungvár/Uzhhorod, and to that end built there a new administrative district in the new Czech national style of architecture, known as rondo-cubism. Transcarpathia's peoples thus found themselves at the bottom of the informal hierarchy of ethnicities that defined interwar Czechoslovakia: the Czechs dominated, the Slovaks had been reduced to a "younger branch" of the "Czechoslovak nation," and the Rusyns – like the Germans – were to be assimilated.

Around twenty years later, this ambitious state-building project had failed. After the Munich settlement of September 1938, the Czechoslovak state found itself in a hopeless position, prompting the resignation of President Edvard Beneš. In early 1939, Beneš devised a highly secret plan whose intent was to "push the republic eastward." He was even prepared to offer Czechoslovakia's Transcarpathian territories to Joseph Stalin in exchange for Soviet military assistance. This sacrifice turned out to be in vain. After the war, Stalin simply took what had been offered to him before it started.[15]

Clearly, then, the fate of the Central and Eastern European states and their borders did not so much depend on the actions of their governments. Of greater import were the decisions of the "Big Three," Winston Churchill, Franklin D. Roosevelt, and Joseph Stalin, reached at the Tehran, Yalta, and Potsdam conferences of 1943–45. Of crucial importance during these talks was the concept of "spheres of influence," which all convening parties accepted as a guiding principle.[16] Famously, Churchill came to a quick agreement with the Soviet dictator during his visit to Moscow in October 1944. This is how Churchill described the incident in his memoirs:

> Let us settle about our affairs in the Balkans. Your armies are in Rumania and Bulgaria. We have interests, agents, and missions there. Don't let us get at cross-purposes in small ways. So far as Britain and Russia are concerned, how would it do for you to have ninety percent predominance in Rumania, for us to have ninety percent of the say in Greece, and go fifty-fifty about Yugoslavia?" While this was being translated, I wrote out on a half-sheet of paper:
> Rumania: Russia 90% the others 10%
> Greece: Great Britain (in accord with U.S.A.) 90% Russia 10%
> Yugoslavia: 50-50%

Hungary: 50-50%
Bulgaria: Russia 75% the others 25%
I pushed this across to Stalin, who by then had heard the translation. There was a slight pause. Then he took his blue pencil and made a large tick upon it and passed it back to us. It was all settled in no more time than it takes to set down.[17]

Indeed, the Russian President Putin has recently called for a return to such ways of managing the geopolitical global order, assigning a decisive historical role to the victorious Allied Powers, which continue to sit as the permanent members on the UN Security Council.[18] From an Eastern European perspective, such a proposal amounts to a step back into an imperial past when the leaders of Great Powers pored over maps and drew borders without interference. For many Poles, "Yalta" is still synonymous with the treachery of the Western Powers, which had deprived interwar Poland of its eastern provinces and now condemned Poland to Soviet satellite status. Similarly, countries like Ukraine and Georgia fear a "new Yalta" that might leave them at the mercy of a Russian great power play.

NOTES

1 Judy Batt, "Transcarpathia: Peripheral Region at the 'Centre of Europe,'" *Regional and Federal Studies* 12 (2002): 155–77.
2 Leslie Waters, *Borders on the Move: Territorial Change and Forced Migration in the Hungarian–Slovak Borderlands, 1938–1948* (Rochester: University of Rochester Press, 2020).
3 Edward Boyle, "Borderization in Georgia: Sovereignty Materialized," *Eurasia Border Review* 7 (2016): 1–18.
4 On the contrary, the process of international recognition and the solidifying of the Polish-Ukrainian border as had been agreed in the aftermath of the Second World War required a significant intellectual effort, championed primarily on the pages of Polish anti-communist opposition and émigré periodicals such as *Kultura*, edited by Jerzy Giedroyc. See Timothy Snyder, *The Reconstruction of Nations: Poland, Ukraine, Lithuania, Belarus: 1569–1999* (New Haven: Yale University Press, 2004), 217–31; Khrystyna Chushak, *Nemaie vil'noï Pol'shchi bez vil'noï Ukraïny: Ukraïna u politychnii dumtsi pol's'koï ópozytsiï (1976–89)* (Lviv: PAIS, 2011); Andrzej Turkowski, "Polish Intelligentsia Totems in Elites' Struggles for Legitimization: The Case of Jerzy Giedroyc and Poland's Eastern Policy," *East European Politics and Societies* 33, no. 1 (2019): 66–88.

5 Georg Jellinek, *Allgemeine Staatslehre* (Berlin: O. Häring, 1905), 386, 391.
6 Ibid., 113.
7 Brian Porter-Szűcs, "The Birth of the Polak-katolik," *Sprawy narodościowe. Seria nowa* 49 (2017): 1–12.
8 Roman Dmowski, *Kościół, naród i państwo* (Wrocław: Ossolineum, 1993), 22.
9 Volodymyr Vynnychenko, *Vidrodzhennia natsii*, 3 vols. (Kyiv and Vienna: Dzvin, 1920), 3:327.
10 Ulrich Schmid, "Volodymyr Vynnyčenko as Diarist, Historian and Writer: Literary Narratives of the 'Ukrainian Revolution,'" *Studi Slavistici* 15 (2018): 111–24.
11 Aleksej Dzermant, "Metafizika 'tutejšesti,'" *Perekrestki. Zhurnal Issledovaniia Vostochnoevropeiskogo Pogranich'ia* 1 (2018): 130–49.
12 Larry Wolff, *Woodrow Wilson and the Reimagining of Eastern Europe* (Stanford: Stanford University Press, 2020), 68, 91.
13 Snyder, *The Reconstruction of Nations*, 64.
14 Wolff, *Woodrow Wilson*, 124.
15 Milan Hauner, "'We Must Push Eastwards!' The Challenges and Dilemmas of President Beneš after Munich," *Journal of Contemporary History* 44 (2009): 628–9.
16 Susanna Hast, *Spheres of Influence in International Relations: History, Theory, and Politics* (London: Routledge, 2014), 114–16.
17 Winston Churchill, *The Second World War* (New York: Rosetta Books, 2010), 227.
18 Vladimir Putin, "The Real Lessons of the 75th Anniversary of World War II," *The National Interest*, 18 June 2020, https://nationalinterest.org/feature/vladimir-putin-real-lessons-75th-anniversary-world-war-ii-162982.

Acknowledgments

The idea of publishing a volume on the making of Ukraine's borders came in September 2018, when, during an international workshop hosted in the Ukrainian city of Uzhhorod, we proposed to look in greater detail, from a historical and comparative perspective, at the historical processes that established Ukraine's borders during the twentieth century. The workshop, "Transcultural Contact Zones in Ukraine: Borders, Conflicts, and Multiple Identities," was organized by the University of St Gallen's Centre for Governance and Culture in Europe (GCE) as the annual conference of the "Ukrainian Regionalism: A Research Platform" network. Several of those attending encouraged us to nurture this plan, given the growing academic interest in this topic following Russia's annexation of Crimea in 2014 and the ongoing war in eastern Ukraine's Donbas region.

We applied for funding to the GCE and in 2019 received financial support to organize another international workshop. We would like to thank Professor Ulrich Schmid, coordinator of the "Ukrainian Regionalism" project at the University of St Gallen, and Dr Sandra King-Savic, Executive Director of the GCE, for embracing this project. The workshop itself, "Making the Borders of Contemporary Ukraine," was hosted by the New Europe College – Institute for Advanced Study in Bucharest, a traditional partner of the GCE and an excellent venue for interdisciplinary scholarship on the wider Black Sea region. Our gratitude goes to Rector Valentina Sandu-Dediu, Academic Coordinator Anca Oroveanu, Executive Director Lelia Ciobotariu, and the entire NEC team, who on 5–6 December 2019 provided participants with such an excellent environment in which to foster fruitful academic debate. The workshop was extremely useful in the preparation of this volume, as it allowed the dozen participants to directly engage with colleagues working on similar topics. We are greatly indebted to our panel discussants, all those who attended from around Europe, and the first readers and reviewers of our draft chapters.

We would like to extend our gratitude to our editor Richard Ratzlaff at McGill-Queen's University Press and to the peer reviewers appointed by the publisher. In addition, we would also like to thank Professors Andrii Portnov, Yaroslav Hrytsak, and Spasimir Domaradzki for their insightful comments received during the annual conference "*Recovering Forgotten History: The Image of East-Central Europe in English-Language Academic Textbooks.*" Their feedback made this volume a better and more solid work of academic scholarship. Finally, and not least, we want to thank Samuel Foster and Matthew Kudelka for their support in editing and proofreading the manuscript.

Olena Palko and Constantin Ardeleanu,
September 2021

Note on Transliteration and Translation

In this volume, the authors follow the simplified Library of Congress system for romanization of Ukrainian, Belarusian, and Russian texts and proper names, except for cases where a commonly accepted English translation exists (for example, Trotsky or Yalta). This system omits the prime (') used to transliterate the Cyrillic soft sign (ь) and, in masculine personal surnames, the final (й) (thus Rudnytsky, not Rudnyts'kyi). The same system is applied in non-bibliographic references to persons and places in the endnotes. In the bibliography and bibliographic references in the endnotes, the full Library of Congress system is used. In endnote bibliographic references, the author's name appears in the language of the given publication. Thus, in references to Rudnytsky's Ukrainian-language publications, his surname appears as Rudnyts'kyi, while the English form, Rudnitsky, is used with his English-language publications.

We have used the parallel Polish/Russian/Ukrainian names for geographical places where it is necessary to highlight the contested nature of those places. Otherwise, the English version of the geographical places is used (e.g., Kyiv, Dnieper) for the sake of consistency.

MAKING UKRAINE

INTRODUCTION

Making the Borders of Contemporary Ukraine

Olena Palko and Constantin Ardeleanu

BORDERS IN FLUX

When Ukrainians took to the streets of their national capital in the winter of 2013, few imagined that their demonstrations would dramatically reshape the country. Even while protesters from across Ukraine were gathering in the heart of Kyiv, soldiers without insignia on their green uniforms were seizing control of Crimea. On 16 March 2014, a referendum was held, under close supervision, regarding the status of the peninsula. Crimean citizens were asked whether they wished to join Russia as federal subjects or restore Crimea's status as a part of Ukraine, granted by its 1992 constitution.[1]

Two days after what is generally regarded as an illegitimate vote, Russia's President Vladimir Putin confirmed the accession of the so-called independent Republic of Crimea to the Russian Federation, signing the necessary legislation that declared Crimea and the city of Sevastopol as federal subjects. Shortly after, another staged referendum in the self-proclaimed Donetsk People's Republic resulted in overwhelming support for self-rule and yet another plea for Russia "to consider the issue of our republic's accession into the Russian Federation."[2] Since April 2014, Russia has been backing the two self-proclaimed people's republics of Donetsk and Luhansk and providing military support in their fight against the Ukrainian government.

One reason for the relative ease with which Russia could occupy Crimea and meddle in the affairs of eastern Ukraine was the porousness of the border. Ukraine's western borders with Poland, Slovakia, Hungary, and Romania follow well-demarcated lines drawn in the aftermath of the Second World War and strengthened since the European Union's eastward enlargements in 2004 and 2007; by contrast, its eastern boundaries exist only on paper. The Soviet authorities had long promoted territorialization, yet the internal borders between the Soviet republics had never been fully demarcated on the ground. As a result, even thirty years after the fall of the Soviet Union, Ukrainian citizens could travel to Russia with internal passports only. All the while, smuggling and illegal crossings posed a severe problem for the Ukrainian border control service.[3]

The occupation of Crimea violated the 1975 Helsinki Accords. As successor states to the Soviet Union, both Ukraine and Russia were signatories of the Final Act of the Conference on Security and Cooperation in Europe (CSCE), according to which the participating states agreed to "regard as inviolable one another's frontiers" and to "refrain now and in the future from assaulting those frontiers." Further down, the signatories agreed to "respect the territorial integrity of each of the participating states" and "likewise refrain from making each other's territory the object of military occupation."[4] Those principles were restated by the Charter of Paris for a New Europe in 1990 that laid the foundation for a post–Cold War Europe.[5]

Ukraine's territorial integrity and the inviolability of its borders were further reassured by the 1994 Budapest Memorandum, whereby Ukraine agreed to transfer all of its nuclear arms to Russia in exchange for Russia, the US, and the UK reaffirming "their obligation to refrain from the threat or use of force against the territorial integrity or political independence of Ukraine."[6]

Crimea's swift occupation established a dangerous precedent for territorial revisionism in Europe, undermining the very foundations of the continent's postwar order. Besides provoking a strong international reaction, the annexation invited parallels to the appeasement of Nazi Germany during the 1930s.[7] The Ukrainian crisis raised questions as to the longevity of political borders and showed that state boundaries are by no means fixed. It also led to the realization that even in this Age of Globalization, in which freedom of movement and mobility has almost become a norm, unguarded state borders can undercut a country's territorial integrity and national security.

Karl Schlögel, a German historian, journalist, and essayist who has done extensive work on Soviet and Russian history and society, writes that the Russian leaders' recent actions in relation to Ukraine are encouraging observers to take "a fresh look at the map and review what we think we might know" about Ukraine and its people.[8] With this in mind, the editors of this book have set out to re-examine Ukraine's borders and investigate how they were drawn and which state and local actors, and natural factors, contributed to that process.⁹ This book asks who agreed on the frontiers, when, and under what conditions, to help us make sense of the current crisis.

In this introduction, we familiarize readers with the state of the field and integrate the findings of the book's contributing authors into the rapidly emerging scholarship on Ukraine. To that end, we will be referring briefly to the emergence of Ukrainian national identity in the eighteenth and nineteenth centuries in the context of competing imperial projects; the role of activist intellectuals in establishing a national historical narrative, culminating in the work of the historian Mykhailo Hrushevsky; the importance of ethnographic and linguistic scholarship in identifying various national features; and the efforts of cartographers to establish the Ukrainian lands as a geographical, cultural, and intellectual concept. In the second part, we present the key findings of the chapters alongside existing historiographical arguments, the aim being to challenge and enrich our understanding of the main drivers of Ukraine's cultural and political boundaries. While it is hard to disagree that Ukraine's borders have been the outcome of "total wars" between major global powers of the first half of the twentieth century,[10] the contributing authors show quite convincingly that the drawing of Ukraine's political borders was no less impacted by economic considerations, competition for natural resources, ideological rivalries, and turf wars between central and local decision-makers, as well as physical and cultural factors.

THINKING UKRAINE INTO BEING

In the mid-nineteenth century, on Europe's political and mental maps, there was no such place as Ukraine. The territories that would come to comprise modern Ukraine were divided between two great empires – Russia and Austria. The three historic partitions of the former Polish-Lithuanian Commonwealth between 1772 and 1795 granted Russia control over vast areas populated by Little Russians (Orthodox peoples inhabiting the territories of modern-day Ukraine who spoke dialects similar to modern-day Ukrainian), on both sides of the Dnieper. These territories were organized administratively into nine provinces or *gubernii*: Chernihiv, Katerynoslav, Kharkiv, Kherson, Kyiv, Podolia, Poltava, Taurida, and Volhynia (see map 0.1). Farther west, the partitions had allowed Austria to acquire the region of Galicia and part of neighbouring Volhynia. There was no national community – imagined or not – called "Ukrainians."[11] In these two imperial contexts – in which national identity was defined in linguistic and religious terms – no "Ukrainian" language was ever listed on census questionnaires or other official surveys.[12] In Habsburg Austria,

0.1 Ukrainian lands as part of the Russian Empire, 1914.

the Ruthenian vernacular was associated with the Ruthenians, the *rus'kyi* (Rus) national group, or *Rusnaks* in Hungary; in the southwestern provinces of the Russian Empire, Little Russians were identified through their use of the Little Russian (*malorusskii*) dialect. The term "Ukraine" already existed, and had been associated with the Cossack territories since the seventeenth century, but its meaning was vague and its connotation somewhat poetic. By the eighteenth century, however, the term "Ukraine" was being applied to the Kharkiv region – that is, "Sloboda Ukraine" (*Slobids'ka Ukraïna*).[13]

Scholars specializing in the late imperial era continue to argue about precisely when Ukrainians began to develop a national consciousness separate from that of the Russians.[14] Alexei Miller's seminal work presents the Ukrainian question as a contest between the emerging all-Russian and Ukrainian identities.[15] He contends that Ukrainian national identity arose in opposition to the idea of an all-Russian nation – an idea that was shaped and ardently promoted by the imperial authorities in the early nineteenth century, with "Great Russians" (Russians), "Little Russians" (Ukrainians) and "White Russians" (Belarusians) defined as three historic branches of a single nation. This notion of competing national movements is also the focus of Faith Hillis's study of the development of Russian nationalism in

Right-Bank Ukraine in the nineteenth and early twentieth centuries.[16] Hillis's thesis differentiates between the Little Russian pro-imperial lobby that contributed to the invention of a Russian nation and the Ukrainian national movement that, she posits, only began to emerge in the second half of the 1870s. In response to these approaches, Johannes Remy dates the beginnings of a separate Ukrainian identity to the mid-1840s, suggesting that the tendency to distance Ukrainians from Russians had its origins in the clandestine activities of the "Brotherhood of Saints Cyril and Methodius," a secret political society that operated briefly from 1845 to 1847.[17]

Most recently, Fabian Baumann's innovative study of the divisions within the politically influential Shulgin/Shulhyn family maintains that the distinctive separation between the Ukrainian and Russian national cultures is itself a comparatively recent phenomenon.[18] Instead of coherent identities, Baumann identifies a complex web of entangled and multilayered loyalties among nineteenth-century Kyiv intellectuals, whose nationalism was not an expression of a pre-existing and essentialized ethnicity, but rather a conscious choice between various nation-building projects, conditioned by their social milieu and based on individual political preferences. Indeed, their self-fashioning as unambiguous members of the Russian or Ukrainian nation occurred in the aftermath of the 1917 revolutions; the emergence of almost completely distinct public spheres among émigré communities was a product of the interwar decades.

That said, the logic of nationalism precipitated by the "national awakenings" of the mid-nineteenth century fundamentally changed the manner in which nationality was understood, for it shifted the emphasis away from pre-modern notions of regional, religious, or historical identities. Central to this was the development of linguistics as a scientific discipline. Having highlighted the presence of separate languages, historians were gradually inspired to conduct research on the ethnic origins of different groups. This often resulted in competing claims over the same territories and historical heritage. In their own search for a separate modern Ukrainian identity, nationalist activists turned to anthropological and ethnographic knowledge, historical writings, and geography to help distinguish Ukrainians from their neighbours. At this point, various linguistic communities began to be imagined as distinct nations, with the extent of their settlements representing their historical homelands.[19] With this in mind, what role did historians, ethnographers, and cartographers play in the creation of modern Ukraine? What lay behind the decision to adopt the name "Ukrainians" for a people living under different imperial regimes, and the perception that the lands where those people lived were a single country, Ukraine?

Constructing a National Past

A major challenge facing the Ukrainian "national awakeners" in the mid-nineteenth century was to come up with a coherent national history. In an age still dominated by imperialism, a clear narrative of origins and development could justify claims that Ukrainians were their own nation, just like their more powerful Polish and Russian neighbours. This construction of a national and historical identity was predicated on two interdependent processes of equal importance: dismantling the existing imperial narratives, and simultaneously building a Ukrainian national one.[20] The first task could be achieved by disentangling the history of Ukraine from those of its neighbours, so as to depict Ukrainians as having followed a historical trajectory separate from that of the Poles and the Russians, albeit with some overlap. The second task was to establish Ukraine's national history as a synthesized totality supported by a developed body of historical scholarship.

This construction of a distinct Ukrainian historical identity was already under way by the eighteenth century. Some of the earliest sources that attempt to trace a separate trajectory for Ukraine's history come down to us from the age of the Cossacks. As a historical phenomenon, "Cossackdom" occupied the southeastern frontiers of the Polish-Lithuanian Commonwealth, to which the name "Ukraine" was originally attributed.[21] In the seventeenth century, the Cossack Hetmanate had gained self-governing autonomy under its first Hetman, Bohdan Khmelnytsky. In their search for military alliances against Poland, the Cossacks turned to the Russian tsar. The resulting Pereiaslav Agreement of 1654 enabled Russia to gradually expand its influence over the Cossack lands. After the Hetman Ivan Mazepa deserted his patrons during the Swedish invasion of Russia in 1708–09, the Hetmanate was threatened with liquidation.[22]

In an effort to preserve their autonomy, the Cossacks' ruling elites had developed a historical argument claiming the "ancient" and therefore legitimate origins of Cossack rights, privileges, and freedoms.[23] This argument was initially pushed by the Cossack Chronicles, three key texts from the early 1700s: the anonymous *Litopys Samovydtsia* (The Eyewitness Chronicle), Hryhorii Hrabianka's *Deistviia* ... (The Events ...), and Samiilo Velychko's *Skazanie* (The Tale ...).[24] While addressing the wider history of Ukraine, all three texts focused on the crucial events surrounding Khmelnytsky's uprising and the emergence of the Hetmanate between 1648 and 1657. Both Hrabianka and Velychko portrayed Hetman Khmelnytsky as the noble leader of his people, fighting a just and heroic struggle against the Polish yoke. Khmelnytsky, so it was said, had the right to rebel against the Polish king since the latter disrespected the rights and liberties of the Little Russians as well as their Orthodox Christian faith. The Chronicles treated the Pereiaslav Agreement, defined by Serhii Plokhy as "the Magna Carta of the Hetman's liberties," in a similar vein.[25] While remaining generally loyal to the Russian tsar, the authors concurred that the agreement of 1654 had been a mutually binding treaty concluded between two equal parties.

Those arguments were made even more explicit in *Istoriia Rusiv* (The History of the Rus), an apocryphal text of unknown authorship that circulated a few years after the Napoleonic Wars.[26] Plokhy defines it as "the most influential – and from the perspective of the Russian Empire, most destructive – historical texts of the modern era."[27] The account depicts the history of Ukraine (the term *Rus'* referred to the Ukrainian Cossacks) from ancient times to 1769, focusing mostly on the era of the Cossacks. Contrary to the emerging imperial narrative of a Russian nation comprising Great Russians, Little Russians, and White Russians, the anonymous author claimed that the Cossacks were of an ancient noble heritage whose privileged status had begun under the medieval principality of Kyivan Rus, which had later joined the Polish-Lithuanian Commonwealth on an equal footing with Poland and Lithuania. This agreement had broken down only when Poland's kings started violating the traditional privileges of the Rus, notably through their attempts to destroy their Orthodox faith through the church union of 1596. The Cossacks, led by Khmelnytsky, had rebelled and subsequently joined the Tsardom of Muscovy of their free will out of a sense of religious and ethnic affinity with the Russian people. Like their Polish counterparts, the tsars had also eventually started breaching the Agreement of 1654, curtailing the privileges of the Cossack elites. In contrast to the previous Cossack chronicles, however, the author of *Istoriia Rusiv* did not hide his anti-Russian and anti-autocratic sentiments.[28]

Plokhy maintains that *Istoriia Rusiv* transformed the history of Cossackdom: no longer did it reflect a social entity and autonomous polity; it now served as a nation-building myth that would help split the monolith of Russian imperial identity and lay the foundation for the modern Ukrainian nation.[29] The Cossack myth thus became instrumental to the Ukrainian national revival. This romanticizing of the Cossack wars of the sixteenth to eighteenth centuries, in defence of the liberties of the Little Russian people, quickly found resonance among the Ukrainian national awakeners. The mid-nineteenth century would be marked by a revived public interest in the Cossack chronicles.[30] According to Frank E. Sysyn, the Cossack Chronicles and *Istoriia Rusiv* had a major impact in the 1840s and 1850s in part because both granted the Ukrainians a voice concerning their own past:

> Unlike sources from the Muscovite government or the Polish nobility that survived in abundance from the seventeenth century and were published in the nineteenth century, few Ukrainian sources survived ... The Ukrainian revivalists longed for their own voice about the events and found it in *Istoriia Rusov* and the earlier Cossack chronicles. That they discovered manuscripts that had passed from hand to hand only added to the texts' authority among the Romantics. The populist revivalists could at least see them as analogous to the voice of the people that they found in historic songs and *dumy*.

This manifestation of the Cossack legacy became especially pronounced during the revolutionary events of 1917–21. In an attempt to legitimize the new political order, the Ukrainian government set out to fashion its own official narrative of the past, claiming a direct link with the Cossack struggle for freedom. This was most overt within the ranks of the new Ukrainian army, which revived the Cossack uniforms of the past (among other cultural touchstones) and reorganized itself along traditional Cossack lines. The first Ukrainianized military units, or "Cossack regiments," were named after famous hetmans and other historical figures who had been lionized by the national awakeners, such as Petro Sahaidachny, Petro Doroshenko, Khmelnytsky, and Mazepa. At the same time, spontaneous attempts were made to form voluntary militia units called *Vilne Kozatstvo* (Free Cossacks).[31] Moreover, during the short-lived Ukrainian state (April–December 1918), the Hetmanate was itself restored, with Pavlo Skoropadsky, a descendant of one of the Cossack hetmans of the early eighteenth century, taking the post of Hetman.[32] As well, the mythologized ideals attributed to Cossackdom were mobilized, albeit to a lesser degree, during the territorial discussions between the Soviet Ukrainian and Russian governments, when the Ukrainian lobby pushed for the Kuban region to be adjoined to Ukraine on the basis that it was populated largely by Ukrainian-speaking Cossacks.[33]

However, this separate Ukrainian historical narrative had developed mainly as a response to the emerging imperial narrative of a unified Russian past.[34] In an early effort to promote this imperial paradigm, the conservative historian Nikolai Karamzin presented Kyivan Rus as an integral part of the Russian past, depicting Kyiv as the original capital of the Russian state and Russian and Ukrainian history as being that of one "Slavic-Russian" people.[35] Roman Szporluk writes that Russia's national historical identity was subsequently built around these notions of an unbroken, thousand-year continuity from Kyiv through to Vladimir, Suzdal, Moscow, and, ultimately, the St Petersburg of the tsars.[36] This neglect of the Ukrainian past, or its representation solely as a province of Russia, provoked the search for a distinct Ukrainian historical paradigm.

The emergence of a separate Ukrainian national narrative began with the work of Mykhailo Maksymovych, the first rector of Kyiv University, who defended the distinctive character of Ukrainian history, which at the time was perceived as synonymous with the territories historically inhabited by Cossacks. Later scholars such as Panteleimon Kulish, Osyp Bodiansky, Mykola Kostomarov, and Volodymyr Antonovych argued that the Ukrainian narrative ought to be expanded in chronological, geographic, and social terms.[37] These founders of Ukrainian historiography asserted a continuity within Ukrainian history and questioned the very concept of a unified "Russian" nation, thus laying the foundation for an organized Ukrainian historical synthesis. This remained underdeveloped in scholarly terms, however, so that Ukrainian history continued to be rejected as a subject of academic inquiry in its own right.[38]

The task of overcoming this mindset fell to Mykhailo Hrushevsky (1866–1934), a history professor and political activist as well as head of the Central Rada, the All-Ukrainian Council of the Ukrainian People's Republic, in 1917–18. Recognizing Hrushevsky's indispensable role in promoting Ukraine's historical and, indeed, political identity, John A. Armstrong declared Hrushevsky "a father of Ukrainian nationalism."[39] Hrushevsky, a disciple of Antonovych, built upon the theoretical findings of his predecessors, creating a coherent national narrative for Ukrainian history. In his writings, he not only laid claim to the heritage of Kyivan Rus but also attempted to appropriate the most ancient period of Eastern Slavic history. Much like "the father of the Czech nation," František Palacký, who "proved" that the Czech nation had existed for at least one thousand years prior to the nineteenth century, in order to make the Ukrainians into a historical nation, Hrushevsky attempted to trace the Ukrainian people's ancestral lines back to the Antes, an early East Slavic tribe that had inhabited the lower Danube and the Black Sea region in the sixth and seventh centuries.[40]

Hrushevsky's views were perhaps questionable; even so, between the early 1890s to the mid-1930s, he largely succeeded in deconstructing the Russian imperial narrative while constructing a separate Ukrainian one. In doing so, he reconfigured the previously disparate and often tangential accounts of earlier scholars to construct a single national epic – the story of the rise, decline, and resurgence of the Ukrainian nation. As summarized by Plokhy, "the formulation of the new historical paradigm, which brought about the 'nationalization' of the Ukrainian past and established Ukrainian history as a separate field of study, provided the young nation with a birth certificate and curriculum vitae sufficiently respectable to support an application for membership in the exclusive club of modern European nations."[41]

Searching for the Ukrainian Ethnicity

Based on the ethnic and linguistic argument, "Ukraine" meant the territory where Ukrainian dialects were spoken.[42] Since no standardized Ukrainian language existed until the late 1920s, however, such a definition remained highly ambiguous.[43] To grant this argument some semblance of scientific validity, during the nineteenth century experts and amateurs alike took to the field in search of cultural commonalities in everyday life, traditions, and folklore that might help distinguish "Ukrainians" from their neighbours.[44] The ethnographic knowledge thereby gathered was then used to draw the first ethnographic maps of Ukraine, encompassing the areas where "Little Russians," as defined by similarities in language, everyday culture (*byt*, or *pobyt*), and sometimes religion, costituted a majority of the population.

The first significant intellectual attempt to map Ukraine in this manner can perhaps be attributed to the mid-nineteenth-century *Hromada* group. *Hromada* was a cultural and semi-political clandestine movement through which the Ukrainophile intelligentsia attempted to promote a Ukrainian national revival in Imperial Russia. Of the various publications associated with the movement, by far the most important was the journal *Osnova* (The Basis), published in St Petersburg in 1861–63 by Vasyl Bilozersky. Anton Kotenko describes *Osnova* as "a Ukrainian 'National Geographic' of the time", featuring articles and various travelogues dealing with the delineation of the Ukrainian national territory. The journal also promoted Ukrainian geographic nomenclature, subtly popularizing the name "Ukraine" over the more commonly used "Southern" or "Little Russia."[45]

Osnova's very first issues included an important contribution from the Ukrainian ethnographer Mykhailo Levchenko titled "The Present-Day Places of Living and Local Names of the Ruthenians." Adhering to the idea of a linguistic commonality, Levchenko described the territories under discussion as being populated by a continuous mass of "the Southern Rus people, Little Russians, or, more correctly, the Ruthenians."[46] According to Levchenko, their vast area of settlement included Poltava, Kharkiv, Kyiv,

Volhynia, and Podolia provinces; parts of Chernihiv, Kursk, Voronezh, Katerynoslav, Kherson, Taurida, Lublin, and Hrodna provinces; the lands of the Black Sea Cossacks; Bessarabia and the city of Azov; disparate communities in Galicia, Hungary, Bukovina, and Dobrudja; and even parts of Siberia between the Volga and Lake Baikal.

This textual description provided the basis for the first Ukrainian ethnographic map, the "Ethnographic Map of Little Russia" (*Karta etnohrafichna Malorusy*), which made its first appearance alongside an anonymously written article, "Ruthenians: Fragments of a Larger Historic-Ethnographic Text," in the pages of the Lviv-based serial *Lvovite*, advertised as a "handy household calendar" for 1862. This black-and-white map clearly demarcated a continuous territory populated by "Little Russians" in the Habsburg, Romanov, and Ottoman empires. It largely corresponded with the borders of the Little Russian ethnic territories as originally proposed by the Hungarian historian and ethnographer Pavel Jozef Šafařik in his 1842 "Slavonic Ethnography" (*Slovanský národopis*) and "Slavonic Geography" (*Slovanský zeměvid*). According to the map, Ukrainians lived on the territory from Poprad (in the Habsburg Empire) to the western districts of Voronezh province and Kuban (in the Romanov Empire), extending south to Dobrudja (in the Ottoman Empire).[47]

The most important attempt at mobilizing such knowledge in the late nineteenth century was an ethnographic and statistical expedition to western Russia (*Zapadno-Russkii krai*) organized in 1869–70 by the Russian Imperial Geographical Society (RGO). Pavlo Chubynsky, a former member of *Hromada*, was named the expedition's leader, having only recently received permission to return from Arkhangelsk, where he had been exiled since 1862 for his "harmful" Ukrainophile activities. By the end of two years, it had gathered extensive information about daily life in the region for the purpose of charting its ethnic make-up. That information included the customs and habits of the peasantry in Kyiv, Volhynia, and Podolia *gubernii* as well as parts of Bessarabia and Minsk, Grodno, Lublin, and Siedlce provinces. The expedition's ethnographic reports, focusing on daily life, local folklore and folk beliefs, customs and dialects, peculiarities of food and clothing, and popular calendar and customary law, were later compiled into seven volumes as "Proceedings of Ethnographic Statistical Expedition to the West Russian Region," published in St Petersburg in 1872–79.[48]

The *Osnova* map reflected Ukraine's ethnic territory as imagined by the Ukrainophile intelligentsia; by contrast, the publications of the RGO expedition largely reflected imperial political concerns. Francine

Hirsch posits that imperial ethnographers played an important role in state-sponsored efforts to promote and celebrate the empire.[49] Government-sponsored ethnographic studies were also seen as providing a scientific basis for underscoring the region's Russian character, thereby repudiating the popular view that Russia's western provinces – specifically those parts of the Romanov Empire acquired after the partition of the Polish-Lithuanian Commonwealth – were "Poland" and that its nobility was "Polish."[50]

Having been assigned the task of negating the narrative of Polish cultural and political dominance, Chubynsky now had to find a way to disentangle complex local identities in a region were language, culture, and religion had been intermixed for centuries.[51] The first step was to divorce ethnicity and religion so that "Catholics" would no longer be equated with "Poles."[52] To that end, linguistic and ethnographic criteria were prioritized. These ethnographic manipulations significantly reduced the size of the area's assumed Polish population by re-categorizing most Catholics as Little Russians. For the imperial authorities, Chubynsky's conclusions were both desirable and necessary. Among the total Catholic population of the West Russian region, Poles suddenly constituted a minority of only 25 per cent; the remaining 75 per cent of Catholics were now regarded as Little Russians.[53]

Another task faced by Chubynsky's team was to map the dominant ethnic group in the region, the Little Russians. By studying the spread of the Little Russian dialect alongside materials gathered during their ethnographic survey, the authors were able to delineate the ethnographic borders of the Little Russian nationality (*narodnost'*):

> The territory enclosing the population which speaks Little Russian, or more correctly the South-Russian language [*rech'*], encompasses the following Russian *gubernii*: Kyiv, Volhynia, Podolia, Chernihiv (except for the Surazh, Mglin, Starodub and Novozybkovsky districts), Kharkiv, Katerynoslav, Kherson, Taurida – up to the Perekop isthmus; the Kobryn and Brest districts, almost all of Pruzhany, the southern corner of Slonim, part of Belsk and the southern part of Belostok – of the Grodno *gubernia*; Pinsk and part of Mozyr – of the Minsk *gubernia*; Sudzhan, Graivoron, Belgorod, Staro-Oskol, Putivl, most of Novo-Oskol and a half of Rylsk – of the Kursk *gubernia*; Biriuchensk, Korotkoiaksk, Ostrogozk, Pavlov, almost the whole of Valuiki and a third of Boguchary – of the Voronezh *gubernia*; Khotyn – of Bessarabia; the eastern half of the

Lublin *gubernia* and the south-eastern half of the Sedlets *gubernia* and the whole of the land of Black Sea Cossacks.

In Austria-Hungary it occupies the following districts: Chortkiv, Ternopol, Zolochev, Zhovkva, third of Bukovina, Kolomyia, Stanislav, Berezhany, Lviv, Stryi, Sambor, Peremyshl, Sianok and the south-eastern corner of Sandech; in Hungary comitats: Marmoros, Bereg, Ugoch, Ungvar and most of Sukmar, Sabolch and Zemlin with a part of Sharosh.[54]

Based on these findings, the linguist Kostiantyn Mykhalchuk was able to prepare a map of "the South-Russian dialects and vernaculars," published in 1871 (see map 0.2). Although widely regarded as the first ethnographic map to provide a scientific basis for the Ukrainian national space, and to feature the continuous national borders of the Ukrainian territory across all three regional empires,[55] it was, at best, imprecise. Because the first imperial census was not conducted until 1897, the authors were able to present only an approximation of the territories inhabited by those who spoke what they labelled "South Russian dialects." Nonetheless, these early attempts at ethnographic mapping prepared the intellectual ground for the "imagining" of Ukraine.

Putting Ukraine on the Map

Robert Kaiser writes that a national movement is "always a struggle for control of land ... The 'land' ... is intrinsic to the very concept of national identity."[56] So it is unsurprising that the age of European nationalism was marked by violent conflicts over land and dramatic territorial reconfigurations. At the same time, it was an age of "passionate and widespread cartophilia," as noted by Catherine Dunlop. In an era when Europeans were intent on discovering, demarcating, and legitimizing new forms of modern national boundaries, the modern map proved an extremely influential medium. To improve the administration and integration of their lands, modernizing governments turned to surveyors, statisticians, and geographers.[57] Such experts used maps to construct national identities and subsequently cement the idea of a "national" homeland for those countries' diverse populations. But how could one map a territory inhabited by a people who – like the Ukrainians in 1917 – had no pre-existing state?[58] In the absence of a unified centre of power, national activists set out to map Ukraine into being.

0.2 South Russian dialects and vernaculars, 1871.

As numerous studies of the historical role of maps have shown, cartographical imagery nearly always provides a biased view of the land it is depicting. Maps do not provide an accurate geographical impression of a territory; they *interpret* that impression.[59] In his innovative study of the history of Thai nationalism, Thongchai Winichakul demonstrated that "[a] map anticipated spatial reality, not vice versa. ... A map was a model for, rather than a model of, what it purported to represent."[60] Hence, before they could become a modern nation, Ukrainians first had to form their "identity space" by mapping out an imagined homeland, the place where Ukrainians lived.[61]

No one did more to territorialize the "imagined" Ukrainian nation than the geographer and cartographer Stepan Rudnytsky (1877–1937).[62] Born in Przemyśl in Austrian Galicia, the son of a local teacher, Rudnytsky majored in history and geography at the universities of Lemberg/Lviv, Vienna, and Berlin. In Lviv, he joined the Shevchenko Scientific Society, established in 1873, where Hrushevsky was his patron. With Hrushevsky's encouragement, Rudnytsky drafted a new ethnographic map of Ukraine for his popular

1910 study "A Brief Geography of Ukraine" (*Korotka heohrafiia Ukrainy*).⁶³ In 1912, he completed the first Ukrainian school atlas (reprinted in 1917, 1919, and 1928), which included maps of Europe's Great Powers as well as a demographic survey of Ukraine based on systematic fieldwork and recent census statistics. As the first Professor of Ukrainian Geography at Lemberg University, Rudnytsky helped elevate his specialty to a legitimate field of academic research. Meanwhile, he prepared the first precise geographic description of the Ukrainian ethnolinguistic territories.

During the First World War, Rudnytsky lived in Vienna, where he joined the Union for the Liberation of Ukraine (SVU), a German-sponsored organization that united Ukrainian émigré scientists, writers, and activists who wished to leverage the war to secure Ukrainian independence. SVU's principal activity was disseminating propaganda among POWs of Ukrainian extraction. Using the pen name "Levenko," Rudnytsky composed a series of patriotic brochures for the SVU, in which he justified self-rule for Ukrainians.⁶⁴ He later served as a consultant to the West Ukrainian People's Republic's government-in-exile. To help familiarize a wider international audience with the Ukrainians' claim to their own state, he also revised his "Brief Geography," translating it into German and having it republished in Berlin in 1916 as "*Ukraina, Land und Volk.*" An edition in English, "Ukraine: The Land and Its People," was released in 1918.⁶⁵ After the war, Rudnytsky helped organize the Ukrainian Free University, based first in Vienna and later in Prague. In 1926, he accepted an invitation from the Soviet Ukrainian government to organize and promote geographic research in Kharkiv. This led to the founding of the "Ukrainian Scientific Research Institute of Geography and Cartography." Rudnytsky was also named the first Chair of Geography at the All-Ukrainian Academy of Sciences, founded in 1918.⁶⁶

Throughout these years, Rudnytsky viewed his work as an extension of the campaign for Ukrainian independence. Much like Hrushevsky with his historical research, he wished to use geography and cartography to promote the international recognition of a Ukrainian homeland.⁶⁷ In a region where identities remained fluid and no standardized language existed, a recognized national territory could, in Rudnytsky's words, become "the main foundation of the nation."⁶⁸ That nation would follow the ethnographic boundaries of a future Ukraine. As Rudnytsky stated in the original preface of his "Brief Geography," "we are Ukrainians, the land where we live is called Ukraine, no matter if it is under Russia, Austria or Hungary. Even if it is divided by borders and torn to pieces, the nation [*narod*] that populates it is one, with one language, psyche [*vdacha*] and traditions."⁶⁹

In a 1916 pamphlet, "Why Do We Want an Independent Ukraine?" (*Chomu my khochemo samostiinoï Ukraïny?*), which appeared in Vienna, Berlin, Lviv, and Stockholm, Rudnytsky elucidated on his political goal of a sovereign Ukraine. He began by defining the land itself: "[Ukraine] is where you hear our native Ukrainian language and song, where people observe Ukrainian traditional rites, where people remember their common historic joy and grief, where people want a free, Ukrainian life." This was followed by a description of Ukraine's territorial extent: "From the rapid Poprad river and the muddy Vepr (Wieprz) [in the west], Ukraine spreads across the remote and red steppes surrounding the Caspian Sea, from the hot Hungarian lowland and Carpathian forests [in the west] to beyond the fish-laden Don, from the dark pine forests of the Bilovezha [in the northwest] to the glacier-capped Caucasus, and from the bottomless swamps of the Polesia [in the north] to the sunny coast of the Black Sea."[70]

The sweeping political changes of 1917 were a major inspiration for Rudnytsky, who especially welcomed the founding of a Ukrainian government in Kyiv. He viewed the national revolutionary upheaval of 1917–18 as a unique opportunity to transform the "identity space" of Ukrainians – defined by the commonality of language, culture, and history – into the "decision space" for a Ukrainian national state. It was around this time that he shifted his research focus from racial to cultural anthropology, expanding on his definition of the Ukrainian lands. This coincided with his growing criticism of the new government for its ignorance of Ukraine's contiguous ethnographic territory and its reluctance to extend Ukrainian territorial claims. From Rudnytsky's perspective, the national leadership was abandoning the pursuit of Ukraine's former historical state boundaries so as not to be perceived as imperialistic.[71] The most egregious example of this was, he thought, a memorandum tabled by the Ukrainian mission to the Paris Peace Conference of 1919 (see map o.3). Rudnytsky claimed that the included map had been drawn spontaneously; in the Sub-Caucasus, for example, some 180,000 square kilometres with a – primarily Ukrainian – population of 3 million had been completely excluded.[72] At the same time, he insisted on the cross-border unity of the Ukrainian lands. This reflected how his definition of Ukraine's territorial integrity shifted as he moved beyond mere ethnography to include those regions of "essential political and economic significance" such as Kuban, Crimea, and Bessarabia.[73]

Steven Seegel calls Rudnytsky "a dreamer" who envisaged a greater Ukraine and thought of Ukrainians not as speakers of a local dialect but as a group possessing a shared language, georgraphic space, and high cultural history.[74] In his strivings for national unity, Rudnytsky defined

0.3 Territories claimed by the Ukrainian People's Republic at the Paris Peace Conference, 1919.

Ukrainians by race, language, history, region, and culture. Like most scholars of the time, he was a social Darwinist who viewed struggles between ethnic groups as a natural process. Yet while he prioritized racial criteria, he did not view them as making a nation. According to Rudnytsky, a nation was

> a large community of people, whose bodies are similar to that of each other, but different from those of other nations, the community of people that has a separate language that is different from other languages, that has its own distinct rites and traditions, that has its own national history, common understanding and a shared experience of good and bad occurrences, that has a common view of the future, that has its own culture, and most importantly, that has somewhere to live – occupying a large and wealthy piece of land together.[75]

To reduce Rudnytsky's role in defining and shaping modern Ukraine to a simple matter of race, as some recent scholarship has tended to do, is to ignore his contributions to geography as a new academic discipline, not just in Ukraine but worldwide.[76] Moreover, such narrow-minded criticism of his achievements disregards the European intellectual climate of the early twentieth century, a time when many scholars, as well as governments, including in established democracies, embraced racial determinism.[77] Rudnytsky contributed greatly to the Ukrainian national movement as a scholar and political thinker, but he was also very much a man of his times.[78]

Regardless, the idealized national boundaries that Rudnytsky presented on his maps were far from reflecting post-1917 political realities (see map 0.4). The Ukrainian national governments were on a very weak footing and never controlled more than a limited amount of territory beyond the capital. Nonetheless, the maps became foundational to the Ukrainian national movement and the spread of Ukrainian nationalism, especially among Ukrainians abroad. Thanks to Rudnytsky, Ukrainians for the first time possessed a cartographical representation of a distinctive space they could claim as their own. Moreover, it was he who popularized the term "Ukrainians," which he used consistently instead of "Rusyns" or "Little Russians."

Fifteen years after Rudnytsky, Volodymyr Kubiiovych, a Ukrainian geographer at the Jagiellonian University in Krakow, further advanced ethnographic understanding of the Ukrainian people with his "Atlas of Ukraine and Adjoining Countries" (*Atlas Ukrainy ta sumezhnykh krain*, 1937) and "Geography of Ukraine and Adjoining Lands" (*Heohrafiia Ukrainy i sumezhnykh zemel*), first published in 1938 and reprinted in 1943. Much like Rudnytsky, Kubiiovych used linguistic and anthropological criteria to represent the geographical reach of the Ukrainian lands. However, in mapping these territories he surpassed previous Ukrainian ethnographic and linguistic research. In the introductory essay to his "Geography of Ukraine," he challenged the frontiers of the Ukrainian nation (*narod*), its language, and its culture. He emphasized that the Ukrainian lands "stretch from Tisza, Danube, the Black Sea and the Caucasus up to the forests and muds of Polesia; from Poprad [in Slovakia], San River, Vepry and Belovezha up to the Caspian desserts and the broad Don, and extends to the Ukrainian colonies across Asia up to the shores of the Pacific Ocean."[79]

In his collective biography of European "map men," Seegel poses a pertinent question: how should one judge a scientific geographer whose "geopolitics" were derived "from maps not made, from sources that were destroyed or never reached the light of day"?[80] Seegel agrees that Rudnytsky's patriotic work might raise troublesome issues. During the Second World War, for example, his understanding of the Ukrainian race, shaped in the context of the 1920s, was appropriated by Ukrainian radical nationalists and those collaborating with the Nazi occupation to argue for a pure Ukrainian race. Central to this was an opposition to mixed marriages with neighbouring peoples, such as Poles, or to minorities, specifically Jews,

0.4 "Map of Ukraine" by Stepan Rudnytsky, 1918.

hence endorsing the ethnic cleansing of the Ukrainian lands.[81] The question of retroactive responsibility becomes especially relevant when the issue is not about the misuse of one's ideas, but about open collaboration with totalitarian regimes. Such was the case with Kubiiovych, who, as a leading member of the Krakow-based Ukrainian Central Committee (UTSK), was responsible for the dissemination of anti-Semitic materials during the Holocaust in Poland and who later participated in ethnic cleansing as an early member of the *Waffen*-ss *Galizien*.[82]

UKRAINE: FROM PEOPLE TO NATION

The making of a distinct Ukrainian political identity can be linked to the wake of the First World War and the Russian revolutions, which resulted in the collapse of the Romanov Empire.[83] The events of February 1917 in Petrograd inspired representatives from pro-Ukraine political parties and national activists in Kyiv to organize themselves. On 4 March 1917, the Ukrainian Central Rada was formed, laying the foundations for future Ukrainian statehood. On 7 November, the Rada announced the founding of an autonomous Ukrainian People's Republic (UNR) and its government – the General Secretariat (see map 0.4).[84] The Third Universal of the Ukrainian Central Rada subsequently defined the UNR's territory as lying within the nine *gubernii* of the former Russian Empire. The new governing authorities also laid claim to the provinces of Kholm/Chełm and Pidliashshia/Podlasie in eastern Poland, as well as parts of Russia's Kursk and Voronezh provinces, where Ukrainians were a significant part of the population.[85]

Parallel to the vision of Ukraine as elaborated by the nationally oriented parties, farther to the east, plans for a Soviet Ukrainian polity were being initiated. By early December, at a congress of the Soviets held in Kharkiv, the Bolsheviks had proclaimed an autonomous Ukrainian People's Republic of Soviets and its government, the People's Secretariat of Ukraine.[86] At the same time, that body sent an ultimatum to the Rada threatening war with the UNR. It was promptly rejected, sparking armed conflict. On 9 January 1918, while the fighting raged, the UNR proclaimed full independence, establishing a separate Foreign Ministry and dispatching its own diplomatic missions abroad. By this point, however, such gestures made little practical difference: the General Secretariat was simply too weak to defend its territory. On 26 January, Bolshevik and local pro-Soviet forces took Kyiv for the first time, forcing the UNR authorities to retreat west to Zhytomyr.

Seeking allies against the pro-Soviet forces, the Ukrainian nationally oriented political elites approached the Central Powers. Though the First World War was still raging, the Central Powers eagerly supported Ukraine's attempts to forge a separate statehood, for they regarded the break-up of Russia as an opportunity to improve their military situation on the Eastern Front.[87] Since December 1917, the nationalist Ukrainian and the Russian Soviet governments had both been negotiating separate peace treaties with the Central Powers. On 9 February 1918, the UNR signed an agreement with its former enemies. Under the terms of that agreement, Germany and Austria-Hungary would recognize Ukraine as a fully independent state and provide military support against Bolshevik Russia in exchange for imports of foodstuffs.[88]

This formal recognition of Ukraine's sovereignty inevitably raised the issue of borders. Pressed for time, Austria-Hungary accepted the territorial demands of the Ukrainian delegation and agreed to the UNR's annexation of Kholm/Chełm as well as to the creation of an autonomous Austrian "crownland" in the Ukrainian-majority regions of Eastern Galicia and Northern Bukovina. The First Treaty of Brest-Litovsk thus defined Ukraine's western border: the old boundary between the Habsburg Monarchy and Russia, as it was prior to the outbreak of the First World War, was

0.5 Territories claimed by the Ukrainian People's Republic, December 1917.

to be respected, and the border with a restored Poland would run from Ternohorod up to Lake Vydonovsk, corresponding to the Ukrainian western ethnographic frontier. Meanwhile, however, the question of Ukraine's northeastern border with Soviet Russia would remain open until negotiations between the two states could take place. However, when the Russian representatives signed the Second Treaty of Brest-Litovsk with the Central Powers on 3 March 1918, no border was clearly established. The Russians merely agreed to conclude a peace with the UNR and to withdraw their forces from its territory.[89]

By the end of February 1918, there were almost half a million German and Habsburg soldiers on the territory of Ukraine. By the end of April, they had occupied its entire territory and installed the Ukrainian authorities back in power in the capital. Yet Germany and Austria-Hungary placed little trust in the left-leaning UNR. Thus, on 29 April, the Central Powers helped stage a military coup that brought the reactionary general Pavlo Skoropadsky to power; Skoropadsky subsequently abolished the UNR and declared himself Hetman of Ukraine (see map 0.6).[90] In return, Skoropadsky was expected to honour the UNR's earlier pledge to deliver substantial

0.6 Territories claimed by the Ukrainian State, June 1918.

quantities of food and raw materials to aid the Central Powers' ongoing war effort. The main burden of this fell on the peasants, who could not comprehend how or why the Germans had come to be in control. Taking advantage of the power vacuum across much of the countryside, many peasant leaders, *otamans*, declared communal self-rule and took control of the land.[91]

After the German surrender on the Western Front in November 1918, Skoropadsky's regime collapsed. Ukraine quickly became a war zone, with the Reds (which included the Bolshevik armies but also those of the Odesa and Donetsk–Kryvyi Rih Soviet Republic), the anti-Bolshevik Whites, and local peasant militias all fighting one another for control. When the erstwhile UNR leader Symon Petliura, backed by the Polish army, returned to Kyiv in May 1920, the anti-Bolshevik uprising he had hoped for failed to materialize through lack of popular support.[92] The government in Kyiv lasted only until 13 June, when it abandoned the city to the Bolsheviks for the final time (see map 0.7).

Although the Ukrainian government never at any time controlled all the territories it claimed to represent, the existence of a separate political authority, and its national and international activities, meant that the

0.7 Territories claimed by the Ukrainian People's Republic, December 1918.

concepts of "Ukraine" and "Ukrainians" gradually became almost universally accepted. Sysyn posits that during the national revolution of 1917–18, "a revolution in perception" had occurred, one more important than the political events commonly associated with the period:

> This "revolution" was the acceptance of the idea of an entity with fairly well-defined borders called the "Ukraine," and the self-identification of the masses living in this area as "Ukrainians." This was a revolution in perception, and it brought about a general recognition that Ukrainians were a separate nation. Even the Russians or Poles, who had hitherto viewed Ukrainians as merely a part of their own nations, came to accept this new view.[93]

Although short-lived, the existence of a separate state entity placed the Ukrainian nation-building project in a position of relative strength in the context of Eastern and Central Europe. The Ukrainian lobby had used the Brest-Litovsk peace talks to push for the incorporation of all territories inhabited by Ukrainians into the new state. This included the Habsburg provinces of Eastern Galicia, Northern Bukovina, and Trans-Carpathian

Rus, as well the territories with mixed Polish-Ukrainian populations of Kholm/Chełm and Pidliashshia/Podlasie, which were also currently under Austro-Hungarian military administration.[94] If accepted, these territorial claims could negatively affect the Dual Monarchy and a future Poland in terms of territories. Recognition of the Ukrainian state, as well as partial approval of their territorial claims at Brest-Litovsk, represented a determined effort to define Ukraine's borders along ethnic lines. This also, albeit for a brief time, made Ukraine a focal point of international politics and boosted Ukrainian government morale, much needed in its fight against the Soviet Red Army.

The collapse of the Central Powers in the autumn of 1918, however, rendered the previous territorial settlement defunct. A new Polish-Ukrainian border was agreed upon in the wake of the Polish-Soviet War of 1920 and formalized under the Riga Peace Treaty, signed on 18 March 1921 by representatives of the Second Polish Republic, Soviet Russia, and Soviet Ukraine (see map 0.8). That border, however, was a compromise that failed to satisfy any of the sides involved and later emerged as a source of future conflict.[95] The new border also sealed the ultimate fate of the UNR, since the idea of anti-Soviet Polish-Ukrainian cooperation, agreed upon in the course of talks earlier that year, was abandoned; it also put an end to Józef Piłsudski's ambitious geopolitical federalist program for Eastern Europe.[96] Moreover, the fact that the "Ukrainian" lands remained divided provided the ideological justification for the Soviet occupation of former Eastern Galicia in 1939 and its subsequent unification with Soviet Ukraine (see map 0.9).

WRITING ABOUT UKRAINE'S BORDERS

With the collapse of the Soviet Union, the former Soviet republics started developing their own historical narratives. Scholars in particular were expected to justify and legitimize the new states' borders.[97] Since 1991, a few general studies examining the definition of Ukraine's territory have appeared within Ukrainian historiography.[98] As a rule, these studies are broad in their geographical and chronological scope; as such, they aim to provide an overview of the history of Ukraine's border formations and its relations with its neighbours. One of the earliest explorations was a study by Vasyl Boiechko, Oksana Hanzha, and Borys Zakharchuk, first published as a journal article in 1992.[99] In 1994, a revised version of their study was released as a separate volume; this one featured relevant maps and documents from the national archives. The study's narrative accounts for

0.8 Soviet Ukraine, 1921.

0.9 Soviet Ukraine, 1939.

various factors involved in delineating the border of the UNR and, later, Soviet Ukraine. Among the episodes explored are the border shifts between Soviet Ukraine and Russia in 1919, with less attention paid to later delineations; the Bessarabian question and the formation of the Moldovan Autonomous Soviet Socialist Republic (MASSR) in the mid-1920s; the incorporation of western Ukraine in 1939; and the transfer of Crimea to Soviet Ukraine in 1954. Another collection of documents that deals with the demarcation of Ukraine's borders is the 2008 volume *Etnichni mezhi i derzhavnyi kordon Ukraïny* (The Ethnic Frontiers and State Border of Ukraine), edited by Ukrainian historian Volodymyr Serhiichuk.[100] The introduction to that work discusses the evolution of representations of the Ukrainian lands by foreign and native cartographers, highlighting the discrepancy between the ethnic and political boundaries of today's Ukraine. The collection offers numerous previously unpublished documents organized (rather oddly, and unpractically for the reader) geographically (south, southeast, east, etc.), but there is no index or document list to aid researchers wishing to consult them.

In 2016, another volume dedicated almost entirely to the discussion of Ukraine's borders was published by a group of "activist historians" affiliated with Ukraine's Academy of Sciences.[101] Published as *Narodzhennia kraïny. Vid kraiu do derzhavy. Nazva, symvolika, terytoriia i kordony Ukraïny* (The Birth of the Country: From Land to State: Name, Symbols, Territory, and Borders of Ukraine), this volume also served as the opening title in a series of popular history books released as part of the new project "Likbez: History without Censorship" launched by historians and political activists in 2015.[102] The historians involved in this initiative engage with highly contested and ideologized events of the past; their declared aim is to refute popular myths and provide an alternative reading of Ukraine's history. The first volume in the series begins with a reconstruction of the names used to define the lands of today's Ukraine, such as Rus Ukraine, Malorosia, and Novorossiya, which gained a new prominence and ideological bias in the wake of the 2014 political crisis. This is followed by a discussion of national symbols and foreign and native maps depicting the lands of today's Ukraine. The book is largely dedicated to exploring territorial definitions of modern Ukraine, examining the border shifts between the country and its neighbours. A separate section is devoted to Crimea and seeks to refute the conventional narrative that the peninsula is a historically Russian territory. Instead, the authors provide an alternative reading of history, one that emphasizes the violent Russification of Crimea's autochthonous populations after it became part of the Russian Empire in 1783.[103]

Ukraine's borders and border regions have also drawn the attention of Russian historians. In 2005, the Russian Academy of Science's Institute of Slavic Studies published a collection of essays dedicated entirely to examining Ukraine's regions and border formations from a historical perspective.[104] While a few contributions discuss the delineation of a physical border, the volume overall, according to its editor Leonid Gorizontov, is first and foremost "a study of regions [*regionalistika*]" and an analysis of the regional factor in Ukraine's history, emphasizing its diversity and the coexistent nature of various regional identities. Among those articles examining the border itself, the most relevant are ones by Elena Borisenok, examining the border contestations between Russia and Ukraine in the 1920s, and V. Lebedeva, examining the negotiations over the Belarusian-Ukrainian border in the spring of 1918.

Ukraine's borders cannot be viewed in isolation.[105] In Polish historiography, for example, the border with Ukraine (among other regions) features prominently. Studies by Roman Wapiński and Piotr Eberhardt examine the concepts and visions of Polish intellectuals and political activists in the nineteenth and early twentieth centuries regarding territorial definitions of the restored Polish state.[106] In the contemporary texts, a common reference was to the first partition of the Polish-Lithuanian Commonwealth in 1772, whereby Poland lost large swathe of its northeastern territory, including Right-Bank Ukraine, to the Russian Empire.[107] However, the territorial imaginations of Polish ideologues often overlapped with those of Ukrainian nationalists – for example, when both laid claim to the same territory, as can be seen in their views about the future of Lviv/Lwów. These irreconcilable views led to direct conflict between the Second Polish Republic and the West Ukrainian People's Republic (ZUNR) in November 1918; this in turn influenced the direction of scholarship, with the border question becoming as much a subject of military as of political history.[108]

One of the most discussed sections of Ukraine's border is the one it shares with Russia. This topic has featured prominently in studies about the territorial expansion of the Russian Empire and the shaping of its western and southeastern borders. It must be said, however, that existing scholarship provides a somewhat one-sided story, an example being studies that highlight the rectitude of Russian territorial acquisitions such as eastern Donbas but neglect to mention the Ukrainian government's claims to areas with large Ukrainian populations within Russia's borders.[109] Such studies are largely concerned with Moscow's role in border delineation. Other historians, though, have chosen to explore Ukrainian perspectives on border-making. Russian historian Borisenok made use of extensive archival

0.10 Soviet Ukraine, 1937.

material to investigate the territorial claims of the Ukrainian government over Voronezh, Kursk, and Briansk *gubernii* and the resultant border shifts in 1924–26.[110] Paralleling this, Ukrainian historian Henmadii Iefimenko has scrutinized the interests of Ukrainian leaders and their position on border delineation, which did not always align with that of the Kremlin.[111] The most recent study, by Stephan Rindlisbacher, highlights the complex interactions between three main hierarchical layers: the party leadership in Moscow, the cadres of the union republics, and local activists, who all played equally important roles in delineating the border between the two Soviet republics.[112]

Another group of authors have indirectly addressed the formation of Ukraine's borders while examining different aspects of Ukraine's modern history. Among these studies are ones that focus on border negotiations during the national revolution;[113] the revolutionary period and the consolidation of Soviet power;[114] territorial changes during the Stalinist era and beyond, notably the incorporation of western Ukraine, Northern Bukovina, and Transcarpathia (*Zakarpattia*);[115] and the transfer of Crimea in 1954.[116]

In this regard, the interwar decades are a key time period, for that is when the Soviet state contributed greatly to the emergence and consolidation of national identities among the numerous peoples of the Soviet Union. This coincided with the new-nationalities policy of *korenizatsiia* (indigenization), with *Ukrainizatsiia* as its Ukrainian version. In his seminal study, Terry Martin maintains that "the Soviet nationalities policy began with the formation of national territories."[117] Similarly, Borisenok in her study of Ukrainian *korenizatsiia* highlights that border delineation was a political prerequisite, since the authorities needed to first define the territories on which their policies would be implemented.[118]

No less contested is the historiography of Ukraine's western border. In 1939, after the signing of the German-Soviet Non-Aggression Pact, the Red Army occupied western Ukraine and Belarus, joining those areas to the Ukrainian and Belorussian SSRs, respectively. (The border with Poland would be finalized only in 1952, following a forced exchange of populations and frontier areas between Ukraine and Poland.[119]) In June 1940, after the withdrawal of the Romanian military and administration from the region, Northern Bukovina and Southern Bessarabia also became part of Soviet Ukraine. Then as a last step during that era, Carpathian Ukraine, which had been occupied by Hungary during the war, was incorporated into Soviet Ukraine in January 1946 (see map 0.11). Soviet scholarship was characterized by a narrative of liberation, asserting that the Red Army pursued a "liberating mission" to free the Ukrainian people from the capitalist countries of Poland, Romania, and Czechoslovakia.[120] In contrast, Ukraine's diaspora historians presented these events as "occupation" and "annexation."[121] More recent scholars have described the division of Poland in 1939 as "the fourth partition," referring to the three partitions of the Polish lands in the late eighteenth century.[122]

Since independence, the main debate among Ukrainian historians has been whether territorial expansion was "incorporation" (*pryiednannia*) or "reunification" (*voz'iednannia*). Ukrainian historians emphasize the complexity and ambiguity of Ukraine's history. Was it the case that the Ukrainian people, who for centuries had been divided among different empires, were finally united within common borders? Or was it the case that unification was achieved through violence, Red Army aggression, brutal Sovietization policies, the shattering of social and cultural systems, and rejection of the norms of international law?[123] The predominant view among Western scholars is that the Nazis and the Soviet dictatorship forged secret agreements that led to unlawful annexation and an ensuing power vacuum.[124]

0.11 Soviet Ukraine, 1940.

STRUCTURE AND KEY THEMES

Borders have long been a prominent theme among scholars. However, many studies refer to boundary lines mainly in order to define their own scope. By contrast, this volume makes Ukraine's physical borders its primary focus. Central to this are the processes of negotiation, delineation, and contestation that led to Ukraine's borders being drawn the way they have been in the twentieth century. The contributors scrutinize all of the borders that Ukraine shares with its seven neighbouring countries, to highlight the complex interactions between international, state, and local actors. They also examine the ethnographic, historical, and geographical factors that contributed to border-drawing, thereby offering a fresh approach to studying the events that resulted in the international borders of today's Ukraine.

The editors have invited the contributors to consider how, when, and under what conditions Ukraine's borders have been drawn. This volume covers every aspect of Ukraine's borders, including the most important peace treaties that led to them. This has often meant prioritizing high politics and international relations at the expense of other methodological approaches. This volume is organized around three main themes: the interstate treaties that brought about the new international order in Eastern Europe; the formation of the internal boundaries between Ukraine and other Soviet republics; and the delineation of Ukraine's borders with its western neighbours.

Part one comprises four chapters that investigate the impact of various peace treaties and the role of the Great Powers in defining Ukraine's territory. These chapters focus on the shifting of Ukraine's western border, mainly shared with a revived Poland in the first half of the twentieth century. Borislav Chernev scrutinizes the interests of the Great Powers in upholding Ukrainian demands for self-determination during the separate peace negotiations at Brest-Litovsk from December 1917 to March 1918. Elżbieta Kwiecińska's chapter investigates the contrasting positions and interests of the Polish and Ukrainian delegations to the Paris Peace Conference, presented as a contest between competing claims for self-determination. The overlapping interests of Poland, Ukraine, and Russia would once again come to the fore during the Polish-Soviet War of 1920. Jan Jacek Bruski focuses on the territorial negotiations between the Second Polish Republic and the UNR, demonstrating how the subsequent territorial arrangements, formalized during the Riga Peace Treaty of March 1921, not only sealed the UNR's fate but also formed the basis of the future Polish-Soviet border that existed up to September 1939. Lastly, Damian Markowski investigates the interests of the Great Powers in Eastern Europe during and shortly after the Second World War, examining their impact on the redrawing of Ukraine's western border.

Part two examines the processes of border delineation between the Soviet republics and has particular relevance to the situation of present-day Ukraine. This includes the contentious issue of Crimea, as well as the various "frozen" post-Soviet territorial disputes, particularly in the case of Moldova. The section opens with a chapter by Dorota Michaluk that scrutinizes negotiations between the Ukrainian and Belarusian governments over the demarcation line between the two people's republics in 1918, as well as the role of experts in the delimitation of the Belarusian-Ukrainian border. Stephan Rindlisbacher's chapter aims to reconstruct the process of border formation between Russia and Ukraine in the early 1920s by examining the constant negotiations among the party leaders, alongside republican and local party cadres and activists in the border regions, concerning the management of Soviet ethnic diversity. Alexandr Voronovici analyzes the process of negotiating and delineating the Ukrainian-Moldovan border in the context of the shifting regional balance of power during the interwar and wartime years. Lastly, Austin Charron discusses the unification of Crimea with Soviet Ukraine in 1954, drawing attention to the discrepancies between the official Soviet rhetoric and more pragmatic considerations of economic practicality and efficiency.

Part three investigates the inter-state contestations behind the formation of the western Ukrainian border, discussing the demarcation of Ukraine's boundaries with Poland and Romania, alongside the territorial definitions of the Transcarpathian region. Serhii Hladyshuk details a largely understudied aspect of the Polish-Ukrainian border delineation in Volhynia between 1918 and 1921. During this period, the region changed hands multiple times, with competing governments articulating differing plans on how best to utilize the local, mostly Ukrainian, population in their propaganda efforts. The Bolsheviks viewed Volhynia as a springboard for spreading the proletarian revolution to Western Europe; the Polish government aspired to annex the province in a bid to recover their nation's "historic" territories to the east. Iaroslav Kovalchuk investigates Ukraine's role in the territorial tensions between the Soviet Union, Hungary, Czechoslovakia, and Romania immediately following the Second World War. In particular, the chapter focuses on Soviet attempts to navigate the competing interests of the other parties, resulting in the eventual unification of Transcarpathia with Soviet Ukraine in 1946. Lastly, Constantin Ardeleanu investigates the making of the current Ukrainian-Moldovan-Romanian border in the area of the Danube Delta. Ardeleanu observes how state actors negotiated conflicting claims inherited from imperial times and how they reacted to environmental crises stemming from the river's economic use. This includes the highly contested issue of delineating the territorial limits along the continental shelf surrounding Serpents Island in the Black Sea.

The discussion of the formation of Ukraine's border concludes with a chapter by Tatiana Zhurzhenko tracing the process of bordering Ukraine since 1991, with a particular focus on the competing visions of future relations between Russia and Ukraine.

Overall, the book's contributors reveal that Ukraine's borders have been the product of several overlapping processes and phenomena, including international treaties concluded during the "continuum of crisis" of 1914–22,[125] as well as interactions between activists representing competing nation-building projects, including the Soviet *korenizatsiia* initiative. No less important has been the interplay of economic, physical, and cultural factors.

Ukrainian statehood became possible in the wider context of redrawing European boundaries, itself a consequence of the demise of the continental empires and the emergence of new nation-states in Eastern and Central

Europe. The governments of these new entities were eager to uphold the principle of national self-determination, which had been prioritized by the Paris Peace Conference as it sought to justify the new territorial arrangements in Europe.[126] But at that international forum, not every nation was seen as equal. In her examination of the Polish-Ukrainian territorial disputes following the First World War, Kwiecińska speaks of "the hierarchy of self-determinations." Ukraine, in that regard, was viewed as a "former client state" of the Central Powers. As a consequence, it was totally ignored during the peace conference: the Ukrainian delegation went unrecognized, and no commission was established for Ukraine, as was the case for the other new Eastern European states.[127]

A growing body of research supports the idea that ethnic-based violence became an unintended consequence of national self-determination and support for the nation-state, as provided by the Versailles system and institutionalized through the League of Nations, a new international organization created in January 1920 with the task of guaranteeing Europe's redrawn state borders while defending the rights of numerous national communities that suddenly found themselves as minorities within those new states.[128] The shift from "the world of empires" to "the world of nations" is often viewed as a key reason why so many borderland populations that had coexisted for centuries descended into internecine violence.[129] Indeed, the old empires had been defined by their ethnic and confessional diversity, whereas the new nation-states had been formed on the basis of ethnic purity, and linguistic and religious homogeneity, with many governments turning to racial anthropology and eugenics to define their national demography.[130]

It was in this context that inter-ethnic conflict, driven by a new sense of exclusive national identity, became widespread. Inspired by the new international climate, national governments started laying competing claims to the same areas with ethnically mixed populations. In this vein, Chernev's contribution to this volume demonstrates the difficulties that faced the Central Powers as they attempted to manoeuvre through the demands and expectations of the Ukrainian, Russian, and Polish parties, given that appeasing Ukrainian demands in the west would mean antagonizing the Poles. Similarly, Kwiecińska examines the intellectual battle between Poles and Ukrainians over the ownership of Eastern Galicia. The Poles' mandate to govern Galicia – a mandate they had received at Versailles – coupled with complete disregard for Ukrainian grievances in the region led to inter-ethnic conflict between Poles and Ukrainians that would last well into the mid-twentieth century.

In many respects, autonomous Ukraine was a result of Great Power politics. As several chapters demonstrate, other European countries' fears, and their hopes of collaboration with Russia, largely shaped international attitudes toward Ukraine's borders in the early twentieth century. Competition over territory with Bolshevik Russia drew the Ukrainian government closer to its former enemies – the Central Powers and Poland; this rapprochement is what led to the treaties of Brest-Litovsk and Riga. At the same time, Ukraine's position between Europe and Russia forced the Western Great Powers to take an interest in local national movements; they promoted the state- and nation-building aspirations of local elites in the hope of weakening their eastern rival. In other instances, those same powers decided on Ukraine's borders without even considering local interests.

Parallel to this, ongoing fear of the Bolsheviks led the Great Powers to support Poland's restoration. They viewed that reborn state as a buffer against "Red" Russia. Inadvertently, the founding of the Second Polish Republic and other new states in Eastern Europe highlighted the issue of minorities within their borders, which increased the incidence and severity of inter-ethnic violence, especially along frontiers. Although the issue of ethnic conflict falls outside this volume's ambit, several chapters provide a better understanding of the underlying issues that saw it reach unprecedented levels before and after the Second World War.

The present volume maintains that the Great Powers' interest in promoting Ukraine's independence, and by extension defining its borders, was twofold. First, in their efforts to accrue economic benefits, the Great Powers often used Ukraine's territorial integrity as a bargaining chip. Second, Ukraine's sovereignty came to be instrumental in the Great Powers' ideological battle with Bolshevik Russia.

Indeed, access to Ukraine's vast resources did much to drive border-making processes and to shape what borders "meant" to local inhabitants. Ukraine had long been the "breadbasket" of imperial Russia, and for the Soviet Union, it was still that; the desire to secure Ukraine's fertile black soil was a major reason why the Soviets engineered a famine in Ukraine in 1932–33, and why Hitler invaded Russia in 1941 (in search of *Lebensraum*).[131] Even before these events, however, Ukraine's economic potential had long shaped processes of border-making and the actual meaning of borders for those living in the frontier regions. In this volume, Chernev shows how Ukraine's abundant resources led the Central Powers to recognize Ukrainian statehood during the First World War. The Central Powers faced severe food shortages during the war; those shortages threatened to ignite revolutions in Germany and the Hapsburg Monarchy; so they recognized Ukraine's independence out of an urgent need for Ukrainian grain to stave off defeat in the war and revolution in its aftermath.[132] Likewise, Bruski posits that the outcome of the Polish-Ukrainian negotiations in 1920 was very much a function of the Ukrainian government's readiness to ensure and protect the legal status of Polish landowners. The privileged status of the Polish landed nobility in Right-Bank Ukraine also defined how this area was perceived in the Polish imagination, as Kwiecińska maintains. Similarly, Ardeleanu highlights that access to both the Black Sea and the Danube was imprinted onto the borders of Southern Bessarabia.

When we turn to how the borders of Soviet Ukraine were shaped, we find that the Soviet government was aware of bonds of language and heritage and paid some heed to them. But when it came to drawing actual borders between Soviet republics, economic considerations were paramount, including desire to maximize access to natural resources.

As early as October 1920, Stalin observed that "central Russia, that hearth of the world revolution, cannot hold out long without the assistance of the border regions, which abound in raw materials, fuel and foodstuffs."[133] Similarly, Lev Kamenev, another Bolshevik leader, underscored the importance of access to raw materials: "The communist society in Moscow cannot be built without establishing a fair relationship with those peoples living around the Donets [coal] basin, or around Baku oil, or Siberian bread, or steppe pastures."[134] The hard lessons learned during the Russian Civil War compelled the Soviet government to reassess its position on the national question and redefine the center/periphery relationship, so that in the end, it conceded a separate status to Soviet Ukraine.[135]

Voronovici highlights that control over resources defined discussions surrounding the formation of the MASSR in 1924, as well as the Moldovan Soviet Socialist Republic during the war years. Charron shows that economic development and integration with mainland Ukraine shaped debates on the territorial status of Crimea. Markowski highlights that economic necessity underpinned border negotiations between the Soviet and Polish communist governments.

At the macro-level, the territorial definition of ethically mixed regions was defined by all-Union economic interests, whereas at the local level, border debates were informed by local communities' access to fields and forests. In his examination of the Russian-Ukrainian border, Rindlisbacher maintains that borders running through some frontier regions were decided based on economic and administrative necessity rather than linguistic and national-ethnographic bonds, with each side attempting to improve its local economic base at the expense of its neighbours. Moreover, borders between Soviet republics did not always correspond with land use – indeed, exchanges of land between border villages remained commonplace until 1991. These small yet frequent alterations contributed to the porousness of the internal Soviet borders, often weakening their meaning in the eyes of local communities.[136]

Competing ideologies also contributed greatly to border-making, as several chapters demonstrate. Much like the Poles, who sought to "civilize" Eastern Galicia, the Soviet government operated within a colonialist trope, pledging to fight backwardness and to modernize the country. These views often underpinned the debate over highly contested regions, such as Transcarpathia, as Kovalchuk's contribution to this volume maintains.

Parallel to this, in the years immediately after the revolution, Ukraine's borders sometimes served as an extension of Moscow's ambition to export the socialist revolution. Several scholars have pointed out that international considerations partly drove the Soviet nationalities policy of *korenizatsiia*.[137] In this context, Ukraine's borders were partly shaped by the Soviet government's desire to create a positive impression among foreigners and to foster international sympathy for the regime. This might in turn attract Ukrainians living in adjacent countries to the socialist cause, while simultaneously destabilizing neighbouring governments. This argument appeared most prominently in the case of Moldova. Voronovici builds on recent historiography to claim that the Bessarabian question gained particular importance for Soviet leaders as they strove to export the revolution to Central Europe and the Balkans by way of Romania.[138] They saw a Moldovan republic playing a crucial international role, not least in weakening Romanian influence in the region. Similar reasoning lay behind Soviet support for the Ukrainian national movement in Polish-controlled Volhynia, as Hladyshuk demonstrates. The region, increasingly regarded as a springboard to Poland, featured prominently in the Bolshevik agenda of the time.

Albeit for a limited time, the strength of the Ukrainian lobby was yet another factor shaping modern Ukraine. The creation of a national Ukrainian government, short-lived though it was, strengthened the Ukrainian project. Ukraine's success in negotiating with the Central Powers at Brest-Litovsk is fairly well-known, yet the Ukrainian government's role in defining the border with Belarus has been largely overlooked. In her study of the negotiations over the Ukrainian-Belarusian border in 1918, Michaluk contends that the resultant border became one of the oldest and most enduring lines of political and administrative division in Eastern Europe.

No less important was the Ukrainian lobby within Soviet institutions. It is commonly believed that border-making in the Soviet Union was exclusively in the hands of the central Communist leadership in Moscow.[139] But as the contributions to this volume make clear, the situation on the ground, at least in the early 1920s, was far more complex. During the crucial decade of the 1920s, the Soviet Ukrainian government, though it had a limited decision-making authority compared to that of Moscow, was instrumental in defining its borders with the other Soviet republics. The strength of the Ukrainian lobby, reinforced by the *korenizatsiia* policy, became especially apparent during the delineation of the Russo-Ukrainian border. Not only did Ukrainian negotiators lay claims on Kursk and Voronezh provinces (much as had the UNR), but they also expressed interest in the Briansk and the Kuban regions, populated mainly by Ukrainian-speaking Cossacks, as Rindlisbacher tells us. While most of these demands for Russian territories were ignored in favour of the "principle of administrative order,"[140] Kharkiv came to play a more significant role in establishing the "Moldovan" territory. Voronovici highlights the importance of republican-level institutions in Soviet Ukraine in devising and later defining the borders of the MASSR.

The decision-making power of Soviet Ukraine was significantly curtailed only as a result of Stalin's "Great Break," which meant that any future territorial alterations would be decided exclusively in Moscow. This was the case with the territorial definition of Transcarpathia; the transfer of the Crimean *oblast* of the RSFSR to Soviet Ukraine in 1954, which symbolically marked the 300th anniversary of the Pereiaslav Council (the Ukrainian Cossacks' decision to ally with Moscow in 1654);[141] and the territorial and population exchanges with Poland in the late 1940s and early 1950s.

Lastly, physical factors played a role. States, Ukraine included, looked to balance national and strategic interests in the pursuit of strong "natural borders" such as seas, rivers, and mountain ranges. Ukraine's founding fathers had this in mind when they defined the extent of the Ukrainian homeland: several of its territories were situated around or in close proximity to historically contested regions, such as the Sea of Azov, the Danube, and Carpathia. At the same time, as Ardeleanu demonstrates in his chapter on the Danubian border, much of the discord related to the challenge of creating borders in a delta region whose physical geography was fluid, whose geopolitical symbolism ran deep, whose economic relevance was great.[142]

Present-day Ukraine was once a frontier region between three empires, each of which left its own legacy. With the disintegration of these Great Powers, the governments of the new nation-states laid claim to the same territories by appealing to history, nostalgia, and a sense of local identity, often resorting to military force in order to draw, or revise, inter-state borders. These "memory wars" have proven especially tangible along Ukraine's western border, as Hladyshuk, Kovalchuk, and Ardeleanu all demonstrate. The drawing of Ukraine's border with the former Soviet republics posed a different kind of challenge. A territory and people that, in both imperial Russian and Soviet narratives, was often presented as a singular whole, was subsequently divided among competing governments after of the First World War and again after the collapse of the Soviet Union.[143] Rindlisbacher, Charron, and Voronovici all show how difficult it was to negotiate the border, especially since all-Union and republic-level interests frequently clashed.

All of the contributors to this volume demonstrate how history and memory can foment disputes between Ukraine and its neighbours. This is particularly apparent in light of the current conflict with Russia. Unresolved historical problems and conflicting national memories have been equally relevant to the shaping of Ukraine's relations with its other neighbours. Regarding Poland, one might recall the Polish-Ukrainian inter-ethnic conflict during and shortly after the Second World War, described by Timothy Snyder as an early example of ethnic cleansing in the twentieth century, and recently defined by the Polish parliament as genocide.[144] This is equally apparent in the Romanian context, wherein the legacy of the 1939 German-Soviet Pact has solidified as the contested issue. That pact's territorial arrangements thwarted Romanian ambitions to gain control over the Black Sea continental shelf around Serpents Island.[145]

This volume is unique in its comprehensive overview of the making of the Ukrainian borders across regions and differing time periods. The contributors cover a diverse set of (trans)national contexts, focusing mainly but not exclusively on the critical years 1917 to 1954. Although its primary aim is to dissect the complex and non-linear project of making modern Ukraine, the chapters' broad geographical and thematical coverage highlights the fact that the dynamics of contemporary border formation cannot be fully understood with reference to any one particular state, border, or ideology. Nowhere does this appear more applicable than in the competing historical narratives used to define Ukraine's borders. The broad palette of national schools and historiographical traditions represented by the contributors makes it a distinctive scholarly endeavour. In this regard, the history of Ukraine's borders elucidates a shared history of territory and state formation in both Europe and the wider modern world.

NOTES

1 The Constitution of the Autonomous Republic of Crimea was adopted on 6 May 1992 and lost its validity on 17 March 1995: https://zakon5.rada.gov.ua/krym/show/rb076a002-92.
2 This query was issued on 12 May 2014 following the referendum held on 11 May 2014: https://www.dp.ru/a/2014/05/12/Doneckaja_respublika_provo/?ShortUrl=a%2F2014%2F05%2F12%2FDoneckaja_respublika_provo.
3 On the contemporary border between Ukraine and Russia, see Taras Kuzio, "Borders, Symbolism and Nation-State Building: Ukraine and Russia," *Geopolitics and International Boundaries* 2 (1997): 36–56; Tatiana Zhurzhenko, *Borderlands into Bordered Lands – Geopolitics of Identity in Post-Soviet Ukraine* (Stuttgart: ibidem-Verlag, 2010); Tatiana Zhurzhenko, "Ukraine's Border with Russia before and after the Orange Revolution," http://www.heeresgeschichtlichesmuseum.at/pdf_pool/publikationen/ukraine_zerissen_zw_ost_u_west_m_malek_ukraines_border_t_zhurzhenko.pdf; Tatiana Zhurzhenko, "Cross-border Cooperation and Transformation of Regional Identities in the Ukrainian-Russian Borderlands: Towards a Euroregion 'Slobozhanshchyna'?," *Nationalities Papers* 32, no. 1 (2004): 207–32, and no. 2 (2004): 497–514.
4 Helsinki Final Act of 1 August 1975: https://www.osce.org/helsinki-final-act.
5 *The Charter of Paris for a New Europe of 21 November 1990*, https://www.osce.org/mc/39516.
6 Memorandum on Security Assurances in Connection with Ukraine's Accession to the Treaty on the Non-Proliferation of Nuclear Weapons: https://www.securitycouncilreport.org/atf/cf/%7B65BFCF9B-6D27-4E9C-8CD3-CF6E4FF96FF9%7D/s_1994_1399.pdf.
7 See, for example: BBC, "Crimea Seen as 'Hitler-style' Land Grab," 7 March 2014, https://www.bbc.com/news/world-europe-26488652; Reuters, "German Minister Compares Putin's Ukraine Moves to Hitler in 1938," 31 March 2014, https://www.reuters.com/article/us-ukraine-russia-germany-idUSBREA2U0S420140331; Pavlo Solod'ko, "Putin – Uchen' Hitlera" [Putin – Hitler's disciple], 21 December 2018, http://texty.org.ua/d/2018/putler.
8 Karl Schlögel, *Ukraine: A Nation on the Borderland* (London: Reaktion Books, 2018), 13.
9 In this, the present volume differs significantly from some transnational histories of East-Central Europe, as well as histories of everyday life that analyze how the Soviet Union's (and Soviet Ukraine's) borders were

sometimes subverted through international travel and smuggling, through the transfer of ideas across borders over the radio and television, and so on. On this, see William Jay Risch, ed., *Youth and Rock in the Soviet Bloc: Youth Cultures, Music, and the State in Russia and Eastern Europe* (Lanham: Lexington Books, 2015); Anne E. Gorsuch, *All This Is Your World: Soviet Tourism at Home and Abroad after Stalin* (Oxford: Oxford University Press, 2011); Sergei Zhuk, *Soviet Americana: The Cultural History of Russian and Ukrainian Americanists* (London: Bloomsbury, 2018); Zbigniew Wojnowski, *The Near Abroad: Socialist Eastern Europe and Soviet Patriotism in Ukraine, 1956–1985* (Toronto: University of Toronto Press, 2017); Zbigniew Wojnowski, "The Pop Industry from Stagnation to Perestroika: How Music Professionals Embraced Economic Reform That Broke East European Cultural Networks," *Journal of Modern History* 92, no. 2 (2020): 311–50; and Zbigniew Wojnowski, "An Unlikely Bulwark of Sovietness: Cross-Border Travel and Soviet Patriotism in Western Ukraine, 1956–1985," *Nationalities Papers* 43, no. 1 (2015): 82–101; Anne Appelbaum, *Iron Curtain: The Crushing of Eastern Europe, 1944–1956* (New York: Doubleday, 2012).

10 George Liber, *Total Wars and the Making of Modern Ukraine, 1914–1954* (Toronto: University of Toronto Press, 2016)

11 The authors agree with Benedict Anderson's maxim that modern nations are in fact imagined communities. See Anderson, *Imagined Communities. Reflections on the Origin and Spread of Nationalism* (London: Verso, 1983).

12 Quoted from Rok Stergar and Tamara Scheer, "Ethnic Boxes: The Unintended Consequences of Habsburg Bureaucratic Classification," *Nationalities Papers* 46, no. 4 (2018), 580. Also on the census: Alexander Pinwinkler, *Historische Bevölkerungsforschungen: Deutschland und Österreich im 20. Jahrhundert* (Göttingen: Wallstein, 2014); Wolfgang Göderle, "Administration, Science, and the State: The 1869 Population Census in Austria-Hungary," *Austrian History Yearbook* 47 (2016): 61–88; Juliette Cadiot, "Searching for Nationality: Statistics and National Categories at the End of the Russian Empire (1897–1917)," *The Russian Review* 64, no. 3 (2005): 440–55; Jerzy Tomaszewski, *Rzeczpospolita wielu narodów* (Warsaw: Czytelnik, 1985).

13 Dmytro Bahalii, *Istoriia Slobids'koï Ukraïny* (Kharkiv: Del'ta, [1917] 1993); Johannes Remy, *Brothers or Enemies: The Ukrainian National Movement and Russia from the 1840s to the 1870s* (Toronto: University of Toronto Press, 2016), 20.

14 Selected scholarship on the Ukrainian national movement in the Russian empire: Fedir Savchenko, *Zaborona ukraïnstva 1876 roku* (Kyiv and

Kharkiv: DVU, 1930; repub. Munich: Suchasnist', 1970); Zenon Kohut, "The Development of a Little Russian Identity and Ukrainian Nation Building," *Harvard Ukrainian Studies* 10, nos. 3–4 (1986): 565–76; David Saunders, "Russia and Ukraine under Alexander II: The Valuev Edict of 1863," *International Historical Review* 17, no. 1 (1995): 23–50; David Saunders, "Russia's Ukrainian Policy (1847-1905): A Demographic Approach," *European History Quarterly* 25, no. 2 (1995): 181–220; Andreas Kappeler, "Einleitung," in *Die Russen: Ihr Nationalbewustsein in Geschichte und Gegenwart*, ed. Kappeler (Cologne: Markus 1990); Andreas Kappeler, *Russland und die Ukraine: Verflochtene Biographien und Geschichten* (Vienna: Böhlau, 2012); Andreas Kappeler, "The Ukrainians of the Russian Empire, 1860–1914," in *The Formation of National Elites: Comparative Studies on Governments and Non-Dominant Ethnic Groups in Europe, 1850–1940*, vol. 6, ed. Andreas Kappeler (in collaboration with Fikret Adanir and Alan O'Day) (New York: NYU Press, 1992), 105–22; Alexei Miller, *The Ukrainian Question: The Russian Empire and Nationalism in the Nineteenth Century* (Budapest: CEU Press, 2003); Serhii Plokhy, *The Origins of the Slavic Nations: Premodern Identities in Russia, Ukraine, and Belarus* (Cambridge: Cambridge University Press, 2006); Serhii Iekelchyk, *Ukraïnofily: Svit ukraïns'kykh patriotiv druhoï polovyny XIX stolittia* (Kyiv: KIS, 2010); Serhiy Bilenky, *Romantic Nationalism in Eastern Europe: Russian, Polish, and Ukrainian Political Imaginations* (Stanford: Stanford University Press, 2012); Faith Hillis, *Children of Rus': Right-Bank Ukraine and the Invention of a Russian Nation* (Ithaca: Cornell University Press, 2014).

15 Miller, *The Ukrainian Question*.
16 Hillis, *Children of Rus'*.
17 Remy, *Brothers or Enemies*; George S.N. Luckyj, *Young Ukraine: The Brotherhood of Saints Cyril and Methodius, 1845–1847* (Ottawa: University of Ottawa Press, 1991).
18 Fabian Baumann, "Diverging Paths: The Shul'gin/Shul'hyn Family and the Emergence of Rivalling Nationalisms in Late Imperial Kiev" (PhD diss., University of Basel, 2020); Fabian Baumann, "Nationality as Choice of Path: Iakov Shul'gin, Dmitrii Pikhno, and the Russian-Ukrainian Crossroads," in *Kritika: Explorations in Russian and Eurasian History* (forthcoming).
19 On the role of elites in nation-making, see Kappeler, *The Formation of National Elites*.
20 Roman Szporluk introduced a paradigm of the "making, unmaking, and remaking" of nations. Roman Szporluk, "Ukraine: From an Imperial Periphery to a Sovereign State," *Daedalus* 126, no. 3 (1997): 85–119. Serhii

Plokhy extends his maxim that that "one nation's fall is another nation's rise" to the realm of imperial and national identities and historical narratives. See Serhii Plokhy, *Unmaking Imperial Russia: Mykhailo Hrushevsky and the Writing of Ukrainian History* (Toronto: University of Toronto Press, 2005).

21 Serhii Plokhy, "Ukraine or Little Russia? Revisiting an Early Nineteenth-Century Debate," *Canadian Slavonic Papers/Revue canadienne des slavistes* 48, nos. 3–4 (2006): 335–53.

22 Zenon Kohut, *Russian Centralism and Ukrainian Autonomy: Imperial Absorption of the Hetmanate, 1760s–1830s* (Cambridge, MA: Harvard Series in Ukrainian Studies, 1988); Frank E. Sysyn, "The Khmel'nyts'kyi Uprising: A Characterization of the Ukrainian Revolt," *Jewish History* 17, no. 2 (2003): 115–39; John Basarab, *Pereiaslav 1654: A Historiographical Study* (Edmonton: Canadian Institute of Ukrainian Studies Press, 1982); Serhii Plokhy, *The Cossacks and Religion in Early Modern Ukraine* (Oxford: Oxford University Press, 2001).

23 Plokhy, *The Origins*, 344–5.

24 For texts of the Eyewitness Chronicle, see *Litopys Samovydtsia* (Kyiv: Naukova Dumka, 1971); for the Hrabianka Chronicle, see Hryhorij Hrabjanka, *"The Great War of Bohdan Xmel'nyc'kyj"* (Cambridge, MA: Harvard University Press, 1990). For a scholarly edition of the first volume of the Velychko Chronicle, see *Samiila Velychka Skazaniie o voini kozatskoi z poliakamy*, ed. Kateryna Lazarevska (Kyiv: Drukarnia UAN, 1926); the complete text was published under the title *Letopis sobytii v Iugo-Zapadnoi Rossii v XVII veke*, 4 vols. (Kyiv, 1848–64).

25 Plokhy, *The Origins*, 346. On the Cossack Chronicles, see Plokhy, *The Origins*, chapter 8; Frank E. Sysyn, "The Cossack Chronicles and the Development of Modern Ukrainian Culture and National Identity," *Harvard Ukrainian Studies* 14, nos. 3–4 (1990): 593–607.

26 Serhii Plokhy, *The Cossack Myth: History and Nationhood in the Age of Empires* (Cambridge: Cambridge University Press, 2012).

27 Plokhy, *The Cossack Myth*, 3.

28 The memory of Cossacks was thereafter mobilized by rival nation-building projects. See Frank Sysyn, "The Changing Image of the Hetman: On the 350th Anniversary of the Khmel'nyts'kyi Uprising," *Jahrbücher für Geschichte Osteuropas* 46, no. 4 (1998): 531–45; Frank Sysyn, "Grappling with the Hero: Hrushevs'kyi Confronts Khmel'nyts'kyi," *Harvard Ukrainian Studies* 22 (1998): 589–609; Amelia M. Glaser, ed., *Stories of Khmelnytsky: Competing Literary Legacies of the 1648 Ukrainian Cossack Uprising* (Stanford: Stanford University Press, 2015).

29 Plokhy, *The Cossack Myth*, 5.
30 Samiilo Velychko's *Skazanie* was republished in 1854, and then again in the crucial years of national awakening 1926, 1986, and 1991. This proves the centrality of the Cossack myth for the reconstruction of historical consciousness. See Sysyn, *Cossack Chronicles*.
31 Volodymyr Lobodaiev, *Revoliutsiina stykhiia. Vilnokozachyi rukh v Ukraïni 1917–18 rr.* (Kyiv: Tempora, 2010).
32 O.W. Gerus, "Manifestations of the Cossack Idea in Modern History: The Cossack Legacy and Its Impact," *Ukrains'kyi istoryk* 1–2 (1986): 22–39; Frank Sysyn, "The Reemergence of the Ukrainian Nation and Cossack Mythology," *Social Research* 58, no. 4 (1991): 845–64; Christopher Gilley, "Fighters for Ukrainian Independence? Imposture and Identity among Ukrainian Warlords, 1917–22," *Historical Research* 90, no. 247 (2017): 172–90.
33 See the contribution of Stephan Rindlisbacher to this volume.
34 For a thorough analysis of the prevalent "tropes" in the Ukrainian historiography from the eighteenth century to the present, see Andrii Portnov, Tetiana Portnova, Serhii Savchenko, and Viktoriia Serhiienko, "Whose Language Do We Speak? Some Reflections on the Master Narrative of Ukrainian History Writing," *Ab Imperio* 4 (2020): 88–129.
35 Nikolai Karamzin, *Istoriia Gosudarstva Rossiiskogo* (St Petersburg, 1816–29).
36 Szporluk, "Ukraine," 95.
37 Serhiy Bilenky, ed., *Fashioning Modern Ukraine: Selected Writings of Mykola Kostomarov, Volodymyr Antonovych, and Mykhailo Drahomanov* (Toronto: CIUS Press, 2013).
38 Plokhy, *Unmaking Imperial Russia*, 153-55.
39 John A. Armstrong, "Myth and History in the Evolution of Ukrainian Consciousness," in *Ukraine and Russia in Their Historical Encounter*, ed. Peter J. Potichnyj, Marc Raeff, Jaroslaw Pelenski, Gleb N. Zekulin (Edmonton: Canadian Institute of Ukrainian Studies Press, 1992): 128.
   The first modern synthesize of Ukrainian history, however, was authored by Oleksandra Yefymenko, whose overview "of Southern Rus' history," albeit first published in 1906, had been submitted more than five years earlier to the Kyiv-based journal *Kievskaia Starina*. See Portnov et al., *Whose Language*, 122–4; Andreas Kappeler, *Russland und die Ukraine: Verflochtene Biographien und Geschichten* (Vienna: Böhlau Verlag, 2012).
40 On the role of Hrushevskyi, see Plokhy, *Unmaking Imperial Russia*; Szporluk, "Ukraine"; Viktoriia Serhiienko, "'Official History' for a Stateless Nation: Mykhailo Hrushevsky's *Illustrated History of Ukraine*," in *Official*

History in Eastern Europe, ed. Korine Amacher, Andrii Portnov, and Viktoriia Serhiienko (Osnabrück, 2020), 15–38.
41 Plokhy, *Unmaking Imperial Russia*, 5.
42 Szporluk, "Ukraine," 98.
43 Roman Horbyk and Olena Palko, "Righting the Writing: The Power Dynamic of Soviet Ukraine Language Policies and Reforms in the 1920s–1930s," *Studi Slavistici* 14 (2017): 67–89; Andrij Hornjatkevych, "The 1928 Ukrainian Orthography," in *The Earliest Stage of Language Planning: The "First Congress" Phenomenon*, ed. J.A. Fishman (Berlin and New York: Mouton de Gruyter, 1993), 293–304; Ivan Ohiienko, *Narysy z istoriï ukraïns'koï movy: Systema ukraïns'koho pravopysu* (Warsaw: s.l., 1927; Kyiv: NBU im. Iaroslava Mudroho, 2018).
44 On the evolution of the term *narod* in imperial Russia, see Nathaniel Knight, "Ethnicity, Nationality, and the Masses: Narodnost' and Modernity in Imperial Russia," in *Russian Modernity: Politics, Knowledge, Practices*, ed. David Hoffmann and Yanni Kotsonis (London: Macmillan, 2000), 41–66. On similar processes in the Balkans, see Samuel Foster, *Yugoslavia in the British Imagination: Peace, War, and Peasants before Tito* (London: Bloomsbury, 2021).
45 Anton Kotenko, "Do pytannia pro tvorennia ukrainskoho natsionalnoho prostoru v zhurnali 'Osnova,'" *Ukraïns'kyi Istorychnyi Zhurnal* (hereafter *UIZ*) 2 (2012): 42–57; Anton Kotenko, "Ukraine's First Ethnographic Map: Made in the Russian Empire," *Nationalities Papers* 48, no. 5 (2020): 931–941.
46 Quoted in Kotenko, "Ukraine's First Ethnographic Map," 935.
47 Kotenko, "Ukraine's First Ethnographic Map," 932.
48 *Trudy etnografichesko-statisticheskoi ekspeditsii v Zapadno-Russkii Krai, snariazhennoi Imperatorskim Russkim Geograficheskim Obshchestvom. Iugo-Zapadnyi otdel. Materialy i issledovaniia*, 7 vols. (St Petersburg: Imperatorskoe Russkoe Geograficheskoe Obshchestvo, 1872–8).
49 Francine Hirsch, *Empire of Nations: Ethnographic Knowledge and the Making of the Soviet Union* (Ithaca: Cornell University Press, 2005), 33. On imperial experts and their role in preserving the empire, see Nathaniel Knight, "Science, Empire, and Nationality in the Russian Geographical Society, 1845–1855," in *Imperial Russia: New Histories for the Empire*, ed. Jane Burbank and David L. Ransel (Bloomington: Indiana University Press, 1998), 108–41; David W. Darrow, "Census as a Technology of Empire," *Ab Imperio* 4 (2002): 145–76; Robert Geraci, "Ethnic Minorities, Anthropology, and Russian National Identity on Trial: The Multan Case, 1892–96," *The Russian Review* 59, no. 4 (2000): 530–54; Joseph Bradley,

Voluntary Associations in Tsarist Russia: Science, Patriotism, and Civil Society (Cambridge, MA: Harvard University Press, 2009), esp. chapter 3 on the RGO, 86–127; Vytautas Petronis, *Constructing Lithuania: Ethnic Mapping in Tsarist Russia, ca. 1800–1914* (Stockholm: Stockholm University, 2007).

50 Anton Kotenko, "The Ukrainian Project: In Search of National Space, 1861–1914" (PhD diss., CEU, 2013), 109; Johannes Remy, "The Ukrainian National Movement and Poland from the 1840s to the 1870s," *Przegląd Wschodni* 14, no. 3 (2017), 535–64. On the role of the "Polish Question" in the development of the Russian national idea, see also Hillis, *Children of Rus'*; Mikhail Dolbilov and Alexei Miller, eds., *Zapadnye okrainy Rossiiskoi imperii* (Moscow: NLO, 2006); Daniel Beauvois, *La bataille de la terre en Ukraine: les polonais et les conflits socio-ethniques* (Lille: Septentrion, 1998); Darius Staliūnas, *Making Russians: Meaning and Practice of Russification in Lithuania and Belarus after 1863* (Amsterdam: Rodopi, 2007).

51 On the region, see Kate Brown, *A Biography of No Place: Ethnic Borderland to Soviet Heartland* (Cambridge, MA: Harvard University Press, 2004).

52 The 1903 instruction for the Governor of Vilna suggested the following equivalents that could be used to reconstitute national composition: Orthodox were Russians, Catholics were Poles or Lithuanians, Protestants were Germans, and *Iudeii* were Jews. See Cadiot, *Searching for Nationality*, 444.

53 Chubinskii, *Trudy etnograficheckо-statisticheskoi ekspeditsii*. vol. 7.1, 281–9. His main theses appeared in the calendar of the South-Western region for 1873, designed for the wider audience: V. Borisov and P. Chubinskii, eds., *Kalendar' Iugo-Zapadnogo Kraia na 1873 god* (Kyiv, 1872): 58–66.

54 Chubinskii, *Trudy etnograficheckо-statisticheskoi ekspeditsii*. vol. 7.2, 454.

55 Kotenko, "The Ukrainian Project," 122.

56 Robert Kaiser, "Geography and Nationalism," in *Encyclopaedia of Nationalism*, ed. Alexander Motyl, vol. 1, 315–33 (San Diego: Academic Press, 2000), 316; Robert Kaiser, *The Geography of Nationalism in Russia and the USSR* (Princeton: Princeton University Press, 1994). On the link between territory and nationalism, see also Jan Penrose, "Nations, States and Homelands: Territory and Territoriality in Nationalist Thought," *Nations and Nationalism* 8, no. 3 (2002): 277–97; Anne Godlewska and Neil Smith, eds., *Geography and Empire* (Oxford: Blackwell, 1994).

57 Catherine T. Dunlop, *Cartophilia: Maps and the Search for Identity in the French–German Borderland* (Chicago: University of Chicago

Press, 2015), 4. On the importance of border-making for the formation of national identity, see the classic study of Peter Sahlins, *Boundaries: The Making of France and Spain in the Pyrenees* (Berkeley: University of California Press, 1989). On the role of mapmaking in the construction of national, religious, and cultural identities in Russia, see Valerie Kivelson, *Cartographies of Tsardom: The Land and Its Meanings in Seventeenth-Century Russia* (Ithaca: Cornell University Press, 2006); Steven Seegel, *Mapping Europe's Borderlands: Russian Cartography in the Age of Empire* (Chicago: University of Chicago Press, 2012); Steven Seegel, *Ukraine under Western Eyes: The Bohdan and Neonila Krawciw Ucrainica Map Collection* (Cambridge, MA: HURI, 2013); Maciej Górny, *Kreślarze ojczyzn: Geografowie i granice międzywojennej Europy* (Warsaw: Instytut Historii PAN, 2017).
58 This was the research question posed by Paul Robert Magocsi when defining the territorial extent of "Rusyny" settlement. See Paul Robert Magocsi, "Mapping Stateless Peoples: The East Slavs of the Carpathians," *Canadian Slavonic Papers/Revue canadienne des slavistes* 39, nos. 3–4 (1997): 301–31.
59 Dunlope, *Cartophilia*, 7. See also Mark Monmonier, *How to Lie with Maps* (Chicago: University of Chicago Press, 1992); as applied to Ukraine: Roman Szporluk, "*Mapping Ukraine*: From Identity Space to Decision Space," *Journal of Ukrainian Studies* 33–4 (2008–9): 441–52.
60 Thongchai Winichakul, *Siam Mapped: A History of the Geo-Body of Siam*, 310, quoted in Anderson, *Imagined Communities*, 173–4.
61 Szporluk, "Mapping Ukraine," 447.
62 Stepan Rudnytsky is one of five "map men" whose intellectual biography was scrutinized by Steven Seegel, *Map Men: Transnational Lives and Deaths of Geographers in the Making of East Central Europe* (Chicago: University of Chicago Press, 2018). See also Górny, *Kreślarze ojczyzn*. Due to his role in Ukrainian nation-building, Rudnytsky has received significant scholarly attention in independent Ukraine, See N.O. Radvans'ka, ed., *Ukraïna prostovora v kontseptsiinomu okreslenni Stepana Rudnyts'koho* (Kyiv: Ukraïns'ka Vydavnycha Spilka, 2003); Oleh Shablii, *Akademik Stepan Rudnyts'kyi: Fundator ukraïns'koï heohrafii*, 2nd ed. (Lviv: Vydavnychyi Tsentr LNU im. Ivana Franka, 2007); Pavlo Shtoiko, *Stepan Rudnyts'kyi, 1887–1937: Zhyttepysno-bibliohrafichnyi narys* (Lviv: NTSh, 1997). In those accounts, the paradigm of national historiography prevails, however. For a similar approach to Rudnytsky in Western historiography, see Ihor Stebelsky, "Putting Ukraine on the Map: The Contribution of Stepan Rudnyts'kyi to Ukrainian Nation-building,' *Nationalities Papers* 39, no. 4 (2011): 587–613; and its revised and expanded version, *Placing Ukraine*

on the Map: Stepan Rudnytsky's Nation-Building Geography (Kingston: Kashtan Press, 2014).
63 Stepan Rudnyts'kyi, *Osnovy zemleznannia Ukraïny* (Prague: Vydavnytstvo Ukraïns'koho Universytetu u Prazi, 1923), i–ii.
64 Serhii Yekelchyk, "Review of Ihor Stebelsky, *Placing Ukraine on the Map: Stepan Rudnytsky's Nation-Building Geography*," *Canadian Slavonic Papers/Revue canadienne des slavistes* 59, nos. 3–4 (2017): 406–8.
65 Stephan Rudnyc´kyj, *Ukraina: Land und Volk* (Vienna: Verlag des Bund zur Befreiung der Ukraina, 1916); Stephen Rudnitsky, *Ukraine, the Land, and Its People: An Introduction to Its Geography* (New York: Rand McNally, 1918).
66 On the Soviet policy toward pro-Soviet émigrés and the relationship between the émigrés and the Bolsheviks during the 1920s, see Christopher Gilley, *The "Change of Signposts" in the Ukrainian Emigration: A Contribution to the History of Sovietophilism in the 1920s* (Stuttgart: ibidem-Verlag, 2009).
67 Seegel, *Map Men*, 24.
68 Stepan Rudnyts'kyi, "Ohliad natsional'noï terytoriï Ukraïny," in *Chomu my khochemo samostiinoï Ukraïny* (Lviv: Svit, 1994), 210.
69 Stepan Rudnyts'kyi, *Korotka heohrafiia Ukraïny* (Kyiv: Lan, 1910), 6.
70 Rudnyts'kyi, *Chomu my khochemo*, 36.
71 Stebelsky, *Putting Ukraine on the Map*, 601.
72 When criticizing the timid demands of the Ukrainian delegation to Paris, Rudnyts'kyi cited *Mémoire sur l'indépendance de l'Ukraine présenté à la Conférence de la paix par la Délégation de la République ukrainienne* (Paris: Imp. Robinet-Houtaix, 1919).
73 Stepan Rudnyts'kyi, *Ohliad natsional'noï terytoriï Ukraïny* (Berlin: Ukraïns'ke Slovo, 1923). Reprinted in *Chomu my khochemo*, 209–70.
74 Seegel, *Map Men*, 54.
75 Rudnyts'kyi, *Chomu my khochemo*, 39.
76 For such accounts, see Grzegorz Rossolinski-Liebe, "Racism and Modern Antisemitism in Habsburg and Russian Ukraine: A Short Overview," in *Modern Antisemitisms in the Peripheries: Europe and Its Colonies, 1880–1945*, ed. Raul Cârstocea and Éva Kovács (Vienna and Hamburg: New Academic Press, 2019), 133–59.
77 Per Anders Rudling, "Eugenics and Racial Anthropology in the Ukrainian Radical Nationalist Tradition," *Science in Context* 32, no. 1 (2019), 67–91, 32; Olga Linkiewicz, "Applied Modern Science and the Self-Politicization of Racial Anthropology in Interwar Poland," *Ab Imperio* 2 (2016): 179–80.
78 Yekelchyk, "Review," 407.

79 Volodymyr Kubiiovych, *Heohrafiia Ukraïny i sumezhnykh zemel'* (Krakiv and Lviv: Ukraïns'ke vydavnytstvo, 1943), 3.
80 Seegel, *Map Men*, 111.
81 Per Anders Rudling, *The OUN, the UPA, and the Holocaust: A Study in the Manufacturing of Historical Myths* (Pittsburgh: Carl Beck Papers, 2011), 5.
82 On Kubiiovych's political involvement and cooperation with the Nazis, see Paweł Markiewicz, "Volodymyr Kubijovych's Ethnographic Ukraine: Theory into Practice on the Western 'Okraiiny,'" *Jahrbücher für Geschichte Osteuropas* 64 (2016): 228–59; Markiewicz, "Historical Memory and Interpretation – the Question of Collaboration in World War II and How to Deal with It," http://www.pac1944.org/featured-stories/historical-memory-and-interpretation-the-question-of-collaboration-in-world-war-ii-and-how-to-deal-with-it; Tarik Cyril Amar, *The Paradox of Ukrainian Lviv: A Borderland City between Stalinists, Nazis, and Nationalists* (Ithaca: Cornell University Press, 2015); Per Anders Rudling, "'The Honor They So Clearly Deserve': Legitimizing the Waffen-SS Galizien," *Journal of Slavic Military Studies* 26 (2013): 114–37.
83 Mark von Hagen, "The Great War and the Mobilization of Ethnicity in the Russian Empire," in *Post-Soviet Political Order: Conflict and State Building*, ed. Barnett R. Rubin and Jack Snyder (London: Routledge, 1998), 34–54. On periodization of the national movements, see Miroslav Hroch, *Social Preconditions of National Revival in Europe: A Comparative Analysis of the Social Composition of Patriotic Groups among the Smaller European Nations* (Cambridge: Cambridge University Press, 1985). See also Alexander Maxwell, "Twenty-five Years of A-B-C: Miroslav Hroch's Impact on Nationalism Studies," *Nationalities Papers* 38, no. 6 (2010): 773–6; and Alexander Maxwell, "Typologies and Phases in Nationalism Studies: Hroch's A-B-C Schema as a Basis for Comparative Terminology,' *Nationalities Papers* 38, no. 6 (2010): 865–80; as well as Hroch's response: "Comments," *Nationalities Papers* 38, no. 6 (2010): 881–90. For the application of Hroch's scheme to the history of the Ukrainian national movement, see Andreas Kappeler, "Die ukrainische Nationalbewegung im Russischen Reich und in Galizien: Ein Vergleich," in Kappeler, *Der schwierige Weg zur Nation Beiträge zur neueren Geschichte der Ukraine* (Vienna: Böhlau Verlag, 2003), 70–87; "Die ukrainische und litauische Nationalbewegung im Vergleich," in *Der schwierige Weg*, 88–98; and Paul Robert Magocsi, "The Ukrainian National Revival: A New Analytical Framework," *Canadian Review of Studies in Nationalism* 16, nos. 1–2 (1989): 45–62; Szporluk, "Ukraine."

84 A comprehensive review of the vast literature on the Ukrainian Revolution and the many historiographical debates is beyond the scope of this volume. For classic studies, see: Volodymyr Vynnychenko, *Vidrozhdennia natsiï*, 3 vols. (Kyiv and Vienna: Dzvin, 1920), Dmytro Doroshenko, *Istoriia Ukraïny 1917–1923 rr.* (New York: Bulava, 1954); Pavlo Khrystiuk, *Zamitky i materiialy do istoriï ukraïns'koï revoliutsiï 1917–1920* (New York: Vydavnytsvo Chartoryis'kykh, 1969). For some recent studies, see Vitalii Smolii et al., *Narysy istoriï ukraïns'koï revoliūtsiï 1917–1921 rokiv*, 2 vols. (Kyiv: Naukova dumka, 2011); Volodymyr Soldatenko, *Ukraïna v revoliutsiinu dobu: Istorychni ese-khroniky: U 4-kh tomakh* (Kyiv: Svitohliad, 2010). For the historiographical debates, see Marko Bojcun, "Approaches to the Study of the Ukrainian Revolution," *Journal of Ukrainian Studies* 24, no. 1 (1999): 21–38; John-Paul Himka, "The National and Social in the Ukrainian Revolution of 1917–20: The Historiographical Agenda," *Archiv für Sozialgeschichte* 34 (1994): 95–110; John S. Reshetar, ed., *The Ukrainian Revolution, 1917–1920: A Study In Nationalism* (Princeton: Princeton University Press, 1972); Stephen Velychenko, *State-Building in Revolutionary Ukraine: A Comparative Study of Governments and Bureaucrats, 1917–22* (Toronto: University of Toronto Press, 2011); Taras Hunczak, ed., *The Ukraine, 1917–1921: A Study in Revolution* (Cambridge, MA: HURI, 1977).

85 "Third Universal of the Ukrainian Central Rada," in *Ukraïns'ka Tsentral'na Rada. Dokumenty i materialy*, ed. Vladyslav Verstiuk (Kyiv: Naukova Dumka, 1996), 1:398–401. The English translation is in Hunczak, *Ukraine*, 382.

86 On the early history of the Soviet regime in Ukraine, see Vsevolod Holubnychy, "Outline History of the Communist Party of Ukraine," in *Soviet Regional Economics: Selected works of Vsevolod Holubnychy*, ed. Iwan S. Koropeckyj (Edmonton: CIUS Press, 1982); Moisei Ravich-Cherkasskii, *Istoria Kommunisticheskoi Partii (bov) Ukrainy* (Kharkov: Gosizdat Ukrainy, 1923); Ivan Maistrenko, *Istoriia Komunistychnoï Partiï Ukraïny* (Munich: Suchasnist', 1979); Mykola Popov, *Narys Istoriï Komunistychnoï Partiï (Bil'shovykiv) Ukraïny* (Kharkiv: DVU, 1928); Stanislav Kul'chyts'kyi, *Komunism v Ukraïni: Pershe desiatylittia (1919–1928)* (Kyiv: Osnovy, 1996); Jurij Borys, *The Russian Communist Party and the Sovietization of Ukraine: A Study in the Communist Doctrine of the Self-Determination of Nations* (Stockholm: Norstedt, 1960); Arthur Adams, *The Bolsheviks in the Ukraine: The Second Campaign, 1918–1919* (New Haven: Yale University Press, 1963).

87 Some recent studies on the German interest in Ukraine: Caroline Milow, *Die ukrainische Frage 1917–1923 im Spannungsfeld der europäischen Diplomatie* (Wiesbaden: Harrassowitz Verlag, 2002); Wolfram Dornik and Stefan Karner, "Die Besatzhung der Ukraine 1918 durch Österreichisch-Ungarische Truppen," in *Die Besatzung der Ukraine 1918: Historischer Kontext, Forschungsstand, wirtschaftliche und soziale Folgen*, ed. Wolfram Dornik and Stefan Karner (Graz, Vienna, and Klagenfurt: Verein zur Förderung der Forschung von Folgen nach Konflikten und Kriegen, 2008), 141–80; Wolfram Dornik, ed., *Die Ukraine zwischen Selbstbestimmung und Fremdherrschaft, 1917–1922* (Graz: Leykam, 2011); Oleh S. Fedyshyn, *Germany's Drive to the East and the Ukrainian Revolution, 1917–1918* (New Brunswick: Rutgers University Press, 1971); and Frank Golczewski, *Deutsche und Ukrainer, 1914–1939* (Paderborn: Schöningh, 2010).

88 On the separate peace negotiations, see Fedyshyn, *Germany's Drive to the East*, 60–86; Borislav Chernev, *Twilight of Empire: The Brest-Litovsk Conference and the Remaking of East-Central Europe, 1917–1918* (Toronto: University of Toronto Press, 2017), 126–38.

89 Magocsi, *A History of Ukraine*, 515–16.

90 On the history of the Hetmanate, see Taras Hunczak, "The Ukraine under Hetman Pavlo Skoropadsky," in Hunczak, *Ukraine*, 61–81; Mark von Hagen, "'I Love Russia, and/but I Want Ukraine,' or How a Russian General Became Hetman of the Ukrainian State, 1917–1918," *Journal of Ukrainian Studies* 29, nos. 1–2 (2004): 115–48. For a first-hand account of the events, see Pavlo Skoropads'kyi, *Spohady (kinets' 1917–hruden' 1918)*, ed. Iaroslav Pelens'kyi (Kyiv and Philadelphia: Instytut ukraïns'koï arkheohrafiï ta dzhereloznavstva im. M.S. Hrushevs'koho NAN Ukrainy, 1995); Immo Rebitschek, "Statebuilding under Occupation: Pavlo Skoropadsky's Hetmanate in 1918," *Revolutionary Russia* 32, no. 2 (2019): 226–50; Mikhail Akulov, "The Third Path or An Imperial Roundabout? Skoropadsky's Ukraine, Technocrats, and the 'Great Russian Lobby'" (forthcoming in *Jahrbücher für Geschichte Osteuropas*, 2022).

91 Gilley, *Fighters for Ukrainian Independence*; A.E. Adams, "The Great Ukrainian Jacquerie," in Hunczak, *Ukraine*, 247–70; Frank Sysyn, "Nestor Makhno and the Ukrainian Revolution," in Hunczak, *Ukraine*, 271–304; G. Kasianov, "Die Ukraine zwischen Revolution, Selbständigkeit und Fremdherrschaft," in Dornik, *Die Ukraine*, 131–79; Serhy Yekelchyk, "Bands of Nation Builders? Insurgency and Ideology in the Ukrainian Civil War," in *War in Peace: Paramilitary Violence in Europe after the Great War*, ed. R. Gerwarth and J. Horne (Oxford: Oxford University Press, 2012), 52–71; Felix Schnell, *Räume des Schreckens: Gewalt und Gruppenmilitanz in der Ukraine, 1905–33* (Hamburg: Hamburger Edition, 2012).

92 For the most recent scholarship on the Warsaw Agreement, see the special issue of *Przegląd Wschodni*, 16, no. 1:61 (2020). For the vast scholarship on Polish-Soviet as well as Polish-Ukrainian relations during the civil war, see Jan Jacek Bruski's contribution to this volume.
93 Sysyn, *Nestor Makhno*, 277.
94 Chernev, *Twilight of Empire*, 165–6.
95 Jan Jacek Bruski, *Między prometeizmem a Realpolitik*, II, *Rzeczpospolita wobec Ukrainy sowieckiej, 1921–1926* (Krakow: Historia Iagellonica, 2010), also available in English translation as *Between Prometheism and Realpolitik: Poland and Soviet Ukraine, 1921–1926* (Krakow: Jagiellonian University Press, 216)
96 On Prometheanism in Polish foreign policy, see Marek Kornat, "Idea prometejska a polska polityka zagraniczna (1921–1939/40)," in *Ruch prometejski i walka o przebudowy Europy Wschoniej 1918–1940* (Warsaw: Instytut Historii PAN, 2012), 35–90; Kornat, "Prometeizm – pol's'ka viziia perebudovy Skhidnoi Ievropy (1921–1939)," *Ukraina Moderna* 17, no. 6 (2010): 131–48; Bruski, *Między prometeizmem*; Andrzej Nowak, "Józef Piłsudski, A Federalist or an Imperialist?" in *History and Geopolitics: A Contest for Eastern Europe*, ed. Andrzej Nowak (Warsaw: Polish Institute for Foreign Affairs 2008), 169–86.
97 For a critical assessment of the cult of *sobornist'* (understood as the unification of all "ethnographically Ukrainian" lands) in the Ukrainian national project, see Portnov et al., *Whose Language*, 107–13.
98 M. Dnistrians'kyi, *Kordony Ukraïny: Terytorial'no-administratyvnyi ustrii* (Lviv: Svit, 1992); Vasyl' Boiechko, Oksana Hanzha, and Borys Zakharchuk, *Kordony Ukraïny: Istorychna retrospektyva ta suchasnyi stan* (Kyiv: Osnovy, 1994); Hennadii Iefimenko and Stanislav Kul'chyts'kyi, "Kordony derzhavni Ukrainy, pryntsypy i istorychna praktyka ikh vstanovlennia," in *Entsyklopediia istoriï Ukraïny*, 10 vols. (Kyiv: Naukova Dumka, 2008), 5: 137–48.
99 Vasyl' Boiechko, Oksana Hanzha, and Borys Zakharchuk, "Kordony Ukraïny: istoriia ta problem formuvannia (1917–1940)," *UIZ* 1 (1992): 56–77.
100 Volodymyr Serhiichuk, *Etnichni mezhi i derzhavnyi kordon Ukraïny* (Kyiv: PP Serhiichuk M.I., 2008). Serhiichuk is a well-established scholar in Ukraine, known for his publications of archival sources. Nonetheless, as Jared McBride suggests, Serhiichuk may not always have the best command of the sources he includes in his documentary collections. See: Jared McBride, "To Be Stored Forever" [Book review of Taras Bul'ba-Borovets': Dokumenty. Statti. Lysty, ed. Volodymyr Serhiichuk (Kyiv, 2011)], *Ab*

Imperio 1 (2012): 434–45. For similar criticism of Serhiichuk's approach, see Hennadii Iefimenko, "Pro osoblyvosti 'istoryko-statystychnoho' metodu vid Volodymyra Serhiichuka," http://www.historians.in.ua/index.php/en/dyskusiya/2838-gennadij-efimenko-pro-osoblivosti-istoriko-statistichnogo-metodu-vid-volodimira-sergijchuka.

101 Kyrylo Halushko et al., *Narodzhennia kraïny. Vid kraiu do derzhavy. Nazva, symvolika, terytoriia i kordony Ukraïny* (Kharkiv: Klub simeinoho dozvillia, 2016).

102 http://likbez.org.ua/ua. Their review: Iryna Vushko, "Historians at War: History, Politics and Memory in Ukraine," *Contemporary European History* 27, no. 1 (2018): 112–24.

103 In her detailed analysis of the Likbez initiative, Yulia Yurchuk shows that the historians involved in the project from the very beginning of the Ukrainian-Russian conflict regarded their profession as a tool in warfare and positioned themselves as civic activists who strived to influence the situation. Thus, Likbez is a political campaign that presented history as a matter of security. It was conceived as a tool for debunking Russian propaganda myths and opposing them with popular history narratives that would align with their securitization strategy. Although the historians involved in the project claim that all Likbez publications undergo peer review, they do not follow traditional academic standards: academic writing references are absent, and only a list of recommended literature is provided. See Yuliya Yurchuk, "Historians as Activists: History Writing in Times of War: The Case of Ukraine in 2014–2018," *Nationalities Papers* 49, no. 4 (2020): 691–709.

104 Leonid Gorizontov, ed., *Regiony i granitsy Ukrainy v istoricheskoi retrospektive* (Moscow: Institut Slovianovedeniia RAN, 2005).

105 On Belarus: Leonid Spatkai, *Rubtsy na tele Belarusi. Kogda i kak izmenialis' granitsy nashykh gosudarstv* (Moscow: Izdatel'skie resheniia, 2018); Serhei Khomich, *Territoriia i gosudarstvennyie granitsy Belarusi v XX veke* (Minsk: Ekonompress, 2011). On Moldova, see A.M. Lazarev, *Moldavskaia sovetskaia gosudarstvennost' i bessarabskii vopros* (Kishinev: Cartea Moldovenească, 1974); Vasyl' Boiechko, "Utvorennia Moldavs'koï Avtonomnoï Sotsialistychnoï Radians'koï Respubliky i 'bessarabs'ke pytannia,'" *Problemy istoriï Ukraïny: Fakty, sudzhennia, poshuky* 3 (1994): 25–32; Alexandr Voronovici, "Justifying Separatism: The Year 1924, the Establishment of the Moldovan ASSR, and History Politics in the Transnistrian Moldovan Republic," *Euxeinos: Governance and Culture in Black Sea Region* 15–16 (2014): 104–17; Voronovici, "The Ambiguities of Soviet 'Piedmonts': Soviet Borderland Policies in the

Ukrainian SSR and the Moldovan ASSR, 1922–1934" (PhD diss., CEU, Budapest, 2016); and Marcel Mitrasca, *Moldova: A Romanian Province under Russian Rule: Diplomatic History from the Archives of the Great Powers* (New York: Algora, 2002).

106 Petr Eberhardt, *Polska i jej granice. Z historii polskiej geografii politycznej* (Lublin: Wydaw. Uniwersytetu Marii Curie-Skłodowskiej, 2004); Peter Eberhardt, "Koncepcje granic państwa polskiego u progu odzyskania niepodległości," *Studia z Geografii Politycznej i Historycznej* 4 (2015): 9–35; Roman Wapiński, *Polska i małe ojczyzny Polaków* (Wrocław–Warszawa–Kraków: Zakład Narodowy im. Ossolińskich, 1994). See also Janusz Kowalczyk, "Granica Polsko-Ukrainska w XX wieku," *Przeglad Geopolityczny* 2 (2010): 153–68.

107 C. Jankowski, *Polska etnograficzna* (Warszawa: B. Wierzbicki, 1914); W. Wakar, "Program terytorialny," *Polska. Pismo Poświęcone Zagadnieniom Ideologii Patriotycznej* 2 (1917): 6–16; 4 (1917): 14–16; 5 (1917): 15–16; W. Wakar, *Rozwój terytorialny narodowości Polskiej*, 3 vols. (Warszawa-Kielce: Wydawnictwo Biura Pracy Społecznej, 1917–18).

108 Michał Klimecki, *Polsko-ukraińska wojna o Lwów i Wschodnią Galicję 1918–1919 r. Aspekty polityczne i wojskowe* (Warsaw: Wojskowy Instytut Historyczny, 1997); Ludwik Mroczka, *Spor o Galicje Wschodnia 1914–23* (Krakow: Wydawnictwo Naukowe WSP, 1998); Benjamin Conrad, *Umkämpfte Grenzen, umkämpfte Bevölkerung: Die Entstehung der Staatsgrenzen der Zweiten Polnischen Republik, 1918–1923* (Stuttgart: Franz Steiner Verlag, 2014); Christoph Mick, *Lemberg, Lwów, L'viv, 1914–1947: Violence and Ethnicity in a Contested City* (West Lafayette: Purdue University Press, 2016).

109 N.A. Diakova and M.A. Chepelkin, eds., *Granitsy Rossii v XVII–XX vekakh. Prilozheniie k istorii Rossii* (Moscow: ShiK, 1995).

110 Elena Borisenok, "Ukraina i Rossiia: spor o granitsakh v 1920-e gody," in Gorizontov, *Regiony i granitsy*, 205–35; Elena Borisenok, "Volost' za volost', uezd za uezd. Vopros o granitsakh mezhdu USSR i RSFSR v 1920-e gody," *Rodina* 8 (1998): 111–15.

111 Hennadii Iefimenko, "Vyznachennia kordonu mizh USSR ta RSFRR," *Problemy istoriï Ukraïny* 20 (2011): 135–76.

112 Stephan Rindlisbacher, "From Space to Territory: Negotiating the Russo-Ukrainian Border, 1919–1928," *Revolutionary Russia* 31, no. 1 (2018): 86–106; as well as his contribution to this volume. See also Igor B. Torbakov, "Russian-Ukrainian Relations, 1917–1918: A Conflict over Crimea and the Black Sea Fleet," *Nationalities Papers* 24, no. 4 (1996): 679–90.

113 O. Boiko, "Problema vyznachennia kordoniv Ukraïny v period Tsentral'noï Rady (1917–1918 rr.)," *UIZ* 1 (2008): 31–46.
114 Iurii Galkin, ed., *Sbornik dokumentov o pogranichnom spore mezhdu Rossiei i Ukrainoi v 1920–1925 gg. za Taganrogsko-Shakhtinskuiu territoriiu Donskoi oblasti* (Moscow: Shcherbinskaia Tipografiia, 2007).
115 On postwar Soviet border-making, see: Tuomas Forsberg, ed., *Contested Territory: Border Disputes at the Edge of the Former Soviet Empire* (Aldershot: Edward Elgar, 1995); Alfred J. Rieber, *The Struggle for the Eurasian Borderlands: From the Rise of Early Modern Empires to the End of the First World War* (Cambridge: Cambridge University Press, 2014); David Wolff, "Stalin's Postwar Border-making Tactics: East and West," *Cahiers de Monde Russe* 52, nos. 2–3 (2011): 273–91; G. Murashko and A. Noskova, "Stalin and National-Territorial Controversies, Part I," *Cold War History* 1, no. 3 (2001): 161–72; Murashko and Noskova, "Stalin and National-Territorial Controversies, Part II," *Cold War History* 2, no. 1 (2001): 145–57. On western Ukraine, see Jan T. Gross, *Revolution from Abroad: The Soviet Conquest of Poland's Western Ukraine and Western Belorussia* (Princeton: Princeton University Press, 1988); Ola Hnatiuk, *Odwaga i strach* (Wroclaw: Wydawnictwo KEW, 2015); For the English translation see Hnatiuk, *Courage and Fear* (Boston: Academic Studies Press, 2019); Wlodzimierz Bonusiak, *Polityka ludnościowa i ekonomiczna ZSRR na okupowanych ziemiach Polskich w latach 1939–1941 ("Zachodia Ukraina" i "Zachodnia Bialorus")* (Rzeszow: Wydawnictwo Uniwersitetu rzeszowskieho, 2006). On Transcarpathia, see Paul Robert Magocsi, *The Shaping of a National Identity: Subcarpathian Rus', 1848–1948* (Cambridge, MA: Harvard University Press, 1978); Frantisek Nemec and Vladimir Moudry, *The Soviet Seizure of Subcarpathian Ruthenia* (Westport: Hyperion Press, 1981); Sabine Dullin, "How the Soviet Empire Relied on Diversity: Territorial Expansion and National Borders at the End of World War II in Ruthenia," in *Seeking Peace in the Wake of War Europe, 1943–1947*, ed. Stefan-Ludwig Hoffmann (Amsterdam: Amsterdam University Press, 2016), 217–46; Valentina Mar'ina, *Zakarpatskaia Ukraina (Podkarpatskaya Rus) v politike Benesha i Stalina. 1939–1945 gg.* (Moscow: Novyi Khronograf, 2003). For social and cultural histories of twentieth-century Ukraine that emphasize that the establishment of new western borders during the Second World War, preceded and accompanied by massive ethnic cleansing campaigns, was legitimated through the "Ukrainization" of the borderlands, see Amar, *The Paradox*; Brown, *A Biography of No Place*; Svetlana Frunchak, "Commemorating the Future in Postwar Chernivtsi," *East European Politics and Societies* 24, no. 3

(2010): 435–63; Frunchak, "The Making of Soviet Chernivtsi: National 'Re-unification,' World War II, and the Fate of Jewish Czernowitz in Postwar Ukraine" (PhD diss., University of Toronto, 2010); William Jay Risch, "A Soviet West: Nationhood, Regionalism, and Empire in the Annexed Western Borderlands," *Nationalities Papers* 43, no. 1 (2015): 63–81, Risch, *The Ukrainian West: Culture and the Fate of Empire in Soviet Lviv* (Cambridge, MA: Harvard University Press, 2012).

116 Gwendolyn Sasse, *The Crimea Question: Identity, Transition, and Conflict* (Cambridge, MA: Harvard University Press, 2007); Sasse, "The Crimean Issue," *Journal of Communist Studies and Transition Politics* 12, no. 1 (1996): 83–100; David R. Marples and David F. Duke, "Ukraine, Russia, and the Question of Crimea," *Nationalities Papers* 23, no. 2 (1995): 261–89; Mikhail Smirnov, "Like a Sack of Potatoes: Who Transferred the Crimean Oblast to the Ukrainian SSR in 1952–54 and How It Was Done," *Russian Politics and Law* 53, no. 2 (2015) 32–46; Paul Robert Magocsi, *This Blessed Land: Crimea and the Crimean Tatars* (Toronto: University of Toronto Press, 2014); Kerstin S. Jobst, *Geschichte der Krim: Iphigenie und Putin auf Tauris* (Berlin: De Gruyter Oldenbourg, 2020); Stanislav Kul'chyts'kyi and Larysa Iakubova, *Kryms'kyi vuzol* (Kyiv: Klio, 2018); Zbigniew Wojnowski, "Soviet Identity Politics in Ukrainian Crimea: Friendship of the Peoples and Internal Borders in the USSR between the 1950s and the 1980s," *Acta Slavica Iaponica* (2020): 125–48; Dmytro Hordiienko, "Crimea within or Outside the Ukrainian borders," *Nash Krym = Our Crimea = Bizim Qirimimiz* IV (2019): 5–49.

117 Terry Martin, *The Affirmative Action Empire: Nations and Nationalism in the Soviet Union, 1923–1939* (Ithaca: Cornell University Press, 2001), 31.

118 Borisenok, *Ukraina i Rossiia*, 206. See also Elena Borisenok, *Fenomen sovetskoi Ukrainizatsii, 1920-30-e gody* (Moscow: Evropa, 2006).

119 Snyder calls the UPA's conflict with the Poles, resulting in the Volhynia massacre, "one of the earliest examples of ethnic cleansing in the 20th century"; Timothy Snyder, *The Reconstruction of Nations: Poland, Ukraine, Lithuania, Belarus, 1569–1999* (New Haven,: Yale University Press 2003), 169; Snyder, "The Causes of Ukrainian-Polish Ethnic Cleansing," *Past and Present* 179, no. 1 (2003): 197–234; Snyder, "'To Resolve the Ukrainian Problem Once and for All': The Ethnic Cleansing of Ukrainians in Poland, 1943–1947," *Journal of Cold War Studies* 1, no. 2 (1999): 86–120. Also see Grzegorz Motyka, *Od rzezi Wołyńskiej do Akcji "Wisła": Konflikt Polsko-Ukraiński 1943–1947* (Krakow: Wydawnictwo Literackie, 2011); Ihor Il'iushyn, *UPA i AK: Protystoiannia u Zachidnii Ukraïni (1939–1945 rr.)* (Kyiv: Kyievo-Mohylians'ka Akademiia, 2009).

On forced population exchanges, see Catherine Gousseff, "Evacuation versus Repatriation: The Polish-Ukrainian Population Exchange, 1944–46," in *The Disentanglement of Populations: Migration, Expulsion and Displacement in postwar Europe, 1944–1949*, ed. Jessica Reinisch and Elizabeth White (London: Palgrave Macmillan, 2011), 91–111; Catherine Gousseff, *Échanger les Peuples – Le Déplacement des Minorités aux Confins Polono-Soviétiques (1944–1947)* (Paris: Fayard Histoire, 2015); Yurii Slivka, ed., *Deportatsii: Zakhidni zemli Ukraïny kintsia 30-kh- pochatku 50kh- rr. Dokumenty, materialy, spohady, vol. 1, 1939–1945* (Lviv: Natsional'na akademiia nauk Ukrainy, 1996); Jan Pisulinski, *Przesiedlenie ludności ukraińskiej z Polski do USRR w latach 1944– 1947* (Rzeszów: WUR, 2009); Grzegorz Motyka, "Postawy wobec konfliktu polsko-ukraińskiego w latach 1939–1953 w zależności od przynależności etnicznej, państwowej i religijnej," in *Tygiel narodów. Stosunki społeczne i etniczne na dawnych ziemiach Wschodnich Rzeczypospolitej 1939–1953*, ed. K. Jasiewicz (Warsaw-London: PAN- RYTM, 2002), 279–407; Eugeniusz Misiło, *Repatriacja czy deportacja. Przesiedlenie ukraińców z Polski do USRR 1944–1946, vol. 1: Dokumenty 1944–1945* (Warsaw: Archiwum Ukrainskie, 1996); Misiło, *Akcja "Wisła" 1947: Dokumenty i materiały* (Warsaw: Archiwum Ukraińskie, 2013); Keith Sword, *Deportation and Exile: Poles in the Soviet Union, 1939– 1945* (London: Macmillan, 1996); S.A. Makarchuk, "Pereselennia poliakiv iz zakhidnykh oblastei Ukraïny v Pol'shchu u 1944–1946 rr.," UIZ 3 (2003):.103–15. On instrumentalization of those issues in contemporary Ukraine and Poland, see David Marples, *Heroes or Villains? Creating National History in Contemporary Ukraine* (Budapest: CEU Press, 2013), 203–37.

120 M. Bril', *Osvobozhdennaia Zapadnaia Ukraina* (Moscow: Politizdat, 1940); V.Ia. Klokov, *Velikii osvoboditel'nyi pokhod Krasnoi Armii (Osvobozhdeniie Zapadnoi Ukrainy i Zapadnoi Belorussii)* (Voronezh: Veronezhskoe oblastnoe knigoizdatel'stvo, 1940); I. Trainin, *Natsional'noe i sotsial'noie osvobozdenie Zapadnoi Ukrainy i Zapadnoi Belorussii* (Moscow: Institut prava AN SSSR, 1939); T.S. Bilousov, *Vozz'ednannia ukraïns'koho narodu v iedynii ukrains'kii radians'kii derzhavi* (Kyiv: Vydavnytsvo AN URSR, 1951); H.I. Koval'chuk, Iu.Iu. Slyvka, and V.P. Chuhaiov, *Podiia velykoho istorychnoho znachennia* (Kyiv: Politvydav, 1979).

121 Milena Rudnyts'ka, ed., *Zakhidnia Ukraïna pid Bol'shevykamy IX. 1939– VI. 1941* (New York: NTSh, 1958); V. Kosyk, *Ukraïna i Nimechchyna u Druhii Svitovii Viini* (Paris, New York, and Lviv: NTSh u Lvovi, 1993).

The accounts of those émigré historians are often distorted due to their involvement in political events in Ukraine themselves. On nationalist predominance in émigré Ukrainian studies, see Rudling, *The OUN, the UPA*, esp. 19–20.

122 Stanislav Kul'chyts'kyi, "Koly i iak vidbulosia vozz'ednannia Zakhidnoï Ukraïny z USSR," *UIZ* 5 (2009): 121–39; Volodymyr Danylenko, "'Chetvertyi podil': Pol'shchi i vstanovlennia radians'koho totalitarnoho rezhymu v Zakhidnii Ukraïni," *Z Arkhiviv VUChK-HPU-NKVD-KGB* 22/23, nos. 1/2 –4 (2004): 59–79.

123 O.S. Rubliov and Iu. A. Chernenko, *Stalinshchyna i dolia zakhidnoukraïns'koï intelihentsii* (Kyiv: Naukova Dumka, 1990); I. Kozlovs'kyi, *Vstanovlennia ukraïns'ko-pol's'koho kordonu 1941–1951* (Lviv: Kameniar, 1998); M.R. Lytvyn, O.I. Luts'kyi, and K.Ie. Naumenko, *1939: Zakhidni zemli Ukraïny* (Lviv: Krytyka, 1999); Volodymyr Serhiichuk, *Pravda pro 'Zolotyi Veresen' 1939-ho roku* (Kyiv: Ukraïns'ka vydavnycha spilka, 1999); Kul'chyts'kyi, *Koly i iak vidbulosia vozz'ednannia*.

124 Gross, *Revolution from Abroad*; Timothy Snyder, *Black Earth: The Holocaust as History and Warning* (London: Bodley Head, 2015); Claudia Weber, *Der Pakt: Stalin, Hitler und die Geschichte einer mörderischen Allianz, 1939–1941* (Munich: C.H. Beck, 2019).

125 The term belongs to Peter Holquist; see Peter Holquist, *Making War, Forging Revolution: Russia's Continuum of Crisis, 1914–1921* (Cambridge, MA: Harvard University Press, 2002).

126 For more recent studies on the Versailles system, the League of Nations, and the minorities rights, see Mark Mazower, "Minorities and the League of Nations in Interwar Europe," *Daedalus* 126, no. 2 (1997): 47–63. Christian Raitz von Frentz, *A Lesson Forgotten: Minority Protection under the League of Nations: The Case of the German Minority in Poland, 1920–1934* (New York: LIT Verlag, 1999); Martin Scheuermann, *Minderheitenschutz contra Konfliktverhütung? Die Minderheitenpolitik des Völkerbundes in den zwanziger Jahren* (Marburg: Herder Institut, 2000); Carole Fink, *Defending the Rights of Others: The Great Powers, the Jews, and International Minority Protection, 1878–1938* (Cambridge: Cambridge University Press, 2004); Eric Weitz, "From the Vienna to the Paris System: International Politics and the Entangled Histories of Human Rights, Forced Deportations, and Civilizing Missions," *American Historical Review* 113 (2008): 1313–43. For a critical assessment of the scholarship on the League of Nations, see Susan Pedersen, "Back to the League of Nations," *American Historical Review* 112, no. 4 (2007):

1091–117. On the impact of the Versailles system on the status of the minority populations, see Olena Palko and Samuel Foster, "Introduction: Contested Minorities in the 'New Europe': National Identities in Interwar Eastern and Southeastern Europe," *National Identities* 23, no. 4 (2021).
127 See the essay by Elżbieta Kwiecińska in this volume.
128 On the links between nation-states, violence, and eventually genocide, see Mark Levene, "Creating a Modern Zone of Genocide: The Impact of Nation- and State-Formation on Eastern Anatolia, 1878–1923," *Holocaust and Genocide Studies* 12, no. 3 (1998): 393–433; Levene, *The Crisis of Genocide*, 2 vols. (New York: Oxford University Press, 2013); Karen Barkey and Mark von Hagen, *After Empire: Multiethnic Societies and Nation-Building: The Soviet Union and the Russian, Ottoman, and Habsburg Empires* (London: Routledge, 1997); Omer Bartov and Eric D. Weitz, *Shatterzone of Empires: Coexistence and Violence in the German, Habsburg, Russian, and Ottoman Borderlands* (Bloomington: Indiana University Press, 2012); Donald Bloxham, *The Final Solution: A Genocide* (New York: Oxford University Press, 2009). For a different treatment of nation-states as protectors of minorities, see Snyder, *Black Earth*. For the analysis of recent historiography, see Raz Segal, "The Modern State, the Question of Genocide, and Holocaust Scholarship," *Journal of Genocide Research* 20, no. 1 (2018): 108–33; Raul Cârstocea, "Historicising the Normative Boundaries of Diversity: The Minority Treaties of 1919 in a Longue Durée Perspective," *Studies on National Movements* 5, no. 37 (2020): 1–37.
129 Bartov and Weitz, *Shatterzone of Empires*, 2.
130 Rudling, *Eugenics and Racial Anthropology*, 68–9.
131 On the links between human-induced environmental catastrophes and mass violence in the modern world, see Snyder, *Black Earth*; Mark Levene and Daniele Conversi, "Subsistence Societies, Globalisation, Climate Change, and Genocide: Discourses of Vulnerability and Resilience," *International Journal of Human Rights* 18, no. 3 (2014): 281–97. See also Mark Levene, "From Past to Future: Prospects for Genocide and Its Avoidance in the Twenty-First Century," in *The Oxford Handbook of Genocide Studies*, ed. Donald Bloxham and A. Dirk Moses (New York: Oxford University Press, 2010), 638–59; Eagle Glassheim, *Cleansing the Czechoslovak Borderlands: Migration, Environment, and Health in the Former Sudetenland* (Pittsburgh: University of Pittsburgh Press, 2016); Ben Kiernan, *Blood and Soil: A World History of Genocide and Extermination from Sparta to Darfur* (New Haven: Yale University Press, 2009).
132 See the essay by Borislav Chernev in this volume.

133 Joseph Stalin, *Sochineniia* (Moscow, 1946–2006), 4: 351.
134 Quoted from Borisenok, *Fenomen*, 67.
135 Olena Palko, "Debating the Early Soviet Nationalities Policy: The Case of Ukraine," in *The Fate of the Bolshevik Revolution: Illiberal Liberation, 1917–1941*, ed. by James Harris, Lara Dauds, and Peter Whitewood (London: Bloomsbury, 2020), 157–72.
136 The internal borders between the Soviet republics gained particular meaning during the famine of 1932–33, when according to Stalin's directive of 22 January 1933, the borders of Ukraine and the North Caucasus were closed so that starving people would be unable to leave the republic. See, for example, Anne Applebaum, *Red Famine: Stalin's War on Ukraine* (New York: Doubleday, 2017); Stanislav Kulchytsky, *The Famine of 1932–1933 in Ukraine: An Anatomy of the Holodomor* (Edmonton: Canadian Institute of Ukrainian Studies Press, 2018); On the meaning of Soviet borders during the famine, see David R. Marples, "Ethnic Issues in the Famine of 1932–1933 in Ukraine," *Europe-Asia Studies* 61, no. 3 (2009): 505–18; Hiroaki Kuromiya, "The Soviet Famine of 1932–1933 Reconsidered," *Europe-Asia Studies* 60, no. 4 (2008): 663–75.
137 Terry Martin, "The Origins of Soviet Ethnic Cleansing," *Journal of Modern History* 70, no. 4 (1998): 813–61; Matthew D. Pauly, "Soviet Polonophobia and the Formulation of Nationalities Policy in the Ukrainian SSR, 1927–34," in *Polish Encounters, Russian Identity*, ed. David Ransel and Bozena Shallcross (Bloomington: Indiana University Press, 2005), 172–88; Alexandr Voronovici, "A Springboard for Revolution? The Establishment of the Moldovan ASSR and the Competing Visions of its International Revolutionary Role," in *New Europe College Yearbook: Pontica Magna Program, 2015–2017* (Bucharest: NEC, 2018), 337–65.
138 For more recent scholarship on Moldova, see Diana Dumitru and Petru Negură, eds., "Moldova: A Borderland's Fluid History," *Euxeinos – Culture and Governance in the Black Sea Region* 15 (2014).
139 For the Cold War–inspired scholarship that treated the Soviet Union as a multinational empire, "a prison of nations" that aimed at a highly centralized state and a unified Soviet people (*sovetskii narod*), see Robert Conquest, *The Last Empire* (London: Ampersand, 1962); Conquest, *Stalin: Breaker of Nations* (London: Weidenfeld and Nicolson, 1991); Hélène Carrère d'Encausse, *The Great Challenge: Nationalities and the Bolshevik State, 1917–1930* (New York: Holmes and Meier, 1992).
140 Hirsch, *An Empire of Nations*, 211.
141 Serhy Yekelchyk uses the example of the transfer of Crimea and its official justification to maintain that twentieth-century Russian and Ukrainian

national identities were projected onto the past. Serhy Yekelchyk, *Ukraine: Birth of a Modern Nation* (New York: Oxford University Press 2007), 154–5.
142 Also on this, see Constantin Ardeleanu, *The European Commission of the Danube, 1856–1948: An Experiment in International Administration* (Leiden: Brill, 2020), Ardeleanu, "Fishing in Politically Troubled Waters: The Fishermen of Vylkove: Romanian Nation-Making and an International Organization in the Danube Delta in the Late 1850s and Early 1860s," *Revue des études sud-est européennes* 55 (2017): 325–38.
143 The success of the project of constructing a unified Soviet identity remains highly debated. Although theorized in various ways, the role of ethnic identities in the future Soviet community was unclear. In the process of the supposed *sliianie* (merging) and *sblizheniie* (coming closer together) of ethnic groups, the "Soviet people" nevertheless was not conceived of as a *natsiia*, *narodnost'* or *natsional'nost'*. As Zbigniew Wojnowski claims, Soviet-ness was a contested and multifaceted identity. For some members of the political and cultural elites in Moscow, the "Soviet people" was often tantamount to ethnic Russians and an idealized vision of a conservative Russian culture. The process of reorienting toward nineteenth-century Russian culture has been examined by David Brandenberger. Whereas for the non-Russian intelligentsia, the "Soviet people" was not only a despised smokescreen for state-sponsored destruction of ethnic cultures (see Heorhii Kasianov), but also a set of institutions that cultivated ethnic languages and cultures (for example, see Serhy Yekelchyk). In approaching the subject of Soviet identity and culture, Martin builds an argument that from the 1920s onwards, the Soviet authorities attempted to decouple high culture and national identity; signs that it was working one can find in the aftermath of the Second World War. See: Heorhyi Kasianov, *Nezhodni: Ukraïns'ka intelihentsiia v rusi oporu 1960kh–80kh rokiv* (Kyiv: Lybid', 1995); Serhy Yekelchyk, *Stalin's Empire of Memory: Russian-Ukrainian Relations in the Soviet Historical Imagination* (Toronto: University of Toronto Press, 2004); D. Brandenberger and A. Dubrovsky, "'The People Need a Tsar': The Emergence of National Bolshevism as Stalinist Ideology, 1931–1941," *Europe-Asia Studies* 50, no. 5 (1998): 873–92; David Brandenberger, *National Bolshevism: Stalinist Mass Culture and the Formation of Modern Russian National Identity, 1931–1956* (Cambridge, MA: Harvard University Press, 2002); David Brandenberger and Kevin Platt, eds., *Epic Revisionism: Russian History and Literature as Stalinist Propaganda* (Madison: University of Wisconsin Press, 2006); Terry Martin, "Modernization of Neo-Traditionalism? Ascribed Nationality and Soviet

Primordialism," in *Russian Modernity*, 161–84. For the analysis of scholarship, see Zbigniew Wojnowski, "The Soviet People: National and Supranational Identities in the USSR after 1945," *Nationalities Papers* 43, no. 1 (2015): 1–7.

144 On the decision of the Polish Sejm, see https://www.sejm.gov.pl/Sejm8.nsf/komunikat.xsp?documentId=2D76E3019FA691C3C1257FF800303676. On the reaction of Ukraine: https://www.unian.info/politics/1432207-polish-sejm-labels-volyn-killings-genocide.html.

145 Romania initially refused to recognize its border with Ukraine unless Ukraine denounced the Molotov-Ribbentrop Pact. The Ukrainian side regarded this demand as a possibility for territorial claims, especially since the two countries had disputes over the continental shelf in the Black Sea around Serpents Island. Romania's wish to enter NATO speeded up the process of mutual recognition of borders. The most difficult part was to agree on the border with the Russian Federation. After numerous interstate treaties were signed, the border contestations between the two countries continued; especially disputed was the border in the Sea of Azov and the Kerch Straits. See Taras Kuzio, *Ukraine: State and Nation Building* (London and New York: Routledge, 2002), 100–18.

PART ONE

Negotiating Borders

Great Power Diplomacy and Ukraine's Borders

1

Ukraine's Borders at the Brest-Litovsk Peace Conference, 1917–18

Borislav Chernev

At two o'clock in the morning on 10 February 1918, representatives of the Central Powers (Germany, Austria-Hungary, the Ottoman Empire, and Bulgaria) signed the first peace treaty of the First World War at the half-burnt Russian fortress of Brest-Litovsk on the Bug River. This was not in the presence of their Russian counterparts, however, but with representatives of a brand-new state, the Ukrainian People's Republic (UNR). The treaty's provisions would be null and void within a year. "The wheel of history crushed it," Pavlo Khrystiuk, a contemporary politician and early historian of the Ukrainian Revolution, would later remark, "[but this] does not lessen [its] importance ... in the history of the Ukrainian people's struggle for national liberation and nation building."[1] The importance of the First Treaty of Brest-Litovsk for modern Ukrainian statehood is undeniable, and the fact that it came to pass is quite extraordinary. When the war began, no one foresaw the emergence of an independent Ukrainian state; as late as January 1917, almost no one did. Yet within months of the collapse of the imperial regime in Petrograd in February 1917, an autonomous and eventually fully independent Ukrainian republic had been established in the southwestern part of the defunct Russian Empire and was making bold territorial claims to the Ukrainian-speaking areas of neighbouring Austria-Hungary.

This chapter argues that the Brest-Litovsk Peace Conference played an important – and somewhat underappreciated – role in the making of Ukraine's contemporary borders. Border-making, which began at Brest-Litovsk and culminated at the Paris Peace Conference of 1919–20, was crucial to the process of territorializing ethnicity in East-Central Europe. The drawing of Ukraine's western borders at Brest-Litovsk proved particularly problematic, for Ukraine's national claims clashed with those of neighbouring Poland over the Kholm region and Habsburg-controlled Eastern Galicia. The negotiations also required the creation of a mental as well as physical map of Ukraine. This meant that by the end of the conference, the fledgling state had entered the European popular imagination with specific – if subject to constant revision – borders based on ethnic lines, an indispensable characteristic of a twentieth-century European nation-state.

Many studies about the Ukrainian Revolution have appeared since Ukraine re-emerged as an independent country in 1991. Notable among these have been Valerii Soldatenko and Vladislav Verstiuk's investigations into aspects of Ukrainian statehood in its various guises between 1917 and 1920; these authors pay special attention to the increasingly complicated relationship between Ukraine and Bolshevik Russia during that period.[2] Also, recent German-language studies of the Central Powers' intervention in Ukraine as it related to Ukrainian state-building have raised important questions about the periodization of the First World War in the east, the course of Soviet history between 1917 and 1922, and the international implications of Ukrainian statehood.[3] This chapter builds on these works by proposing a connection between Brest-Litovsk, the origins of modern Ukrainian statehood, and the first concerted attempt to define Ukraine's borders along ethnic lines.

THE CENTRAL POWERS AND UKRAINE BEFORE BREST-LITOVSK

After the First World War broke out, the Central Powers paid close attention to events in Dnieper Ukraine while attempting to foment revolution in the Russian Empire. This was part of a larger process of the imperial mobilization of ethnicity. That concept, first developed by Mark von Hagen in a groundbreaking article, points to the active involvement of the Romanov, Habsburg, and Hohenzollern imperial establishments in the very same nationalizing processes that contributed, inadvertently, to their own demise.[4]

Ukrainian elites on both sides of the Zbruch River participated in these same processes, which necessitated a mental delimitation of Ukraine's borders, which at this point were still somewhat vague. One illustration of this can be found in a detailed memorandum to the Austro-Hungarian Foreign Office that Metropolitan Andriy Sheptytsky, the long-time leader of the Ukrainian Greek Catholic, or Uniate, Church between 1901 and 1944, composed in August 1914.[5] This remarkable document discussed the organization of military, socio-legal, and ecclesiastical affairs in a future Ukrainian state, which would be separate from the Russian Empire and closely affiliated with Austria-Hungary. Basically, it envisioned the unification of Eastern Galicia with Dnieper Ukraine through the extension of the Greek Catholic Church's jurisdiction to all Ukrainian-populated territories and that church's transformation from a regional to a Ukrainian national institution that would serve as the foundation of Ukrainian national identity.

In the wake of the February Revolution of 1917, the Central Powers kept a keen eye on the territorial fragmentation of the Russian Empire and the emergence of the Central Rada (Council) in Kyiv. However, Berlin and Vienna remained ambivalent about Ukraine's independence – and hence its borders – as the overall military situation in the east remained uncertain. What is more, the collapse of the Russian Empire had the potential to spread west, which would have devastating consequences for the multinational Habsburg Monarchy in particular. Full-blown support for national revolution during what appeared to be a fluid, transitional phase (*Zwischenstadium*) in relations along Russia's western border (*Neuordnung der Verhältnisse an der russische Westgrenze*) would be hazardous at best – so warned the German Foreign Office as late as mid-December 1917.[6] The same office further argued that early recognition of Ukrainian independence would not be beneficial for Germany.[7] Yet as the Russian Empire continued to fragment, the question of borders became more and more pressing in the minds of diplomats.

The removal of the imperial centre in Petrograd had an immediate impact on nationalist activists in the borderlands, who began to demand greater national autonomy and cultural rights within the framework of a decentralized Russian federation. On 18 March, the Russian-language daily *Kievskaia mysl'* reported on a large gathering of various Ukrainian national organizations in Kyiv the previous day. Those groups duly created a Central Rada to serve as a local governing body. While recognizing the authority of the Provisional Government in Petrograd, the Rada immediately set about securing its own power base by arranging the return of exiled members of the Ukrainian intelligentsia, reopening the historic cultural society Prosvita (Enlightenment), and founding an official newspaper, *Rada*.[8] As the connection between the centre and the periphery grew increasingly tenuous over the following months, and the Bolsheviks overthrew the Provisional Government, the Rada proclaimed the existence of a sovereign Ukrainian People's Republic within a reorganized All-Russian Federation, which it wished to see created. So stated the so-called Third Universal of 20 November.[9]

However, the Central Powers chose to prioritize events in Petrograd, with the goal of knocking Russia out of the war so that they could transfer their forces to the Western and Italian fronts. In fact, Ukraine was not even mentioned in the policy conferences of early December held in Berlin, Kreuznach, and Vienna in the lead-up to Brest-Litovsk. Indeed, as Oleh S. Fedyshyn has pointed out, the negotiations between the Central Powers and the UNR reveal how improvised and reactive the Central Powers' entire *Ospolitik* (eastern policy) in 1917–18 really was.[10] It was Kyiv, not Berlin or Vienna, that initiated the negotiations that led to the Brest-Litovsk system.

EARLY EXCHANGES IN BREST-LITOVSK

After some hesitation, the Central Rada decided to dispatch a small delegation to the armistice negotiations, which arrived too late to participate in the talks. The Russian delegates treated the Ukrainians with suspicion and refused to share any of the details of the discussions. Subsequently, on 24 December the General Secretariat of the Central Rada resolved to send a full delegation to Brest-Litovsk, which would deal with the Central Powers separately. The four representatives arrived at Brest-Litovsk late on 1 January 1918. They had intended to steer a middle course, holding preliminary meetings with both sides. However, this proved impossible, as the Bolsheviks' goal of world revolution could not be reconciled with the Ukrainian quest for national statehood and clearly drawn borders. Keen observers were quick to notice this at the time. For instance, Colonel Dzhon Fokke, a military expert in the Russian delegation, wrote in his memoirs: "The conflict between the Ukrainian Rada and the Soviet delegation in Brest was inevitable by the very nature of things."[11]

So Kyiv quickly began to shape its foreign policy in opposition to that of Petrograd. In his memoirs, Volodymyr Vynnychenko, who served as prime minister of the UNR through most of the negotiations, remarked that the Ukrainian delegation's "proper, peaceful, and even friendly at times" behaviour was in sharp contrast to the hostile attitude of the Russians. He also asserted that Ukraine had wanted to secure the support of the Great Powers in order to buttress its national statehood and achieve appropriate borders.[12] This would entail incorporating all territories inhabited by native Ukrainian-speakers into the new state. Vynnychenko himself hoped for the backing of the Western Entente, but Britain and France were reluctant to offer any support, for they still hoped to keep Russia in the war. This meant that the Central Powers were Ukraine's only possible supporters.

Habsburg and Hohenzollern diplomats were quick to appreciate the benefits of separate negotiations with the Ukrainians, especially once they realized that the Bolsheviks intended to treat the negotiations as a staging ground for their cherished world revolution. Thus, a preliminary meeting between the two sides took place on the morning of 4 January, with Ambassador Friedrich Hans von Rosenberg of the German Foreign Office being the most senior diplomat of the Central Powers present. The Ukrainians affirmed that they would continue negotiating at the present location, even if the Russians failed to return after the ten-day adjournment. They hoped to do so as part of an All-Russian delegation, representing all successor states of the former Russian Empire, but this seemed unlikely, given that the Bolsheviks claimed to be the sole representatives of Russia.[13] Consequently, the leaders of the Austro-Hungarian and German delegations, Count Ottokar Czernin and Baron Richard von Kühlmann, decided to attend the second meeting later that day. They were keen to learn more about Ukraine's political and military situation and its relations with Russia. There was also the legal claim to sovereignty and Kyiv's willingness to conclude peace on the basis of non-interference in the Central Powers' domestic affairs. The latter was an especially sensitive point for the Austrians, who wished to avoid the fraught question of the Dual Monarchy's Ukrainian population in Galicia, Bukovina, and Trans-Carpathian or Ugric Rus.[14]

SETTLING UKRAINE'S JURIDICAL STATUS AND BORDERS

These preliminary meetings showed that the two sides could work together, and a formal session between delegations from the Central Powers and the UNR took place on 6 January. The most important item on the agenda was Ukraine's juridical sovereignty and, by extension, its borders. When the Ukrainians insisted that the Central Powers formally recognize their independent state, Kühlmann responded with three conditions. First, the negotiations should continue straight away. Second, there should be no interference in domestic affairs. Third, the Rada must sign all agreements concluded at the peace conference up to that point. The Ukrainian delegates were somewhat taken aback but agreed to consider these conditions before withdrawing.[15]

The ensuing incident very nearly brought the negotiations to a premature end. To make matters worse, the Central Powers could not agree among themselves whether to accept Ukrainian independence "purely and simply" or stick to their conditions. Uncharacteristically, the German and Habsburg chief diplomats found themselves disagreeing on this issue. While Kühlmann and the Bulgarian Minister of Justice embraced the "pure and simple" approach, Czernin, the Ottoman Foreign Minister, and the representative of the German High Command, Major-General Max von Hoffmann, argued that Ukraine should be treated as a confederate state of the Russian Republic for the time being. It took a second conference for a compromise of sorts to be reached. The Central Powers would prepare a joint declaration recognizing Ukraine's independence "purely and simply." However, they would keep this secret until a junior German diplomat persuaded the Ukrainians in private to accept the aforementioned conditions. The apparent unwillingness of the Central Powers to recognize the UNR as a fully independent entity did not go down at all well with the Ukrainian delegates, who were, of course, unaware of these private discussions. During dinner on 6 January, one of them even told the Bulgarian Minister of Justice that his delegation might choose to return to Kyiv and leave it to the Ukrainian people to secure their independence on their own.[16]

This impasse threatened to play into the hands of the Russian delegation, which in the meantime had returned to Brest-Litovsk led by the People's Commissar for Foreign Affairs, Leon Trotsky. Trotsky viewed the Rada's delegates with repugnance, dismissing them in his memoirs as "the Ukrainian variety of Kerenskyism and differed from their Great Russian prototype only in that they were even more provincial."[17]

Moreover, by this point the armed forces of Kyiv and Petrograd had been fighting in eastern Ukraine since the end of December. Tensions between the two combatants' delegations came to a head during the very first joint plenary session at Brest-Litovsk, on 10 January. Trotsky was visibly displeased when the Ukrainian State Secretary for Commerce and Industry, Vsevolod Holubovych, read out a lengthy note from the General Secretariat of the Central Rada that proclaimed the UNR to be a fully independent country. When questioned on this by Kühlmann, Trotsky had no alternative but to agree that "in full accord with the fundamental recognition of the right of self-determination of every nation, even to complete severance, [the Russian delegation] sees no obstacle to the participation of the Ukrainian Delegation in the peace negotiations."[18] But that did not end the matter. By pointedly using the term "the Ukrainian delegation" instead of "the delegation of the Ukrainian People's Republic," Trotsky had left the issue sufficiently open to allow him to recruit his own Ukrainian delegation representing the Ukrainian Soviet Republic, proclaimed in late December 1917 in Kharkiv.

THE EASTERN GALICIA AND KHOLM/CHEŁM TERRITORIAL DISPUTES

Trotsky's acknowledgment appeared to be a clear victory for the Ukrainian representatives, who could now move on to discuss Ukraine's borders. However, they were unhappy that the Central Powers had not immediately proffered an official vote of recognition. "They did not want to tie recognition to the conditions we gave them, not because they think the conditions are unfair, but because they consider this connection between the two an insult," the Bulgarian military representative wrote to Prime Minister Vasil Radoslavov on 11 January.[19] However, a private meeting between the German and Ukrainian delegates the following day delivered a mutually agreeable solution. The Central Powers would recognize the UNR as a fully independent state *de facto*, but *de jure* recognition "depends on the peace treaty [*bleibt dem Friedensvertrag vorbehalten*]."[20] Now that the vexatious question of Ukraine's juridical status had been resolved, surely the two sides would be able to conclude a swift peace in the face of Bolshevik intransigence.

It was Ukraine's borders that threatened to pose insuperable obstacles. As the representatives of an emerging nation, the Rada intended to incorporate all Ukrainian-inhabited territories into the new state. This included the four or so million Ukrainians living in the Habsburg lands of Eastern Galicia, Northern Bukovina, and Trans-Carpathian or Ugric Rus. To this end, the delegates seized on the idea of national self-determination, supposedly one of the guiding principles of the entire peace conference.[21] Holubovych raised this matter during a secret meeting with the Germans on 13 January, where he asked for the annexation of Eastern Galicia and Kholm/Chełm. A part of Congress Poland until 1912, the latter region, with its mixed Polish-Ukrainian population, was currently under Austro-Hungarian military administration as part of the Military Government Lublin. Perhaps, Holubovych added, Eastern Galicia might be evacuated in order to allow for the population to decide which state they would rather be part of. Naturally, Kühlmann refused to entertain the notion of bargaining with the territory of his country's closest ally.[22]

In the meantime, Count Czernin was suffering from one of his recurrent nervous breakdowns, his condition having been exacerbated by the latest dispatches from the Dual Monarchy on the outbreak of the so-called Great January Strike on 15 January. This explained why the Austro-Hungarian Foreign Minister did not wish to negotiate with the young Ukrainian delegates directly, even though that offered the best way out of the diplomatic quagmire. Fortunately for both sides, General Hoffmann decided to intervene, consulting with the Ukrainians privately. During that meeting, he agreed to the transfer of Kholm/Chełm but refused all Ukrainian claims to Eastern Galicia. "I looked upon the demand for Austrian-Hungarian territory as a piece of impudence and I gave the two men to understand as much, in a somewhat rough manner," he later wrote.[23] The Ukrainian negotiators promised to reconsider.

It is impossible to know with any certainty whether the Ukrainians truly thought they would be able to annex Eastern Galicia. The minutes from the meetings of the Rada and the General Secretariat offer little in the way of concrete information. What is more, ongoing struggles with the government's Hughes wireless apparatus significantly hampered communications between Kyiv and Brest-Litovsk. Considering how quickly they dropped their demands, one might deduce that the Ukrainians were prepared to abandon their claim from the very beginning, so long as the Austrians offered something in exchange. Hoffmann had a different explanation, writing that "it apparently had dawned upon the Rulers in Kyiv that the defeated side could not demand the cession of territory from the other party."[24] Regardless, by 16 January, they had accepted the proposed offer of free national, cultural, and political development for their Galician compatriots in Austria. Meanwhile, the Habsburgs agreed in secret to the creation of an autonomous Austrian crownland from the Ukrainian-majority regions of Eastern Galicia and Northern Bukovina – though not in Hungary (Trans-Carpathian or Ugric Rus).[25]

While this measure did not affect Ukraine's borders directly at the time of the peace conference, it would have significant implications for the future. First, in spite of all attempts at secrecy, it quickly became public knowledge. Second, it legitimated Ukrainian claims to these territories and ultimately contributed to the proclamation of a second Ukrainian state, the West Ukrainian People's Republic, at the end of the war.[26] The Ukrainians' focus on borders might appear odd, given that the Central Rada was in politically dire straits by the second half of January. The Bolsheviks' military advance from the north and east, led by Vladimir Antonov-Ovseenko, threatened the very existence of the UNR. However, clearly defined political and linguistic borders are of vital importance to successful nation-state-building: they are indispensable for defining the imaginary national community, especially in the multi-confessional, multi-ethnic, entangled spaces of East-Central Europe.[27]

A major purpose of border-making in Kholm/Chełm and Eastern Galicia was to clearly separate a Ukrainian national space from its Polish and

Russian counterparts. These efforts would continue, *mutatis mutandis*, during the early Soviet period. As Francine Hirsch has argued, the delimitation of the borders of the Soviet Union's constituent republics played an important role in the formation of Soviet national identities in the 1920s and 1930s, including that of Soviet Ukraine.[28]

Yet even the reduced demands for a Ukrainian crownland and the annexation of Kholm/Chełm placed Czernin in an extremely difficult spot. As previously noted, Kholm/Chełm had been part of Congress Poland before 1912, besides which it had a large Polish population. So the Poles considered it part of their national space, and this made them at least as sensitive as the Ukrainians to the political and cultural aspects of border-making. If the Habsburgs assigned Kholm/Chełm to Ukraine, they would lose Polish support overnight, which would make any future implementation of the Austro-Polish Solution extremely difficult.[29] Thus, any advantages to be gained from appeasing the Ukrainians would come at the cost of antagonizing the Poles, and vice versa.

However, Czernin had little room to manoeuvre. The Ukrainian negotiations between 15 and 20 January coincided with the worst phase of the Great January Strike in Austria, the purpose of which was to force a quick agreement at Brest-Litovsk and to relieve the Dual Monarchy's food crisis. Only peace with Ukraine, famously the breadbasket of the former Russian Empire, might achieve both. With the Dual Monarchy teetering on the brink of revolution, Czernin decided to prioritize negotiations with Ukraine over those with Russia, securing whatever concessions he could from the Austrian and Hungarian governments.[30]

To that end, the Foreign Minister asked Vienna to convene an Imperial Council to consider establishing an autonomous Ukrainian crownland. "The question of East Galicia I will leave to the Austrian Ministry; it must be decided in Vienna," Czernin wrote in his diary. "I cannot, and dare not, look on and see hundreds of thousands starve for the sake of retaining the sympathy of the Poles, so long as there is a possibility of help."[31] This was a sensible line of reasoning. Also, the Poles' pro-Habsburg sentiments were strictly transactional, resting largely on the fact that the monarchy was the most accommodating partitioning power – but a partitioning power, nonetheless. If the Central Powers won the war, Polish preferences would still lean toward the flexible Habsburgs rather than the more rigid Hohenzollerns. If they lost, the Poles would demand outright independence within the historical borders of the Polish-Lithuanian Commonwealth, as was to occur within a matter of months. With such deliberations in mind, Czernin returned to Vienna on 21 January.

The Imperial Council of 22 January proved a challenge for Czernin, who faced stern opposition from some of his fellow ministers. Nevertheless, the Austrian Prime Minister Ernst von Seidler reassured the Count that the government would obtain the two-thirds parliamentary majority required to implement the constitutional changes inherent in the establishment of a Ukrainian crownland, even if the Polish Club tried to block this action. However, the Hungarian Prime Minister Sándor Wekerle and Joint Finance Minister István Burián were firmly against such a proposal, arguing that "no external interference in the affairs of the Monarchy could be tolerated." This could set a dangerous precedent that might unravel the delicate inter-ethnic relations holding the Dual Monarchy together. Czernin had anticipated this Hungarian opposition and elaborated that only urgent shipments of Ukrainian grain could avert severe food shortages in Austria, especially since Hungary could not spare its own supplies. While the policy threatened unforeseen consequences, the foreign minister preferred "the risk of death to the certainty of the same." After much angry wrangling, the Imperial Council decided in favour of Czernin's proposal, acquiescing to the establishment of a Habsburg Ukrainian crownland.[32] By the time the Foreign Minister returned to Brest-Litovsk on 28 January, he was free to conclude a swift peace with Ukraine.

Clearly, the Great January Strike had forced the Habsburgs to offer unprecedented concessions. As it transpired, however, the Monarchy was far from the only country represented at the conference that was suffering from an increasingly fractious domestic climate. Petrograd's financial and military support of the Ukrainian Bolshevik uprising in eastern Ukraine had caused numerous problems for the Rada, which lacked reliable troops. In late January, Kyiv intercepted a message from Joseph Stalin, then the People's Commissar of Nationalities, to the leaders of the Ukrainian Soviet Government in Kharkiv, promising the transfer of two million rubles. "In case the bank refuses to honor it, arrest the staff," Stalin ordered. "This is not the time to whine, this is the time to act in a revolutionary manner!"[33] Meanwhile, Trotsky had instructed his Red Guards stationed along the Romanian frontier to do everything possible to undermine the Rada's hold on the local Ukrainianized forces.[34] Before long, the advance of the Bolshevik forces on multiple fronts had prompted the UNR's government to evacuate to the western town of Zhytomyr. Back in Brest-Litovsk, Trotsky seized the opportunity this presented and recruited two Ukrainian Bolsheviks, "voiceless and meaningless pawns," as one of the Russian military experts described them, to serve as delegates.[35] He then sent Kühlmann a note to the effect that the Rada had fallen, the Ukrainian

Soviets were now in control of the country, and their representatives would be joining the Russian delegation.[36]

FINAL NEGOTIATIONS AT BREST-LITOVSK

At this juncture, it was not just Ukraine's borders that appeared uncertain – Ukrainian national statehood itself was in jeopardy. The Rada desperately needed foreign military assistance against the Bolshevik onslaught, and the Central Powers were the only feasible option. Yet Berlin and Vienna needed *Ukrainian* support if they were to avoid the complete breakdown of the Brest-Litovsk negotiations and the potentially grave repercussions this could have on their respective home fronts. In these circumstances, it was Russian intransigence that bought the Central Powers and Ukraine together.

To accelerate the process, the Austrian and German delegations facilitated a showdown between Trotsky and the Rada, which duly took place on 2 February, when Mykola Liubinsky delivered a fiery speech denouncing the Bolsheviks.[37] This had a stunning effect on all those present. General Hoffmann described it as "an excellent speech,"[38] and Czernin gave the following account of it in his diary entry for the day:

> I have tried to get the Ukrainians to talk over things openly with the Russians and succeeded almost too well. The insults hurled by the Ukrainians to-day against the Russians were simply grotesque and showed what a gulf is fixed between the two Governments. Trotsky was so upset it was painful to see. Perfectly pale, he stared fixedly before him, drawing nervously on his blotting paper. Evidently, he felt deeply the disgrace of being abused by his fellow citizens in the presence of the enemy.[39]

Immediately after Liubinsky's speech, Czernin declared that the Central Powers would not withdraw their recognition of the Rada and closed the sitting. The Foreign Minister had every reason to be happy with his little theatrical coup. After his return from the subsequent conference in Berlin, he quickly worked out the details of the treaty with Ukraine. Nevertheless, he was under no illusion as to the severity of the situation. "I wonder if the Rada is still really sitting at Kieff [sic]?," he mused in his diary on 8 February, the day before the treaty was scheduled to be signed.[40] Although his musings turned out to be justified, it did not prevent the two sides from signing the first peace treaty of the war on the night of the 9–10 February 1918.

A full accounting of the Ukrainian Treaty of Brest-Litovsk and the considerable (and growing) literature on the subject is beyond the scope of this chapter. Suffice it to say that the treaty was subject to multiple interpretations at the time and continues to be subject to heated debates to the present day. As Frank Golczewski has observed: "The [First] Brest Peace is an excellent example of a controversial historical event, which one can evaluate as one sees fit."[41] For our purposes here, it is important to emphasize that the treaty boosted the UNR's juridical claim to independent statehood through its legal recognition by the countries of the Quadruple Alliance. It also established close economic relations between Ukraine and the Central Powers based on Ukrainian deliveries of at least one million tons of foodstuffs in exchange for German and Austrian manufactured goods. The ratification of the treaty by Germany and Austria-Hungary was contingent on such deliveries. These close political and economic relations required Austro-German military intervention on behalf of the Rada in order to control the territories it claimed.

THE FIRST TREATY OF BREST-LITOVSK AND UKRAINE'S BORDERS

The treaty itself certainly included significant discussion about Ukraine's borders. Article 2, Paragraph 1, covered the southern portion of the western boundary, stipulating that "the frontiers which existed between the Austro-Hungarian Monarchy and Russia prior to the outbreak of the present war will be preserved."[42] Article 2, Paragraph 2, detailed the northern portion of this border as running from Tarnogród/Ternohorod through Biłgoraj/Bilgoray, Szczebrzeszyn/Shchebzheshyn, Krasnystaw/Krasnostav, Radzyń Podlaski/Radzyn, Międzyrzecze, Sarnaki, Mielnik, Wysokie Litewskie/Vysoke, Kamieniec Litewski/ Kamenets Litevsky, and Pruzhany up to Lake Vydonovsk. A further clarification added that "this frontier will be delimited in detail by a mixed commission, according to the ethnographical conditions and after taking the wishes of the inhabitants into consideration."[43]

This final point was obviously an attempt to placate the Poles, who were bound to protest against the inclusion of Kholm in the new Ukrainian state. However, this segue proved to be too little too late, as the actual Polish reaction was far worse than anything Czernin had feared. Indeed, when the Austro-Hungarian Foreign Office Representative in Warsaw presented the details of the treaty to the representatives of the Polish Regency Council on 10 February, one of its members, Prince Zdisław Lubomirski, shook violently in a wordless rage before denouncing the treaty as a Fourth

The Ukrainian Boundary as described in the Peace Treaty of Brest-Litovsk, 9 February, 1918, Article II, Paragraph 2.

1.1 Northwestern boundary of Ukraine by the Treaty of Brest-Litovsk, 1918.

Partition of Poland, as did his associates, all of whom resigned within days.[44] The Polish Prime Minister, Jan Kucharzewski, retained his composure, but was no less despondent, arguing that Ukrainians only made up 7 per cent of the disputed region's population.[45] As the backlash intensified over the subsequent weeks, the Polish Legion in the Habsburg Army mutinied, and a wave of popular demonstrations against the treaty took place in Krakow, Warsaw, and other large Polish cities.[46]

A subsequent attempt at damage limitation, involving the signing of a protocol on 4 March regarding the interpretation of Article 2, Paragraph 2, of the treaty – explaining that "the said mixed Commission shall be composed of representatives of the contracting parties and of the representatives of Poland, and each one of these parties shall designate an equal number of parties to the Commission" – failed to assuage Polish objections.[47] The establishment of Ukraine's western borders also involved the implicit – though no less real – settlement of Poland's borders. Ultimately, the claims of both national movements proved impossible to reconcile: the border question fuelled inter-ethnic conflict in the region and would lead to a series of bloody wars over the next few years.

The First Treaty of Brest-Litovsk did not specify Ukraine's northern or eastern borders. Neither did the Second or Russian Treaty of Brest-Litovsk, signed between the Central Powers and Bolshevik Russia on 3 March, which merely stipulated that Russia agreed to withdraw its troops from Ukrainian territory and conclude a peace treaty with the UNR forthwith.[48] However, this never transpired: General Pavlo Skoropadsky overthrew the Rada at the end of March and established a Hetmanate (officially, Ukrainian State) in its stead. Thus, it was the Hetman's representatives who met with Bolshevik Russian diplomats to negotiate a peace treaty and address Ukraine's borders over the following months. The border question was one of the main talking points – in the official transcripts of the negotiations, the word "borders" would appear no fewer than two hundred times![49] Even so, the debates proved largely academic and were eventually abandoned without an agreement, let alone a peace treaty, having been signed.[50]

The use of maps was not limited to the negotiating table at Brest-Litovsk. The First World War in general, and the Brest-Litovsk period in particular, saw a proliferation of maps published in popular newspapers on both sides of the Atlantic. In a meticulous study of sixty-two maps of Ukraine published in Austria-Hungary and the United States in 1917–18, Alexander Maxwell convincingly argues that "wartime maps helped raise the 'Ukrainian question' in the era of national questions."[51] What is more, they ensured that the reading public encountered the issue within a particular geographic space, complete with specific borders.

The system established by the Brest-Litovsk Peace Conference did not last long enough to establish a definitive set of borders for twentieth-century Ukraine. The collapse of the Central Powers in the autumn of 1918 meant that the territorial settlement was once again subject to constant revision. As additional players, such as the newly independent Poland, entered the fray, Ukrainian-populated territories once again became a key battleground in the struggle for supremacy in East-Central Europe. With Ukrainian forces fighting multiple foes against overwhelming odds on several fronts, this second phase of the 1914–23 continuum of violence could bring no permanent solution to the Ukrainian Question. Ethnic Ukrainians would remain divided between the borders of the Soviet Union, Poland, and Czechoslovakia during the interwar period.

NOTES

1 Pavlo Khrystiuk, *Zamitky i materialy do istoriï ukraïns'koï revoliutsii* (Vienna: Sotsiologichnyi ukrains'kyi instytut, 1921), 115.
2 A comprehensive review of the vast literature on the Ukrainian Revolution and the many historiographical debates is beyond the scope of this chapter. Some of the more important recent works include V.A. Smolii et al., *Narysy istoriï ukraïns'koï revoliūtsiï 1917–1921 rokiv*, 2 vols. (Kyiv: Naukova dumka, 2011); V.F. Soldatenko, *Grazhdanskaia voina v Ukraine (1917–1920 Gg.)* (Moscow: Novyi khronograf, 2012); V.F. Soldatenko, *Ukraïna v revoliutsiinu dobu: Istorychni ese-khroniky: U 4-kh tomakh* (Kyiv: Svitogliad, 2010); V.F. Soldatenko, *Ukraïns'ka revoliutsiia: Kontseptsiia ta istoriohrafiia* (Kyiv: Poshukovo-vydavnyche ahenstvo "Knyha pam'iati Ukraïny, 1997). In addition to Khrystiuk's émigré study, a classic early work on the subject is Volodymyr Vynnychenko, *Vidrozhdennia natsiï*, 3 vols. (Kyiv and Vienna: Dzvin, 1920).
3 Wolfram Dornik and Stefan Karner, eds., "Die Besatzung der Ukraine 1918 durch Österreichisch-Ungarische Truppen," in *Die Besatzung der Ukraine 1918: Historischer Kontext, Forschungsstand, Wirtschaftliche und soziale Folgen* (Graz, Vienna, and Klagenfurt: Verein zur Förderung der Forschung von Folgen nach Konflikten und Kriegen, 2008), 141–80; Wolfram Dornik, ed., *Die Ukraine zwischen Selbstbestimmung und Fremdherrschaft 1917–1922* (Graz: Leykam, 2011); Caroline Milow, *Die ukrainische Frage*

1917–1923 im Spannungsfeld der europäischen Diplomatie (Wiesbaden: Harrassowitz Verlag, 2002).

4 Mark von Hagen, "The Great War and the Mobilization of Ethnicity in the Russian Empire," in *Post-Soviet Political Order: Conflict and State Building*, ed. Barnett R. Rubin and Jack Snyder (London and New York: Routledge, 1998), 34–57; Borislav Chernev, "The Habsburg Mobilisation of Ethnicity and the Ukrainian Question during the Great War," in *Österreich-Ungarns Imperiale Herausforderungen: Nationalismen und Rivalitäten im Habsburgerreich um 1900*, ed. Bernhard Bachinger, Wolfram Dornik, and Stephan Lehnstaedt (Göttingen: Vandenhoeck & Ruprecht, 2020), 139–56.

5 "Erzbischof Szeptycki an Urbas: Pro memoria über die Organisierung der Ukraine in militärischer, sozial-rechtlicher und kirchlicher Hinsicht mit dem Ziehl ihrer Loslösung von Russland, 15 August 1914," in *Ereignisse in der Ukraine 1914–1922, deren Bedeutung und historische Hintergründe.*, vol. 1, ed. Theophil Hornykiewicz (Philadelphia: W.K. Lypynsky East European Research Institute, 1966), 8–11.

6 "Übersicht über die Russische Fremdbevölkerung. Stand vom 12 Dezember 1917," National Archives and Records Administration (NARA), RG 242, Microcopy no. T 120: Records of the German Foreign Office Received by the Department of State, roll 1792, D 818464–D 818471.

7 Rosenberg to the Foreign Ministry, no. 96, 16 December 1917, NARA, RG 242, T 120, roll 1792, D 818456–D818457.

8 "V ukraïnskykh organizatsiiakh," *Kievskaia Mysl'* 5:18, March 1917, in *Ukraïns'ka Tsentral'na Rada: Dokumenty i materialy u dvokh tomakh*, vol. 1: *4 bereznia–4 hrudnia 1917 r.*, ed. V.F. Verstiuk, 2 vols. (Kyiv: Naukova dumka, 1996).

9 "Proclamation of the Ukrainian People's Republic," in *Documents of Soviet Foreign Policy: The Triumph of Bolshevism, 1917–1919*, vol. 1, ed. Rex A. Wade, Documents of Soviet History (Gulf Breeze: Academic International Press, 1991), 38–40.

10 Oleh S. Fedyshyn, *Germany's Drive to the East and the Ukrainian Revolution, 1917–1918* (New Brunswick: Rutgers University Press, 1971); see also Jerry Hans Hoffman, "The Ukrainian Adventure of the Central Powers, 1914–1918" (PhD diss., University of Pittsburgh, 1967); for the opposite view, see Peter Borowsky, *Deutsche Ukrainepolitik 1918 unter besonderer Berücksichtigung der Wirtschaftsfragen* (Lübeck and Hamburg: Mathiesen Verlag, 1970).

11 D.G. Fokke, "Na stsene i za kulisami Brestskoi tragikomedii: Memuary uchastnika Brest-Litovskikh mirnykh peregovorov," *Arkhiv Russkoi Revolucii* 20 (1930): 162.

12 Vynnychenko, *Vidrozhdennia natsiï*, 2:202–3.
13 Protokoll der ersten Vorbesprechung mit den ukrain. Delegierte, 4 January 1918, in *Ereignisse in der Ukraine 1914–1922, deren Bedeutung und historische Hintergründe*, vol. 2, ed. Theophil Hornykiewicz (Philadelphia: W.K. Lypynsky East European Research Institute, 1966): 49–52.
14 Protokoll der zweiten Vorbesprechung mit den ukrain. Delegierten, 4 January 1918, in *Ereignisse in der Ukraine 1914–1922*, 52–5.
15 Protokoll der gemeinsamen Sitzung der verbündeten Delegationen mit den ukrain. Delegierten, 6 January 1918, in *Ereignisse in der Ukraine 1914–1922*, 58–64.
16 Popov to Radoslavov, unnumbered, 6 January 1918, Tsentralen Durzhaven Arkhiv, fond 313k, opis 1, arkhivna edinitsa 2463, list 185–7.
17 Leon Trotsky, *My Life: An Attempt at an Autobiography* (Mineola: Dover, 2007), 376.
18 *Proceedings of the Brest-Litovsk Peace Conference: The Peace Negotiations between Russia and the Central Powers 21 November, 1917–3 March, 1918* (Washington, DC: Government Printing Office, 1918), 56–9.
19 Ganchev to Radoslavov, no. 2300, 11 January 1918. TSDA, f. 313k, op. 1, a.e. 2465, l. 34.
20 Ibid.
21 Borislav Chernev, "The Brest-Litovsk Moment: Self-Determination Discourse in Eastern Europe before Wilsonianism," *Diplomacy and Statecraft* 22, no. 3 (September 2011): 369–87.
22 Protokoll der allgemeinem vertraulichen Besprechung zwischen der deutschen und der ukrain. Delegation, 13 January 1918, in *Ereignisse in der Ukraine*, ed. Theophil Hornykiewicz, vol. 2, 80–7.
23 Max Hoffmann, *The War of Lost Opportunities* (New York: International Publishers, 1925), 220–1.
24 Ibid., 222.
25 Ibid. Protokoll der Besprechung zwischen der deutschen, österr.-ung, und ukrain. Delegation, 16 January 1918, in *Ereignisse in der Ukraine*, ed. Theophil Hornykiewicz, vol. 2, 106–10.
26 See Vasyl Rasevych, "Die Westukrainische Volksrepublik von 1918/19," in *Die Ukraine zwischen Selbstbestimmung und Fremdherrschaft 1917–1922*, ed. Wolfram Dornik (Graz: Leykam, 2011), 181–200.
27 On the importance of border-making for the formation of national identity, see the classic study of Peter Sahlins, *Boundaries: The Making of France and Spain in the Pyrenees* (Berkeley: University of California Press, 1989).
28 Francine Hirsch, *Empire of Nations: Ethnographic Knowledge and the Making of the Soviet Union* (Ithaca: Cornell University Press, 2005).

29 On the Austro-Polish Solution, see Clifford F. Wargelin, "The Austro-Polish Solution: Diplomacy, Politics, and State Building in Wartime Austria-Hungary 1914–1918," *East European Quarterly* 42, no. 3 (Fall 2008): 253–73.
30 Czernin to Müller (for Demblin, resp. His Majesty), unnumbered, 19 January 1918. Haus- Hof- und Staatsarchiv, Politisches Archiv I: Allgemeines I, Karton 1077.
31 Diary entry for 20 January 1918. Ottokar Czernin, *In the World War* (New York: Harper & Brothers, 1920), 241.
32 Protokoll eines am 22 Jänner 1918 unter Seiner k.u.k, Apostolischen Majestät abgehalten Kronrates, in *Protokolle des Gemeinsamen Ministerrates der Österreichisch-Ungarischen Monarchie (1914–1918)*, ed. Miklósné Komjáthy (Budapest, Akadémiai Kiadó, 1966), 627–33.
33 The Royal Legation in Stockholm to the Ministry of Foreign Affairs and Confessions in Sofia, no. 169, 25 January 1918, TSDA, f. 176k, op. 3, a.e. 700, l. 106.
34 Karakhan to Kuzmin and Reizon, January 1918, Houghton Library, MS 13, Leon Trotsky Soviet Papers, box 1, T 5.
35 Fokke, "Na stsene i za kulisami Brestskoi tragikomedii," 128.
36 Trotsky to Kühlmann, unnumbered, 3 February 1918, NARA, RG 242, T 120, roll 1787, D 815344.
37 *Proceedings of the Brest-Litovsk Peace Conference*, 135–8.
38 Hoffmann, *The War of Lost Opportunities*, 224–5.
39 Czernin, *In the World War*, 246.
40 Ibid., 249.
41 Frank Golczewski, *Deutsche und Ukrainer 1914–1939* (Paderborn: Schöningh, 2010), 322–3.
42 *Texts of the Ukraine "Peace": With Maps* (Washington, D.C.: Government Printing Office 1918), 10.
43 Ibid., 11.
44 Von Ugron to the Foreign Office, no. 62, 10 February 1918, HHStA, PA I, K 1080.
45 Von Ugron to the Foreign Office, no. 65, 11 February 1918,. HHStA, PA I, K 1080.
46 Clifford F. Wargelin, "Bread, Peace, and Poland: The Economic, Political, and Diplomatic Origins of Habsburg Policy at Brest-Litovsk, 1914–1918" (PhD diss., University of Wisconsin at Madison, 1994), 371–2.
47 *Texts of the Ukraine "Peace,"* 28.
48 Ibid.

49 O.I. Lupandin et al., eds., *Myrni perehovory mizh Ukraïns'koiu Derzhavoiu ta RSFRR 1918 r.: Protokoly i stenohramy plenarnykh zasidan': Zbirnyk dokumentiv i materialiv* (Kyiv and New York: M.P. Kots, 1999).
50 For an overview of the most relevant issues, see O. Boiko, "Heopolitychni problemy Ukraïny v konteksti myrnykh perehovoriv Ukraïns'koï Derzhavy z RSFRR (Analitychna zapyska D. Dontsova "O granicakh Ukraïns'koï Derzhavy pid vzgliadom politychnym")," *Visnik KNLU* 19 (2014). 78–88
51 Alexander Maxwell, "Ukrainian Frontiers in Austro-Hungarian and American Popular Cartography, 1917–1918," *New Zealand Slavonic Journal* 47–8 (2013): 125–53, quotation on 147.

2

Poland's "Civilizing Mission" and Ukrainian Statehood at the Paris Peace Conference

Elżbieta Kwiecińska

The claim of a "civilizing mission" is usually associated with Western colonialism and the establishment of the mandate system after the First World War. This chapter aims to show how such "civilizing mission" discourses were used in another geographic region, East-Central Europe, and how they collided with the principle of national self-determination. I will first detail how influential members of the Polish delegation at the Paris Peace Conference in 1919, and other Polish statesmen, employed the argument of a "Polish civilizing mission" to contest the establishment of a Ukrainian state and claim control over territories, where Polish rule would secure the development of other nations through Poles' supposed cultural superiority. I will also consider the response of Ukrainian statesmen and authors who, while appropriating nativist and anti-colonial rhetoric, portrayed their nation as a victim of Polish occupation and colonization.[1]

References to the idea of a "Polish civilizing mission" emerge from primary sources, meaning that it is not simply a modern research term imposed on the past. For contemporary authors, "mission" referred to transferring the cultural tenets of "civilization" from an allegedly "superior" to an "inferior" nation. As Maciej Janowski notes, the "civilizing mission" was often evoked to legitimize political power in modern East-Central European history. The quality of being a so-called *Kulturnation* brought with it the entitlement to bring "civilization" to "non-civilized" peoples and to retain their territories under a paternal administrative regime that sought to promote progress.[2] I will be using a broad range of source materials, including international legal documents, diplomatic correspondence, newspaper articles, philosophical literature, and map collections, in order to examine this political and legal discourse and how it was used to shape the post-1919 Polish-Ukrainian border.

When the borders of the newly established nation-states in East-Central Europe were discussed at the Paris Peace Conference in Versailles, there was no formal international regulation regarding state recognition. A standard legal definition of the state was only established fourteen years later, with the Montevideo Convention on the Rights and Duties of States, concluded in the Uruguayan capital on 26 December 1933 and still in use today. The criteria for state recognition are: a permanent population, a clearly defined territory, an established government, and the capacity to enter into relations with other states.[3] Although this definition did not exist in 1919, some of its elements were used in formulating international law and public discourse when Polish and Ukrainian national independence were discussed following the First World War.

Given the multi-ethnic populations of Eastern Europe, it was difficult to draw borders between states where different nations had often coexisted on the same territories for centuries. The Ukrainians argued that they held a majority in the "Ukrainian ethnic territory," while the Poles claimed to be the dominant ethnicity in the larger Ukrainian cities – a situation that resembled that of Hungarians in Transylvania.

Poles were not a numerically dominant population in Ukraine, so they needed to find other arguments to defend their claims to Ukrainian territory. They therefore came to rely on the argument that Ukrainians as a nation were not "mature enough" to establish a modern nation-state themselves. The Poles set out to discredit the Ukrainians as incapable of governing themselves and thus incapable of meeting the essential state criterion of possessing an effective government.

The principle of self-determination was proclaimed at the Paris Peace Conference as a basic tenet of the future international order. In theory this meant that every nation had an equal right to establish its own nation-state. In practice, however, there was a hierarchy of nations, based on a prerequisite level of "civilization," which was often directly associated with perceived state-building capacity. Polish delegates at Versailles thus argued that Ukraine needed a "Polish civilizing mission" to bring order to its anarchical territory. This chapter will demonstrate that the international law principle of national self-determination was infused with colonial ideas, which, in the Polish-Ukrainian case, expressed themselves as Poland's "civilizing mission" in East-Central Europe.

WHO COMES FIRST? A HIERARCHY OF SELF-DETERMINATIONS

As mentioned earlier, the principle of self-determination was acknowledged at the Paris Peace Conference, but not all nations were deemed culturally capable of maintaining a functioning nation-state. Point Thirteen of Woodrow Wilson's famous Fourteen Points, delivered to the US Congress on 8 January 1918, referred to the establishment of a Polish state, and on 11 February 1918 the American president further stated that "national aspirations must be respected; people may now be dominated and governed only by their own consent. 'Self-determination' is not a mere phrase; it is an imperative principle of action."[4] While Wilson made no reference to Ukraine, both Poland and Ukraine were mentioned as nations entitled to self-determination by Vladimir Lenin and the Central Powers in the Treaty of Brest-Litovsk, signed in March 1918.

Ukraine had aligned itself with the Central Powers during the war, which meant that after the war, when its delegates arrived in Versailles to negotiate the borders of the Ukrainian state, it bore the political stigma of having once been a client state of the enemy. Thus, the Entente powers looked with more favour on Polish demands when establishing the Polish-Ukrainian border. Indeed, the Polish delegation enjoyed official recognition; its Ukrainian counterpart did not. Moreover, the Polish state had been fully recognized by the victors (setting aside the final settlement of borders), in contrast, again, to the West Ukrainian People's Republic (ZUNR) and the Ukrainian People's Republic (UNR).[5] This issue of international recognition was resolved, however, after the Bolsheviks invaded the UNR's territory and a government-in-exile was established in Poland.

In his book about the Ukrainian cause at the Paris Peace Conference, Polish historian Przemysław Żurawski vel Grajewski points out that the victors did not regard the Ukrainian question as an independent one, but only as a side-question to Austria-Hungary's dissolution and the Russian question. It is also worth noting that no commission was established for Ukraine during the conference, though commissions were established for Poland, Czechoslovakia, Romania, and the Kingdom of Serbs, Croats, and Slovenes (Yugoslavia).[6]

From the perspective of the victorious Entente, it was necessary to establish an independent Polish or Ukrainian state in order to confront the threat of a Bolshevik invasion. France and the United States maintained that Poland would represent a stronger bulwark, while Great Britain advocated for Ukraine.

British support for the Ukrainian cause flowed from London's backing of Germany and a possible post-Bolshevik Russia under monarchist White General Anton Denikin as a counterweight to France, which was Britain's competitor in European politics. British Prime Minister David Lloyd George wanted to keep Poland within its "ethnic borders," which would not include Vilnius, Eastern Galicia (today western Ukraine), and Silesia. His position against Poland closely resembled Roman Dmowski's own arguments against Ukrainian independence: that the Poles' own "barbarism" inhibited their state-building capabilities. Famously, Lloyd George declared that giving "the Silesian industry to the Poles is like giving [a] monkey a watch."[7] Norman Davies writes that in Lloyd George's view, European civilization extended to the German-Polish border, beyond which only barbarous space existed. Davies also points out that British politics aside, the prime minister's Welsh identity influenced his views on Polish-Ukrainian matters, which he considered through the lens of English-Welsh-Irish relations. While he sympathized with "small nations' patriotism," he viewed any grander international aspirations as the preserve of the established Great Powers. Thus, he condemned Polish claims to Eastern Galicia as "imperialism" while failing to see anything "imperialistic" about Britain ruling over some 450 million non-British subjects.[8]

It was in this context that the British delegation proposed a Polish-Soviet border called the "Curzon Line," mistakenly named after Foreign Secretary George Curzon. In fact, the Curzon Line had been conceived by Lewis Bernstein Namier (1888–1960), a British historian of Polish-Jewish origin (born and raised in Galicia) and a member of the British delegation to the Paris Peace Conference. As was the case with Lloyd George, Namier's views on the border were shaped by his identification with an oppressed minority – in particular, by his experience of Polish antisemitism. He resented the Poles for how they had dominated Habsburg Galicia's Ukrainians and Jews after 1867. So he lobbied for a Polish-Soviet border that would follow the Bug and San Rivers, thus keeping Lwów/Lviv out of Polish hands. He argued that the territory's landowning class consisted of Ukrainian Poles who were alien to the indigenous population over whom they wished to continue holding power. However, he did not support Ukrainian independence, considering Ukrainians to be part of the Greater Russian nation.[9]

Curzon proposed the Curzon Line in a diplomatic note sent to Georgy Chicherin on 11 July 1920 (see map 2.1). The idea would re-emerge after the Second World War, serving as the basis for the Polish-Soviet border in 1945 and thus depriving Poland of both Lwów/Lviv and Wilno/Vilnius. After the First World War, however, the Paris Peace Conference simply

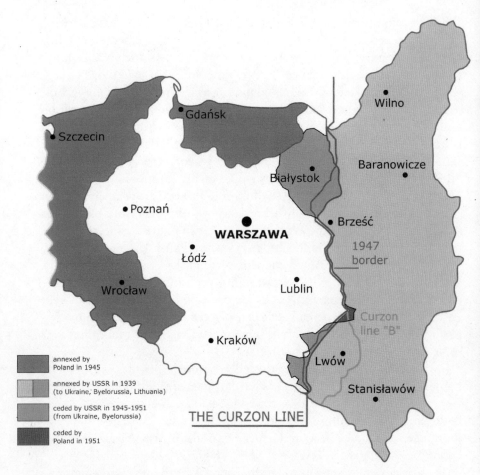

2.1 The Curzon Line between the Second Polish Republic and the Soviet Union, first proposed in 1919.

approved the *fait accompli* that had resulted from fighting among the Poles, the Ukrainians, and the Soviets. After the Polish army seized Galicia in July 1919, it recognized Poland's temporary administration of that province as well. Moreover, until 14 March 1923, the Great Powers treated Eastern Galicia itself as a disputed territory, one in which sovereignty was exercised by the victors, according to the 1919 Treaty of Saint-Germain-en-Laye.

On 20 November 1919, the Great Powers proposed a new plan for Eastern Galicia. It would grant Poland a twenty-five-year mandate to administer the region, with a provision for territorial autonomy and with sovereignty transferred to the Entente. Once the mandate expired, a local plebiscite would be organized, as in the Polish-German borderlands in Silesia, Warmia, Masuria, and Powiśle. The intent here was to encourage the Poles to fight the Bolsheviks, since Poland was viewed as a more "reliable" and "civilized" power in the region, one that would preserve order in Eastern Galicia until the Whites' expected victory in the Russian Civil War.[10]

Warsaw, however, was not satisfied with this decision, for it meant that sovereignty over Galicia would in the end be surrendered to the Entente and that the border between Poland and Galicia would remain fixed at the Curzon Line. The Polish delegation at Versailles now made several attempts to establish the provisional Polish-Ukrainian border along the Zbruch River as the permanent one. Paradoxically, their arguments complied with the ideas underpinning the postwar international mandate system. That system had been adopted after the First World War primarily to administer the former Asian and African colonies of imperial Germany and the Ottoman Empire on behalf of the newly founded League of Nations. Article 22 of the League's founding convention referred to territories that were no longer ruled by their previous sovereigns but whose inhabitants were not considered "able to stand by themselves under the strenuous conditions of the modern world"; they would be "entrusted to *advanced nations* [my emphasis] who by reason of their resources, their experience or their geographical position can best undertake this responsibility."[11] The same article provided that the system would be based on two governing principles: non-annexation of the territory and its administration, and "the sacred trust of civilization" to develop the territory for the well-being of its native people.[12]

The Polish mandate in Eastern Galicia was modelled on the one created for Czechoslovakian rule in Sub-carpathian Rus. In the end, neither came into force, and both countries subsequently annexed the occupied territories.[13] The plan to establish a Polish mandate in Eastern Galicia failed to materialize; even so, after the Whites were defeated in the Russian Civil War, the Polish delegation used the idea of a "civilizing mission" to justify their rule in Galicia.

CONCEPTUALIZING THE "POLISH CIVILIZING MISSION" AND CLAIMING EASTERN GALICIA

Poland's border with Germany was essentially drawn by the war's victors, whereas the Polish-Ukrainian border was drawn through military and diplomatic action. Poland's position on this was most clearly articulated by two of its leading statesmen, and political rivals – Roman Dmowski and Józef Piłsudski.

Dmowski was an ethnonationalist who opted for the "incorporation idea" – in other words, the Polish nation-state should contain as few national minorities as possible.[14] Piłsudski, by contrast, supported the federalist or Jagiellonian tradition, which envisioned Poland leading a new federation of those East-Central European countries that had once formed the Polish-Lithuanian Commonwealth (Lithuania, Belarus, and Ukraine).[15] However, this rivalry between Dmowski and Piłsudski did not manifest itself in relation to the shape of the Polish-Ukrainian border and the "Polish civilizing mission." Both politicians agreed that Wilno/Vilnius and Lwów/Lviv should stay within Poland's borders. Piłsudski acted in the region by military means, while Dmowski, together with Jan Paderewski,[16] led Polish diplomacy at the Paris Peace Conference, signing the Treaty of Versailles on behalf of the Second Polish Republic.[17] Unlike Piłsudski, Dmowski sought allies for Polish independence in Russia, which he regarded as "less civilized" and therefore less dangerous to Poland than the "more civilized" and militarily stronger Germany.[18]

Another key difference between Dmowski and Piłsudski related to their views on whether the Ukrainians should be recognized as a separate nation. Piłsudski saw them as such, being descended from the Polish-Lithuanian Commonwealth tradition; Dmowski did not. In his Memorandum on the Recognition of Poland's Independence, submitted to the Russian government in March 1917, Dmowski noted that Ukrainian nationality had largely been formulated with Habsburg and German support; Ukrainians were in fact a fraction of the Russian people, the Malorussians ("Little Russians"). Piłsudski, by contrast, argued that Poland was the most important national element in East-Central Europe since "the Poles occupy the first place there, both by their number and by the degree of their civilization and their political traditions."[19]

For Dmowski, the Ukrainian question was merely an aspect of Polish-Russian relations. In his wartime pamphlet *Problems of Central and Eastern Europe* (1917), addressed to the British public, he insisted that Ukraine needed to be partitioned between Poland and Russia along the Dnieper, which had served as the border between the Polish-Lithuanian Commonwealth and the Russian Empire in 1793. According to Dmowski, the Dnieper divided Ukraine into two civilizations: the Polish and the Russian. The Right-Bank Ukrainian elites were Poles, while those on the Left Bank were Malorussians – an ethnically mixed population of Russians, Tatars, Greeks, Armenians, Romanians, and Germans. Dmowski argued that the only thing Ukrainians shared was a distinct language. However, some scholars considered it a dialect of Russian, literary Ukrainian having only developed since the mid-nineteenth century. Another argument for the partition of Ukraine was, Dmowski believed, the lack of a common history, for which reason the Russian and the Ukrainian regions very different politically and culturally.[20]

Piłsudski, for his part, recognized the Ukrainians as a distinct nation, although he defined Ukraine's borders differently from Ukrainian national activists. Piłsudski, and Polish public opinion, viewed Eastern Galicia and the city of Lwów/Lviv as indisputably Polish. Indeed, in April 1919 the Polish parliament adopted a resolution calling on the government to take all measures "to ensure the union of those lands in which either the Polish population held a demographic majority or showed the *civilizational work* [my emphasis] that marked the Polish character." The same resolution emphasized that the government should "persistently take care" and "make every effort to re-establish the voluntary union between Poland and Lithuania, Belarus, Ruthenia" that had been in place several centuries earlier.[21] The Commonwealth had ceased to exist in 1795, yet in 1919 Polish public opinion continued to view Ukraine through the lens of this former union.[22]

So the Polish delegation's core argument at Versailles was that the Ukrainians were incapable of self-government and needed a more "civilized" Polish administration to rule them – the so-called "Polish civilizing mission." In their "Note of the Polish Delegation regarding the Eastern Border of Poland," submitted to the chair of the conference's Committee for Polish Affairs on 3 March 1919,[23] the delegates depicted the Lithuanian and Ruthenian territories as rife with political and social anarchy and claimed that the local Polish minority "represents the country's only intellectual and economic strength." This contrasted with the Russian cultural influence, which was spreading "anarchy and Bolshevism."[24]

In another note, dated 3 March 1919, the delegation argued that including Lithuanian and Ruthenian lands in the Polish state would represent a historical "re-vindication." The note referred to the 1772 borders of the former Polish state, which had extended along the Dnieper and reached the Daugava River farther to the north. These territories had subsequently become "a land of Polish Western civilization," where the local elites had adopted Polish customs, language, and even nationality, and where the masses, though they retained their own language, remained loyal to the Polish state. Poland was also presented as the historic victim of Russian policies aimed at erasing Poland's influence in its former Lithuanian-Ruthenian territories. As a consequence, due to Russian governance and a stronger cultural influence in the easternmost parts of the Lithuanian-Ruthenian territories, "there is no element strong enough and capable of forming a permanent government." Therefore, the Polish delegation did not demand the full "re-vindication" of the 1772 borders; instead it proposed to acquire the former Russian Kingdom of Poland, excluding the northern Suwałki region; the *gubernii* of Vilnius, Grodno, and Minsk; the western portion of Vitebsk; Volhynia and the western parts of Podolia; and the entire Galician region; in addition to most of the former Habsburg province of Cieszyn Silesia, northern Spiš, and Orava.[25] Dubbed the "Dmowski Line," this newly proposed Polish border would extend a further two hundred kilometres eastwards from what was finally agreed upon in 1923 (see map 2.2).

Yet Dmowski's plan for Poland's borders was not "ethnonationalist," as it is commonly described in the historiography. His proposals extended far beyond the territory on which Poles formed an ethnic majority and even beyond the Curzon Line. An argument for Poland's extended eastern border was that the Poles were the only "civilized" element in Poland's border regions or *kresy* – an observation repeated in other documents produced by the delegation. As Dmowski further argued in *Problems of Central and Eastern Europe*: "Nations who are too weak or whose national development is not advanced enough should not be organized into separate states, but included in those capable of ensuring their progress."[26] He therefore believed that Poland should encompass the entire territory between Russia and Germany, as a means of ensuring Ukraine's progress. Similarly, his Memorandum on the Polish State Territory, which he submitted to President Wilson on 8 October 1918, asserted that Galicia did not possess a native Ukrainian intelligentsia capable of ruling the country, making a Polish administration the only guarantee of progress. In the Russian western borderlands (*Ziemie Zabrane*), Poles were "the only cultural element because the rest consist of petty merchants and priests." Therefore, Dmowski believed, the establishment of independent Lithuanian and Ukrainian states would only invite anarchy and further invasion by the Germans. As "the only intellectual and economic power there," the Poles should rule Lithuania and Ukraine.[27] Being the only "civilized" element in the *kresy*, the Poles could not be replaced by anyone else.

Dmowski often contrasted Polish "civilization" with Russian "barbarism." In *Problems of Central and Eastern Europe* he highlighted the "Eastern character" of the Russian state, by which he intended to convey "lack of democracy." In Russia, he declared, there were no institutions, the people did not take part in public matters, and the central authorities looked upon their subjects as slaves rather than citizens. Non-governmental initiatives were criminalized, the law was routinely abused by the state, and respect for the rule of law did not exist. By contrast, Poland could ensure proper governance of Lithuania and Ruthenia and lead them toward "progress."[28]

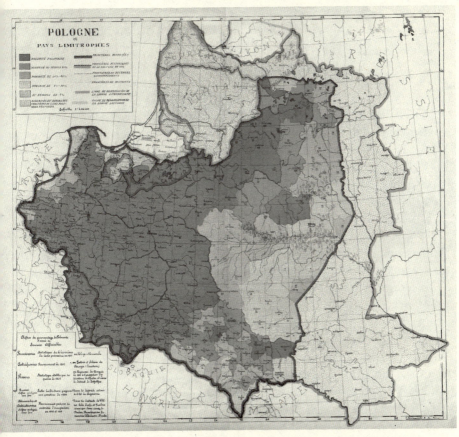

2.2 Territories claimed by the Second Polish Republic at the Paris Peace Conference, 1919.

Apart from this line of argumentation, which resorted to colonial rhetoric about Poles' civilizational superiority over Ukrainians and Russians, the delegation reflected on the principle of national self-determination, arguing that the shape of Poland's borders could be based neither on linguistic principles nor on historical grounds (specifically the border of 1772). This claim was repeated in every document in which Polish territories were discussed.[29] Several justifications were made for this modified interpretation. The first reason for not including the entire historical territory of the Polish-Lithuanian Commonwealth was that it would be a cultural burden for the newly re-established state. Dmowski believed that "the basis for Poland's strength is the area where the mass of the population speaks Polish, is aware of its Polish nationality and is attached to the Polish cause."[30] According to Dmowski, Galicia, western Podolia, and Volhynia fulfilled those conditions;

however, most of the population farther east, although of "Polish civilization," was vulnerable to Russian agitation. Such a large territory would threaten the state's cohesion.[31] Furthermore, striving for the restored borders of 1772 would imply expansionist ambitions, while Poland aimed at peace. In his memorandum to Wilson, who was known to be a liberal when it came to international relations, Dmowski described Poland as holding "a duty to civilized humanity, the mission as a defender of high ideals of justice, freedom and peace." Dmowski hoped that the Poles' contribution to peace would make it a worthy and useful member of the future League of Nations.[32]

His second reason was that although in the *kresy* (that is, in Lithuania, western Podolia, western Volhynia, and Galicia), ethnic Poles were a minority, the majority had adopted the trappings of "Polish civilization."[33] As mentioned, Dmowski proposed the partition of Ukraine between Russia and Poland as being between two civilizations, with Ukrainians not featuring among the "civilized" nations.[34] Besides this, he noted that the census conducted by the imperial authorities in the *kresy* was not objective and that it discriminated against the Polish population. Dmowski estimated that there were 6 million Poles in *Ziemie Zabrane*[35] and that Poles were 25 per cent of the population in Eastern Galicia. He calculated that overall, there were 70 per cent Poles in the *kresy*. However, in presenting these statistics, he was defining Polishness very broadly, as "a population of Polish language, culture, thoughts and feelings."[36]

His third reason was that the *kresy* needed to be included as Polish territory to help strengthen Poland as a truly independent state. The *Memorandum on the Polish State Territory* further argued that Poland "must become a great, creative democracy in Eastern Europe, a bulwark against German pressure to the east, and at the same time it must defend itself against destructive influences."[37] There were three prerequisites to all of this: Poland must cover a vast territory and have a large population; said population must be sufficiently homogeneous to ensure internal cohesion; and the borders must meet certain geographical requirements to ensure independence from Poland's neighbours.[38] A strong Poland would be needed to maintain a European balance of power and especially to counterbalance Germany in East-Central Europe.[39] This was especially true with regard to Ukraine, where Dmowski perceived Poland's role as that of a counterweight to "German intrigue," which he believed was perpetuating support for the Ukrainian national idea.[40] In 1925, Dmowski wrote in his memoirs that while negotiating the eastern borders in 1919, he had hoped to establish Poland as a counter-empire to Germany, one that would provide "support for the smaller nations of Central Europe."[41]

UKRAINIAN RESPONSES TO THE "POLISH CIVILIZING MISSION"

The Polish delegation based its claims to Eastern Galicia on the "Polish civilizing mission"; the Ukrainian delegates responded with the demographic argument. Ukrainian demands were based on Mykhailo Hrushevsky's idea of "Ukrainian ethnic territories," which encompassed those lands inhabited by "ethnic" Ukrainians stretching to the San River in the west. Hrushevsky had formulated these ideas in the first of his ten volumes on the *History of Ukraine-Rus* (1898). During the war, he elaborated on his arguments for Ukrainian independence in a popular book aimed at an English-speaking audience, *The Historical Evolution of the Ukrainian Problem* (1915), in which he broached ideas about "civilization" and "expansion" to support Ukrainian independence. Answering allegations that Ukrainians were "barbaric," he argued that it was a high level of civilization, rich natural resources, and fertile lands that had encouraged Poland and Russia to "conquer" Ukraine in the first place. He also mentioned repeatedly that Ukraine was "cultured" or "civilized" enough to become an independent state. And he noted that through colonial expansion, the medieval state of Kyivan Rus had assimilated cultural influences from the east, north, and south.[42]

The Ukrainian delegation in Paris was not formally recognized; even so, it strove to convince the victors of the righteousness of the Ukrainian cause. Between February and April 1919, its members vigorously lobbied the conference, demanding recognition as an official delegation (just like the Poles and the Romanians) and that this recognition be extended to the UNR as the only legitimate entity representing the Ukrainian nation.[43] To justify independence, the Ukrainians referred to the principle of national self-determination, which they interpreted differently than the Poles. While the Poles at Versailles highlighted their "higher degree of civilization," the Ukrainians pointed to a well-defined population as the proper basis of self-determination. In a note dated 10 February 1919, Hryhorii Sydorenko, who headed the delegation, argued that the Ukrainian population made up the majority in Ukraine, with smaller minorities of Poles, Russians, and Jews, and already existed as a great nation of some 45 million people. Sydorenko also noted that Ukraine had large amounts of natural resources, such as wheat, coal, iron, and oil, and the ability to export them through its Black Sea ports.[44]

Moreover, Sydorenko named the current Polish regime in Galicia as one of aggression, conquest, and occupation. The Ukrainian delegation also protested the conference's support for (the Polish) "Haller's Army" in its purported conflict with the Bolsheviks. According to the Ukrainians, the Poles were in fact deploying that army to re-establish "Great Poland" rather than to counter the Soviet threat.[45]

Meanwhile, the Ukrainian National Committee of the United States expressed its objection to the Polish mandate in Galicia in a telegraphic note, titled *The Polish Atrocities in Ukrainian Galicia* (July 1919), which it sent to French President Georges Clemenceau, even though he was backing Poland. (Clemenceau also oversaw the Paris Peace Conference.)[46] The report began by accusing the Supreme Council of the Paris Peace Conference of allowing "an occupation of a great portion of the Western Territory of the Ukrainian Republic, that is to say, East Galicia up to the Zbruch River," in that it had authorized the Warsaw government in the resolution of 25 June 1919 to take action against the Bolshevik threat. The Ukrainian Committee considered this an outright violation of the principle of self-determination and of the UNR's territorial sovereignty. It then argued for national self-determination for all Ukrainian territory, providing both ethnographic and historical arguments and claiming that until the sixteenth century there had existed an independent Ukrainian state, which had been annexed by Poland. Since then, Ukrainians had endured oppression yet refused to consent to the occupation. The Polish state was now pursuing an imperialist policy, which made the Ukrainians victims who had a right to defend themselves. Regarding the ethnographic argument, Poles in Galicia were "an insignificant minority" and therefore had no right to rule lands that had never been Polish. Furthermore, there were Ukrainians who fought with the Bolsheviks and thus the mandate was a mistake, as it was not directed against the Red Army, but mainly as "a dream of exterminating Ukrainian people" and imposing denationalization. The committee added that Poles had never respected their existing treaties with Ukraine, and it was highly doubtful whether Warsaw would even permit the Galician plebiscite in twenty-five years.[47]

In addition to indicating the unlawfulness of Polish military actions in Galicia, the Ukrainian Committee demonstrated that the Poles were abusing the mandate of the pacification, which had nothing to do with the "civilizing mission." It then provided a lengthy account of "Polish atrocities." While the Poles justified their rule as a "civilizing mission," the Ukrainians adopted an anti-colonial vocabulary, portraying themselves as victims of colonialism.[48] The "crowning argument" for this was the colonization of Eastern Galicia by Polish legionaries and disabled soldiers, permitted under agrarian reforms introduced by the Polish parliament. These were compared to Prussia's policy of "internal colonization" and similar measures adopted by the Austrian Germans, with the Polish colonization of Galicia labelled a means "to propagate their culture."[49]

While the Polish delegation highlighted their "civilizing mission" and Ukrainian barbarism, the Ukrainian Committee accused the Poles of being the true "barbarians" against the "civilized" Ukrainian nation. Poles in Galicia were using the political situation "as means to destroy educated Ukrainians and the civilizing work of the Ukrainian people."[50] The Ukrainian delegation also mentioned a Polish "barbarous policy of annihilation, as Ukrainian prisoners are treated worse than beasts, they have an appearance of living corpses[51] and the atrocities are on a par with the barbarous cruelties perpetrated in the Balkans and Armenia, such as the massacre of the patriotic village of Cherche."[52]

The opposite of these "barbarous cruelties," according to the committee, was represented by the UNR, where Poles and Jews enjoyed full national rights.[53] The committee portrayed Galicia under Ukrainian rule as a multicultural paradise. It rejected Polish accusations that the Polish minority in the *kresy* was in danger, and it debunked photographs of claimed Ukrainian cruelty taken during the ongoing Polish-Ukrainian war. In this regard, its portrait of Galicia amounted to a mirror image of Piłsudski's idealized *kresy*:

> East Galicia has always enjoyed, under Ukrainian rule, order and tranquility; that there have been no troubles, no uprising, no pogroms, that all the inhabitants without considering race or creed, and all classes of society have found equal protection under the law; and that the Poles in particular have possessed full liberty and freedom to develop their cultural and national activities according to the just and impartial laws then existing.[54]

The Ukrainian delegation had protested the Polish mandate for Galicia in 1919. However, the 1921 Polish-Soviet Treaty of Riga effectively ended any prospect of Ukrainian independence. The delegates even demanded that the Polish mandate in Galicia be implemented so as to transfer its sovereignty to the League of Nations; in this way, direct annexation by Poland would be avoided. The Entente powers ignored these Ukrainian protests and demands, arguing that the UNR's government did not control any of the territories it claimed were "ethnically Ukrainian." As a result, on 15 March 1923, the League's Council of Ambassadors approved the Polish-Soviet border agreed to in the Treaty of Riga. Under its terms, Poland acquired Vilnius and Lviv, which the Polish delegation had considered "the minimum." The 1921 border itself would follow the former eastern boundary of the Polish-Lithuanian Commonwealth after the second partition of 1793 (with the additional territories of Volhynia, Polesia, and the city of Pinsk). Russia and Ukraine renounced their claims to Eastern Galicia. Furthermore, the council did not formally link Polish independence to respecting the Galician region's autonomy, thus preventing it from coming into force at a later date.[55]

MAPPING THE "CIVILIZING MISSION"

Maps played an important role during the peace negotiations at Versailles. Besides being an objective depiction of reality, they were rhetorical acts. The main cartographers and political geographers who served the Polish and Ukrainian delegations were Eugeniusz Romer and Stepan Rudnytsky, respectively. Both had been educated in Lviv and Vienna, where they studied under Professors Antoni Rehman and Albrecht Penck. At the time, the concept of the "German civilizing mission" was already present in German geographical parlance, and Romer and Rudnytsky would later appropriate that concept for their own countries' respective national "missions."[56]

The Polish delegation produced several maps to support its territorial claims (see map 2.2). These were drawn up by Romer, who provided his expertise both to the Paris negotiations and later to those in Riga. His approach was to merge cartography with geopolitics, and he used the claims of a Polish "civilizing mission" to further his country's interests. In *Podstawy przyrodnicze Polski historycznej* [Natural Bases of Historical Poland] (1912), he espoused the belief that the Polish lands represented a "bridging location" in the Baltic–Black Sea region. The Poles' claim to have been the masters of all territory between the two seas was justified by the region's physiographic features. A subsequent title, *The Land and the State* (1917), indicated four routes for Poland's expansion, which he termed *Drang nach Osten*: the first followed the "great valleys," the second ran southeast toward Kyiv, the third southwest as far as the Danube, and the fourth extended to the Baltic Sea. In the introduction to his *Geographical-Statistical Atlas of Poland* (1916), Romer described the Polish geopolitical situation in the east in terms of its "civilizing mission": "Having strengthened the western borders of his country, Bolesław [king of Poland, 967–1025] pointed out to Poland the way to expand towards the east, where Poland was led by natural geographical conditions. There, in the Ruthenian lands, Poland was rich in land and held the noble mission of spreading Western culture."[57]

Romer's *Atlas* was published in Polish, German, and French and circulated throughout Europe. It included various maps illustrating the former Polish-Lithuanian Commonwealth, the partitions of Poland, the region's current ethnographic composition, and the production of certain goods such as livestock and grain. During the Versailles negotiations, Romer produced further ad hoc maps to support certain Polish claims, republished in 1921 as *The Polish Congress Atlas*.[58] One of these maps, titled "The Density of Poles," illustrated the "density" of the Polish population within the historical borders of the former Commonwealth after the First World War (see map 2.3).

For this, Romer used four scales of density, indicated by varying shades of red: 0–50 per cent, 50–75 per cent, 75–100 per cent, and nearly 100 per cent. The first scale covered a vast territory, a tactical manoeuvre to avoid showing that Poles represented a minority in Galicia and Lithuania. Another map presented the density of the Ruthenian population within the borders of the former Ruthenian voivodeship of the Polish-Lithuanian Commonwealth. The map suggests that the Ruthenians and the Greek Catholics did not overlap: the former were a majority (over 75 per cent) in only a small area of the voivodeship.[59]

Romer also produced numerous maps of the *kresy wschodnie* that pointed out Polish schools, libraries, publishing houses, Roman Catholic churches, and battles fought during the Polish national uprising of 1863–64. These elements contributed to what Dmowski identified as the presence of "Polish civilization" in Ukraine. Although Poles did not represent a majority, the maps supported a prevailing image of Polish "civilizing activity."

Another map shows the locations of schools organized in Volhynia and Podolia by the Polish administration from 1918 to April 1919. This demonstrated one of the Polish delegation's key arguments: Poland's ability to preserve good governance in Ukraine, exemplifying, according to Dmowski, its higher "civilization."[60]

Similar maps were produced by Rudnytsky to demonstrate "the ethnic territory of Ukraine" with reference to Hrushevsky's earlier ideas (see map 0.4, page 21 of this volume). Like Romer, Rudnytsky argued that Ukraine was a bridge between East and West in the basin of the Dniester, Dnieper, and Don Rivers. However, although he conceptualized Ukraine as occupying the same geopolitical location, his geographical arguments were founded on the principle of population.

The Ukrainian delegation proposed a bold vision for Ukraine's borders, which, besides Galicia, included a considerable part of contemporary

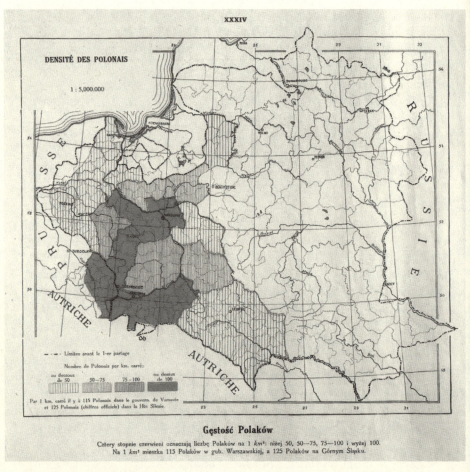

2.3 Density of Poles in 1921.

Belarus and Russia. Interestingly, like Dmowski and Romer, Rudnytsky used the argument of the "civilizing mission" and "expansion" in territories where the Ukrainian population did not represent an ethnic majority. This was particularly notable in the Kuban region, where he saw prospects for Ukrainian colonization.[61]

As Grzegorz Rossoliński-Liebe recently noted, Rudnytsky strengthened his geopolitical argument with racism. He responded to the Polish allegations of Ukrainian civilizational inferiority with a claim about the superiority of the Ukrainian race over the Polish and Russian ones. Rudnytsky provided examples of a higher fertility rate among Ukrainians. Also, in his view, "settlements, buildings, costumes, the nourishment and mode of life of the Ukrainian peasant stand much higher than those of the Russian, White Russian and Polish peasant."[62]

In 1915, Rudnytsky published his map, with a historical-geographical description, in a popular English-language edition titled *The Ukraine and the Ukrainians*, and in German under the title *Die Ukraine und die Ukrainer*. Although Ukraine did not win its "ethnic borders" in 1919, these author's works crystalized in the Ukrainian national conciseness a mental map of their country's "true" boundaries.

CONCLUSION

The Polish mandate to govern Galicia never came into force. Poland later annexed the region. The Riga Treaty of 1921, concluded between Poland and the Russian, Ukrainian, and Belarusian Soviet Republics, confirmed the new status quo. The Polish-Ukrainian border on the Zbruch River was recognized by the Conference of Ambassadors with the provision that Eastern Galicia would receive regional autonomy, which also never came into force.[63]

With a border established along the Zbruch, Poland achieved its aim of incorporating Vilnius and Lviv without establishing an eastern border based on historical or linguistic claims. Notwithstanding their political views, Piłsudski and Dmowski agreed that Eastern Galicia should be annexed to Poland. The concept of the "civilizing mission" was an ideological tool for legitimizing Polish sovereignty over an already annexed territory. For Ukraine, the "Polish civilizing mission" was simply a ploy to demonstrate Poland's strength as a newly re-established country and to justify its claimed ability to rule in the eyes of the Entente powers. In response, the Ukrainian delegation argued that the Poles were the "barbarians" who were "occupying" Ukraine and that the Ukrainian government was the only legitimate power in Eastern Galicia. Although the colonial discourse of the "Polish civilizing mission" was appropriated for Galicia, its aim was national rather than colonial – to justify territorial claims and establish a nation-state.

NOTES

1 For other publications on Polish-Ukrainian relations during this period, see Jan Jacek Bruski, *Między Prometeizmem a Realpolitik*, II, *Rzeczpospolita wobec Ukrainy Sowieckiej 1921–1926* (Kraków: Historia Iagiellonica, 2010); Aleksy Deruga, *Polityka wschodnia Polski wobec ziem Litwy, Białorusi i Ukrainy, 1918–1919* (Warszawa: Książka i Wiedza, 1969); Zbigniew Karpus, *Wschodni sojusznicy Polski w wojnie 1920 roku: Oddziały wojskowe ukraińskie, rosyjskie, kozackie i białoruskie w Polsce w latach 1919–1920* (Toruń: Wydawnictwo Uniwersytetu Mikołaja Kopernika, 1999).
2 Maciej Janowski, *Justifying Political Power in 19th Century Europe: Habsburg Monarchy and Beyond*, in *Imperial Rule*, ed. Alexei Miller and Alfred J. Rieber (Budapest: CEU Press, 2006), 70.
3 "Convention on Rights and Duties of States, Adopted by the Seventh International Conference of American States, Uruguay, on December 26, 1933," https://treaties.un.org/doc/Publication/UNTS/LON/Volume%20165/v165.pdf.
4 "President Wilson's Address to Congress, Analyzing German and Austrian Peace Utterances," 11 February 1918, https://wwi.lib.byu.edu/index.php/President_Wilson%27s_Address_to_Congress,_Analyzing_German_and_Austrian_Peace_Utterances.
5 Karol Grünberg and Bolesław Sprengel, *Trudne sąsiedztwo. Stosunki polsko-ukraińskie w X-XX wieku* (Warsaw: Książka i Wiedza, 2005), 264–5.
6 Przemysław Żurawski vel Grajewski, *Sprawa ukraińska na Konferencji Pokojowej w Paryżu w roku 1919* (Warszawa: Wydawnictwo Naukowe Semper, 2017), 140.
7 Michael Howard, "The Legacy of the First World War," in *Paths to War: New Essays on the Origins of the Second Word War*, ed. R. Boyce and E.M. Robertson (London: Macmillan, 1989), 46.
8 Norman Davies, "Lloyd George and Poland, 1919–20," *Journal of Contemporary History* 6, no. 3 (1971): 132–54.
9 Piotr Eberhardt, "The Curzon Line as the Eastern Boundary of Poland: The Origins and the Political Background," *Geographia Polonica* 85, no. 1 (2012): 5–12; Bartłomiej Rusin, "Lewis Namier a kwestia 'linii Curzona' i kształtowania się polskiej granicy wschodniej po pierwszej wojnie światowej," *Studia z Dziejów Rosji i Europy Środkowo-Wschodniej* 48 (2013): 95–116; Andrzej Nowak, *Lewis Namier – albo zemsta na (polskiej) mapie*, in *Pierwsza zdrada Zachodu. 1920 – zapomniany appeasement* (Kraków: Wydawnictwo Literackie, 2015), 229–66.

10 Grunberg and Sprenger, *Trudne sąsiedztwo*, 264–6.
11 "Peace Treaty of Versailles, Articles 1–30, and Annex: The Covenant of the League of Nations," http://net.lib.byu.edu/~rdh7/wwi/versa/versa1.html.
12 Peace Treaty of Versailles and Annex.
13 See Paul Robert Magosci, "The Ukrainian Question between Poland and Czechoslovakia: The Lemko Rusyn Republic (1918–1920) and Political Thought in Western Rus'-Ukraine," *Nationalities Papers* 21, no. 2 (1993): 95–103.
14 See Krzysztof Kawalec, *Roman Dmowski: Biografia* (Poznań: Zysk i S-ka, 2006).
15 See Marian K. Dziewianowski, *Joseph Piłsudski: A European Federalist, 1918–1922* (Stanford: Hoover Institution Press, 1969); Włodzimierz Suleja, *Józef Piłsudski* (Wrocław: Ossolineum, 2004).
16 Roman Wapiński, *Ignacy Paderewski* (Wrocław: Zakład Narodowy im. Ossolińskich, 1999).
17 See Andrzej Walicki, "The Troubling Legacy of Roman Dmowski," *East European Politics and Societies* 14, no. 1 (2000): 12–46.
18 Roman Dmowski, *Myśli nowoczesnego polaka*, 5th ed. (Warsaw: Wydawnictwo Zachodnie, 1934), 110–11.
19 Roman Dmowski, "Memoriał w sprawie uznania niepodległości Polski. Złożony przez R. Dmowskiego Rządowi Rosyjskiemu na ręce ambasadora w Paryżu, w marcu 1917," March 1917, in *Polityka polska i odbudowanie państwa z dodaniem memorjału "Zagadnienia środkowo- i wschodnio-europejskie" i innych dokumentów polityki Polskiej z lat 1914–1919* (Warszawa: Perzyński, Niklewicz, 1925), 512–13.
20 Dmowski, *Zagadnienia środkowo- i wschodnio-europejskie*, 569.
21 Józef Piłsudski, *Pisma zbiorowe Józefa Piłsudskiego*, ed. Kazimierz Świtalski, 5 vols. (Warszawa: Instytut Józefa Piłsudskiego Poświęcony Badaniu Najnowszej Historii Polski, 1937), 5:7.
22 See Juliusz Bardach, "Krewo i Lublin: z problemów unii polsko-litewskiej," *Kwartalnik Historyczny* 76, no. 3 (1969): 583–619; Tomasz Kempa and Krzysztof Mikulski, eds., *Unia Lubelska z 1569 roku. Z tradycji unifikacyjnych i rzeczypospolitej* (Toruń: Wydawnictwo Adam Marszałek, 2011); Elżbieta Kwiecińska, *Dzieje Rusi – Dzieje Ukrainy w historiografii Polskiej XIX – początku XX wieku*, MA thesis, University of Warsaw, 2004.
23 "Nota Delegacji polskiej w sprawie granicy wschodniej Polski, złożona przewodniczącemu Komisji dla spraw polskich dnia 3 marca 1919," in *Akty i dokumenty dotyczące sprawy granic Polski na Konferencji Pokojowej w Paryżu 1918–1919*,pt1,131–3.https://polona.pl/item/akty-i-dokumenty-dotyczace-sprawy-granic-polski-na-konferencji-pokojowej-w-paryzu,MjI5NTU5Mw/2.

24 "W kraju tym nie ma pierwiastka dostatecznie silnego i zdolnego do utworzenia stałego rządu ... Silna mniejszość polska reprezentuje jedyną siłę intelektualną i ekonomiczną kraju," in *Akty i dokumenty*.
25 Ibid.
26 Dmowski, *Zagadnienia środkowo - i wschodnio-europejskie*, 590.
27 Roman Dmowski, *Memoriał o terytorium Państwa Polskiego, złożony przez Romana Dmowskiego Prezydentowi Wilsonowi w Waszyngtonie d. 8 października 1918 r.*, in *Polityka polska i odbudowanie państwa*, 608–14.
28 Ibid., 559, 576.
29 Dmowski, *Memoriał o terytorium Państwa Polskiego, złożony Sekretarzowi Stanu, Balfourowi w Londynie w końcu marca 1917*, 525; Dmowski, *Zagadnienia środkowo- i wschodnio-europejskie*, 576, 589; Dmowski, *Memoriał o terytorium Państwa Polskiego, złożony przez Romana Dmowskiego Prezydentowi Wilsonowi w Waszyngtonie d. 8 Października 1918 r.* 599; Dmowski, *Nota Delegacji Polskiej na Konferencję Pokojową w sprawie granic wschodnich Polski*, 624.
30 Dmowski, *Memoriał o terytorium Państwa Polskiego, złożony Sekretarzowi Stanu, Balfourowi w Londynie w Końcu Marca 1917*, 525.
31 Ibid.
32 Dmowski, *Memoriał o terytorium Państwa Polskiego, złożony przez Romana Dmowskiego Prezydentowi Wilsonowi w Waszyngtonie d. 8 Października 1918 r.*, 615–16.
33 Dmowski, *Memoriał o terytorium Państwa Polskiego, złożony Sekretarzowi Stanu, Balfourowi w Londynie w Końcu Marca 1917*, 524.
34 Dmowski, *Zagadnienia środkowo- i wschodnio-europejskie*, 569.
35 Dmowski, *Memoriał o terytorium Państwa Polskiego, złożony przez Romana Dmowskiego Prezydentowi Wilsonowi w Waszyngtonie d. 8 Października 1918 r.*, 611.
36 Dmowski, *Zagadnienia środkowo- i wschodnio-europejskie*, 586.
37 Dmowski, *Memoriał o terytorium Państwa Polskiego złożone przez R. Dmowskiego Prezydentowi Wilsonowi w Waszyngtonie 8 Października 1918 r.*, 599.
38 Ibid. For similar arguments, see Dmowski, *Memoriał o terytorium Państwa Polskiego złożony Sekretarzowi Stanu, Balfourowi w Londynie w końcu marca 1917*, in *Polityka polska i odbudowanie państwa*, 524–5.
39 Dmowski, "Memoriał w sprawie uznania niepodległości Polski. Złożony przez R. Dmowskiego Rządowi Rosyjskiemu na Ręce Ambasadora w Paryżu, w marcu 1917," in *Polityka polska i odbudowanie państwa*, 512; Dmowski, *Memoriał o terytorium Państwa Polskiego, złożony Sekretarzowi Stanu, Balfourowi w Londynie w Końcu Marca 1917*, 524–5; Dmowski,

Nota Komitetu Narodowego Polskiego w Paryżu do ministrów spraw zagranicznych państw sprzymierzonych, przed konferencją międzysojuszniczą r. 1917, in *Polityka polska i odbudowanie państwa*, 598; Dmowski, *Zagadnienia środkowo- i wschodnio-europejskie*, 537, 563, 584–5, 594.

40 Dmowski, *Zagadnienia środkowo- i wschodnio-europejskie*, 590.

41 Dmowski, "Polityka polska i odbudowanie państwa," in *Polityka polska i odbudowanie państwa*, 483–4.

42 Mykhailo Hrushevsky, *The Historical Evolution of the Ukrainian Problem* (London: SVU, 1915), 6–8.

43 *Notes Présentées par la Délégation de la République Ukrainienne à la conférence de la paix à Paris*, 11 April 1919, February–April 1919 (Paris, 1919), 37.

44 Ibid., 7–8.

45 Ibid., 39.

46 *Polish Atrocities in Ukrainian Galicia: A Telegraphic Note to M. Georges Clemenceau, President of the Peace Conference, from Vladimir Temnitsky, Minister of Foreign Affairs of the Ukrainian Republic and Joseph Burachinsky, Minister of Justice of the Western Territory of the Ukrainian Republic* (New York: Ukrainian National Committee of the United States, 1919).

47 *Polish Atrocities in Ukrainian Galicia*, 3, 5, 6–8.

48 This Ukrainian delegation employed particularly emotive terms such as "invasion," "occupation," "chauvinism," "slavery," "imperialism," "extermination," "annihilation," "massacres," "corruption," "violence," and "persecution" (of the Ukrainian intelligentsia). They also referred to "nationalist peasants," "national leaders," and attacks on the Greek Catholic Church (stating that many of their churches had been sacked by Poles, with more than one thousand Greek Catholic priests arrested). The behaviour and actions of Polish soldiers were also condemned, with mentions of "deportation," "internment," the "assassination" of Ukrainian soldiers, the "murder" of the sick and wounded, sexual violence against Ukrainian women (especially from the upper classes), and the burning of Ukrainian villages. They accused the Polish authorities of overt cultural and ethnic discrimination such as burning Ukrainian books, forbidding the use of the Cyrillic alphabet or speaking Ukrainian in public, censoring the Ukrainian press, dismissing Ukrainian officials, and closing down Ukrainian theatre, schools, and scientific institutions. Public gatherings had also been banned, as was the singing of Slavic hymns in church. See *Polish Atrocities*, 4–15.

49 Ibid., 10, 16.

50 Ibid., 9.

51 Ibid.
52 Ibid., 13.
53 Ibid., 4.
54 Ibid., 6.
55 Żuławski vel Grajewski, *Sprawa ukraińska na Konferencji Pokojowej*, 130–3.
56 Maciej Górny, *Kreślarze ojczyzn. Geografowie i granice międzywojennej Europy* (Warsaw: Instytut Historii PAN, 2017), 7–9, 114–15, 173–5. For the role of cartographers in border-making, see Steven Seegel, *Map Men: Transnational Lives and Deaths of Geographers in the Making of East Central Europe* (Chicago: University of Chicago Press, 2018).
57 Eugeniusz Romer, *Geograficzno-statystyczny atlas Polski* (Warsaw, Kraków: Gebethner i Wolff, 1916), 8.
58 Eugeniusz Romer, *Polski Atlas Kongresowy* (Lwów: Książnica Polska Towarzystwa Nauczycieli Szkół Wyższych, 1921).
59 Eugeniusz Romer, *Polski Atlas Kongresowy* (1921), board nr 27, https://www.wbc.poznan.pl/dlibra/publication/557987/edition/474602/content.
60 Ibid., board nr 24.
61 Stefan Rudnitsky, *The Ukraine and the Ukrainians* (Jersey City: Ukrainian National Council, 1915), 7.
62 Grzegorz Rossoliński-Liebe, "Racism and Modern Antisemitism in Habsburg and Russian Ukraine," in Raul Cârstocea and Éva Kovács, eds., *Modern Antisemitisms in the Peripheries: Europe and Its Colonies 1880–1945* (Vienna and Hamburg: New Academic Press, 2019), 140–7. See also Per Anders Rudling, "Eugenics and Racial Anthropology in the Ukrainian Radical Nationalist Tradition," *Science in Context* 32, no. 1 (2019): 67–91.
63 "Decision Taken by the Conference of Ambassadors with Regard to the Eastern Frontiers of Poland," Paris, 15 March 1923, http://www.worldlii.org/int/other/LNTSer/1923/36.html.

3

The Path to the Treaty of Riga

The Establishment of the Polish-Ukrainian Border, 1918–21

Jan Jacek Bruski

In November 1918, after 123 years' absence, a sovereign Poland reappeared on the political map of Europe. Its restoration was not a surprise. Toward the end of the First World War, the Polish question had been actualized in the international arena, and in late 1916 the germs of Polish statehood started to appear under the aegis of the Central Powers, albeit initially as a rump territory. The re-established Kingdom of Poland neighboured the new-born Ukrainian state, which first took the form of the Ukrainian People's Republic (UNR) and later a quasi-monarchy under Hetman Pavlo Skoropadsky. In the autumn of 1918, both emerging states faced an urgent need to define their mutual relations. A number of factors, most notably the threat posed to both by Bolshevik Russia, encouraged closer cooperation. However, nascent Polish-Ukrainian relations would soon be overshadowed by territorial conflict.

The conflict was initially related to the allocation of ethnically mixed Polish-Ukrainian areas that prior to 1914 had been part of the Russian Empire. However, the division of the former Habsburg province of Galicia quickly emerged as the main point of contention. That disagreement gave rise to a prolonged military confrontation followed by an even longer diplomatic tussle, from which Poland would emerge the victor. Ultimately, however, the decisive influence on the course of the Polish-Ukrainian border was exerted by another armed conflict – the war against Soviet Russia. The peace treaty that ended it, signed in Riga in 1921, would solidify the borders in Eastern Europe until the outbreak of the Second World War.

The Polish-Ukrainian territorial dispute that followed the end of the First World War has been the subject of extensive scholarly analysis, and some earlier studies from the interwar period are still relevant today.[1] The most important publications on the subject, however, have appeared in the last three decades, since the collapse of Communist rule in Poland and the emergence of an independent Ukraine. These works focus mainly on the conflict over Eastern Galicia, overshadowing other Polish-Ukrainian territorial controversies.[2] Another issue frequently addressed in the literature is the political rapprochement between Poland and the UNR, which led to the Piłsudski-Petliura alliance in April 1920 and the joint Kyiv expedition. In this context, the challenges surrounding the negotiations over the border between Poland and the UNR have been discussed at length.[3] Scholars have also been interested in the international aspects of Polish-Ukrainian relations, including Polish-Ukrainian rivalry during the Paris Peace Conference and the Great Powers' attitude toward the conundrum of Eastern Galicia.[4] That said, the Polish-Soviet war of 1919–20 and the Treaty of Riga have undoubtedly received the most attention, besides generating the largest body of literature in English. While not always particularly insightful, such research has gone some way toward addressing the Ukrainian theme.[5]

In this chapter, I examine the problem of establishing the border between Poland and Ukraine in 1918–21 in a synthetic manner, using the extensive literature mentioned earlier and my own earlier studies, which were based on research conducted in Polish and Ukrainian archives. I try to identify the main stages of the processes discussed and the factors that determined them, paying particular attention to the differences in strategic positions and international conditions that favoured the Polish side. I also endeavour to show the role played by other nations in the Polish-Ukrainian conflict: the Western Powers on the one hand, and Bolshevik Russia on the other. I also note the negligible impact that the principle of self-determination had on the process of establishing the Polish-Ukrainian border.

The chapter has five parts. First, I present the reasons behind the Polish-Ukrainian territorial dispute and the opening stage of the conflict, which broke out in the autumn of 1918 and concerned the allocation of the Chełm/Kholm region, southern Podlachia, and western Volhynia. Second, I separately discuss the events of the military and diplomatic conflict over Eastern Galicia up until the province's capture by the Polish army in July 1919. The third and fourth sections are devoted to the political relations and negotiations over the border that the governments of Poland and the UNR conducted until April 1920. Two important outcomes were a Ukrainian declaration on the border on 2 December 1919 and the signing of the Piłsudski-Petliura alliance. The final section discusses the weaknesses of the joint Polish-Ukrainian offensive against Kyiv, and its consequences. In this context, I present the circumstances in which the concept of the so-called Curzon Line emerged. I am also interested in the impact the Ukrainian factor had on the Polish-Soviet peace negotiations conducted at Riga in the autumn of 1920, and I endeavour to answer the question of what lay behind the ultimate demarcation of the border between Poland and the Soviet republics of Ukraine, Russia, and Belarus. Ultimately, the Riga border was a compromise, with which none of the parties was satisfied and which would be a source of future conflict.

THE CHEŁM/KHOLM REGION, PODLACHIA, VOLHYNIA, AND THE BEGINNINGS OF THE POLISH-UKRAINIAN CONFLICT

For the Ukrainian government in Kyiv it seemed obvious in the autumn of 1918 that the border with the restored Polish state should follow the prewar border between the Southwestern Krai and the Kingdom of Poland, incorporating into Ukraine the Chełm/Kholm region and southern Podlachia, which had been allocated to the UNR in the Treaty of Brest-Litovsk.[6] This particular border was generally viewed by the Ukrainian side as the most favourable, although some contended it was not altogether fair since it still left large Ukrainian communities on the Polish side.[7] The head of the Central Council (Central Rada) of Ukraine, Professor Mykhailo Hrushevsky, lamented that Drohiczyn/Dorohychyn (the coronation town of King Danylo of Halych) remained in Polish hands, and that the Ukrainians had failed to secure the "old ethnographic boundary."[8] Generally speaking, however, this aspect of relations with Poland did not weigh heavily on the minds of Dnieper Ukrainian politicians.

Relations with Ukraine provoked much greater emotion on the Polish side. The territorial decisions made at Brest-Litovsk were frequently condemned, and the wave of outrage they generated had led, in the closing months of the war, to the breakdown of some Polish circles' previous orientation toward Germany and Austria-Hungary.[9] It should also be noted that a great number of Poles – influenced by the nationalist ideas of the National Democratic Party – remained hostile toward the very notion of an independent Ukraine. They perceived its emergence as a threat to the future Polish state, and preferred a direct boundary with Russia. That would move Poland's borders much farther east, approximately up the line of the Second Partition of Poland of 1793. National Democracy (Endecja) supporters understood that in the eastern territories, Ukrainians and Belarusians outnumbered Poles; but they believed that Poland had a "civilizing mission" on these territories, which could be Polonized relatively quickly.[10]

On the international stage, this position was represented by the Polish National Committee (KNP), residing in Paris and led by Roman Dmowski, the leader of the National Democrats. That committee aspired to the role of a Polish government-in-exile, but in the event, it was the so-called Pro-Independence Left that would gain political power in the newly reconstituted country. The latter group had gathered around the influential figure of Józef Piłsudski, who became the head of the civilian authorities (Chief of State) and Supreme Commander of the Army of the newly proclaimed Republic of Poland. However, Piłsudski and the KNP then forged a compromise, with the latter being granted considerable powers in the realm of foreign policy. Dmowski himself would lead the Polish delegation at the Paris Peace Conference. On 3 March 1919, he addressed a note setting out Poland's territorial demands in the east to the Supreme Council of the Allies. Regarding the Ukrainian stretch of the border, the so-called Dmowski Line left not only the Podlachia and the Chełm/Kholm regions but also all of Polesia, most of Volhynia, and western Podolia in Polish hands as well (see map 2.2, page 95 of this volume).[11] The Piłsudski camp, which initially determined Poland's eastern policy, represented a different view. The Chief of State's adherents wanted to support the aspirations for national sovereignty on the peripheries (*okrainy*) of the former Russian Empire (Ukraine, Belarus, Lithuania, the Baltic provinces), hoping they would later join Poland in a federation or a close political alliance. This would ensure that the power of the Russian state would not be restored; in Piłsudski's vision, that state would be pushed much farther east and enclosed within the borders of the sixteenth-century Grand Duchy of Moscow.[12] The Piłsudskiites had modest ambitions with regard to the Ukrainian lands, but they also assumed that the Chełm/Kholm region and western Volhynia would belong to Poland.

These frontier territories would be the setting of an undeclared armed conflict between Poland and Ukraine in the autumn of 1918. The situation on the Ukrainian side was made even more difficult by a simultaneous revolt against Hetman Skoropadsky, led by the Directory of the revived UNR. "However the fight in Central Ukraine will end, however one views it," stated Oleksandr Skoropys-Ioltukhovsky, the Ukrainian *starost* of the *gubernia* of Chełm/Kholm, "in the Polish-Ukrainian borderland we must continue to work towards strengthening the Ukrainian state and national positions ... The Chełm/Kholm region must be Ukrainian."[13] However, declarations like these remained wishful thinking, since Skoropys-Ioltukhovsky's rule and the powers at his disposal were limited. It should therefore be mentioned that the Central Powers never actually followed through on the commitments they had made to Ukraine at Brest-Litovsk. A rudimentary Ukrainian administration could be established only in Podlachia, then under occupation by the German army. The Chełm/Kholm region proper, captured by Austro-Hungarian forces, was not controlled by Kyiv at all; the occupiers instead supported the emerging local Polish authorities.[14] After the Central Powers were defeated in November 1918, the former *gubernia* of Chełm/Kholm passed into Polish hands with relative ease. No serious Polish-Ukrainian clashes took place west of the Bug River, and the Ukrainian administrative apparatus was evacuated to Brest. The territories of Brest and Kobryn counties were subsequently captured by Polish forces in early February 1919.[15] Fighting was also taking place in Volhynia at that time, having broken out in November 1918, when Polish troops captured Volodymyr-Volhynsky. Armed clashes between the Polish army and the UNR's forces would continue until May 1919, leaving a victorious Poland in control of western Volhynia.[16]

THE GALICIAN KNOT

The future of Eastern Galicia – the eastern part of the former Austrian crownland, inhabited mainly by Ukrainians but with a large Polish minority that dominated its political, economic, and cultural life – emerged as the most serious impediment in Polish-Ukrainian relations.[17] Even before the collapse of Habsburg rule, both sides had aspired to take control of the entire region. The issue of how Lwów/Lviv, the capital of the province, as well as the important oil fields near Drohobycz/Drohobych and Borysław/Boryslav, should be allocated provoked especially strong emotions. On 19 October 1918, the Ukrainian National Council summoned in Lwów/Lviv had announced its intention to establish a Ukrainian State on the territories that had previously belonged to the Austro-Hungarian Monarchy. This state was to include all of Eastern Galicia up to the San River as well as the Lemko region – a part of Western Galicia densely populated by Ruthenians that stretched as far as the Poprad River and the environs of Nowy Sącz.[18] The Ukrainians captured Lwów/Lviv on the night of 31 October, surprising their Polish counterparts, who had been preparing to do the same. A similar scenario played out in other towns across Eastern Galicia. Two weeks later, the West Ukrainian People's Republic (ZUNR) was proclaimed on these territories. Having initially been caught unawares, the Poles were quick to recover the initiative. Indeed, an anti-Ukrainian uprising had broken out in Lwów/Lviv on 1 November.[19] The intensity of Polish emotions at the time can only be comprehended if we remember the city's hold on the Polish national consciousness. It was not simply the capital of a formerly Austrian-ruled province; it was also a centre of Polishness whose significance across all of the partition zones was comparable only to that of Warsaw and Kraków. However, Lwów/Lviv had an equally important symbolic meaning for the Ukrainians, even though they were a minority in the city itself, for it was there that all of the most important institutions of the Ukrainian national movement were located; it was also the place of residence of the Metropolitan of Halych, the head of the Ukrainian Greek Catholic Church.[20]

The Polish insurgents, who knew the city's topography very well and were supported by the civilian populace, were much more successful at street fighting than their opponents. As a result, after a few days of clashes, the western part of Lwów/Lviv found itself under Polish control. Two weeks later, relief reached the city, and the Ukrainians were forced to abandon it. Although the siege would continue for almost four more months, the fact that the Poles held on to Lwów/Lviv in November had a decisive psychological impact. Regular units of the Polish army soon joined the fighting, which meant that the newly created government in Warsaw had formally joined the conflict. Conversely, on 22 January 1919, the ZUNR and the UNR were united. Although this new federation remained politically loose and mostly theoretical, its creation meant that Warsaw and Kyiv found themselves officially at war.

The fighting in Eastern Galicia lasted until mid-July 1919. For the first few months, the front line remained stable, running roughly along the San River. The strategic railway linking Lwów/Lviv with Przemyśl/Peremyshl was also in Polish hands, along with a strip of adjacent land. West of the San, despite initial successes, the Ukrainians were unable to hold on to more permanent positions. In particular, the Lemko region remained outside their control, apart from a brief episode during which the so-called Komancha Republic briefly existed along its eastern edge. Local activists, most of whom were affiliated to the Russophile camp, distanced themselves from the ZUNR and devised plans to secede, together with the Transcarpathian Ruthenians, and unite with neighbouring Czechoslovakia.[21]

On the Galician territories they controlled, the Ukrainians created a well-organized administrative structure and mobilized a strong, disciplined army of more than fifty thousand soldiers. Even so, the ZUNR's chances of long-term survival were slim, largely because it lacked reserves. In the absence of external support, be it armed or diplomatic, the Galician Ukrainians stood no chance in their conflict with the Poles. Such assistance could not be offered to the ZUNR by Dnieper Ukraine, which had its own opponents and internal problems with which to deal. For both sides of the conflict, it was vital to win the backing of the victorious Entente Powers, which were seeking a peaceful resolution to the conflict. The first step in that endeavour would be to bring the two sides on the Galician front to the table and sign an armistice as soon as possible. However, efforts in this direction were routinely sabotaged by either the Poles or the Ukrainians, depending on how the fighting was going; both sides were justifiably concerned that a temporary armistice line would eventually become permanent. The most serious attempt at Entente mediation was a French mission led by General Joseph Barthélemy. In February 1919, the mission arrived in Lwów/Lviv, where it presented a proposal for an armistice in Eastern Galicia and a provisional division of the territory until a more permanent settlement could be reached at the Paris Peace Conference. The so-called Barthélemy Line ran along the Bug River to Kamionka Strumiłowa/Kam'ianka (leaving this town and Sokal on the Polish side), then south toward Bóbrka/Bibrka and Mikołajów/Mykolaiv, halting at the railway line from Stryj/Stryi to Ławoczne/Lavochne, which was to remain in Ukrainian hands. Poland was to keep Lwów/Lviv and the Polish army was to take the Drohobycz/Drohobych and Borysław/Boryslav basin. This would, however, be governed by an international commission, and the Ukrainians were promised a 50 per cent share of the field's oil production.[22] These proposals undoubtedly favoured the Poles, but accepting them gave the Ukrainians a unique opportunity to have the ZUNR officially recognized by the Entente Powers. Nevertheless, during the negotiations conducted on 28 February in Chodorów/Khodoriv, the Ukrainian delegation rejected the Entente's terms. The conflict was to be settled by "blood and iron," as stated by the order issued by the command of the Ukrainian Galician Army.[23] A final attempt to reach a compromise in the Polish-Ukrainian dispute was made by the Inter-Allied Armistice Commission, established in Paris and presided over by the South African General Louis Botha. In early May 1919, the commission presented new terms for an armistice in Galicia to the Polish and Ukrainian delegations with a proposed demarcation line more favourable to the ZUNR. It left Lwów/Lviv on the Polish side, and the Drohobych oil fields on the Ukrainian one. This time it was the Poles who categorically rejected the agreement.[24]

Throughout the conflict, only a few sporadic Polish and Ukrainian voices called for a permanent division of the contested territory. It is therefore all the more notable that this solution was granted serious consideration by Piłsudski himself. Unlike most Polish politicians, he regarded Eastern Galicia as a region of secondary importance and the conflict there as "an ... unnecessary struggle" or even "an idiotic war," as one of his close aides, Leon Wasilewski, put it.[25] This followed from the Chief of State's deep conviction that Poland needed to reach an agreement with the emerging Ukrainian state and that "the source of the Ruthenian question" was in Kyiv, not in Lwów/Lviv. However, he too had to take into consideration the uncompromising position of Polish public opinion when it came to Eastern Galicia, which was that Poland must hold on to Lwów/Lviv and the Borysław/Boryslav oilfields. For strategic reasons, Piłsudski opted for a border that would leave the Drohobycz/Drohobych–Lwów/Lviv–Kowel/Kovel railway in Polish hands. The desire to gain a suitable defensive advantage in the east also led him to demand that western part of Volhynia be awarded to Poland.[26] Piłsudski's vision corresponded with the broader concept, put forward by the Piłsudkiites and other groups, of creating a border based on the so-called line of ethnic balance. That vision assumed that the number of Ukrainians remaining on the Polish side would be the same as the ultimate number of the Poles within Ukrainian borders.[27] The problem was specifying the criteria for resolving the ethnicity of the individual groups inhabiting the contested territory.

Politicking aside, the conflict was eventually settled by force: Polish troops captured all of the contested territories, first the western part of Volhynia and then all of Galicia. The breakthrough was possible because, in clear violation of the Entente's orders, Poland sent in an superbly equipped and well-disciplined army led by General Józef Haller that had been formed in France toward the end of the First World War. The Supreme Council of the Paris Peace Conference criticized Poland's actions; even so, on 25 June 1919 it formerly authorized the Polish occupation of Eastern Galicia. However, this remained a provisional solution: the Western Powers reserved the right to decide the province's fate in the future. Initially, they intended to give Poland a mandate for governing this territory for only twenty-five years, but this idea was subsequently abandoned in the face of protests from Warsaw. However, the Polish authorities administering Eastern Galicia were expected to give this region a special autonomous status.[28]

POLAND-UNR:
STAGES OF RAPPROCHEMENT IN 1919

The Western Powers left unresolved the matter of allocating the eastern part of Galicia. They were also unwilling to recognize Polish claims to those areas of the former Russian Empire east of the Bug River. In a declaration issued by the Supreme Council of the Allies on 8 December 1919, the temporary boundary between Poland and a future Russia was drawn along the Bug and, farther north, along the eastern boundary of the former Białystok/Belostok *oblast*.[29] In this situation, the Polish government tried to protect its territorial interests in two ways: by conducting military operations in the east and creating *faits accomplis* in this manner, and by opening (behind the backs of the Entente Powers and the Galician Ukrainians) direct negotiations with representatives of Dnieper Ukraine. The UNR was now being weakened by fighting on several fronts: not only against Poland but, more importantly, against the forces of "White" Russia and the Bolsheviks, who had formed a Communist government under their aegis in Kharkiv, from where they had progressively occupied more and more Ukrainian territory. This situation made the UNR a convenient partner for negotiations, for it was increasingly inclined to make territorial concessions to Poland as its own political circumstances deteriorated. In return, it expected support in combating the existential threat posed by Russia. On the Ukrainian side, the main proponents for an agreement with the Poles were the Chief *Otaman* (Commander) of the UNR's military and, after February 1919, the Chairman of the its Directory, Symon Petliura, who realized that the price for a rapprochement with its western neighbour was to renounce, as he expressed it, "territorial maximalism."[30] For this, he had found a cooperative ally in Piłsudski, for whom an anti-Russian alliance with Ukraine was the fundamental element in his long-term plan for transforming Eastern Europe.[31]

First talks with representatives of the UNR's Directory, led by the politician and historian Viacheslav Prokopovych, opened in Warsaw in January 1919. Both sides were eager to reach an agreement, but negotiations broke down over the issue of the Polish-Ukrainian border. The UNR delegates agreed to Poland retaining the Chełm/Kholm region, Podlachia, and parts of Polesia, but they rejected the division of Eastern Galicia, which would have left Lwów/Lviv and the Borysław/Boryslav Basin in Polish hands. Direct negotiations now collapsed for several months. An agreement was signed on 24 May 1919 by the Polish Prime Minister Ignacy Jan Paderewski and the Directory's representative, Borys Kurdynovsky, but this should be viewed as an act of political subversion conceived by the Polish side to impress the Western Powers. Indeed, the inside story of Kurdynovsky's mission remains unclear to this very day. There is much to suggest that the Ukrainian emissary, having been given only very general instructions, far exceeded the mandate granted to him and attempted to play an independent political role, with the result that his personal ambitions were exploited by the Polish side. In the agreement itself, Kurdynovsky consented – in return for Poland recognizing Ukraine's sovereignty and the promise of a military alliance – to the UNR renouncing all of Eastern Galicia as well as the western part of Volhynia as far as the Styr River. The treaty of 24 May also included the Ukrainian side's obligation to coordinate its foreign policy with the Warsaw government and to guarantee, albeit on a mutual basis, the rights of the Polish minority in Ukraine. This would have effectively turned the UNR into a Polish protectorate. It is no surprise, then, that the agreement was disavowed by the Ukrainian government. Nevertheless, its signing strengthened the Polish tactical position at the Paris Peace Conference, and it became a reference point during the subsequent negotiations between Poland and the UNR.[32]

By mid-July 1919, the government of the ZUNR and the Ukrainian Galician Army had been driven back across the Zbrucz/Zbruch River (the former Austria-Russian border) into UNR-controlled Podolia. The end of the conflict in Galicia opened the way for further Polish-Ukrainian talks. In mid-August a Ukrainian mission led by the UNR's former Minister of Railways, Pylyp Pylypchuk, arrived in Warsaw to broach the prospect of Polish cooperation against the Bolsheviks; the delegates carried a personal letter from the Chief *Otaman* Petliura addressed to Piłsudski.[33] Official talks began on 20 August, having been preceded by a declaration in which the Ukrainian side agreed to a provisional border with Poland along the rivers Zbrucz/Zbruch (meaning the *de facto* cession of Eastern Galicia), Turia/Turiia, and Pripyat (giving Poland a fragment of western Volhynia, albeit smaller than that offered in the Paderewski-Kurdynovsky agreement). Additionally, it was announced that there would be a possible revision of the principles of the UNR's agrarian reforms, specifically in regard to the large Polish-owned landed estates.[34] It turned out, however, that these concessions were no longer deemed satisfactory. In particular, the Poles demanded that a larger portion of Volhynia, including the Brody–Zdołbunów/Zdolbuniv–Sarny railway, be subject to Polish administration "for the duration of the war." Unauthorized to decide whether to accept these terms, after a few days of talks Pylypchuk decided to return to Kamianets-Podilsky, where the UNR government was residing at the time, for fresh instructions.

Pylypchuk's report on the declaration was met with sharp criticism. Pylypchuk himself was reprimanded for a careless interview he had given to the Polish press in which he had stated, among other things, that the matter of Eastern Galicia "had clearly been decided in Paris" in Poland's favour and that "the Galician government and army have ceased to exist." This latter point drew particular opprobrium. The Galician leader, Ievhen Petrushevych, had continued to cooperate with the Directory, and the army under his command was, at that time, also the UNR's main armed force.[35]

The August mission did not end in complete failure, however. It improved Polish-Ukrainian relations, paving the way for future agreements. Only a few days later, on 1 September, the representatives of the Polish and Ukrainian armies signed an armistice, which thereafter was extended every ten days. Also, economic relations were soon established with the signing of a Polish-Ukrainian trade agreement on 7 October.[36] This rapprochement also saw political talks continue. In late September 1919 the UNR's government decided to send a new diplomatic mission to Warsaw. Its unenviable task was to establish closer relations with Poland (preferably through a military pact) while at the same time reversing the concessions previously made by Pylypchuk. Moreover, it was purposefully given a more representative character. The mission was led by the head of the Ukrainian Ministry of Foreign Affairs, Andrii Livytsky, who was to be seconded by political counsellors, delegated from different political parties, and a group of independent experts. The mission was also joined by representatives of the Eastern Galician government. According to the directives given to Livytsky, the issue of the border was to be avoided, and if this proved impossible, Eastern Galicia was to be defended at all costs. It was to be emphasized that only the Paris Peace Conference could determine the region's future. The maximum concession that the delegates were permitted to offer was the conditional relinquishing of the Chełm/Kholm region and Podlachia.[37]

The new round of talks in Warsaw began in the latter half of October 1919. From the beginning, the Poles placed the Ukrainians in a difficult position by clearly stating that they regarded the current negotiations as a continuation of the talks with Pylypchuk. As far as Warsaw was concerned, all agreements reached in August remained in force. The opening declaration presented by the UNR's delegates was returned by the Poles with demands that it be modified according to Poland's wishes. This was hardly surprising. The revised document, which the Ukrainians resubmitted on 28 October, was very different from the earlier agreement reached with Kurdynovsky, as well as from Pylypchuk's declaration. Regarding the border issue, it defended the ethnographic principle; left the agrarian problem to a future Ukrainian constituent assembly; and demanded sharply that Ukraine's sovereignty be recognized and that the UNR be treated as an equal partner.[38] Further talks proceeded with considerable difficulty. In response to the Ukrainian side's demands, the issue of the border was delegated to a special commission. This proved completely fruitless.

By late November, the Poles had started to apply even greater pressure.[39] Its effectiveness was compounded by grievous news from the UNR regarding the situation facing Petliura's government. After a brief period of military success in August 1919, the Ukrainian forces had found themselves in retreat again, pushed back both by the Bolsheviks and by General Anton Denikin's Volunteer Army. However, the UNR's greatest enemy proved to be a horrific typhoid epidemic, which decimated its army. In November 1919, only the westernmost portions of Podolia and Volhynia remained under its control. The Directory's situation was made all the worse when units of the Ukrainian Galician Army switched sides and joined Denikin's Volunteers.[40] This decision had been forced in those units by the tragic situation on the front line, but it also resulted from underlying discrepancies between the Galician and Dnieper Ukrainians. These tensions could be traced back to opposing attitudes toward the looming rapprochement between the UNR and Poland at the expense of Eastern Galicia. Vasyl Paneiko, an Eastern Galician delegate to the Paris Peace Conference, had long lobbied for cooperation with "White" Russia. In late August 1919, he had even sent a letter to Petrushevych in which, allegedly quoting the words of an official from the French Ministry of Foreign Affairs, he argued: "You ally yourself with states of secondary importance, such as Poland or Romania, you pay them in provinces, such as Galicia, the Chełm/Kholm region, Bessarabia, and yet if you joined the Russian federation you could keep all of those provinces."[41] The Galician Ukrainians' agreement with the "White" Russians was undoubtedly a major blow to the UNR government. At the same time, however, untied the hands of the Dnieper Ukrainians, making further negotiations with the Poles considerably easier.

The Polish side demanded that talks in Warsaw be brought to an end, threatening to break off relations with the Directory and not prolong the armistice by the agreed ten days. The Ukrainian negotiators still endeavoured to avoid a final settlement on the Galician issue. Indeed, a prepared draft of its political declaration stated that the Zbrucz/Zbruch River was the UNR's western border without even specifying the neighbouring state.[42] This ploy obviously did not escape the Poles' attention, prompting them to issue an ultimatum: the declaration must emphasize the allocation of Eastern Galicia to Poland. Consequently, the final text, presented on the evening of 2 December 1919, was not far from the declaration signed by Pylypchuk a few months earlier. Besides relinquishing the UNR's rights to Galicia and specifying that the Polish-Ukrainian border would run through northwestern Volhynia (its exact placement would depend on decisions reached in Paris), this new declaration also announced that "the legal status of the landowners of Polish ethnicity in Ukraine would be regulated by a special agreement between the Ukrainian and Polish governments." Livytsky's one modest success was that attached to the document was a list of Ukrainian demands, which had been verbally accepted by the Polish side. These included postulates from Poland officially recognizing the UNR; agreements on military, trade, and consular conventions; support for Ukrainian diplomacy abroad; the release of persons interned by the Poles; and assisting the UNR's ongoing war effort by sending military equipment.[43]

TOWARD THE PIŁSUDSKI-PETLIURA ALLIANCE

The declaration of 2 December 1919 sealed the split between the governments of the UNR and the ZUNR. However, it was met with protests, and not only by the Galician Ukrainians. The territorial concessions to Poland outraged many Dnieper Ukrainian groups, who openly contested Petliura's policies, the Chief *Otaman* having been leading the Directory almost single-handedly at the time.[44] However, Petliura had no choice but to accept the outcome of Livytsky's mission. By late November, at the behest of the UNR government, Polish forces had captured Kamianets-Podilsky, where only a handful of Ukrainian ministers remained, alongside the government's plenipotentiary, Professor Ivan Ohiienko. The Ukrainian Prime Minister Isaak Mazepa, accompanied what remained of the UNR's army on a guerrilla raid against the "Whites" while Petliura himself sought refuge on Polish territory. On 7 December, he arrived in Warsaw to oversee further talks with the Poles. He also met with Piłsudski, and the two conferred throughout the night. Most of the UNR forces were now completely unfit to continue fighting; they were disarmed and placed in Polish internment camps or military hospitals.

After the December declaration, talks in Warsaw were halted for more than three months. Meanwhile, the Ukrainian armed forces had secretly started to rebuild themselves on the territories controlled by Poland. Negotiations did not resume until March 1920, when Poland's own ongoing hostilities with Soviet Russia started to escalate in severity. During this time, Moscow was preparing an offensive with the intention of spreading the fire of world revolution "over Poland's corpse" to Western Europe; this prompted Warsaw to feverishly prepare its own countermeasures. Poland, which did not have the backing of the Great Powers and was readying itself for a major clash against the Bolsheviks in Ukraine, now strongly desired, for political as well as military reasons, a formal alliance with the UNR. Yet it was also understood in Warsaw that the fledgling Ukrainian state, having been deprived of its territory and now largely dependent on Polish help, was weak – a situation the Poles were eager to exploit.

Once again, the principle controversies arising from these new Polish-Ukrainian talks concerned the border separating Poland from the UNR. Since Eastern Galicia's allocation had already been resolved, these disputes centred on the border in Volhynia. After prolonged and rather futile negotiations, the Poles presented their draft agreement as an ultimatum on 3 April, demanding that it be approved within four days. Both the contents of this document and the form in which it was presented were an unpleasant surprise for the UNR delegates. The issue of the Volhynia border, which apparently had been heading toward an amicable resolution during Pylypchuk's and Livytsky's earlier negotiations, was now brought to a head. The seven westernmost counties of Volhynia were to be attached to Poland; and moreover, the Poles refused to accept the Pripyat River as Ukraine's northern border, insisting instead on a line along the border of the former *gubernia* of Minsk. Presented with these terms, Livytsky personally intervened with Piłsudski, but the Polish delegation showed minimal willingness to compromise through further talks. The Ukrainians attempted to move the provisions related to the border from the political agreement to the planned military convention, but this manoeuvre failed as well. General Stanisław Haller, who headed the Polish General Staff, appraised this proposal as insincere and demanded that it be rejected. In an opinion passed on to the government, he stressed that moving the issue of the Polish-Ukrainian border to the military convention "would give this important matter a provisional character" and, once the Bolsheviks had been defeated, "would create a pretext for starting new negotiations about the state's borders, which would then be conducted in circumstances less favourable to us."[45]

The negotiations, conducted in a tense atmosphere, came to an end in the early hours of 22 April 1920 with the signing of a Polish-Ukrainian political agreement.[46] The treaty's future was on a knife edge until the very last moment and was finally secured only after a five-hour conference between Petliura and Piłsudski, who subsequently ordered that some concessions be made to the Ukrainian side. The most important provision of the agreement was that Poland recognized Ukrainian sovereignty and the Directory headed by Petliura as the UNR's supreme authority. The border between Poland and Ukraine was to run in the south along the Zbrucz/Zbruch River, through Volhynia along the line from Wyszogródek/Vyshhorodok, then north over the Krzemieniec/Kremenets' Mountains, east of Zdołbunów/Zdolbuniv, and finally along the eastern border of the Równe/Rivne county. This was more or less the same as the provisions of the Polish draft of the agreement written in early April, but the Ukrainian side had managed to introduce a provision that would allow for revision of the border in the counties of Równe/Rivne, Dubno, and Krzemieniec/Kremenets'.[47] Of particular importance was Article III of the treaty, in which the Polish government declared that Ukraine would be allocated all territories up to the historical border of the former Polish-Lithuanian Commonwealth prior to the partitions – essentially to the Dnieper River – "which Poland already possesses or shall recapture from Russia by military or diplomatic means." Much historical misunderstanding has since arisen around this provision. It is claimed in the literature that the Polish side wanted to limit the UNR's territory to Right-Bank Ukraine.[48] In fact, the quoted provision was a consequence of the position the Poles had taken in their negotiations with the Bolsheviks – that is, the stipulation that the partitioning treaties of the eighteenth century were no longer in force. Consequently, Poland, as heir to the former commonwealth, could dispose of all territories stretching as far as the 1772 border, to which Russia, whether "Red" or "White," could not lay claim.[49]

Two days later, on 24 April, the Polish-Ukrainian military convention was signed. The treaty provided for joint actions against the Bolsheviks, with the UNR army being placed under Polish command. For their part, the Poles agreed that Petliura could raise fresh troops on their territory and promised to equip three new Ukrainian divisions. Immediately after signing the convention, the UNR's central offices were to be reopened in Kamianets-Podilsky and on those territories that had been occupied by the Poles; administration would gradually be handed over to the Ukrainians. This was a very important provision, because the Polish authorities in the occupied Podolian counties had previously behaved in a way that suggested there was a plan to annex this territory to Poland. In addition, the civilian and military administration of the territories gradually liberated from the Bolsheviks was to be placed under the Ukrainian authorities.[50]

FROM THE WARSAW AGREEMENT TO THE TREATY OF RIGA

The April agreement, more often remembered as the Piłsudski-Petliura pact, faced harsh criticism from its inception from both the Polish and Ukrainian sides. The Polish National Democrats protested against an alliance with Ukraine, but the treaty had even more opponents among Ukrainian politicians. The Galician Ukrainians, understandably, viewed it as a betrayal and as renouncing the idea of a united (*soborna*) Ukraine, but Petliura was also criticized by his compatriots from Dnieper Ukraine for capitulating to Polish demands.[51] It should be noted, however, that the signed agreement, although undoubtedly unequal and asymmetrical, closely reflected the balance of power in Polish-Ukrainian relations. "The weaker side," according to the Polish-American historian Piotr Wandycz, "paid in concessions for the help and support it received."[52] Yet overall, the alliance promised to benefit both parties. Indeed, for the Directory it was probably the last chance to return to its own territory and save the UNR's independence.

The treaties were also the trump card Piłsudski needed to launch his plan for countering "Red" Russia. In late April 1920, Polish-Ukrainian forces launched an attack in the direction of Kyiv. This first operational stage ended in spectacular success – with the seizing of the Ukrainian capital on 7 May – but the tide quickly turned. The allied armies failed to achieve their greater strategic goal of crushing the main Soviet forces, which had retreated east of the Dnieper without major losses. At the end of May, the Bolsheviks launched a successful counter-attack that forced the allies to evacuate Kyiv and retreat back to the west. By the latter half of June, the Polish and Ukrainian forces had been pushed back to the point from which the offensive had been launched in April.[53] And they continued to retreat after that – by August, all the way into Eastern Galicia. The Poles and Ukrainians, so recently competing with each other for control over that province, now found themselves fighting side by side to prevent the Red Army from taking Lwów/Lviv. The Bolsheviks made clear their intentions for the region, proclaiming a "sovereign" Galician Soviet Socialist Republic. They announced its temporary capital in Tarnopol/Ternopil, and the Revolutionary Committee for Galicia (so-called *Halrevkom*) was established there in early August.[54] As well, a separate Polish Soviet Republic was to be created on territory limited to ethnically Polish lands.

The Great Powers were also in favour of trimming Poland's territory. In July 1920, at a conference in the Belgian town of Spa, the Polish Prime Minister Władysław Grabski, seeking international mediation in the

Polish-Soviet conflict, had to agree to the proposal that a line of demarcation between the fighting sides. What would later be known as the Curzon Line was roughly the same as the provisional Polish border specified in the Allied Powers' declaration of 8 December 1919 but elongated to include Eastern Galicia. While the original version had left Lwów/Lviv and the oilfields on the Polish side, the final draft, presented to the Bolsheviks on 11 July, moved the border west, running slightly east of Przemyśl/Peremyshl. However, the Soviet side, believing victory to be near, rejected these proposals.[55] The Curzon Line would re-enter the vocabulary of international relations and European public discussion during the Second World War.

The Bolsheviks' predictions of a decisive victory proved to be premature. In mid-August 1920, the Polish army launched a surprise counteroffensive, pushing the Soviet forces back from Warsaw and precipitating a general retreat by the Red Army. The Poles' success was sealed at the Battle of the Niemen River in late September. Polish-Ukrainian forces also gradually pushed the Bolsheviks out of Eastern Galicia and continued their operations east of the Zbrucz/Zbruch River. By now, both sides' armies were exhausted and a decisive victory for either seemed highly unlikely. There was growing readiness on both sides to make peace as quickly as possible; indeed, negotiations had already started, in mid-August 1920. The first round of talks took place in Minsk, then under Red Army control. The Soviet negotiators attempted to force the Poles to accept terms that amounted to capitulation. The radical change in military fortunes saw the negotiations moved to Riga, the capital of neutral Latvia, where they resumed in the second half of September.[56] The UNR delegates were not allowed to participate, the Soviets having categorically rejected their presence. Moreover, the prolonged negotiations that Piłsudski had anticipated did not come to pass.

The Polish Chief of State had been politically marginalized since mid-July 1920, having been removed from key decisions made on the matter of a peace treaty. He was further hampered by the National Defence Council, most of whose members were critics of his federalist program for Eastern Europe. This body had the decisive influence on the instructions given to the emissaries sent to the peace talks and on the composition of the delegation itself. It was far from coincidental that its central figure was a leader of the National Democrats, Stanisław Grabski. The Chief of State's adherents were a minority in the delegation. During the negotiations, which began in late September 1920, the issue of the UNR was swiftly abandoned: the Polish delegates recognized the mandate of Dmytro Manuilsky, representing Soviet Ukraine, who had been co-opted into the Russian delegation for tactical reasons.[57] For all intents and purposes, this meant that Poland had broken its alliance with Petliura's government. The Bolsheviks blackmailed the Polish negotiators, threatening to demand a plebiscite in Eastern Galicia if the Poles were adamant about defending the UNR's interests. The chief Soviet negotiator, Adolf Ioffe, presented this in no uncertain terms: "Eastern Galicia is being referred to for tactical reasons, as a counter in the event of the Poles bringing up the question of a Petliura Ukraine. Russia appreciates that Poland needs Galician oil, but Russia needs Ukrainian wheat."[58]

The Bolshevik side was equally prepared to make considerable territorial concessions on the condition that the Poles renounce their federalist ambitions for the wider region. The Soviets' position was improved by the stance adopted by most of the Polish delegation, including Grabski. During an internal discussion, they rejected the option of demanding those areas of Belarus, including Minsk, which the Polish army had captured toward the end of the campaign. The Chief of State's opponents feared that annexing this territory would enable the Piłsudskiites to play the Belarusian card and perhaps even establish a sovereign state federated with Poland.[59] The delegates also rejected the idea of claiming the Podolian counties of Kamieniec/Kamianets' and Płoskirów/Proskuriv. These areas were controlled by the Polish forces and their allies in combat, Petliura's army, but it was decided to renounce them on the grounds that "it was necessary to give Russia clear proof that Poland was really leaving Ukraine wholly to the Russian sphere of interest."[60]

On 12 October 1920 the Preliminary Peace and Armistice Agreement was signed, which became binding three weeks later, after the exchange of ratification papers. Its signatories were the Republic of Poland and the Soviet Republics of Russia and Ukraine.[61] The delineation of the Polish-Soviet border was its most important feature. Regarding Volhynia, the border was moved slightly east of the line that had been established in the Polish-Ukrainian agreement of April 1920, and farther down along the Zbrucz/Zbruch River, the prewar border between the Russian Empire and Austria-Hungary. The western counties of Podolia, still controlled by Polish forces and the UNR army, remained on the Soviet side. A particularly important passage in the treaty spoke of the Polish-Soviet border as "the border between Poland on the one hand, and Ukraine and Belarus on the other hand." This indicated clearly that Poland had abandoned its federalist plans and was leaving the initiative, in this regard, to the Soviets.[62]

The armistice obliged the Polish army to withdraw to the border that had been agreed upon. Also, the anti-Bolshevik allied forces – Russian, Ukrainian, and Belarusian – were required to leave the territory of the Republic of Poland. The Ukrainian army subsequently retreated to Podolia, to which the UNR's government institutions had also been evacuated. This Podolian foothold was to serve as the basis for one last desperate attempt to launch an offensive against the Bolsheviks. Petliura's army was secretly receiving assistance from the Polish command, but in the event, it was unable to withstand the Red Army on its own. The Bolsheviks pre-empted Ukrainian preparations and attacked UNR troops gathering in Podolia. In late November 1920, after a few days of fighting, the Ukrainians were forced to retreat to the western bank of the Zbrucz/Zbruch River. On entering Polish territory, their units were disarmed and interned.[63]

Further talks in Riga resulted in only minor adjustments to the Polish-Soviet border. The final peace agreement, signed on 18 March 1921, mostly confirmed the territorial provisions of the preliminary treaty.[64] An important remaining task was to delimit the exact border in the field. This work, beginning in July 1921, was given to the Delimitation Commission, led by the former Polish Minister of Foreign Affairs, Leon Wasilewski, and a Bolshevik of Polish descent, Stanisław Pestkowski (Stanislav Pestkovskii). The commission supervised the activities of four mixed sub-commissions, each of which dealt with a separate section of the border. The work proceeded quite satisfactorily, although not completely so; most notably, the Soviets refused to take economic considerations into account when determining the border's exact course. It was not uncommon, for example, for peasants to suddenly find themselves separated from their fields, which had ended up on the other side of the border. This led to numerous protests, with the residents of frontier villages petitioning the delegates acting on behalf of their respective countries. One such peasant delegation met with the Polish Minister of Foreign Affairs, Konstanty Skirmunt, in Warsaw in January 1922.[65] However, Polish diplomatic interventions were rarely successful. There were also technical complications: "The maps were so bad," the Delimitation Commission reported, "that in some places we made real geographical discoveries. For instance, in Polesia, on an area of approximately 30 sq. km, marked on the map as uninhabitable swamp, we found up to a thousand human settlements and a whole network of roads."[66] The delimitation was completed in November 1922. Three months later, on 15 March 1923, the Conference of Ambassadors acknowledged Poland's eastern boundary, symbolically tying up the question of the Polish-Soviet (and Polish-Ukrainian) border. The Western Powers had accepted the status quo in Eastern Europe as it stemmed from the Treaty of Riga. From the Ukrainians' point of view, recognizing Poland's sovereignty over Eastern Galicia was of particular importance, as it ultimately buried the hopes of the ZUNR government-in-exile, which had been working toward making Galicia an international problem.

CONCLUSION

The drawing of the Polish-Ukrainian border during the tumultuous years following the First World War was the result of prolonged military clashes and diplomatic battles involving Poland, both national Ukrainian republics, the forces of "White" Russia, the Bolsheviks (with the façade government of Soviet Ukraine subordinated to them), and the Western Powers. The Wilsonian principle of self-determination, supposedly the foundation and guarantee of the permanence of the new postwar international order, did not play a significant role in this conflict, despite being frequently invoked by all sides. Ultimately, strategic and geopolitical considerations were decisive, with military power proving to be the strongest form of argument.

In the dispute over Eastern Galicia, the Western Powers (notwithstanding some differences between Britain and France) tended to sympathize with Poland. London and especially Paris viewed Warsaw as the more reliable ally in Eastern Europe and saw a revived Polish Republic as crucial to obstructing Bolshevism's spread to Western Europe. This does not mean they supported Warsaw's far-reaching territorial ambitions in the east. The Entente Powers wanted to delineate the eastern border of Poland in accordance with the ethnographic principle. But in this, they were not guided by the interests of Ukrainians or Belarusians, but rather by their reluctance to antagonize a future, non-Bolshevik Russia. The Entente's role in demarcating the borders in Eastern Europe ultimately proved insignificant. Those borders would be determined by an armed confrontation between Soviet Russia and Poland and sealed in Riga.

The way the events finally unfolded could not have satisfied Ukrainian nationalists. Their struggle for a sovereign state ended in failure; they were also unable to achieve the ideal of *soborna* Ukraine. It was not without reason that the Ukrainians saw the Treaty of Riga as a repeat of the seventeenth-century Truce of Andrusovo that had divided the Ukrainian lands between Russia and the Polish-Lithuanian Commonwealth.[67] As for Poland, it had been rewarded with substantial territorial gains in Riga. Yet in the long run, it would be difficult to regard the peace treaty with the Soviets as a Polish success. In terms of politics, it meant abandoning the idea of Polish-Ukrainian cooperation, which had been beginning to develop despite many obstacles, and which had been the most important element of Piłsudski's ambitious geopolitical plans. The Treaty of Riga also failed to guarantee the young Polish state a lasting peace. As would become evident in the events of 1939, this was merely a reprieve before another round in Poland's deadly game with its eastern neighbour.

NOTES

1 See Mykhailo Lozyns'kyi, *Halychyna v rr. 1918–1920* (Vienna: Institut Sociologique Ukrainien [Ukraïns'kyi Sotsiologichnyi Instytut], 1922); Witold Hupert, *Zajęcie Małopolski Wschodniej i Wołynia w roku 1919* (Lwów and Warsaw: Książnica – Atlas, 1928); Hupert, *Walki o Lwów (od 1 listopada 1918 do 1 maja 1919 roku)* (Warsaw: Księgarnia Wojskowa, 1933); Wasyl Kutschabsky, *Die Westukraine im Kampfe mit Polen und dem Bolschewismus in den Jahren 1918–1923* (Berlin: Junker und Dünnhaupt, 1934). The last one was translated into English as *Western Ukraine in Conflict with Poland and Bolshevism, 1918–1923* (Edmonton: Canadian Institute of Ukrainian Studies Press, 2009).

2 Maciej Kozłowski, *Między Sanem a Zbruczem: Walki o Lwów i Galicję Wschodnią 1918–1919* (Krakow: Wydawnictwo Znak, 1990); Ludwik Mroczka, *Spór o Galicję Wschodnią 1914–1923* (Krakow: Wydawnictwo Naukowe Wyższej Szkoły Pedagogicznej im. Komisji Edukacji Narodowej, 1998); Mykola Lytvyn, *Ukraïns'ko-pol's'ka viina 1918–1919 rr.* (L'viv: Instytut ukraïnoznavstva im. I. Kryp'iakevycha NAN Ukraïny, 1998); Orest Krasivs'kyi, *Skhidna Halychyna i Pol'shcha v 1918–1923 rr.: Problemy vzaiemovidnosyn* (Kyiv: Vydavnytstvo Akademii Derzhavnoho Upravlinnia pry Prezydentovi Ukraïny, 1998); Krasivs'kyi, *Stosunki ukraińsko-polskie w latach 1917–1923* (Poznań and Gniezno: Wydawnictwo Polskiego Towarzystwa Przyjaciół Nauk, 2010); Michał Klimecki, *Polsko-ukraińska wojna o Lwów i Wschodnią Galicję 1918–1919 r.* (Warsaw: Oficyna Wydawnicza Volumen, 2000); Rafał Galuba, *"Niech nas rozsądzi miecz i krew ...": Konflikt polsko-ukraiński o Lwów i Galicję Wschodnią w latach 1918–1919* (Poznań: Wydawnictwo Poznańskie, 2004); Damian Markowski, *Dwa powstania: Bitwa o Lwów 1918* (Krakow: Wydawnictwo Literackie, 2019).

3 See Marian Kamil Dziewanowski, *Joseph Piłsudski: A European Federalist, 1918–1922* (Stanford: Hoover Institution Press, 1969); Piotr Stefan Wandycz, "Z zagadnień współpracy polsko-ukraińskiej w latach 1919–20," *Zeszyty Historyczne* 12 (1967): 3–24; Józef Lewandowski, "U źródeł wyprawy kijowskiej," *Zeszyty Naukowe Wojskowej Akademii Politycznej im. Feliksa Dzierżyńskiego*, no. 26, Seria Historyczna 7 (1962): 90–111; Michael Palij, *The Ukrainian-Polish Defensive Alliance: An Aspect of the Ukrainian Revolution* (Edmonton: Canadian Institute of Ukrainian Studies Press, 1995); Bohdan V. Hud' and Viktor Ie. Holubko, *Nelehka doroha do porozuminnia: Do pytannia genezy ukraïns'ko-pol's'koho viis'kovoho spivrobitnytstva 1917–1921 rr.* (L'viv: Vydavnytstvo "Ukraïns'ki

tekhnolohiï", 1997); Jan Jacek Bruski, *Petlurowcy: Centrum Państwowe Ukraińskiej Republiki Ludowej na wychodźstwie, 1919–1924* (Krakow: Arcana, 2000); and Jan Pisuliński, *Nie tylko Petlura: Kwestia ukraińska w polskiej polityce zagranicznej w latach 1918–1923* (Wrocław: Wydawnictwo Uniwersytetu Wrocławskiego, 2004).

4 Zofia Zaks, "Sprawa Galicji Wschodniej w Lidze Narodów (1920–1922)," *Najnowsze Dzieje Polski: materiały i studia z okresu 1914–1939* 12 (1967): 127–53; Zaks, "Walka dyplomatyczna o naftę wschodniogalicyjską (1918–1923)," *Z Dziejów Stosunków Polsko-Radzieckich: studia i materiały* 4 (1969): 37–60; Zaks, "Problem Galicji Wschodniej w czasie wojny polsko-radzieckiej," *Studia z Dziejów Rosji i Europy Środkowo-Wschodniej* 8 (1972): 79–109; Ihor B. Datskiv, "Dyplomatiia ZUNR na Paryz'kii myrnii konferentsiï 1919 r.," *Ukraïns'kyi Istorychnyi Zhurnal*, no. 5 (2008): 121–37; Aleksandra J. Leinwand, "Walka dyplomatyczna Polski o Galicję Wschodnią 1918–1923," *Studia z Dziejów Rosji i Europy Środkowo-Wschodniej* 46 (2011): 85–98; Przemysław Piotr Żurawski vel Grajewski, *Sprawa ukraińska na Konferencji Pokojowej w Paryżu w roku 1919*, 2nd rev. ed. (Warsaw: Wydawnictwo Naukowe Semper, 2017).

5 The most important works on this subject include Piotr Stefan Wandycz, *Soviet-Polish Relations 1917–1921* (Cambridge, MA: Harvard University Press, 1969); Norman Davies, *White Eagle, Red Star: The Polish-Soviet War, 1919–20*, foreword by A.J.P. Taylor (New York: St Martin's Press, 1972); Wojciech Materski, *Na widecie: II Rzeczpospolita wobec Sowietów 1918–1943* (Warsaw: Oficyna Wydawnicza Rytm, 2005); Adam Zamoyski, *Warsaw 1920: Lenin's Failed Conquest of Europe* (London: HarperCollins, 2008); Andrzej Nowak, *Pierwsza zdrada Zachodu: 1920 – zapomniany appeasement* (Krakow: Wydawnictwo Literackie, 2015). The issue of the Ukrainian army's participation in the 1920 campaign is addressed in Zbigniew Karpus, *Wschodni sojusznicy Polski w wojnie 1920 roku: Oddziały wojskowe ukraińskie, rosyjskie, kozackie i białoruskie w latach 1919–1920* (Toruń: Wydawnictwo Uniwersytetu Mikołaja Kopernika, 1999); Jacek Legieć, *Armia Ukraińskiej Republiki Ludowej w wojnie polsko-ukraińsko-bolszewickiej w 1920 r.* (Toruń: Wydawnictwo Adam Marszałek, 2002); and Andrii O. Rukkas, "*Razom z pol's'kym viis'kom*": *Armiia Ukraïns'koï Narodnoï Respubliky 1920 r. (struktura, orhanizatsiia, chysel'nist', uniforma)*, 2nd ed. (Kyiv: Oleh Filiuk, 2015), and the place of the Ukrainian problem in the Polish-Soviet peace negotiations in Riga in Tamara V. Halyts'ka-Didukh, "Ukraïns'ke pytannia na Mins'kii konferentsiï (17 serpnia–2 veresnia 1920 r.)," *Visnyk Prykarpats'koho Universytetu: Istoriia* 2 (1999): 85–94; Halyts'ka-Didukh, "Dyplomatychna borot'ba

navkolo problemy ukraïns'koho predstavnytstva na myrnii konferentsiï v Ryzi (veresen' 1920–berezen' 1921 rr.)," *UIZ* 6 (2006): 100–9; Mykola P. Het'manchuk, *Mizh Moskvoiu ta Varshavoiu: Ukraïns'ke pytannia u radians'ko-pol's'kykh vidnosynakh mizhvoiennoho periodu (1918–1939 rr.)* (L'viv: Vydavnytstvo Natsional'noho Universytetu L'vivs'ka Politekhnika, 2008), 90–121; Jan Jacek Bruski, *Between Prometheism and Realpolitik: Poland and Soviet Ukraine, 1921–1926* (Krakow: Jagiellonian University Press, 2016), 36–46. The most complete discussion of the Riga Conference and the problems related to establishing the borders, which were its subject, can be found in Jerzy Borzęcki, *The Soviet-Polish Peace of 1921 and the Creation of Interwar Europe* (New Haven: Yale University Press, 2008). See also Jerzy Kumaniecki, *Pokój polsko-radziecki 1921: geneza – rokowania – traktat – komisje mieszane* (Warsaw: Biblioteka Narodowa, 1985); A.A. Kovalenia et al., eds., *Rizhskii Mir v sud'be belorusskogo naroda 1921–1953 gg. V dvukh knigakh* (Minsk: Belaruskaia navuka, 2014).

6 These territories essentially corresponded with the *gubernia* of Chełm/Kholm, which had been separated from the Kingdom of Poland and incorporated directly into the Russian Empire before the First World War. The *gubernia* was officially established in 1912, but it was not actually detached from Congress Poland until three years later, just before the armies of the Central Powers invaded the territory. It was an ethnically diverse area, but reconstructing the exact proportions of the Polish and Ukrainian population in the entire *gubernia* and in its individual counties is very difficult. This is because of the inaccuracy and bias of the censuses carried out first by the Russian authorities and then by the Austro-Hungarian and German occupiers' administration. It is also problematic to identify the ethnicity of individual religious denominational groups. Especially dubious is the ethnicity of some Greek Catholics and the so-called *kalakuty*: Ruthenian-speaking Latin Catholics. It should be added that ethnic relations for the Polish communities in the Chełm/Kholm and Podlachia provinces were significantly improved following the evacuation of the Orthodox population, carried out in 1915 by the Russian authorities. In 1918, 45 per cent of the population of these areas was Catholic, 36 per cent was Orthodox, and 15 per cent Jewish. Pisuliński, *Nie tylko Petlura*, 22–3n4.

7 Volodymyr Serhiichuk, *Etnichni mezhi i derzhavnyi kordon Ukraïny*, 3rd rev. ed. (Kyiv: PP Serhiichuk M.P, 2008), 453–4.

8 Mykhailo Hrushevs'kyi's speech at the Small Council meeting, 15 March 1918, in Vladyslav F. Verstiuk et al., eds., *Ukraïns'ka Tsentral'na Rada: Dokumenty i materialy: u dvokh tomakh*, (Kyiv: Naukova dumka, 1997), 2:203–6.

9   See Leon Grosfeld, "Sprawa Chełmszczyzny w 1918 r.," *Kwartalnik Historyczny*, no. 1 (1974): 33–43; Jarosław Cabaj, "Postawy ludności Chełmszczyzny i Podlasia wobec kwestii przynależności państwowej swych ziem (1912, 1918–1919)," *Kwartalnik Historyczny*, no. 4 (1992): 63–91.
10 Roman Wapiński, "Endecka koncepcja polityki wschodniej w latach II Rzeczypospolitej," *Studia z Dziejów ZSRR i Europy Środkowej* 5 (1969): 65.
11 Dmowski's note of 3 March 1919, in Remigiusz Bierzanek and Józef Kukułka, eds., *Sprawy polskie na Konferencji Pokojowej w Paryżu w 1919 r.: Dokumenty i materiały* (Warsaw: Państwowe Wydawnictwo Naukowe, 1965), 1: doc. 23, 105–7; Pisuliński, *Nie tylko Petlura*, 113–14.
12 See Dziewanowski, *Joseph Piłsudski*, passim; Andrzej Nowak, "Józef Piłsudski: A Federalist or an Imperialist?," in Andrzej Nowak, *History and Geopolitics: A Contest for Eastern Europe* (Warsaw: Polish Institute for Foreign Affairs, 2008), 169–86.
13 Minutes of the Chełm/Kholm *gubernia* council meeting of 17 November 1918, in Oleksandr Il'in, ed., "Zakhidne Polissia v Ukraïns'kii Derzhavi het'mana Skoropads'koho (Istoriia v dokumentakh)," *Nad Buhom i Narvoiu*, no. 5 (2013): doc. 23, 41–2.
14 Skoropys-Ioltukhovs'kyi's letter to Skoropads'kyi, 30 November 1918, in Il'in, "Zakhidne Polissia," doc. 24, 43; Cabaj, "Postawy ludności," 74–87. Incidentally, Austria-Hungary, unlike Germany and the other signatories of the Quadruple Alliance, never ratified the February 1918 treaty with Ukraine.
15 Ievhen Pasternak, *Narys istoriï Kholmshchyny i Pidliashshia (Novishi chasy)* (Winnipeg and Toronto: Instytut Doslidiv Volyni, 1968), 181–2.
16 Henryk Jabłoński, "Z dziejów genezy sojuszu: Piłsudski-Petlura (Początki konfliktu zbrojnego, XI. 1918 – III. 1919 r.)," *Zeszyty Naukowe Wojskowej Akademii Politycznej im. Feliksa Dzierżyńskiego*, no. 21, Seria Historyczna 5 (1961): 46–9. In the former *gubernia* of Volhynia, Poles were a decisive minority, constituting between 6 and 10 per cent of the population, depending on whether the adopted criterion was linguistic or religious (Roman Catholic faith). On the other hand, almost half (45.7 per cent) of agricultural land in Volhynia was in Polish hands. Pisuliński, *Nie tylko Petlura*, 24.
17 The name Eastern Galicia was traditionally applied to the area under the jurisdiction of the appeal court in Lwów/Lviv, which included fifty counties. Ethnicity on this territory largely corresponded with individuals' affiliation with the Byzantine (Greek Catholic) or Latin rite of the Catholic Church. In 1910, Greek Catholics (who can be by and large identified with the Ukrainian population) made up 61.7 per cent, while Roman Catholics (mostly Poles) constituted 25.3 per cent of the area's population. Henryk

Batowski, "Pojęcie polityczne Galicji Wschodniej," in: Michał Pułaski, ed., *Ukraińska myśl polityczna w XX wieku* (Krakow: Uniwersytet Jagielloński, 1993), 33–43; Mroczka, *Spór o Galicję Wschodnią*, 15–16.

18 Krasivs'kyi, *Skhidna Halychyna*, 71–2; Klimecki, *Polsko-ukraińska wojna*, 47–50.

19 On the events that took place in Lwów/Lviv on 1 November 1918, and subsequent battles for the city, see Kozłowski, *Między Sanem a Zbruczem*, 134–83; Lytvyn, *Ukraïns'ko-pol's'ka viina*, 31–106; Klimecki, *Polsko-ukraińska wojna*, 67–145; Markowski, *Dwa powstania*, passim.

20 Before the outbreak of the First World War, Poles constituted 51.2 per cent of Lviv's residents, Jews 27.8 per cent, and Ukrainians 19.1 per cent. Mroczka, *Spór o Galicję Wschodnią*, 23.

21 Bogdan Horbal, *Działalność polityczna Łemków na Łemkowszczyźnie, 1918–1921* (Wrocław: Wydawnictwo Arboretum, 1997), 38–70; Jarosław Moklak, *The Lemko Region in the Second Polish Republic: Political and Interdenominational Issues, 1918–1919* (Krakow: Jagiellonian University Press, 2013), 28–33.

22 General Barthélemy's draft truce agreement of 15 February 1919, in *Sprawy Polskie* (Warsaw: Państwowe Wydawnictwo Naukowe, 1967), 2: doc. 19, 241–2.

23 John S. Reshetar, *The Ukrainian Revolution, 1917–1920: A Study in Nationalism* (Princeton: Princeton University Press, 1952), 273–4; Galuba, "*Niech nas rozsądzi miecz i krew...*," 107–18; Datskiv, "Dyplomatiia ZUNR," 130–2.

24 Klimecki, *Polsko-ukraińska wojna*, 208–9; Galuba, "*Niech nas rozsądzi miecz i krew*," 183–93; Datskiv, "Dyplomatiia ZUNR," 127–9; Żurawski vel Grajewski, *Sprawa ukraińska*, 43–8.

25 Wasilewski's report no. 1, Paris, 3 April 1919, in Sławomir Dębski, ed., *Polskie dokumenty dyplomatyczne: 1919: styczeń-maj* (Warsaw: Polski Instytut Spraw Międzynarodowych, 2016), doc. 255, 588; Wandycz, "Z zagadnień współpracy," 5.

26 Andrzej Nowak, *Polska i trzy Rosje: Studium polityki wschodniej Józefa Piłsudskiego (do kwietnia 1920 roku)* (Krakow: Arcana, 2001), 208–9; Jan Pisuliński, "Józef Piłsudski a Ukraina (1918–1922)," *Arcana*, no. 2 (2006): 104–5.

27 See Pisuliński, *Nie tylko Petlura*, 88–9.

28 Reshetar, *The Ukrainian Revolution*, 295–8; Krasivs'kyi, *Skhidna Halychyna*, 117–27; Galuba, "*Niech nas rozsądzi miecz i krew*," 204–20, 240–60; Datskiv, "Dyplomatiia ZUNR," 132–5; Żurawski vel Grajewski, *Sprawa ukraińska*, 49–52.

29 The Supreme Council declaration of 8 December 1919, in Weronika Gostyńska et al., eds., *Dokumenty i materiały do historii stosunków polsko-radzieckich* (Warsaw: Książka i Wiedza, 1961), 2: doc. 269, 481–3. The declaration did not address the question of Eastern Galicia's allocation.
30 Bruski, *Petlurowcy*, 141.
31 Aleksy Deruga, *Polityka wschodnia Polski wobec ziem Litwy, Białorusi i Ukrainy (1918–1919)* (Warsaw: Książka i Wiedza, 1969), 232–5; Pisuliński, *Nie tylko Petlura*, 97–100. Also: Dangiras Mačiulis and Darius Staliūnas, *Lithuanian Nationalism and the Vilnius Question, 1883–1940* (Marburg: Verlag Herder-Institut, 2015); Per Anders Rudling, *The Rise and Fall of Belarusian Nationalism, 1906–1931* (Pittsburgh: University of Pittsburgh Press, 2015); Klaus Richter, *Fragmentation in East Central Europe: Poland and the Baltics, 1915–1929* (Oxford: Oxford University Press, 2020); Felix Ackermann, *Palimpsest Grodno: Nationalisierung, Nivellierung und Sowjetisierung einer mitteleuropäischen Stadt 1919–1991* (Wiesbaden: Harrassowitz, 2011).
32 On Kurdynovs'kyi's mission, see Jacek Legieć, "Misja Borysa Kudrynowskiego w Warszawie (kwiecień-sierpień 1919 r.)," *Studia z Dziejów Rosji i Europy Środkowo-Wschodniej* 33 (1998): 53–62; Bruski, *Petlurowcy*, 104-10; Pisuliński, *Nie tylko Petlura*, 124–40. The Kurdynovs'kyi-Paderewski treaty of 24 May 1919, in: Witold Stankiewicz and Andrzej Piber (eds.), *Archiwum Polityczne Ignacego Paderewskiego, 1919–1921*, (Wrocław: Zakład Narodowy im. Ossolińskich, 1974), 2: doc. 136, 167–8.
33 Petliura's letter to Piłsudski, 9 August 1919, in: Taras Hunczak (ed.), *Poland and Ukraine in Documents 1918–1922* (New York: Shevchenko Scientific Society, 1983), 1: doc. 66, 237–8.
34 The Pylypchuk mission's declaration of 19 August 1919, in Oleksander Dotsenko, *Litopys Ukraïns'koï Revoliutsiï: materiialy i dokumenty do istoriï ukraïns'koï revoliutsiï*, 2, part 4 (Kyiv, L'viv, 1923), 51–3.
35 Palij, *The Ukrainian-Polish Defensive Alliance*, 68-9; Bruski, *Petlurowcy*, 114–15; Pisuliński, *Nie tylko Petlura*, 154–7.
36 Rafał Galuba, "Pertraktacje polityczno-wojskowe między Polską a Ukraińską Republiką Ludową (lipiec-sierpień 1919 roku)," *Mars: Problematyka i Historia Wojskowości: Studia i Materiały*, 2 (1994): 53–67; Bruski, *Petlurowcy*, 115–17; Pisuliński, *Nie tylko Petlura*, 158–69.
37 Isaak Mazepa, *Ukraïna v ohni i buri revoliutsiï, 1917–1921*, ed. Vasyl' Iablons'kyi (Kyiv: Tempora, 2003), 286–7.
38 The declaration of 28 October 1919, in Valentyn Kavunnyk, ed., *Arkhiv Ukraïns'koï Narodnoï Respubliky: Ministerstvo Zakordonnykh Sprav: dyplomatychni dokumenty vid Versal's'koho do Ryz'koho myrnykh*

dohovoriv (1919–1921) (Kyiv: Instytut ukraïns'koï arkheohrafiï ta dzhereloznavstva im. M.S. Hrushevs'koho, 2016), 557–8.

39 It was decided that, until the Ukrainians announced a declaration that would meet Polish expectations, the issuing of visas for Ukrainian passports would be suspended; it was also threatened that the agreement on the transit of banknotes printed for the UNR in Germany would be rescinded. Livyts'kyi's report to Premier Isaak Mazepa, 3 December 1919, in *Arkhiv Ukraïns'koï Narodnoi Respubliky*, 561.

40 Reshetar, *The Ukrainian Revolution*, 288–90.

41 Qtd in Zofia Zaks, "Galicja Wschodnia w polityce Zachodnio-Ukraińskiej Republiki Ludowej i Ukraińskiej Republiki Ludowej w drugiej połowie 1919 r.," in Tadeusz Cieślak et al., eds., *Naród i państwo: Prace ofiarowane Henrykowi Jabłońskiemu w 60 rocznicę urodzin* (Warsaw: Państwowe Wydawnictwo Naukowe, 1969), 397.

42 The Galician counsellors submitted their own version of the project. They proposed to declare that the Zbrucz/Zbruch River would separate the territory of the UNR from Eastern Galicia, "which in accordance with the decision of the Paris Peace Conference shall remain under the government of the Republic of Poland for twenty-five years." In Dotsenko, *Litopys* , 50.

43 The declaration of 2 December 1919, in *Arkhiv Ukraïns'koï Narodnoï Respubliky*, 566–9. For more on the October–December talks in Warsaw, see Bruski, *Petlurowcy*, 117–19; Pisuliński, *Nie tylko Petlura*, 169–83; Viktor Matviienko, "Storinky diial'nosti Ukraïns'koï dyplomatychnoï misiï u Varshavi (zhovten' 1919 r.–kviten' 1920 r.)," *Naukovyi Visnyk Ukraïns'koï Dyplomatychnoï Akademiï Ukraïny* 10, no. 2 (2004): 502–8.

44 See Jan Jacek Bruski, "Porozuminnia ta soiuz z Pol'shcheiu v otsinkakh ukraïns'kykh politychnykh elit (1918-1920 rr.)," in *Pratsi ukraïns'ko-pol's'koï komisiï doslidzhennia vzaiemyn 1917–1921 rr.*, ed. Jan Jacek Bruski and Vladyslav Verstiuk (Kyiv: Instytut istoriï Ukraïny NANU, 2019), 1:35–9.

45 General Haller to the Presidium of the Council of Ministers, Warsaw, 14 April 1920, in *Sąsiedzi wobec wojny 1920 roku: Wybór dokumentów*, ed. Janusz Cisek (London: Polska Fundacja Kulturalna, 1990), doc. VIII 4:164–5.

46 The text of the Polish-Ukrainian treaty of 21 April 1920, in *Dokumenty i materiały*, 2, doc. 379, 745–7 (in Polish); Dotsenko, *Litopys*, 2, pt 5: 270–1 (in Ukrainian); Reshetar, *The Ukrainian Revolution*, 301–2 (English translation). For more on the negotiations preceding the treaty, see Bruski, *Petlurowcy*, 135–7; Pisuliński, *Nie tylko Petlura*, 210–21; Matviienko, "Storinky," 508–12; Olena Mykhailova, "Pol's'ko-ukraïns'kyi perehovornyi

protses ta pidpysannia Varshavs'koho dohovoru (berezen'-kviten' 1920 r.),"
Ukraïna XX st.: kul'tura, ideolohiia, polityka 9 (2005): 154–75.
47 The Polish consent to this point was perhaps related to the previously formulated plans for a possible exchange of the aforementioned counties for the western part of Podolia.
48 See Ihor Kamenets'kyi, "UNR i ukraïns'ka zahranychna polityka mizh dvoma svitovymy viinamy," *Ukraïns'kyi Istoryk*, nos. 1–4 (1993): 79.
49 However, John S. Reshetar is right to observe that "the third article placed Ukraine in a subservient position because it recognized a prior claim of the Poles to their 1772 frontier and made the Ukrainians appear to be the objects of Polish beneficence." Reshetar, *The Ukrainian Revolution*, 305.
50 The text of the military convention of 24 April 1920, in *Dokumenty i materiały*, 2, doc. 381, 749–53 (in Polish); Palij, *The Ukrainian-Polish Defensive Alliance*, 72–5 (English translation).
51 J.J. Bruski, "Porozuminnia ta sojuz z Pol'shcheiu," 43–8.
52 Wandycz, "Z zagadnień współpracy," 20.
53 On the Kyiv offensive see Tadeusz Kutrzeba, *Wyprawa kijowska 1920 roku* (Warsaw: Gebethner i Wolff, 1937); Lech Wyszczelski, *Kijów 1920* (Warsaw: Bellona, 1999); Tomasz Grzegorczyk, *Wyprawa kijowska* (Toruń: Wydawnictwo Adam Marszałek, 2014). On the UNR Army's participation in this campaign see Karpus, *Wschodni sojusznicy*, 25–42; Legieć, *Armia Ukraińskiej Republiki Ludowej*, 71–105; Rukkas, "Razom z pol's'kym viis'kom," 41–76.
54 For the Galician Soviet Socialist Republic episode, see Vasyl' Veryha, *Halyts'ka Sotsialistychna Soviets'ka Respublika, 1920 r.* (New York: Naukove Tovarystvo im. T. Shevchenka, 1986); and Michał Klimecki, *Galicyjska Socjalistyczna Republika Rad: Okupacja Małopolski (Galicji) Wschodniej przez Armię Czerwoną w 1920 r.* (Toruń: Wydawnictwo Uniwersytetu Mikołaja Kopernika, 2006).
55 For more on this, see Materski, *Na widecie*, 78–80; Nowak, *Pierwsza zdrada Zachodu*, 394–405. On the genesis of the Curzon Line see Roman Syrota, "'Liniia Kerzona' chy 'Liniia Nem'iera'?: Kordon i modernizatsiia u bahatoetnichnomu rehioni," *Visnyk L'vivs'koho Universytetu. Seriia Istorychna* 39–40 (2006); 314–48; Bartłomiej Rusin, "Lewis Namier a kwestia 'linii Curzona' i kształtowania się polskiej granicy wschodniej po I wojnie światowej," *Studia z Dziejów Rosji i Europy Środkowo-Wschodniej* 48 (2013): 95–116.
56 Materski, *Na Widecie*, 88–90; Borzęcki, The *Soviet-Polish Peace*, 96–104.
57 Halyts'ka-Didukh, "Dyplomatychna borot'ba," 102.

58 Jan Dąbski, *Pokój Ryski: Wspomnienia, pertraktacje, tajne układy z Joffem, listy* (Warsaw: Kulerski, 1931), 106.
59 It is disputable whether the Soviet side would have consented to such a demand, with the most recent study on the Treaty of Riga being unequivocally negative in its analysis. See Borzęcki, *The Soviet-Polish Peace*, 130–3. For an alternative view see Bruski, *Between Prometheism and Realpolitik*, 306n30.
60 Stanisław Grabski, *Pamiętniki*, ed. Witold Stankiewicz (Warsaw: Czytelnik, 1989), 2:171–2.
61 The Russian delegation also officially represented the interests of Soviet Belarus. For the text of the treaty of 12 October 1920, see *Dokumenty i materiały*, 3, doc. 236, 465–75.
62 Materski, *Na widecie*, 110. The consent to introduce such a provision "undoubtedly meant," as Stanisław Grabski recollects, "that we agreed to settle the question of buffer states 'to the advantage' of Russia." Grabski, *Pamiętniki*, 2:175.
63 Bruski, *Petlurowcy*, 223–37; Legieć, *Armia Ukraińskiej Republiki Ludowej*, 158–96.
64 In comparison to the preliminary treaty, Poland gained approximately 3,400 square kilometres, comprising mostly woodlands. Borzęcki, *The Soviet-Polish Peace*, 221.
65 Borzęcki, *The Soviet-Polish Peace*, 246–9.
66 The Delimitation Commission's report of 15 February 1922, qtd in Bruski, *Between Prometheism and Realpolitik*, 72.
67 See for example Volodymyr Kedrovs'kyi's memoirs: *Ryzhs'ke Andrusovo: spomyny pro rosijs'ko-pol's'ki myrovi perehovory* (Winnipeg: Ukrains'ka Vydavnycha Spilka v Kanadi, 1926).

4

From the Molotov-Ribbentrop Pact to the Territorial Agreement of "the Big Three"

Redrawing the Polish-Ukrainian Border in 1939–52

Damian Karol Markowski

After the Second World War broke out, the Polish-Ukrainian ethnic borderland, extending from the eastern Carpathians through Eastern Galicia and the northern edge of Volhynia, was subjected to a number of administrative divisions. The most notable of these were a consequence of the German-Soviet aggression against Poland, which culminated in the division of Poland's territories in September 1939, with the demarcation lines being drawn by the aggressors; the division of areas populated by peoples of mixed ethnicity by the German occupying administration in the summer of 1941; and the reoccupation of the Polish-Ukrainian ethnic borderland by the Soviet Union and the Polish Communist authorities installed by the Soviet Union in the final stages of the war. The last of these events would legally determine the postwar border between Poland and the Ukrainian Socialist Soviet Republic. The traumatic, often violent, processes whereby the final, and still internationally valid, state border between Poland and Ukraine was eventually established would impact the lives of hundreds of thousands of Poles and Ukrainians along the border zone. The "exchange of people" between Poland and the Soviet Union in 1944–46, and the subsequent "Vistula" campaign of 1947, resulted in waves of refugees and mass deportations by the Polish and Soviet governments. For many of these inhabitants, the border in its final form represented a tragedy; their forced departure amounted to an abandonment of the "little homelands" where their families had lived for generations.

By drawing on the key points underpinning current Polish and Ukrainian historiography, this chapter offers a cross-sectional and synthetic outline of the events and political developments that led to the demarcation of the border between Poland and Soviet Ukraine in the aftermath of the Second World War. Among the scholars dealing with the postwar formation of the Polish-Ukrainian border, one should mention Piotr Eberhardt, whose work focuses on the relationship between state borders and regional geography, with particular attention paid to the so-called Curzon Line, regarded as a key legal element in the creation of the postwar Polish-Soviet border; Andrzej Wawryniuk, who scrutinizes the technical aspects surrounding the new border's delimitation; Iurii Soroka, who examines the formation of the border from the Ukrainian perspective; and Ivan Kozlovsky, who examines the administrative processes behind the border's delineation.[1]

This chapter argues that the contemporary border between Ukraine and Poland was not a result of the Great Power politics whereby Western allies, seeking to appease Moscow, conceded to Stalin's territorial claims in Eastern Europe. Soviet territorial claims were determined by a combination of political, economic and ideological considerations. The Soviet authorities insisted that their border with the newly established Polish People's Republic be drawn along the so-called Curzon Line. By adhering to that line, which had first been proposed in 1919, the Soviets ensured that they would maintain control over vast areas of western Ukraine and western Belarus, as agreed earlier by the Molotov-Ribbentrop Pact of 1939. In this way, the Soviet government would maximize Soviet access to natural resources, especially the oilfields of Eastern Galicia. The final border was equally impacted by the desire of the Soviet and Polish governments to establish ethnically homogeneous communities on both sides of the new border, so as to obviate the need to deal with potentially less loyal minority populations.

This chapter highlights the most significant stages in the complex process of negotiating and delineating the Polish-Ukrainian border between 1939 and 1951. It briefly discusses how the boundaries, agreed upon by the wartime Soviet and German occupation authorities, were administered. Then it examines the interests and motives of the Great Powers in delineating the western Soviet border. This discussion is enhanced by an investigation of the prewar Polish government's political response to proposed changes to the border during the war. The chapter concludes with an outline of the postwar amendments to the Polish-Ukrainian border. In parallel, the chapter discusses popular reactions to border revisions and the social impact of shifting borders on Ukrainian and Polish communities.

THE GERMAN AND SOVIET SPHERES OF INTEREST, SEPTEMBER 1939 TO JUNE 1941

A supplementary protocol to the Molotov-Ribbentrop Pact, signed in Moscow on 23 August 1939, allowed the Third Reich and the Soviet Union to divide Central and Eastern Europe into separate spheres of influence. As the German and Soviet invasions drew to a close, new diplomatic arrangements led to an adjustment of the occupied territories' demarcation lines, included in the Boundary and Friendship Treaty of 28 September 1939.[2] This new boundary followed the Bug River, thus separating the Lublin region (Lubelszczyzna), organized by the German occupation authorities into the Lublin district of the General Government (GG), from Volhynia, which remained in the Soviet Union. Accordingly, the border ran along the Bug to the mouth of the Solokiia/Sołokija River and past the city of Uhniv/Uhnów toward the area surrounding the city of Krystynopil/Krystynopol (renamed Chervonohrad in 1951). It then turned sharply to the west and southwest, leaving the former Rava-Ruska/Rawa Ruska *poviat* areas, inhabited mostly by Ukrainians, on the Soviet side. The final section ran along the upper San River to its source at the foot of the Uzhok/Użok Pass, on the border of the western and eastern Bieszczady Mountains.

This partition of occupied Poland was informally acknowledged by foreign statesmen, who hoped that the resulting, albeit temporary, border would become a new front line in the near future, when the new front against Nazi Germany would be opened, involving German troops in Central and Eastern Europe. On 1 October 1939, an expert at the British Foreign Office proposed that upon the victory in the war against Germany this line become the basis for the future Polish-Soviet border.[3] Three days later, on 4 October, the First Secretary of the Communist Party of Bolsheviks of Ukraine (KP(b)U), Nikita Khrushchev, the chairman of the Ukrainian Union of the Soviet Writers, Oleksandr Korniichuk, and the commander of the Ukrainian Front, Marshal Semyon Timoshenko, arrived in Lviv for a "working rally" (*rabochii vizit*) to launch the "election campaign" for the so-called Ukrainian People's Assembly. This body then sent a request for incorporation to the Soviet authorities.[4]

On the orders of the Council of People's Commissars, the areas annexed by the Soviet Union were divided into new administrative districts and regions. The newly established Volhynia and Lviv *oblasti* bordered on the Lublin district of the GG across the Bug River and Roztochchia/Roztocze, respectively. The Lviv *oblast*'s border with the GG's Krakow district ran from the vicinity of Lubachiv/Lubaczów (leaving the town on the Soviet side) to the San River and then south, dividing Peremyshl/Przemyśl in two before

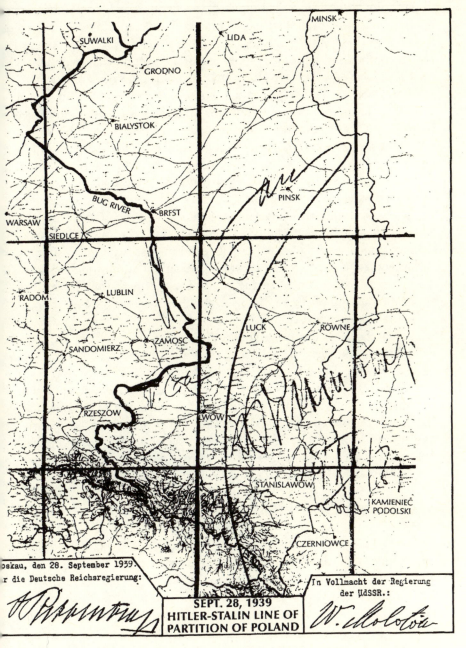

4.1 The map from the secret appendix to the Molotov-Ribbentrop Pact showing the new German-Soviet border. The map is signed by Joseph Stalin and German Foreign Minister Joachim von Ribbentrop.

running along the river to its source next to the prewar Polish-Hungarian border, and, prior to Carpathian Ruthenia's annexation by Hungary in March 1939, the Polish-Czechoslovakian border. In February 1940, a mixed border commission composed of German and Soviet officials and military personnel formally established the new border along this demarcation line.[5]

Meanwhile, the Polish government-in-exile, which had fled to France and then relocated to Britain following France's defeat in 1940, expended its limited diplomatic energies on attempts to maintain the idea of keeping Poland's prewar eastern border intact in the eyes of their Western allies. However, the lack of any convincing geopolitical arguments meant that any actions taken by the Polish government were merely symbolic. Moreover, after the fall of France, Britain's now internationally isolated wartime government sought rapprochement with the Soviet Union by undermining the Hitler-Stalin Pact. This was done, *inter alia*, via a memorandum issued to the British Ambassador in Moscow, Stafford Cripps, declaring that "until consultations were pending," London would recognize the "de-facto sovereignty" of the Soviet Union "in Estonia, Lithuania, Latvia, Bessarabia, Northern Bukovina and those parts of the former Polish State now under Soviet control."[6]

The Soviet occupation of western Ukraine, which continued to be regarded by both Poles and Ukrainians as integral to their respective countries, was viewed by both sides as merely temporary. In fact, the newly established demarcation line between Nazi Germany and the Soviet Union was legally recognized only by the two occupying powers and a part of the Ukrainian community that welcomed the incorporation of Volhynia and Eastern Galicia into Soviet Ukraine. Although still hostile to the Soviet regime, this segment of Ukrainian society could appreciate that they now lived in one state with their fellow nationals, rather than under foreign rule.

THE NAZI DIVISION OF OCCUPIED POLAND, AUGUST 1941–AUTUMN 1944

On 22 June 1941, the German-led Axis Powers commenced their invasion of the Soviet Union, code-named Operation Barbarossa; after only a few weeks of fighting, the whole of prewar Poland was under German occupation. While this meant that the demarcation line of September 1939 effectively no longer existed, Allied diplomats would continue to recognize it as the western border of the Soviet Union. During the summer of 1941, German plans for the future administrative status of Eastern Galicia were also redefined. Originally, Galicia was to remain a separate Reich

Commissariat with its capital at Lviv/Lwów/Lemberg, based on directives formulated by Alfred Rosenberg, Reich Minister for the Occupied Eastern Territories. It is not known what the boundaries of this new administrative entity would have looked like.[7] However, following Hitler's intervention, it was decided that Eastern Galicia would be incorporated into the future German settlement zone, under the General Government, as the Galicia district. Governed by the head of the GG, Hans Frank's brother-in-law, Dr Karl Lasch, the new district was divided into *poviaty* or *Kreishauptmannschaften* (counties) and separate cities (*Kreisfreistadt*). German was introduced as the official language; Ukrainian and Polish were retained as auxiliary languages.[8] The district covered a vast area – more than 48,081 square kilometres – including most of the three southeastern provinces of prewar Poland: Lviv/Lwów, Ternopil/Tarnopol, and Stanyslaviv/Stanisławów. It boasted a population of 4,789,000.[9]

The new German administration expanded the district's boundaries by several hundred square kilometres so as to include Uhniv/Uhnów, which had been separated from the Lublin district, and a fragment of the central Roztochchia/Roztocze region. To the south, from Peremyshl/Przemyśl toward the Carpathians, the new border between these districts extended several kilometres east of the original demarcation line to encompass areas near the former Polish-Hungarian border, namely the Peremyshl/Przemyśl foothills and the northeastern edge of the Bieszczady Mountains. Concurrently, the German forces incorporated Volhynia/Wołyń into the newly founded *Reichskommissariat Ukraine* (RKU) as part of the Volhynia-Podolia Commissariat (*Generalbezirke Volhynia-Podolia*). The border between the RKU and the Galicia district was thus determined largely by the course of the prewar southern administrative borders between the Volhynia/Wołyń, Lviv/Lwów, and Ternopil/Tarnopol provinces.[10]

The boundaries between the RKU and the administrative units of the GG were closely guarded by a network of *Grenzschutz* outposts, although the latter's internal borders were under a less strict regime of surveillance. To some extent, the border between the Galicia district and the Krakow district was regarded by Poles and Ukrainians as only a temporary barrier to their respective interests. The Poles were reluctant to abandon their already privileged position, while the Ukrainians perceived the Krakow district as part of occupied Poland, despite it comprising several *poviaty* with significant Ukrainian populations, such as Peremyshl/Przemyśl, Iaroslav/Jarosław, and Sianik/Sanok. Thus, even the division imposed by the Third Reich failed to establish a border between areas with a Polish majority and those with a largely Ukrainian population.

4.2 Ukrainian lands during the Second World War, 1942.

Unsurprisingly, the occupation authorities' decision to merge the district with the GG – recognized as the main Polish occupation zone – was met with great disappointment among parts of the Ukrainian community. Indeed, both the Ukrainian underground and a part of the intelligentsia perceived its incorporation as a forced redistribution of lands that should have been allocated to an independent Ukrainian state. The artificial division of areas cohabited by Ukrainians and Poles, therefore, represented another form of the "divide and conquer" strategy; the Nazis were seeking to consolidate their rule by precipitating conflict between the two communities.[11]

THE CURZON LINE AS THE BASIS FOR A NEW POLISH-SOVIET BORDER (THE TEHERAN ARRANGEMENTS)

After the Germans launched Operation Barbarossa, the Soviet Union exerted diplomatic pressure on Britain – and on the United States, following the latter's entry into the war in December 1941 – to establish a new Western Front as quickly as possible. However, until 1944 the Western leaders remained largely focused on the conflict's African, East Asian, and

Mediterranean theatres instead of committing troops to an invasion of German-occupied northwest Europe. So after the war, they bowed to Stalin's demand that the Soviet Union, which had borne the brunt of Nazi Germany's war effort, be "rewarded" by being allowed to keep at least some of its territorial conquests from the years 1939–40.[12]

As discussed earlier, one of the main foreign-policy vectors for Poland's legal government-in-exile had been to retain the Second Polish Republic's eastern territories. Those Polish politicians who had fled abroad after 1939 viewed themselves as the most loyal members of the anti-fascist coalition, and they could not conceive that even a small portion of their country's former eastern provinces might be incorporated into the Soviet Union. However, the Soviets sent clear signals to the Poles that they would not consider any Polish claims that referred to cities like Lviv/Lwów, Stanyslaviv/Stanisławów, and Ternopil/Tarnopol as part of occupied eastern Poland.[13]

It was only when the prime minister of the government-in-exile, Stanisław Mikołajczyk, was prevented from attending a meeting with US President Franklin Roosevelt and British Prime Minister Winston Churchill prior to their departure for the Tehran Conference in 1943 that the Polish authorities expressed serious concerns. Mikołajczyk's uneasiness that Poland might lose its eastern territories was reinforced when the commander-in-chief of the Polish Armed Forces, General Kazimierz Sosnkowski, wrote to him that the Soviets, with British support, would be seeking to reconfigure the new border along the 1919 Curzon Line; as compensation, the Poles *might* be offered Gdansk, East Prussia, and Silesia in the west. As Sosnkowski accurately predicted, the Soviet Union that would have the greatest say in establishing the borders of postwar Central and Eastern Europe.[14]

These speculations became a reality at the "Big Three" meeting in Tehran on 1 December 1943. The question of the postwar Polish-Soviet and thus Polish-Ukrainian border emerged as a major stumbling block during discussions between the British delegation, represented by Churchill and the British Foreign Minister Anthony Eden, and their Soviet interlocutors – Stalin and the People's Commissar for Foreign Affairs Vyacheslav Molotov. At Tehran, Stalin insisted that the new border be configured according to a "fair ethnic principle" and be based on the western border of the Soviet Union as had been established under the 1939 partition. The Soviet delegation insisted that this new Polish-Ukrainian ethnic border be based on the old Curzon Line (see map 2.1, page 90 of this volume). Eden protested, pointing out that although that line mainly followed the Bug River, its course farther to the south was less precise. With his insistence on the 1919 demarcation line, the Soviet Foreign Secretary most likely wished to leave the door open in regard to Poland's key territorial demands, which were for Lviv/Lwów, Drohobych/Drohobycz, and Boryslav/Borysław regions with their rich oilfields. Stalin concurred, stating that Lviv/Lwów should remain on the Soviet side and that the border should run through the Peremyshl/Przemyśl region farther west. He also declared that there should remain no Polish population cluster on the Soviet side of the border. Roosevelt suggested that this could be achieved through a "voluntary" resettlement of the border populations, a motion eagerly accepted by Stalin. Churchill agreed to leave Lviv/Lwów, including the much-coveted Galician oil basin, to the Soviets on condition that postwar Poland be compensated for this loss of territory at Germany's expense. He also promised to deal with the Polish government's protests against such arrangements. Moscow's demands regarding the postwar border proved to be convenient, since in April 1943, Polish-Soviet diplomatic relations were beginning to deteriorate in the wake of the discovery of mass graves containing the victims of the 1940 Katyn Forest massacre.[15]

Poland's government-in-exile and those Poles living in the former eastern provinces were shocked and appalled by the outcome of the Tehran Conference. At the same time, the Ukrainian inhabitants of Eastern Galicia and Volhynia were buoyed by the hope that the Tehran decisions would make it possible for them to reside in a single contiguous state with their compatriots.

On 11 January 1944, the Soviet Telegraph Agency announced that the new Polish-Soviet border would be based on the 1939 demarcation line. It added that the new boundary was not yet set in stone and suggested that the border might be adjusted in such a way that "the areas where the Polish population predominates would be transferred to Poland." Significantly for Ukrainians, this continued adherence to the former demarcation line that followed in places the course of the San River would leave Lviv/Lwów on the Soviet side, as indicated by the Soviet map first published in the *Izvestiia* newspaper on 13 January 1944.[16]

But the Soviet announcement, in conjunction with the crossing of the prewar Polish-Soviet border by the Red Army a few days earlier, was negatively received by the Polish government-in-exile. A much-anticipated meeting between Mikołajczyk and Churchill did not take place until 20 January 1944. During that meeting, the British Prime Minister announced that Poland should be "strong, free, and independent," albeit with its borders defined by the Curzon Line in the east and the Oder River in the west. As recalled by Mikołajczyk, Churchill explained that neither Great Britain nor the United States will go into war to defend Poland's eastern borders. Once the agreement on these borders has been reached, they will be guaranteed by both the United Kingdom and the Soviet Union. President Roosevelt will not be in a position to provide such guarantees, however, since the American constitution does not allow for this. That is why I advise you to approve of the Curzon Line as the eastern border of Poland. If you accept, we will start negotiations that, I am certain, will lead to the revival of Polish-Soviet relations.[17]

The Polish government thus found itself in double jeopardy. First, it had lost the assurances of its most powerful allies regarding the shape of the postwar Polish state. Second, the lack of diplomatic relations between the Soviet Union and the London-based government-in-exile proved far more advantageous for the Soviets, for it allowed Moscow to deal with the Western Powers independently of the Poles.

The postwar Polish-Ukrainian border also proved to be the deadliest point of conflict between the Polish and Ukrainian resistance organizations. During talks with the Organization of Ukrainian Nationalists (OUN) in Warsaw and Lviv between 1942 and 1943, representatives of the Polish Underground State demanded that their Ukrainian counterparts swear loyalty to the Polish state. In return, the Poles offered only vague promises of equal rights and the possibility of partial autonomy in areas where the Ukrainian population predominated. These areas included Volhynia and Eastern Galicia, as well as much of Lublin province, Lemkivshchyna/Łemkowszczyzna, and part of the Peremyshl/Przemyśl. However, such an offer carried no specific assurances regarding a possible change in the internal policies of a revived Polish state toward its Ukrainian citizens.

The Ukrainians viewed all of this as a continuation of Poland's prewar domestic policy of relegating non-Poles to the status of second-class citizens, deprived of any real opportunities for social and economic advancement. The German occupation undoubtedly fed into these perceptions, thus strengthening a radical Ukrainian nationalism as well as the conviction that Ukrainians would only achieve full rights within the borders of a separate Ukraine. This further heightened ethnic tensions between the two communities, resulting in bloody inter-communal violence and ethnic cleansing in the region between 1943 and 1945. During those years, between sixty and ninety thousand Poles fell victim to the Ukrainian nationalists' drive to erase the Polish population within the disputed territories;

meanwhile, between eight and eleven thousand Ukrainians died at the hands of the Polish underground, mainly in the Lublin and Nadsiannia/Nadsanie regions.[18]

CREATING A NEW REALITY: PROMOTING THE SOVIET INTEREST IN DRAWING THE BORDER

Disregarding the nationalist violence on the ground, the Soviet authorities acted by *faits accomplis*, installing their own administrations in the areas occupied by the Red Army. In a bellicose speech to the First War Session of the Supreme Council of the Soviet Union on 5 March 1944, Khrushchev went as far as to suggest that even the Curzon Line would not represent the limits of Soviet Ukraine's future territorial demands: "The Ukrainian people will live to see the completion of the great historical reunification of their Ukrainian lands in one Soviet Ukrainian state. The Ukrainian nation will live to see the incorporation into the Ukrainian Soviet state of the ever-Ukrainian lands, the Cholm province, Hrubeshiv, Zamostia, Tomashiv and Iaroslav!."

Clearly, Khrushchev intended to retain the lands incorporated into Soviet Ukraine in 1939 and to push that border even farther west, almost to the centre of prewar Poland. To that end, he skillfully appropriated the propagandistic phrasing of the Soviet Ukrainian historian Nikolai Petrovsky, who had earlier defined the disputed western territories as "ever-Ukrainian" (*spokonvichno ukraïns'ki*), in order to legitimize their annexation by the Red Army. Encouraged by the high-level endorsement of his "scholarly" claims, Petrovsky further pressed his assertions in an article on the "ever-Ukrainian territories" published in the newspaper *Radians'ka Ukraïna* on 30 April 1944.[19]

Ultimately, though, it was Soviet military strength and the Soviet Union's place among the victorious Allies that served as its key advantage. Through the Red Army's reoccupation of Poland's former eastern territories, Stalin unceremoniously restored the status quo established in the autumn of 1939 with the *de facto* consent of London and Washington. Moreover, the efforts of the exiled Polish leadership to politically outmanoeuvre the Soviet Union proved disastrous for Poland's Home Army resistance movement. The failure of Operation Tempest, during which the Home Army had attempted to seize control of the German-occupied cities, including those in the disputed border areas, was compounded by the subsequent arrests of resistance members by the People's Commissariat for Internal Affairs (NKVD) and the Military Counter-Intelligence agency SMERSH (an abbreviation of *Smert' Shpionam* – Death to the Spies) within a few days of the Third Reich's withdrawal.[20]

The importance of the Soviet Union's reoccupation of the territories seized in September 1939 was evidenced by Khrushchev's visit to Lviv, where he attended a meeting held in front of the Grand Theatre on 30 July 1944. The secretary of the party's municipal committee, Mykola Chupis, reported that local Ukrainians appeared significantly more relaxed following a speech by the First Secretary, in which he declared that Lviv would remain a "Soviet and Ukrainian" city.[21] The city's Soviet status was also confirmed by the Polish Committee of National Liberation (PCNL), a quasi-political body founded in July 1944 by pro-Soviet Polish activists and affiliates of prewar Poland's main communist organizations, which served as the primary vehicle for accomplishing the Polish section's goal as outlined by Stalin, which was to make Poland a socialist state closely affiliated with Moscow. From the start, the PCNL approved the Curzon Line as the basis for the eastern border of postwar Poland.

On 12 October 1944, Mikołajczyk arrived in Moscow for a summit with Stalin, which was due to commence the following day. Churchill and Eden, as well as the US Ambassador to Moscow, Averell Harriman, were also present. Poland's eastern border once again dominated discussions, with Stalin declaring an agreement between the "Lublin" (referring to the PCNL) and "London" (the government-in-exile) Poles to regard the border defined by the Curzon Line "as reality."[22] Churchill welcomed the Soviet leader's speech and, addressing the Polish delegation, reassured them that Britain and the Soviet Union would guarantee "that you will be compensated for the losses suffered in Germany, East Prussia, and Silesia." Mikołajczyk, invoking the PCNL, stated that "they had not lost hope of saving Lwów for Poland" (without specifying who had actually said this). Stalin dismissed this "rumour" as "unfounded" and curtly informed the Polish Prime Minister that "we don't trade Ukrainian lands." Churchill, still in support of Stalin's position, reiterated his earlier promise of granting Poland an even greater share of the Baltic coast, including the seaport of Stettin/Szczecin.[23]

When Mikołajczyk continued to refuse to accept the Curzon Line, Molotov interrupted him by saying, "After all, it all has been settled in Tehran." He then turned to Churchill and Harriman, reminding them that the decision concerning the eastern Polish border had been made during the first "Big Three" conference. This brought the meeting to an end, with Stalin having made it clear that his position was final. It is believed that he concluded the negotiations by stating, "If you, gentlemen, wish to have relations with the Soviet Government, then it will not be possible without recognizing the Curzon Line as principle." He continued that the "new version" of the Curzon Line would leave Białystok, Łomża in northern

Poland, and all of Peremyshl/Przemyśl within the Polish state borders, as opposed to their 1939 variant. After his return to London, Mikołajczyk communicated Stalin's conditions for reaching an "agreement" to the other members of the government-in-exile. They rejected those conditions, forcing Mikołajczyk to resign.[24]

In the areas under Soviet administration, Lviv/Lwów emerged as a bastion of Polish resistance to the new reality. When Soviet officers gathered as part of the honorary tribune in front of the Grand Theatre, they were met with shouts from the crowd: "Poland is not yet lost!," "Long live the Polish Lwów!," "Lwów unto Poland!."[25] On 9 September 1944, Ivan Grusecky, the head of the Lviv *oblast* party committee, informed Khrushchev of the popular sentiments in Lviv: "The majority of the city's Polish intelligentsia are rapidly adopting nationalist positions, orienting themselves towards Mikołajczyk and the Polish government-in-exile, and expect Lviv to be handed over to Poland in the near future, otherwise they intend to leave for Poland."

Meanwhile, the Polish underground in Lviv/Lwów also continued to wage the war on symbols that it had started during the first Soviet occupation in 1939–41. On 15 and 16 September 1944, members of the underground set fire to maps depicting the new Polish-Soviet border, which had probably been hung on advertising pillars. These actions were repeated around the city, despite the presence of armed guards.[26]

On 1 November 1944, members of the Home Army continued with their symbol acts of defiance by graffitiing the Cemetery of the Defenders of Lwów with slogans such as "We will not give up Lwów to the Soviet Union"; "Glory to the fighters for the Polish city of Lwów"; "What the foreign force has taken from us, we shall retrieve with sabre," and a map of Poland showing its pre-1939 eastern borders. Around five p.m., Poles began to gather at the Tomb of the Unknown Soldier. Over the following hours, according to Soviet informants, the crowd, numbering some three to four thousand, sang *Rota* ("The Oath," a Polish poem once proposed as a national anthem) and Dąbrowski's *Mazurka* ("Poland Is Not Yet Lost"), while shouting chants honouring the Home Army and Mikołajczyk, before dispersing at around nine p.m. NKVD officers eventually arrived and detained six people, mainly young adults aged eighteen to twenty, deemed responsible for inciting those who had gathered.[27]

The new border had similarly negative repercussions for a significant part of the western Ukrainian community, including the nationalist underground. For example, a new boundary based on the Curzon Line would mean abandoning areas with predominant Ukrainian populations farther to the west, such as Lemkivshchyna/ Łemkowszczyzna, Boikivshchyna/

Bojkowszczyzna, and the eastern parts of the Lublin and Cholm/Chełm regions. Propaganda issued by the OUN and its paramilitary wing the Ukrainian Insurgent Army (UPA) portrayed the territorial settlement as dividing the living body of the Ukrainian nation and declared that the UPA would continue to fight any such changes. The UPA also called for general resistance to the resettlement of Ukrainians from the Polish lands. That resistance would take a far more violent form than the forced departure of Poles from the Soviet Union. Nationalist propaganda was translated into action and led to armed resistance of the Ukrainian formations against Polish communist rule until the end of 1947.[28]

TOWARDS A RESOLUTION: YALTA, POTSDAM, AND THE NEW BORDER TREATY

After the Yalta Conference on 12 February 1945, the "Big Three" issued a declaration concerning postwar Europe in which any doubts about the course of the new Polish-Soviet and thus Polish-Ukrainian border were finally dispelled. It read: "The three representatives of the governments concerned consider that the Polish eastern border should run along the Curzon Line with deviations of five to eight kilometers in favor of Poland."[29]

Based on this settlement, postwar Poland would include about half of the prewar Lviv/Lwów province, leaving the city of Lviv/Lwów to the Soviets. A memorandum from the government-in-exile proposing that decisions on the shape of the borders be postponed until the end of the war, distributed prior to the Yalta Conference, was met with silence. A similar reaction met a later memorandum issued on 13 February 1945, in which the new Prime Minister, Tomasz Arciszewski, protested against the conference's decisions concerning Poland while declaring that "the separation of the eastern half of Poland's territory from the Polish people would be regarded as a new partition of Poland."[30]

Around the same time, the PCNL made weak attempts to retain Lviv/Lwów and the oil-rich Boryslav/Borysław region for the new Polish state. These were decisively halted by Stalin himself. Moreover, by signing the "Agreement on the Exchange of People" on 9 September 1944, the PCNL had granted the Soviets their tacit consent to continue their purge of the Polish population of the prewar eastern territories. Poland's shift to the west as part of the British-sponsored "balance of power," which was in line with the Soviet policy of annexing the lands originally conquered in 1939, led to a radical change in both the political system and the regional social and economic order.[31]

The recognition granted by Britain and the United States to the communist-dominated Provisional Government of National Unity (PGNU), formed on 28 June 1945, and the immediate withdrawal of support for the Polish government-in-exile in London a week later, validated the decision previously reached on the postwar Polish-Soviet border in Yalta, making it officially binding.[32] Thus, the revised 1939 demarcation line remained the basis for establishing Poland's new eastern boundaries. The subsequent decisions regarding the new border's southern section reached at the Potsdam Conference simply reinforced what had already been formulated at Tehran and Yalta. The border was to run along the Curzon Line (according to the "adjusted" Soviet version), with some symbolic deviations from its eastward course that favoured Poland.[33]

The precise and final shape of the border was to be determined by another conference of representatives from the Polish and Soviet sides, scheduled to take place in Moscow on 12–16 August 1945. The Polish representatives continued to cherish the hope that the Soviets would make significant concessions to their prior territorial claims; perhaps Poland might even retain Lviv/Lwów. Their more realistic expectations, however, were at least to secure the region of Truskavets/Truskawiec and Boryslav/Borysław in exchange for areas on the western side of the Bug River and the northern Salakas/Sołokija, between the Variazh/Waręż and Sokal (from the so-called Bug River twist), which had been granted to Poland in July 1944. Eberhardt points out that the Polish delegation also expected revisions to the section of the border with Czechoslovakia and in the region of Belz/Bełz.[34]

According to the Polish project, the new border would run from the Uzhock/Użok Pass, near the village of Sianki. It would then head northeast, leaving Skhidnytsia/Schodnica and Truskavets/Truskawiec on the western side and Stryi and Medenychi/Medenice on the east. The Poles wanted to leave Sambor on their side, farther to the north, as well as Krukenychi/Krukienice village. This adjusted border would then arrive at the previously established boundary line north of Medyka. This new demarcation would continue along the western side of the border established in July 1944, with the Soviets obtaining the area of Velyki Ochi/Wielkie Oczy, Horynets'/Horyniec, Liubycha/Lubycza, and areas to the east of Narol, excluding the small city of Kryliv/Kryłów on the Bug River's western bank. In economic terms, Poland would receive a large part of the oil basin while retaining some local traffic routes.

The Soviets deemed all of this completely unacceptable. Their experts and delegates had no intention of discussing the matter any further. It became clear to the Polish side that the Soviets' political patience should not be tested. So the Polish delegation presented a more humble request: it asked to annex the rail and road junction at Khyriv/Chyrów, which was important for its two parallel railway lines. An additional request for Rava Ruska/Rawa Ruska, around four kilometres east of the Curzon Line, was issued, owing to this town being at the conjunction of three Polish lines and one Ukrainian. Unsurprisingly, these requests were promptly rejected, with Poland only managing to achieve a slight shift of the border eastwards, near Peremyshl/Przemyśl, Korchova/Korczowa and Horynets'/Horyniec. Thanks to the position of Polish experts, Medyka also remained on the Polish side. Moreover, following some skillful negotiations by the Polish delegate Stanisław Leszczycki, the area covered by the Bieszczady Mountains, stretching over three hundred square kilometres, and dominated by the peaks of Halicz and Tarnica, was recognized as the southernmost part of communist Poland.[35]

During those discussions in Moscow, it soon became apparent that the Soviet delegates were going to ignore all attempts by the Polish delegation to negotiate any adjustments to the already existing border agreements, which had been reached with the PCNL in July 1944, and would only engage in talks on relatively minor border revisions. Thus, this meeting was used to legitimize the state of affairs that had existed for almost a year now. As Leszczycki later reflected:

> In the end, all Polish revisions were rejected. The Soviet Union adopted the interpretation of the Curzon Line that was the most favorable for their leadership, and in their greed they crossed the limits of decency; here again, Soviet imperialism, ruthlessness, lack of magnanimity, and their very strong advantage manifested itself. In fact, the border was dictated with no substantial discussion and no consideration of Poland's interests at all.[36]

Under international law, the future of the disputed Polish-Ukrainian ethnic border areas was decided on 16 August 1945, when the PGNU concluded the "Polish-Soviet Border Agreement" with the Soviet Union in Moscow. This agreement stipulated that the new border would come into force – in its agreed form – from the beginning of 1946. Work on the more localized aspects of its course was delegated to the three subcommittees of the "Mixed Delimitation Committee" that had been established for this purpose. An exchange of documents certifying the course of the borders took place on 6 February 1946 in Warsaw, although the committee continued its work until March 1946. The unwavering stance of the Soviet negotiators had left Rava-Ruska/Rawa Ruska, Khyriv/Chyrów and Dobromyl/Dobromil on the Soviet side.[37]

The shifting of the Polish-Ukrainian border and the associated ethnic cleansing by means of resettlement affected around 787,000 Poles still living in what was now Soviet Ukraine; at the same time, more than 500,000 Ukrainians were violently displaced from the territory of postwar Poland.[38] The expulsion of about 1.3 million people represented a kind of "matching," with both countries seeking to recalibrate their demographic compositions to align with the newly created border. The establishment of cross-border relations between the states was, in turn, finalized with the signing of an agreement on 8 July 1948, granting Poland the much-desired village of Medyka along with parts of the Lviv and Drohobych *oblasts*, including a border strip approximately six hundred metres wide and less than thirty-five kilometres in length, that stretched along the Błotnia Streak.[39]

THE 1951 BORDER "ADJUSTMENT" AND THE END OF POSTWAR BORDER-SHAPING

In 1951, less than five years after the last revision of the border presented by communistic propaganda as final and "fair" to both Poles and Ukrainians, the Polish and the Soviet authorities conducted yet another territorial exchange in Lubelszczyzna and the Bieszczady Mountains. The reason for this new revision was the discovery of coal deposits in the eastern Lubelszczyzna region, which the Soviet government wanted to profit from. As a result, much to the benefit of the Soviet Union, Poland renounced the southeastern part of the Lublin province, along with the towns of Belz/Bełz, Krystynopil/Krystynopol, Variazh/Waręż, and Khorobriv/Chorobrów. The border adjustment affected seven municipalities, one of which (Krystynopil/Krystynopol) was incorporated into the Soviet Union in its entirety. The Soviet Union, in turn, renounced its sovereignty over the western part of the Drohobych/Drohobycz *oblast*, including the towns of Ustryki Dolyshni/Ustrzyki Dolne, Liutovyska/Lutowiska, Charna/Czarna, and Krostenko/Krościenko, as well as the entire railway line connecting Peremyshl/Przemyśl with Zagórze. The 1951 territorial exchange between Poland and the Soviet Union would become one of the largest direct geopolitical alterations of its kind in postwar Europe (see map 4.3).[40]

4.3 Soviet Ukraine, 1952.

As a result, thousands of social bonds were broken, as were many family ties. However, the communist decision-makers had little interest in the social costs of their actions. As Roman Czmełyk writes, "the adequate and characteristic signs of any cultural and ethnic borderland, thus multiculturalism, multi-ethnicity, multilingualism, coexistence of a number of religions or creeds, have virtually disappeared from the said areas [covered by the 'exchange']."[41] According to some Polish historians, the border adjustment proved extremely unfavourable for communist Poland, depriving it of numerous and rich coal deposits. Indeed, the exchange's only real material value may have been in allowing the Poles to complete the Myczkowce-Solina hydroelectric dam and power plant complex on the San River.[42] From a humanitarian perspective, thousands of individual and family tragedies, the trauma of forced resettlement, and the harm done to both Polish and Ukrainian border communities was concealed under the notion of "border adjustment."[43]

In the autumn of 1952, the governments of both countries began planning another, much larger exchange of territories involving the "transfer" of around 1,300 square kilometres. Poland was to hand over the eastern outskirts of Lubelszczyzna with Hrubeshiv/Hrubieszów and part of the Tomashiv/Tomaszów Lubelski *poviat* to the Volhynia *oblast* of Soviet Ukraine, while receiving the areas around Nyzhankovychi/Niżankowice, Khyriv/Chyrów, and Dobromyl/Dobromil, located in Soviet Ukraine's Drohobych/Drohobycz *oblast*. However, Stalin's death in March 1953 rendered these proposals obsolete. Consequently, since the autumn of 1951, the border between Poland and Ukraine has remained unchanged, running 535 kilometres from Sobibór by the Bug River on the border between the outskirts of Lubelszczyzna with Volhynia/Wołyń to the Kremenets/Krzemieniec peak in the Bieszczady Mountains.

In summary, the continuous redrawing of the postwar Polish-Ukrainian border was determined by economic considerations and the Soviet leadership's desire for access to natural resources. The Soviet authorities wanted to incorporate territories rich in natural resources, such as the oil basin near Drohobych/Drohobycz and the coal basin nearby Sokal, alongside what would become the largest urban and cultural centre in western Ukraine – the city of Lviv/Lwów. In compensation, the western border of Poland was "moved" significantly to the west. The process of negotiating and delineating the new borders of communist Poland and Soviet Ukraine exposed the sharp discrepancy between the territorial visions of the more powerful governments and more localized views of the Polish and Ukrainian leaders.

After the collapse of communism at the beginning of the 1990s, the existing border between Poland and independent Ukraine was again granted formal recognition on 24 August 1992, becoming a pillar of mutual trust and a basis for future political and economic cooperation between the two states. The border, which had been the site of much inter-ethnic resentment and hostility for decades, has become a bridge to better coexistence and mutual understanding between Poles and Ukrainians.

NOTES

1 Piotr Eberhardt, "Formowanie się polskiej granicy wschodniej po II wojnie światowej," *Dzieje Najnowsze* 2 (2018): 87–118; Eberhardt, *Polska granica wschodnia 1939–1945* (Warsaw: Editions Spotkania, 1992); Eberhardt, "Linia Curzona jako wschodnia granica Polski. Geneza i uwarunkowania polityczne," *Studia z Dziejów Rosji i Europy Środkowo-Wschodniej* 46 (2011): 127–58; Eberhardt, "The Curzon Line as the Eastern Boundary of Poland: The Origins and the political Background," *Geographia Polonica* 85, no. 1

(2012): 5-21; A. Wawryniuk, "Delimitacja wschodniej granicy Polski po II wojnie światowej a sprawa Medyki," *Rocznik Przemyski* 48 (2012): 119-42; Wawryniuk, *Granica polsko-sowiecka po 1944 roku (na odcinku z Ukrainą)* (Chelm: Państwowa Wyższa Szkoła Zawodowa, 2015); Iu. Soroka, "Demarkatsiia ukraïns'ko-pol's'koho kordonu u 1946-1948 rokach," *Etnichna Istoria Narodiv Ievropy* 35 (2011): 4-8; I. Kozlovskyi, *Vstanovlennia ukraïns'ko-pol'skoho kordonu, 1941–1951 rr.* (Lviv: Kameniar, 1998).

2 S. Dębski, *Między Berlinem a Moskwą. Stosunki niemiecko-sowieckie 1939–1941* (Warsaw: Polski Instytut Spraw Międzynarodowych, 2007).

3 D. Boćkowski, *Na zawsze razem. Białostocczyzna i Łomżyńskie w polityce radzieckiej w czasie II Wojny Światowej (IX 1939–VIII 1944)* (Warsaw: Wydawnictwo Neriton, Instytut Historii Polskiej Akademii Nauk, 2005), 22.

4 Ukrainian Central Historical State Archive (Lviv): F. 859, op. 1, case 1, p. 18, transcript of National Assemblies of Western Ukraine. Lviv, 26 October 1939.

5 Eberhardt, *Polska granica wschodnia*; V. Danilenko, "Likvidatsiia Pol's'koï derzhavy ta vstanovlennia radians'koho rezhymu v Zakhidnii Ukraïni," *Ukraïns'kyi Istorychnyi Zhurnal'* 3 (2006), 114-15.

6 M. Hułas, "Memorandum Stafforda Crippsa z 22 października 1940 r. Polskie aspekty," *Dzieje Najnowsze* 4 (1993): 85.

7 W. Bonusiak, *Małopolska Wschodnia pod rządami Trzeciej Rzeszy* (Rzeszów: Wyższa Szkoła Pedagogiczna, 1990), 56–60, D. Schenk, *Noc morderców. Kaźń polskich oficerów we Lwowie i Holokaust w Galicji Wschodniej* (Kracow: Wysoki Zamek, 2012).

8 The Decree of General Gouvernment Reign, L'viv, 1 August 1941, in *Radianskyi L'viv 1939–1955. Dokumenty i materialy*, ed. M.K. Ivasiuta, V.I. Paschenko, and H.S. Syzonenko (Lviv: Knyzhkovo-zhurnal'ne vydavnytstvo, 1956), 177–8.

9 H. Stefaniuk, "Polityka natsysts'koï okupatsiinoï vlady shchodo Skhidno-halyts'koho sotsiumu u 1941-1944 rr.," *Storinky Voiennoï Istoriï Ukraïny. Zbirnyk Naukovykh Statei* 12 (2009), 171–2.

10 See more in G. Hryciuk, *Przemiany narodowościowe i ludnościowe w Galicji Wschodniej i na Wołyniu w latach 1931–1948* (Toruń: Wydawnictwo Adam Marszałek, 2005); D. Pohl, *Niemiecka polityka ekonomiczna na okupowanych terenach wschodniej Polski w latach 1941–1944*, "Pamięć i Sprawiedliwość" 2009, nr 1 (2014): 93–4.

11 See more in R. Torzecki, *Kwestia ukraińska w polityce III Rzeszy 1933–1945* (Warsaw: Książka i Wiedza, 1972).

12 S. Berthon and J. Potts, *Warlords: The Heart of Conflict, 1939–1945* (London: Politico, 2005); Hułas, *Memorandum*, 85–8.
13 More in: M. Hułas, "Brytyjskie próby rozwiązania problemu granicy polsko-radzieckiej od lutego do kwietnia 1943 roku," in *Europa nieprowincjonalna. Przemiany na ziemiach wschodnich dawnej Rzeczypospolitej (Białoruś, Litwa, Łotwa, Ukraina, wschodnie pogranicze III Rzeczypospolitej Polskiej) w latach 1772-1999*, ed. K. Jasiewicz (Warsaw and London: Instytut Studiów Politycznych Polskiej Akademii Nauk, 1999), 104–16; *Lwów i Wilno*, London, 19 October 1947, 1.
14 The telegram of the main commander of Polish Armed Forces to the commander of Polish Home Army, London, 29 October 1943, in *Armia Krajowa w dokumentach 1939–1945*, vol. 3, kwiecień 1943–lipiec 1944 [April 1943–July 1944] (Wroclaw, Warsaw, and Krakow: Studium Polski Podziemnej – Zakład Narodowy im. Ossolińskich, 1990), 190; S. Mikołajczyk, *Polska zgwałcona* (Warsaw: De Facto, 2005), 42.
15 Eberhardt, *Polska granica wschodnia*; W. Materski, *Teheran, Jałta, San Francisco, Poczdam* (Warsaw: Wydawnictwa Szkolne i Pedagogiczne, 1987); *Teheran–Jałta–Poczdam. Dokumenty konferencji szefów rządów trzech wielkich mocarstw* (Warsaw: Polski Instytut Spraw Międzynarodowych, 1972).
16 *Izvestiya*, 12 January 1944.
17 Mikołajczyk, *Polska zgwałcona*, 46.
18 G. Motyka, *Od rzezi wołyńskiej do akcji „Wisła." Konflikt polsko-ukraiński 1939–1947* (Kracow: Wydawnictwo Literackie, 2016); Motyka, *Tak było w Bieszczadach. Walki polsko-ukraińskie 1943–1948* (Warsaw: Oficyna Wydawnicza Volumen, 1999); Motyka, *Ukraińska partyzantka. Działalność Organizacji Ukraińskich Nacjonalistów i Ukraińskiej Powstańczej Armii* (Warsaw: Oficyna Wydawnicza Rytm – Instytut Studiów Politycznych Polskiej Akademii Nauk, 2006).
19 *Radians'ka Ukraïna*, 6 March 1944; S. Iekel'chyk, *Imperia pam'iati. Rosiisko-ukraïns'ki stosunky v radianskii istorychnii uiavi* (Kyiv: Krytyka, 2008), 91; Mykola Petrovs'kyi, *Vozz'iednannia ukraïns'koho narodu v iedynii ukraïns'kii radians'kii derzhavi* (Kyiv and Kharkiv: DVU, 1944); Mykola Petrovs'kyi, *Zakhidna Ukraïna (Istorychna dovidka)* (Kyiv: DVU, 1945).
20 D. Markowski, *Płonące kresy. Operacja „Burza" na ziemiach wschodnich II Rzeczypospolitej Polskiej* (Warsaw: Oficyna Wydawnicza Rytm, 2008); D. Markowski, *Anatomia strachu. Sowietyzacja obwodu lwowskiego 1944–1953. Studium zmian polityczno-gospodarczych* (Warsaw: Instytut Pamięci Narodowej, 2018).

21 L'viv Oblast' State Archive (DALO), F. P-; op. 1, case 6; p. 70: information about the situation in the town, written by a local leader of the (Ukrainian) Bolshevik Party (Chupis), L'viv, after 29 July 1944.
22 Mikołajczyk, *Polska zgwałcona*, 79.
23 The Report of Polish Foreign Affairs Minister Romer from the Moscow Conference, after 13 October 1944, in *Armia Krajowa w dokumentach*, vol. 5, październik 1944–lipiec 1945 [October 1944–July 1945] (Warszaw, Kraków, and Wrocław: Studium Polski Podziemnej – Zakład Narodowy im. Ossolińskich, 1991), 64–5.
24 The Report of Polish Foreign Affairs Minister Romer from Moscow Conference, after 13 October 1944, in *Armia Krajowa w dokumentach*, vol. 5, 66; E. Duraczyński, *Stalin: twórca i dyktator supermocarstwa* (Pułtusk and Warsaw: Akademia Humanistyczna im. Aleksandra Gieysztora, 2012), 509.
25 G. Hryciuk, "Dwa dokumenty radzieckie z roku 1944. Spojrzenie na polską inteligencję we Lwowie. Jak ukrainizować 'stare ukraińskie miasto'?," *Wrocławskie Studia Wschodnie* 2 (1998), 196.
26 Markowski, *Anatomia strachu*, 141–50.
27 DALO, F. P-3, op. 1,, case 6; p. 55–7: information about the anti-Soviet riots organiszed by Polish nationalists, Lviv, 5 November 1944.
28 More in Motyka, *Tak było w Bieszczadach*.
29 Mikołajczyk, *Polska zgwałcona*, 91.
30 The Statement of Polish Government in London, 13 February 1945, in *Armia Krajowa w dokumentach*, vol. 5, 277.
31 B. Martin, "Sytuacja międzynarodowa w lecie 1944 roku: współpraca aliantów – początki zimnej wojny," in *Powstanie Warszawskie 1944: Praca zbiorowa pod redakcją Stanisławy Lewandowskiej i Bernda Martina* (Warsaw: Wydawnictwo Polsko-Niemieckie, 1999), 31–2.
32 See more in Materski, *Teheran, Jałta, San Francisco, Poczdam*.
33 *Foreign Relations of the United States: Diplomatic Papers: The Conference of Berlin (the Potsdam Conference)*, 1945, vol. 1, 1945, 760–6, https://search.library.wisc.edu/digital/APOWN6XXJYOWIY8X.
34 Eberhardt, *Formowanie się polskiej granicy*, 91.
35 Ibid., 91–2.
36 Ibid., 202.
37 Dziennik Ustaw 1947, nr 35, poz. 167, http://isap.sejm.gov.pl/DetailsServlet?id=WDU19470350167; Eberhardt, *Formowanie się polskiej granicy*, 100–10.
38 J. Kochanowski, "Przesunięcie granic," *Karta* 24 (1998), 67.

39 The Republic of Poland Foreign Affairs State Archive (Warsaw), F. 6, vol. 559; case 35, p. 31–2, letter from the Law Bureau Main Director to the I. Soviet Department, Warsaw, 28 December 1948; Wawryniuk, *Delimitacja wschodniej granicy Polski*; Soroka, *Demarkatsiia*, 4–8.
40 I. Kozlovs'kyi, *Vstanovlennia ukraïns'ko-pol'skoho kordonu*.
41 R. Chmelyk, "Stavlennia meshkantsiv ukraïns'ko-pol's'koho pohranychia do kordonu," *Narodoznavchi Zoshyty* 1 (2012), 37.
42 A. Gawryszewski, *Ludność Polski w XX wieku* (Warsaw: Instytut Geografii i Przestrzennego Zagospodarowania im. Stanisława Leszczyckiego Polskiej Akademii Nauk, 2005), 49.
43 T. Pron', "Radians'ko-pol's'kyi obmin diliankamy terytoriï 1951 r. u perekazakh boikiv stepu Ukraïny," *Naukovi Zapyski. Zbirnyk prats' molodykh vchenykh ta aspirantiv* 2 (2009): 264–73.

PART TWO

Establishing the Borders
of the Soviet Republics

5

Emerging States and Border-Making in Times of War

Negotiating the Ukrainian-Belarusian Borders in 1918

Dorota Michaluk

The First World War aggravated unresolved issues in the Russian Empire's domestic affairs; this led to the February Revolution of 1917 and, soon after, the political transformation of the state. Social and national issues took centre stage, awakening political forces that not only demanded the extension of individual rights but also generated increasingly brazen ultimatums from those nations on Russia's peripheries. In early 1917, these demands focused on political autonomy; later, they were extended to territorial autonomy within a loose, democratic federation; by the end of 1917, they had escalated even further into outright calls for independence. These developments were hastened by the activities of the Bolsheviks, a faction within the Russian Social Democratic Labour Party (RSDLP) that had splintered off in 1903. In early November 1917, after losing an election to the Socialist Revolutionary Party, they overthrew the post-tsarist Provisional Government and dissolved, by force, the All-Russian Constituent Assembly.

In the context of the dissolving imperial Russian state, this chapter delves into how the border came to be drawn between the emerging states of Ukraine and Belarus. As the leaders of both nations attempted to consolidate their new polities, one of the most important bilateral negotiations concerned the creation of a shared border. This chapter examines the context in which delegations from both sides met in Kyiv in April 1918 and how their discussions were shaped and influenced by external factors, from the volatile international climate in the wake of the First World War to changing regional power relations in East-Central Europe. It will also touch upon how cartographic expertise was recruited in support of territorial claims. It utilizes a range of sources, including archival materials and contemporary maps and publications, while building on the existing historiography.[1]

The Ukrainians and Belarusians followed similar paths toward independence, paths that were similar to those taken by other nations – such as Georgia and the Baltic states – as they sought political independence from the crumbling Russian Empire. On 17 March 1917,[2] the Central Council of Ukraine was established in Kyiv under the leadership of Mykhailo Hrushevsky, a renowned historian and the leader of the Ukrainian national movement. On 23 June 1917 the Rada published its First Universal, which proclaimed Ukraine's political autonomy within Russia. On 20 November 1917, after the Bolsheviks seized power in Petrograd and overthrew the Provisional Government, the Rada released its Third Universal, which proclaimed the formation of the Ukrainian People's Republic (UNR) in federation with Russia. This was followed on 25 January 1918 by the Fourth Universal, which proclaimed the UNR's outright independence.[3]

The Belarusians had also started to organize themselves politically in February 1917, but their various factions did not begin to cooperate closely until the following autumn, shortly before the Bolshevik takeover in Petrograd.[4] An All-Belarusian Congress gathered in Minsk in December but did not discuss separation from Russia. That question was not raised until after the congress was brutally dispersed by the Bolsheviks. The situation was then exacerbated by the signing of the Treaty of Brest-Litovsk between the Central Powers and Soviet Russia, which was deeply unfavourable to Belarus. On 21 February 1918, on the initiative of the pro-independence faction, the First Constituent Charter (*I Gramata*) proclaimed the establishment of a provisional government for Belarus – the People's Secretariat. On 9 March, the Second Constituent Charter announced the creation of a Belarusian People's Republic (BNR) in federation with Russia. On 25 March 1918, the Third Constituent Charter proclaimed the full independence of Belarus, mirroring the UNR.[5]

EXPERTS, MAPS, AND THE EARLY PROJECTS FOR THE BORDERS OF BELARUS AND UKRAINE

Drawing national borders was a key priority for both Ukraine and Belarus.[6] Toward the end of the war, as emancipated nations began to establish their own states on the ruins of Central and Eastern Europe's former multi-ethnic empires, ethnicity became a common criterion for border-making. The assumption here was that a state should incorporate the area where the nation was demographically predominant. In the terminology of the time, such territories were "ethnic" or "ethnographic" lands. Socialist activists realized that ethnically mixed border regions were a fact on the ground, but they still believed that borders could be drawn according to the local inhabitants' will. This belief was encouraged by the spread of the principle of self-determination, which was promoted independently (albeit with slightly different meanings) by both US President Woodrow Wilson and the leader of the Russian Bolsheviks, Vladimir Lenin. Soon enough, the realities of international politics and the competing territorial aspirations of the various emerging states challenged this optimistic approach.

Scholarly knowledge played an important part in shaping the claims of the parties involved. The contours of the Belarusian borders emerged to a certain degree from the "Ethnographic Map of the Belarusian People" (*Etnograficheskaia karta belorusskogo plemeni*), prepared by Professor Iefim Karski, a linguist from Petrograd University, which illustrated the area where the Belarusian language was spoken (see map 5.1). It should be emphasized that Karski's scholarship was purely linguistic and that, while he used the term "ethnographic," he considered no other criteria (such as ethnography or traditions) besides linguistic ones. Even so, Karski's research had a significant impact, for it framed Belarusian as an independent language rather than a dialect of Russian (which many other contemporary linguists thought it was).[7]

Karski included several regions in this Belarusian linguistic space. These included the northern part of the Belsk district;[8] the Pruzhany district in the Grodno/Hrodno Governorate; a portion of the northern Pinsk district; the northern and eastern parts of the Mozyr district; the Rechitsa and Gomel districts in the Minsk Governorate; the southern part of Horodnia district; a small portion of the southern part of the Sosnytsia district; and the northwestern part of the Novhorod-Siversky district of the Chernihiv Governorate.

In 1917, Karski's map was reprinted with some minor revisions. This newer version indicated the external border only, thus rendering it as a map of the ethnic Belarusian lands. In March 1917, Karski was appointed to a special committee, established at the congress of Belarusian national organizations in Minsk, to delineate Belarus's national borders. Its members included the historians Matvey Lubavski from Petrograd University and Mitrofan Doŭnar-Zapolski from the Imperial University of Kyiv, as well as Karski's fellow linguist Alexei Shakhmatov from the Petrograd Academy of Sciences.[9] The committee did not undertake any joint actions, however, with the result that the BNR's territory, as defined by the Third Constituent Charter, was based largely on Karski's map. The Belarusian state was to include all areas where the Belarusian people was demographically

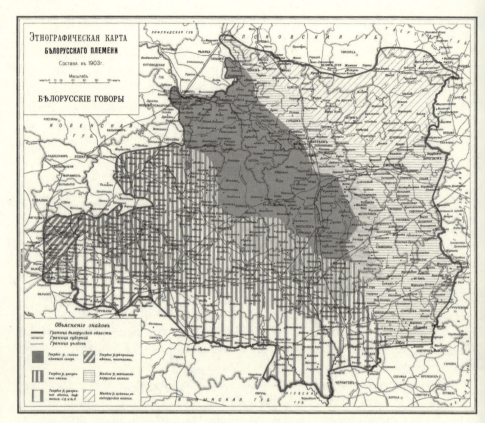

5.1 Ethnographical map of the Belarusian tribe, 1903.

predominant: the Mogilev Governorate, and parts of the Governorates of Minsk, Grodno (with Grodno and Białystok), Vilnius (including the city of Vilnius), Vitebsk, Smolensk, and Chernihiv, as well as the fringe areas of neighbouring governorates inhabited by ethnic Belarusians.[10]

At this time, the Ukrainians were able to draw on a far broader base of local scientific research. The first contours of Ukraine's borders were influenced by the works of geographer and cartographer Stepan Rudnytsky, an alumnus of the University of Lviv/Lemberg.[11] He was a member of the Union for the Liberation of Ukraine, and his motto "a national territory is the nation's main foundation," was no mere platitude, but carried cognitive and political value.[12] Rudnytsky had studied the physical geography of Ukraine and the location of its natural resources; in doing so, he had laid the foundations for the development of Ukrainian political geography and cartography.[13] His involvement in the Ukrainian independence movement was reflected in much of his work.[14]

Rudnytsky's book *Ukraine und die Ukrainer* (1914), published at the outbreak of the First World War, included a coloured map titled *Etnographische Übersichtskarte der Ukraine* (Ethnographic Overview Map).[15] This same map appeared in his next study, *Ukraina, Land und Volk* (1916). A year later, a more detailed version was printed as the *Ohliadova karta ukraïns'kykh zemel'* (Overview Map of the Ukrainian Lands) and was featured in the Ukrainian-language textbook *Ukraïna nash ridnyi krai* (Ukraine: Our Motherland). It was republished again in 1918, as a separate large-scale wall map, by the Viennese cartographic publisher G. Freytag and Berndt (see map 0.4, page 21 of this volume). Rudnytsky presented Ukraine's borders as incorporating the southern part of the Belsk district in the Grodno Governorate as well as the Brest and Kobrin districts. Continuous Ukrainian settlements were spread along both sides of the Pripyat River and reached the southern and central parts of the Pinsk district (including the city of Pinsk) and the southern part of the Mozyr district (including the titular capital). The Horodnia, Novozybkov, Starodub, Surazh, and Mglin districts constituted a continuous area where Ukrainians were a majority. Rudnytsky considered the lands above the Pripyat – specifically the southern part of the Pruzhany district, the northern peripheries of the Pinsk district, the northern part of the Mozyr district, and all of the Rechitsa and Gomel districts – to be an area of mixed Belarusian-Ukrainian settlement, represented on his map with intermittent pink lines. Similar diversity was also shown to exist in parts of eastern Polesia (a triangular area delimited by the cities of Mozyr, Sokolovka, and Loiev and the southwestern Mglin area). This was an entirely novel approach, for neither linguists nor ethnographers had doubted that the population of eastern Polesia was predominantly Belarusian: cartographical works by Karski, Dietrich Schäffer, and other members of the dialectological committee of the Imperial Academy of Sciences had indicated as much. However, it should be noted that Rudnytsky had not created a linguistic map, but – as a singular case among the above-mentioned authors – one that represented the reach of those lands that, according to his ethnic views, should belong to Ukraine and serve its geopolitical needs.[16]

In its Third Universal, the Central Rada presented the territory of the UNR in very general terms. The People's Republic was to include Podolia and Volhynia along with the Kyiv, Chernihiv, Poltava, Kharkiv, Katerynoslav, Kherson, and Taurida Governorates, but excluding Crimea,[17] following the declaration of an independent Crimean People's Republic by local Crimean Tatars in November 1917. It was suggested that the fates of the Kursk, Kholm, and Voronezh Governorates, as well as parts of those neighbouring governorates and districts inhabited by Ukrainians, should be decided by the "will of the nations" (most likely through plebiscite). In its Fourth Universal, the Central Rada stated that it wished to live in concord and friendship with all neighbouring states, such as Russia, Poland, Austria, Romania, and Turkey, but that none of them would be allowed to interfere in the life of independent Ukraine.[18] This list of neighbours did not include Belarus, which would announce its founding only on 9 March 1918, several weeks after the Third Universal was published. The UNR and the BNR proclaimed their independence merely two months apart; however, during that time the political tide had turned dramatically against the Belarusians, making it difficult for them to gain support for their new state even from the UNR.

On 9 February 1918, a separate peace was reached between the Central Powers and the UNR. The recognition of the UNR's government by Germany and Austria-Hungary meant that the former now had to take the latter's views into account. On 3 March 1918, Germany, Austria-Hungary, Bulgaria, and Turkey signed the Treaty of Brest-Litovsk with Soviet Russia. Belarusian territory subsequently remained under German occupation until Russia had paid its agreed reparations. For Belarus, another unfavourable provision was Berlin's promise to Petrograd that it would deny recognition to any new state that attempted to proclaim independence from the former territories of the Russian Empire. This obligation made it difficult for Belarus to secure recognition from Germany, and from the UNR as well, which could not afford to take any steps in this direction without the approval of its German patron.

After the BNR proclaimed its independence, its leaders attempted to place their state under Germany's influence, counting on the support of Ukrainian politicians. The two nations were strongly linked, a fact noted by Rudnytsky, who in 1917 described Ukraine's neighbours this way: "to the north ... lives no Pole, but our nearest dear brother Belarusian, or, as it often said here, Lithuanian."[19]

Having been recognized as the lawful government of Ukraine by the Central Powers in January 1918, the Central Rada planned a conference in Kursk to meet with Russian representatives.[20] The Ukrainian-Russian border was among the pressing topics for discussion. Through their contacts in the Central Rada, representatives from Belarus also intended to be present in Kursk, hoping that Soviet Russia would recognize the eastern and southern borders of Belarus and, by extension, the state itself.[21] These negotiations were to be preceded by the settlement of the Ukrainian-Belarusian border in the east, which would require Soviet Russia to extend its recognition to the BNR. The border in that area would be delimited through a three-party agreement.

Some decisions had already been made about western Polesia. On 9 February 1918, Germany, Turkey, Austria-Hungary, Bulgaria, and the Central Rada signed an agreement regarding the UNR's northern border. The first section was similar to the prewar border between Austria-Hungary and Russia; the second followed the line connecting the towns of Bilgoray, Shebreshin, Krasnystaw, Pugachev, Radzyn, Miedzyzhec, Sarnaki, Melnik, Vysokoe Litevskoe, Kamenets Litevsky, and Pruzhany, ending at Vydonovsk Lake.[22] Thus, the UNR was to include part of southern Podlachia to the Narev River (the Belsk district in the Grodno Governorate) as well as all of western Polesia, including the Pripyat River basin (the Brest and Kobrin districts of the Grodno Directorate). The agreement did not cover eastern Polesia; it was expected that the fate of the southern districts of Mogilev and Minsk Governorates would be settled when the border was drawn between Ukraine and Soviet Russia. The establishment of the BNR's government in March 1918, however, saw the political situation change dramatically: Ukraine's northern neighbour might now be Belarus instead of Russia or Poland, the two states posing the greatest danger to Ukrainian sovereignty. Given that, a region of mixed Belarusian and Ukrainian settlement might well become highly contested. In western Polesia, that region included the Brest, Kobrin, and Pruzhany districts of the Grodno Governorate, and in eastern Polesia the Pinsk, Mozyr, and Rechitsa districts of the Minsk Governorate as well as the Homel district of the Mogilev Governorate.

POLESIA: A BELARUSIAN-UKRAINIAN BORDERLAND

Ethnographically, Polesia was important for both Ukraine and Belarus. Western Polesia in particular was ethnically diverse, and the national consciousness of its inhabitants was still relatively weak, though it had been strengthening since the turn of the twentieth century. The language spoken by the local peasantry is today classified as "West Polesian," a dialect incorporating elements of Ukrainian and Belarusian. In 1897, the first fully national census conducted in the Russian Empire found that the majority of inhabitants in the districts of Brest (64.38 per cent), Kobrin (79.57 per cent), and Pinsk (74.30 per cent) spoke "Little Russian" (Ukrainian), with most of them probably using the Polesian dialect.[23] Based solely on this linguistic criterion, the population of these districts was assigned Ukrainian nationality.

Yet many scholars researching nationality and ethnographic questions (such as Julian Talko-Hryntsewich, Mitrofan Doŭnar-Zapolski, and Ivan Ieremich) contended that language should not be the sole factor when determining nationality.[24] Polesia's inhabitants, whose customs, folklore, and mentality shared many features with the Belarusian population of Central Belarus, were presented as prime example. In the mid-nineteenth century, several researchers (including Pavel Shpilevsky and Pavel Bobrovsky) maintained that Polesians were a separate ethnographic and linguistic group.[25] The acculturation of this community to the Belarusian nationality and culture was accelerating by the end of the nineteenth century, especially in western Polesia. Between 1857 and 1897, the percentage of people declaring Belarusian as their mother tongue increased in the Kobrin, Brest, and Pruzhany districts, yet the share of Ukrainians in these districts remained higher (as the western Polesian language continued to be viewed as a dialect of Ukrainian). Interestingly, linguistic developments did not appear to parallel the development of national consciousness: most Russian army conscripts from western Polesia declared themselves Belarusians.[26] In the censuses conducted during the interwar period, following the area's annexation by the Republic of Poland, most of its inhabitants leaned toward claiming Belarusian rather than Ukrainian nationality.[27]

Eastern Polesia was less ethnically mixed: the Belarusian population exceeded the Ukrainian one and counted a higher proportion of urban-dwellers.[28] The importance of this region for Belarus was stressed by Doŭnar-Zapolski, who was a specialist in Polesian ethnography and who was involved in codifying the core tenets of Belarusian statehood. According to him, the eastern Belarusians had been Russified, while those in the west were mostly Polonized, making their southern areas highly valuable, both nationally and economically. From a historical and ethnographic perspective, it was important that the BNR not relinquish any lands to the south.[29]

As state borders were defined, references to historical territorial divisions gained rhetorical prominence. In seeking out their state's origins, Belarusian scholars increasingly pointed to the Principality of Polotsk, the Principality of Turov and Pinsk, and the Gediminas dynasty. Doŭnar-Zapolski believed that the areas populated by Belarusians and Ukrainians had been separated by the southern border of the Principality of Turov and Pinsk and the Grand Duchy of Lithuania, as well as by the southern borders of two voivodeships (provinces) – Minsk and Brest-Lithuania (previously Podlachia) – in their pre–Union of Lublin form.[30] This idea was criticized by Rudnytsky, who showed that it was impossible to establish a chronology of "Belarusian" and "Ukrainian" settlements in the upper Pripyat and

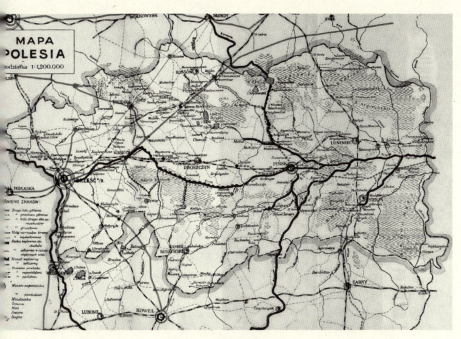

5.2 Map of Polesia, 1935.

Pinsk. He also pointed to the administrative divisions of the Grand Duchy of Lithuania, but his delimitation ran differently – he contended that under Lithuanian rule the former Principality of Turov and Pinsk had been divided into two provinces – Novhorod and Podlachia (or Brest)[31] – with the boundary between them corresponding to the modern-day Belarusian-Ukrainian border.[32]

UNR politicians were equally aware of the ethnic situation in eastern Polesia. They declared that the Belarusians would certainly enjoy personal autonomy and that Ukraine would watch over the "Belarusian Piedmont" that was to take shape in the Rechitsa, Gomel, and Mozyr districts, though Ukraine's administrative and educational systems would be imposing policies of Ukrainization.[33] These actions would be guided not by romantic ideals but by consistent pragmatism: Polesia had a significant role to play in securing the Ukrainian state due to a branch of the Brest-Moscow railway that ran parallel to the Pripyat River. That railway linked Brest and Gomel, passing through Kobrin and Luninets, and was essentially the only year-round communication route between western and eastern Polesia. Other forms of overland travel were only possible during the dry summer and cold winter months.

The importance of the railway was noted by Hetman Pavlo Skoropadsky, who viewed the junction at Gomel as the pivotal link to both Chernihiv and Kyiv, and thus all of Ukraine.[34] Years later, this matter was commented on by Dmytro Doroshenko, the Minister of Foreign Affairs in Skoropadsky's short-lived Ukrainian State government: "We would have felt safe only if that railway had belonged to a strong, independent Belarusian state. However, we could not be sure whether in those circumstances such a state (though formally proclaimed) could be strengthened and consolidated; on the contrary, it was most likely that the railway would be taken over by Soviet Russia or Poland."[35]

NEGOTIATING THE BELARUSIAN-UKRAINIAN BORDER

One of the earliest decisions by the People's Secretariat of the BNR was to establish diplomatic relations with the UNR.[36] On 22 March 1918, an extraordinary delegation, sent by the Rada of the BNR, headed for Kyiv, tasked with obtaining Ukrainian recognition for the BNR and with delimiting the Belarusian-Ukrainian border. Several meetings of the Joint Committee organized for this matter were held between 19 and 29 April 1918.[37] The Belarusian side was represented by two members of the Rada, Alyaksandr Tsvikievich, who served as its chair, and Symon Rak-Mikhailoŭski. They were accompanied by five consultants: Ivan Kurylovitch, Jazep Farbotka, Lavon Leuchenko, Ivan Kraskoŭski, and Mitrofan Doŭnar-Zapolski, who, significantly, was selected to join the Belarusian delegation following the initial negotiations. The UNR was represented by two members of the All-Ukrainian Council of Military Delegates, Tymofii Petrivsky and Mykola Svidersky, and led by Anastas Likhniakevich, the only participant with any connection to the government as a member of the Central Rada's review committee.[38] The lack of symmetry within the committee was quite evident, which suggests that the Central Rada viewed the talks as *pro forma*. They did not wish to be bound by obligations toward representatives of a government with an uncertain future, but at the same time, the Central Rada itself needed foreign recognition and acceptance, even from the People's Secretariat of the BNR.

The minutes of the meetings reveal that the Belarusian delegation was poorly prepared and had yet to formulate a proposition regarding the border. The challenges facing Tsvikievich and Rak-Mikhailoŭski were compounded by the fact that their advisers were absent from the opening meetings. Thus, from the very start of the negotiations, the Ukrainian side took the lead.

At the initial meeting, it was decided that the Joint Committee would be guided mainly by the criterion of ethnicity and, as proposed by the Ukrainian side, would consider the geographical and economic needs of both states.[39] Maps were selected to aid the discussions. The Belarusians proposed the second (1917) edition of Karski's map and Rudnytsky's "Overview Map of Ukrainian Lands." The Ukrainian delegates wanted to use statistical data and German maps, including Schäffer's 1918 map *Länder- und Völkerkarte Europas*. However, as these ethnographic maps depicted the territory under negotiation without showing population data, the committee elected to work on a physical map, using ethnographic maps as auxiliary. Before a final decision, the Belarusian delegation changed its mind and declared that Karski's map would be used to delineate Belarus's southern border. This proved beneficial for Ukraine: while the map incorporated the Rechitsa, Mozyr, Gomel, and Pinsk districts within the Belarusian linguistic region, the Brest and Kobrin districts were located outside of the designated border.

The Belarusian delegates attempted to commence the delimitation in the east, at a place called Hremach, where the River Sudost flowed into the River Desna. The Ukrainians insisted that the starting point be Mglin, a district town in the Chernihiv Governorate; as Mglin was located farther north, the northern districts of this governorate would belong to Ukraine. The map presented by the Ukrainians showed two hand-drawn lines beginning at Vydonovsk Lake, the end of the Ukrainian border as confirmed by the agreement reached with the Central Powers,[40] as alternative proposals for the northern border. The first, a red line, was drawn according to the ethnographic criterion and overlapped with the northern reaches of continuous Ukrainian settlement depicted on the maps of Rudnytsky and Schäffer. The second, a blue line, ran approximately 50 to 150 kilometres farther north and was defined by the UNR's strategic needs. Thus, Ukraine would incorporate not only the area marked by Rudnytsky as one of mixed ethnicity, but also the southern portion of the Slutsk district and the southern and central parts of the Bobruisk district in the Minsk Governorate, the southern part of the Rogachev district in the Mogilev Governorate, and all of the Surazh and Mglin districts of the Chernihiv Governorate. The borders of Ukraine would include not only all of Polesia and the Brest-Gomel railway line but also the areas north of these regions. This border, which ran near Bobruisk and Rogachev (which would remain in Belarus), would enable Ukraine to control an important hard-surface road connecting the towns (including the fortified areas) of Brest, Kobrin, Slutsk, Bobruisk, and Rogachev.

This "strategic" borderline was rejected outright by Tsvikievich and Rak-Mikhailoŭski; the Ukrainian interpretation of the "ethnographic" line also raised doubts among the Belarusian delegates. From their perspective, the border should leave the BNR with the Pripyat basin, the Brest-Gomel railway, and the northern districts of the Chernihiv Governorate. Presenting this version of the eastern section of the border, Tsvikievich reminded the committee that the BNR's Rada had not recognized the peace treaty signed between Ukraine and the Central Powers and thus would not consent to the border between Strabla and Vydonovsk Lake since it had been delimited by said agreement.[41]

The second round of talks, initiated on 20 April, involved a discussion on the fate of the Pripyat basin and the Homel area.[42] Rak-Mikhailoŭski and Tsvikievich argued that most of the population in the Mglin area, in the districts of Gomel, Rechitsa, and Mozyr, and in southwestern Chernihiv Governorate were Belarusian, as indicated by their language's characteristic features. However, this argument was presented without statistical evidence. It was ultimately agreed that Ukraine would receive part of the Chernihiv Governorate in the northwest, but in exchange for the area between the mouth of the Pripyat (where it flows into the Dnieper) in the east and the town of Vlodava in the Brest district in the west.

Svidersky protested this, referring to Karski's earlier linguistic studies, which had concluded that the area of Mglin belonged within the boundaries of the Ukrainian-speaking zone. In this he was supported by Petrivsky, who quoted the findings of Nikolai Durnovo, Nikolai Sokov, and Dmitrii Ushakov, as well as Schäffer, as evidence that the border of the Ukrainian ethnographic area lay far to the north of Pripyat. Likhniakevich did not even attempt to hide his doubts as to whether the BNR would survive, arguing that Ukraine's northern peripheries should be secured against Russia or Poland by including the strategic Brest–Pinsk–Gomel railway line. In response, Rak-Mikhailoŭski suggested that a free Ukrainian-Belarusian zone be created in Polesia under the joint protectorate of both states, with equal access to the disputed railway line. This idea, which was not new (having been discussed in 1903 at a joint meeting of Belarusian and Ukrainian socialists), was criticized by Svidersky.

However, the talks focused mainly on eastern Polesia, with less attention paid to the western part of the border. The definition of this part of the border did not raise any particular protests from Tsvikievich and Rak-Mikhailoŭski, whose position, however, would shift following consultations with Kraskoŭski and Doŭnar-Zapolski two days after the talks with the Ukrainian party began. Both advisers not only rejected the border delimitations proposed by the Ukrainians but also criticized Tsvikievich and Rak-Mikhailoŭski's general stance in the negotiations.[43] They requested that the Belarusian delegation renege on all matters that had been settled so far and that a new proposal for delimitation of the Belarusian-Ukrainian border be put forward. To achieve this end, Doŭnar-Zapolski suggested several solutions, including organizing a plebiscite in Polesia and submitting written statements and protests against, as he put it, the annexation of the Polesian districts by the UNR.[44] He also demanded that talks with Ukraine be suspended while Minsk established its own direct relations with Berlin through Germany's envoy to Kyiv, Alfons Mumm von Schwarzenstein.[45]

Under pressure from their own expert advisers, the Belarusian delegation presented Likhniakevich, Svidersky, and Petrivsky with the following declaration:

> The borderline drawn by us at one of the meetings was merely our personal, premature position; when establishing the border, we should note that the Grodno area with Brest, Dorohychyn, Belsk, Kobrin and Pruzhany is considered by all Belarusians to be Belarusian territory. Basically, as far as we know it, Belarus's southern border follows the border of the Minsk and Grodno provinces, except in the southern corner of the Brest district. Therefore, during the negotiations it is vital for Belarus as well as for Ukraine to set normal ethnic borders in the east and north, so it is important and indispensable that Ukraine helps in all possible ways to secure active participation for our delegation to [the meeting in] Kursk. On our side, we will spare no efforts to conclude the negotiations on our border with Ukraine.[46]

This was accepted by the Ukrainian side, and the relatively brief minutes contain no note of any discussion.

On 25 April, Tsvikievich and Rak-Mikhailoŭski asked the Ukrainian Minister of Foreign Affairs to inform the government of Soviet Russia that the UNR was negotiating the border delineation with BNR representatives. They also requested that Kyiv convince Moscow to abandon its territorial claims to Polesia in the districts where Belarus bordered Ukraine. Moreover, they insisted that Ukraine's delegation in Kursk demand – issuing an ultimatum if necessary – that Soviet Russia recognize the BNR's independence. The Belarusian delegation's request was accompanied by a submitted "Preliminary Agreement between the UNR and the BNR on the matter of the state borders" in which they committed themselves to consider Ukrainian needs during the border delimitation.[47] These were very ambitious plans, to say nothing about their implementation, given that the UNR government had to prioritize own objectives.

Following this, there were no further discussions on these proposals, nor was a joint statement agreed upon by the representatives of the BNR and the UNR. This was owing to General Skoropadsky's *coup d'état* on 29 April 1918. With German support, Skoropadsky renounced his allegiance to the Central Rada, nominated himself as Hetman of a new Ukrainian State, and established an anti-socialist government in Kyiv. During his rule, state administration was strengthened, becoming more domestically and diplomatically proactive, including in its approach toward the BNR. The Belarusian delegates, who were preparing to leave Kyiv, were suddenly invited to a meeting by representatives of the new government, Prime Minister Fedir Lyzohub and Dmytro Doroshenko.[48] This resulted in agreements on economic and diplomatic cooperation (such as trade, nomination of consuls, and support for Belarusian refugees), but talks on the delimitation of the Ukrainian-Belarusian border were not reopened.[49] Another BNR delegation, led by Prime Minister Anton Lutskevich, that visited Kyiv in September 1918 attempted to return to this question, but without success, although it did succeed in negotiating financial support.[50]

PLANS FOR POLESIA AND OPINIONS OF ITS INHABITANTS

Meanwhile, the Ukrainian government moved decisively to delimit its territory and organize its administration. The border-making project was handled by a commission led by Serhii Shelukhin. The northern border was to be established with state security in mind. In the west, it would begin in Sarnaki and Mielnik on the River Bug and run through Vysokoe Litevskoe, Kamenets Litevsky, and Pruzhany to Vydonovsk Lake; beyond the Grodno Governorate it would follow the Shtshara River to Lubashev, Male Krugoviche, Loktyshe, Tshepele, Pogost, Uzhetshe, Pasyeki, Glusk, Voroby, and Nove Stepy in the Minsk Governorate. In the Mogilev Governorate, it would reach the Dnieper four *viorsts* above Zhlobin, then run toward Rohyn and Shepetoviche, along the Sozh River to Beseda Creek; from there, it would run along the administrative border of the Chernihiv Governorate to Krasny Roh railway station in Mglin district, then toward Semen and Trubchevsk along the Nerusa and Siva Rivers, to the Tarina River, and toward Oleshkovitse and Oryol.[51] This delimitation of the border was illustrated on a colour map of Ukraine, *Karta Ukraïny*, printed in 1918 in Vienna by the publisher Freytag and Berndt, with Ukraine's northern neighbours being Lithuania and Belarus. The Ukrainian-Lithuanian border followed the delimitation between the UNR and the Central Powers drawn up in Brest, running from Strabla on the Narev to Lake Vydonovsk. The map's legend described all of this as "settled borders." The same map showed the border with Belarus; however, it was marked differently as it had yet to be settled.

The Ministry of Foreign Affairs also developed new administrative divisions for Ukraine that changed the territorial structure inherited from the Russian Empire. The Ukrainian Volhynia Governorate was to include the Pinsk district from the Minsk Governorate, as well as Brest-Litovsk and Kobrin districts from the Grodno Governorate. The Mogilev Governorate's Mozyr district and the Minsk Governorate's Rechitsa district were both included in the Kyiv Governorate, while the Gomel district, also from the former Mogilev Governorate, was added to the Chernihiv Governorate. Further plans were to include appropriate administrative units for those districts that were to become Ukrainian territory. This included transferring part of the Pruzhany district from the Grodno Governorate to Kobrin district; parts of the Slutsk and Bobruisk districts from the Minsk Governorate to the Rechitsa district; parts of the Rogachev district from the Mogilev Governorate to the Gomel district; and a part of the Syenno district from the Oryol Governorate to the Glukhov district of the Chernihiv Governorate.[52]

The inhabitants of these contested territories held different opinions as to their state affiliation. Some wanted Polesia to be incorporated into Ukraine, while others appealed for help and protection from the BNR's People's Secretariat in Minsk or to the Regency Council in Warsaw. Some counted on federation with democratic Russia, while others sympathized with the Bolsheviks. For example, the chairman of the City Duma (Council) in Gomel and the Land Assembly of Gomel District demanded a plebiscite to decide the affiliation of both.[53] Railway workers in Gomel considered their area to be part of Russia, but when faced with the Bolshevik threat they elected to join Ukraine. Meanwhile, people protesting the incorporation of eastern Polesia into Ukraine (such as members of the Gomel Belarusian Association) petitioned the Belarusian Prime Minister Iazep Varonka, demanding that a Belarusian administration be established in the territory.[54] However, unlike the UNR government, the People's Secretariat of the BNR lacked capital, German support, and its own armed forces. Varonka appointed Ian Nietsietsky as Belarusian plenipotentiary to "Polesia and Gomel area, i.e. Pinsk, Mozyr and Rechitsa districts of the Minsk Governorate; Chernihiv, Novozybkov, Novhorod-Siversky, Surazh and

Mglin districts of the Mogilev Governorate; and Bryansk district of the Oryol Governorate," but this post existed in name only.[55]

Local Poles also expressed opinions on the affiliation of the Polesian districts. In December 1917, the landowners Bohdan Orda, Michał Fedorowski, a certain Pusłowski, Henryk Dąbrowski, and a certain Miedzianowski of Nevel, as well as Ursyn Niemcewicz, sent to the Regency Council in Warsaw (established by the German occupiers) a "Declaration of the Poles from Polish and the Polish-Belarusian part of Lithuania." The document requested that Polesia, with the entire historical territory of Lithuania as far as the Dvina/Daugava and Berezina Rivers, be included in the future Polish state.[56]

The archives also include an untitled black-and-white map of Russia's western areas (the Ukrainian, Belarusian, and Lithuanian lands), produced by the Topographic Division of the Central Directorate of the General Staff of the Russian Army and published in an unknown year.[57] The map presents three version of Ukraine's proposed northern border. Two of them do not differ from the previously discussed versions presented by the Ukrainian representatives at the meetings of the joint Belarusian-Ukrainian committee; the green line represents the ethnographic border and the red line the strategic one. However, it also includes a third line, marked in yellow, that is most likely another proposed version of the border that was not discussed. This is unsurprising given that the implementation of such a border would have resulted in the partition of Belarus's entire national territory! Indeed, this third line most likely represented the border between Ukraine and Bolshevik Russia, and possibly Lithuania (state names are not mentioned on the map). Beginning just north of Minsk, it would have run through Borisov below Orsha, north of Horki, then approximately seventy kilometres east of the Orsha-Starodub railway line, near Trubchevsk, ending at Novhorod-Siversky.

It should be assumed that this map and the "third version" were connected to the planned conference with the plenipotentiaries of Soviet Russia, at which the UNR's representatives were to discuss the Ukrainian-Russian border. Kyiv did not attempt to include a Belarusian delegation at this conference, being aware that with such divergent opinions about the Belarusian-Ukrainian border, the presence of a third party would further complicate Ukrainian efforts to establish a border in the southeast that would allow the UNR to retain the Polesian districts located in that area.[58]

Talks with Russia on this issue had been conducted in several rounds, from late spring to the autumn of 1918. During one of these meetings, held in Kyiv in August 1918, Shelukhin, serving as chairman of the

Ukrainian party, warned his Russian counterparts that "if there is a Belarusian state, we will do the delimitation together, perhaps differently than with you."[59]

The BNR delegation did not reach an agreement on the border. However, they did leave Kyiv having concluded significant agreements with Skoropadsky's government and having developed their own ideas regarding the course of the Belarusian-Ukrainian border. This can undoubtedly be credited to Kraskoŭski and Doŭnar-Zapolski. After the Kyiv talks, Belarusian political activists of various stripes became convinced that the entire Pripyat basin, and all of Polesia, should fall within Belarus's borders for ethnographic, historical, and strategic reasons. This conception was very soon translated into the language of cartography. By the beginning of 1919, an unknown author had prepared a colour map, *Karta Belaruskaĭ Narodnaĭ Respubliki/Carte de la République Democratique Blanche-Ruthénienne* (Map of the Belarusian People's Republic), published by Wilhelm Hartmann in Berlin (see map 5.3).[60] This depicted the Belarusian-Ukrainian border along the southern borders of the Grodno, Minsk, and Mogilev Governorates. Belarusian territory included the northern districts of the Chernihiv Governorate; the northern part of Horodnia district (without Horodnia) and all of Novozybkov, Starodub, Surazh, and Mglin districts; and the eastern parts of the Trubchev district (with Trubchev) and the Briansk district (with Briansk) from the Oryol Governorate. Moreover, the southern border of the BNR was placed much farther south than had been assumed in the Ukrainian representatives' project.

However, these separate concepts of the Belarusian-Ukrainian borderline were not discussed. In December 1918, the Hetmanate fell, being replaced – at the initiative of the Central Rada – with the Directory of the UNR. Ukrainian politicians were, it seemed, not only attempting to do state-building in Kyiv. On 1 November 1918, the West Ukrainian People's Republic (ZUNR) was proclaimed in Lviv, claiming the "ethnographic Ukrainian territories" within the borders of the former Habsburg Monarchy: Bukovina, Galicia, and Lodomeria, as well as several *comitates* in Carpathian Ruthenia. In determining the extent of ZUNR territorial holdings, its founders referred to Karl Czernig's map *Ethnographische Karte der osterreichischen Monarchie* (Vienna, 1855).[61] Nevertheless, the ZUNR itself did not border on the territory claimed by the BNR Rada. On 22 January 1919, the unification of the UNR and the ZUNR was signed in Kyiv,[62] with the latter becoming a province of the former.

The Ukrainian delegation did not attach much importance to border talks with BNR representatives in 1918. The meeting revealed the lack of

5.3 Territories claimed by the Belarusian People's Republic, 1918.

preparation by the Belarusians, whose position, in any case, was weak (due to a lack of support for their independence by other countries). Before negotiations commenced, Ukrainian politicians from both the UNR and the Ukrainian State shared a clear view of the course of the Belarusian-Ukrainian border. A meeting with their BNR counterparts in April 1918 in Kyiv appeared to confirm their belief that the Belarusians did not have a developed concept of their state's southern border. Nevertheless, both Ukrainian governments wanted an independent Belarus to be Ukraine's northern neighbour. So it was decided to offer a financial loan to the Belarusian government and establish diplomatic relations, including the appointment of diplomatic representatives and provisions for trade agreements. With the defeat of the Central Powers, however, it was the victorious Entente countries that would redefine the new political boundaries of Eastern Europe. For the purposes of the Paris Peace Conference in 1919, Ukraine's borders were depicted on the map as *La République Ukraïnienne* (The Republic of Ukraine), with the new country being bordered by Lithuania and Belarus in the north. Furthermore, the Belarusian-Ukrainian border was drawn according to the strategic criterion presented to the

Belarusians during the talks in Kyiv in the spring of 1918. Within the borders of Ukraine itself laid the entire Brest *poviat* with Brest, Kobryń, and Pruzhany, the Belsk *poviat* with Belsk and Drokhichyn from the former Grodno governorate, and all of western and eastern Polesia. Maps from 1918–19 reveal how the concept of the Belarusian-Ukrainian border developed, following the approach established by Rudnytsky.

EPILOGUE

After the First World War, neither the UNR or the BNR – for both internal and external reasons – succeeded in gaining independence.[63] Instead, on the initiative of the Bolshevik government in Moscow, a Ukrainian People's Republic of Soviets was proclaimed as early as 24–25 December 1917 in Kharkiv, while a Socialist Soviet Republic of Byelorussia was established on 1 January 1919[64] and re-established on 30 July 1920 as the Byelorussian Soviet Socialist Republic (BSSR), just before the Red Army's offensive against Warsaw. Both continued to survive as constituents of the Soviet Union.

The borders in this part of Europe were shaped by the Treaty of Riga, signed on 21 March 1921, which ended the Polish-Soviet War, with the Belarusian-Ukrainian borderland divided between Poland and Russia (acting also on behalf of Soviet Belarus) and Soviet Ukraine. Consequently, western Polesia became the Polish Polesie Voivodeship, comprising the districts of Brześć, Pińsk, Kobryń, Pruzhany, Drohiczyn, Kamień-Koszyrski, Stolin, Łuniniec, Sarny, and Kosów (according to the pre-1935 territorial division of Poland).

Although now including Minsk, which was returned by Poland in accordance with the Treaty of Riga, the BSSR consisted of only six districts. In 1924, at the request of the leadership, its territory was expanded with the inclusion of fifteen districts of the Vitebsk Governorate, six northern districts of the Mogilev Governorate, and one from the Smolensk Governorate; these lands had been part of Soviet Russia. In 1926, the BSSR's borders were expanded again by three districts from the Pskov Governorate, as well as the Gomel and Rechitsa districts, which had been part of the Soviet Union.[65]

In this way, eastern Polesia became part of the BSSR's territory, and the border of the Byelorussian and Ukrainian Soviet republics took on a new form.

A new stage in the formation of the Belarusian-Ukrainian border was, unsurprisingly, the Second World War. In September 1939, Germany and the Soviet Union commenced military operations against Poland. In accordance with the previously concluded Molotov-Ribbentrop Pact, the eastern voivodeships of the Republic of Poland were incorporated into the Soviet Union. The Polesie Voivodeship was divided: its southern part with Kamień

Koszyrski was included in the Soviet Union, and its northern part with Brest, Pruzhany, and Pinsk was incorporated into the BSSR as Brest and Pinsk districts. Their administrative affiliation changed in 1941, after these territories were occupied by the Germans. Brest district and the southern part of Pinsk district (now as *Kommissariat*) were included into the Volhynia-Podolia district of the *Reichskommissariat* Ukraine. Its northern border ran approximately twenty kilometres north of the Pripyat, encompassing a significant part of western Polesia. The former Rechitsa and Mozyr districts were included in Zhytomyr district of the *Reichskommissariat* Ukraine.

As a result of the decisions reached by the Soviet Union, Great Britain, and the United States at the Yalta Conference in February 1945, the prewar eastern voivodeships of the Republic of Poland, including the Polesie Voivodeship, were once again placed within the Soviet Union's borders after the war. Western Polesia was divided between the Ukrainian SSR (the former Kamień Koszyrski district) and the Byelorussian SSR (formerly the Brześć, Pińsk, Pruzhany, and Kobryń districts). In the east, the territorial division that had been in place from before the German occupation was reintroduced so that Rechitsa, Gomel, and Mozyr were also incorporated into the BSSR's borders.

After Ukraine and the Republic of Belarus proclaimed their independence in 1991, the borders of the former Soviet republics were retained as the new state borders. Today's Belarusian-Ukrainian border seems to be one of the oldest and most enduring lines of political and administrative division in Eastern Europe, reflective of the proposals drawn up by Doŭnar-Zapolski and Kraskoŭski. Its traditions date back to the early Middle Ages, when this area formed the southern edge of the Principality of Turov and Pinsk, while it mostly follows the southern borders of the old Minsk and Brest-Litovsk (previously Podlachian) voivodeships. From 1569 until the Partitions of Poland at the end of the eighteenth century, the borders of those voivodeships separated the Grand Duchy of Lithuania and the Kingdom of Poland – the latter (the Crown) included also the territory of Ukraine. After the incorporation of the former Polish lands into the Russian Empire, this was also the southern border of the Grodno, Minsk and Mogilev Governorates.

NOTES

1 D. Michaluk, *Białoruska Republika Ludowa 1918–1920. U podstaw białoruskiej państwowości* (Toruń: Wydawnictwo Naukowe Uniwersytetu Mikołaja Kopernika, 2010), 130–220 (Belarusian language version: D. Mikhaliuk, *Belaruskaia Narodnaia Rėspubika ŭ 1918–1920 gg, Lia vytokaŭ belaruskai dziarzhaŭnastsi* (Smalensk: Inbielkult 2015), 108–85); D. Mikhaliuk, "Rozmowy o przebiegu granicy państwowej pomiędzy Białoruską Republiką Ludową a Ukraińską Republiką Ludową," in *Nad Bałtykiem. W kręgu polityki, gospodarki, problemów narodowościowych i społecznych w XIX i XX wieku*, ed. Z. Karpus, J. Kłaczkow, and M. Wołos (Toruń: Wydawnictwo Uniwersytetu Mikołaja Kopernika, 2005), 891–911; V.M. Matvienko, *Ukraïns'ka dyplomatiia 1917–1921 rokiv na terenakh postimpers'koï Rosiï* (Kyiv: Vydavnytstvo Kyïvs'koho universytetu in. Tarasa Shevchenka, 2002).
2 The dates are presented in the new style (except when separately marked).
3 "Tretii Universal Ukraïns'koï Tsentral'noï Rady," in: *Ukraïns'ka Tsentral'na Rada. Dokumenty i materialy u dvokh tomakh*, ed. V.F. Verstiuk et al (Kyiv: Naukova Dumka, 1996), 1:398–401; "Chetvertyi Universal Ukraïns'koï Tsentral'noï Rady," in *Ukraïns'ka Tsentral'na Rada*. ed. Verstiuk et al., 2:102–4.
4 See Michaluk, *Białoruska Republika Ludowa*, 130–220.
5 *Natsyianalny Arkhiŭ Rėspubliki Belarus'* (NARB), f. 582, op. 2, sp. 2, l. 2a–b; "[I-ja] Ustaŭnaja Gramata da narodaŭ Belarusi Vykanachaga Kamitetu Rady Piershaga Usebielaruskakha Z'iezdu," in S. Shupa, ed., *Arkhivy Belaruskai Narodnaĭ Rėspubliki*, vol. 1, pt 1 (Mensk-Praga: Nasha Niva Vil'nia-N'iu Iork, 1998) (hereafter ABNR), 46–7; "III Ustaŭnaia Gramata Rady Belaruskai Narodnai Rėspubliki," ABNR, vol. 1, pt 1, 62–3.
6 On the borders of Ukraine and Belarus, see P.I. Sossa, *Istoriia kartohrafuvannia terytoriï Ukraïni vid naidavnishykh chasiv do 1920 r. Korotkyi narys* (Kyiv: Lybid', 2007); E.E. Shiriaev, *Rus' Belaia, Rus' Chernaia, i Litva v kartach* (Minsk: Navuka i tekhnika, 1991); L. Kazloŭ and A. Tsitoŭ, *Belarus' na siami rubiazhakh* (Minsk: Belarus', 1999).
7 On the issue of maps, see N. Durnovo, N. Sokolov, and D. Ushakov, *Dialektologicheskaia karta russkago iazyka v Evrope* (Moscow, 1914); as a map in N. Durnovo, N. Sokolov, and D. Ushakov, "Opyt dialektologicheskoĭ karty russkogo iazyka v Evrope s prilozheniem ocherka russkoĭ dialektologii," in *Trudy Moskovskoi Dialektologicheskoi Kommissi*, vol. 5 (Moscow: Tipografiia, 1915), s. 123; D. Schäffer, *Lände- und*

Völkerkarte Europas (Berlin: Dietrich Reimer/Ernst Vohsen, 1916); L. Niederle, *Nàrodopisnà mapa slovanstva* (Praha: Tůna, 1912). This last title was also published in Russian. For the role of cartographers, see Steven Seegel, *Map Men: Transnational Lives and Deaths of Geographers in the Making of East Central Europe* (Chicago: University of Chicago Press, 2018).

8 I omit here the issue of Belarusian-Ukrainian nationality in the Belsk district of the Grodno Governorate because its affiliation was not discussed during the work of the Ukrainian-Belarusian committee in 1918.

9 "Pratakol z'iezdu belaruskikh natsyanal'nykh arhanizacyï u Minsku 25–27 III 1917 g," *Lietuvos Centrinis Valtsybės Archyvas*, f. 582, ap. 1, b.1, l. 49.

10 "III Ustaŭnaia Gramata Rady Belaruskaï Narodnaï Rėspubliki," *ABNR*, vol. 1, pt 1, 62–3.

11 For the full reference list, see P. Shtoiko, "Problemy kartohrafiï doby Ukraïns'koï Narodnoï Respubliky," in *Kartohrafiia ta istoriia Ukraïny. Zbirnyk naukovykh prats'* (L'viv, Kyiv, and New York: Vydavnytstvo MP Koc', 2000), 126.

12 O. Shablii, *Suspil'na heohrafia. Teoriia, istoriia, ukraïnoznavchi studiï* (Lviv: L'vivs'kii natsional'nyi universitet im. Ivana Franka, 2001), 425.

13 Before the First World War, Rudnytskyi had published such works as *Korotka heohrafia Ukraïny. Fizychna heohraiia* (Kyiv: Lan, 1910); *Morze Bałtyckie i Morze Czarne* in *Encyklopedya Polska*, vol. 1: ss. 1 and 2: *Geografia fizyczna ziem polskich i charakterystyka fizyczna ludności* (Kraków: Wydawnictwo Akademii Umiejętności, 1912), 299–311. For the full reference list, see P. Shtoiko, *Stepan Rudnyts'kyi 1877–1937. Zhyttiepysno-bibliohrafichnyi narys* (Lviv: NTSh, 1997).

14 His concepts regarding the geopolitical location of Ukraine were summarized in his 1920 work: *Ukraïns'ka sprava zi stanovyshcha politychnoï heohrafiï*. Reprint: Stepan Rudnyts'kyi, *Ukraïna – nash ridnyi krai. Ukraïns'ka sprava zi stanovyshcha politychnoï heohrafiï*, ed. P. Shtoiko (Lviv: NTSh, 1998).

15 I. Rowenczak and Ł. Ciuciura, "Prace kartograficzne Stefana Rudnickiego oraz związki ich autora z geografią i kartografią polską," *Polish Cartographical Review* (a supplement in Polish) 1, no. 2 (2017): 73–8. Rudnytsky's work was also published in Rome, Berlin, and Jersey City.

16 M. Górny, "'Futurystyczna geografia.' Rola geografów w kształtowaniu granic Europy Środkowo-Wschodniej i Południowo-Wschodniej w latach 1914–1920," *Studia z Dziejów Rosji i Europy Środkowo-Wschodniej* 48 (2013): 117–39.

17 *Ukraïns'ka Tsentral'na Rada*, 1:398–401.
18 Ibid., 2:102–4.
19 Stepan Rudnyts'kyi, *Ukraïna – nash ridnyi krai* (Lviv: Zahal'na Ukraïns'ka Kul'turna Rada, 1917), 13. Until the beginning of the twentieth century, the term "Lithuanian" was used to denote inhabitants of Lithuania and Belarus (former Grand Duchy of Lithuania) without differentiating their ethnic roots. Considered in terms of residence, a Lithuanian could be not only an ethnic Lithuanian but also a Belarusian or a Pole living on these lands.
20 Matvienko, *Ukraïns'ka dyplomatiia*, 136.
21 Ibid.
22 *Ukraïns'ka Tsentral'na Rada*, 2:138.
23 N.A. Troinickii, ed., *Piervaia vseobshchaia perepis' naseleniia Rossiiskoi Imperii 1897 g.* (Sankt-Petersburg: Izd. Centr. Stat. Komitetom Ministerstva Vnutrennykh Del, 1897–1905).
24 Iu. Tal'ko-Grincevich, "K antropologii narodnosteĭ Litvy i Belorusii," *Trudy Antropologicheskogo Obshchestva pri Voenno-Meditsinskoi Akademii*, vol. 1 (Sankt Peterburg: Voiennaia tipografiia 1894); M. Dovnar-Zapol'skii, *PesniPinchukov, Sbornik etnograficheskikh materialov* (Kyiv: Tipografiia Imperatorskogo universiteta Cv.Vladimira, 1895); I. Eremich, "Ocherki belorusskogo Poles'ia," *Vestnik Zapadnoi Rossii* [Vil'no] 1876, vol. 8.
25 P. Shpilevskiĭ, *Puteshestvie po Poles'iu i belorusskomu kraiu* (Minsk: Polymia, 1992), 39–51 (reprint of the 1858 work published in Petersburg); P. Bobrovskiĭ, *Grodnienskaia Gubernia. Materialy po geografii i statistikie Rossii, sobrannye oficerami general'nogo shtaba* (Sankt Peterburg: Tipografiia departamenta general'nogo shtaba, 1863), 623, 647.
26 P. Tereshkovich, *Etnicheskaia istoriia Belarusi XIX – nachala XX v. v kontekste Tsentral'no-Vostochnoi Evropy* (Minsk: BGU, 2004), 86, 179.
27 P. Eberhardt, *Przemiany narodowościowe na Białorusi* (Warsaw: Editions Spotkania, 1993), 21–2. In the interwar censuses, the forms often included the option of "local" *(tuteishy)* in the nationality column. Jerzy Tomaszewski, an expert on nationality in this area, considers all such persons *(tuteishy)* to be Belarusian: J. Tomaszewski, *Rzeczpospolita wielu narodów* (Warsaw: Czytelnik, 1985), 29–37.
28 Tereshkovich, *Etnicheskaia istoriia*, 93–7.
29 "Pratakol no 6 pasadzhan'nia Dėlegacyi NS BNR u sprave peramovaŭ za 20.04.1918," *ABNR*, vol. 1, pt 1, no. 263, 112. It should be added that toward the end of the First World War, the population of Polesia, in particular of its western part, had decreased dramatically due to the

evacuation, both forced and voluntary, of the Orthodox population to central Russia in the face of the German offensive in the summer of 1915.
30 Doŭnar-Zapol'ski's opinions were also quoted by Rudnytskyi; see Rudnyts'kyi, *Ukraïna*, 24.
31 This refers to the administrative division of the Grand Duchy of Lithuania, introduced in 1513, which established a very large Podlachian province. In 1565–66 the Brest-Litovsk province was separated from this territory.
32 Rudnyts'kyi, *Ukraïna*, 23–4.
33 "Pratakol no 6 pasadzhan'nia Dėlegacyi NS BNR u sprave peramovaŭ za 20.04.1918," *ABNR*, vol. 1, pt I, no. 263, 110, 112.
34 Matvienko, *Ukraïns'ka dyplomatiia*, 140.
35 Ibid.
36 See D. Mikhaliuk, "Dyplomatychni znosyny Bilorus'koï Narodnoï Respubliky ta Ukraïns'koï Narodnoï Respubliky i Het'manatu u svitli dokumentiv (berezen'-gruden' 1918 r.)," *Studiï z arhivnoï spravy ta dokumentoznavstva* (Kyiv, 2004), 12:107–14.
37 I discuss the course of these talks in further detail in D. Michaluk, "Rozmowy o przebiegu granicy państwowej pomiędzy Białoruską Republiką Ludową a Ukraińską Republiką Ludową," in *Nad Bałtykiem*, 891–911; D. Michaluk, "Sprechka adnosna Palessia i sproba vyznachennia dziarzhaŭnaĭ miazhy pamizh BNR i UNR viasnoĭ 1918," *Arche* 3, no. 102 (2011): 329–55.
38 Matvienko, *Ukraïns'ka dyplomatiia*, 132–3.
39 Tsentral'nyi Derzhavnyi Arkhiv Vyshchykh Orhaniv Vlady i Upravlinnia Ukraïny (hereafter TSDAVOU), f. 2592, op. 1, d. 62, a. 25–26v, 43–4; Pratakol no. 6, *ABNR*, vol. 1, pt 1, no. 263, 108–13.
40 It was probably a black-and-white map *Dorozhnaia karta Ukrainy* ("Road Map of Ukraine") published in 1918 by the Cartography Division of the Central Surveying Office at the scale 1:1 million, kept in TSDAVOU, f. 2592, op. 1, d. 103.
41 Pratakol no. 6, *ABNR*, vol. 1, pt 1, no. 263, 108–13.
42 Ibid., 108.
43 Ibid., 108–13.
44 "Pratakol no. 7 pasadzhan'nia Dėlegacyi NS BNR u sprave peramovaŭ za 21.04.1918," *ABNR*, vol. 1, part 1, no. 273, 117–20.
45 Pratakol no. 6, 121–3.
46 TSDAVOU, f. 2592, op. 1, d. 62, a. 50–1.
47 Matvienko, *Ukraïns'ka dyplomatiia*, 132–3.
48 "Pratakol no 11," *ABNR*, vol. 1, pt 1, no. 369, 146.

49 "A report on the work of the Ukrainian consul from 30 May 1918," TSDAVOU, f. 3766, op. 1, d. 33, a. 1–2; "A report from the Belarusian Trade Chamber on goods turnover with Ukraine from 17 August 1918," TSDAVOU, f. 3766, op. 1, d. 139, a. 14–14v; *ABNR*, t. 1, pt 1, no. 173, 75. See also: Mikhaliuk, *Dyplomatychni znosyny*, 107–14.
50 "Pratakol drugoga skhodu Nadzbychaĭnaĭ Delegatsyi Rady BNR dzelia zamezhnykh peramovaŭ za 29.09.1918," *ABNR*, vol. 1, pt 1, 1022, 261–2; "Pratakoly pershaga skhodu Nadzvychaĭnaĭ Delegacyi Rady BNR dzelia zamezhnykh peramovaŭ za 29.09.1918," *ABNR*, vol. 1, pt 1, no. 1006–7, 258–9.
51 "Mezhi Ukraïny vyrosleni komisiieiu pid holovuvanniam S. Shcharukhina za het'mana Skoropads'koho," TSDAVOU, f. 3696, op. 1, sp. 178, a. 7.
52 TSDAVOU, f. 3766, op. 1, sp. 186, a. 15–19.
53 *ABNR*, vol. 1, pt 1, no. 323 and no. 324, 139.
54 *Homan*, no. 38 (234), 10.05.1918 (Vilnius), 1; "Pasadzhan'nia Dėlegatsyi NS BNR u sprave peramovaŭ za 07.05.1918," *ABNR*, vol. 1, pt 1, no. 395, 156: no. 13.
55 Qtd from V. Lebedzeva, "BNR i Gomel'shchyna," *Spadshchyna* 4 (1996): 68–9.
56 "Deklaracja Polaków z polskiej i polsko-białoruskiej części Litwy," http://biblioteka.teatrnn.pl/dlibra/dlibra/docmetadata?id=18825&from=pubindex&dirids=13&lp=5.
57 TSDAVOU, f. 2592, op. 3696, op. 1, d. 103.
58 Matvienko, *Ukraïns'ka dyplomatiia*, 141.
59 Ibid.
60 It was also added to the following works: M. Downar-Zapolski, *Podstawy państwowości Białorusi* (Grodno: Ministerstwo Spraw Białoruskich przy rządzie Litwy, 1919); W. Jäger, *Weissruthenien: Land, Bewohner, Geschichte, Volkswirtschaft, Kultur, Dichtung Mit 93 Abbildungen und einer Karte* (Berlin: Verlag Karl Curtius, 1919); enclosed in the *Petition Presented by the Delegation of the Government of the White Ruthenian Democratic Republic* addressed by the Prime Minister Antoni Lutskevich to the Versailles Peace Conference in January 1919.
61 "Tymchasovyi Osnovnyi Zakon pro derzhavnu samostiinist' ukraïns'kykh zemel' buvshoï avstro-uhors'koï monarkhiï ukhvalenyi Ukraïns'koiu Natsional'noiu Radoiu na zasidanni dnia 13 padolista 1918," art. II, http://www.hai-nyzhnyk.in.ua/doc2/1918%20(11)%2013.konstytutsiya.php.
62 For the original document, see: TSDAVOU, f. 1429, op. 1, d. 5, k. 5.
63 See: D. Michaluk, ed., *Drogi do Niepodległości Narodów Europy Wschodniej 1914–1921* (Ciechanowiec: Muzeum Rolnictwa im. K. Kluka, Archiwum Główne Akt Dawnych, 2018).

64 In February the Byelorussian SSR was united with the Lithuanian Soviet Socialist Republic into the Lithuanian-Byelorussian SSR.

65 The change of borders of Soviet Belarus in 1926 was recently presented by Per Anders Rudling, *The Rise and Fall of Belarusian Nationalism, 1906–1931* (Pittsburgh: University of Pittsburgh Press, 2013), 209–21. For a polemical piece, see A. Marková, "Pakarać śmierccju nieĺha zlitavacca: bielaruski nacyjanalizm u dasliedvanni Pera Andersa Rudlinga," *Bielaruski Histaryčny Ahliad* 23, nos. 1–2 (2016): 167–90.

6

Contested Lines

The Russo-Ukrainian Border, 1917–29

Stephan Rindlisbacher

The Russo-Ukrainian border is a product of territorialization processes that date back to the earliest years of Soviet power. In this respect, I use the term *territory* as one analytical basis for this chapter. According to current debates on *spatial history*, I conceive it as a product of social interaction similar to *space*. Whereas s*pace* itself is something diffuse and vague (like Eastern Europe),[1] *territory* is something clearly defined by recognized borders for the actors who are involved (such as a football pitch). *Territorialization* is the result of social processes that create territory within a certain space. In this way, structures of power are given a geographic shape. At the end of such processes, *borders* define what or who is inside and what or who is outside a certain territory. Thus, analyzing territorialization always implies analyzing structures of power.[2]

Previous Western scholarship on the Ukrainian Soviet Socialist Republic (UkrSSR) had to rely on printed documents; today, greater access to archival sources allows more comprehensive insights. Documents from the Russian and Ukrainian State Archives (GARF and TsDAVO) show clearly that the creation of national borders within the Soviet state did not reflect some insidious form of "divide and rule," as some researchers formerly concluded;[3] rather, it was part of a strategy for managing the ethnic and cultural diversity of the Soviet space. The Communist Party leadership provided a rough, macroscopic framework; republican and local cadres then shaped the processes more locally. When confronted with top-down decisions, activists in the border regions entered this debate at a micro level by linking basic economic needs with national-ethnographic self-perceptions, demonstrating their own agency within these territorialization processes.

On the macro level, this territorial negotiation process was closely linked with the so-called *korenizatsiia* policies and their implementation during the mid- and late 1920s. It was at this time that the "centrist" faction around party leaders such as Mykola Skrypnyk and Oleksandr Shumsky became particularly influential within the Ukrainian Communist Party (KP(b)U). Despite opposition from the rival "leftist" and "Katerynoslav (Ekaterinoslav)" factions, this early generation of leaders worked to promote Ukrainization policies while seeking to unite all Soviet Ukrainians within the UkrSSR. Stalin's rise to power led to the downfall of these "centrists" and halted most of the affirmative *korenizatsiia* policies. In this chapter, I provide a brief overview of the formation of the Russo-Ukrainian border between the February Revolution in 1917 and 1929, focusing on the Soviet period (see map 6.1).

PUTTING A SHATTERING EMPIRE TOGETHER AGAIN

After the collapse of the tsarist government in February 1917, the Central Rada, an assembly of Ukrainian political and social activists in Kyiv, claimed to represent the interests of all Ukrainians within the Russian state, yet its deputies initially advocated for political autonomy rather than independence. At the request of the Provisional Government in Petrograd, the future borders were not defined at this time.[4] In November 1917, however, following the Bolshevik Party's October coup, the Rada acted to define its territory unilaterally. In doing so, the deputies acted with prudence, describing their new polity as follows: "All lands [*hubernii*] that are by majority populated by Ukrainians belong to the territory of the Ukrainian People's Republic [UNR]. Kyiv, Podolia, Volhynia, Chernihiv, Poltava, Katerynoslav, Kherson, Taurida (without Crimea). All further borders of the Ukrainian People's Republic, i.e. parts of Kursk, Kholm, Voronezh as well as border lands where the majority is Ukrainian, will be defined by plebiscites."[5] Two months later, they formally proclaimed the independence of the UNR.

During the Russian Civil War, a unified Ukrainian state with a defined territory existed only on paper, as rival armies and political factions fought one another for dominance between the Dniester and the Don. Over the course of 1918–19, these forces included not only the troops of the UNR, Skoropadsky's Hetmanate, and the Donetsk–Kryvyi Rih Soviet Republic, but also Anton Denikin's White Volunteer Army and imperial German and Austro-Hungarian forces that had occupied Ukrainian lands since 1917–18. In addition, after the collapse of the Habsburg Monarchy in

Contested Lines

6.1 The formation of the Russo-Ukrainian border between 1919 and 1928.

November 1918, local leaders formed a West Ukrainian People's Republic in Galicia.[6] Hence, a Ukrainian state was formed outside the former Russian Empire, though it was soon overrun by the newly born Second Polish Republic.[7]

Amid this chaos, the Bolsheviks attempted to export their revolution to the Ukrainian lands. In early 1919, with Moscow's support, Ukrainian communists proclaimed their own satellite state in the south, the Ukrainian Socialist Soviet Republic (UkrSSR).[8] After failing several times to seize power in Kyiv, this new Soviet government was obliged to establish its capital at Kharkiv, which lay within the borderlands adjacent to the Russian Socialist Federative Soviet Republic (RSFSR).[9] Being more accessible from Moscow, Kharkiv remained the capital until 1934, even though Kyiv was larger and perceived as Ukraine's principal city in historic terms.

At the beginning of 1919, the RSFSR and the UkrSSR entered official negotiations over Ukraine's future borders. The result was the border convention signed on 10 March 1919, for which the above-mentioned definition provided by the Central Rada served as the blueprint. The negotiators defined the Ukrainian territory alongside the *gubernia* (province) borders of the former Russian Empire. However, there were two major differences: the agreement did not adopt the idea of plebiscites in the contested areas, and the Chernihiv *gubernia* was divided between the two Soviet republics.[10] Those involved in the negotiations knew that these borders were only preliminary and open for later debate.

In these opening years, the Soviet space did not yet seem fixed. During the Polish-Soviet War in April 1920, the first territorial transfer between the RSFSR and the UkrSSR took place, with the latter acquiring the western portion of the Don Cossack Host. The idea behind this decision was to unite the industry of the Donets Basin (*Donets'kyi basein*, Donbas) that had been divided between the RSFSR and the UkrSSR under the administration of one Soviet republic. In this way, the war effort against Poland would be coordinated as efficiently as possible.[11] This transfer took place following the Red Army's victory over the White forces in this region. Due to the ongoing war, this territorial revision was not discussed with any local authorities, whose interests will be discussed later in this chapter.[12]

REORDERING SOVIET SPACE

The territory the Ukrainian Soviet government controlled in 1920 was the result of wars as well as decisions taken by the party leadership in Moscow. At this time, the Soviet state was still relatively chaotic regarding territorial matters. Entities inherited from the old regime such as the Kursk *gubernia* continued to exist alongside new nationally defined territories (*oblasti*) or formally independent republics (*respubliki*). After the Soviet Union was established on 30 December 1922, it was far from clear what powers the four founding republics should have in practice.[13] Besides the UkrSSR and the RSFSR, the union consisted only of Belarus and the Transcaucasian Federation; the Central Asian territories had yet to receive the status of union republics.[14] In the mid-1920s, territories' and regional authorities' powers were still a matter of negotiation.[15]

Furthermore, the Ukrainian communists were far from being a homogeneous group. Since 1918, they had split into three competing factions: the "leftists" around Iurii Piatakov and Dmytro Manuilsky; the "centrists" around Mykola Skrypnyk;[16] and the "Katerynoslav group" (or "rightists"), informally headed by Emanuil Kviring. In the early years of Soviet power in Ukraine, these factions struggled for influence and control, resulting in frequent changes in the Ukrainian Communist Party's First Secretary. The leftists were mostly convinced internationalists and insisted on an independent Ukraine under the aegis of the recently established Communist International, yet they abstained from crafting a "nationalist" policy. By contrast, the "Katerynoslav group" championed closer association with the Russian Communist Party. The rightists and leftists were, for their own different reasons, critical of Ukrainian nationalism and the Ukrainization of the party and state institutions, whereas the centrists saw in the national issue an asset for the UKRSSR. In 1920, the centrists received a boost in support when the *borot'bysty* – left-wing Ukrainian Socialist Revolutionaries – joined the ranks of the KP(b)U.[17]

Political changes in Moscow also helped the centrists gain greater influence, and by the mid-1920s they had become the dominant faction within the KP(b)U.[18] Power struggles within the central leadership served to weaken first the leftists, allied to Leon Trotsky, and then the rightists, who were linked to Grigorii Zinov'ev and Lev Kamenev. The centrists also benefited from the so-called *korenizatsiia* policies. During its XII Congress in April 1923, the Russian Communist Party adopted a comprehensive approach to the union's non-Russian peoples. This program, later labelled *korenizatsiia* (rootedness or indigenization), was expected to mobilize these peoples for the Soviet project, while allowing Soviet power to "take root" in the border regions. However, non-Russian delegates to the Congress denounced "Russian great power chauvinism" as oppressive and imperialist. Thus, a distinction between "imperial" and "non-imperial" nations was also implemented.[19] In the UKRSSR, *korenizatsiia* became broadly known as *Ukrainization*; in other non-Russian regions of the Soviet state it led to analogous nation-building processes called *Uzbekization* or *Belarusization*.[20] The wording of the resolutions reached at this Congress provided the discursive background for the territorialization debate that followed.

The centrists' rise to power provided opportunities for younger party activists like Panas Butsenko, who had been a close supporter of Skrypnyk and the Ukrainization policy. In 1923, he became secretary of the Ukrainian Central Executive Committee (VUTSVK) and thus the nominal head of the state administration. This placed him in charge of territorial reforms, the national minorities, and the border revision with the RSFSR. Being a supporter of *korenizatsiia*, he encouraged the formation of national rural soviets and *raiony* (districts) in the UKRSSR while also claiming the same rights for Ukrainian-speaking people in the RSFSR.[21]

In the context of *korenizatsiia*, many regional and national actors were quick to recognize opportunities to augment their power. A particular point of tension was how to (re)distribute Soviet space. Besides the South Caucasus and Central Asia, this territorial renegotiation involved the

Russo-Ukrainian borderlands. For instance, Nikolai Eizmont, Party Secretary in the North Caucasus (*Severokavkazskii krai*), presented claims to parts of eastern Ukraine, particularly the port of Taganrog/Tahanrih and the coal mines of Shakhty. Eizmont argued that the inclusion of these two towns, and their Russian inhabitants, in the RSFSR would guarantee the best possible development for the regional economy.[22]

Leading centrist members of the KP(b)U lobbied successfully to further discuss border revisions in a bilateral Russo-Ukrainian commission. Butsenko and his comrade Mykhailo Poloz, from the Ukrainian planning commission (*UkrDerzhplan*) and previously one of the leading *borot'bysty*, were especially adamant in opposing any changes in the southeast. They also proposed rectifications to the border in the northeast in favour of the UkrSSR.[23] Butsenko and Poloz argued that the population in these northern areas was Ukrainian by majority and that the regional sugar industry should be united under the Ukrainian Republic. Their proposals were, like those of representatives from the North Caucasus, an attempt to improve their local economic base at the expense of their neighbours, and they did not raise national-ethnographic questions.[24] However, some Ukrainian claims did go further. In early 1924, Mykhailo Hrushevsky,[25] the respected Ukrainian historian and statesman, presented a memorandum to the Ukrainian Soviet government in which he argued that the Kuban region should be made part of the UkrSSR because it was populated mainly by Ukrainian-speaking Cossacks.[26] The Ukrainian and Russian party leaderships agreed to discuss these territorial claims, albeit with the least possible publicity.[27]

REDEFINING NATIONAL BORDERS

A bilateral commission on which sat representatives from the Russian and Ukrainian Soviet Republics was tasked with finding feasible solutions for these conflicting territorial claims. Aleksandr Cherviakov, at this time head of the Belarusian Central Executive Committee, was named to lead this bilateral border commission, on which he was to play the role of a neutral broker while representing the interests of the entire union (i.e., Moscow).[28] The Ukrainian representatives, Butsenko and Poloz, had high expectations as they entered negotiations with their Russian colleagues. They claimed not only parts of the Kursk *gubernia* but also parts of Briansk and Voronezh. In these areas, the ethnographic classification of the population proved difficult. The local inhabitants spoke a dialect somewhere between standard Ukrainian and Russian. Overall, the Ukrainian representatives claimed 35,000 square *versta* (about 38,500 square kilometres) with a population of almost 2 million. According to their statistical data, 65 per cent of these people were Ukrainians and 35 per cent were Russians.[29] The Politburo of the KP(b)U supported their claims in the northeast but gave Butsenko and Poloz strict orders not to discuss the Kuban issue. Kuban, that is, was taboo.[30]

Even in the mid-1920s, Kuban was not a safe issue to discuss publicly. Pavlo Burba's case is revealing in this regard. Originally hailing from the Kuban region, in 1924, Burba had received a scholarship to study at Kharkiv University. In 1925 and 1926 he and ten other students from Kuban had publicly campaigned for their native region's transfer to Ukraine for economic and cultural reasons. These claims set alarm bells ringing in Moscow. The OGPU, the Soviet Union's then secret police, ordered that the students be arrested immediately. Burba, who could not understand what had happened, was sentenced as a "counterrevolutionary organizer" to a three-year sentence in a labour camp. His fellow campaigners were exiled to different provinces.[31] Clearly, the Bolsheviks feared Ukrainian "national deviation."[32]

The Cherviakov Commission's first meeting took place on 1 July 1924. The conflicting standpoints were immediately revealed as both sides struggled to agree on the criteria for the revision. The two Ukrainian representatives emphasized the national-ethnographic criterion, whereas their colleagues from the RSFSR, Aleksandr Beloborodov and Martyn Latsis, focused on economic and administrative aspects. The latter were obliged to stick to an economic line: for the sake of avoiding accusations of "Great Russian chauvinism," they could not rely openly on Russian "national" arguments.[33] Both sides tried to present their proposals as the most "efficient" (*tselesoobrazno*) way to address the issues. *Tselesoobrazno* was a Soviet buzzword similar to "kulak": an empty but convenient term that was flexible enough to suit differing contexts; those in power could use it to legitimize their policies. Thus, the main debate within the Cherviakov Commission circled around the question of what to perceive as "efficient."[34]

A few days after the fraught opening meeting on 1 July, the Ukrainians encountered their first setback, indicative of the internal decision-making processes and the power structures within the Soviet state. The Politburo in Moscow, the highest political authority, had decided that parts of eastern Ukraine around the towns of Taganrog/Tahanrih and Shakhty would have to be joined to the RSFSR. This bypassed the newly established bilateral commission under Cherviakov; it also embraced Eizmont's claims exclusively. The party leadership had made this decision even though

Taganrog/Tahanrih and Shakhty were part of the territories that had been transferred from the RSFSR to the UkrSSR only four years earlier. The Politburo justified this re-revision by stating that the North Caucasus required a deep-sea port.[35] Representatives from the Ukrainian state and party protested in vain.[36]

Facing this severe setback, Butsenko and Poloz reasserted their claims to the northern and eastern border territories. Relying on the proclamations of the XII Party Congress, Poloz had already argued that "the Ukrainian population forms a large majority in the border areas [of the Kursk, Voronezh, and Briansk *gubernii*]. The base of our national policy is to serve the cultural needs of these people."[37]

After months of work, reports, and memorandums, the Cherviakov Commission met for its decisive sessions in late November. However, instead of arriving at a compromise, the Russian and Ukrainian representatives continued their dispute and even escalated it into open antagonism. Butsenko underscored his claims with a fervent nationalism: "We talk about territories that are populated by Ukrainians. This Ukrainian population encompasses about one million people. Administrative borders that were created under Catherine II now constrain the cultural development of the Ukrainian population. [They cannot] profit from the same national institutions as the Ukrainians do in Ukraine."[38] Here Butsenko was insinuating that the RSFSR's institutions were not providing for the Ukrainian minorities as they were expected to according to the official party line. Such accusations provoked even more resistance from the RSFSR representatives. Aleksandr Smirnov, People's Commissar for Agriculture, who had replaced Latsis, criticized his Ukrainian colleagues' statistics and tables: "I warn you, if you search according to the national criterion for Ukrainians, then you will not find any Ukrainians. We all know very well, and we do not have to pretend: even in Ukraine, those who speak Ukrainian are a minority. It is a 'pipe dream' [*polneishaia fantasiia*] to assume that we are able to define the borders in these areas only according to national criteria."[39]

Following this outburst, Cherviakov was obliged to intervene and calm the aroused passions of his colleagues and find a feasible compromise between the two camps. As the commission consisted of five members entitled to vote (two Ukrainian and two RSFSR representatives as well as the Belarusian chairman), it was Cherviakov who held the decisive voice. He had argued earlier that Soviet power had to support national minorities and provide an alternative to the Versailles order in Central Europe. In contrast to Poland, where Ukrainians and Belarusians faced repression, the Soviet Union should serve as an example of a state that supported its differing nationalities.[40] Thus, in accordance with the official *korenizatsiia* policies, he adopted most of the Ukrainian claims and voted in favour of a large-scale revision. Among other things, the town of Belgorod/Bilhorod should be given to Ukraine due to its close economic connection to Ukraine and the mostly Ukrainian-speaking inhabitants in the surrounding area.[41]

Unsurprisingly, this infuriated the RSFSR representatives, who now accused their Ukrainian colleagues of being voracious and "imperialist." Here they were using the party's own political vocabulary against any pro-Ukrainian decision.[42] Their protest was noted in the minutes,[43] alongside their alternative solution, which was that only minor parts from the Kursk, Briansk, and Voronezh *gubernii* should be transferred from the RSFSR to the UkrSSR. According to them, in all these areas, national-ethnographic composition or the local administrative context clearly favoured a border revision.[44]

The RSFSR representatives had already received indications from the state and party leadership that the commission should not favour the Ukrainian side too much. Avel' Enukidze, Secretary of the All-Union Central Executive Committee (Tsentral'nyi Ispolnitel'nyi Komitet SSSR, TSIK) and Stalin's intimate, told them frankly to make concessions wherever the interests of the RSFSR were not in jeopardy.[45] This prompted the RSFSR representatives to support the transfer of the Putyvl *uezd* (pre-reform county). Despite possessing a Russian-speaking majority, this area was basically an isolated enclave on UkrSSR territory and was well-integrated with it economically.[46] Enukidze had also hinted that Ukraine was already a powerful state and that larger territorial transfers could harm the interests of the entire union.[47] It was no coincidence that, from Enukidze's perspective, the interests of the union happened to be congruent with those of the RSFSR.

The RSFSR was an exceptional republic within the Soviet framework, since it was not a nationally defined entity. Many of its institutions were identical to those of the union or were filled with the same party cadres.[48] Mikhail Kalinin, for instance, was chairman of both the TSIK and the All-Russian Central Executive Committee (Vserossiiskii Tsentral'nyi Ispolnitel'nyi Komitet, VTSIK). It was therefore unsurprising that party and state activists in Moscow often struggled to distinguish between the interests of the union and those of the RSFSR. This was a principal reason why the Cherviakov Commission's recommendations were dismissed. Notwithstanding the party's slogans, the Ukrainian Republic received no support, for the leading communists feared that a too powerful UkrSSR could destabilise their own power base.

In her seminal book *Empire of Nations*, Francine Hirsch has pointed to the unequal policies toward Ukraine and Belarus. Belarus was territorially promoted in 1924 and 1926 as Belarusian nationalism was viewed as "undeveloped," whereas Ukraine was *not* promoted as the party leadership viewed Ukrainian nationalism as already "developed."[49] This is also one reason why the party treated the Kuban issue as taboo. Strengthening the UkrSSR and Ukrainian nationalism too much could easily lead to "national deviation" and endanger party discipline, which was the wellspring of Bolshevik power.[50]

Party discipline was such that the Cherviakov Commission had to accept this second setback. Thus, it adopted a downsized territorial revision in January 1925 for which the RSFSR representatives' proposal served as a revised blueprint.[51] As a result, many territories that were expected to be joined to Ukraine remained within the RSFSR. In the end, Ukraine gained in spring 1926 only about 6,000 square kilometres inhabited by around 300,000 people, far less than it had "lost" after the transfer of Shakhty and Taganrog/Tahanrih in the southeast.[52]

After the legal transfer of these 6,000 square kilometres, the territorial issues between Ukraine and Russia were not yet over. The TSIK tasked a commission under Saak Ter-Gabrielian, an esteemed Armenian party member, with supervising the border revision's implementation. The chairman was yet another activist perceived as nationally "neutral," and his commission would be permitted to make adjustments if necessary.[53] Moreover, it would be expected to deal with petitions arriving from different sides in favour of or against specific aspects of the redrawing.

THE IMPLEMENTATION ON THE GROUND

Villages in the areas impacted by the revision often reacted critically to Moscow's decisions. In mid-April 1926, for instance, a letter from Znob, on the southern edge of the Briansk *gubernia*, reached the office of the VTSIK. The Cherviakov Commission had previously decided that Znob should be attached to Ukraine for administrative reasons, as the village currently existed almost as an RSFSR enclave within UkrSSR territory.[54] The locals met this plan with utmost opposition. As the chair of the rural soviet, P. Danechkin, stated in the letter to the VTSIK: "The planned transfer of our village from the RSFSR to the UkrSSR puts the citizens' vital interests in jeopardy ... It would be disastrous for its agricultural development and social life. Thus, the population is worried."[55] According to Danechkin, the village had no affiliation to Ukrainian national culture as its ethnographical composition was "100% Great Russian" [*velikorosy*]. The people also feared that the taxes in Ukraine would be higher and that the local peasantry would be unable to afford them since, unlike its neighbouring villages, Znob's principal economic activity was not grain-growing but forestry. Moreover, the forests from which they derived their incomes were expected to remain in the RSFSR. Finally, Danechkin underscored that the administrative centre in Ukraine (Glukhov/Hlukhiv) was farther away than the nearest Russian one (Pochep).[56]

The people of Znob were not the only locals who feared forced Ukrainization after a territorial transfer. People living in the territories expected to change from the RSFSR to Belarus were also afraid of being subject to such policies.[57] The Soviet government tried to dispel these local worries. Thus the Politburo in Moscow ordered that Russian- and Yiddish-speaking villages to be transferred from the RSFSR to Soviet Belarus were not to be subjected to Belarusization.[58] Regarding the UkrSSR, Butsenko emphasized that non-Ukrainian-speaking villages (including Russian-speaking ones) could freely form a national rural soviet with schools and administrations in their native language.[59]

The VTsIK sent the petition from Znob to the Ter-Gabrielian Commission, where it was discussed. After studying the details, its members approved the locals' arguments, as Ter-Gabrielian underscored: "[Comrades], you all know that the TsIK decision is no fetish. It must be implemented efficiently [*tselesoobrazno*], but in this case functionality [*tselesoobraznost'*] indicates that [the people from Znob] do not fit into Ukraine at all, neither according to the national nor the territorial principle. They would be needless victims of a border correction [*zria stanovitsia zhertvoi vypriamleniia granits*]."[60]

Correspondingly, around Miropol'e/Myropillia in southwestern Kursk *gubernia*, the situation was reversed: under the planned new border, the fields, pastures, and forests of seven Ukrainian-speaking villages would end up in the UkrSSR, yet the villages themselves would remain within the RSFSR. The peasants feared they would lose access to their land and that the neighbouring villages across the new border might claim it for their own use, leaving the peasants from these seven villages without hay and other essential resources. Local petitioners believed there might even be bloodshed if no feasible solution was found.[61] They repeatedly urged party and state institutions on different levels to take direct action.[62] As the villages around Miropol'e/Myropillia were economically linked to the region of Sumy, the commission accepted their transfer to Ukraine. The VTsIK and the VUTsVK gave consent for the villages to change their designated republican affiliation in 1927.[63] That same year, a further 200 square kilometres with a population of about 22,500 people was transferred from the RSFSR to the UkrSSR.[64]

The above two examples – Znob and Miropol'e/Myropillia – illustrate how local communities perceived the republican borders as having an immediate impact on their daily life. Moreover, any concerns expressed were typically rooted less in national rather than economic considerations.

The case of Chertkovo/Milove provides another striking example of potential conflict. Here, the border mostly followed the local railway line, and divided the settlement, with the station itself being split between the two republics. On the Ukrainian side, in Milove, there was a large bazaar that regularly attracted peasants from the surrounding villages. During the NEP era, when money was in short supply, the local Ukrainian administration could collect all the market taxes. This prompted functionaries on the Russian side to try to compete with their Ukrainian colleagues by reducing their own taxes so as to entice merchants to sell their products in Chertkovo.[65]

Dmytro Kozachkov, The first Party Secretary in the Starobilsk *okruha* (post-reform county), of which Milove was a part, complained about such border incidents. In a letter to the First Secretary of the KP(b)U, Lazar Kaganovich, he observed:

> The bazar moved partly to spots near the rail tracks due to the repeated border crossing [by merchants and customers] ... That is why the number of people crossing the tracks greatly increased. One day, an accident occurred as a steam train ran someone down. The legs of the body were found on our [Ukrainian] side, whereas the head fell down on the side of the North Caucasus [RSFSR]. Surrounded by a huge crowd, an argument between our [Ukrainian] and the Russian police forces erupted. They were quarrelling about who was in charge of the report and taking care of the body.[66]

According to Kozachkov, such incidents were symptomatic of a much broader problem. Institutional competition between the Ukrainian and Russian sides, for example, had led to the crop harvest being left to rot in front of the railway station building.[67] The two sides could not agree on how to proceed with the shipment. They had also failed to reach a compromise and revise the border accordingly since neither the Ukrainian nor the Russian side was willing to give up territory. As Moscow saw no further risk to its own interests and did not wish to show preference to one side, it remained neutral. Thus, no resolution was reached on the precarious situation in Chertkovo/Milove.

In principle, borders between Soviet republics could be crossed without issue, but they were nevertheless visible in people's daily lives. They separated administrations, taxation systems, official languages, and access to state property and institutions. Furthermore, they had an impact on career opportunities, as it was difficult to get access to a job outside one's "own" union republic unless you had received permission from the centre. On the ground, locals frequently complained of the practical impacts, such as access to a certain field or woodland. Thus, groups otherwise assumed to be indifferent to nationalism adopted national-ethnographic categories as one strategy for upholding their local economic interests.

The politicians and experts who had drawn these borders were well aware of implications like these. Local field commissions sent to survey and mark these boundaries were careful not to cause any economic disruption, instead adopting the boundaries that already separated the fields, woods, and pastures of neighbouring villages. Ensuring that peasants from a border village in the RSFSR did not have to worry about their fields or forests suddenly being located in the UkrSSR, and vice versa, tended to serve as the guiding principle.[68]

Local commissions and the central institutions in Kharkiv and Moscow even tried to establish a mechanism for future border correction. They had good reasons to do so, given that in the mid-1920s the Soviet government had encouraged measures for land use amelioration (*zemleustroitel'stvo*).[69] Among other things, land use between neighbouring villages was to be "rectified" and rationalized. Clearly, the experts involved in demarcating the borders expected that in the coming years, fields might be exchanged between border villages. When this happened, the republican border would no longer correspond with land use. So field surveying commissions decided that every exchange of land between border villages would also be viewed as a change of the border between the two Soviet republics.[70]

It seems that these small border alterations, following amelioration measures, were a common phenomenon until 1991. This was most notable in the Central Asian republics, where local authorities often "forgot" to inform their superiors about these changes. This significantly contributed to the confusion over the exact placing of national borders in this region after 1991.[71]

THE DECLINE OF *KORENIZATSIIA* AND THE FALL OF THE "CENTRISTS" IN THE UKRSSR

As VUTSVK Secretary, Butsenko continued to lobby for a large-scale border revision in favour of the UKRSSR and to send reports to the Politburo of the KP(b)U asking for support:

> The realization of the national policies demands the creation of exact borders between the different Soviet republics. This issue concerns not only our internal policies, but also our foreign ones. Abroad, not only our friends, but also our enemies observe how we handle the nationality question. Relying on exact national-ethnographic data, we have to conclude that the existing borders of the UKRSSR – formed upon administrative considerations – are barely exact and righteous. Of course, we do not speak here about the part of the Ukrainian population (about 4½ million people) living under the yoke of Poland, Romania and Czechoslovakia, we speak about the borders of the UKRSSR within the Soviet Union.[72]

However, Stalin's rise to power saw the decline of *korenizatsiia* policies all over the union. Ideas for revising the republics' borders, as well as petitions to do so, fell off the political agenda. This became especially apparent in February 1929, when Stalin invited a delegation of Ukrainian writers to the Kremlin for a debate on Soviet nationality policy. During the meeting, the Ukrainians highlighted what they saw as an unsatisfactory border between the UKRSSR and the RSFSR, particularly in the east. The party's Secretary General first tried to avoid entering such a debate, but his Ukrainian visitors insisted that he provide an answer. The supreme leader's response was unambiguous: "We have discussed the [border issue] several times; but we change the borders too often … Too often, we change the borders – this makes a bad impression within and outside our country."[73] From Stalin's perspective, changing borders fomented unnecessary conflicts between the republics and impeded socialist construction and industrialization. Subsequently, people and groups who publicly demanded border revisions risked censure or persecution.[74]

Beginning with the campaign against the Ukrainian People's Commissar for Education, Oleksandr Shumsky, in 1927, the centrist faction began to lose political influence within the KP(b)U. In 1928, Butsenko was removed from his position as VUTSVK Secretary. This was followed by many more centrists losing their jobs to loyal Stalinists. Ukrainian national policies and institutional Ukrainization were once again pushed to the bottom of the political agenda. In December 1932, pro-Stalinist party members launched a campaign against the centrists, accusing them of "national deviation" and ultimately driving Skrypnyk to suicide.[75] Many others fell victim to the Great Terror four years later, including Poloz, who was shot in 1937, and Butsenko, who was sent to the Vorkuta labour camp. After Stalin's death, he was rehabilitated, but he never regained his political influence.

CONCLUSION

As I stated at the beginning, analyzing territorialization processes requires an assessment of power relations. The intricate (re)negotiation of the Russo-Ukrainian border after 1920 is a salient example of how functionaries tried to manage the diversity of Soviet space on the macro, meso, and micro levels. On the one side the political promises from Moscow to support *korenizatsiia* policies and the rise of the "centralist" faction in the KP(b)U encouraged plans for a large-scale border revision in favour of Ukraine. However, these negotiations were never a matter of public debate; rather, they entailed administrative decisions by commissioned party functionaries. Moreover, strategic considerations within the party leadership opposed any large-scale concessions to the Ukrainian nationalist claims, the 1924 Cherviakov Commission being the most striking example of this. Even in the mid-1920s, public debates on territorial revisions could easily be perceived as "national deviation" by the Moscow authorities. Stalin's ascension to power presaged the downfall of many national communist activists across the union, the Ukrainian "centralist" faction being no exception. After the so-called Skrypnyk affair in 1932–33 – the denunciation campaign that drove him to suicide – Ukrainian politicians would have been putting their lives at risk had they made nationalistic-sounding statements, included ones that concerned border revision with the RSFSR.

From a micro perspective, the implementation of the Russo-Ukrainian border followed its own rationales, with land use by border villages being key. The basic thinking was that the republican border should not separate a village from its fields, pastures, and woods. The field surveying commissions even tried to implement mechanisms for future amelioration measures: any transfer of fields between border villages was expected to result in an automatic revision of the republican border.

Border-making is never easy. When such changes are implemented, power relations translate into geography. Taking the border negotiations between the RSFSR and the UkrSSR as a starting point, they provide us with insights into *korenizatsiia* as being, to some extent, a means of promoting and perpetuating Soviet power in non-Russian regions. As soon as implementing affirmative measures placed Moscow's power base at risk, the party leadership intervened. Analyzing border formation on a micro level also hints at local perceptions that construed republican borders more often as economic barriers. In doing so, they linked economic considerations with nationalist claims.

NOTES

1 F. Benjamin Schenk, "Eastern Europe," in *European Regions and Boundaries: A Conceptual History*, ed. Diana Mishkova and Balázs Trencsényi (New York and Oxford: Berghahn Books, 2017), 188–209.
2 Nick Baron, "New Spatial Histories of 20th-Century Russia and the Soviet Union: Exploring the Terrain," *Kritika: Explorations in Russian and Eurasian History* 9, no. 2 (2008): 433–47; Henry Lefebvre, *La Production de l'Espace* (Paris: Anthropos, 2000), 35–57; Béatrice von Hirschhausen et al., eds., *Phantomgrenzen: Räume und Akteure in der Zeit neu denken* (Göttingen: Wallstein Verlag, 2015), 9–10; Charles S. Maier, "Consigning the Twentieth Century to History: Alternative Narratives for the Modern Era," *American Historical Review* 105, no. 3 (2000): 808; Steffi Marung and Katja Naumann, eds., *Vergessene Vielfalt: Territorialität und Internationalisierung in Ostmitteleuropa seit der Mitte des 19. Jahrhunderts* (Göttingen: Vandenhoeck & Ruprecht, 2014), 14–16; Matthias Middell and Katja Naumann, "Global History and the Spatial Turn: From the Impact of Area Studies to the Studies of Critical Junctures of Globalization," *Journal of Global History* 5 (2010): 149–79; David Newman, "Boundaries," in *A Companion to Political Geography*, ed. John Agnew, Katharyne Mitchell, and Gerard Toal (Malden: Blackwell, 2008), 123–37; Aanssi Paasi, "Territory," in *A Companion to Political Geography*, ed. Agnew, Mitchell, and Toal, 109–22; Karl Schlögel, *Im Raume lesen wir die Zeit: Über Zivilisationsgeschichte und Geopolitik* (Munich and Vienna: Carl Hanser Verlag, 2003), 393.
3 George Joffé, "Nationalities and Borders in Transcaucasia and the Northern Caucasus," in *Transcaucasian Boundaries*, ed. John F.R. Wright et al. (London: UCL Press, 1996), 15–33; Olaf Caroe, *Soviet Empire: The Turks of Central Asia and Stalinism* (London: Macmillan, 1967), 145–9; Oliver Roy, *The New Central Asia: Geopolitics and the Birth of Nations* (London: I.B. Tauris, 2000), 68.

4 Hennadii Yefimenko, "Die Grenzziehung zwischen der Sowjetukraine und Russland. Kriterien, Verlauf, Ergebnisse," *Nordost-Archiv* 27 (2018): 172–8.
5 Third Universal of the Central Rada, 7–20 November 1917, Central State Archive of the Highest Ukrainian State and Government Organs (*Tsentral'nyi Derzhavnyi Arkhiv Vyshchykh Orhaniv Vlady ta Upravlinnia Ukraïny*, hereafter TsDAVO), f. 1115, op. 1, spr. 4, ark. 9.
6 Stephen Velychenko, *State Building in Revolutionary Ukraine: A Comparative Study of Governments and Bureaucrats, 1917–1922* (Toronto: University of Toronto Press, 2011), 208–23; Jon Smele, *The 'Russian' Civil Wars, 1916–1926: Ten Years That Shook the World* (London: Hurst, 2015), 91–103.
7 Torsten Wehrhahn, *Die Westukrainische Volksrepublik: Zu den polnisch-ukrainischen Beziehungen und dem Problem der ukrainischen Staatlichkeit in den Jahren 1918 bis 1923* (Berlin: Weissensee Verlag, 2004), 223–7; Benjamin Conrad, *Umkämpfte Grenzen, umkämpfte Bevölkerung: Die Entstehung der Staatsgrenzen der Zweiten Polnischen Republik, 1918–1923* (Stuttgart: Franz Steiner Verlag, 2014), 99–102, 204–9.
8 Decision of the Ukrainian Sovnarkom, 6 January 1919, TsDAVO, f. 2, op. 1, spr. 4, ark. 11.
9 Protocols of the Ukrainian Sovnarkom, 28 November 1918–31 January 1919, TsDAVO, f. 2, op. 1, spr. 14.
10 Meeting of representatives from the RSFSR and the UkrSSR, 25 February 1919, TsDAVO, f. 2, op. 1, spr. 4, ark. 11.
11 Telegram of the chairman of the Donetsk Gubrevkom to the VTsIK, 14 March 1920, State Archive of the Russian Federation (Gosudarstvennyi Arkhiv Rossiiskoi Federatsii, hereafter GA RF), f. 5677, op. 1, d. 83, l. 19.
12 Hennadii Iefimenko, "Vyznachennia kordonu mizh URSR ta RSFRR," *Problemy Istoriï Ukraïny* 20 (2011): 155–65; Yurii Galkin, *Sbornik dokumentov o pogranichnom spore mezhdu Rossiei i Ukrainoi v 1920–1925 gg. za Taganrogsko-Shakhtinskuiu Territoriiu Donskoi oblasti* (Moscow: Shcherbinskaia Tipografiia, 2007), 7–15; telegraphic correspondence between the Ukrainian and the Russian Soviet governments, TsDAVO, f. 2, op. 1, spr. 47.
13 L.S. Gatagova, ed., *TsK RK(b)-VKP(b) i Natsional'nyi Vopros*, 2 vols. (Moskau: Rosspen, 2005–09), 1:120–9.
14 Uzbekistan and Turkmenistan gained Union Republic status in October 1924, Tajikistan in 1929, Kazakhstan and Kirgizstan in 1936.
15 See, for instance, the decision of the XII Party Congress on *raionirovanie*: *Dvenadtsatyi s"ezd RKP(b). 17–25 aprelia 1923. Stenograficheskii otchet* (Moscow: Izdatel'stvo politicheskoi literatury, 1968), 697–8.

16 I take the term "centrist" from Panas Butsenko, who used it to describe his faction within the KP(b)U: Afanasii [Panas] Butsenko, "Particular Impressions of the 1st Congress of the KP(b)U," 1927, TSDAVO, f. 1, op. 3, spr. 2504, ark. 167.

17 Butsenko, "Particular Impressions," TSDAVO, f. 1, op. 3, spr. 2504, ark. 167–70; Elena Borisenok, *Fenomen sovetskoi Ukrainizatsii. 1920–1930-e gody* (Moscow: Evropa, 2006), 40, 52–4; on the impact of korenizatsiia in Ukraine in general, see Jurij Borys, *The Russian Communist Party and the Sovietization of Ukraine: A Study in the Communist Doctrine of the Self-Determination of Nations* (Stockholm: P.A. Norstedt, 1960); James E. Mace, *Communism and the Dilemmas of National Liberation: National Communism in Soviet Ukraine, 1918–1933* (Cambridge, MA: Harvard University Press, 1983).

18 Borisenok, *Fenomen sovetskoi Ukrainizatsii*, 163–5.

19 Dvenadtsatyi sezd RKP(b), 691–7; Terry Martin, *The Affirmative Action Empire: Nations and Nationalism in the Soviet Union, 1923–1939* (Ithaca: Cornell University Press, 2001), 19–20; 75, 274–6; Francine Hirsch, *Empire of Nations: Ethnographic Knowledge and the Making of the Soviet Union* (Ithaca: Cornell University Press, 2005), 94–8.

20 On *korenizatsiia* in different parts of the Soviet state, see Per Anders Rudling, *The Rise and Fall of Belarusian Nationalism, 1906–1931* (Pittsburgh: Pittsburgh University Press, 2015), 123–63; Ronald G. Suny, *The Revenge of the Past: Nationalism, Revolution, and the Collapse of the Soviet Union* (Stanford: Stanford University Press, 1993), 102–12; Adeeb Khalid, *Making Uzbekistan: Nation, Empire, and Revolution in the Early USSR* (Ithaca: Cornell University Press, 2015), 280–6.

21 See for instance, Afanasii [Panas] Butsenko, Speech at the Central Commission for National Minority Affairs on Re-election Campaigns in Localities with National Minorities, 27 April 1927, State Archive of the Mykolaiv Oblast (*Derzhavnyi Archiv Mykolaivskoi Oblasti*), f. R-161, op. 1, spr. 701, ark. 4–5.

22 Nikolai Eizmont's letter to the Administrative Commission of the NKVD RSFSR, 14 April 1923, GA RF, f. 5677, op. 4, d. 393, l. 1.

23 *UkrDerzhplan* report to the VUTSVK, 22 May 1923, GA RF, f. 5677, op. 4, d. 393, l. 18–19.

24 Maps with the Ukrainian territorial claims, 1923, TSDAVO, f. 1, op. 2, spr. 1049, ark.1–4; Decision of *UkrDerzhplan* to review the borders in the north and the east of the UkrSSR, 3 August 1923, Russian State Archive for Economy (*Rossiiskii Gosudarstvennyi Arkhiv Ekonomiki*), f. 4352, op. 15, d. 328, l. 25.

25 On Mykhailo Hrushevsky and his relation to Soviet Ukraine, see Christopher Gilley, *The "Change of Signposts" in the Ukrainian Emigration: A Contribution to the History of Sovietophilism in the 1920s* (Stuttgart: ibidem-Verlag, 2009), 200–18.
26 Mykhailo Hrushevsky's memorandum, "On the Ukrainian Borders in the East," 1924, GA RF, f. 5677, op. 5, d. 27, l. 30.
27 Avel' Unukidze's Note to Avram Zolotarevskii, July 1924, GA RF, f. 6892, op. 1, d. 5, l. 32.
28 Decision of the TSIK SSSR, 11 April 1924, GA RF, f. 3316, op. 17, d. 32, l. 87.
29 Minority report of the Russian representatives of the Cherviakov Commission, 29 November 1924, GA RF, f. 3316, op. 17, d. 322, l. 3.
30 Minutes of the Politburo TSK KP(b)U, 27 July 1924, Central State Archive of Public Organisations of Ukraine (Tsentral'nyi Derzhavnyi Arkhiv Hromads'kykh Ob'edan' Ukraïny, hereafter TSDAHO), f. 1, op. 6, spr. 48, ark. 95.
31 Pavlo Burba's letter to Ivan Klymenko, second secretary of the KP(b)U, 1927, TSDAHO, f. 1, op. 20, spr. 2522, ark. 58–60.
32 Jeremy Smith, *The Bolsheviks and the National Question, 1917–1923* (New York: St Martin's Press, 1999), 236.
33 *Dvenadtsatyi s"ezd RKP(b)*, 691–6.
34 Konstantin Egorov, ed., *Raionirovanie SSSR. Sbornik materialov po raionirovaniiu s 1917 po 1925 god* (Moscow and Leningrad: Planovoe khoziaiztvo 1926), 8–12; see also the stenographs of the Cherviakov Commission, July to November 1924: GA RF, f. 3316, op. 17, d. 322, ll. 55–73; GA RF, f. 5677, op. 5, d. 26, ll. 33–65; GA RF, f. 6892, op. 1, d. 19, ll. 21–35; GA RF, f. 6892, op. 1, d. 20, ll. 3–30.
35 Letter of Nikolai Eizmont to the Administrative Commission of the NKVD RSFSR, 14 April 1923, GA RF, f. 5677, op. 4, d. 393, l. 1.
36 Galkin, ed., *Sbornik dokumentov*, 60.
37 Stenographs of the Cherviakov Commission, 1 July 1924, GA RF, f. 3316, op. 17, f. 322, l. 56.
38 Stenographs of the Cherviakov Commission, 28 November 1924, GA RF, f. 6892, op. 1, d. 20, l. 17.
39 Stenographs of the Cherviakov Commission, 27 November 1924, GA RF, f. 5677, op. 5, d. 26, l. 45.
40 Ibid., l. 3.
41 Protocol of the Cherviakov Commission, 28 November 1924, GA RF, f. 5677, op. 5, d. 26, ll. 30–1.

42 Stenograph of the Cherviakov Commission, 28 November 1924, GA RF, f. 6892, op. 1, d. 20, ll. 20 and 27.
43 Minutes of the Cherviakov Commission, 28 November 1924, GA RF, f. 3316, op. 17, d. 322, l. 6.
44 Minority report of the Russian representatives in the Cherviakov Commission, 29 November 1924, GA RF, f. 3316, op. 17, d. 322, l. 5.
45 Minutes of the VTSIK, 17 November 1924, GA RF, f. 3316, op. 17, d. 718, l. 41.
46 Minutes of the Cherviakov Commission, 27 November 1924, GA RF, f. 3316, op. 17, d. 322, l. 8.
47 Stenograph of the commission on *raionirovanie* RSFSR, 14 November 1924, GA RF, f. 6892, op. 1, d. 19, l. 17.
48 Martin, *Affirmative Action Empire*, 356–7; Yuri Slezkine, "The USSR as a Communal Apartment, or How a Socialist State Promoted Ethnic Particularism," *Slavic Review* 53, no. 2 (1994): 443.
49 Hirsch, *Empire of Nations*, 158–60.
50 Smith, *The Bolsheviks and the National Question*, 237; Martin, *Affirmative Action Empire*, 356–62.
51 Minutes of the Cherviakov Commission, 25 January 1925, GA RF, f. 3316, op. 17, d. 718, ll. 70–1.
52 Afanasii [Panas] Butsenko's report on the Russio-Ukrainian border to the Politburo KP(b)U, May 1927, TSDAVO, f. 1, op. 3, spr. 2524, ark. 6–7.
53 Minutes of the bilateral commission to implement the border changes between the RSFSR, the UkrSSR, and the BSSR, 17 July 1926, GA RF, f. 6892, op. 1, d. 24, ll. 1–2.
54 Afanasii [Panas] Butsenko, Table with all areas that asked to be transferred from the RSFSR to the UkrSSR, 1924, GA RF, f. 3316, op. 17, d. 322, l. 81.
55 Petition from P. Danechkin to the VTSIK, 15 March 1926, GA RF, f. 3316, op. 17, d. 720, l. 12.
56 Petition from P. Danechkin to the VTSIK, 15 March 1926, GA RF, f. 3316, op. 17, d. 720, l. 12.
57 Minutes of the Voronezh Gubispolkom, 15–18 November 1924, GA RF, f. 6892, op. 1, d. 17, l. 25.
58 Minutes of the commission to transfer parts of Vitebsk *Gubernia* to the BSSR, 2–14 April 1924, in V.E. Snapkovskii et al., eds., *Gosudarstvennye granitsy Belarusi. Sbornik dokumentov i materialov v dvukh tomakh*, 2 vols. (Minsk: BGU, 2012–13), 1:282–3; Decision of the Politbureau TsK VKP(b), 18 November 1926, in V.E. Snapkovskii et al., eds., *Gosudarstvennye granitsy Belarusi*, 2:10-11; see also Hirsch, *Empire of Nations*, 149–55; Rudling, *The Rise and Fall of Belarusian Nationalism*, 209–21.

59 Panas Butsenko, Presentation at the Central Bureau for National Minority Affairs at VUTSVK, 14 December 1927, State Archive of the Mykolaiv Oblast (*Derzhavnyi Arkhiv Mykolaïvs'koï Oblasti*), f. 161, op. 1, spr. 701, ark. 4–5.
60 Stenograph of the border commission between the BSSR, UkrsSR, and RSFSR, 17 July 1926, *GA RF*, f. 6892, op. 1, d. 24, l. 14.
61 Nikon Seroshtan's petition to the VTSIK, 20 August 1926, *GA RF*, f. 3316, op. 17, d. 720, l. 9.
62 Nikon Seroshtan's petition to Territorial Commission of the Sumy *okruha*, 15 March 1926, State Archive of the Sumy Oblast (*Derzhavnyi Arkhiv Sums'koï Oblasti*, hereafter *DASO*), f. 32, op. 1, spr. 72, ark. 139–40.
63 The transfer of parts of the Miropol'e *volost'*, 21 March–10 October 1927, *DASO*, f. 32, op. 1, spr. 72, ark. 1.
64 Transfer act of a part of the Miropol'e *volost'* from the RSFSR to the UkrsSR, 2 September 1927, *DASO*; f. 32, op. 1, spr. 389, ark. 398.
65 Afanasii [Panas] Butsenko's report to the Politburo KP(b)U, 3 December 1926, *TSDAVO*, f. 1, op. 2, spr. 1809, ark. 3–4.
66 Dmytro Kosachkov's letter to Lazar Kaganovich, 26 October 1926, *GA RF*, f. 3316, op. 17, d. 721, ll. 49–50.
67 Ibid., l. 50.
68 Minutes of the 6th bilateral Russo-Ukrainian border commission (Graivoron *uezd*), 2 April 1926, *TSDAVO*, f. 1, op. 3, spr. 630, ark. 14.
69 P. Ya. Lizhnev-Fin'kovskii, "Uchastie zemleustroitelei v kul'turno-prosvetitel'noi rabote," *Zemleustroitel'* 1, 1 (1924): 6–8.
70 Report of the 6th bilateral Russo-Ukrainian border commission (Graivoron *uezd*), 2 April 1926, *TSDAVO*, f. 1, op. 3, spr. 2546, ark. 52.
71 Christine Bichsel, *Conflict Transformation in Central Asia: Irrigation Disputes in the Ferghana Valley* (London: Routledge, 2009), 106–12.
72 Afanasii [Panas] Butsenko, Regulation of the State Borders between the UkrsSR and the RSFSR, Report to the Politburo TSK KP(b)U, 9 July 1927, *TSDAVO*, f. 1, op. 3, spr. 2504, ark. 200.
73 Stenograph of Stalin's meeting with Ukrainian writers, 12 February 1929, Russian State Archive of Socio-Political History (Rossiiskii Gosudarstvennyi Arkhiv Sotsial'no-Politicheskoi Istorii), f. 558, op. 1, d. 4490, l. 19; Leonid Maximenkov, "Stalin's Meeting with a Delegation of Ukrainian Writers on 12 February 1929," *Harvard Ukrainian Studies* 16, nos. 3–4 (1992): 361–431.
74 Martin, *The Affirmative Action Empire*, 291–302.
75 Ibid., 345–56.

7

Overlapping Spaces

Negotiating and Delineating the Ukrainian-Moldovan Border during the Interwar and Wartime Years

Alexandr Voronovici

The history of Ukrainian-Moldovan border-making in the interwar years is linked primarily to the so-called Bessarabian question. That question related to questions of state belonging as well as to competition for the territory between the Prut and Dniester Rivers and the delineation of the overlapping Ukrainian and Moldovan ethnolinguistic and imaginary spaces within the Soviet framework. During the interwar years, this territory was also a source of tension between rival political projects, most notably the Romanian national and Soviet ones. Importantly, the role of the riverside region on the left bank of the Dniester (Transnistria/Pridnestrov'e) in the struggle over the borderlands gained particular prominence. The establishment of the Moldovan Autonomous Soviet Socialist Republic (Moldovan ASSR) within the Ukrainian Soviet Socialist Republic (UkrSSR) in 1924 would have important and long-lasting consequences for, among other things, the delineation of the Ukrainian-Moldovan border. Eventually, the negotiation and establishment of the borders of the Moldovan ASSR (and later, during the Second World War, of the Moldovan Soviet Socialist Republic [Moldovan SSR]) involved a number of actors operating at different levels of the Soviet party and state bureaucracy, as well as pro-Soviet figures across the Soviet border. Thus, the contemporary Ukrainian-Moldovan border is to a significant extent the outcome of a prolonged struggle over the Soviet Union's southwestern borderlands and decisions made in the decades prior to the Cold War.

This chapter focuses on the Soviet actors, for in the long run their decisions were of greater importance in the evolution of the contemporary

Ukrainian-Moldovan border. It traces the establishment of the Moldovan ASSR and the history of its borders, concentrating on the negotiations and conflicts among various actors, who included the central Moscow authorities, local Moldovan party activists on the left bank of the Dniester, Romanian Communist émigrés in the Soviet Union, and representatives of the Bessarabian underground. In particular, I highlight the role of Kharkiv and the Soviet Ukrainian authorities, who played a crucial role in founding the Moldovan ASSR, as well as the underlying power struggles that were taking place throughout this period.

The chapter traces some of the key moments in the history of the Ukrainian-Moldovan border during the interwar and wartime years. The form that border eventually took was very much the product of Soviet territorial delineation processes. However, that form also took shape within the framework of broader transnational developments in the first half of the twentieth century. A brief account of the Bessarabian question, and of competing visions for that region, from the Russian Revolution to the founding of the Moldovan ASSR, will contextualize the history of border-making within the framework of post–First World War territorial changes and competition over the Eastern European borderlands.[1] Soviet nationality policies that emerged in these years and a belief that internal and foreign policies were interconnected set the stage for the next phase in administrative and territorial changes: the establishment of the Moldovan ASSR and the delineation of its borders as an autonomous republic. Finally, the territorial revisions along the Soviet southwestern border – in particular, the establishment of the Moldovan SSR – were the product of the Second World War and its outcome. The chapter mostly follows these three episodes. It covers the actual delineation of the borders but also highlights the contested nature of Soviet decision-making, with its many unrealized territorial claims, ambitions, and alternatives.

THE BESSARABIAN QUESTION AND THE SOVIET STRUGGLE OVER THE BORDERLANDS BEFORE 1924

The unification of Bessarabia and Romania was largely the consequence of revolutionary changes within the former Romanov empire and territorial revisions following the First World War. Russia's 1917 revolutions in particular spurred the mobilization of political forces in the former imperial borderlands. This process intertwined with the mobilization of ethnicity that took place during the war.[2]

In the southwestern regions of the former Romanov empire, these developments saw the emergence of local autonomous bodies. The national principle played an important though not exclusive role in these. At the same time, it is crucial to keep in mind that these new bodies, though they aspired to autonomy, initially saw themselves as existing within a new "democratic and federative Russia," and that their political imaginary was framed largely in the context of the Russian state. In Bessarabia, these processes culminated in the declaration of the Moldovan Democratic Republic in December 1917, a few months after the Ukrainian People's Republic (UNR) was proclaimed in Kyiv.

However, territorial issues had come to the fore even before these declarations. During the summer of 1917, the Ukrainian Central Rada asserted a claim over Bessarabia. Although the Bessarabian leadership's appeal to the Provisional Government in Petrograd managed to counter these Ukrainian ambitions, this episode demonstrated that the territorial aspirations of at least some Ukrainian political leaders included the incorporation of Bessarabia. At the same time, the Bessarabian leaders had their own territorial claims – albeit less pronounced – involving the areas along the left bank of the Dniester where there was a significant Romanian/Moldovan-speaking population.[3] In response to the Bolshevik Revolution, however, the Ukrainian and Moldovan leaderships agreed to suspend these territorial disputes.[4]

In the years that followed, territories on both sides of the Dniester quickly emerged as diplomatic flashpoints between various political entities.[5] This was exacerbated by widespread political unrest that transformed the UNR into a vast battlefield for various local and external forces. Social, national, and international conflicts became the driving force behind the territory's political landscape.[6] After the October Revolution, Bessarabia's governing legislative body in Chișinău, the Sfatul Țării, became increasingly preoccupied with maintaining security and stability in the face of local social unrest, the Bolshevik threat, and Ukrainian expansionism.[7] To counter the spreading chaos, some of the council's members decided to call upon the support of the Romanian government and its army. On 27 March 1918, in the presence of Romania's prime minister and army, the Sfatul Țării voted for unification with Romania.

This dramatic act did not go uncontested at the regional and international levels. Importantly, the UNR's leadership protested the unification, expressing particular concern about the Ukrainian-speaking population in northern and Southern Bessarabia. The decision had also divided the local elites. Indeed, even within the Sfatul Țării, certain groups, notably those representing ethnic minorities, had opposed unification.[8] Moreover, some of those who had voted in favour quickly became disillusioned with their decision, having viewed the prospects of Bessarabia within Romania through the lens of their expectations of the post-February "democratic" Russia, and possibly their prewar imperial experience. These expectations had included broad regional autonomy, respect for the interests of local elites, and ambitious agrarian and social reforms.[9] Unsurprisingly, not all of these expectations were likely to be reciprocated within the political confines of interwar Romania's national unitary project.[10]

Indeed, some local actors openly challenged the unification of Bessarabia with Romania and, by extension, the new Romanian state border. Bessarabia's former imperial elite – including the leader of the local nobility, Alexander Krupensky, and the former mayor of Chișinău, Karl Schmidt – largely refused to accept the province's joining with Romania; some even organized a campaign against its international recognition. They were joined in this by influential anti-Bolshevik Russian émigrés. During the Paris Peace Conference, prior to the Bolsheviks' victory in the civil war, these representatives of Bessarabia's former imperial elites had even called for their homeland to remain part of the Russian state.[11] A similar approach was adopted by anti-Bolshevik Russian émigrés in relation to other former imperial borderlands, for they were eager to preserve the old territorial borders in anticipation of an imminent Bolshevik defeat.

These attempts at reversing the territorial changes ultimately failed, owing to the defeat of the anti-Bolshevik White armies. As it turned out, the Bolsheviks would play a crucial role in the evolution of the Ukrainian-Moldovan border. The Bolsheviks' decision to create and preserve Soviet Ukraine as a republic proved to be decisive in many ways, highlighting the contrast between their approach and that of the White forces, which largely stood for a "united and indivisible" Russia and, by extension, non-recognition of Ukraine and Ukrainians as a separate nationality.

The Bolsheviks had not recognized Bessarabia's absorption into a Greater Romania. They viewed its unification with Romania as an unlawful act and demanded through their diplomats that a plebiscite on the issue be organized. Interwar Soviet maps drew the state border along the Prut River rather than the Dniester, adding a note that Bessarabia was "occupied." After March 1918, Bessarabia, despite its contested status, had unchangeably been part of Romania; however, the territories on the left bank of the Dniester had fallen under the control of a number of political forces. As the Bolsheviks succeeded in establishing control over the Left Bank of the Dniester, they nurtured ambitions to spread their influence and power to Bessarabia and farther west.

The first important Romanian-Soviet encounter over the Bessarabian issue took place in early 1918, shortly before the province joined Romania. In early March 1918, Christian Rakovsky (at that time a leader of the Rumcherod, the Central Committee of the Soviets of Romanian Front, Black Sea Fleet, and Odesa) negotiated a much-debated agreement with the Romanian Prime Minister, Alexandru Averescu, that envisaged the withdrawal of Romanian troops from Bessarabia over a two-month period.[12] Fearing further military advances by the Bolsheviks, the Romanian government had decided to accept their demands. Nevertheless, Bucharest would quickly renege on these diplomatic obligations as the Soviets' rapidly shifting diplomatic and military fortunes made the agreement largely irrelevant from the Romanian perspective. However, while its terms were not realized, it gave the Soviets a legal and diplomatic pretext for not recognizing the union;[13] it also allowed them to question the delineation of the Romanian-Soviet (and eventually, by extension, the Soviet Ukrainian) state border and to consider the Romanian administration in Bessarabia an occupying force.

Another major Bolshevik attempt to change the Romanian-Soviet border by non-diplomatic means took place in mid-April 1919. Having defeated its opponents in the region, the Red Army divisions stationed in Ukraine began to advance toward the left bank of the Dniester. Its military success raised the prospect of Russia's "return" to Bessarabia, and local Bolsheviks, under the guidance of Moscow and the Ukrainian leadership, began to organize toward this end. From late April to early May, two key policy decisions were made. The first was to establish a temporary Bessarabian "workers' and peasants'" government led by Chairman of the Soviet Ukrainian Sovnarkom Christian Rakovsky and chaired by I.N. Krivorukov, a prominent Bessarabian revolutionary. That government was intended to form the new Soviet administrative structures of "liberated" Bessarabia. According to a telegram sent to its Ukrainian counterpart, the Bessarabian government was expected to proclaim the region for the Soviet Union and issue a manifesto once the first settlement on the right bank of the Dniester had been occupied.[14] As it happened, the manifesto was made public before any such occupation had taken place.

By the beginning of May 1919, the temporary Bessarabian government had issued a manifesto proclaiming a Bessarabian Soviet Socialist Republic as a part of the Russian Socialist Federative Soviet Republic.[15] This outlined a program of future legislation, which differed little from other early examples of Bolshevik lawmaking: the requisition of land and its redistribution among the peasants, the nationalization of all industrial and financial units, the emancipation of workers and peasants, and the autonomy of nationalities in national and cultural administration. In reality, though, the temporary government never controlled any sizable areas of land on either the left or the right bank of the Dniester. The government itself, initially founded in Odesa, was headquartered in Tiraspol. In August 1919, the Red Army was driven from the region, leading to the dissolution of the Bessarabian temporary government in early September.[16] However, actual political power was largely wielded by the Bessarabian *obkom* of the RKP(b), which mostly united the underground revolutionary groups of Bessarabia, and the Bessarabian Red Army, established on 28 April 1919[17] and consisting largely of émigrés as well as the local population of the left bank of the Dniester.

These Bessarabian divisions of the Red Army were overseen by Rakovsky himself.[18] Through them, and with the support the local Bolsheviks, he set out to "revolutionize" Bessarabia and thereby provoke social upheaval in other parts of Romania. These developments might in turn help realize Rakovsky's long-cherished dream of a Communist Balkan Federation.[19] In the spring of 1919, one more consideration came into play: Béla Kun's revolution in Hungary and that country's subsequent war with Romania necessitated the involvement of the Red Army to keep the prospects for a "world revolution" alive. While the Bessarabian Red Army was being established, the bulk of Romanian troops were in the west of the country, conducting a major offensive against the Hungarians.[20] Bolshevik military operations were mostly a failure; nevertheless, they were deemed a significant enough threat to prompt the redeployment of some Romanian divisions to Bessarabia. Organizing the Soviet attack on Romania, Rakovsky came under criticism from Vladimir Lenin for what he viewed as a premature move. The Soviet leader believed that it was much more important to secure the industrially rich Donbas region. Nevertheless, these practical considerations did not prevent Lenin from sending a telegram to Kun at the start of the Red Army's campaign in Bessarabia.[21]

Some historians have portrayed the Bessarabian SSR as the first example of Moldovan Soviet statehood,[22] though there still existed certain ambiguities owing to the provisional character of the temporary Bessarabian government. Other historians reject this conclusion, emphasizing that the Bessarabian SSR was just a cover for Bolshevik expansionist plans.[23] The Bessarabian SSR was part of a campaign to export the revolution through Romania to Central and Southeastern Europe. While similar considerations were important in the process of establishing the Moldovan ASSR in 1924, the context and dynamics of the interactions between the actors were quite different. It is telling that the Bolshevik leadership decided to call the envisaged republic "Bessarabian," not "Moldovan." The non-ethnic and regional denomination "Bessarabian" highlighted the Bolshevik leadership's uneasiness about the mobilizational potential of the ethnic "Moldovan" factor and the convoluted national question that might arise as a result. The borders of the envisioned republic, and, consequently, the issue of the southwestern border of Soviet Ukraine that might emerge if the "Bessarabian SSR" project proved a success, were not clearly specified.[24] These imaginary Bessarabian borders[25] were unlikely to have included the territory on the left bank of the Dniester, which would place the border of Soviet Ukraine along the river. At the same time, for possibly the first time in their history, the population of the future Moldovan ASSR had been exposed to a mass propaganda campaign stressing their proximity to the Bessarabian population as well as the necessity of the "liberation of Bessarabia from Romanian capitalists and landlords."

After these early attempts at "liberation" failed, the Bolsheviks kept looking for ways to redraw the Romanian-Soviet border by diplomatic means, in tandem with clandestine revolutionary activities. The Bolsheviks, as well as pro-Soviet groups on the other side of the border, attempted to spur revolutionary activities through acts of infiltration and sabotage, organizing pro-Soviet revolts and attacking officials in neighbouring states. The Soviet leaders saw this as a potentially useful strategy for destabilizing – and ideally overthrowing – these countries' governments; their hope was to bring Soviet-controlled political forces to power or (in some cases) directly annex border areas. Some of the most famous Communist actions of this kind in Bessarabia included the revolts in Bender/Bendery in 1919 and Tatarbunar/Tatarbunary in 1924.[26] Yet by the mid-1920s, the Soviet leadership's support for such tactics had dwindled, for they were hindering diplomatic efforts to normalize relations with regional neighbours. In the perception of the Soviet leadership, these foreign regimes were beginning to stabilize, which suggested that the strategy of (para)military and clandestine revolutionary activity – which had largely failed even in more unstable years – was increasingly unlikely to bring the anticipated results. In addition, Soviet leaders were becoming more preoccupied with the threat of external intervention by the Great Powers as well as paranoid about "capitalist encirclement."[27]

On 25 February 1925, the Politburo of TSK (Central Committee) RKP(b) elected to curtail the Soviet Union's more overt revolutionary activities, which oftentimes were launched on the initiative of local subversive groups.[28] Such initiatives were denounced as having "harmed our diplomatic work and complicated the work of the respective communist parties."[29] This decision reflected the Politburo's willingness to diplomatically dissociate the Soviet Union from the clandestine and illegal actions of foreign communist partisans and activists, especially in Poland and Romania; indeed, some of these groups were disbanded altogether.[30] The Politburo transferred control over all remaining groups to their respective Communist parties and subordinated them to their specific national movements. In addition, financial support to these groups was expected to not come directly from Soviet institutions, but only from the Communist parties in their respective countries.[31] In fact, this didn't happen: as evidenced by the Politburo's subsequent decisions, pro-Soviet activities across the border continued to be financed by both the All-Union and Ukrainian institutions.[32]

ESTABLISHING THE MOLDOVAN ASSR'S BORDERS AND COMPETING SOVIET VISIONS OF TRANSNISTRIA

The founding of the Moldovan ASSR in 1924 played a key role in the evolution of the Ukrainian-Moldovan border and its contemporary state. Importantly, it also crystallized notions of a connection between Bessarabia and Transnistria among the Soviet Union's leadership. At the same time, the Moldovan ASSR, and the process of its creation, highlighted the existence of competing (and overlapping) visions for the territory.

The creation of the Moldovan ASSR was instigated by the "Memorandum on the Necessity of the Creation of the Moldovan Soviet Socialist Republic," sent to TSK RKP(b) and TSK KP(b)U – (Communist Party (Bolshevik) of Ukraine) – on 5 February 1924.[33] The document's authors were mostly Romanian émigré communists, stationed in Moscow in various Comintern divisions, and representatives of the Bessarabian Communist underground. Grigory Kotovsky, a famous Red Army commander of Bessarabian origin, was another notable signatory. According to the Memorandum, the Moldovan republic was expected to serve the cultural and economic needs of the local population:

> 1. The organization of the Moldovan population in a political and administrative unit would contribute to raising economic and cultural levels. The consolidation of the latter for the Soviet Union is the more necessary, and likely, in the event of military conflict, for which one requires a secure, settled rear border (*pogranichnyi tyl*).[34]

As the cited passage demonstrates, the cultural development of the local population was not the ultimate aim. It was also important for military and defence purposes in the border region. The other purpose of the proposed Moldovan republic was a central aspect of the Memorandum:

> 2. The Moldovan republic can play the same political and propaganda role, as that of Belarusian Republic in relation to Poland, or Karelian to Finland. It would serve to attract the attention and sympathies of the Bessarabian population and reinforce our claims to the reunification of *Zadnestrov'e*.
>
> From this point of view, it is imperative to create a socialist republic, not an autonomous region within the UkrSSR. Uniting *Pridnestrov'e* and *Zadnestrov'e* would serve as a strategic wedge in the Balkans (via Dobrudja) and in Central Europe (via Bukovina and Galicia), which the Soviet Union could use as a springboard for military and political purposes.[35]

Clearly, the Memorandum's authors saw a Moldovan republic as playing a crucial international revolutionary role. The same document suggested the possibility of border revisions and the unification of *Zadnestrov'e* and *Pridnestrov'e*. The choice of *Zadnestrov'e* instead of Bessarabia is noteworthy. Bessarabia by this time was a much more clearly defined region in European symbolic geography, one with settled geographical borders. *Zadnestrov'e*, by contrast, was a vague and politically ambiguous concept whose boundaries were unclear. While some could read it as a synonym for Bessarabia – and generally speaking, the Memorandum suggests this interpretation to its readers – one could also understand *Zadnestrov'e* as a territory extending farther west, beyond Bessarabia.

The reference to other cases of the Soviet instrumentalization of "divided communities" – such as the Belarusian SSR (BSSR) in relation to Poland or the Karelian ASSR in relation to Finland – for political and propaganda purposes highlights the "Piedmont principle" in Soviet nationality policies[36] and its role in the founding of the Moldovan ASSR. The Karelian ASSR is of particular importance for comparative purposes, as it was also a case in which relations with the titular nationality of the neighbouring country were ambiguous. There was little debate in the Soviet Union about Belarusians as a national minority in Poland or Ukrainians as a national minority in Poland or Czechoslovakia.[37] At the same time, the extent to which Moldovans were different from Romanians or Karelians from Finns[38] – and by extension could be viewed as national minorities in Romania and Finland respectively – was a point of debate between various Soviet groups. Competing visions of the Moldovan identity and language and their relation to the Romanian identity and language were also on display when the Moldovan ASSR was being established. That debate was intertwined with discussions about the administrative status of the republic within the Soviet Union.

In that sense, of greater significance for this chapter is that the Memorandum suggested creating a fully-fledged Soviet Republic, not an autonomous one within the UkrSSR. That would have meant carving out a "Moldovan" territory on the left bank of the Dniester at the expense of Soviet Ukraine, thus depriving Kharkiv of any control or say in the future of both this lost territory and Bessarabia, were it to be annexed by the Soviet Union at a future point. This also presupposed changes to the western Soviet-Ukrainian border.

The outcome of the internal debates and struggles for power in the process of establishing the Moldovan ASSR did not, however, fall in favour of the Memorandum's authors. Their initiative had triggered the decision to establish the Moldovan ASSR, yet soon after this the Romanian émigrés found themselves quickly marginalized – the Soviet Ukrainian authorities would have the upper hand in the decision-making.[39] Moscow was unwilling to push the issue too much over Kharkiv's heads, especially while it was lobbying for the transfer of the Shakhty and Taganrog regions from the UkrSSR to the RSFSR for economic reasons.[40] Therefore, while Moscow would determine some of the more general issues, many crucial details remained in the hands of the Ukrainians. For instance, when selecting leadership candidates for the emerging Moldovan ASSR, Kharkiv decided to support local Moldovan Communists[41] while marginalizing Romanian émigrés. This would have long-lasting consequences, as the former advocated a separate Moldovan nationality and language, while the latter viewed it as a branch of Romanian national identity.[42] The local Moldovan Communists also accepted Kharkiv's supervision, since Soviet Ukrainian leaders would assist them in their struggle for power with the Romanian émigrés.

However, some Soviet Ukrainian leaders were skeptical about establishing an autonomous republic in such a sensitive border region, especially as it was clear from the start that it would contain a sizable Ukrainian population.[43] While the logic of *korenizatsiia* and international considerations favoured the creation of a Moldovan autonomous region, not all Ukrainian leaders were prepared to surrender territory they considered Ukrainian, especially as it entailed the issue of control over power and resources. Undoubtedly, the *korenizatsiia* and Soviet Ukrainian ambitions inside and outside the Ukrainian republic were important in Kharkiv's understanding of its own interests.[44]

Mikhail Frunze, a Bolshevik with Moldovan roots[45] who held government positions in both Moscow and Kharkiv, understood the existing balances of power quite well. He was one the first officials to react to the initiative, offering the following verdict to the TSK RKP(b) and TSK KP(b)U: "I am personally for [the initiative], that the Moldovan republic be included in the UkrSSR."[46] The decision to create an autonomous republic within Soviet Ukraine reinforced Kharkiv's decisive role in the fate of the Moldovan ASSR and by extension Soviet Ukrainian interests in Bessarabia. At the same time, the creation of the Moldovan ASSR made the national dimension in the Transnistria and Bessarabian questions much more explicit. In both cases, the Moldovan argument became central in revisionist territorial claims, while also making Soviet Ukrainian interests more pronounced.

After the first phase of internal party discussions in Kharkiv and Moscow, in which Frunze played a major role, the Ukrainian authorities took the first steps toward creating the Moldovan ASSR. On 6 March 1924, the Odesan section of the KP(b)U proclaimed the formation of a Moldovan branch.[47] The following day, the Politburo of the KP(b)U issued a decree stating that it "considered reasonable from the political point of view to delimitate an Autonomous Moldovan region as part of the UkrSSR."[48] These two decisions officially launched the organizational process of Soviet Moldovan autonomy. In addition, Plugarul Roşu (Red Ploughman), the Moldovan party section's official gazette, was launched on 1 May 1924.

Yet many issues remained murky, most notably the demographic and geographical extent of the Moldovan population in the region and, consequently, the borders of their future polity. By 18 April 1924, the Ukrainian Politburo had started to view the decision to establish a Moldovan SSR as unreasonable owing to a lack of ethnographic and territorial data.[49] That decision may have reflected reservations about the idea of a Moldovan republic within the KP(b)U. It may also have illustrated Kharkiv's uneasiness over the activities of the ambitious Romanian Communist émigrés, whom the Soviet Ukrainian leadership attempted, with eventual success, to isolate from further involvement in Soviet Moldovan affairs. Yet, subsequent Ukrainian decisions also demonstrate that this decree did not presuppose an all-out rejection of Moldovan autonomy, only its momentary postponement.

On 29 April 1924, the Ukrainian authorities in Odesa ordered a broadening of national-cultural activities among the Moldovan populace.[50] At the same time, the central Ukrainian authorities organized a special commission to gather and evaluate ethno-territorial data in southwestern Ukraine, underscoring the fact that the question of Moldovan autonomy had been reopened. Parallel to this, the Red Army cavalry commander Grigory Kotovsky, who was then stationed in Transnistria, began his own inquiry. In July 1924, a report from the Territorial Commission reached VUTSVK; the results of the commission's calculations differed dramatically from Kotovsky's. While Kotovsky's calculations resulted in a total of 283,398 Moldovans, the Ukrainian commission claimed there were only 147,410.[51] Even Kotovsky's figures were far from the 500,000 to 800,000 mentioned in the original Memorandum of February 1924. Basing on these discrepancies, the Ukrainian authorities reiterated their previous decision to postpone the formation of a Moldovan territorial unit.

That decision prompted Moscow to intervene. On 25 July 1924, Frunze wrote to Stalin to inform him of the Ukrainian authorities' decision, which he described as erroneous:

> I consider the last decision of the TSK KP(b)U erroneous. I have personally visited Transnistria numerous times and I can ascertain that to the North of Tiraspol there is a continuous strip with a predominantly Moldovan population ... Finally, one should take into account the international dimension. The establishment of even a small Moldovan republic or region will become a means of influencing the peasant and working masses of Bessarabia in the sense of strengthening their hopes for deliverance from the Romanian yoke. I recommend revisiting the issue.[52]

Four days later, the Politburo of the RKP(b) decided that it was necessary to create a Moldovan autonomous republic and suggested that the TSK KP(b)U issue the necessary directives.[53] There are several possible reasons for Moscow's insistence. First, the Ukrainian discussion of the Moldovan issue was subject to several opposing viewpoints. Second, a Moldovan ASSR would be crucial for applying pressure on Romania, especially after the failed negotiations on the Bessarabian question in Vienna. Third, because the future republic was an internationally contested borderland, the Soviet authorities could not simply abandon their intention to create a Moldovan Republic, given that it had already been granted official support. Abandoning the Moldovan project would both diminish the Soviet state's prestige in the eyes of foreign governments and provide Romania with additional diplomatic ammunition in the dispute over Bessarabia. This would be the final time that Moscow intervened directly in the establishment of the Moldovan ASSR, which meant that thereafter it would effectively leave key details of the republican leadership and borders in Kharkiv's hands. Shortly before the Moldovan ASSR's formation, the Romanian Communist émigrés expressed their indignation at the decisive role the Soviet Ukrainian authorities had been granted. Among other things, the Romanian Communist émigrés would reiterate the need to create a fully-fledged Moldovan republic that would have a stronger international presence.[54] A tacit idea behind this suggestion was that it would neuter Soviet Ukrainian involvement and remove the Moldovan republic from Kharkiv's jurisdiction.

Nevertheless, the problem of the borders and the ethnic composition of the future Moldovan ASSR remained contested issues before and after the republic's creation.[55] A key challenge was the presence of various nationalities on the left bank of the Dniester. Also, almost all the towns on the left bank of the Dniester were inhabited primarily by Jews, Ukrainians, and Russians; Moldovans were only a small fraction of the urban populace. This made it almost impossible to create a relatively homogeneous Moldovan autonomous republic while maintaining the administrative and geographic unity of its territory and without disrupting economic and cultural development.

Not until 1926 was the all-Soviet census able to provide the authorities with fairly precise data on the population of the Moldovan republic. Prior to this, the authorities could rely only on estimates, which resulted in some politically awkward situations. On the day of its founding, the Moldovan ASSR comprised only a narrow strip of land along the Dniester. The border itself was delineated through a cooperative endeavour involving Kharkiv, the local Soviet Ukrainian authorities, the party and Soviet leaders of the Odesa and Podolia *gubernii*, and the leaders of the emerging Moldovan Soviet Republic itself. This suggested that it would be possible to creatively reinterpret the demographic balance of the Moldovan population. During the Third Session of the VUTSVK, on 11 October 1924, the Chair of the Ukrainian Sovnarkom, V.Ia. Chubar, declared that Moldovans constituted 58 per cent of the 400,000 inhabitants of the newly established republic.[56] As a later census conducted in 1926 demonstrated, Chubar had miscalculated significantly both the share and the total number of Moldovans, who in fact comprised 30.1 per cent of the Moldovan ASSR's 572,338 recorded inhabitants. Ukrainians were 48.6 per cent, Russians 8.56 per cent, and Jews 8.5 per cent.[57] Clearly, Moldovans were not a majority in the republic; they were not even the largest ethnic group.[58]

РЕСПУБЛКА АУТОНОМЫ СОЧИАЛИСТЫ СОВЕТИКЫ МОЛДОВИНАСКЫ

7.1 Map of the Moldovan ASSR, 1929.

The situation may have been slightly less dramatic than these figures suggest. That said, the territorial revisions carried out between 1924 and 1926[59] had reduced an already unimpressive population share. During those years, the local Soviet territorial commissions, comprising representatives from the Moldovan ASSR and the Odesa and Podolia *gubernii*, had increased the territory and by extension the population of the Moldovan ASSR by more than 20 per cent. In September 1926, the VUTSIK Presidium confirmed the final borders of the autonomous republic. It should be noted that the relatively low number of Moldovans in the region, coupled with the overlapping settlement of other ethnic groups, made it impossible to delineate the borders by following strict linguistic and ethnic criteria.[60] Also, some Soviet Ukrainian leaders harboured reservations about including localities where Ukrainians were a clear majority, such as Kodyma (4 Moldovans and 3,209 Ukrainians), Budei (5 Moldovans and 4,506 Ukrainians), and Serby (4 Moldovans and 3,492 Ukrainians). Nevertheless, the argument often prevailed that the strict use of the ethnic principle would leave the Moldovan ASSR without a sizable continuous territory or basic economic potential.

The greatest and most significant territorial expansion of the Moldovan ASSR took place less than two months after its creation. On 26 November 1924, the VUTSVK and the Ukrainian Sovnarkom, following the decision of the TSK KP(b)U's Politburo, abolished the Balta region and transferred the town of Balta, and part its surroundings, to the Moldovan ASSR to serve as its capital.[61] Some of the reasons for this were economic, particularly as they related to the region's remoteness from its newly designated urban centre (Pervomaisk) following the establishment of the Moldovan ASSR.[62] Yet the fact that the town became the capital of the republic demonstrates that additional considerations necessitated this redrawing of borders. At first, there were three candidates for the Moldovan ASSR's capital. Tiraspol was the most logical choice, given the size of the Moldovan population in the town and its environs. However, Birzula (later Kotovsk) was the "economic centre of the Republic"[63] and therefore the "centre of the proletariat ... vanguard of the Republican development."[64] In this respect, Balta's only real advantage was that it was farther from the Romanian border than Tiraspol and Birzula. Yet Balta was largely a Ukrainian- and Russian-speaking town, and this created significant problems for its planned Moldovanization. Choosing it as the capital also intensified the conflict over Ukrainization. Throughout the interwar years, the need to carry out both Moldovanizing and Ukrainizing cultural campaigns on the same territory complicated the implementation of both efforts and significantly limited the impact of the nationality policies elaborated by the Moldovan leadership. Thus, the commission leading the practical implementation of *korenizatsiia* in the Moldovan ASSR found itself bearing the somewhat contradictory title "Commission of Ukrainization and Moldovanization." Interestingly, plans drafted for 1927 indicated that the local controlling bodies in the Balta region would only have been Ukrainianized, whereas the regions were to be both Ukrainianized and Moldovanized.[65]

As the radical Moldovanizers became increasingly influential in the local leadership, questions about territorial revision emerged. At the Second Moldovan Congress of Soviets, held in May 1926, some of the speakers noted that the Moldovan borders were somewhat ambiguous.[66] In September of that year, the Moldovanizers, particularly Pavel Chior-Ianachi, were more explicit, declaring the Balta region an "eyesore" and a "blind that encloses us from the Moldovan masses."[67] In 1927, at the Fourth Moldovan Party Conference, Chior-Ianachi stated that owing to the situation in Balta, the town should be returned to Ukraine so that Moldovanization could be the primary objective of the Moldovan ASSR.[68] This debate should be viewed in the context of the ongoing political rivalry between the Moldovan ASSR's two most influential leaders – Iosif Badeev and Grigorii Staryi. The former supported the radical Moldovanizers; the latter opposed excessive and – in his opinion – sometimes artificial Moldovanization, and any overt attempt to culturally subsume the republic's other ethnic groups. Ultimately, the Moldovanizers failed to convince the Ukrainian authorities, or their opponents within the Moldovan ASSR, to give up the Balta region in order to make the republic more Moldovan. It is possible that for some Ukrainian and Moldovan leaders the inclusion of Balta served as a sort of counterweight and insurance policy against the overly ambitious Moldovan national activists in what was still a highly precarious border region. However, in the face of sustained political pressure, the capital was eventually moved to Tiraspol in 1929.

Regardless, the Soviet authorities viewed Balta and Tiraspol as only temporary capitals. Presumably, the future capital was to be Chişinău. When the Ukrainian Soviet authorities were establishing the Moldovan ASSR, they declared the Soviet state border to be the western boundary of the autonomous republic, placing it on the Prut River rather than the Dniester.[69] On Soviet interwar maps, where hatching was used to highlight Bessarabia as an occupied territory, the latter was essentially included within Ukraine as part of the Moldovan ASSR.

SEPARATING THE UKRAINIAN AND MOLDOVAN SPACES

The border of the Moldovan ASSR, save for a few minor changes, remained unchanged until the Second World War. On 26 June 1940, the Soviet government issued an ultimatum to Romania. That diplomatic note requested the transfer of Northern Bukovina since its "fate is linked mainly with Soviet Ukraine by the commonality of its historical fate, language and ethnic composition"; this would serve as small "compensation" for "twenty years of Romanian domination in Bessarabia." The same document stated that "in 1918, Romania, benefiting from the military weakness of Russia, forcibly annexed from the Soviet Union (Russia) a part of its territory – Bessarabia. Thus, it [Romania] violated the unity of Bessarabia, inhabited mainly by Ukrainians, with the Ukrainian Soviet Republic."[70] The note's claim that Bessarabia was inhabited mainly by Ukrainians may well have been an example of cynical Soviet manipulation. However, the exact wording was unlikely to have been a coincidence. This was an indication of the Soviet failure to establish a clear division between Moldovans and Romanians despite almost sixteen years of the existence of the Moldovan ASSR.[71] The Soviet leaders apparently lacked confidence in the "Moldovan" justification for their expansionist project; perhaps they feared that it could lead to counter-claims; thus, they preferred a more consolidated "Ukrainian" argument for the unification of Ukrainian lands.[72] In this sense, the note was also construed around their understanding of their existing Ukrainian interests in Bessarabia and even its inclusion within a Ukrainian imaginary space. The Moldovan ASSR's sixteen years of existence within Soviet Ukraine had only consolidated this vision.

This narrative also aligned with the existing administrative order. On 2 July 1940, after Romania accepted the Soviet ultimatum, the Politburo extended the jurisdiction of Soviet Ukraine's administrative bodies to Bessarabia.[73] This essentially made what had previously been symbolic claims surrounding the Moldovan ASSR's (and by extension Soviet Ukraine's) borders an administrative reality; those borders now extended to the Prut River. This almost immediately raised the issue of establishing a fully-fledged Moldovan SSR, driven, most likely, by those Soviet Moldovan leaders who saw an opportunity to enhance their political status. Moscow could also see benefits to this: it would be a means of consolidating power over a contested borderland. A new Soviet republic could legitimize its territorial acquisition, locally and internationally. Thus, the Moldovan SSR was established on 2 August 1940. This decision drew little sympathy from the Soviet Ukrainian leadership, for it was at the cost of their own republic's territory. In addition, Ukrainian leaders viewed the left bank of the Dniester and northern (Hotin/Khotyn region) and Southern Bessarabia as regions with sizable Ukrainian populations.

Soviet Ukrainian and Moldovan leaders subsequently outlined their competing visions for the Ukrainian-Moldovan border.[74] The main disagreements concerned those territories on the left bank of the Dniester and in Southern Bessarabia, with the Moldovans proposing that nearly the entire left bank of the Moldovan ASSR be absorbed into the new Moldovan SSR except for the Balta, Kodyma, and Pishchanka regions. Conversely, the Ukrainian proposal claimed eight regions of the Moldovan ASSR, leaving the Moldovan SSR with only a strip of territory along the Dniester, in addition to the three already mentioned, as well as the Kotovsk, Ananyiv, Valegotsulovo, Krasni Okny, and Chorna regions. The Soviet Ukrainian authorities argued that these regions were populated mainly by Ukrainians.

The Moldovan leadership also laid claim to parts of Southern Bessarabia along the Danube, including the town of Ismail/Izmail, as well as the Reni and Bolhrad regions, arguing that the majority of the population was Moldovan and that Ismail/Izmail was a cultural and economic centre for these areas. The Ukrainians countered this, arguing that Moldovans did not form a majority in Southern Bessarabia. These territories were, in fact, populated by "Ukrainians and Russians" as well as by other minority groups such as Gagauz and Bulgarians. To strengthen the Ukrainians' demographic arguments, the author of the report, who was also Chairman of the Ukrainian Supreme Soviet, Mykhailo Grechukha, counted Ukrainians and Russians together as one statistical group, while also claiming that Gagauz and Bulgarians were "Slavic tribes that have culturally more in common with Ukrainians than with Moldovans."[75] Sensing the ambiguities of such an approach, Grechukha further argued that the Russian and Ukrainian cultures were more closely linked to each other than to Moldovans and that their communities tended to inter-mix, in contrast to the Moldovans. Crucially, according to him, Romanian policies had forced many Ukrainians to identify themselves in official statistics as "Romanians" or "Russians" – the latter due to Romanian concerns about large numbers of Ukrainians and the Russifying heritage of the Romanov Empire.[76]

Moscow would, however, largely endorse the Ukrainian proposal. Under the directive of the Supreme Soviet, just under half of the left-bank Moldovan ASSR was annexed by the UkrSSR (six out of fourteen districts); so was about one third of Bessarabia (three out of nine districts). When delineating the Ukrainian-Moldovan border, the Soviet authorities attempted to stick to ethnographic and linguistic criteria, though economic considerations were also referenced. Even so, it was on these very territories that Ukrainian and Moldovan (alongside other nationalities) ethnolinguistic and – as the competing claims demonstrate – imaginary cultural spaces overlapped. Ukrainian involvement in Bessarabian-Moldovan affairs during the interwar years consolidated the perception among Soviet Ukrainian leaders that this space was part of their sphere of political and administrative interest.

The situation was aggravated by contestations over the national identities of the population, which even the Ukrainian proposals admitted to. This even appeared to be the case in Transnistria, despite two decades of the Soviet enforcement of strict national categories. In Bessarabia, due to its contested character, the change of power, and the experience of different nationality policies, the situation was even more complex. In the cited document, Grechukha attempted to mask this issue by placing blame on Romanian policy and the manipulative nature of Bucharest's statistics, which the Soviet authorities had resorted to in 1940.

In contestations over the Ukrainian-Moldovan border, the ethnolinguistic data could be interpreted in favour of either position, but Ukrainian leaders carried more influence in the Soviet administration. Due to the Moldovan ASSR's subordination to Soviet Ukraine in the interwar period, the Moldovan leadership had fewer connections in Moscow, having communicated largely through their immediate Ukrainian superiors. This likely created a latent bias in favour of the Ukrainian proposition. Although the international dimension granted some advantages in terms of border expansion for the Moldovan ASSR in the 1920s (albeit creating similar issues in regard to nationality policies), this did not carry the same weight for the Moldovan SSR. As a result of various Ukrainian-Moldovan territorial commissions, some minor changes were made to the border in the upcoming months and after the restoration of Soviet power in 1944, particularly in northern and southeastern Bessarabia. It would largely remain unchanged after that until the collapse of the Soviet Union.

EPILOGUE

By the end of the Second World War, the Soviet authorities and territorial commissions had largely finished establishing the Ukrainian-Moldovan border, with some additional changes in favour of the UkrSSR in 1947. Nevertheless, attempts were still made to alter it significantly. In 1946, the Soviet Moldovan leadership sent a letter to Stalin asking for the inclusion of the Bessarabian territories, ceded to Ukraine in 1940 (the Hotin/Khotyn, Cetatea Albă/Akkerman, and Ismail/Izmail districts), within the Moldovan

SSR.[77] This claim was supported by several appendices on ethnolinguistic, economic, and historical data. One of these even outlined the idea of unifying all Moldovan people within a Soviet Moldova, which would inevitably mean annexing historical territories of the Moldavian principality to the west of the Prut.[78] Interestingly, the appendix on the ethnolinguistic situation used the same data as in 1940 but did not place Ukrainians and Russians into the same category, as Grechukha had. This allowed Soviet Moldovan leaders to claim that Moldovans were more numerous than Ukrainians in Southern Bessarabia. Unsurprisingly, this appeal for border revisions went unanswered. Nevertheless, it highlights the attempted instrumentalization of the national question as part of a wider struggle for power within the Soviet framework. It was in some respects similar to previous discussions over the Ukrainian-Moldovan border, but the changing circumstances also happened to affect the choice of emphasis.

The interwar and wartime history of the contemporary Ukrainian-Moldovan border is a story of overlapping and sometimes imposed ethnolinguistic and imaginary cultural spaces. Different competing national and social projects and visions clashed on these territories during the interwar years. The Ukrainian-Moldovan border was largely defined by the Soviet actors, but this was not in isolation from other influences. As much as this is the story of administrative delineation, it is also one of local Soviet activists trying to recruit border-making to their struggles for power and resources. The contested character of Bessarabia and Transnistria, and Soviet attempts to use the national question and cross-border cultural ties for international purposes, further complicated the issue of the Ukrainian-Moldovan border. Importantly, as this chapter has shown, border-making was not simply imposed arbitrarily from Moscow, nor did it follow clear, scientifically defined, ethnolinguistic data. Rather, it was the culmination of a series of struggles between different Soviet actors, changing balances of power, contrasting political ambitions, ethnographic and statistical calculations, and international developments, all of which played out during various periods and framed the key decisions. Some of these decisions would have long-lasting consequences for the region's contemporary borders and their (still) contested nature, such as in the case of the Transnistrian separatist region.

NOTES

The publication was prepared within the framework of the Academic Fund Program at the HSE University in 2021 (grant no. 21-04-061).

1. For a broader chronological and comparative analysis of the struggle over the borderlands, see Alfred J. Rieber, *The Struggle for the Eurasian Borderlands: From the Rise of Early Modern Empires to the End of the First World War* (Cambridge: Cambridge University Press, 2014); Alfred J. Rieber, *Stalin and the Struggle for Supremacy in Eurasia* (Cambridge: Cambridge University Press, 2015).
2. Mark von Hagen, "The Great War and the Mobilization of Ethnicity in the Russian Empire," in *Post-Soviet Political Order: Conflict and State Building*, ed. Barnett R. Rubin and Jack Snyder (London: Routledge, 1998), 34–54; see also Eric Lohr, *Nationalizing the Russian Empire: The Campaign against Enemy Aliens during World War I* (Cambridge, MA: Harvard University Press, 2003); Eric Lohr and Joshua Sanborn, "1917: Revolution as Demobilization and State Collapse," *Slavic Review* 76, no. 3 (2017): 703–9.
3. Whether their language and identity were identical to Romanian or formed a separate Moldovan one was a contested issue and would soon become a matter of fierce political debate. Among other things, it was a key issue in the struggle for power in the Moldovan ASSR during its establishment and first years of existence.
4. Vasyl' Boiechko, Oksana Hanzha, and Borys Zakharchuk, *Kordony Ukraïny: Istorychna retrospektyva ta suchasnyi stan* (Kyiv: Osnovy, 1994), 36.
5. On the diplomatic history of the Bessarabian question during the interwar period, see Marcel Mitrasca, *Moldova: A Romanian Province under Russian Rule: Diplomatic History from the Archives of the Great Powers* (New York: Algora, 2002).
6. On the various regimes in Ukraine and the chaotic circumstances of 1917–21, see Georgiy Kasianov, "Ukraine between Revolution, Independence, and Foreign Domination," in Wolfram Dornik et al., *The Emergence of Ukraine: Self-Determination, Occupation, and War in Ukraine, 1917–1922* (Edmonton and Toronto: Canadian Institute of Ukrainian Studies Press, 2015), 76–132; Stephen Velychenko, *State Building in Revolutionary Ukraine: A Comparative Study of Governments and Bureaucrats, 1917–1922* (Toronto: University of Toronto Press, 2010); Stanislav Kul'chyts'kyi, *Chervonyi vyklyk: Istoriia komunizmu v Ukraïni vid ioho narodzhennia do zahybeli*, vol. 1 (Kyiv: Tempora, 2013); on local level, see Mark R Baker, *Peasants, Power, and Place: Revolution in the Villages of Kharkiv Province, 1914–1921* (Cambridge, MA: Harvard Ukrainian Research Institute, 2016).

7 Charles King, *The Moldovans: Romania, Russia, and the Politics of Culture* (Stanford: Hoover Institution Press 2000), 34–5.
8 Eighty-six voted for, thirty-six abstained, three voted against, and thirteen were absent.
9 For arguments along similar lines, see Andrei Cusco, "Nationalism and War in a Contested Borderland: The Case of Russian Bessarabia (1914–17)," in *The Empire and Nationalism at War*, ed. Eric Lohr, Vera Tolz, Alexander Semyonov, and Mark von Hagen (Bloomington: Slavica, 2014), 158–61.
10 On the interwar Romanian national project and the problems in the newly added provinces that it produced, see Irina Livezeanu, *Cultural Politics in Greater Romania: Regionalism, Nation Building, and Ethnic Struggle, 1918–1930* (Ithaca: Cornell University Press, 2000).
11 Svetlana Suveică has written several articles about the international struggle of those factions within the Bessarabian elite who opposed unification with Romania: Svetlana Suveică, "'Russkoe Delo' and the 'Bessarabian Cause': the Russian Political Émigrés and the Bessarabians in Paris (1919–1920)," *Institut für Ost- und Suedosteuropaforschung Regensburg, 10s Mitteilungen. Arbeitsbereich Geschichte*, no. 64 (February 2014); Suveică, "The Bessarabians 'between' the Russians and the Romanians: The Case of the Peasant Party Deputy Vladimir V. Țîganko (1917–1919)," in *Politics and Peasants in Interwar Romania. Perceptions, Mentalities, Propaganda*, ed. Sorin Radu and Oliver Jens Schmitt (Newcastle upon Tyne: Cambridge Scholars, 2017), 215–50; Suveică, "Against the 'Imposition of the Foreign Yoke': The Bessarabians Write to Wilson (1919)," *Journal of Romanian Studies* 1, no. 2 (2019), 89–113.
12 This document was published in *Bessarabiia na perekrestke evropeiskoi diplomatii: Dokumenty i materialy* (Moscow: Indrik, 1996), 216–17. For the English translation, see Andrei Popovici, *The Political Status of Bessarabia* (Washington, DC: Pub. for the School of Foreign Service, Georgetown University, 1931), 245–50. For Rakovsky's own take on the issue, see C.G. Rakovsky, *Roumania and Bessarabia* (London: W.P. Coates, 1925), 34–47.
13 Romanian diplomacy interpreted the terms of the agreement differently.
14 Vitalie Ponomariov, "Considerations Regarding the Communist Activities in Bessarabia between 1918–1921," *Danubius* 30 (2012): 334.
15 *Kommunisticheskoe podpol'e Bessarabii. Sbornik dokumentov i materialov v 2-h tomah, 1918–1940* (Chișinău, 1987–88), 1:82.
16 RGASPI, f. 17, op. 3, d. 26, l. 2.
17 Ponomariov, "Considerations Regarding the Communist Activities," 335. As the author also outlines, the Bessarabian issue during these several months

ended up at the centre of political and institutional struggles among several (pro-)Soviet groups within Soviet Russia, Soviet Ukraine, and Bessarabia.

18 On the role of Rakovsky in military and diplomatic attacks on Romania in 1919, see Stelian Tănase, ed., *Racovski: Dosar secret* (Iași: Polirom 2008), 113–17.

19 Rakovsky was one of the founding members and the First Secretary of the Central Bureau of the Revolutionary Balkan Social Democratic Labor Federation, established in 1915.

20 On Racovsky's understanding of the Hungarian implications in the Soviet offensive in Bessarabia, see *Bessarabiia na perekrestke evropeiskoi diplomatii*, 267–8.

21 *Kommunisticheskoe podpol'e*, 89.

22 A.M. Lazarev, *Moldavskaia sovetskaia gosudarstvennost' i Bessarabskii vopros* (Chișinău: Cartea Moldovenească, 1974), 558–9; S. Afteniuk, *Leninskaia natsional'naia politika Kommunisticheskoi Partii i obrazovanie sovetskoi gosudarstvennosti moldavskogo naroda* (Chișinău: Cartea Moldovenească, 1971), 200–1. More recently, historians in Transnistria have started to debate the role of the Bessarabian SSR as the "first statehood" of the unrecognized separatist Transnistrian Moldovan Republic: Alexandr Voronovici, "Justifying Separatism: The Year 1924, the Establishment of the Moldovan ASSR, and History Politics in the Transnistrian Moldovan Republic," *Euxeinos: Governance and Culture in Black Sea Region* 15–16 (2014): 115–16.

23 Ludmila Rotari, *Mișcarea subversivă din Basarabia în anii 1918–1924* (București: Editura Enciclopedică, 2004), 124–6; Mihail Bruhis, *Rusia, România și Basarabia. 1812, 1918, 1924, 1940* (Chișinău: Editura Universitas, 1992), 211.

24 Due to geographical proximity, Soviet Ukrainian authorities were quite actively engaged in Bessarabian affairs, maintaining contacts with and providing support to Bessarabian Communists. But it is unlikely that at that moment Soviet leaders would have supported the idea of incorporating Bessarabia into Soviet Ukraine, among others, due to international considerations. On Soviet Ukrainian support for the Bessarabian communist movement in the early 1920s, see V.S. Sidak, ed., *Zakordot v systemi spetssluzhb Radians'koï Ukraïny. Zbirnyk dokumentiv* (Kyiv: Vydavnytstvo Natsional'noi Akademii SB Ukrainy, 2000), 88, 90–1.

25 On the evolution of "Bessarabia" from the point of view of symbolic geography, see Andrei Cusco and Victor Taki (with the participation of Oleg Grom), *Bessarabia v sostave Rossiiskoi Imperii (1812–1917)* (Moscow: Novoe Literaturnoe Obozrenie, 2012).

26 On the Soviet Union's clandestine activities in Bessarabia, see Rotari, *Mișcarea subversivă din Basarabia*.
27 James Harris, "Encircled by Enemies: Stalin's Perceptions of the Capitalist World, 1918–1941," *Journal of Strategic Studies* 30, no. 3 (2007): 513–45; James Harris, *The Great Fear: Stalin's Terror of the 1930s* (Oxford: Oxford University Press, 2016).
28 RGASPI, f. 17, op. 162, d. 2, l. 79–81.
29 Ibid., l. 79.
30 Some scholars have emphasized the connection between failed pro-Soviet subversive activities and the shift in Soviet support for various clandestine groups in neighbouring countries; see David R. Stone, "The August 1924 Raid on Stolpce, Poland, and the Evolution of Soviet Active Intelligence," *Intelligence and National Security* 21, no. 3 (2006): 331–41; Igor Cașu, "Exporting Soviet Revolution: Tatarbunar Rebellion in Romanian Bessarabia (1924)," *International Journal of Intelligence, Security, and Public Affairs* 22, no. 3 (2020): 224–43.
31 RGASPI, f. 17, op. 162, d. 2, ll. 79–80.
32 For instance, RGASPI, f. 17, op. 162, d. 4, l. 66; RGASPI, f. 17, op. 162, d. 6, l. 147.
33 RGASPI, f. 495, op. 289, d. 1, ll. 14-19. The memorandum's text can also be found in Argentina Gribincea, Mihai Gribincea, and Ion Șișcanu, eds., *Politica de moldovenizare in R.A.S.S. Moldovenească: Culegere de documente și materiale* (Chișinău: Civitas, 2004), 28–32.
34 *Politica de moldovenizare*, 30.
35 Ibid.
36 Terry Martin, *The Affirmative Action Empire: Nations and Nationalism in the Soviet Union, 1923–1939* (Ithaca: Cornell University Press, 2001), 8–9.
37 Per Anders Rudling, *The Rise and Fall of Belarusian Nationalism, 1906–1931* (Pittsburgh: University of Pittsburgh Press, 2015); Timothy Snyder, *Sketches from a Secret War: A Polish Artist's Mission To Liberate Soviet Ukraine* (New Haven: Yale University Press, 2005).
38 Nick Baron, "The Language Question and National Conflict in Soviet Karelia in the 1920s," *Ab Imperio* 2 (2002): 349–60; Baron, *Politics, Planning, and Terror in Stalin's Russia, 1920–1939* (London: Routledge, 2007); Mark Lawrence Schrad, "Rag Doll National and the Politics of Differentiation on Arbitrary Borders: Karelia and Moldova," *Nationalities Papers* 32, no. 2 (2004): 457–96.
39 Alexandr Voronovici, "A Springboard for Revolution? The Establishment of the Moldovan ASSR and the Competing Visions of its International Revolutionary Role," *New Europe College Yearbook: Pontica Magna*

Program, 2015–2017 (2018): 337–65; see also Gheorghe E. Cojocaru, ed., *Cominternul și originile "moldovenismului"* (Chișinău: Civitas, 2009).

40   On the dispute over the Shakhty and Taganrog districts, see TSDAHO, f. 1, op. 20, spr. 1813, ark. 70–2, 77–8; Iu. Galkin, *Sbornik dokumentov o pogranichnom spore mezhdu Rossiei i Ukrainoi v 1920–1925 gg. za Taganrogsko-Shakhtinskuiu territoriiu Donskoi oblasti* (Moscow: Shcherbinskaia Tipografiia, 2007); more broadly on the border-making between Soviet Ukraine and the RSFSR, see Stephan Rindlisbacher, "From Space to Territory: Negotiating the Russo-Ukrainian Border, 1919–1928," *Revolutionary Russia* 31 (2018): 86–106.

41   TSDAHO, f. 1, op. 16, spr. 2, ark. 77. The Ukrainian Politburo would later reconfirm their choice and request the disbandment of the "initiative group," TSDAHO, f. 1, op. 20, spr. 2144, ark. 2.

42   In September 1924, the Ukrainian Politburo confirmed the necessity to focus on the development of the "popular (narodnyi) Moldovan language," TSDAHO, f. 1, op. 16, spr. 2, ark. 103, 104zv.

43   Others, however, perceived the establishment of the Moldovan ASSR within the Ukrainian SSR as an opportunity to strengthen Kharkiv's influence in Bessarabian affairs.

44   See V.A. Smolii, ed., *'Ukraïnizatsiia' 1920–30-h rokiv: Peredumovy, zdobutky, uroky* (Kyiv, 2003); Matthew D. Pauly, *Breaking the Tongue: Language, Education, and Power in Soviet Ukraine, 1923–1934* (Toronto: University of Toronto Press, 2014); K.S. Drozdov, *Politika Ukrainizatsii v tsentral'nom chernoziom'e, 1923–1933 gg.* (Moscow and Saint-Peterburg: Tsentr Gumanitarnyh Iniciativ, 2012). More broadly on interwar Soviet nationality policies, see Martin, *The Affirmative Action Empire*; Ronald Grigor Suny and Terry Martin, ed., *A State of Nations: Empire and Nation-Making in the Age of Lenin and Stalin* (New York: Oxford University Press, 2002); Francine Hirsch, *Empire of Nations: Ethnographic Knowledge and the Making of the Soviet Union* (Ithaca: Cornell University Press, 2005); Rudling, *The Rise and Fall of Belarusian Nationalism*.

45   Mikhail Frunze was born in Bishkek. His father was of Moldovan origin; his mother, of Russian. It is unclear whether Frunze had identified himself as a Moldovan or had been ethnically conscious in any sense. At the same time, the documents suggest that he did play an important role in the process of establishing the Moldovan ASSR, among others, as a liaison between Kharkiv and Moscow on that issue; RGASPI, f. 17, op. 3, d. 453, l. 3. At least once the discussion on the Moldovan ASSR was postponed due to Frunze's absence; clearly, then, his presence was obligatory; RGASPI, f. 17, op. 3, d. 452, l. 1.

46 Cojocaru, *Cominternul și originile "moldovenismului,"* 96.
47 *Nachalo bol'shogo puti. Sbornik dokumentov i materialov k 40-letiiu obrazovaniia Moldavskoi SSR i sozdaniia Kompartii Moldavii* (Chișinău, 1964), 33.
48 TSDAHO, f. 1, op. 6, spr. 48, ark. 40.
49 TSDAHO, f. 1, op. 6, spr. 50, ark. 59.
50 A. Repida, *Obrazovanie Moldavskoi ASSR* (Chișinău: Știința, 1974), 51–2.
51 Oleg Galushchenko, *Naselenie Moldavskoi ASSR (1924–1940 gg.)* (Chișinău: Tipografiia Akademii Nauk, 2001), 7.
52 Cojocaru, *Cominternul și originile "moldovenismului,"* 136–7. The narrative of the "yoke" that national minorities experienced in contested borderlands was a recurrent part of the Soviet rhetoric and propaganda.
53 RGASPI, f. 17, op. 3, d. 453, ll. 2–3.
54 TSDAHO, f. 1, op. 20, spr. 1821, ark. 7–9.
55 Soviet border-making in the 1920s rarely went uncontested; see, for instance, Francine Hirsch, "Toward an Empire of Nations: Border-Making and the Formation of Soviet National Identities," *Russian Review* 59, no. 2 (2000): 201–26; Arne Haugen, *The Establishment of National Republics in Soviet Central Asia* (Basingstoke and New York: Palgrave Macmillan, 2003); Beatrice Penati, "Life on the Edge: Border-Making and Agrarian Policies in the Aim District (Eastern Fergana), 1924–1929," *Ab Imperio* 2014, no. 2 (2014): 193–230.
56 *Alcătuirea Republicii Autonome Sovetice Moldovenești: Darea de seamă stenografică a Sessiei a 3-a a vutik-ului*, 8–12 Octombrie 1924 (Harkiv, 1924), 9–10.
57 Galushchenko, *Naselenie Moldavskoi ASSR*, 10, 13.
58 This situation created a discursive paradox in the usage of the term *natsmen*. Politically, Ukrainians should have been a national minority within the Moldovan ASSR; however, numerically they were not. Local authorities were therefore always careful to avoid attributing the term national minority to the Ukrainian population.
59 For a detailed description of administrative-territorial changes in the Moldovan ASSR, see K. Stratievskii, "Izmeneniia v administrativno-territorial'nom delenii i v sostave naseleniia Moldavskoi ASSR (1924–1940 gg.)," *Revista de Istorie a Moldovei* 2 (1995): 24–37.
60 To say nothing of the fluidity of identities, which the local Bolsheviks were well aware of. Moldovans for instance, were considered quite a Russified nationality, and thus not always interested in using the vernacular or organizing a national Soviet territorial unit.
61 *Nachalo bol'shogo puti*, 79.

62 *Darea de samă a Congresului Întîi al Sfaturilor din RSSA Moldovenească de Deputaţi, Muncitori, Ţărani şi Ostaşi Roşi (19–23 Aprilie 1925)* [The Report of the First Congress of Soviets of Deputies, Toilers, Peasants, and Red Soldiers from Moldovan ASSR] (Balta, n/a), 21.
63 Badeev's speech at the First Moldovan Party Conference, AOSPRM, f. 49, inv. 1, d. 15, f. 7. Badeev added that the centre of economic management should be moved to Birzula, since Balta was deemed unsuitable as an economic center.
64 Staryi's speech at the *Darea de samă a Congresului Întîi*, 13.
65 *Politica de moldovenizare*, 49.
66 *Darea de samă stenografică a S'Ezdului al Doilea al Sfaturilor de Deputaţi, Muncitori, Ţărani şi Ostaşi Roşi din RASSM (9–14 Mai 1926)* [Stenographic Report of the Second Congress of Soviets of Deputies, Toilers, Peasants, and Red Soldiers from Moldovan ASSR] (Balta, 1926), 16–17.
67 AOSPRM, f. 49, inv. 1, d. 516, f. 44.
68 *Politica de moldovenizare*, 72.
69 RGASPI, f. 17, op. 3, d. 465, l. 1.
70 *Bessarabiia na perekrestke evropeiskoi diplomatii*, 348–9.
71 In sixteen years, Soviet nationality policies in the Moldovan ASSR went from the use of the Cyrillic alphabet and an almost complete rejection of the Romanian linguistic and literary canon, to the Latinization and use of the Romanian norm and then switching back to the Cyrillic alphabet, albeit with less anti-Romanianism than in the early years of the republic; King, *The Moldovans*; King, "The Ambivalence of Authenticity, or How the Moldovan Language Was Made," *Slavic Review* 58 (1999): 117–42.
72 A crucial underlying argument behind this project was the Soviet decision to consider various labels of identification for the local populace – such as Ruthenians, Hutsuls, Malorosy – within the framework of the "Ukrainian" umbrella.
73 Galushchenko, *Naselenie Moldavskoi ASSR*, 28.
74 For both leaderships' reports to Moscow, see Boiechko, Hanzha, and Zakharchuk, *Kordony Ukraïny*, 161–8.
75 Ibid., 164. For an analysis of Grechukha's arguments, see also Sabine Dullin, *Uplotnenie granits: K istokam sovetskoi politiki. 1920–1940-e* (Moscow: Novoe literaturnoe obozrenie, 2019), 366–8.
76 Ibid., 165–6.
77 See Igor Caşu and Virgil Pâslariuc, "Chestiunea revizuirii hotarelor RSS Moldoveneşti: de la proiectul 'Moldova Mare' la proiectul 'Basarabia Mare' şi cauzele eşecului acestora (decembrie 1943 – iunie 1946)," *Archiva Moldaviae* 2 (2010): 297–334.

78 As scholars have suggested, this proposition was likely to have been elaborated upon in the context of the 1943 Teheran conference. Caşu and Pâslariuc, "Chestiunea revizuirii hotarelor RSS Moldoveneşti," 286–8.

8

Crimea's 1954 Transfer to Ukraine

A Practical yet Contested Union

Austin Charron

Ukraine's territorial evolution was completed in 1954 when the Crimean *oblast* was transferred from the Russian Soviet Federative Socialist Republic to the Ukrainian Soviet Socialist Republic of the Soviet Union. Given that the Crimean Peninsula is physically separated from Russia by the narrow Strait of Kerch and attached to Ukraine by the equally narrow Isthmus of Perekop, including Crimea within Ukraine would appear more logical and efficient in administrative terms. Moreover, Crimea has long been socio-economically connected to the Ukrainian mainland. At the same time, though, as a once-prized colonial possession of the Russian Empire, Crimea is steeped in a centuries-old narrative portraying it as essentially Russian in its socio-cultural character, and consequently it has been populated mainly by ethnic Russians since the early twentieth century, making it the only region of Ukraine with a Russian majority.

The question of whether Crimea rightfully belongs within the borders of Ukraine or Russia has been highly contentious since the dissolution of the Soviet Union, in both popular and academic discourses. As such, much of the scholarly work pertaining to Crimea in recent decades approaches the region from one of three general perspectives: the imperialist view that Crimea is fundamentally Russian in character despite its status as part of Ukraine, found mostly in Russian-language academic sources;[1] the counter-imperialist view that Crimea is an integral part of Ukraine despite Russian claims, by dint of the normative rules of state sovereignty or some deeper historical trends;[2] and the anti-colonial view that Crimea is fundamentally the homeland of the indigenous Crimean Tatars and other small minorities.[3] The clash between Russian- and Ukrainian-centric perspectives on

Crimea has only grown more intense since the Russian Federation forcefully annexed the peninsula on 18 March 2014, and the 1954 transfer that formally placed Crimea within Ukrainian borders has again become a topic of great scrutiny and contention.[4]

Crimea's deep socio-cultural entanglements with Russia helped ensure its initial placement within the Russian republic of the Soviet Union despite the lack of physical contiguity. But Crimea's transfer to the Ukrainian republic was nevertheless in keeping with the common Soviet practice of adjusting administrative borders for reasons of socio-economic expediency (*tselesoobraznost'*).[5] The transfer was also held up rhetorically as a symbolic gesture of friendship and unity between the Russian and Ukrainian people, with the explicit goal of strengthening that bond. Ironically, Russian resentment in the post-Soviet period toward the transfer, and the Russian Federation's forced reversal of it sixty years later with the annexation of Crimea, would contribute to the seismic undoing of that very bond, and the administrative re-severing of Crimea from Ukraine would bring predictable socio-economic consequences to the contested peninsula. This chapter explores the historical, socio-economic, and political contexts of the transfer of Crimea to Ukraine in 1954 and describes the bureaucratic procedures through which the transfer was first proposed and approved. The chapter ends with a discussion of the transfer's tumultuous afterlife that culminated in 2014 with the Russian annexation of Crimea, and points to some of the consequences of the annexation that demonstrate why the peninsula's transfer to Ukraine was so prudent in the first place.

HISTORICAL CONTEXT: CRIMEA'S SHIFTING TERRITORIAL PLACEMENT

From 1441 the Crimean Peninsula formed the central territory of the Crimean Khanate, a successor to the Golden Horde. The Crimean Khanate was ruled and populated primarily by the indigenous Crimean Tatars, a Turkic Muslim people who had emerged as a distinctive ethnic group within Crimea through intermixing and cultural interfusion among the descendants of various settlers and nomadic tribes that had arrived on the peninsula over the preceding millennia. From 1475 the Crimean Khanate was a protectorate of the Ottoman Empire, but with the Treaty of Küçük Kaynarca that ended the Russo-Turkish War (1768–74), the Russian Empire emerged as a powerful new force in the Black Sea region, and the Khanate was pulled into its sphere of influence. Russia formally annexed and colonized the territory of the Crimean Khanate in 1783, thereby expanding its empire into the Crimean Peninsula along with lands the Khanate had controlled to the north and east of the peninsula.

The colonized territory was quickly integrated into the Russian Empire's administrative structure. In 1784, together with adjacent portions of the mainland extending to the Dnieper River, Crimea was organized into the Taurida (Tavricheskaia) *oblast* – a title derived from the ancient Greek name for Crimea, *Tauris*, where a number of Greek city-states had once established small colonial outposts. The Taurida *oblast* was abolished only twelve years later in 1796 and merged with other recently acquired lands in what is now southern and eastern Ukraine to form a reconstituted Novorossiya Governorate (*gubernia*) – an entity that had existed in a different territorial formation without Crimea from 1764 to 1783. This arrangement was also short-lived, for in 1802 the Novorossiya Governorate was split into three smaller administrative units, including the Taurida Governorate, whose territorial delimitation closely resembled that of the earlier Taurida *oblast*. The Taurida Governorate remained intact until the beginning of the Bolshevik Revolution in 1917.

Significantly, from the annexation of the Crimean Khanate in 1783 until 1917, the shifting boundaries of the Russian Empire's first-order administrative territories containing Crimea – that is, *oblasts* and governorates – always extended beyond the Crimean Peninsula itself; thus, administrative contiguity with parts of mainland Ukraine was maintained throughout the time Crimea was ruled by the Russian Empire. However, the Taurida Governorate was further subdivided into seven second-order administrative units known as *uezds*, and a short border cutting through the Isthmus of Perekop separated the mainland Dnieper *uezd* from the peninsular Perekop *uezd*. However minor, this marked the first instance of a formal administrative division between the Crimean Peninsula and mainland Ukraine.

The administrative decoupling of the Crimean Peninsula from the mainland first occurred provisionally in the early stages of the Bolshevik Revolution; in coordination with the nascent, Bolshevik-led Russian Soviet Federative Socialist Republic (RSFSR), on 7 November 1917 the Central Rada of the recently formed Ukrainian People's Republic declared sovereignty over all territories where Ukrainians were a majority of the population, explicitly including the mainland *uezds* of the Taurida Governorate but excluding Crimea, where Russians and Crimean Tatars outnumbered Ukrainians. On 13 December the newly formed *qurultay* (council) of the Crimean Tatar People declared the formation of an independent Crimean People's Republic, whose territory included only the Crimean Peninsula itself. Neither of these political entities would survive for long, but their

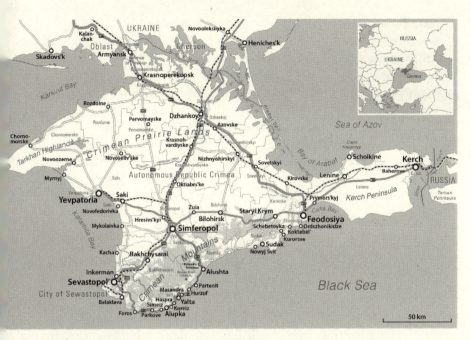

8.1 Map of Crimea.

division of territory along the Isthmus of Perekop would set a precedent for how Crimea and mainland Ukraine would be separately contested during the Russian Civil War, and how they would later enter the hierarchy of administrative territories within the Soviet Union.

Having been captured by the Red Army in February 1920, Crimea entered the territory of the RSFSR and was later declared the Autonomous Crimean Soviet Socialist Republic (Crimean ASSR) on 18 October 1921.[6] In adherence to the early Soviet principle of *korenizatsiia* (root-making) aimed at accelerating the development of national identity among ethnic minorities through territorial autonomy, Crimea was given the status of an autonomous republic on behalf of its indigenous Crimean Tatar community, even though Russians already far outnumbered them.[7] In the declaration announcing the formation of the Crimean ASSR, the republic is described as "a part of the RSFSR within the borders of the Crimean Peninsula."[8] However, the task of delineating the republic's border with the UkrSSR was purposefully left unfinished, with the decree calling for a committee of relevant authorities to convene at a future date to determine exactly where the administrative boundary between the peninsula and the mainland should be drawn.

Despite the republic's declared limitation to the Crimean Peninsula, some Crimean authorities involved in negotiating the placement of the border pushed for the inclusion of parts or all of the mainland portions of the former Taurida Governorate. A February 1923 report by the Commission on the Administrative-Economic Zoning of Crimea recommended that the entirety of the former Taurida Governorate be included within the Crimean ASSR, offering a number of arguments for why the peninsula should not be administratively severed from the mainland: the peninsula relied on the mainland for much of its cereals, dairy, livestock, and other agricultural products; the republic would have insufficient resources to support Crimea's all-important tourism industry; it would disrupt the salt-mining industry spanning the two sides of the Syvash;[9] the republic would be easier to defend militarily if it included mainland territory; and it would disrupt the social and economic lives of those living on and around the Isthmus of Perekop.[10] While some of these arguments were questionable and may be chalked up simply to efforts to extend the republic's territory as much as possible, there were nonetheless sound arguments to be made regarding the socio-economic interdependence of the Crimean Peninsula and adjacent mainland territories that would resurface in the coming decades.

Crimea's Central Executive Committee issued its decision on 22 March 1923 that the Crimean ASSR should annex from the mainland only ten *volosts* – small administrative units one tier below *uezds* – along the Syvash in order to keep the region's salt-mining industry intact within the republic.[11] However, this decision was rendered moot by a decree handed down by the Presidium of the Central Executive Committee of the USSR on 16 October 1925, which officially fixed the borders between the UkrSSR, the Belarusian SSR (BSSR), and the RSFSR and listed precisely where transfers of extant territories were to take place; that decree made no mention of the border between the Crimean ASSR and the UkrSSR. With this omission, the border was thus fixed along the same line cutting through the Isthmus of Perekop that once separated the mainland and peninsular portions of the Taurida Governorate.

The next major change to Crimea's administrative status came in 1945 when it was downgraded from an autonomous republic to an *oblast* for reasons that were altogether tragic and senseless. Citing dubious allegations that the Crimean Tatars had engaged in collective treason against the Soviet Union by aiding and collaborating with the Nazi occupiers during the Second World War, Stalin ordered that all Crimean Tatars be immediately deported from Crimea as punishment.[12] On 18 May 1944, only six days after recapturing the peninsula, Red Army soldiers summarily rounded up every single Crimean Tatar in Crimea, forced them all into cattle cars, and sent them to distant corners of the Soviet Union for permanent resettlement, primarily in Uzbekistan and other parts of Central Asia. An estimated 46 per cent of the Crimean Tatar population perished in the packed and unventilated cattle cars during the long journey,[13] and the trauma surrounding their deportation from their homeland has since become a cornerstone of Crimean Tatar national identity.[14] With the Crimean Tatars completely removed, Crimea's remaining population was almost entirely Slavic. In 1939 the Crimean ASSR's population was 49.6 per cent Russian, 19.4 per cent Crimean Tatar, and 13.7 per cent Ukrainian;[15] by 1959, Russians were 71.4 per cent of Crimea's population, with Ukrainians making up most of the rest at 22.3 per cent.[16] With Russians now the outright majority and in the absence of a titular national minority, Crimea no longer qualified as an ethnonational republic, and its autonomous status was thus revoked by decree of the Presidium of the Supreme Council of the USSR on 30 June 1945.

Steady and persistent Russification was perhaps Crimea's defining trend between the time of its annexation to the Russian Empire in 1783 and the mid-twentieth century. Once the realm of the Crimean Tatars (though many other minority communities were present), Crimea slowly morphed into a colony populated predominantly by ethnic Russians, who by 1945 had completely displaced the Crimean Tatars to become the outright majority of the regional population. But just as importantly, Crimea had been imbued over that time with a potent mythology of Russian sociocultural significance. As the supposed site of Prince Vladimir I's baptism in 988, Crimea had been proclaimed the birthplace of Eastern Orthodoxy. Crimea had also inspired generations of Russia's most celebrated authors, poets, and painters, resulting in many artistic representations of Crimea that were renowned and beloved throughout the Russian-speaking world. The Crimean port of Sevastopol was home to the Russian (later Soviet) Black Sea Fleet and had twice been destroyed while serving as a critical stronghold of resistance against invading armies during the Crimean and Second World Wars; thus Crimea was deeply associated with Russian/Soviet military glory. Although Ukrainians had the same right as Russians to revere Crimea for these same reasons, Russian hegemony within the Soviet cultural sphere helped ensure that this mythology was coded and perceived as innately Russian.[17]

SETTING THE STAGE FOR CRIMEA'S TRANSFER TO UKRAINE

By the early 1950s, Crimea was still struggling to recover economically from the destructive impacts of the Second World War. Its infrastructure, industry, and agriculture had been devastated during the war, and its population had suffered a massive reduction due to wartime casualties and the complete removal of the Crimean Tatars and other small minorities. From a total of 1,126,429 in 1939, Crimea's population had fallen to only around 780,000, a loss of around 31 per cent.[18] A severe drought in 1946 had decimated agricultural production in the north of the peninsula, resulting in crop failures in 1947.[19] In an effort to offset local labour shortages and assist Crimea in its economic recovery, central authorities ordered the relocation of entire collective and state farms to Crimea from other regions of the UkrSSR and RSFSR beginning in 1944. In 1944 alone some 17,040 families totalling 62,104 people were resettled in Crimea from the Kyiv, Vinnytsia, Zhytomyr, and Podolia *oblasts* of the UkrSSR and from several *oblasts* of the RSFSR.[20] The influx of Ukrainian and Russian collective farmworkers continued throughout the 1950s, albeit at a declining pace, with a total of 57,000 individuals arriving between 1950 and 1954.[21]

Facing a lack of resources, intolerable living conditions, inadequate support, and inexperience farming in Crimea's warmer climate, many of the resettled farmers eventually returned home, but those who stayed contributed to the gradual recovery of Crimea's population, which by 1959 had surpassed its prewar total by about 75,000 people, reaching 1,201,517. Ethnic Russians saw the largest increase over their 1939 population, with a total of 858,273 in 1959 compared to 558,481 twenty years earlier, an increase of 53.7 per cent. Crimea's Ukrainian population also increased significantly during this period, from 154,123 in 1939 to 267,659 according to the 1959 census, an increase of 73.7 per cent.[22] The removal of the Crimean Tatars between 1939 and 1959 did a lot to skew the relative proportions of Russians and Ukrainians on the peninsula, and it was Russians who certainly made the greatest gains despite the higher rate of increase among Ukrainians. Nevertheless, the steady rise in Crimea's Ukrainian population between the mid-1940s and early 1950s helped strengthen the cultural and ethnolinguistic ties between the peninsula and the Ukrainian mainland and would ultimately help justify the transfer of the Crimean *oblast* to the UkrSSR.

Despite efforts to stimulate Crimea's flailing economy through population transfers, recovery was disappointingly slow. By 1950, industrial and agricultural output in most of Crimea was still far lower than it had been before the war; relative to levels of productivity in 1940, textile production was operating at 63 per cent and shoe manufacturing at only 49 per cent, while iron ore extraction had reached 78 per cent but ferrous metallurgical output an abysmal 3.7 per cent. By 1950 the output of Crimea's fish products had reached 83 per cent of 1940 levels, vegetable and fruit cultivation 66 per cent, and bread production 41 per cent (but flour production only 37 per cent).[23] Separated from the rest of the RSFSR by the Kerch Strait, Crimea grew more economically reliant on the UkrSSR during the struggling postwar years, both as a reliable source for products its lagging industries were unable to produce sufficiently and as a destination for raw materials that local industries were unable to process. During this time a large portion of the food Crimeans consumed came from the UkrSSR, and the iron ore mined in Crimea was mostly sent to Ukrainian industrial centres to be turned into steel.[24]

But of all the resources that Crimea lacked in sufficient volume, water was the most critical. Northern and central Crimea are part of the same steppe ecosystem that covers much of southern and eastern Ukraine, boasting the same rich chernozem soil that has earned Ukraine the moniker "the breadbasket of Europe." But at the same time, northern Crimea and adjacent parts of the mainland feature some of the lowest precipitation rates in all of Europe and thus rely heavily on irrigation to support local agriculture and industry. Flowing southward through central Ukraine and emptying into the Black Sea about one hundred kilometres northwest of Crimea, the Dnieper River has long been a crucial source of irrigated water for the dry but otherwise fecund reaches of southern Ukraine; but as a small peninsula isolated from the rest of the steppe by the Syvash, Crimea has no significant rivers capable of supporting large-scale irrigation. The devastating drought of 1946 further demonstrated the peninsula's precarious reliance on irrigation, and solving this problem became a major component of Crimea's postwar recovery.

Led by a Ukrainian engineering enterprise, two new reservoirs were built in Crimea between 1951 and 1957 in an effort to provide the peninsula with more reliable hydrological resources, but both reservoirs were quite small and together could not meet Crimea's growing demand for water.[25] Thus, a bold new solution was announced in 1951: the construction of a canal that would direct water from the Dnieper through the Isthmus of Perekop and along Crimea's northeastern flank all the way to the city of Kerch near the peninsula's eastern tip. Designed by the same Ukrainian enterprise responsible for Crimea's new reservoirs, the canal would provide a reliable and substantial new source of water for both Crimea and the Kherson *oblast*. Along with a major hydroelectric dam at the city of Kakhovka built in conjunction with the canal, the North Crimean Canal would constitute a major infrastructural linkage between the peninsula and the mainland that would make Crimea's agricultural, industrial, and socio-economic framework fundamentally dependent on Ukraine's hydrological and energy resources. The project would also mean that the water of the Dnieper – so central to the history, culture, and economy of Ukraine[26] – would water Crimea's crops and sustain its people and industries for the first time, forging a symbolic new bond between Crimea and Ukraine.

POLITICAL CONTEXT OF THE TRANSFER

Although Crimea and Ukraine shared a long history of interconnectivity that was only growing stronger by the early 1950s, the decision to transfer the Crimean *oblast* to the UkrSSR was ultimately a product of a very particular set of circumstances converging at a unique moment in Soviet history. For one, the transfer occurred during an auspicious year for Russian-Ukrainian relations: 1954 marked the three hundredth anniversary of the Treaty of Pereiaslav, which had created the first military alliance between the Tsardom of Russia and the Cossack Hetmanate under Bohdan Khmelnytsky and by the twentieth century had become historicized as the moment of unification – or, as it was often deemed, "reunification" – of Russia and Ukraine under Russia's authority. As the origin point of what was perceived to be the strongest and most enduring partnership underlying the rhetoric of "friendship" and "fraternal bonds" among Soviet nationalities, the 1654 Treaty of Pereiaslav was the subject of frequent commemoration throughout the Soviet period, and the 1954 tricentennial was marked by events, speeches, and celebrations in both republics throughout the year. Not entirely coincidentally, it was against this important socio-historical backdrop that an exchange of territory between the Russian and Ukrainian republics – in the form of Crimea – would take place.

By all accounts, the chief protagonist behind the transfer was Nikita Khrushchev, a stalwart figure in Soviet politics since the 1920s who had worked his way into Stalin's inner circle in the years leading up to the leader's death, during which time Khrushchev served as First Secretary of the Moscow Regional Committee of the Communist Party. Khrushchev was Russian by birth but had lived in the Ukrainian city of Iuzovka (modern-day Donetsk) from a young age and had thus developed deep Ukrainian roots – a fact that helped earn him the position of First Secretary of the Communist Party of Ukraine (KP(b)U) between 1938 and 1949. In 1943, while serving in this position, Khrushchev had commissioned a report on Crimea's socio-political, ethnonational, and administrative profile, which suggests that he may have been eyeing the peninsula for possible inclusion within the UkrSSR from an early date.[27] However, this idea would not come to fruition until after Stalin's death in March 1953.

Stalin died without appointing a successor to take up his position as General Secretary of the Communist Party of the Soviet Union, and his death initiated a period of collective leadership among the Presidium of the Central Committee (formerly the Politburo) of the Communist Party of the Soviet Union as its key members jockeyed for power. A relatively low-ranking member of this body at the time of Stalin's death, Khrushchev leveraged his deep patronage network within the Soviet political apparatus to quickly rise within the ranks of the Presidium, becoming the First Secretary of the Central Committee in September 1953. By the beginning of 1954, Khrushchev's influence within the Presidium was rivalled only by that of Georgy Malenkov, then the Chairman of the Council of Ministers of the Soviet Union. The question of transferring Crimea to the UkrSSR was first raised within the Presidium of the Central Committee in January 1954, amid this power struggle between Khrushchev and Malenkov.

While there are no records that concretely verify Khrushchev's role in bringing the question of Crimea's transfer before the Presidium, anecdotal and speculative accounts point to him as the initiator. With his deep personal and political roots in Ukraine, Khrushchev relied heavily on his Ukrainian colleagues for support during his ongoing power struggle within the Presidium of the Central Committee, and he likely viewed the transfer of Crimea to the UkrSSR as a means of further shoring up the support of the Ukrainian party leadership as he prepared to challenge Malenkov for supreme authority. The transfer also adhered to many of the policies that were central to Khrushchev's political and economic vision for the state as he vied for power, including economic decentralization and administrative efficiency.[28] Moreover, the placement within Ukraine of a region that had become indelibly coded as culturally Russian and with a Russian majority population would necessarily pull Kyiv and Moscow into a tighter socio-political bond – an objective that would further benefit Khrushchev politically as the pre-eminent "Ukrainian" figure at the top of the Soviet Union's political pecking order.[29]

Members of Khrushchev's family have also pointed to factors that likely motivated him to initiate the transfer: his great-granddaughter, Nina Khrushchev, believes that his personal affinities for Ukraine played a key role,[30] and his son Sergei Khrushchev has argued that the impending construction of the North Crimean Canal motivated his father to streamline the chain of command surrounding the project by placing Crimea within the UkrSSR.[31] In one notorious account, Khrushchev's son-in-law Aleksei Adzhubei claims that the idea for the transfer came to Khrushchev during their vacation to Crimea in October 1953. According to Adzhubei, Khrushchev had requested a tour of northern Crimea and was appalled to see that it had barely recovered from the destruction of the Second World War. Khrushchev also supposedly met with a group of collective farmers recently resettled in Crimea, who informed him of their woeful living conditions and struggles to grow crops in the dry climate. Spotting a plane on the tarmac of a small airport, Khrushchev reportedly located the pilot and demanded to be flown directly to Kyiv so that he could meet with Ukrainian party officials and raise the issue of Crimea's stagnating recovery, although Adzhubei claims no overt proposal to transfer Crimea was made at the ensuing meeting.[32] These remarkable claims have never been verified, but they have nevertheless contributed to the widely held and likely accurate perception that Khrushchev personally spearheaded the transfer of Crimea both for practical purposes and calculated political gain.

THE BUREAUCRATIC PROCEDURE BEHIND THE TRANSFER

The transfer of Crimea was initiated on 25 January 1954 with a decree issued by the Presidium of the Central Committee of the Communist Party of the Soviet Union – signed by First Secretary Khrushchev – on "the transfer of the Crimean Oblast from the RSFSR to the UkrSSR," calling for a special session of the Presidium of the Supreme Council of the USSR to be convened in order to approve the transfer.[33] A draft of a corresponding decree was issued the same day by the Presidium of the Supreme Council of the USSR; it echoed the call for a special session, further noting that the transfer was necessary, "considering [Ukraine and Crimea's] common economy and economic expediency, as well as the historically established cultural ties between the populations of the Crimean Oblast and the UkrSSR" (see map 7.2).[34]

On the direction of the Soviet of Ministers of the RSFSR, the Presidium of the Supreme Council of the RSFSR dutifully approved the transfer on

8.2 Soviet Ukraine, 1954.

5 February, acknowledging the "common economy, territorial proximity, and close economic and cultural ties between the Crimean Oblast and the UKRSSR" as the reason for the transfer.[35] On or around the same day a joint statement in support of the transfer was issued by the Presidiums of the Supreme Councils of the RSFSR and UKRSSR, citing their peoples' "fraternal ties" and "mutual struggle against oppression and foreign invaders" dating back to the Treaty of Pereiaslav.[36] After the Presidium of the Supreme Council of the RSFSR approved the transfer on 5 February, the corresponding body of the UKRSSR followed suit eight days later on 13 February, declaring the proposed transfer "quite appropriate" and "a testament to the Russian people's boundless trust in the Ukrainian people."[37]

The fateful meeting of the Presidium of the Supreme Council of the USSR to approve the transfer was convened on 19 February. Among those in attendance were the Chairmen and First Secretaries of the Presidiums of the Supreme Councils of both the RSFSR and UKRSSR, as well as representatives from the Executive Committee of the Crimean Oblast and the City Councils of Simferopol and Sevastopol. Since the transfer had already been initiated and approved by the highest authorities within the party leadership, the purpose of this meeting was little more than to confirm the consent of all relevant parties and to give the transfer the necessary rubber stamp. But the meeting was also an opportunity for attendees to provide commentary as to why Crimea's inclusion within the UkrSSR was necessary or prudent, and the reasons offered reveal both a concern for economic and administrative practicality and obsequious reverence for the Soviet rhetoric of fraternal union between Russia and Ukraine.

Several speakers pointed to the same geographic, economic, and sociocultural links between Ukraine and Crimea that had been the basis for earlier calls for administrative continuity between the peninsula and the mainland. The Chair of the Presidium of the Supreme Council of the RSFSR, Mikhail Tarasov, stated that

> the Crimean Oblast, as we know, occupies the entire Crimean Peninsula and is territorially adjoined to the Ukrainian Republic, as if it were a natural extension of the southern steppe of Ukraine. The economy of the Crimean Oblast is closely linked with the economy of the UkrSSR. For geographic and economic reasons, the transfer of the Crimean Oblast to the brotherly Ukrainian republic is practical and corresponds with the common interests of the Soviet government.[38]

One member of the Presidium of the Supreme Council of the USSR, Nikolai Shvernik, spoke further to Crimea's economic importance and connection with Ukraine:

> The Crimean Oblast plays a significant role within the national economy of the Soviet Union as a region of ferrous metallurgy, viticulture, winemaking, canning and fish industries, animal husbandry, and a paradise of high-quality wheat cultivation. The Crimean Oblast borders the territory of the UkrSSR. This fact led to the development of common cultural and economic ties between the Crimean Oblast and Soviet Ukraine.[39]

Shvernik added that the transfer would help develop Crimea's agricultural and health resort industries. The Chairman of the Presidium of the Supreme Council of the UkrSSR, Demian Korotchenko, similarly deemed the transfer "quite appropriate" due to the "commonalities of economic development, territorial proximity, and growing economic and cultural ties between the Ukrainian Republic and the Crimean Oblast."[40]

That the transfer was guided chiefly by pragmatic considerations was further underscored by repeated praise for the Soviet Union as a state in which such decisions were thoughtfully made and smoothly executed. Otto Kuusinen, a Vice Chairman of the Presidium of the Supreme Soviet of the USSR from the Karelo-Finnish Republic, remarked that

> only in our country is it possible that such important issues as the territorial reallocation of individual regions to one particular republic or another are resolved without any difficulty and with full coordination, guided solely by considerations of practicality and economic and cultural development, and by the general interests of the Soviet state and the interests of further strengthening friendship and trust between peoples.[41]

His statement was echoed by Kliment Voroshilov, the Chairman of the Presidium of the Supreme Council of the USSR, who declared that

> only under the conditions of the Union of Soviet Socialist Republics is it possible to come to such a fair solution for all territorial issues between Union Republics, one based on economic considerations and economic practicality, and with the complete mutual friendship and fraternal cooperation of their peoples.[42]

Indeed, mention of economic and other practical rationales was frequently couched in effusive declarations of the "fraternal bond" between the Russian and Ukrainian people under socialism, and how the transfer of Crimea would further strengthen this bond. "The Ukrainian people long ago tied their fate with the Russian people," declared Tarasov:

> Over the course of many centuries they fought together against common enemies – Tsarism, feudalists, and capitalist – and also against foreign invaders. The centuries-old friendship between the Ukrainian and Russian peoples was further strengthened with the victory of the great October socialist revolution, as was strengthened the economic and cultural ties between Crimea and Ukraine.[43]

Voroshilov went even further, arguing that Crimea served as an historical emblem of friendship and cooperation between Russians and Ukrainians in their struggle against malevolent forces and that the transfer would reinforce this bond:

Due to its historical development and to its territorial and economic position, the Crimean Oblast has important meaning for the whole Soviet state. And in the distant and not-so-distant past, enemies have repeatedly tried to take the Crimean Peninsula away from Russia, to use it for the robbery and plunder of Russian and Ukrainian lands, building military bases there to assault Russia and Ukraine. But more than once, in their common struggle the Russian and Ukrainian peoples ferociously beat back the impudent invaders and threw them out of Ukraine and Crimea. Ukraine and Crimea are closely connected by common economic interests ... [and] cultural ties between Crimea and Ukraine in particular have grown and deepened. Undoubtedly, the transfer of the Crimean Oblast to the UkrSSR will further strengthen these traditional connections.[44]

As the Ukrainian representative, Korotchenko was particularly effusive in his praise of the "Russian people" for their gift of Crimea, affirming that the body he represented "expresses its heartfelt gratitude to the great Russian people for this exceptionally wonderful act of fraternal aid."[45] To which he added:

With a feeling of deep satisfaction and warm appreciation, the Ukrainian people greet the decision of transferring Crimea to the UkrSSR as a bright new manifestation of the boundless trust and sincere love of the Russian people for the Ukrainian people, and as new evidence of the inviolable fraternal friendship between the Russian and Ukrainian people.[46]

Tellingly, four of the six attendees to offer extended commentary – including Tarasov, Korotchenko, and Voroshilov – referred to the symbolic fact that the transfer was taking place during the tricentennial of the "reunification" of Russia and Ukraine through the Treaty of Pereiaslav, which, according to Tarasov, played "an enormous, progressive role in the political, economic, and cultural development of the Ukrainian and Russian peoples."[47]

As expected, the movement to approve the transfer passed unanimously and with no abstentions. With Voroshilov's signature the decree was sent to the full Supreme Council of the USSR for final approval and entry into Soviet law on 26 April – again with Voroshilov's signature as the chairman of that body's presidium. Despite all indications that Khrushchev had played the paramount role in initiating the transfer, he offered no commentary during the 19 February meeting, and it was ultimately Voroshilov's signature that made the transfer official. Also conspicuously silent during the proceedings were the three representatives from Crimea, who, likely invited to convey the impression of regional support for the transfer but powerless to object, may well have intended to signal disapproval through their silence.[48] Regardless, Crimea officially became a part of the UkrSSR on 26 April 1954, thus completing the republic's territorial expansion and fixing the borders with which Ukraine would become an independent state in 1991.

Construction on the North Crimean Canal began in 1961 and took ten years to complete, reaching its eastern terminus in Kerch in 1971. The project proved instrumental in the recovery and expansion of Crimea's agricultural and industrial sectors: it provided Crimea with an abundant new source of water, while the Kakhovka Power Station at the canal's source provided the peninsula with a reliable new source of energy, thus making Crimea heavily dependent on its integration into Ukraine's electrical and hydrological infrastructures.[49] Despite a decades-long, brazenly persistent campaign for the right to live in their homeland, the deported Crimean Tatars were consistently denied the right to return to Crimea until the Soviet Union's final years. They began returning in droves on the eve of Ukrainian independence.

THE TRANSFER'S CONTENTIOUS AFTERLIFE

The transfer of Crimea to the UkrSSR in 1954 was a fairly banal event for residents of the region, who remained within the centralized Soviet state regardless of the union republic to which they were assigned. Although the transfer coincided with the tricentennial of the Treaty of Pereiaslav, it was never presented to the public as a component of this celebration and was barely covered by the Soviet press. However, the consequences of the transfer would prove significant after the collapse of the Soviet Union in December 1991, when, to the horror of many ethnic Russians in Crimea, Ukraine and Russia became two separate states with Crimea stranded on the "wrong" side of the new international border. In a first for the Soviet Union, Crimea had regained the status of an autonomous republic by popular referendum in January 1991 as local politicians scrambled to consolidate their regional authority ahead of Ukraine's possible independence – although stymieing the returning Crimean Tatars' efforts to reclaim their lost land and property was likely another factor in this push for regional autonomy. Ukraine's sovereignty over Crimea was further complicated by the fact that Sevastopol was a vitally important Soviet naval base, which the Russian Federation intended to keep.

The early and mid-1990s were a turbulent period for Crimea. An influential pro-Russian separatist movement and tensions between Slavic Crimeans and returning Crimean Tatars threatened to plunge the peninsula into ethno-territorial conflict. Miraculously, Crimea weathered this tense period, and through painstaking negotiations between Simferopol and Kyiv an agreeable compromise was met wherein Crimea retained wide regional autonomy within Ukraine.[50] Kyiv similarly reached an agreement with Moscow over the fate of the Black Sea Fleet at Sevastopol, dividing the fleet between the two states and granting Russia a long-term lease of its facilities in the port city. By the late 1990s, Crimea's pro-Russian political movement had lost momentum and gone into a period of dormancy, while the Crimean Tatars had regained some footing in their homeland and were once again an integral component of Crimean society.

But bitterness among Russian Crimeans continued to simmer, and the 1954 transfer that had fated their exclusion from the Russian Federation became the subject of great resentment and vitriol. The events and deliberations surrounding the transfer underwent new scrutiny, and some began to argue that the transfer had been executed illegally according to Soviet law. The crux of this argument comes down to interpretations of Article 18 of the 1936 Soviet constitution, which states that changes to the territorial composition of union republics may not be made without the consent of the republic(s) being affected. Critics of the transfer claimed that a republic's consent to territorial changes could only be issued by its highest governing authority – its Supreme Council – and hence the transfer of Crimea was unconstitutional because it had been approved only by the Presidium of the Supreme Council of the RSFSR and not by the entire assembly.[51] Similar language in the constitutions of the RSFSR and UkrSSR has also been cited to bolster claims that the transfer was unconstitutional.[52] Others have argued that Sevastopol – which had been given the status of a federal city outside the administration of the Crimean *oblast* in 1948 – was never actually transferred to Ukraine in the first place and thus still rightfully belonged to Russia, even though the city had been administratively integrated into Ukraine along with the rest of Crimea since 1954.

These interpretations are selective and self-serving, besides ignoring the fact that Soviet constitutional norms were frequently flouted in the course of policy formation. That said, the apparent haste and procedural abnormalities associated with Crimea's transfer have rendered it illegitimate in the eyes of many pro-Russian Crimeans.[53] While the true extent of his role in the transfer has still not been determined, Khrushchev has been singled out and vilified for his assumed bias and apparent frivolity in "gifting" Crimea to his beloved Ukraine without considering the consequences – supposedly, according to some critics, in a drunken stupor.[54] Such spurious accusations ignore the fact that Khrushchev had not yet secured power in 1954 and was thus in no position to single-handedly affect such changes; they also ignores the practical considerations on which the transfer was ultimately based.

Nevertheless, the myth of illegitimacy surrounding the transfer of Crimea has persisted well into the twenty-first century. That myth took on a powerful new significance in 2014, sixty years after the transfer took place, when it was used to help justify Russia's illegal annexation of Crimea, which effectively nullified and reversed the transfer. Indeed, Russian President Vladimir Putin referred directly to elements of the myth surrounding the 1954 transfer in his speech marking Russia's reabsorption of Crimea on 18 March 2014:

> In 1954, a decision was made to transfer [the] Crimean [*oblast*] to Ukraine, along with Sevastopol, despite the fact that it was a federal city. This was the personal initiative of the Communist Party head Nikita Khrushchev. What stood behind this decision of his – a desire to win the support of the Ukrainian political establishment or to atone for the mass repressions of the 1930's in Ukraine – is for historians to figure out. What matters now is that this decision was made in clear violation of the constitutional norms that were in place even then. The decision was made behind the scenes. Naturally, in a totalitarian state nobody bothered to ask the citizens of Crimea and Sevastopol. They were faced with the fact. People, of course, wondered why all of a sudden Crimea became part of Ukraine.[55]

Crimea has remained under Russian occupation since 2014, although most of the international community continues to recognize Ukraine's sovereignty over the peninsula. Along with the war in the Donbas region of eastern Ukraine that also began in 2014, the Russian occupation of Crimea has precipitated a major social, political, economic, and cultural schism between Russia and Ukraine, marking an enormous shift in their centuries-long history of close interaction and interdependence. That this schism occurred due in part to lingering contentions over the decision to transfer Crimea in 1954 – a decision that was explicitly presented at the time as a means of *strengthening* the bond between Russia and Ukraine – is tremendously ironic.

With Crimea once again under Russia's *de facto* rule, the idea that the peninsula bears some inherent and natural Russian character has sadly become normalized. The Russian Federation partly overcame the restrictive fact of its physical detachment from Crimea with the completion of the Crimean Bridge in 2018, linking the peninsula to the Krasnodar Krai across the Strait of Kerch and integrating it directly into Russia's transportation infrastructure for the first time. But history has shown consistently that Crimea's physical, economic, and cultural linkages with Ukraine are not only substantial but also essential to the peninsula's prosperity and the well-being of its residents. Recent developments in Russian-occupied Crimea continue to bear this out. Crimea's crucial tourism industry has taken a tremendous blow since the annexation, as millions of Ukrainian citizens who once visited every summer now go elsewhere for their vacations. In 2015, Ukrainian activists initiated a grassroots commercial blockade of Crimea and destroyed key pieces of infrastructure delivering power to the peninsula, resulting in increased prices for commercial goods as well as frequent blackouts that have exacerbated Crimea's economic woes. But perhaps most critically, Ukrainian authorities blocked the flow of water from the Dnieper into the North Crimean Canal shortly after the annexation in 2014, cutting the peninsula off from over 85 per cent of its available water resources. As of 2021 Crimea is experiencing another severe drought that has again devastated the region's agriculture, leaving Russian officials scrambling to find new solutions to the same problem that Soviet engineers solved decades earlier when they first built the canal that delivered water from Ukraine. Thus, while the 2014 annexation sought to reverse Crimea's 1954 transfer to Ukraine based on ethnocultural and socio-political grievances, the consequences of the annexation serve as a poignant reminder of the socio-economic conditions and practical administrative considerations that motivated Soviet officials to place Crimea under Ukrainian administration in the first place.

NOTES

1 See Andrei Zorin, "Krym v istorii russkogo sazmosoznaniia," *Novoe Literaturnoe Obozrenie* 31 (1998): 123–43; Andrei Mal'gin, *Krymskyi uzel* (Simferopol: Novyi Krym, 2000); Vasily Andriiash, *Golos Kryma k Rossii (Pravda o Kryme)* (Simferopol: Tavriia, 2005).

2 See Serhii Plokhy, "The City of Glory: Sevastopol in Russian Historical Mythology," *Journal of Contemporary History* 35, no. 3 (2000): 369–83; Taras Kuzio, *Ukraine–Crimea–Russia: Triangle of Conflict* (Stuttgart: ibidem Verlag, 2007).
3 See Edward A. Allworth, ed., *The Tatars of Crimea: Return to the Homeland* (Durham: Duke University Press, 1998); Paul Robert Magocsi, *This Blessed Land: Crimea and the Crimean Tatars* (Toronto: University of Toronto Press, 2014); Natalia Belitser, *Kryms'ki Tatary iak korinnyi narod* (Kyiv: Natsional'ne gazetno-zhurnal'ne vidavnytsvo, 2017).
4 See Volodymyr I. Holovchenko, "Vkliuchennia Krymu do skladu Ukraïns'koï RSR: Mizhnarodno-politychni i ekonomichni pidstavy," *Aktual'ni Problemy Mizhnarodnykh Vidnosyn* 121, no. 1 (2014): 5–14; Dmytro Hordiienko, "Crimea Within or Outside the Ukrainian Borders," in *Nash Krym = Our Crimea = Bizim Qirimimiz*, vol. 4, ed. H. Papakin et al. (Kyiv: National Academy of Sciences of Ukraine, 2019), 5–49; Mikhail Smirnov, "Like a Sack of Potatoes: Who Transferred the Crimean Oblast to the Ukrainian SSR in 1952–54 and How It Was Done," *Russian Politics and Law* 53, no. 2 (2015): 32–46.
5 For other examples of the role of socio-economic *tselesoobraznost'* in the formation of Ukraine's modern borders, see Stephan Rindlisbacher's chapter in this volume.
6 The name of the autonomous republic was formally changed to the Crimean Autonomous Soviet Socialist Republic in 1936.
7 According to the first Soviet census in 1926, Russians in Crimea numbered 301,398 and Crimean Tatars only 179,094. "Vsesoiuznaia perepis' naseleniia 1926 goda. Natsional'nyi sostav naseleniia po regionam RSFSR," *Demoskop Weekly*, 2013, http://www.demoscope.ru/weekly/ssp/rus_nac_26.php?reg=788.
8 "Dekret Vserossiiskogo Tsentral'nogo Ispolnitel'nogo Komiteta i Soveta Narodnykh Komissarov," *Sobranie uzakonenii i rasporiazhenii Rabochego i Krest'ianskogo Pravitel'stva* no. 69, 22 November 1920, https://pravo.ru/store/interdoc/doc/464/18.10_Crimea.pdf.
9 The Syvash is a system of highly saline inland waterways connected to the Sea of Azov and bracketed by the Isthmus of Perekop to the west and the Arabatska Spit to the east. This vast network of salty lakes and pools forms the maritime barrier between Crimea and the mainland.
10 V.O. Borshevan, "Granitsa mezhdu Krymom i Ukrainoi," 2017, https://proza.ru/2017/01/01/1639.

11 Borshevan, "Granitsa mezhdu Krymom i Ukrainoi." See also Vasyl' Boiechko, Oksana Ganzha, and Borys Zakharchuk, *Kordony Ukraïny: Istorychna retrospektyva ta suchasnyi stan* (Kyiv: Osnovi, 1994), 88–9.
12 See Brian Glyn Williams, *The Crimean Tatars: From Soviet Genocide to Putin's Conquest* (London: Hurst, 2015), 91–8.
13 Brian Glyn Williams, "A Community Reimagined: The Role of 'Homeland' in the Forging of National Identity: The Case of the Crimean Tatars," *Journal of Muslim Minority Affairs* 17, no. 2 (1997): 225–53.
14 See Greta Uehling, *Beyond Memory: The Crimean Tatars' Deportation and Return* (New York: Palgrave Macmillan, 2004).
15 "Vsesoiuznaia perepis' naseleniia 1939 goda. Natsional'nyi sostav naseleniia po regionam Rossii," *Demoskop Weekly*, 2013, http://www.demoscope.ru/weekly/ssp/rus_nac_39.php?reg=68. Two other groups in Crimea that were sizable minorities in 1939 were also removed from the region just before or during the Second World War: ethnic Germans made up 4.6 per cent of Crimea's population in 1939 but were removed by order of Stalin shortly before the advancing German Army reached Crimea, while Jews represented 5.8 per cent of the regional population before their tragic eradication under Nazi occupation.
16 "Vsesoiuznaia perepis' naseleniia 1959 goda. Gorodskoe i sel'skoe naselenie oblastei SSSR (krome RSFSR) po polu i natsional'nosti." *Demoskop Weekly*, 2013, http://www.demoscope.ru/weekly/ssp/resp_nac_59.php?reg=9.
17 See Austin Charron, "Whose Is Crimea? Contested Sovereignty and Regional Identity," *Region* 5, no. 2 (2016): 225–56.
18 Boiechko, Ganzha, and Zakharchuk, *Kordony Ukraïny*, 89.
19 Ibid., 89–90.
20 M.M. Maksymenko, "Pereselennia v Krym sil's'koho naselennia z inshykh raioniv SSR (1944–1960 rr.)," *Ukraïns'kyi Istorychnyi Zhurnal* no. 11 (1990): 52–8.
21 Maksymenko, "Pereselennia v Krym," 55.
22 "Vsesoiuznaia perepis' naseleniia 1959 goda ..."
23 Boiechko, Ganzha, and Zakharchuk, *Kordony Ukraïny*, 90.
24 Ibid.
25 Ibid.
26 See Roman A. Cybriwsky, *Along Ukraine's River: A Social and Environmental History of the Dnipro* (Budapest: CEU Press, 2018).
27 Gwendolyn Sasse, *The Crimea Question: Identity, Transition, and Conflict* (Cambridge, MA: Harvard University Press, 2007), 116.
28 Ibid., 118–20.
29 Ibid., 120–1.

30 Krishnadev Calamur, "Crimea: A Gift to Ukraine Becomes a Political Flashpoint," NPR, 27 February 2014, https://www.npr.org/sections/parallels/2014/02/27/283481587/crimea-a-gift-to-ukraine-becomes-a-political-flash-point.
31 André de Nesnera, "Khrushchev's Son: Giving Crimea Back to Russia Not an Option," *Voice of America*, 6 March 2014, https://www.voanews.com/europe/khrushchevs-son-giving-crimea-back-russia-not-option.
32 Aleksei Adzhubei, "Kak Khrushchev Krym Ukraine otdal," *Novoe Vremia* no. 6 (1992): 20–1.
33 O.V. Volobueva and G.N. Iofis, "'Iskliuchitel'no zamechatel'nyi akt bratskoi pomoshchi.' Dokumenty i materialy o peredache Krymskoi oblasti iz sostava RSFSR v sostav USSR (ianvar'–fevral' 1954 g.)" *Istoricheskyi Arkhiv* no. 1 (1992): 39–54. This source compiles and reproduces several key archival documents related to the bureaucratic proceedings that led to and culminated in the transfer of Crimea.
34 Volobueva and G.N. Iofis, "'Iskliuchitel'no zamechatel'nyi,'" 41.
35 Ibid., 43–4.
36 Ibid., 44–5.
37 Ibid., 46.
38 Ibid., 48.
39 Ibid., 50.
40 Ibid., 49.
41 Ibid., 51.
42 Ibid., 52.
43 Ibid., 48.
44 Ibid., 52.
45 Ibid., 49.
46 Ibid., 50.
47 Ibid., 48.
48 Sasse, *The Crimea Question*, 110-11.
49 As one demonstration of this reliance, a 2013 report indicated that the North Crimean Canal accounted for 86.65 per cent of Crimea's available water resources. "Doklad o sostoianii i okhrane okruzhaiushchei sredi Respubliki Krym v 2013 godu," *Reskomprirody Kryma* (2013): 17, https://meco.rk.gov.ru/rus/file/doklad_eco_2013.pdf.
50 See Sasse, *The Crimea Question*.
51 A.V. Fedorov, *Pravovoi status Kryma. Pravovoi status Sevastopolia* (Moscow: Izdatel'stvo Moskovskogo Universiteta, 1999).
52 Edward Ozhiganov, "The Crimean Republic: Rivalries for Control," in *Managing Conflict in the Former Soviet Union*, ed. Alexei Arbatov, Abram

Chayes, Antonia Handler Chayes, and Lara Olson (Cambridge, MA: MIT Press, 1997): 83–135.
53 Sasse, *The Crimea Question*, 107–12.
54 Sergei Grabovsky, "Trezvye resheniia 'p'ianogo Nikity': Krymskoe izmerenie," *Krym. Realii*, 7 January 2017, https://ru.krymr.com/a/28204358.html.
55 "Address by President of the Russian Federation," 18 March 2014, http://en.kremlin.ru/events/president/news/20603.

PART THREE

Delineating Ukraine's Western Border

9

The Formation of the Polish-Ukrainian Border in Volhynia, 1918–21

Serhii Hladyshuk

Over the centuries, Ukraine's western border has been revised numerous times. Volhynia has been the region of today's Ukraine possibly most affected by these changes: it has switched state affiliation more often than any other territory with an ethnic Ukrainian majority. In medieval times, it had been a constituent territory of Kyivan Rus; then it became part of the Grand Duchy of Lithuania after the former's political fragmentation. After the Union of Lublin in 1569, Volhynia, along with neighbouring Eastern Galicia, which also had a large Ukrainian population, was absorbed into the Polish-Lithuanian Commonwealth, or *Rzeczpospolita*. Then after the three partitions of Poland in the late eighteenth century, Volhynia's inhabitants found themselves under the rule of the Russian Empire, unlike Eastern Galicia, which had become part of the Habsburg Monarchy. These various imperial legacies would have a strong impact on the political, social, and economic trajectories of both "Ukrainian" territories.

The newly formed Volhynia province consisted of twelve counties. In economic terms, agrarian Volhynia was one of the least developed Ukrainian provinces in the Russian Empire. Two thirds of the inhabitants were Orthodox Ukrainian, and most of them were illiterate: Ukrainian schools did not begin to appear until the First World War. A rigid social hierarchy had locked in place a largely static, ethnically based class structure: Ukrainian peasants, Polish landowners, and a Russian or Jewish intelligentsia. Unlike Eastern Galicia, which became a cradle of the Ukrainian national movement, the vast majority of Ukrainians in Volhynia had no firm national identity.[1] The Ukrainian national movement, understood as a movement for political rights within a Ukrainian state, was at a rudimentary stage in Volhynia. To explain the situation there, the three-stage model of nationalist mobilization as proposed by the Czech historian Miroslav Hroch is especially useful. According to Hroch, during the initial Stage A ("the period of scholarly interest"), the local intelligentsia gather folklore and use it to create a national language and culture; during Stage B ("the period of patriotic agitation"), institutions are established that promote the national idea and spread it among the population; during Stage C ("the rise of a mass national movement"), national political parties appear and the national movement becomes a popular one, which enables its leaders to demand political autonomy or national independence.[2] This A-B-C schema has enjoyed great popularity among historians of nationalism in the Habsburg, Russian, and Soviet empires. Applying it to the nineteenth-century Russian Empire, Andreas Kappeler, for instance, argued that by the beginning of the twentieth century the Ukrainian national movement had only entered Stage B.[3] At the imperial western frontiers, national mobilization lagged even farther behind, especially in Volhynia, given its provincial status, distance from the centres of political life, low level of literacy, and dearth of a Ukrainian intelligentsia who could champion and channel a national movement. In addition to all this, the Russian Orthodox Church had done much to Russify the region, gradually turning it into a hotbed of the empire's radical monarchist movement.[4]

During the First World War and the revolutionary years 1917–21, Volhynia changed hands frequently as different governments competed for control. The newly restored Poland sought to regain its lost eastern borderlands, or *kresy*, and the Ukrainian government in Kyiv wished to gather all ethnic Ukrainian lands within a single state. Meanwhile, the Soviet government in Moscow saw Volhynia as a possible springboard for spreading the revolution to Western Europe; when that project failed, it continued to interfere in the region's politics in the hope of weakening the rival Polish government. In accordance with the 1921 Treaty of Riga between Soviet Ukraine and Poland, however, western and central Volhynia were ceded to Poland, where they formed the Volhynia voivodeship (*województwo wołyńskie*). Soviet Ukraine retained eastern Volhynia.[5]

Volhynia/Wołyń remains a somewhat understudied region in the historiography of interwar Eastern Europe.[6] Ukrainian scholars tend to discuss its border delineation in the context of the revolutionary events of 1917–21, paying attention to particular aspects of Volhynia's history; or they treat it as one aspect of broader regional studies (*kraieznavstvo*).[7] Similarly, Polish researchers focus mainly on Eastern Galicia between 1918 and 1923, largely ignoring the Polish-Ukrainian border delimitation in Volhynia.[8] The region's history has tended to remain the preserve of military historians and of those studying the formation of the Polish administrative apparatus.[9]

Similarly, this region remains largely overlooked by Western historians, who have tended to concentrate on developments in Eastern Galicia.[10] Timothy Snyder and Cornelia Schenke are among the few scholars who have examined the Volhynia/Wołyń issue. Schenke's *Nationalstaat und nationale Frage. Polen und die Ukrainer in Wolhynien* (2004) is a comprehensive study of Ukrainian-Polish relations in the interwar period.[11] In his famous study *The Reconstruction of Nations: Poland, Ukraine, Lithuania, Belarus, 1569–1999*, Snyder sets out to reconstruct the modern national projects, including those in Volhynia and Eastern Galicia between 1914 and 1939.[12] In his other work, he focuses on the "Volhynia experiment" implemented under *wojewoda* Henryk Józewski between 1928 and 1938.[13] That program's objective was to create a tolerant multinational society by promoting ethnic, linguistic, and religious coexistence among the region's inhabitants. Unlike the communists, who wished to build a classless society, or the nationalists, who strove for an ethnically pure nation, Józewski envisaged a multicultural community in which ethnic, linguistic, and religious differences would be tolerated and even promoted. The interwar Polish-Ukrainian rapprochement in Volhynia was viewed as a prerequisite for the formation of this new multicultural society.[14] Unlike eastern Galicia, where the interwar decades were marked by intensifying inter-ethnic confrontation, ethnically diverse Volhynia, with its underdeveloped political culture and weak national movements, was seen by the Polish authorities as a suitable testing ground for such experiments. By examining local responses to the region's incorporation into Poland, the present chapter seeks to demonstrate how the foundations for Polish-Ukrainian dialogue and mutual understanding were established between 1918 and 1921. At the same time, the failure of the "Volhynia experiment," accompanied by the fraying of the Polish-Ukrainian relationship in the late 1930s, contributed to the ethnic cleansing from which the region suffered during the Second World War.

This chapter also examines the delineation of the Polish-Ukrainian border in Volhynia/Wołyń, starting with the end of the First World War and the withdrawal of the Central Powers in late 1918, through the formation of the Wołyń Voivodeship, and concluding with the signing of the Treaty of Riga in the spring of 1921. Particular attention is paid to examining the reasons for, and the process of, forging a compromise between the local Ukrainian population and the local Polish authorities and civic organizations. As the region was being acceded to Poland, the Polish authorities sought opportunities for intercultural dialogue within the multinational population of Wołyń that were practically impossible to find in neighbouring Eastern Galicia, where Polish-Ukrainian relations grew ever more tense throughout the same period.

This chapter begins by examining the territorial changes that took place during the First World War in Volhynia, as well as the evolution of Polish-Ukrainian relations in 1917–18. It then deals with the occupation of Volhynia by the Polish army (*Wojsko Polskie*) in 1918–19 and the establishment of a Polish administration in the region. It then explores the drawing of the Polish-Ukrainian border in 1920–21. The final section scrutinizes local perceptions of Volhynia's final accession to Poland as outlined by the Treaty of Riga.

Note that toward the end of the First World War, in Polish public parlance, the word "Ukraine" almost always referred solely to those Ukrainian lands lying within Poland's historical borders before the first partition in 1772 – that is, all of Right-Bank Ukraine, including Kyiv. However, "Ukraine" was occasionally used to define, along with Volhynia and Podolia, the Kyiv province, which Poland had lost during its second partition in 1793.[15] By contrast, a majority of Ukrainian politicians conceived of Ukraine as existing on both sides of the Dnieper River. This included the whole of the former Russian Empire's Volhynia *gubernia*, which was to join the future Ukrainian state. In this chapter, by Volhynia I mean first and foremost the western and central counties of the Volhynia *gubernia*, namely Volodymyr-Volhynsky, Dubno, Kovel, Kremenets, Lutsk, Ostrih, and Rivne counties. During 1918–21 these administrative areas gradually came under the control of the Polish army and civil administration, thus forming the Polish-Ukrainian and, after 1921, Polish-Soviet border that would remain in place until 1939.

VOLHYNIA/WOŁYŃ DURING THE FIRST WORLD WAR

During the First World War, Volhynia became a battlefield for the Austro-Hungarian and Russian imperial armies. Until the end of 1916, the region's eastern counties, centred around Lutsk, were controlled by Russian troops, while the western part of Volhynia, which included the cities of Kovel and Volodymyr-Volhynsky, remained under the authority of the Dual Monarchy.[16] From the autumn of 1916, the front line in Volhynia was fixed along the Stokhid River. It would remain relatively unchanged until February 1918.[17]

In August 1914, at the initiative of the Legion of Ukrainian Sich Riflemen – a Ukrainian military formation established within the Austro-Hungarian army and consisting mainly of Galicians – Volhynia's western counties witnessed the inception of the Ukrainian national movement, during which schools were opened across the region that conducted cultural and educational work. In 1915–17, Hnat Martynets, an educator and public figure from Galicia, served as a city commander (*mis'kyi komendant*) for Volodymyr-Volhynsky.[18] Another local activist, Marko Lutskevych, championed cultural and educational activities in Kovel; he emphasized the need to Ukrainianize the local Orthodox Church and expand the network of Ukrainian schools as a counterweight to Polish educational initiatives.[19] Meanwhile, relations between Volhynia and the Ukrainian authorities in Kyiv started to crystallize. In 1917, Samiilo Pidhirsky, a prominent regional public figure, was elected to the Ukrainian Central Rada (Council), a representative body of the Ukrainian people formed in Kyiv in March 1917. By the end of the First World War, local representatives of the Ukrainian intelligentsia had begun to establish political connections with Eastern Galicia and Dnieper Ukraine; they were also beginning to form their own political agenda regarding the region's future.

During the war, the local Polish elites intensified their political activities in the region. Although a minority – only some 9 per cent of the population – Poles were still the dominant social class, and local Polish landowners sought to maintain that dominance by preparing the ground for a future Polish regime in the region. This took the form of public committees. Within those committees, Tadeusz Krzyżanowski and Tadeusz Dworakowski advocated for Polish educational initiatives.[20] At the same time, in late 1917 and early 1918, Bolshevik activists appeared in Volhynia with the aim of destabilizing the political situation there. In November 1917, after the October Revolution in Petrograd and their early successes in the other Ukrainian lands, the Bolsheviks proclaimed Soviet power in Lutsk, though they lacked grassroots support.[21] Over the following months, sporadic bands of so-called people's (*narodni*) Bolsheviks were formed, occupying themselves mainly by plundering the estates of Polish landowners.[22] Not until the Polish-Soviet War of 1920 did the Bolsheviks begin properly organizing themselves as a political force in the region. It was at this time that the Bolshevik leadership in Moscow attempted to promote the idea of exporting the revolution to Poland through Volhynia, and from Poland to Western Europe.

Grounds for the future territorial demarcation of Volhynia/Wołyń were laid in Kyiv and Warsaw. Over the course of 1917, Polish-Ukrainian relations evolved from attempted cooperation to outright confrontation. In March 1917 a congress of Polish civic organizations was held in Kyiv representing Polish communities in that city as well as the provinces of Kyiv, Volhynia, and Kamianets-Podilsky. During that congress, the Polish Executive Committee of the Association of Polish Organizations was formed, later renamed the Polish Executive Committee on the Rus (*Polski Komitet Wykonawczy na Rusi*).[23] Initially, the committee was supportive of Ukrainian state-building initiatives, which commenced in the spring of that year. In particular, on 30 March 1917, the committee addressed the Central Rada with a declaration urging Ukrainians and Poles to live in peace and work together for the common good.[24] Polish representatives were later brought into the Central Rada, which established a Secretariat of Polish Affairs. Mieczysław Mickiewicz, a Ukrainian politician and lawyer of Polish descent, was appointed Secretary General of Polish Affairs.[25] Overall, Poles supported the Ukrainians' efforts to achieve national self-determination, recognizing that within a Ukrainian state – be it independent or autonomous within a federated Russia – they would have greater influence on political and economic life than they would in a multinational but still centralized Russian state.[26]

The Central Rada was dominated by socialist-leaning parties that called stridently for social and economic justice. A key initiative of the new Ukrainian authorities was radical agrarian reform; they envisaged the breaking up of large landed estates and the redistribution of land among the peasantry.[27] Toward the end of 1917, spurred by the prospect of acquiring their own smallholdings, peasant mobs began spontaneously attacking estates in Right-Bank Ukraine, most of which were owned by Poles. Left unprotected by the authorities in Kyiv, the majority of Poles began to re-evaluate their political allegiances and their attitudes toward Ukrainian independence.

Territorial contestations further overshadowed Polish-Ukrainian relations. In early 1918, a delegation from the newly proclaimed Ukrainian People's Republic (UNR) travelled to Brest-Litovsk to conduct separate peace negotiations with Germany and Austria-Hungary. Under the resultant Treaty of Brest-Litovsk, signed on 9 February 1918, the Central Powers were to provide the UNR with military support against the Bolsheviks. In the years to come, the UNR's political development would largely be defined by German and Austro-Hungarian occupation of the Ukrainian lands. In addition, the Central Powers sided with the Ukrainian delegation regarding sovereignty over the Kholm/Chełm and Pidliashshia/Podlasie region. It was during the Brest-Litovsk negotiations that the Volhynia province was recognized as part of the UNR – later, the Ukrainian State under the rule of Pavlo Skoropadsky. It is also worth noting that at first, the Poles only opposed the Kholm/Chełm region's accession to the UNR, while accepting the UNR's acquisition of those territories to the east of the Bug River.[28] As of early 1918, the question of Volhynia/Wołyń's state affiliation had not yet been raised during Polish-Ukrainian discussions. This was to change, however, following Poland's declaration of independence in November that year, which led to intensified hostilities between Poles and Ukrainians in the region.

Not until late 1918 did Poland's eastern borders begin to take shape. Although they yearned for it, most political factions in Warsaw understood that it would be impossible to resurrect Poland's 1772 borders: the Poles simply lacked the military capability to achieve such an ambition, and international support for it was inadequate. Conversely, there existed a consensus that the newly restored Poland should not be restricted to its ethnographically defined homelands. Poland's vision of its eastern border was outlined in a speech given by Roman Dmowski, the leader of the right-wing National Democracy movement, at the Paris Peace Conference in January 1919. In that speech, Dmowski described Eastern Galicia, western Volhynia (including Volodymyr-Volhynsky, Kovel, and Lutsk counties), western and central Polesie, Wilno/Vilnius, and parts of the Minsk province as historical Polish territories, but not Podolia and the Kyiv region, which had also been part of Poland before the partitions.[29]

No agreement on Poland's eastern borders was reached at Paris. The Polish Foreign Minister, Leon Wasilewski, stated there that the Chief of State (*naczelnik państwa*), Józef Piłsudski, generally agreed to the eastern line proposed by Dmowski, while also emphasizing that "since our borders go along the rivers, we should make sure that both of their shores belong to Poland."[30] At that time, Piłsudski maintained that "in the east, we can only rely on ourselves, our own forces. Gradually we need to reach beyond the borders of the Kingdom of Poland – towards Wołyń and Polesia, and then to Wilno/Vilnius."[31] It is worth mentioning at this point that the easternmost border of the Kingdom of Poland, as of 1569, had been the Lublin Voivodeship, bordering on Volhynia to the east. It was beyond these medieval boundaries that the Polish army began to encroach as early as November 1918, after the gradual retreat of the German and Habsburg troops. Indeed, Piłsudski was right: the delineation of the Polish-Ukrainian border in Volhynia/Wołyń would not be settled through diplomatic negotiations. Instead, it would be the front line laid down during Poland's subsequent wars with the UNR and Soviet Union that laid the real foundations for the regional border demarcation.

THE OCCUPATION OF VOLHYNIA/WOŁYŃ
BY THE POLISH ARMY IN 1918–19

At the end of the First World War, the eastern border of the newly restored Poland ran through the Lublin and Białystok districts; the regions of Kholm/Chełm, Volhynia/Wołyń, Polissia/Polesie, and Podolia/Podole were still controlled by the Central Powers. In late November 1918, with little difficulty, the Polish army occupied the Kholm/Chełm region; from there, it continued its offensive. Major Wladyslaw Boncz-Uzdowski was assigned to lead Polish forces into Volhynia and occupy its western districts. Volodymyr-Volhynsky quickly fell, allowing those forces to advance farther east.[32] These military operations took place without Poland having declared war against the UNR, which on 20 November 1917, in the Third Universal of the Central Rada, had declared its jurisdiction over the now Polish-occupied territories.[33] After Poland occupied the western parts of Volhynia/Wołyń, activists from the Piłsudski camp were sent to the region with the aim of promoting Volhynia's voluntary accession to Poland. It would lobby for the multi-ethnic population's consent by engaging with representatives of the Ukrainian, Jewish, German, and Czech minorities.

The Society of Borderland Guards (*Towarzystwo Straży Kresowej*), founded in Lublin in early 1918, became the main vehicle for these efforts. This non-governmental organization worked closely with Polish military intelligence to implement Piłsudski's federative conception for the eastern borderlands.[34] Proponents of his project formulated ideas about how to divide the Romanov empire into independent Belarusian, Lithuanian, and Ukrainian states, which would later join Poland in a loose federation.[35] Following this strategy, Warsaw initially sought to unite the Kholm/Chełm and Pidliashshia/Podlasie regions with Poland, while maintaining formal procedures for expressing the will of the local population. This same approach would also be tested in Volhynia. Based on the federalist idea, and in response to the Bolsheviks' occupation of large swathes of the former Russian Empire, a new concept, "Prometheism," quickly gained traction in Polish politics. Proponents of Prometheism, many of whom belonged to Piłsudski's governing circle, advocated lending support to the "enslaved peoples" of Soviet Russia (including Ukrainians) in their state-building initiatives. This would ultimately weaken Soviet power and help Poland gain supremacy in the region.[36]

At the end of 1918, *Towarzystwo Straży Kresowej* was established in Volhynia/Wołyń under the leadership of a local activist, Henryk Orłowski, although many local representatives had previously participated in its covert activities while the territory was still controlled by the UNR. As for Volhynia/Wołyn itself, the society pursued the following objectives: "In contacts with local population to avoid mentioning the idea of an independent Ukraine. In discussions with the intelligentsia, to emphasize Poland's interest in the emergence of an independent Ukraine. In the matter of Ukraine's independence, it is important to distinguish between Halych-Volhynia Rus and the Kyivan Rus. Kyiv should become the center of the Ukrainian state."[37] As seen from these instructions, the Polish authorities supported an independent Dnieper Ukraine with Kyiv as its capital but did not envisage Volhynia/Wołyń as one of its constituent provinces. The mention of Kyivan Rus as its historical predecessor was significant, for this particular medieval polity, even at its greatest territorial extent, had not included Volhynia/Wołyń, that had in fact been part of the Halych-Volhynia principality, later joining the Grand Duchy of Lithuania and Polish-Lithuanian Commonwealth.

During this period, in light of the ongoing military conflict, the activities of the Towarzystwo Straży Kresowej remained largely clandestine. Nevertheless, its members continued working to develop a positive image of Poland and prepare the ground for a Polish administration in the region. Activities like these received approval from representatives of the Polish Army in early January 1919, during talks with the leadership of the organization, represented at the time by Polish activist Zdzisław Lechnicki.[38]

Towarzystwo Straży Kresowej adopted the well-known Polish slogan "The free with the free; equals with equals" (*Wolni z wolnymi, równi z równymi*). This slogan dated back to the Union of Lublin in 1569 and had been used by nineteenth-century Polish insurgents attempting to revive the independence of *Rzeczpospolita* in their struggle against the Russian Empire. During the January (1830–31) and November (1863–64) risings, Poles had attempted to convince the local population of Right-Bank Ukraine, especially Ukrainians, to join their revolutionary struggle. Consequently, *Towarzystwo Straży Kresowej* also strove to establish cooperation, not only with Ukrainians but also with the German, Russian, and Czech minorities that made up a large portion of Volhynia/Wołyń's population.[39] The society planned to establish people's councils (*ludowe*) in each county that would include representatives of all these national and social groups. Such councils were to act as democratically as possible, shaping a positive image of Poland in the eyes of the local populace and promoting the region's annexation by Poland.

However, not all Poles supported the society's outlook, nor did they its activities in the region. More radical elements among the Polish public rejected this reconciliatory strategy, electing instead to throw their weight behind Dmowski and the National Democrats. Dmowski called for all territories in which Poles were an ethnic majority or in which they enjoyed economic and cultural domination to be annexed to Poland.[40] Such proposals held a particular appeal for Volhynia/Wołyń Polish landowners and the region's urban intelligentsia. Both social segments believed that the region's Poles should promote national solidarity and defend Polish interests exclusively, without taking other national groups into account. Instead of people's *(ludowe)*, they proposed national *(narodowe)* councils, which were to be made up of Poles exclusively.[41] These national councils would provide support to the Polish army in Volhynia/Wołyń and demand a favourable border for Poland, disregarding the interests of the non-Polish population. Representatives of this nationally exclusive strategy would lay the foundation for the Polish civil administration in Wołyń.

From 19 February 1919, Wołyń and other occupied territories began to be administered by the Civil Administration of Eastern Lands (*Zarząd Cywilny Ziem Wschodnich*).[42] On 22 April 1919, during a speech in Wilno/Vilnius, Piłsudski outlined the new administration's principal tasks in governing the eastern territories. These included "free elections to local self-governing bodies; assistance to all who need it; freedom of religion; and equality of all nationalities living in the region."[43] This speech served as a blueprint for the agenda of the new Commissioner General of the Eastern Land, Jerzy Osmołowski.[44]

At the beginning of 1919, after all German and Austro-Hungarian troops had finally left the region, the Polish army launched another offensive against the UNR. Volhynia, especially its eastern part, descended into chaos, with violence becoming the norm. *Towarzystwo Straży Kresowej* recorded the activities of the "people's Bolsheviks" – local gangs who looted the estates of Polish landowners and who most likely had no organizational link with the Bolsheviks. Apart from the Polish landed nobility, Jews suffered enormously in early 1919 during these campaigns of plunder and pogroms. Jews were some 10 per cent of Volhynia's population, and they lived mostly in the cities. Jews were often accused of supporting the Bolsheviks and serving as their agents. However, as noted by Henry Abramson, only a very small number of Bolsheviks were of Jewish origin, and even fewer Jews belonged to the Bolshevik Party.[45] Territorially, most Jewish pogroms (80 per cent of the 1,300 documented) occurred in the regions of Kyiv, Podolia, and Volhynia, where 80 per cent of Ukraine's total Jewish population lived. The pogroms involved all regular and irregular military formations active in this area, although the largest number of pogroms (40 per cent of those recorded) were linked to the UNR army headed by Petliura.[46] Among that army's allies were numerous local *otamans* (peasant leaders), who were often driven by personal gain. The biggest Jewish pogrom of that time took place in February 1919 in Proskuriv in neighbouring Podolia province, organized by the *otaman* Ivan Semesenko.[47] "The Joint" (American Jewish Joint Distribution Committee) recorded similar pogroms, although much smaller in scale, in eastern Volhynia at the turn of 1918–19. For instance, the Jewish pogrom in Novohrad-Volhynsky in May 1919 was organized by the *otamans* Sokolovsky, who were in control of the territory around Korets.[48]

At this point, the Polish-Ukrainian border was being determined by the war's front line, extending through Kovel, Volodymyr-Volhynsky, Poritsk, and Sokal, as well as by the displacement of local populations on both sides.[49] The UNR army, led by its Chief *Otaman* (Supreme Commander) Symon Petliura, was fighting on several fronts. To the east, the Soviet Red Army, in an effort to weaken the new government in Kyiv, attacked Ukrainian forces in the Polesie region, pushing them back to the Sarny-Korosten-Kovel line. Taking advantage of the UNR's escalating conflict with the Bolsheviks, the Poles launched a general offensive in the northern sector of the Polish-Ukrainian front.[50]

After taking Kovel, Polish troops advanced farther east, crossing the Stokhid River in March 1919 and threatening the city of Lutsk. To reinforce the Polish advance, the army of General Józef Haller was transferred from France in May, forming a special strike force under the command of General Aleksander Karnicki. Its orders were to take Lutsk and defeat the UNR army in the region. Sightings of the Polish army near Lutsk's city walls caused the local UNR garrison to panic. On 16 May 1919, the Polish army entered the city, encountering almost no resistance. At the behest of the local *otaman*, Oleksandr Osetsky, the Ukrainian troops capitulated; the Poles disarmed them and interned them in camps. On 18 May, the triumphant Polish army advanced on the River Styr to the north.[51]

In the aftermath of these military defeats, a special envoy of the UNR government, Boris Kurdynovsky, arrived in Warsaw to hold negotiations with the Polish Foreign Minister, Ignacy Paderewski, regarding a possible resolution to the conflict. Consequently, on 24 May 1919, a political agreement was signed between the two parties according to which Eastern Galicia and part of Volhynia up to the Styr would remain under Polish control. In addition, the Ukrainians pledged to coordinate their foreign policy with Warsaw. Poland reciprocated by recognizing Ukraine's independence.[52] The treaty, though it was rejected by Kyiv two days later, marked the first official attempt to outline the Polish-Ukrainian border in Volhynia in mid-1919.

Meanwhile, the UNR continued its fight against the Bolsheviks. Toward the end of May, Petliura launched a fresh offensive against the Red Army from the districts of Dubno and Kremenets', and Ukrainian troops succeeded in recapturing much of southeastern Ukraine. However, the Polish army quickly moved into the territories vacated by the UNR army, intervening in the military conflict against the Bolsheviks.[53] By August, Polish troops had occupied Dubno, Kremenets', Rivne, and Sarny. These military achievements were followed soon after by an administrative reorganization. On 7 June 1919, within the Civic Administration of the Eastern Lands, the Wołyń District Administration (*Zarząd Powiatów Wołyńskich*) was established, headquartered in Kovel and with authority over the Volodymyr, Kovel, and Lutsk counties of the former Volhynia province.[54] As early as 9 September, the Wołyń District Administration was transformed into the Wołyń district (*okręg wołyński*), incorporating the following counties of the former Volhynia province: Volodymyr, Kovel, Lutsk, Dubno, Rivne, Kremenetsky, Ostrih, Saslavsk, and Zviahel.[55]

From October 1919, a UNR diplomatic mission, headed by the Ukrainian Foreign Minister, Andrii Livytsky, was established in Warsaw.[56] In tandem with this, a military delegation under General Viktor Zelinsky, whose main task was to organize the Ukrainian troops in Poland and prepare a joint Polish-Ukrainian offensive in Ukraine against the Bolsheviks, took up residence in the Polish capital.[57] However, in return for military assistance, Warsaw demanded significant territorial concessions. Initially, the Ukrainians agreed to the temporary inclusion of only the Kholm/Chełm and Pidliashshia/Podlasie regions within Poland. However, mounting military setbacks forced them to concede to a demarcation line farther to the east along the Zbruch River. Thus, the UNR lost not only Eastern Galicia but also western and central Volhynia/Wołyń.

By the autumn of 1919, the Ukrainian state was fighting a war on several fronts and suffering defeat at the hands of the Polish Army, the Bolsheviks, and Anton Denikin's White Volunteers. This was compounded by an outbreak of typhus that further weakened the UNR army, which paid the price in territorial losses. The Ukrainian government now controlled only part of the southwestern Podolia region, and even that was proving difficult to hold. In mid-November, Petliura requested that the Polish military leadership take partial control of Podolia; this would allow the UNR's forces to regroup and launch a counteroffensive against the Red and White armies. This new operation, known as the First Winter Campaign, was aimed at retaining limited control over the Ukrainian territories. While in Warsaw, Petliura sought to negotiate with Piłsudski on future Polish-Ukrainian military cooperation. The occupation of Podolia by the Polish army in late 1919 saw further revision of the Polish-Ukrainian border and the formation of a new administrative unit on the territories of Wołyń and Podole.

DELINEATING THE POLISH-UKRAINIAN BORDER IN 1920–21

Following an order from Piłsudski, issued on 17 January 1920, a new political and administrative unit, headed by Antoni Minkiewicz, was established on the territories of Wołyń and Podole: the Civilian Authority of the Lands of Wołyń and the Podole Front.[58] In addition to the Wołyń district, the Civilian Authority's jurisdiction extended to the four districts of Podole: Starokonstiantyniv, Proskuriv, Kamianets, and Ushytsia. Stanisław Stempowski, the Political Secretary of the new administration, suggested that those Podolian counties would, in future, be expected to serve as the basis of a Podolia Voivodeship (*województwo podolskie*).[59] These newly acquired lands were treated as genuinely Polish territories. During their meetings with military leaders, local officials stated that "we are not on occupied lands, but on Polish lands, local people of other nationalities and religious denominations are Polish citizens and should be treated accordingly."[60] It is worth noting that in the official documentation, the head of the Wołyń district, Stefan Smólski, was also referred to as voivode (*wojewoda*).

On 1 March 1920, a letter from the head of the political section of the Wołyń front was published in Równe, outlining the Polish army's policy concerning the territory of Wołyń:

> Currently, *Rzeczpospolita* is trying to support the Ukrainian national movement in its desire to form an independent Ukraine ... Based on the verified sources, we can say that Wołyń will remain a part of Poland, but the issue of the eastern border has not yet been resolved ... *Otaman* Petliura, who is in Warsaw at the moment, has agreed to the incorporation of the disputed territories of Eastern Galicia and Wołyń into Poland ... In all disputes between Ukrainians and Russians, we should support the former. On the territories occupied by Polish troops, no manifestations of the Ukrainian national character should be allowed, yet we should treat the Ukrainian population favorably, promoting their economic development and campaigning for an independent Ukraine, as well as Polish-Ukrainian cooperation against Russia.[61]

As the above-cited source illustrates, by the spring of 1920, both the regional Polish administrative apparatus and the Polish military leadership had started to regard western Volhynia as Polish territory.

Petliura, who had been in Warsaw since December 1919 and had taken part in the Polish-Ukrainian negotiations on a future agreement, was well aware that in order to continue the war against the Bolsheviks the UNR would have to concede Volhynia and Eastern Galicia to the Poles. These territorial concessions were captured in the terms of the Polish-Ukrainian Alliance signed in Warsaw on 21 April 1920. In exchange for territorial gains, the Polish authorities pledged their military support to the UNR army.

In the wake of these agreements, the Polish government began the region's accession process. Based on orders issued by the Chief of State on 29 March 1920, from 10 June 1920 the following counties were withdrawn from the control of the Civilian Authority of the Lands of Wołyń and the Podole Front: Volodymyr, Kovel, Lutsk, Dubno, and Rivne counties, as well as part of Ostrih county, which lay within the Rivne district (*powiat*), and northwestern Kremenets county. Administration of these counties was transferred to the Council of Ministers of Poland.[62]

The Polish-Ukrainian union drew various reactions among Ukrainians and Poles. The local Ukrainian population remained ambiguous about the shifting border and the transfer of part of Volhynia to the Polish state. The *Towarzystwo Straży Kresowej*'s instructor in Dubno county, Wacław Sąchocki, observed that Petliura's manifesto to the Ukrainian people regarding the Polish-Ukrainian Alliance "was generally welcomed with great joy and enthusiasm. However, some people remained dissatisfied. Special agitators are spreading rumors in the villages that *Otaman* Petliura is the son of the former Austrian Emperor and wants to unite with Poles to establish serfdom in Ukraine."[63] While many in Ukraine harshly criticized the territorial concessions that Petliura had made in Warsaw, among Poland's left- and right-wing circles, the Piłsudski-Petliura Alliance was favourably received.

The Polish-Ukrainian alliance also gained much support from the government of Prime Minister Leopold Skulski and the leaders of Socialist opposition. At the beginning of June 1920, the latter proposed a conference in Warsaw to which would be invited Ukrainian representatives from the territories recently ceded to Poland. On 6 June 1920, invitations, signed by the Polish ambassadors Zygmund Dreszer, Irena Kosmowska, and Jan Dębski, were sent out.[64] The conference took place on 9 June. Sixteen Ukrainian delegates were present representing Chełm, Podlachia, western Polesia, and western Volhynia (represented by Kowel, Łuck, and Włodzimierz counties). The delegation from Volhynia was headed by a local activist from

Kovel, Marko Lutskevych. Lutskevych, together with another activist from Chełm, Antin Vasynchuk, led the Ukrainian delegation. The Polish side was represented by 185 delegates representing five political clubs. All those attending the conference received a bilingual text of the memorandum, which was to form the basis of the discussion.[65] The introduction stated that "due to political circumstances, a part of the Ukrainian population finds itself within Poland's borders and, given such state of affairs, expresses its readiness to cooperate loyally towards the improvement of social life within the *Rzeczpospolita*."[66]

This was followed by a list of the general terms that were to form the basis for Polish-Ukrainian cooperation, equality, and mutual respect:

> The Ukrainian population, equal to the Polish population, should enjoy all civil rights, such as freedom of speech, press, assembly, and so on. Previous initiatives by the local administration aimed to impede the Ukrainian movement and encourage pro-Moscow sentiment should be stopped immediately. All those who had participated in the Polish–Ukrainian war are to receive amnesty. On those territories populated by Ukrainians, the military occupation authorities must be abolished. The issue of free choice of state affiliation must be settled once and for all.[67]

The Polish political crisis of June 1920, which brought about the resignation of the Skulski government, interrupted the conference, and its postulates were never put into practice.

THE POSITION OF THE LOCAL POPULATION AND THE FINAL DEMARCATION OF THE BORDER IN VOLHYNIA

The Polish population of Volhynia/Wołyń treated the formation of the new administration as proof of the region's final inclusion within Poland.[68] By 18 June 1920, in Włodzimierz/Volodymyr-Volhynsky, a committee for the inclusion of Volhynia/Wołyń into Poland, headed by the local mayor Franciszek Twerd, had been formed. Despite its pro-Polish leanings, the committee included representatives from other national communities: Ukrainians were represented by Ia. Berezovsky, Jews by B. Strasberg, and the Polish population by Rapczewski. There was also a separate representative from the Orthodox clergy, Demian Gershtanskyi. The committee marked its formation by issuing an appeal stating that: "By order of the Chief of the Polish Forces, the administration of Wołyń was transferred to the Government of *Rzeczpospolita*. We welcome the fact of Wołyń's final unification with Poland." Echoing the slogans of the *Towarzystwo Straży Kresowej*, its members also maintained that the peoples of Wołyń had joined Poland through collective consent – "the free with the free; equals with equals"[69] – in this way highlighting their desire to seek compromise among the representatives of each nationality.

Even so, the inclusion of the region within the Polish state would depend heavily on outcome of the fighting. On 7 May 1920, a Polish-Ukrainian army captured Kyiv. However, the situation changed dramatically the following month: the Bolsheviks launched a counter-offensive that saw the Red Army gradually take over Volhynia/Wołyń. The Polish administration of Wołyń now ceased operations and was evacuated west to the central provinces of Poland. Then on 3 July 1920, the Poles were driven out of Lutsk and that city came under the occupation of the Red Army, commanded by Semion Budionnyi.[70] By 10 August 1920, the entire Volhynia/Wołyń district was in Bolshevik hands.[71] In the cities and villages of Volhynia, revolutionary committees started to appear, forming new Bolshevik strongholds at a local level.

However, in the Battle of Warsaw on 16 August 1920, the Poles turned back a Soviet invasion commanded by Mikhail Tukhachevsky. Moreover, the remaining UNR forces, led by Colonel Mark Bezruchko, succeeded in halting Red Army reinforcements near Zamostia that were attempting to move on Warsaw in support of Tukhachevsky.[72] On 2 September 1920, the Soviets abandoned Kovel; on 6 September, Budionnyi's First Cavalry Army retreated to Volodymyr-Volhynsky. Six days later, the Polish Third Army under General Władysław Sikorski, together with units commanded by Generals Franciszek Krajewski and Stanisław Bułak-Bałachowicz, occupied Kovel, and later Volodymyr, Lutsk, and Rivne. At the same time, units commanded by General Lucjan Igeligowski were approaching Kremenets from Sokal.[73]

These military events led to the final delineation of the Polish-Soviet border in Volhynia/Wołyń. On 12 October 1920, the Poles and Soviets commenced border negotiations in Riga that were to last until the early spring of 1921. Though the Red Army had been defeated, the Bolsheviks still hoped to acquire sovereignty over the Ukrainian population in western Ukraine. Evidence of that enduring aspiration can be found in a letter, dated 30 November 1920, sent by the Soviet Ukrainian representative at Riga, Emanuil Kviring, to the chairman of the Soviet Ukrainian Council of Ministers, Christian Rakovsky. Kviring noted that ceding western Volhynia and Eastern Galicia, which contained millions of Ukrainians, would allow them to build a localized revolutionary movement in the region under their ideological and organizational control. Such a movement would inevitably emerge, given the oppressive nature of the Polish regime. Kviring even suggested that a special committee be formed immediately with the task of carrying out partisan activities in western Ukraine. To avoid being accused by Warsaw of violating international law, this organization would function on an independent basis, with propaganda and agitational activities being carried out under the pretext of "state unification of all Ukrainian lands." These activities would presage an eventual armed uprising, as well as the establishment of new revolutionary committees.[74]

Meanwhile, Volhynia/Wołyń was being integrated into the Polish state. Shortly after the talks in Riga began, numerous Polish government delegations visited the region and Polish-Ukrainian conferences were organized. On 12 November 1920, one such delegation, headed by Prime Minister Wincenty Witos, Skulski (now Minister of Internal Affairs), and the head of the Provisional Office of the Front and Front Territories, Władysław Raczkiewicz, arrived in Lutsk to evaluate the educational and economic situation and to meet with local community leaders. One of the more interesting questions was posed to the representatives by the editor of the Ukrainian weekly *Nash Holos* (Our Voice), Danylo Shulha, who asked whether members of the local Ukrainian intelligentsia would be able to participate in local government bodies. Skulski's reply was suitably vague: "We can assure you that this will happen in the near future. At present, this question is being deliberated in the relevant committees, which have been tasked with preparing a law that would allow the local Ukrainian intelligentsia of Wołyń to work in the regional administration."[75]

Skulski added that the administration's key purpose, first and foremost, was to defend the interests of Poland. Those who would interfere with the state's broader goals would be deprived of opportunities to work in the state apparatus.[76] The government delegation then visited Rivne, Volodymyr-Volhynsky, and Kowel, where they met with local cultural and educational figures, representatives of the clergy, various civic organizations, and member of the Ukrainian public.

On 12 and 13 December 1920, following local public pressure, a congress of civic activists representing all nationalities in Volhynia/Wołyń gathered in Lutsk. The purpose of the meeting was to establish the grounds for future cooperation between local communities and the Polish authorities. The congress was attended by representatives of the Ukrainian intelligentsia, who spoke in favour of a Polish-Ukrainian dialogue. After these joint discussions, the delegates approved political, economic, and educational proposals advanced by activists from Kovel and Lutsk counties.[77]

To ensure the national, economic, and cultural development of the region's entire population, Volhynia/Wołyń's public leaders agreed to work closely with the Poles under the slogan "the free with the free; equals with equals." Ukrainian representatives sought the right to use the Ukrainian language freely in local administration, self-government, the courts, and the schools, which would position them as the equals of Poles. In addition, plans were made to erase the border between Volhynia/Wołyń and the provinces of central Poland. The most urgent issue, however, was regional self-government. It was argued that positions in civil administration should be accessible to the entire population of Volhynia/Wołyń, regardless of nationality and religion. In determining candidates for administrative roles, the opinion of the Ukrainian population as the largest group had to be considered.[78] Unfortunately, the slogans of the Polish administration were for the most part declarative in nature and were never fully implemented. Similarly, despite the outpouring of positive rhetoric, the local Ukrainian intelligentsia had not been granted the right to participate in administering the region.

Following the December congress, a commission that included Ukrainian, Czech, and Polish representatives was formed to present its findings to the Polish government and lower House of Parliament (*Sejm*) in Warsaw. Because Witos was absent from the capital, the delegation was received by Skulski and the Minister of Education, Maciej Rataj. In addition, negotiations were held with parliamentary representatives and some Warsaw periodicals.[79] Skulski praised the Congress's resolutions as a step toward the much-coveted promise of Polish-Ukrainian cooperation in the region.

During the meeting in Warsaw, the minister inquired about the attitudes of Wołyń activists toward the national movement in Eastern Galicia. The commission's Ukrainian representative, Ivan Vlasovsky, took the floor and assured the Polish state leadership that "the Ukrainian movement in Wołyń is developing completely independently and is not a subject of influence from Eastern Galicia." The different aims of the two movements were linked to differing circumstances faced by the Ukrainians in Wołyń and Eastern Galicia.[80] Thanks to previous inter-state agreements, western Wołyń was now administered directly by the Polish central government; the status of Eastern Galicia still required legal registration and recognition.[81] In the circumstances, public figures in Wołyń needed to agree only on the status of the lands within Poland, and not its legal state affiliation, as this had already been determined, albeit without their participation. Thus, Vlasovsky hoped that Polish-Ukrainian relations in western Wołyń would have better prospects than those in the neighbouring region. Indeed, the Polish government had put great effort into preventing possible negative influences from spilling over into Wołyń from Eastern Galicia. To facilitate this, a strengthened administrative border had been established between the two Ukrainian territories, the so-called Sokal border, which hindered communication between these regions.

Following a decree from the Council of Ministers on 4 February 1921, three new voivodeships in the eastern territories of Poland came into existence on 1 March 1921: Wołyń, Polesie, and Nowogródek.[82] The Wołyń Voivodeship had nine counties: Dubno, Gorokhiv, Kovel, Kremenets, Luboml, Lutsk, Rivne, Volodymyr, and Ostrih. Also, Wołyń's administration was placed under the direct control of the Polish Ministry of Internal Affairs. The Treaty of Riga, signed on 18 March 1921 between Poland, the Soviet Union, and the governments of Soviet Ukraine and Belarus, legally enshrined Wołyń as a Polish province, finally ending the prolonged discussion over its legal status that had lasted from 1918 to 1921. According to the agreements, the border between Poland and Soviet Ukraine passed from the village of Bukcha (in Soviet Belarus) to the Olevsk-Sarny railway line. It then continued through Goryn, Korets, and Ostroh, following the Viliia River, then through Belozyrka, arriving at the Viliia's confluence with the Dniester.[83] The eastern districts of Volhynia remained within Soviet Ukraine, where they formed the Volhynia province. According to Włodzimierz Mędrzecki, in signing the Treaty of Riga with the Bolsheviks, the Poles had agreed on the division of the Belarusian and Ukrainian national territories; in doing so, they had effectively abandoned the idea of Prometheism. In addition, by signing the treaty with the government of Soviet Ukraine, Poland had breached the tenets of the Polish-Ukrainian Union from April 1920.[84]

CONCLUSIONS

The delineation of the Polish-Ukrainian border in Volhynia/Wołyń had started at the end of 1918, following the retreat of the German and Habsburg armies from the region. The demarcation line between Poland and the UNR in 1919–20 corresponded with the front-line advances of the Polish army. In general, Polish public opinion viewed western Volhynia/Wołyń, with its predominantly Ukrainian population, as lying exclusively within Poland's borders. Views differed over how this region was to be integrated, however. As Head of State, Piłsudski called for a peaceful incorporation based on a possible plebiscite as well as cooperation between representatives of different nationalities. Until now, however, Piłsudski's true intentions regarding his eastern policy remain disputed. Nonetheless, it is possible to state that an independent Ukraine first and foremost would have helped the Poles protect their interests in the region. To that end, the task of implementing such a policy had fallen on *Towarzystwo Straży Kresowej*, which aimed to establish cooperation with leading Ukrainian public figures in the region and to shape a positive image of Poland among the local population.

However, representatives of Poland's more radical political tendencies called for a system of regional governance through which they could begin the Polonization of other nationalities. Under the terms of the Polish-Ukrainian Alliance of April 1920, UNR representatives had agreed to abandon western Volhynia to Poland. The Polish-Soviet War in the summer of that year led to the short-term occupation of the region by the Bolsheviks and the erasure of the Polish-Ukrainian border in Volhynia/Wołyń. A counteroffensive by the Polish army and the beginning of negotiations in Riga between Poland and the Soviet government in October 1920 marked the beginning of the Polish-Soviet border's delineation. That line would divide the region into Soviet Volhynia, part of the Ukrainian Soviet Republic, and Polish Wołyń, incorporated into the Wołyń Voivodeship of the Second Polish Republic.

The inclusion of western Volhynia/Wołyń within Poland was recognized by the Ukrainian population, who acquiesced to (possible) Polish-Ukrainian cooperation in exchange for language rights (cultural and educational) and administrative representation. The national consciousness of Volynian Ukrainians was less developed than in Eastern Galicia, and they were less ambitious to achieve statehood, given that they lacked a native intelligentsia. In the early 1920s, the Ukrainian national movement in Volhynia/Wołyń was weak, and its leaders had only started to articulate their attitudes toward the Polish state. The lack of a developed network of the Ukrainian political parties, coupled with the local population's desire to cooperate with the central government, meant that Volhynia/Wołyń became the only region in Poland where a tolerant multicultural society was deemed possible. Polish-Ukrainian dialogue, nonetheless, served as the precondition for such an experiment. This is why the Polish state, beginning in the early 1920s, increasingly implemented measures to distance Volhynia from possible negative political influences emanating from Eastern Galicia, where far fewer opportunities existed for Polish-Ukrainian rapprochement. In Volhynia, the development of the communist movement in the 1920s and the nationalist movement in the 1930s, coupled with the incoherence of the Polish government's policies in the late 1930s, aggravated Polish-Ukrainian relations, with the result that Volhynia became a place of ethnic cleansing during the Second World War.

NOTES

1 On the concept of national "indifference," see Tara Zahra, "Imagined Noncommunities: National Indifference as a Category of Analysis," *Slavic Review* 69, no. 1 (2010): 93–119.
2 Miroslav Hroch, *Social Preconditions of National Revival in Europe: A Comparative Analysis of the Social Composition of Patriotic Groups among the Smaller European Nations* (Cambridge: Cambridge University Press, 1985).
3 Andreas Kappeler, *Rußland als Vielvölkerreich: Entstehung – Geschichte – Zerfall* (Munich: C.H. Beck, 2008). Here the quote is from Kappeler, "Natsional'nyi rukh ukraïntsiv u Rosiï ta Halychyni: sproba porivniannia," in *Ukraïna: kul'turna spadschyna, natsional'na svidomist', derzhavnist'*, Zbirnyk naukovykh prats', vol. 1 (Kyiv: Naukuva Dumka, 1992), 105–9.
4 More in Klymentii K. Fedevych and Klymentii I. Fadevych, *Za Viru, Tsaria i Kobzaria. Malorosiis'ki monarkhisty i ukraïns'kyi natsional'nyi rukh (1905–1917 rokiv)* (Kyiv: Krytyka, 2017), 308.
5 These are Zhytomyr, Zaslavsk, Novohrad-Volynskyi, Ovruch, and Starokonstiantyniv *povity* of the Volhynia *gubernia* of the former Russian Empire.
6 In this text, I will use Wołyń when referring to the Polish administrative unit in the interwar years, and Volhynia when referring to the imperial/Ukrainian/Soviet administrative unit, or referring to the region in more general terms.
7 For the most recent comprehensive overview of the Ukrainian historiography about the revolutionary events in Volhynia in 1917–21, see Oleh Razyhraev, "Revoliutsyonnye sobytyia 1917–1921 hh. na Volyne v svete ukrainskoi istoriohrafii," in *Dni, które wstrząsnęły światem. Rewolucje w Imperium Rosyjskim w 1917 r.*, ed. P. Cichoracki, R. Klementowski, and M. Ruchniewicz (Wrocław and Warsaw: Instytut Pamęci Narodowej, 2019), 209–27.
8 Przemysław Żurawski vel Grajewski, *Sprawa ukraińska na Konferencji Pokojowej w Paryżu w roku 1919* (Warsaw: Septer, 2017), 178; Ludwik Mroczka, *Spór o Galicję Wschodnią 1914–1923* (Kraków: Wydawnictwo Naukowe WSP, 1998), 228; Michał Klimecki, *Polsko-ukraińska wojna o Lwów i Wschodnią Galicję 1918–1919* (Warszawa: Wojskowy Instytut Historyczny, 1997), 279; Jan Pisuliński, *Nie tylko Petlura. Kwestia ukraińska w polskiej polityce zagranicznej w latach 1918–1923* (Toruń: Wydawnictwo naukowe Uniwersytetu Mikołaja Kopernika, 2013), 476.

9 Włodzimierz Mędrzecki, *Województwo Wołyńskie 1921–1939. Elementy przemian cywilizacyjnych, społecznych i politycznych* (Wrocław, Warszawa, Kraków, Gdańsk, and Łódź: Wydawnictwo Polskiej Akademii Nauk, 1988), 203; Włodzimierz Mędrzecki, "Przemiany społeczne i polityczne na Wołyniu w latach 1917–1921," in *Metamorfozy społeczne: Badania nad dziejami społeczeństwa polskiego w XIX i XX wieku*, ed. J. Żarnowskiego (Warsaw: Neriton, 1997), 1137–70.

10 Some recent scholarship on the region includes Katheryn Ciancia, *On Civilization's Edge: A Polish Borderland in the Interwar World* (Oxford: Oxford University Press, 2020); Ciancia, "The Local Boundaries of the Nation: Borderland Guard Activists in Polish-Occupied Volhynia, 1919–1920," *Slavic Review* 78 no. 3 (2019): 671–93; Jeffrey Burds, *Holocaust in Rovno: The Massacre at Sosenki Forest, November 1941* (New York: Palgrave Macmillan, 2013); Jared McBride, "Neighborly Violence and the Undoing of Multi-Ethnic Western Ukraine, 1941–1944" (PhD Diss., UCLA, 2014); see also Jared McBride, "Contesting the Malyn Massacre: The Legacy of Inter-Ethnic Violence and the Second World War in Eastern Europe," *Carl Beck Papers in Russian and East European Studies*, no. 2405 (2016); and McBride, "Peasants into Perpetrators: The OUN-UPA and Ethnic Cleansing of Volhynia, 1943–1944," *Slavic Review* 75, no. 3 (2016): 630–55.

11 Cornelia Schenke, *Nationalstaat und nationale Frage. Polen und die Ukrainer in Wolhynien (1921–1939)* (München: u.a., 2004).

12 Timothy Snyder, *The Reconstruction of Nations: Poland, Ukraine, Lithuania, Belarus, 1569–1999* (New Haven: Yale University Press, 2003).

13 Timothy Snyder, *Sketches from a Secret War: A Polish Artist's Mission to Liberate Ukraine* (New Haven: Yale University Press, 2005).

14 Yaroslav Hrytsak, *Strasti za natsionalizmom: stara istoriia na novyi lad* (Kyiv: Krytyka, 2011), 202.

15 Pisuliński, *Nie tylko Petlura*, 43.

16 For a detailed analysis of the history of the region under Russian and Austro-Hungarian control during the First World War, see Oleh Razyhraiev, *Po obydva boky frontu. Hromads'ki orhanizatsiï na Volyni v roky Velykoï Viiny: 1914–1918 rr.* (Luts'k: Vezha-Druk, 2018), 242.

17 Iaroslav Shabala, "Persha svitova viina. Ukraïns'ka revoliutsiia (1914–1921 rr.)," *Zakhidne Polissia: Istoriia ta kul'tura* (L'uts'k: Volyns'ka oblasna drukarnia, 2012), 294–302.

18 Vitalii Skal's'kyi, "Mis'ki holovy Volodymyra-Volyns'koho 1915–1923 rr.," *Mynule i suchasne Volyni ta Polissia. Naukovyi zbirnyk* 55 (2015): 211–18.

19 Roman Koval', *Mykhailo Havrylko: i stekom, i shableiu: Istorychnyi narys* (Vinnytsia: Derzhavna kartohrafichna fabryka, 2012), 371–80.
20 Joanna Gierowska-Kallaur, *Zarząd cywilny ziem wschodnich (19 lutego 1919–9 września 1920)* (Warsaw: Neriton, 2003), 339.
21 Serhii Lys, *Volyn' v Ukraïns'kii Revoliutsiï 1917–1921 rokiv: Peredumovy, perebih, podii, naslidky* (Luts'k: Terezy, 2017), 5.
22 *Archiwum Akt Nowych* (AAN) Zesp. 55. Sygn. 337. K. 62. Raporty instruktorów Straży Kresowej na powiat łucki. 1919 r.
23 Vitalii Skal's'kyi, "Politychne zhyttia pol's'koi hromady pid chas ukraïns'koï revoliutsiï (berezen' 1917–kviten' 1918 rr.)," *UIZ* 11 (2008), 186.
24 Yurii Kramar, *Pol's'kyi chynnyk u perebihu podii Ukraïns'koï Revoliutsiï na Volyni. Volyn' v roky Ukraïns'koï Revoliutsiï 1917–1921 rokiv* (Luts'k: Vezha-Druk, 2019), 78.
25 Kramar, *Pol's'kyi chynnyk*, 78.
26 Skal's'kyi, *Politychne zhyttia pol's'koï hromady*, 189.
27 Maksym Potapenko, "Ukraïns'ke pytannia v politychnykh proektakh poliakiv Naddniprianschyny u 1917–1918 rokakh," *Studia Politilogica Ucraino-Polona* 2 (2012), 150.
28 Włodzimierz Mędrzecki, *Kresowy kalejdoskop. Wędrówki przez ziemie wschodnie Drugiej Rzeczypospolitej, 1918–1939* (Kraków: Wydawnictwo Literackie, 2018), 51.
29 Mędrzecki, *kresowy Kalejdoskop*, 52.
30 Leon Wasilewski, *Piłsudski jakim go znałem.* (Warszawa: Muzeum Historii Polski, 2013), 215.
31 Wasilewski, *Piłsudski jakim go znałem*, 216.
32 Pisuliński, *Nie tylko Petlura*, 94.
33 "Third Universal of the Ukrainian Central Rada," in *Ukraïns'ka Tsentral'na Rada. Dokumenty i materialy*, ed. V. Verstiuk (Kyiv: Naukova Dumka, 1996), 1:398–401.
34 Volodymyr Komar, "Skhidna polityka Pol'shchi 1918–1921 rr.: vid federalizmu do prometeizmu," in *Ukraïna: Kul'turna spadschyna, natsional'na svidomist', derzhavnist'*, vol. 18 (L'viv: Instytut ukraïnoznavstva im. Ivana Kryp'iakevycha, 2009), 43.
35 Komar, "Skhidna polityka Pol'shchi," 23.
36 Ibid., 47. On Prometheism in Poland's foreign policy, see Volodymyr Komar, *Kontseptsiia prometeizmu v politytsi Pol'shchi (1921–1939 rr.)* (Ivano-Frankivs'k: Misto NV, 2011); Marek Kornat, "Prometeizm – pol's'ka viziia perebudovy Skhidnoi Ievropy (1921–1939)," *Ukraina Moderna* 17, no. 6 (2010): 131–48; Jan Jacek Bruski, *Między prometeizmem a realpolitik. II Rzeczpospolita wobec Ukrainy Sowieckiej, 1921–1926* (Krakow: Historia

Iagellonica, 2010); Sergiusz Mikulicz, *Prometeizm w polityce II Preczpospolitej* (Warsaw: Ksiazka i Wiedza, 1971).
37 AAN, Zesp. 55. Sygn. 182. K. 18. Instrukcja dla p. Henryka Orłowskiego kierownika Okręgu Wołyńskiego (5 września 1919 r.).
38 *Instytut Józefa Piłsudskiego w Ameryce*. Zesp. 701/2. Sygn. 3. Styczeń – kwiecień 1919 r. K. 239, http://archiwa.pilsudski.org/teczka.php?nonav=0&nrar=701&n.
39 Yaroslava Varmenych, "Volyns'ka huberniia," *Entsyklopediia istoriï Ukraïny*: vol. 1: A-V. (Kyiv: Instytut istoriï Ukraïny NAN Ukraïny, 2003), 606; For more on separate aspects of social and economic development of the Volhynia *gubernia*, see Valerii Bortnikov, *Orhany derzhavnoï vlady ta mistsevoho samovriaduvannia na Volyni (kinets' XVIII–pochatok XX st.)*. (Luts'k: SNU im. Lesi Ukraïnky, 2015), 480; Olena Pryschepa, *Mista Volyni u druhii polovyni XIX – na pochatku XX st.* (Rivne: PP DM, 2010), 287.
40 Komar, "Skhidna polityka Pol'shchi," 43.
41 Mędrzecki, *Kresowy kalejdoskop*, 74.
42 Waldemar Kozyra, "Zemia Wołynska w okresie funkcjonowania administracji Zarządu Cywilnego Ziem Wschodnich i Zarządu Cywilnego Ziem Wołynia i Frontu Podolskiego (1919–1921)," *Ukrainica Polonica* 1 (2004), 170.
43 Joanna Gierowska-Kallaur, *Straż kresowa a Zarząd Cywilny Ziem Wschodnich. Współdziałanie czy rywilizacja?* (Warszawa: Neriton, 1999), 9.
44 Kozyra, "Ziemia Wołynska," 171.
45 Henry Abramson, *A Prayer for the Government: Ukrainians and Jews in Revolutionary Times, 1917–1920* (Cambridge, MA: Harvard University Press, 1999); here the quotes are from the Ukrainian translation: *Molytva za vladu. Ukraïntsi ta ievrei v revoliutsiinu dobu, 1917–1920* (Kyiv: Dukh i litera, 2017), 29–79; see also Christopher Gilley, "Beyond Petliura: The Ukrainian National Movement and the 1919 Pogroms," *East European Jewish Affairs* 47, no. 1 (2017): 45–61; Joshua Sanborn, *Imperial Apocalypse: The Great War and the Destruction of the Russian Empire* (New York: Oxford University Press, 2014).
46 Abramson, *A Prayer for the Government*, 184.
47 Ibid., 193.
48 Appendix of report by Abraham Shohan on JDC activities in Polish Ukraine (Wolyn and Podolia), 1919–1920. JDC Archives. 1919–1921, New York Collection. Poland: Administration, NY AR191921/4/34/1/230.1., 11.
49 Oleksandr Dem'ianiuk, "Volyn' ta Halychyna v ukraïns'ko-pol's'kykh stosunkakh u 1919 r.," *Visnyk Natsional'noho Universytetu «L'vivs'ka Politekhnika»* (L'viv: L'vivs'ka politekhnika, 2007), 114.

50 Mykola Kucherepa, "Volyn' u kontseptsiiakh derzhavnoho budivnytstva Pol'schi v dobu natsional'noho vidrodzhennia," in *Volyn' u roky Ukraïns'koï Revoliutsiï 1917–1921 rr.* (Luts'k: Vezha-Druk, 2019), 63.

51 Kucherepa, *Volyn' u kontseptsiiakh derzhavnoho budivnytstva Pol'schi*, 65.

52 Pisuliński, *Nie tylko Petlura*, 151.

53 Stanislav Stempien', "Holovnyi Otaman Symon Petliura – derzhavnyi muzh i tvorets' modernoï ukraïns'koï armiï," in *Volyn' u roky Ukraïns'koï Revoliutsiï 1917–1921 rr.* (Luts'k: Vezha-Druk, 2019), 30.

54 *Dziennik Urzędowy Zarządu Cywilnego Ziem Wschodnich* (1919), no. 5, Poz. 41, S. 37. Zarządzenie Komisarza Generalnego Ziem Wschodnich z dnia 7 czerwca 1919 r. dotyczące utworzenia Okręgów administracyjnych: Wileńskiego, Brzeskiego, oraz Zarządu powiatów wołyńskich.

55 *Dziennik Urzędowy Zarządu Cywilnego Ziem Wschodnich* (1010), no. 17, Poz. 153, S. 161. Zarządzenie Komisarza Generalnego Ziem Wschodnich z dnia 9 września 1919 r. dotyczące utworzenia okręgu administracyjnego Wołyńskiego i uprawnień komisarza Okręgowego Wołyńskiego.

56 *Arkhiv Ukraïns'koï Narodnoï Respubliky. Ministerstvo Zakordonnykh Sprav. Dyplomatychni dokumenty vid Versal's'koho do Ryz'koho myrnykh dohovoriv (1919–1921)* (Kyiv: Instytut ukraïns'koï arkheohrafiï ta dzhereloznavstva im. M.S. Hrushevs'koho, 2016), 41.

57 Stempien', *Holovnyi Otaman Symon Petliura*, 31.

58 Oleh Razyhraiev, *Pol's'ka derzhavna politsiia v zakhidnii Volyni u 1919–1926 rr.* (Luts'k: Volyns'ki starozhytnosti, 2012), 99.

59 Stanisław Stempowski, "Ukraina (1919–1920)," *Zeszyty Historyczne* (Paryż: Instytut Literacki, 1972), 85.

60 Ibid.

61 *Instytut Józefa Piłsudskiego w Ameryce*. Styczeń–marzec 1920 r. Zesp. 701/2. Adiutantura Generalna Naczelnego Wodza. Sygn. 7, K. 303–6, http://archiwa.pilsudski.org/teczka.php?nonav=0&nrar=701&n.

62 *Dziennik Ustaw Zarządu Cywilnego Ziem Wołynia i Frontu Podolskiego*, (1920), no. 3, Poz. 167, S. 93. Rozkaz Naczelnego Wódza wojsk Polskich z dnia 29 maja 1920 r. w przedmiocie przekazania zarządu powiatów Wołyńskich Rządowi Rzeczpospolitej Polskiej.

63 AAN, Zesp. 55, Sygn. 328 K. 8. Raport instruktora Straży Kresowej na powiat dubieński (kwiecień 1920 r.).

64 *Przymierze*, no. 13 (7 November 1920), 4.

65 Ibid.

66 Mirosław Szumiło, *Antoni Wasyńczuk 1883–1935. Ukraiński działacz narodowy i polityk* (Lublin: Wydawnictwo Uniwersytetu Marii Curie-Skłodowskiej, 2006), 129.

67 *Przymierze*, no. 13 (7 November 1920), 5.
68 Kozyra, *Ziemia Wołyńska*, 180.
69 Ibid.
70 For more on the Bolshevik occupation of Volhynia in summer of 1920, see Serhij Hladyshuk, "Agitacja bolszewicka i ruch komunistyczny na Wołyniu w okresie formowania polskiej administracji (1919–1921)," *Komunizm: system-ludzie–dokumentacja. Rocznik naukowy*, 4 (2015): 3–18.
71 Lys, *Volyn' v Ukrains'kii Revoliutsiï 1917–1921 rokiv*, 20.
72 Ibid.
73 Nina Zielińska, "Postawy mieszkańców Wołynia w czasie wojny polsko-bolszewickiej (na podstawie raportów Towarzystwa Straży Kresowej)," in *Społeczeństwo polskie w dobie Pierwszej Wojny Światowej i Wojny Polsko-Bolszewickiej 1920 roku*, ed. Ryszard Kołodziejczyk (Kielce: Kieleckie Towarzystwo naukowe, 2001), 278.
74 N.S. Rubliova and O.S. Rubliov, eds., *Ukraïna–Pol'shcha 1920–1939 rr.: z istoriï dyplomatychnykh vidnosyn USRR z Druhoiu Richchiu Pospolytoiu: dokumenty i materialy* (Kyiv: Dukh i litera, 2012), 75.
75 *Nash Holos*. No. 9 (21 November 1920), 5.
76 Ibid.
77 AAN. Zesp. 55, Sygn. 251, K. 9, Wydział organizacyjny. Naczelna Rada Ludowa Ziemi Wołyńskiej, 1919–21.
78 *Nash Holos*. No. 12, 19 December 1920, 2.
79 Centralne Archiwum Wojskowe, Zespół I.301.8, Oddział II NDWP, Sygn. I.301.8.325 K. 13 Raport sytuacyjny Wydziału Organizacyjnego Straży Kresowej dotyczący powiatów: włodzimierskiego, łuckiego, nowogródzkiego, świąciańskiego i wołyńskiego (styczeń 1920 – kwiecień 1921 rr.).
80 *Nash Holos*, no. 18, 27 February 1921, 4.
81 Only on 15 March 1923 did the Entente's Council of Ambassadors reach a final decision regarding the inclusion of Eastern Galicia within the borders of Poland, based on the promise of Warsaw granting autonomy to the local Ukrainian population. This provision however, only ever existed on paper and was never realized during the interwar period.
82 Kozyra, *Ziemia Wołynska*, 183.
83 Ivan Zavada, *Ryz'kyi Dohovir i Ukraïna* (Kyiv: Prosvita, 2000), 138–41.
84 Mędrzecki, *Kresowy kalejdoskop*, 78.

10

To Reach beyond the Carpathians

The Integration of Transcarpathia into Soviet Ukraine, 1944–45

Iaroslav Kovalchuk

Transcarpathia became Ukraine's westernmost territory after the Second World War, completing the Soviet consolidation of power over the Ukrainian lands in the west. Thirty years prior, during the Russian offensive in the winter of 1914–15, the Russian Empire, seeking to reverse the disastrous setbacks of the First World War's opening months, attempted to cross the Carpathians under a rallying call to unify all Russians under one state. The Russians failed in their objective, and the Transcarpathian lands remained outside the empire. In 1944, the Soviet Union reached beyond the mountains, but unlike the imperial government, the Communist leadership called for the unification of Ukrainians, not Russians. However, Transcarpathia's population was comprised of multiple and sometimes competing national identities: some claimed to be Ukrainians, while others identified as Russians. Additionally, local activists had by then popularized the idea of a separate Rusyn nation, and an influential Hungarian minority was present that had enjoyed the privileges of Magyar rule in the region between 1939 and 1944. To complicate things further, the region was to be returned to Czechoslovakia according to an agreement between Moscow and the Czechoslovak government-in-exile, whereby the Soviet leadership would restore the country to its pre-October 1938 borders. With the Soviet Union's attempts to annex new territory beyond the Carpathians, all of these complexities required solutions.

In late 1944, in the month following Hungary's loss of control over the territory and the Czechoslovak administration's failure to regain its sovereignty over the region, Transcarpathian communists supported by the Red Army quickly organized a movement to join Soviet Ukraine. On

26 November, local Communists gathered representatives from various Transcarpathian towns and villages in the city of Mukachevo[1] and proclaimed the reunification of Transcarpathia with the Ukrainian homeland across the Carpathian Mountains. Under the protection of the Red Army, the Mukachevo Congress established the temporary quasi-independent state of Transcarpathian Ukraine, with the intention of eventually joining it to Soviet Ukraine. Its leaders attempted to establish institutions similar to those of their Soviet counterparts, including the Communist Party of Transcarpathian Ukraine, or KPZU, which would come to play role similar to that of the Communist Party in the Soviet Union. More importantly, the local Communists pursued nationality policies that privileged Ukrainians and Russians at the expense of the Hungarians and Germans. The new state also made territorial claims against Slovakia and Romania based on the Ukrainian nationality of many peasants living within the latter countries' borders. They viewed the nationality principle as essential to Transcarpathia's eventual inclusion in Soviet Ukraine.

This chapter explores the role played by the Transcarpathian pro-Soviet actors in the delineation of what was to become the westernmost border of Soviet Ukraine, with a particular focus on local policies and discourses related to Transcarpathia's political integration. I will interrogate two aspects of this process: the border aspect, dealing with the conflict between the Czechoslovak administration on the one side and pro-Soviet activists and the Soviet leadership on the other; and failed attempts by pro-Soviet Ukrainians to annex territories from Slovakia and Romania. Overall, I argue that the local Transcarpathian Communist activists were highly active and influential in the making of the Soviet-Ukrainian border in the west, albeit always within the parameters set by Moscow, and satisfied both their own interests and those of the leadership.

CARPATHIAN RUS, 1848–1944

Using Paul Robert Magocsi's approach to the region's history, I will refer to Carpathian Rus when describing a broader region that includes the Transcarpathian *oblast* of Ukraine, formed by the Soviet Union. In addition to Transcarpathia, Carpathian Rus includes northeastern Slovakia (Prešov region) and a small part of northern Romania (Maramureș county). Magocsi's explanation for the vague borders of Carpathian Rus is based on the shared ethnicity of the local peasantry – termed "Rusyn" or "Carpatho-Rusyn" by Magocsi – who were exposed to various nationalist movements throughout the nineteenth century. Magocsi distinguishes three national orientations of Carpatho-Rusyns – Ukrainophile, Russophile, and Rusynophile – which subsequently divided the Carpatho-Rusyn population into three different nations.[2] Although the construction of a common ethnic identity might be interpreted as a nationalist claim,[3] his work successfully tracks the competition among these political orientations as they sought to impose a particular national identity on the general Carpatho-Rusyn population. Furthermore, Magocsi's definition of Carpathian Rus, with its imprecise borders, implicitly acknowledges the rivalries among local nationalists, regardless of their orientation, as well as with the Hungarian, Romanian, and Slovak nationalist projects.

These orientations will serve as markers for ascribing national identity to the local population: Ukrainian, Russian, or Rusyn. Yet not all activists were political allies simply because they supported the same national project. Ukrainian nationalists in particular – among whom could be found conservatives like Avhustyn Voloshyn and radicals from the Organization of Ukrainian Nationalists (OUN) – as well as pro-Soviet Ukrainophiles regarded the Carpatho-Rusyn population as Ukrainians and aspired to unify them within a single Ukrainian polity, yet they fought bitterly with one another over conflicting ideas as to what Ukrainian national identity actually meant. This also applied to Russophiles, who shared the common idea of belonging to a single Russian culture and nationality but who variously followed either the Soviet or anti-Soviet idea of "Russianness." By contrast, the Rusynophiles seemed to be the least politically developed orientation; among that group, there were few competing factions.

Carpathian Rus occupied a fairly marginal position in the Ukrainian and Russian nationalist projects, with the result that the development of its national identity took a somewhat idiosyncratic path.[4] Here, contrast Carpathian Rus with eastern Galicia. John-Paul Himka presents an explanation for the success of the Ukrainian national orientation among eastern Galician peasants over the competing Polish and Russian national projects. He argues that political support from Vienna had been a critical factor in allowing Ukrainian nationalism in Galicia to survive and partly defeat its opponents, specifically the Russophiles.[5] The Carpathian situation differed from the Galician one, however: the Hungarian authorities opposed all other nationalist movements in Transcarpathia and attempted to Magyarize the local Slavs, leaving the Russophile project weak and the Ukrainophile and Rusynophile projects underdeveloped.[6] In summarizing nineteenth-century nationalist politics in Carpathian Rus, Himka acknowledges the region's peripheral status and heavy dependence on the successes of the major regional players as well as on inter-imperial competition.

10.1 Carpathian Rus', 1919–38.

After the First World War, Carpathian Rus was absorbed into Czechoslovakia, losing Maramureș county to Romania and the Prešov region to Slovakia. The region acquired the official name of Subcarpathian Rus and received new territories populated not only with Carpatho-Rusyns but also with Hungarians, who dominated the western and southern areas and the cities. There were also Romanians on the border with Romania, as well as more geographically diffuse Jewish and Romani communities. Overall, Carpatho-Rusyns, regardless of their national orientation, were placed in a single administrative unit within which they enjoyed formal titular status, while coexisting alongside other national groups.

In its politics, interwar Czechoslovakia allowed a limited pluralism, unlike many states in the region, which prohibited opposition parties. Nevertheless, Subcarpathian activists clashed with Prague over the status of Subcarpathian Rus and the Carpatho-Rusyns within Czechoslovakia. According to Magocsi, local nationalists, regardless of their orientation, faced two main problems: the borders of Subcarpathian Rus as an administrative unit of Czechoslovakia, and the degree of *de facto* versus *de jure* autonomy.[7] These issues unified local activists of various political orientations, who demanded that eastern Slovakia's Prešov region, home to a significant number of Carpatho-Rusyns, be folded into Subcarpathian Rus, which they maintained should enjoy the same level of autonomy (i.e., an elected local diet and governor) as other administrative units of Czechoslovakia.

Before the 1938 partitions of Czechoslovakia, divisions among Subcarpathia's various political orientations were not overly pronounced. Activists found common ground in their demands for border changes and greater autonomy. After the Munich Treaty, when France, Britain, and Italy agreed that Germany had a right to occupy those Czechoslovak lands with a German majority, Prague created a Subcarpathian regional government and promised to hold elections for a local diet, thus granting the autonomy that Carpatho-Rusyn activists had been demanding throughout the 1920s and 1930s. The first government was a mix of Ukrainophiles and Russophiles, led by one of the latter: Andrei Brodii. However, the Czechoslovak government quickly discovered that Brodii had secretly begun preparations for a Hungarian annexation of Subcarpathian Rus. He was subsequently imprisoned, and the Ukrainophile leader Avhustyn Voloshyn became the new head of the local government. Voloshyn was a conservative Ukrainian nationalist, yet he relied on the support of the radical OUN, which had recently formed its own paramilitary organization, "Carpathian Sich." This was to serve as a counterpart to the Czechoslovak military forces and would become the basis for the violence that would characterize Ukrainian nationalist rule (during which of Czech and Russian schools were shut down, political opponents were imprisoned, and elections were rigged) and their eventual separation.[8]

The Ukrainophiles completely controlled the Subcarpathian government in the final months of Czechoslovakian independence, yet an independent Ukrainian state in Transcarpathia risked being annexed by Hungary unless it attracted support from Nazi Germany. Indeed, in November 1938, Hungary annexed those regions with a Hungarian majority, including Subcarpathia's three largest cities – Uzhhorod, Mukachevo, and Berehovo – and the Subcarpathian government was compelled to relocate to the town of Khust. On 15 March 1939, an independent state of Carpatho-Ukraine was proclaimed. However, the Carpatho-Ukrainian government did not receive the expected German support. The following day, the new state was occupied by Hungarian troops, with little resistance from the Carpathian Sich. Most of the government members emigrated, and the Hungarian administration, together with loyal Russophiles who, like Brodii, had been collaborating with Hungarian intelligence in hopes of support for their

Russophile agenda, took control of the region.[9] Thus, the territory of Subcarpathian Rus ended up as part of Hungary, while the Prešov region remained in Slovakia. The status of Maramureş county, however, was not addressed in mainstream debates about the unification of the Carpatho-Rusyns.

Under Hungarian rule, Russophiles expected to gain autonomy and to Russify the local population. However, Hungary's leaders had different plans for Carpathian Rus. Initially, the Russophiles proposed limited autonomy, but Budapest refused to consider it. In the end, the Hungarian parliament even rejected initial plans for limited local autonomy. The Hungarians were fearful of the Communists' popularity in the region and did not fully trust the local Russophiles, especially Stepan Fentsik, who had strong ties with White Russian émigrés, particularly from the Russian Fascist Party, which dreamed of building a fascist Greater Russia, which would mean Carpathian Rus's eventual separation from Hungary.[10] So the local elites' aspirations for greater autonomy came to nothing; they even lost what they had had when they were part of Czechoslovakia.

Hungary also betrayed the Russophiles' expectations regarding cultural policy and support for Russian national identity. Miklós Kozma, Commissioner of the Subcarpathian Territory (Hungary's official name for Carpathian Rus), expressed his full support for the Rusyn political orientation and encouraged the use of the local ethnonym Rusyn instead of Russian, as well as the teaching of the local vernacular in the region's schools, which had been codified by Ivan Haraida, a member of the local intelligentsia.[11] Russophiles were allowed to publish in Russian and were not subjected to repressions like Ukrainophiles, who were associated with Soviet and nationalist clandestine groups. However, Kozma did recommend that Brodii change the language of his journal, *The Russian Messenger*, from Russian to Rusyn.[12] Moreover, teachers and school administrators of Russophile orientation were constantly under suspicion, especially after Hungary entered the war against the Soviet Union in 1941.[13] Thus, Russophiles became marginal cultural actors, while their Rusynophile counterparts received Hungary's full support.

TRANSCARPATHIAN UKRAINE AND ITS BORDERS: THE SOVIET NATIONALITY POLICIES

The Soviet Union was a multinational polity with a complex political structure. Its leadership aimed to rule through national diversity, albeit under a highly centralized system of decision-making controlled by the

Communist Party. Terry Martin labels this form of polity "the affirmative action empire." Basically, each nationality received its territorially demarcated homeland, where the national language enjoyed official status. Another critical factor was the promotion of the local inhabitants to leadership positions, notably within the Communist Party. These two measures were intended to make Soviet rule appear natively organic and close to the people.[14] Thus, newly annexed territories, including Transcarpathia, were to be assigned a specific national republic, and cadres were to be drawn from the identified titular nationality – Ukrainians, in the Transcarpathian case.

At the same time, the Bolsheviks wanted to foster the loyalty of all to the project of building socialism. Joseph Stalin defined All-Union socialist culture simply as "socialist in content, but national in form." This heavy emphasis on unity became increasingly pronounced as Bolshevik paranoia about foreign intervention intensified throughout the 1930s. As a result, transnational socialist culture gradually acquired characteristics that were distinctively Russian in substance, and national minorities that had transborder ties were subject to repression.[15] The unity of the Soviet nations was a challenging issue that required balancing the preservation of national distinctions and All-Union solidarity. For Transcarpathia, such a policy meant that both Russophiles and Ukrainophiles would be able to find their place in the Soviet Friendship of the Peoples.

In the Ukrainian Soviet Socialist Republic, the Ukrainian language enjoyed official status and ethnic Ukrainians held leading positions. However, the public sphere was bilingual, with the Russian language dominating those institutions of All-Union significance, such as industry, while Ukrainian prevailed in culture and education.[16] Moreover, as Serhiy Yekelchyk has shown, Ukrainians shared special symbolic connections with Russians through the Friendship of the Peoples, corresponding to the Stalinist construction of a Ukrainian national literary canon and history. As was the case with Russian national identity, Soviet representations of "Ukrainianness" took symbols from the pre-revolutionary national tradition and changed their meaning to emphasize the country's peasant origins, political radicalism, and ties with Russians and Russian culture.[17] This cultural policy evoked Russification for some Ukrainophiles, especially those with a strong Ukrainian national movement as in Galicia. However, those in Transcarpathia already faced severe competition with Russophiles and Rusynophiles, so the mere identification of locals as Ukrainians represented a significant victory for pro-Ukrainians despite their conflict with the Soviet project.

The erasure of borders in Central and Eastern Europe during the Second World War gave the Soviet Union an opportunity to rearrange its western border. Alfred Rieber proposes that the Soviet Union's wartime role be interpreted as involving multiple civil wars along its western borderlands. He asserts that Stalin viewed the war as a "civil war" and that he had a territorial rather than internationalist view of revolution. In this regard, the war represented an opportunity for him to secure the Soviet revolution from external interventions, and that included removing groups perceived as threatening from the border regions.[18] Stalin's desired outcome was the full integration of these western borderlands into the Soviet Union, leaving no place for external influence. In this context, the Ukrainian question in Transcarpathia was an opportunity for territorial enlargement as well as a chance to eliminate any potential transborder influence from other, mainly nationalist, competing visions of Ukrainian nationhood.

The first example of bringing Ukrainian lands into the Soviet fold during the war was the annexation of the eastern Polish territories of Galicia and Volhynia in October 1939. Jan T. Gross's exploration of the logic of Sovietization (i.e., the integration of Poland's former eastern borderlands into the Soviet system) presents an image of the Soviet state as utilizing ultra-violent methods when wiping away previous institutions and replacing them with Soviet ones. This initially involved empowering oppressed local groups, namely Ukrainian and Belarusian peasants, and granting them opportunities to seek revenge on their Polish oppressors. The result was often anarchy. However, these localized cadres were later taken over by the central authorities, with many being purged. There was also a crucial difference between rural areas, where the previous order was wiped away radically and suddenly, and urban areas, where a gradual replacement of local bureaucrats with new Soviet cadres selected from the local population was adopted.[19] The idea behind this initial lawlessness was to bring about the "self-subjugation" of local populations to the Soviet system; all previous ties were to be destroyed so that people found their lives completely changed.[20] Gross's approach fits into the totalitarian paradigm of Soviet studies: the atomization of society precedes the totalitarian movement, which supersedes previous communal links between individuals. This also explains how and why the Transcarpathian Communists could have agency in the integration of their region into the Soviet system.

The nationality issue was equally relevant in these processes. The Soviets framed the annexation as a unification of the Ukrainian and Belarusian nations and encouraged the non-Polish population to attack representatives of the old order, particularly the *pans* (Polish gentry). The victims possessed both class and ethnic distinctions, but it was ethnic Poles, whatever their class affiliation, who suffered the most, especially in villages. Although many representatives of the Ukrainian, Belarusian, and Jewish communities were later purged, the national dimension to those actions was not as prominent as with the Poles.[21] In Transcarpathia, the Czechs, Hungarians, and Germans were similarly scapegoated for past misfortunes.

Overall, the Soviet acquisition of Ukrainian lands involved harnessing the grievances of local Ukrainians and Soviet sympathizers to overthrow the previous order and clear the way for the Soviet revolutionary project. This allowed locals to exert a degree of political agency, in that they were able to pursue their national interests within the wider framework of Soviet nationality policies.

THE CZECHOSLOVAK ADMINISTRATION VERSUS THE SOVIETS

Soviet troops pushed the Wehrmacht westwards in 1944 and were soon approaching the Soviet Union's prewar western borderlands. Moscow was now faced with the question of how to administer the liberated non-Soviet territories. The lands within the prewar Soviet borders simply fell back under the domain of Soviet administration, but what of the lands of the prewar Central European states? Their borders would have to be negotiated between the Soviet Union and the respective national governments. Edvard Beneš's Czechoslovak government-in-exile agreed with the Soviet Union that Czechoslovak territory would be recognized according to its pre-Munich borders. This meant that Slovakia together with the lost territories of the Sudetenland, Cieszyn Silesia, and Subcarpathian Rus would once again be part of Czechoslovakia. The treaty between the Soviet and Czechoslovak governments stated that the Red Army would administer the territory close to the front; a Czechoslovak civic administration would oversee the liberated territory in the rear.[22] Transcarpathia, being part of interwar Czechoslovakia, was to be governed initially by both administrations. This would be followed by the gradual restoration of Czechoslovak sovereignty over the region.

Yet there were indications that Beneš was prepared to cede Subcarpathian Rus to the Soviet Union for the sake of a robust postwar Czechoslovak-Soviet alliance. In negotiations with Soviet representatives, Beneš even used the official Soviet Ukrainophile name of the region, Transcarpathian Ukraine, instead of the more neutral Czechoslovak name, Subcarpathian Rus.[23] From this point, I will use the names Transcarpathian Ukraine or Transcarpathia because the change in how people called it marked a crucial shift in the region's national affiliation. In other words, it indicated the beginning of a transition from a nationally contested Carpathian Rus to the Ukrainophile idea of Transcarpathia. Although the Czechoslovak government made specific symbolic preparations, such as changing the name of the region, the eventual transition of Transcarpathia to Soviet Ukraine was expected to happen only after a Czechoslovak administration had been established.

In October 1944, when the troops of the Fourth Ukrainian Front took Transcarpathia under their control, the Czechoslovak administration arrived in Khust to begin reconstructing eastern and northern Transcarpathia. However, the military administration continued to control the region's larger cities (Uzhhorod, Mukachevo, and Berehovo), located in its western and southern parts. The Czechoslovak delegation consisted of party representatives from the government-in-exile and was led by the Social Democratic representative František Němec. While it travelled from London to Khust via Moscow, Ivan Turianytsia, a member of the Communist Party of Czechoslovakia who had not been part of the government-in-exile, joined the delegation. Turianytsia was a Transcarpathian Communist, born and raised in Carpathian Rus, who had studied at the party school in Kharkiv in the 1930s and fled to the Soviet Union in March 1939, when Hungarian troops entered Carpatho-Ukraine.

Almost immediately upon arrival, Turianytsia left Khust and launched a campaign for Transcarpathia's unification with Soviet Ukraine, agitating in the towns and villages of Transcarpathia independently from the Czechoslovak delegation and ignoring their administrative zone. Magocsi contends that this was not entirely Turianytsia's initiative and that the Soviets had been planning to annex Transcarpathia by repeating their earlier pattern in other western Ukrainian territories. Basically, that meant agitating among locals to support Sovietization.[24] Self-organized people's committees, which the Czechoslovak administration encouraged locals to create, became a basis for Turianytsia's activism. The presence of the Red Army ensured that these committees consisted of local Communists or activists loyal to the idea of unification with Soviet Ukraine. Another initiative crucial for Turianytsia was the establishment of the separate Communist Party of Transcarpathian Ukraine (KPZU) in Mukachevo on 19 November 1944. The last step in building a parallel structure to the Czechoslovak civic administration came with the First Congress of the People's Committees of Transcarpathian Ukraine, which gathered the week after the establishment of KPZU on 26 November, when the Act of Reunification with Soviet Ukraine was proclaimed.

Symbolically, the act meant that Soviet Ukrainophiles would control Transcarpathia. From a legal perspective, it established the People's Council of Transcarpathian Ukraine, or NRZU, parallel to the Czechoslovak administration. This indicates how the congress finished its preliminary preparations for integrating Transcarpathia into Soviet Ukraine. Such measures meant that the territory and its population could not simply become part of the Soviet Union after signing a formal treaty, as President Beneš had envisioned.[25] According to Gross, integration into the Soviet Union presupposed deep social and political changes, which symbolically had to come from below with assistance from the Party.[26] In this manner, the Bolsheviks strove to prepare a suitable basis for these transformations and set up local pro-Soviet groups.

These first steps were completed even before Soviet troops entered Transcarpathian territory, when groups of partisans were dispatched to the region in the summer of 1944. According to Oleksii Korsun, their main tasks were to prepare the locals to greet Soviet troops and to organize people's committees that would send representatives to the Reunification Congress. Partisans were also involved in the formation of local militias and eventually served as a pool of reliable cadres for the incoming Soviet administration. (However, only one of these actors, Vasyl' Rusyn, gained a position in the NRZU; the rest continued to operate at the local level.[27]) In this way, the Bolsheviks established a strong organizational presence even before the arrival of the Red Army, which Turianytsia only later mobilized.

The Red Army's role was crucial in separating Transcarpathian Ukraine from Czechoslovakia. Mobilization into the Soviet military proved the most efficient way of connecting locals with the Soviet Union. As Němec noted in his memoirs, this approach sparked the first major conflict between the Czechoslovak delegation and the Soviets. Formally, the Transcarpathians were Czechoslovakian citizens, and a Czechoslovak citizen who wished to serve in a foreign army required the permission of the Czechoslovak president. Indeed, the Soviet-Czechoslovak treaty stated that the population on the territory of interwar Czechoslovakia had to join Czechoslovak military units. Nevertheless, Transcarpathians found themselves serving in the Red Army.[28] According to Vasyl' Markus', an eyewitness and later Ukrainian diaspora nationalist activist who worked for the CIA, the Red Army enlisted around ten thousand Transcarpathians, using both threats and the promise of material rewards.[29] The main reason for this mobilization was the Soviet Union's need for more soldiers to sustain its offensive against the Third Reich and its satellites. That said, it also played an essential role in severing the region from Czechoslovakia. As Amir Weiner shows, from the perspective of the Soviet leadership the Red Army was one of the most powerful institutions in the Soviet Union, and over the course of the Second World War it served as the principal bond between the population to the Soviet regime.[30] After joining the Red Army, Transcarpathians gradually cut their ties with Czechoslovakia; moreover, they could expect to be materially supported after the war due to their elevated status in the community and the material goods this would bring them and their families. In practical terms, the presence of Transcarpathians in the Soviet Army meant that Czechoslovakia was beginning to lose both its citizens and territory.

TERRITORIAL DISPUTES WITH SLOVAKIA AND ROMANIA

Parallel to the Red Army's mobilization, local Communists and intelligentsia planned to spread their control over the neighbouring territories of eastern Slovakia and Maramureş county in Romania. The Temporary Constitutional Law of Transcarpathian Ukraine adopted by the NRZU during the Mukachevo Congress claimed that it "would automatically have power over the Carpatho-Ukrainian lands of Hungary, Slovakia, and Romania, which would unite with Transcarpathian Ukraine later."[31] This statement was indicative of the shifting state borders during the war, or, at least, expectations among local pro-Soviet activists that the territory of Transcarpathian Ukraine would be enlarged with the backing of the Red Army and Soviet Union, which had already helped end the Czechoslovak administration.

Eastern Slovakia or the Prešov region amounted to the biggest territorial claim in Transcarpathian Ukraine. Immediately after the Red Army's arrival, local Russophiles in the Prešov region organized a rally demanding that the Soviet leadership take over Transcarpathian Ukraine.[32] Then after the Mukachevo Congress, the Prešov activists sent a letter to the NRZU asking for unification with Transcarpathian Ukraine. Although Prešov's Communists used the name Transcarpathian Ukraine, they interchangeably described themselves as Russians or Rusyns, indicating their Russophile orientation.[33] Exploiting events in eastern Slovakia, the NRZU sent a letter to Beneš that praised the unification rally in the eastern Slovak city of Prešov.[34] Mikhail Shmigel' and Valentina Mar'ina interpret the NRZU's actions as part of a wider Soviet game against the Czechoslovak government-in-exile, playing on the latter's fears of losing further territory in Slovakia as a means to inveigle it into a quick agreement to abandon any efforts to keep Transcarpathia.[35] In other words, the Bolsheviks pragmatically used sentiments in favour of the unification of the Ukrainian lands that went beyond Transcarpathian Ukraine in order to secure their claims over

Transcarpathia. This dismissal of local Ukrainophile or Russophile sentiments exemplified how the Ukrainian question served the greater power interests of the Soviet Union, helping it shift its borders and obtain access to the Central European states on the western side of the Carpathians.

Under pressure from the NRZU and pro-Soviet activists, Němec left Khust for Moscow on 11 December 1944 to clarify the situation in Transcarpathia. Czechoslovak Communists, who were in Moscow at the time told Němec that Beneš had accepted that Transcarpathia would become part of the Soviet Union. However, in a later conversation with Němec, Beneš denied any previous agreements existed about Transcarpathia joining the Soviet Union; he instructed Němec to follow the previous agreement about the division of military and civil administrations, but to do so without intervening in the activities of Transcarpathian Communists.[36] After Moscow, Němec travelled to Slovakia to establish a Czechoslovak administration there, leaving a small staff led by a Transcarpathian Soviet Ukrainophile named Ivan Petrushchak in Transcarpathian Ukraine. Later, the Red Army political commissar Mikhail Pronin, who played a significant role in the Soviet annexation of the region, noted that it was important that Němec left ethnic Ukrainians in Transcarpathian Ukraine, which was in line with the Ukrainization of the local administration.[37] More importantly, Petrushchak, the remaining representative of the Czechoslovak delegation, was himself a Communist, which meant that the region was fully under Soviet rule the moment Němec departed. The Czechoslovak delegation had thus made it very clear that it did not wish to claim the territory for Czechoslovakia; however, it saved face by being formally present on its pre-Munich territory. The Czechoslovak delegation had ceased to be a threat. Formally, the bilateral treaty between Czechoslovakia and the Soviet Union in June 1945 finalized the transition of Transcarpathian Ukraine and secured most of the territory of eastern Slovakia, except for the village of Chop, which had strategic value for the Soviet railway connection but no ethnic Ukrainians that could justify its annexation (see map 10.2).

Transcarpathian Ukraine was also locked in a territorial dispute with Romania over Maramureș county. The Ukrainians viewed this as an opportunity for further territorial enlargement. Maramureș's significance revolved around the town of Sighet, which was strategically important, for the railway connection with the eastern, mountainous parts of Transcarpathia ran through it. According to Nikita Khrushchev, it was the local Communist leader Turianytsia who conceived of the idea of annexing Maramureș county; he wanted to capitalize on the uncertainty caused by the war. Khrushchev, who was head of the Communist Party of Ukraine at that

10.2 Soviet Ukraine, 1945.

time, was certainly not opposed to adding more land to the growing Soviet Republic.[38] Clearly, the formation of the borders of Transcarpathian Ukraine was being driven not only by the interests in Kyiv and Moscow but also by local initiatives.

In February 1945, people's committees under the jurisdiction of the NRZU were established in Maramureș county and its unification with Transcarpathian Ukraine was proclaimed.[39] However, the local Romanian population and representatives of Bucharest resisted this, backing the local Romanian administration and rejecting any claims by the NRZU. The Romanians were prepared to use violence to defend their territorial integrity. This led to the Ukrainian Maramureș delegates being severely beaten immediately after the rally in Sighet. Khrushchev was informed by local Communists that the Romanians' actions risked provoking a conflict between the Romanian authorities and the two thousand Red Army soldiers mobilized from Maramureș.[40] In the end, the NRZU did not risk challenging Romania's control over the county, and Turianytsia abandoned any attempts to annex the territory.

According to Aleksandr Stykalin's interpretation of these events, Moscow had unleashed Ukrainophile sentiments in order to legitimately annex

Transcarpathia. This sometimes had unforeseen consequences, given that the Soviet leadership had not anticipated the annexation of Maramureş county. Stalin had to intervene personally to prevent additional annexations to Transcarpathian Ukraine. Initially, the Bolsheviks were ready to annex Maramureş, but when the left-wing government of Petru Groza came to power in Romania, the Soviet Union did not wish to risk a conflict around a small piece of land that was important only to Transcarpathian Communists. The Soviet leader therefore told Khrushchev to inform Turianytsia that he had to halt any attempts to annex that territory to Transcarpathian Ukraine.[41] In the end, the Soviet Union and Romania divided the contested area around Sighet along the Tisza River. As a result, some of the villages and towns along the river were divided into Romanian and Ukrainian sectors – for example, the town of Tiachiv – which disrupted local life.[42] Local interests would not be permitted to impact the settling of Ukraine's western borders, and they remained hostage to the Soviets' broader plan for rearranging the postwar order in Central Europe.

Though he accepted Maramureş county as part of Romania, Turianytsia tried to help the Red Army soldiers who had been drafted from Maramureş's Carpatho-Rusyn population return to their home villages. Soon after being demobilized, however, they found themselves being discriminated against by the local Romanian administration, and they complained about this to the KPZU. In his letter to the Ukrainian Commissar of Foreign Affairs of Soviet Ukraine, Turianytsia asked that he be allowed to negotiate with the Romanian government for equal treatment of Red Army as well as Romanian war veterans.[43] Local Communists had been trying to exert influence over the Maramureş affair as they pursued Ukrainophile irredentism. While this may have been instigated from above, it quickly became strongly self-propelled at the local level.

This local nationalist activism contradicts Magocsi's interpretation – that Transcarpathia became part of Soviet Ukraine solely through decisions made in Moscow. It also points to a more complex picture of local activists' promotion of a Ukrainian irredentist agenda, as well as to a more pragmatic and flexible approach by the Soviet leadership. The wider interests of the Soviet Union shaped the border of Transcarpathian Ukraine, with local interests and nationalist sentiments testing the limits of what was allowed. The Prešov and Maramureş affairs illustrate how local initiatives could enlarge Ukrainian territory in the west and correspond with the Soviet policy of Ukrainian national unification. However, the Soviet Union always remained cautious: it did not seek to trigger anti-Soviet nationalist sentiments in Central European countries, and it placed limits on the scope for

Ukrainian unification. Overall, the Soviet authorities merely pursued minor changes in the borders originally established by the Czechoslovaks.

CONCLUSIONS

The Soviet Union transformed the amorphous concept of Carpathian Rus, contested by multiple nationalist movements, into the idea of Transcarpathia, which gained clear administrative borders within Soviet Ukraine. This transformation was primarily the result of the Great Powers' aspirations, the Soviets' approach to resolving the Ukrainian territorial question, and the national orientations of local pro-Soviet activists, notably Soviet Ukrainophiles. First, the activists compelled the Czechoslovak administration to leave; then they used Soviet institutions like the Red Army to detach local populations from Czechoslovakia and join them to Soviet Ukraine. The Transcarpathian Communists attempted to enlarge Ukraine's territory along the Slovak and Romanian borderlands, but pragmatic considerations in Moscow blocked these regional irredentist aspirations. In the end, the Ukrainophile sentiments of local activists played a legitimizing role in the annexation of Transcarpathian Ukraine to Soviet Ukraine. The Soviet Union signed a treaty with Czechoslovakia in June 1945 and another with Romania in February 1947, officially settling the disputes over the borders of the Transcarpathian *oblast*.

Overall, the Soviets' gathering all the Ukrainian lands within a single set of borders served to defuse Ukrainian nationalist claims and to make the new borderlands in the west a platform for future revolutions in Central Europe. This would have a lasting affect on national politics in the territories under discussion. Maramureş's Ukrainians mostly remained as peasants, with only one Ukrainian-language school in Sighet, while Rusynophiles became a dominant national orientation in eastern Slovakia after the collapse of the Socialist bloc. One can say that out of the three regions discussed in this chapter, only in Transcarpathia, which remains part of Ukraine to this day, did Ukrainian national identity dominate, clearly defining the region as Ukrainian.

NOTES

1 For the sake of consistency, and the paper's historical focus on the period 1944–45, I will be using the Ukrainian names when referring to

Transcarpathian cities, such as *Mukachevo*, rather than the Hungarian *Munkács*.

2 Paul Robert Magocsi, *The Shaping of a National Identity: Subcarpathian Rus', 1848–1948* (Cambridge, MA: Harvard University Press, 1978), 12.
3 Magocsi is a Rusynopile activist himself.
4 Magocsi, *The Shaping of a National Identity*, 67.
5 John-Paul Himka, "The Construction of Nationality in Galician Rus': Icarian Flights in Almost All Directions," in *Intellectuals and the Articulation of the Nation*, ed. Ronald Grigor Suny and Michael D. Kennedy (Ann Arbor: University of Michigan Press, 1999), 135–6.
6 Suny and Kennedy, *Intellectuals and the Articulation of the Nation*, 147–8.
7 Magocsi, *With Their Backs to the Mountains: A History of Carpathian Rus' and Carpatho-Rusyns* (Budapest: CEU Press, 2015), 193–4.
8 Ibid., 276–78.
9 Vikentii Shandor, *Carpatho-Ukraine in the Twentieth Century: A Political and Legal History* (Cambridge, MA: Harvard University Press, 1997), 220–5.
10 Andrei Pushkash, *Tsivilizatsiia ili varvarstvo: Zakarpat'ie 1918–1945* (Moscow: Evropa, 2006), 320–1.
11 Magocsi, *With Their Backs to the Mountains*, 287–8.
12 Pushkash, *Tsivilizatsia ili varvarstvo*, 362.
13 Ibid., 363.
14 Terry Martin, *The Affirmative Action Empire: Nations and Nationalism in the Soviet Union, 1923–1939* (Ithaca: Cornell University Press, 2001), 10–13.
15 Peter A. Blitstein, "Cultural Diversity and the Interwar Conjuncture: Soviet Nationality Policy in Its Comparative Context," *Slavic Review* 65, no. 2 (2006): 279.
16 Martin, *The Affirmative Action Empire*, 123.
17 Serhiy Yekelchyk, *Stalin's Empire of Memory: Russian-Ukrainian Relations in the Soviet Historical Imagination* (Toronto: University of Toronto Press, 2004), 109.
18 Alfred J. Rieber, "Civil Wars in the Soviet Union," *Kritika: Explorations in Russian and Eurasian History* 4, no. 1 (2003): 139–40.
19 Jan Tomasz Gross, *Revolution from Abroad: The Soviet Conquest of Poland's Western Ukraine and Western Belorussia* (Princeton: Princeton University Press, 1988), 51.
20 Ibid., 67–70.
21 Ibid., 35–41.
22 Valentina Mar'ina, *Zakarpatskaia Ukraina (Podkarpatskaya Rus) v politike Benesha i Stalina. 1939–1945 gg.* (Moscow: Novyi Khronograf, 2003), 41.
23 Ibid., 37.

24 Magocsi, *With Their Backs to the Mountains*, 295.
25 Mar'ina, *Zakarpatskaia Ukraina*, 39.
26 Gross, *Revolution from Abroad*, 51.
27 Oleksii Korsun, "Vid Uporiadnyka," in *Posylennia politychnykh represii proty meshkantsiv Zakarpattia na zavershalnomu etapi ioho radianizatsii. 1947–1953 rr.*, ed. Oleksii Korsun (Uzhhorod: Karpaty, 2016), 10.
28 František Němec and Vladimir Moudrý, *The Soviet Seizure of Subcarpathian Ruthenia* (Westport: Hyperion Press, 1981), 95–7.
29 Vasyl' Markus', *Pryiednannia Zakarpats'koï Ukraïny do Radianskoï Ukraïny 1944–1945* (Kyiv: Intel, 1992), 40. Keeping in mind Markus's bias as a Ukrainian nationalist who worked with one of the branches of the OUN (*dviikari*) and the US government, his memoirs should be used carefully. In this case, how he describes the mobilization to the Red Army through benefits and coercion seems plausible, although the exact number of Carpatho-Rusyns mobilized to the Red Army requires further research.
30 Weiner, *Making Sense of War*, 362.
31 Derzhavnyi Arkhiv Zakarpats'koï Oblasti (State Archive of Transcarpathian Oblast, or DAZO) f. P-14, op. 1, spr. 12, ark. 2.
32 Mikhail Shmigel', "Dvizhenie za prisoedinenie Severo-Vostochnoi Slovakii k Sovetskoi Ukraine (1944–1945) v kontekste aneksii Zakarpat'ia SSSR," *Codrul Cosminului* 16, no. 2 (2010): 138.
33 DAZO f. 4, op. 1, spr. 11, ark. 1.
34 DAZO f. P-14, op. 1, spr. 13, ark. 1.
35 Shmigel', "Dvizhenie za prisoedinenie": 142; Mar'ina, *Zakarpatskaia Ukraina*, 135.
36 Němec and Moudrý, *The Soviet Seizure*, 128–36.
37 Tsenatral'nyi Arkhiv Ministerstva Oborony Rossiiskoi Federatsii (The Central Archives of the Ministry of Defence of the Russian Federation, or TSAMO RF) f. 244, op. 2980, d. 97, l. 351–3.
38 Nikita Khrushchev, *Vospominaniia*, 3 vols. (Moscow: Moskovskiie Novosti, 1999), 1:573.
39 DAZO f. 4, op. 1, spr. 103, ark. 1.
40 DAZO f. 4, op. 1, spr. 78, ark. 6–7.
41 Aleksandr Stykalin, "Pochemu ne realizilovalis novye plany po rasshireniiu Sovetskoi Ukrainy za schet Rumynii v 1945 g.," in *Slavianskyi mir v tretiiem tysiacheletii: Chelovek, obshchestvo, narod v istorii, iazyke i kulture*, ed. Elena Uzeneva (Moscow: Institute of Slavic Studies of the Russian Academy of Sciences, 2014), 210–12.
42 DAZO f. 4, op. 1, spr. 93.
43 DAZO f. 4, op. 1, spr. 104, ark. 5.

11

The Making of the Romanian-Ukrainian-Moldovan Border at the Maritime Danube in the Nineteenth and Twentieth Centuries

Constantin Ardeleanu

"DEPOSITS OF NATIONAL PRIDE"

On 3 February 2009, the International Court of Justice (ICJ) in The Hague delivered its judgment in a dispute between Romania and Ukraine. This proposed a way to establish the boundaries of the continental shelf around Serpents Island (Ostriv Zmiiny/Insula Șerpilor), an islet in the Black Sea some forty kilometres east of the Danube Delta.

Because the line proposed by the ICJ awarded Romania around 79 per cent of the disputed shelf, Romanian patriots hailed the decision as a great national and international success. For Bogdan Aurescu, Romania's chief negotiator during the dispute – and the current Romanian Foreign Minister, as of September 2021 – the line marked "the most important extension of Romania's sovereign jurisdiction for more than 90 years, since the Great Union of 1918."[1] Although diplomats tried to make it clear that Romania had no territorial claims from Ukraine and that the islet's sovereignty had never been in play, the ruling gave Romanians more than hypothetical access to the significant oil and gas resources of its newly recognized exclusive economic zone. This had "soothed" one of "Romania's open wounds," in reference to the territories that Greater Romania had lost in 1940. For the most ardent Romanian patriots, and for several nationalist political parties and organizations, the ICJ's ruling was a triumph worthy of Romania's high aspirations as a new EU member-state.

In Kyiv, by contrast, the decision was rather badly received, although Ukraine's representative at the ICJ, Volodymyr A. Vassylenko, tried to "sell" the judgment as a fair compromise, given that Ukraine kept most of the known oil and gas reserves on the disputed continental shelf. Opposition forces, however, presented the verdict as a shameful defeat for the Ukrainian government, which they viewed as too incompetent to defend the country's interests and as paving the way for the partition of Ukraine.[2] A confidential diplomatic report from the US Embassy in Kyiv pinpointed the symbolic relevance of the dispute: the Black Sea's continental shelf was rich in hydrocarbons, and besides that, it contained "important deposits of national pride" for both contenders.[3]

The American report mentioned a second economic and symbolic dispute that tested diplomatic relations between the two states in 2010. This one involved "navigation, dredging, and pollution" in the Danube Delta borderland, "where each side claims that its interests are harmed by the economic activity of the other."[4] In this second apparent zero sum game, the government in Bucharest seemed again to be in a better position: with loud support from transnational environmental groups, the Romanians succeeded in blocking (or at least postponing) a major infrastructural project on the Ukrainian side of the delta: the Bystroe (Bystre/Bîstroe) Canal, a deep-water canal in Ukrainian territorial waters that according to its opponents threatened the fragile ecosystem of a UNESCO-protected biosphere reserve.[5]

In an age in which mineral resources and transportation infrastructures are vital for regional development and national competitiveness, both disputes, beyond their clear economic and geopolitical relevance, had deeper historical roots. A notable component of these two episodes has been the frequent border changes in the region of the Maritime Danube, the memory of which is still fresh in both countries. The seeds of contention were planted in imperial times, when the Danube Delta was a Russian-Ottoman borderland (see map 11.1) and played a strategic role in the European balance of power. In fact, Ukraine's counter-memorandum submitted to the ICJ in 2006 noted that "the relevant historical developments related to the problem of recent maritime delimitation in the Black Sea between Ukraine and Romania started in the 19th century." The two contenders did not exist "as independent States and played no active role in international politics" at that time, but "the geopolitical struggle which developed in the area periodically triggered important changes concerning Ukrainian and Romanian ethnic territories and borders."[6] The current riparian countries – Romania, Ukraine, and Moldova – inherited these disputes, which resurface periodically and which these states have integrated into their historical narratives. The source of the discord is largely to be found in the complexity of drawing borders through a deltaic region with a fluid geography, as well as rich geopolitical symbolism and major economic relevance.

INTERNATIONAL RIVERS AS STATE BORDERS

It is generally considered that large rivers are among the most coveted borders that states can aspire to have. A recurring leitmotif in historical writing is that empires have always aimed for clear physical borders, like those provided by rivers. Yet rivers, especially long ones ending in deltaic marshes, are intricate hydrographic systems, and drawing borders through such labyrinths can be a fraught exercise. When delineating state borders along rivers, several principles have been used,[7] and choosing between them is a function of the power relations between the interested parties.

This has clearly been the case for the Danube, Europe's second longest waterway (after the Volga) and the world's most international river, flowing as it does through ten countries. At the end of its long journey, the Danube forms a delta as it branches into three main distributaries, Kiliia (Kiliiske *hyrlo*/Chilia), Sulina (Sulynske *hyrlo*/Sulina), and St George (Heorhiyivske *hyrlo*/Sf. Gheorghe), which together carry the river's sediments into the Black Sea. Secondary school geography textbooks in Romania describe the Danube Delta as the nation's "newest land." It is not only that the Delta is relatively young in geological terms, but also that the tens of millions of tons of alluvia carried along its 2,850-kilometre course extend it farther into the Black Sea each year. The delta thus amounts to a magical workshop in which nature keeps producing fresh land,[8] so that problems arise when borders need to be drawn through it.

This chapter highlights the interplay of geopolitical, economic, and environmental factors that have contributed to the making of the border that separates Ukraine, Moldova, and Romania in the region of the Maritime Danube. Laura di Fiore has recently observed "that border studies have a relatively small historical component" and has called for border-making to be analyzed from a more comparative perspective. Her recent research examines border creation processes in the nineteenth century, regarding them not simply as the product of institutional decision-making by emerging modern states but also as the result of a dialectic between state institutions and actors inhabiting borderlands.[9] One such actor, this chapter claims, has been the river itself. Because of its fluid geography, the Danube has required cartographers to regularly update their maps; it has also forced engineers to rethink projects meant to "tame" its course. Anthropologists have focused on the agency of nature in human affairs, and in this regard, "with its dynamics, rhythms and whims," the Danube has been viewed as a strategic agent that has long triggered serious border disputes between riparian states.[10]

11.1 The Danube estuary in 1867.

This chapter describes the making of three borderlines that have been drawn and redrawn in the Maritime Danube region over the past two centuries: the "riverine borderline" along the tortuous river itself, the "buffer borderline" aiming to secure the Danube's political and economic relevance, and the "maritime boundary" or the jurisdiction over Serpents Island and its continental shelf, control of which has usually been linked to the Danube Delta. I will follow a thematic/chronological structure, touching on the making of the three borders at several critical junctures. Given the long-term perspective and aims of this chapter, I will rely largely on international treaties and secondary literature in describing the history of the Danubian borders. Through this historical interpretation, the chapter aims to move beyond the rather rich literature on the issue published in Romanian and Ukrainian, by authors who usually parrot the official claims of their states. Various factors will be considered – geopolitical and economic, legal and ethnic – but an important element of my perspective relates to how the fluctuating geography of the region has resulted in various political interpretations as to its bordering, most often than not inspired by power relations between riparian states and by larger geopolitical calculations.

BORDERING THE MARITIME DANUBE IN THE NINETEENTH CENTURY: RIVAL EMPIRES, AN INTERNATIONAL ORGANIZATION, AND FISHING DISPUTES

When the Russian Empire annexed the eastern half of the principality of Moldavia in 1812, it inched one step closer to the Turkish Straits, seen by many observers as imperial Russia's main political goal in southeastern Europe. With the annexation of Bessarabia, Russia reached the mouths of the Danube, which it also gradually annexed. Through the Treaty of Adrianople (1829), it gained control over the entire Danube Delta. The new Russian-Ottoman border ran along the Maritime Danube and its southern branch, the St George, but the "functional" border, along which the imperial authorities established a rigorous quarantine system, followed the Sulina branch, the main transportation corridor used for international navigation toward inland Danubian ports. From this time on, a serious problem with bordering the area was accommodating the river's role as a well-guarded strategic inter-imperial border with its function as a busy transportation corridor for international trade.

Rising imperial rivalries turned the Danube into a symbolic red line against the Russian Empire's anti-Ottoman drives as well as a barometer for European stability. Russia now started to be held accountable for failing to improve the river's navigability through hydraulic works in its territorial waters. The legal argument was that according to the 1815 Vienna principles, the Danube was an international river, and riparian countries were expected to carry out engineering works to secure the safe passage of ships in their respective territorial waters.[11]

A dispute about Russian Sulina, a choke point where navigation was suffocated equally by a sandbank and the corruption of local authorities, played a significant role in Crimean War diplomacy. At the 1856 Paris Peace Congress, the Western victors discussed several solutions aimed at securing the freedom of the Danube and at buttressing the region against Russia's political and economic aggression. Two decisions inscribed in the 1856 Paris Peace Treaty would be crucial to the making of the "riverine border." The first of these compelled Russia to cede both the Danube Delta and a portion of Southern Bessarabia, which were handed over to the principality of Moldavia, an autonomous state under Ottoman suzerainty. In 1857, through an additional agreement among Europe's powers, the Danube Delta was transferred to the Ottoman Empire, which would exercise direct sovereignty. The second decision was to create the European

Commission of the Danube (ECD), an international organization comprising delegates from the seven contracting powers. This institution was tasked with designating and executing the hydraulic works necessary "to clear the mouths of the Danube, as well as the neighbouring parts of the sea, from the sands and other impediments which obstruct them." It had a term of two years to complete its tasks,[12] but the ECD was regularly prolonged, and the organization started to act not only as a body of technical experts but also as a bulwark for the Great Powers' political and economic interests in the region.

Problems with the new Danubian border soon emerged. Unhappy with the "loss" of the Danube Delta, Moldavian (Romanian)[13] statesmen protested the decision and tried to find a better channel linking the Southern Bessarabian mainland to the Black Sea. The establishment of the border between Moldavia and the Ottoman Empire created additional disputes related to local fishing communities. Thus, Lipovan fishermen from Vylkove/ Vâlcov lost access to their fishing grounds, and their protests lengthened to the list of issues that finally convinced several powers to examine the border between Moldavia and the Ottoman Empire. In 1861, the ECD was tasked with finding a solution, and commissioners started to collect information on the geography and hydrography of the Danube Delta. However, disagreements soon emerged when they tried to organize this corpus of knowledge into a coherent system of principles, as these officials failed to agree on even simple definitions: What characteristics define the separate "identity" of a branch of the river in such a labyrinthine area? How deep should a river channel be to be considered navigable? For how many months of a year should its physical characteristics be recorded? Eventually, a border was drawn along the thalweg of "the most northern branch of the Danube," but excluding "all and every one of the Islands of the Delta from Moldavia."[14] This consecrated the special regime of the Danube Delta border, whose status was different from that of all the other borders between the Ottoman Empire, Wallachia, and Moldavia along several hundred kilometres of the Danube. This gave it a distinctive political character, resulting from the asymmetric power relations between local riparian states rather than from a purely technocratic solution based on mutually agreed juridical principles.

In 1878, at the end of the Russian-Ottoman War, Russia re-annexed Southern Bessarabia, in exchange for which it provided Romania, its former ally, with ample territorial compensation: Romania received the Danube Delta and the province of Dobrudja (Dobrogea), which imperial Russia had just received as war indemnities from the Ottoman Empire.

Russia showed little interest in retaining the delta, where the ECD was still carrying out hydraulic works along the navigable Sulina branch. An article in the Treaty of San Stefano, later duplicated in the Berlin Treaty (1878), clearly mentioned the contours of the new riverine border between the Russian Empire and Romania: it was to follow "the mid-channel of the Kiliia Branch and the Old Stambul [Starostambulske] mouth." Through this provision, Russia claimed the very border that had been denied to Moldavia (Romania), one that allowed it a safer channel of communication between Southern Bessarabian ports and the Black Sea.[15]

In the coming decades the Russian authorities managed to remove the ECD's jurisdiction from its portion of the Danube Delta. Russian engineers now intended to carry out hydraulic works in the Kiliia sub-delta so as to complete a deep-water canal; this would increase river traffic toward the Southern Bessarabian ports. In 1894, after several conflicts between Russian and Romanian fishermen, discussions began over a new delineation of territorial waters in the Old Stambul mouth, with the Russians claiming that changes in the thalweg required a renegotiation of the border. A joint commission of experts analyzed the problem, but no agreement was reached. A new fishing convention between the two states did manage to reduce the frequency of conflicts between local fishermen.[16]

Establishing borders in the Danube Delta proved extremely complicated given the various actors involved in the decision and their conflicting views on the function of borders. The border finally agreed upon was a compromise between the hydro-political ambitions and vanities of an imperial power (Russia), the procedures of an international bureaucracy (the ECD), and the fears and political vanities of a young nation-state (Romania). This asymmetric riverine border divided the delta into political units that did not consider the dynamics of an environmental machine that followed the laws of nature.

DISPUTED ISLANDS, SHIFTING CHANNELS, CHANGING BORDERS

The border question returned to the Danube Delta in 1940, after the Soviet Union annexed Bessarabia, which in the murky revolutionary context of 1918 had joined Romania, despite protests from representatives of the emergent Ukrainian state. The events of 1918 and 1940 are still controversial, and, as I will briefly present below, historical narratives differ considerably in Romanian and Ukrainian historiographies, as well as in Moldova.

The border between Romania and the Soviet Union was delineated by a joint commission that met in Moscow in September 1940. The Romanian delegation was led by General Constantin Sănătescu and the Soviet one by General German Malandin. The delimitation started with a map attached to Vyacheslav Molotov's June ultimatum note sent to the Romanian authorities, through which the Soviet Union demanded the evacuation of the Romanian military and civil administration from Bessarabia and Northern Bukovina, territories that, it was noted, were either "mainly populated by Ukrainians" or linked "with Soviet Ukraine by the community of historical fate, and by the community of language and ethnic composition."[17]

The delineation proceeded with little controversy along most of the new border. In the Maritime Danube the border followed the main riverbed. Complications arose, however, in several sections of the Danube Delta, where further assistance was requested from a joint commission of hydraulic experts, who conducted additional surveys in October 1940. Nevertheless, disputes developed over which was the main navigable channel and which the main thalweg. The Romanian side wanted to return to the border of 1878; Soviet negotiators requested several islands that had formed since changes in the delta's hydrography. A second dispute concerned the border in the Old Stambul area: the Soviet side requested control over a channel that exited unobstructed into the sea. Their claim to have the border follow the Musura Channel was rejected by Romania, since it had not existed in 1878. Between 1878 and 1940, alluvial deposits had extended the shoreline by 8–10 kilometres in the region of Old Stambul, an advance that had contributed to the formation of the Musura Channel. This was an appropriate border, Soviet negotiators contended, given that Romania already had a good exit to the sea, either at Sulina or at St George. However, in late October 1940, before this argument had a chance to end, Soviet troops occupied the disputed islands (total area of twenty-four kilometres square). The Soviet diplomat Vladimir Dekanozov explained this action in the context of the Soviets' strategic interest in securing a strong position along the Kiliia branch of the Danube, at a time when Romania had just moved toward closer economic and military cooperation with Nazi Germany. The new border, Dekanozov continued, was hardly a problem for Bucharest, given that Romania remained in full possession of most of the Danube Delta, including the branches of Sulina and St George.[18]

Romania joined the Second World War in May 1941 as an ally of Nazi Germany, occupying its former provinces, including the Danube Delta region, and extending its rule in the "Transnistria Governorate," a

Romanian-administered territory between the Dniester and Bug Rivers, where Romanian soldiers committed atrocious war crimes.[19] In 1944, the Soviet Union returned to Bessarabia and the 1940 Danubian border was re-established. Eventually, the 1947 Paris Treaty fixed the Soviet-Romanian frontier in accordance with the Soviet-Romanian Agreement of 28 June 1940 and the Soviet-Czechoslovak Agreement of 29 June 1945.[20]

On 4 February 1948, Molotov and the Romanian Prime Minister Petru Groza signed in Moscow the Treaty of Friendship, Collaboration and Mutual Assistance between Romania and the USSR, as well as a protocol detailing the course of the border between the two states. Where there were inconsistencies between the textual description of the border and the border as rendered on maps, the text was to enjoy pre-eminence. In the Danube Delta region, the border was to follow "the Danube River from Pardina to the Black Sea, leaving the islands of Tătaru Mic [Tataru], Daleru Mic and Mare [Velykyy Daler and Malyy Daler], Maican [Maikan], and Limba [Ostriv Limba] on the Soviet side, and Tătaru Mare, Cernovca and Babina on the Romanian side." Demarcation on the ground was carried out from October to December 1948 by a joint commission of experts, and once again disputes emerged regarding the ownership of several islands. Demarcation documents were drawn up, and in 1949 a bilateral treaty was negotiated that regulated the Soviet-Romanian border and introduced instruments of cooperation and mutual assistance in border issues.[21]

A new border treaty was concluded in 1961, and throughout the socialist period regular surveys of the border were conducted by joint commissions of experts. Although bilateral treaties stipulated that "the border route had to be changed according to the natural shift of the middle of the main waterway," technical experts and political negotiators never agreed to alter the border. One of the longest-lasting disputes concerned Maikan/Maican Island in the Danube Delta. The Romanians claimed that after a shift of the main waterway the island now fell on Romania's side; Soviet delegates to the mixed commission rejected this interpretation. A similar controversy surrounded the Musura Channel. The Soviet negotiators had concluded that the treaty provisions were contradictory, outdated, and open to interpretation; moreover, according to the principle of the main waterway, the Soviet-Romanian border should run along the Sulina branch.[22] The Russian Empire and the interwar Soviet Union had stayed away from the Sulina Canal, probably because of its status as the main transportation corridor for international trade and shipping, regulated by an international organization. That situation changed only in 1948, with the dissolution of the ECD.[23]

Since the 1990s, Romanian-Ukrainian border negotiations in the Danube Delta have been conducted along much the same lines. When in 1991 a Ukrainian ship – the *Rostock* – sank in a narrow section of the Sulina Canal, many in Romania regarded this as an act of sabotage meant to divert river traffic toward the Ukrainian portion of the river. Romania had similar concerns when the Ukrainian authorities started to build the Bystroe Canal, which supposedly would have impacted the protected ecosystem of the Danube Delta. Romania contested the project in front of international organizations; after being labelled as an "environmental threat," the deep-water canal was received with resistance.[24]

Romania and Ukraine have also discussed Maikan/Maican Island, but no agreement has been reached either by joint commissions or by politicians. The problem is that any change to the border would contradict the principle of border inviolability upheld in the Ukrainian-Romanian basic treaty of 2003; moreover, Ukraine's experts contend that borders in the Danube Delta "were determined following other principles, namely the principle of the three-meter isobar."[25] Ukrainian authors regard Romania's claims as part of the revisionist ethos that has come to characterize the foreign policy of Romania, which has been emboldened by its "success" regarding Serpents Island.[26]

As this section has tried to show, one of the main challenges in the Danube Delta has been how to align bordering principles for international rivers with the economic value of the Danube and its function as a major European transportation artery. In this regard, the Soviet Union – and, later, Ukraine – set out to establish a strategic border that would allow access to a deep-water channel linking Southern Bessarabia and the Black Sea. Romania has long been in possession of the main navigable branch of the Danube Delta, the Sulina Channel, and for economic reasons has resisted attempts to change the morphology of the delta. In recent times, the region's status as a protected bioreserve has placed new hurdles in front of Ukraine's efforts to develop navigation in its territorial waters. As for the Danubian islands, they are more important for nationalist than for economic reasons. For young states fighting to maintain their territorial integrity, the inviolability of borders is a crucial principle, one that overrides any efforts to correct the border so as to reflect permanent shifts in a dynamic environmental system.

BUFFER BORDERING: THE BUDJAK AND ITS CONNECTION TO THE DANUBE

This section examines the "buffer border" that aimed to secure the Danube's political and economic relevance. This division line across Southern Bessarabia or the Budjak has a long history, entangled in that of the "riverine border" described in previous sections.

At the end of the Crimean War, the Western victors set out to secure Danubian navigation by pushing imperial Russia away from the river. To that end, the 1856 Paris Peace Treaty stripped Russia of a large portion of the Bessarabian province. Using a French map copied from a Russian original, negotiators outlined the course of the new border from the Black Sea to Cotul Morii, on the Prut River.[27] Demarcation started in the summer of 1856, at which time the commissioners of five empires noticed that the maps used in Paris had been mistaken and misinterpreted. The town of Bolgrad/Bolhrad was one of the main bones of contention, as it seemed to communicate to the Danube; the strategic value of the treaty would have been ruined had that town been left in Russian hands.[28] A compromise was mediated by France, and the new border was consecrated during an ambassadorial conference that convened in Paris in 1857. Russia received additional territorial compensation in the Lake Ialpuh area as well as the town of Comrat in the Gagauz district, while Bolgrad/Bolhrad remained in Moldavia to preserve the strategic value of the 1856 Paris Treaty.[29]

Southern Bessarabia was integrated into Moldavia (Romania), but its function as a buffer region proved to be a double-edged sword. The Moldavian authorities had numerous reasons to be dissatisfied with the borders of their new province, as the Budjak was one of the most ethnically mixed parts of Bessarabia and its integration into the Romanian nation-state would prove to be a challenge. Russia re-annexed the area in 1878, and the Budjak would stay in the empire until 1918, when it again was returned to Romania. With its multicultural identity and poor transportation infrastructure, it lagged economically, and after the formation of the Moldovan Autonomous Soviet Socialist Republic (MASSR) in the Ukrainian territories on the left bank of the Dniester in 1924, it served as a wedge for contesting Romanian control of the entire Bessarabian region.

When Bessarabia, Northern Bukovina, and the Hertza region were annexed by the Soviet Union in June 1940, the fate of these territories had yet to be decided by the Soviet leadership. Tense discussions followed in Moscow and Kyiv, and eventually it was agreed to establish an "independent" Moldovan Soviet Socialist Republic (MSSR), separated from Soviet

Ukraine along ethnic and linguistic lines.[30] In July 1940, negotiations between Moldovan and Ukrainian delegates continued, with the Ukrainian side insisting that all territories inhabited by ethnic Ukrainians be included in Soviet Ukraine. Three counties were targeted – Khotyn/Hotin, Bilhorod-Dnistrovskyi/Cetatea Albă, and Izmail/Ismail. Moldovan leaders resisted the inclusion of Izmail/Ismail, a county where, they claimed, a non-Ukrainian majority existed: only 5 per cent of the population was supposedly Ukrainian, with a multi-ethnic majority consisting of Russian, Moldavian, Bulgarian, and Gagauz people. Ukrainian leaders Nikita Khrushchev, Mykhailo Grechukha, and Leonid Korniyets insisted on getting the urban centre of Izmail/Ismail and the area of Budjak, as "by law and customs" Ukrainians and Russians in the region cohabitated well.[31]

The main reason, however, had more to do with the strategic location of the Budjak region and with its economic value. The Soviet leadership considered it crucial to have a single administrative unit in control of the entire riverbank: with its link to the Black Sea, the Danube could be more efficiently exploited by the fluvial and maritime fleet of the ukrSSR, "which is why there is no point in dividing the Danube into spheres of influence, both economically and strategically."[32]

Moldovan leaders tried to resist this division of Bessarabia, but by August 1940 the decision had been taken. Further negotiations took place in Chișinău between A. Mezherin, Secretary of the Supreme Soviet of the ukrSSR, and Feodor Brovko, Chairman of the Moldovan SSR. Documents were signed on 22 August 1940 with a preliminary agreement for the division line in northern Bessarabia, Transnistria, and the Budjak. In the coming weeks, several changes were made, mainly along ethnic lines, but disputes continued regarding Budjak, especially in relation to the delineation of the border in the Bilhorod-Dnistrovskyi/Cetatea Albă region. Bolgrad/Bolhrad, the "capital" of Southern Bessarabian Bulgarians, was again disputed, and it eventually remained on the Ukrainian side. The new border was accepted by Moscow in early September and legalized on 4 November 1940, when the Supreme Soviet of the USSR voted for a decree titled "On the establishment of the border between the ukrSSR and the Moldovan SSR." A description detailed the new border, which remained to be demarcated on the ground.[33]

According to several pro-Moldovan sources, a strategic reason for this border change in the Budjak region was to cut off Soviet Moldova from any access to the Danube and the Black Sea while also mitigating any attempts at independence, or union with Romania.[34] However, details about this are lacking, since the protocols on the joint Moldovan-Ukrainian discussions and the maps used to delineate the new border are unavailable to historians. As both republics were part of the Soviet Union, this administrative border was not believed to be especially burdensome for local people.

Disputes over the border continued into the Soviet period, with several Moldovan leaders petitioning Moscow for the reunification of Bessarabia. In 1946, Nichita Salogor, the interim Prime Secretary of the Moldovan Communist Party, submitted several documents to Moscow to support his claim. These included reports on Moldova's ethnic composition and economy and a history of its borders, as well as an account of the boundaries of the Moldavian people and language. As most inhabitants were ethnic Moldavians, it was only natural to make the republic a single administrative unit within the Soviet Union. Salogor also insisted on the ethnic composition of Izmail/Ismail, where Moldavians held a majority, and on the need for a proper connection to the Danube, given its importance for the republic's economy. Similar requests followed throughout the coming decades, but to little avail.[35] Moreover, in 1947 the Moldovan SSR lost about 460 hectares of arable land at Palanca, including five kilometres of Black Sea coast and access to the estuary of the Dniester.[36]

With the dissolution of the Soviet Union and the formation of the independent states of Ukraine and Moldova, internal administrative borders were turned into hard borders in the early 1990s. A bilateral treaty signed in 1992 recognized the pre-dissolution status quo. A further protocol was concluded in 1999 to resolve two outstanding issues: the Reni-Odesa highway, which crosses Moldovan territory at Palanca, and Moldova's Danubian riverfront. The two states negotiated an exchange of territories that would have given Ukraine full possession of the area where the Ukrainian Reni-Odesa highway crosses Moldovan territory (a total of 10.5 kilometres square) in exchange for a similar portion of land between Giurgiulești and Reni, an area that has access to the Danube. However, the protocol was blocked when a dispute arose in relation to jurisdiction over a territory called "Rîpa de la Mîndrești" (the Ravine from Mîndrești). The Ukrainian side was inclined to give it to the Moldovans, but the latter pretended it was legally Moldovan territory, as it had been part of Soviet Moldova. Moldova now possesses a 340-metre stretch of Danubian bank and hopes to get an extension from Ukraine that would allow it to further develop its Danubian port of Giurgiulești. In 2012, negotiations between the two countries led to an agreement to maintain the status quo, as nationalist forces in both countries oppose any exchange of territories.[37]

For similar reasons, Europe's Great Powers and the Soviet Union supported the separate identity of the Budjak region. It was presented as a cosmopolitan area in an inter-imperial periphery, but for all parties concerned its main value derived from the geopolitical, economic, and symbolical relevance of the Danube. When the region's borders were drawn in 1856 and 1940, strategic reasons weighed at least as much as ethnic ones, with the result that the Bulgarian or Gagauz villages, colonized in the Budjak in the nineteenth century, were split between the two sides of the border. Bolgrad/Bolhrad was part of Moldavia (Romania) between 1856 and 1878, while Comrat, the centre of the Gagauz community, remained within the Russian Empire. With the new division in 1940, Comrat ended up in the Moldovan SSR while Bolgrad/Bolhrad became part of the UkrSSR. Significant numbers of Bulgarians and Gagauzes were separated on the two sides of the border. Concerning strategic calculations, the state controlling the Budjak has always found it crucial to secure unimpeded access to a navigable channel of the Danube.

AN ISLAND IN HISTORICAL AND DIPLOMATIC DISPUTE

This section touches on the making of the "maritime boundary" or the jurisdiction over Serpents Island, the control of which has usually been linked to the Danube Delta. I will be referring to the arguments Romanian and Ukrainian negotiators brought before the ICJ, as their memorandums provide a clear summary of the clashing official narratives of both states regarding their shared border over the past century.

Serpents Island, an islet of 0.17 hectares, was "rediscovered" in the 1820s by Russian scholars from Odesa, who took an interest in its ancient ruins and biological diversity. As the decades passed, it became increasingly prominent in navigational atlases; with the development of Black Sea navigation, it started to be used as a landmark for ships navigating the western Pontic coast from Istanbul to ports in the Danubian Principalities and the Ukrainian provinces of the Russian Empire. In the 1840s the Russian authorities built a lighthouse there.[38]

The 1856 Paris Peace Treaty made no reference to Serpents Island. At the end of the Crimean War, Russia laid claim to it but found it was already occupied by Ottoman troops supported by the British navy.[39] A diplomatic dispute followed, with the Western Powers insisting that jurisdiction over the islet be linked to that of the Danube Delta. As the latter had been taken from the Russian Empire, the island should go to its new master, too. Through an appended protocol of January 1857, Serpents Island was given to the Ottoman Empire. As noted earlier, Russia received additional territorial compensations in Southern Bessarabia.[40]

In 1878, Serpents Island was transferred to Romania together with the Danube Delta. The local lighthouse was serviced by the European Commission of the Danube, which thus controlled most of the islet's economic life.[41] The islet, however, occupied an interesting place in the Romanian geographical imagination for its rich mythology and as destination for scholarly or artistic excursions to Romania's "only colony."[42]

The 1947 Paris Peace Treaty again made no reference to the islet. However, the Soviet Union mentioned it in a protocol signed in February 1948 in Moscow. For Romanian patriots, the arrangement that made official the transfer of this territory to the Soviet Union was not sanctioned by the Romanian parliament and thus had no legal value.[43] The Soviets, making an argument subsequently taken over by Ukraine, contended that possession of the island derived from the 1948 delineation of the "riverine border," as presented earlier. The strategic value of the island had increased with the development of radiocommunication and radar systems,[44] not to mention its value for navigation along major Black Sea routes and the important hydrocarbon reserves discovered on its continental shelf.

Attempts to demarcate the boundary of maritime spaces between Romania and the Soviet Union lasted throughout the communist era. Bilateral discussions were initiated at the expert level, but the delimitation of the continental shelf and the establishment of exclusive economic zones in the Black Sea proved impossible due to failure to agree on the basic principles for governing such an agreement.[45] In 1996, Romania denounced the 1948 Protocol, which had facilitated the transfer of Serpents Island to the Soviet Union. Eventually, Romanian-Ukrainian bilateral relations were normalized, with the treaties of 1997 and 2003 recognizing the border between the two states.[46]

When Romania and Ukraine agreed to go before the ICJ to settle the dispute regarding the territorial limits of the continental shelf in the Black Sea around Serpents Island, the memorandums submitted by the two sides showed that beyond disagreements of a technical nature, historical polemics made any possible dialogue all the more problematic.[47] Some basic historical facts were understood in completely different ways, and narratives of the events of 1917–18, 1939–41, 1944, and 1947–48 as they emerged from the official positions of the two delegations showed that the two countries adhered to two alternative versions of history.

In their memorandum, Romania's delegates made ample references to history. Chapter 3 outlined the historical background, insisting on the "strategic significance accorded to Serpents Island since at least the nineteenth century and detailing the circumstances surrounding its peremptory seizure by the Soviet Union in 1948." The main phases in Danubian diplomatic history were mentioned, as well as the fact that the islet had been part of Romania between 1878 and 1948. It had been the scene of several naval battles in both world wars, and Serpents Island was neither included on the list of territories claimed by the Soviet Union in June 1940 nor part of the negotiations for the new border settlement in the autumn of that year. Territorial losses in 1940, the Romanians argued, had been a direct result of the Ribbentrop-Molotov Pact and its secret additional protocol. The islet was eventually annexed in 1948 "against the provisions of the 1947 Paris Peace Treaty." It was turned into a military outpost, with an uncertain legal status, "under the direct control of the central military authorities in Moscow" – a fact that underscored the Soviet Union's geostrategic reasons for annexing Serpents Island, in line with those of all imperial powers during the previous centuries. In another chapter, titled "The Influence of History," more historical content was provided. The two documents that transferred the island to the Soviet Union, it was claimed, had not been authorized and ratified by the Romanian parliament and thus were legally void; they were also morally flawed, as the documents were not the result of "free negotiations" between the two signatory parties. This was because Romania had been occupied by the Red Army, which imposed an illegitimate communist government under the leadership of Petru Groza, the very person who had agreed to cede the island. In their conclusion, the Romanian negotiators pointed out that Romania placed value on "the need for order and stability of the international community" and that it made no territorial claims on the Soviet Union or Ukraine. However, "the flawed transaction of 1948 should not be prolonged and extended in space, beyond the actual language of the 1949 delimitation agreements, to the manifest disadvantage of Romania." Finally, "an equitable solution should take into account any historical or political prejudice previously inflicted."[48]

Ukraine's memorandum responded in detail to Romania's "distorted version of events" and insisted on its own version of history. Imperial Russia's control of Bessarabia in the nineteenth century constituted an important gain, given that "Southern Bessarabia was mostly ethnically Ukrainian," and Romania's ill will was quite evident throughout the first half of the twentieth century. Ukrainian diplomats then focused on developments in the First World War in connection with another contested territory in Romanian-Ukrainian relations: Bukovina. Secret negotiations between Romania and Russia (in 1914) and then with all the Entente Powers (in 1916) stipulated the division of Bukovina along ethnic lines should Austria-Hungary be defeated in the war. However, in 1918, taking advantage of the disintegration of its imperial neighbours, Romania had "illegally seized the ethnic Ukrainian territories of Southern Bessarabia and northern Bukovyna." The emerging Ukrainian states protested this decision, while Soviet Ukraine and Russia opposed the recognition of Romanian sovereignty over Bessarabia, which had also become part of Greater Romania in 1918. The Romanian occupation of ethnic Ukrainian territories had been accompanied by severe denationalization of the Ukrainian population, while Romania's "obstinate refusal to negotiate and reach a fair and equitable territorial settlement" with its eastern neighbours resulted in there being "no legally established State border between the Soviet Union and Romania: before 1940 their territories were divided by a provisional demarcation line."[49]

A favourable geopolitical alignment followed, and Ukraine's "legitimate rights to Northern Bukovyna and Southern Bessarabia" were restored by the Soviet Union in 1940. The Ribbentrop-Molotov Pact and its secret additional protocol played no role in this. An article did mention the Soviet interest in Bessarabia, which, however, existed long before the said agreement was concluded. The new Romanian-Soviet border was almost settled in the summer of 1941, and only "some issues remained unsettled, relating mainly to the islands in the Danube Delta, including Serpents Island." Romania had joined Nazi Germany in the war of aggression against the Soviet Union and over the next three years had occupied large parts of Ukrainian territory, where Romanian troops committed atrocious war crimes. In 1944 Romania was occupied by Soviet troops as it was an "aggressor State," and in the aftermath of the war the border was settled based on the 1940 agreement. There was no mention of Serpents Island in this agreement or in the 1947 Paris Peace Treaty, as both documents "were concerned essentially with the mainland frontiers of Romania." The map annexed to the treaty was, as noted, a very small-scale one.[50]

Beyond these alternative views of the past, the ICJ analyzed the broader national and international implications. Romanian nationalists saw in a positive resolution of the dispute a strengthening of the country's geopolitical role in the region; Ukrainian patriots hoped to gain additional momentum to denounce Romania's revisionist schemes. Bilateral treaties in 1997 and 2003, signed in the context of Romania's negotiations for accession to NATO and the EU, made the Romanian government's requests for a solution even more geopolitically and politically loaded. Some analysts, often mobilized by their own political biases, regarded the ICJ's decision as having stemmed from such strategic power struggles, thus challenging the postwar order on which European stability rested.[51]

CONCLUSIONS

The three borders that have been drawn and redrawn in the Maritime Danube region over the past two centuries underscore the complexities of bordering a deltaic region with a strategic and symbolic function at the junction of geopolitical tectonic plates.

The riverine border changed after every major conflict in the region: in 1812, 1829, 1856, 1878, 1918, and 1947 the same pattern of division is visible, each time reflecting an interest in balancing the international character of the Sulina branch, regulated for navigation by an early international organization, with the desire of the state that owns the Budjak region to secure a navigable channel within the Kiliia sub-delta. The river itself has played a major role in political negotiations, as the continuous fluctuations of its hydrography have made border-drawing a complex process in which not only geographical and hydrographical knowledge and juridical principles count, but also power relations. Romania and Ukraine inherited a riverine border that came with the same bones of contention as those of their predecessor states.

Farther north, the buffer border in the Budjak was drawn, this chapter has claimed, to serve geopolitical calculations in relation to the Maritime Danube. In 1856, Europe's victors had the river's economic value in mind when they decided to push imperial Russia farther from a busy international transportation infrastructure. In 1940, the UkrSSR drew the division line separating it from the Moldovan SSR in a manner that privileged not only ethnic arguments but also strategic ones – specifically, securing access to the Danube. According to Moldovan sources, economic factors, but also defensive reasons in relation to Romanian revisionism, were the basis of the border delineation between the two Soviet republics.

Not the least of these issues was jurisdiction over Serpents Island, which has changed often over the past two centuries. From a landmark for shipping in the western Black Sea, the islet became a military communication outpost and the centre of a region rich in hydrocarbons, but all the while, its possession has been linked to the Danube Delta and different states' national historical narratives.

Borders are vital to fixing the territories and identities of young states. The current borders of Moldova, Romania, and Ukraine reflect painful histories of nation- and state-making as well as wounds that have yet to heal. All three countries respect the principle of border inviolability upheld in bilateral and multilateral treaties; that said, borders within hybrid geographical spaces have proven as dynamic as these states' volatile histories.

As the case brought before the ICJ made clear, the dispute between Romania and Ukraine was more than about controlling the resources buried in the vicinity of an island or a rock. It also involved sentiments such as "national pride" and efforts to come to terms with "historical frustrations" rising from troubled histories.

NOTES

1 Bogdan Aurescu, "Cuvânt introductiv," in *Delimitarea maritimă dintre România și Ucraina la Curtea de la Haga: documentele scrise și pledoariile României în cauza România c. Ucraina privind delimitarea spațiilor maritime în Marea Neagră, soluționată de Curtea Internațională de Justiție la 3 februarie 2009*, ed. Bogdan Aurescu, Cosmin Dinescu, and Liviu Dumitru (Bucharest: Editura Academiei Române, 2009), 7.
2 See, for example, Vladimir Dergachev's analysis of the geopolitical implications of the settlement: *Chernomorskiy ostrov Zmeinyy v zerkale geopolitiki. Kto vyigral i proigral konflikt vokrug kontinental'nogo shel'fa?*, http://dergachev.ru/geop_events/05.html.
3 "Ukraine's 'Other' Security Threat – Romania," confidential report from the US Embassy in Kyiv, 25 January 2010, https://wikileaks.org/plusd/cables/10KYIV120_a.html.
4 "Ukraine's 'Other' Security Threat – Romania."
5 "Bystroe Canal Project under International Scrutiny, overviews of activities addressing the Bystroe Canal project under multilateral environmental agreements and by intergovernmental organizations," 9 May 2008, https://www.ramsar.org/news/bystroe-canal-project-under-international-scrutiny.
6 ICJ, *Case Concerning Maritime Delimitation in the Black Sea (Romania v. Ukraine). Counter-Memorial Submitted by Ukraine* 1, no. 18, May 2006, 66–7, https://www.icj-cij.org/files/case-related/132/14699.pdf.
7 François Schroeter, "Le système de délimitation dans les fleuves internationaux," *Annuaire français de droit international* 38 (1992): 948–82.
8 Tanya Richardson, "Where the Water Sheds: Disputed Deposits at the Ends of the Danube," in *Watersheds: The Poetics and Politics of the Danube River*, ed. Marijeta Bozovic and Matthew Miller (Boston: Academic Studies Press, 2016), 307.
9 See Laura Di Fiore, "The Production of Borders in Nineteenth-Century Europe: Between Institutional Boundaries and Transnational Practices of Space," *European Review of History/Revue européenne d'histoire* 24, no. 1 (2017): 36–57.

10 Ștefan Dorondel, Stelu Șerban, and Daniel Cain, "The Play of Islands: Emerging Borders and Danube Dynamics in Modern Southeast Europe (1830–1900)," *Environment and History* 25, no. 4 (2019): 521–47.
11 Constantin Ardeleanu, *International Trade and Diplomacy at the Lower Danube: The Sulina Question and the Economic Premises of the Crimean War (1829–1853)* (Brăila: Editura Istros, 2014).
12 *Congrès de Paris 1856* (Paris: Impr. Impériale, 1856), 12–13.
13 The union of Moldavia and Wallachia, after the double election of Prince Alexandru Ioan Cuza in 1859, led to the creation of modern Romania.
14 Constantin Ardeleanu, "Fishing in Politically Troubled Waters: The Fishermen of Vylkove, Romanian Nation-Making, and an International Organization in the Danube Delta in the Late 1850s and Early 1860s," *Revue des Études Sud-Est Européennes* 55 (2017): 325–38.
15 Dimitrie A. Sturdza, *Recueil de documents relatifs à la liberté de navigation du Danube* (Berlin: Puttkammer und Mühlbrecht, 1904), 123–4.
16 Gr. Antipa, *Dunărea și problemele ei științifice, economice și politice* (Bucharest: "Cartea românească," Tipografia Rasidescu, 1921), 145–6; Ion Ionescu, "Chestiunea Stari-Stambul, o tentativă de violare a frontierelor tânărului stat independent român," *Anuarul Muzeului Marinei Române* 29, no. 8 (1998): 69–72.
17 Ion Șișcanu, "Trasarea frontierei pe Dunăre – obiectivul tratativelor româno-sovietice de la Moscova, 1940," *Revista istorică* 6, nos. 5–6 (1995): 477–96.
18 Șișcanu, "Trasarea frontierei pe Dunăre."
19 Vladimir Solonari, *A Satellite Empire: Romanian Rule in Southwestern Ukraine, 1941–1944* (Ithaca: Cornell University Press, 2019).
20 Charles I. Bevans, ed., *Treaties and Other International Agreements of the United States of America 1776–1949*, vol. 4: *Multilateral, 1946–1949* (Washington, DC: Department of State Publication, 1970), 404.
21 Grigore Stamate, *Frontiera de stat a României* (Bucharest: Editura Militară, 1997), 77–9.
22 Laurențiu-Cristian Dumitru, "România și frontierele la Dunăre și Marea Neagră 1948–1961," *Buletinul Universității Naționale de Apărare Carol I*, no. 1 (2011): 271–81; Dumitru, "Frontiera României la Marea Neagră 1966–1991," *Buletinul Universității Naționale de Apărare Carol I*, no. 2 (2011): 423–33; Dumitru, "Romanian-Soviet Disputes Regarding the Maritime Boundary Delimitation during the Postwar Period," in *Black Sea: History, Diplomacy, Policies and Strategies*, ed. Gavriil Preda and Gabriel Leahu (Bagheria: Mineo Giovanni Editore, 2012), 41–52.

23 P.G. Fandikov, *Mezhdunarodno-pravovoi rezhim Dunaia: istoricheskii ocherk* (Moscow: Gosiurizdat, 1955), 21.
24 Mirela Șofineți and Cristina Dobrotă, "Controversa româno-ucrainiană în problema Canalului Bîstroe," *Revista Transilvană de Științe Administrative* 6, no. 12 (2004): 158–62; Mari Koyano, "Effective Implementation of International Environmental Agreements: Learning Lessons from the Danube Delta Conflict," in *Public Interest Rules of International Law: Towards Effective Implementation*, ed. Teruo Komori and Karel Wellens (London: Routledge, 2009), 275–308; Richardson, "Where the Water Sheds," 307–36.
25 Anatolii Kruglashov, "Troublesome Neighborhood: Romania and Ukraine Relationship," *New Ukraine: A Journal of History and Politics* 11 (2011): 114–25.
26 Andrey Ganzha, *Rumyny "predlagayut vernut'*," https://odnarodyna.org/content/rumyny-predlagayut-vernut.
27 *Congrès de Paris*, 12–13.
28 W.E. Mosse, "Britain, Russia, and the Question of Serpents Island and Bolgrad: Two Incidents in the Execution of the Treaty of Paris," *Slavonic and East European Review* 29, no. 72 (1950): 86–139; Dumitru Vitcu, "The Treaty of Paris and the Bolgrad Crisis of Its Execution," *Anuarul Institutului de Istorie A.D. Xenopol* 43–4 (2006–7): 335–53.
29 The protocol of 6 January 1857 in *Hertslet's Commercial Treaties: A Collection of Treaties and Conventions, Between Great Britain and Foreign Powers*, 31 vols. (London 1859), 10:553–4.
30 Vitalie Văratec, "The Political-Territorial Division of Bessarabia in 1940," *Arhivele Totalitarismului* 13–14, nos. 4–1 (1996–7): 105–8.
31 Ibid., 109–13.
32 Ibid., 114.
33 Ibid., 118–22.
34 Nicolae Enciu, "Decretul Prezidiului Suprem al URSS din 4 noiembrie 1940 (3)," http://www.art-emis.ro/istorie/1981-decretul-prezidiului-suprem-al-urss-din-4-noiembrie-1940-3.html.
35 Igor Cașu and Virgil Pâslariuc. "Chestiunea revizuirii hotarelor RSS Moldovenești: de la proiectul 'Moldova Mare' la proiectul 'Basarabia Mare' și cauzele eșecului acestora (decembrie 1943–iunie 1946)," *Archiva Moldaviae* 2 (2010): 275–370.
36 Ion Varta, "Cum ni s-a furat accesul la Marea Neagră: Documente ale istoriei," *Literatura și arta* (5 August, 23 August, and 9 September 2010): 1–3.

37 Vlad Cubreacov, "Legătura între Palanca și Canalul Bâstroe, Insula Șerpilor," http://www.moldova.org/legatura-intre-palanca-si-canalul-bastroe-insula-serpilor-204717-rom.
38 More on the history of the island in Romulus Seișanu, *Dobrogea: Gurile Dunării și Insula Șerpilor* (Bucharest: Tipografia Ziarului "Universul," 1928).
39 Mosse, "Britain, Russia, and the Question," 86–139; Vitcu, "The Treaty of Paris," 335–53.
40 The Protocol of 6 January 1857, in *Hertslet's Commercial Treaties*, 10:553–4.
41 Adrian Pohrib, "Farurile Comisiei Europene a Dunării din Delta Dunării și de pe Insula Șerpilor (1856–1939)," in Aurel-Daniel Stănică and Cristian Leonard Micu, eds., *Istro-Pontica 2. Studii și comunicări de istorie a Dobrogei* (Brăila: Editura Istros, 2014), 71–84.
42 Ethel Greening Pantazzi, *Roumania in Light and Shadow* (Toronto: Ryerson Press, 1921), 122.
43 Dumitru, "Romanian-Soviet Disputes," 43–4.
44 *Ukraina i naslediye Rossii i SSSR: ostrov Zmeinyy v proshlom i nastoyashchem*, unsigned analysis by Russian Regnum News Agency, 12 February 2009, https://regnum.ru/news/polit/1124215.html.
45 Dumitru, "Romanian-Soviet Disputes," 47–51.
46 See Kruglashov, "Troublesome Neighborhood," 114–25.
47 For different scholarly approaches, see Mihai Mereuță, "Delimitation of the Continental Shelf and Exclusive Economic Zone of the Sea Border between Romania and Ukraine," *Codrii Cosminului* 17, no. 1 (2011): 211–22; L. Tymchenko and V. Kononenko, "The Delimitation of Ukrainian Maritime Boundaries," *Law of Ukraine* 2 (2013): 184–200.
48 ICJ, "Memorial Submitted by Romania," 19 August 2005, 20–30, 51–60, https://www.icj-cij.org/files/case-related/132/14697.pdf.
49 ICJ, "Counter-Proposal Submitted by Ukraine," 65–80.
50 Ibid.
51 Dergachev, *Chernomorskiy ostrov Zmeinyy v zerkale geopolitiki. Kto vyigral i proigral konflikt vokrug kontinental'nogo shel'fa?*, online at http://dergachev.ru/geop_events/05.html.

CONCLUSION

Making and Unmaking the Ukrainian-Russian Border since 1991

Tatiana Zhurzhenko

With the collapse of the Soviet Union in 1991, Ukraine appeared on Europe's political map as one of fifteen newly independent states. As the Soviet Union disintegrated along the administrative boundaries of its republics, the newly independent Ukrainian state inherited the territory that had been the Ukrainian Soviet Socialist Republic (Ukrainian SSR). Ukraine's borders, which had been largely shaped during the first half of the twentieth century when Eastern Europe was reordered in the aftermath of two world wars, now turned into international boundaries. Among other priority tasks, the new Ukrainian state-in-the-making had to negotiate the terms of separation with the Soviet and Russian governments, to secure international recognition and guarantees of its territorial sovereignty and integrity, to reconfirm its borders with neighbouring countries through bilateral treaties, and to organize a system of border control.

The challenges facing Ukraine at its "old" and "new" borders were, however, of a different nature. Ukraine's borders with the countries of the "socialist camp" – that is, with Poland, Hungary, Slovakia, and Romania – had been part of the Soviet external border and thus were well protected and hardly permeable. By contrast, Ukraine's borders with the former Soviet republics – the Russian Federation, Belarus, and Moldova – had been mere administrative lines that were neither demarcated nor controlled. Moreover, they hardly mattered in terms of the labour market, social provisions, or the education system.

Ukraine thus needed to modernize the infrastructure of its western border to answer the needs of growing cross-border traffic and to facilitate contacts between the residents of these border regions. At the "new" borders of Ukraine with the former Soviet republics, delimitation and demarcation had to be carried out and an infrastructure of border and customs controls needed to be built practically from scratch. Additional challenges arose with the Ukrainian-Moldovan border, where the frozen conflict in Transnistria had become a source of instability and economic crime. Moreover, Ukraine's regions bordering Belarus, though thinly populated and not very busy in terms of traffic, had become heavily polluted as a result of the Chernobyl nuclear accident in 1986.

The main challenge for Ukraine, however, was the border with the Russian Federation. As the main stakeholder of the Soviet Union and later its successor, Russia is more than a neighbour: a former imperial centre, it is still a great power with geopolitical ambitions in the "near abroad." In the wake of the Soviet collapse, Ukraine's ambitions for independence seemed to risk a military conflict, given that Ukraine still had Soviet troops stationed on its territory (including the Black Sea Fleet in Crimea), hosted Soviet nuclear weapons, and, last but not least, was home to millions of ethnic Russians. Moreover, for many in both countries, Ukrainians and Russians were "one people" with close cultural and historical ties. Together with the Belarusians, they constituted the "Slavic core" of the Soviet state, which Moscow viewed as fundamental to a new supranational reintegration project. During the first post-Soviet decade, Russian nationalists and the Communist opposition in both countries denounced the new international border between Ukraine and Russia as a "wound" slashing through the collective body of East Slavic civilization and as an artificial barrier imposed on "brotherly peoples" by "corrupted pro-Western elites."[1]

Nevertheless, despite some tensions, setbacks, and moments of crisis, the Ukrainian state succeeded rather well at ensuring its territorial integrity and settling border issues with its neighbours, including Russia. By the mid-1990s, Ukraine had given up its nuclear weapons stockpile, the third largest in the world, in exchange for security assurances offered by Russia, the United States, and the United Kingdom, as stipulated in the Budapest Memorandum of 1994. The three signatories pledged to respect the independence and sovereignty of Ukraine within its existing borders and to refrain from any threat or use of force against it. In the first half of the 1990s, Kyiv signed agreements on cooperation regarding the borders with Poland, Slovakia, and Hungary.[2] A similar agreement was signed with Romania in 2003.[3] The accession of these countries to NATO and the European Union served to further stabilize Ukraine's western border. Moreover, the problem of Sevastopol and the Black Sea Fleet was settled through the Treaty on Friendship, Cooperation, and Partnership between Ukraine and the Russian Federation (1997). Then in 2003, presidents

Vladimir Putin and Leonid Kuchma signed the Treaty on the State Border between Ukraine and Russia. Both countries agreed on the delimitation of the land part of their border; the remaining issues regarding the Azov Sea and the Kerch Strait seemed more economic than political.

Had this book been published a decade ago, this account of the new Ukrainian state's border-making would have been viewed as one of success. In the spring of 2014, however, the country faced an unprecedented challenge. Exploiting the political crisis in Ukraine that had resulted from the Euromaidan protests and the fall of Viktor Yanukovych's regime, Russia seized control of the Crimean Peninsula and swiftly annexed it after a hastily organized and internationally unrecognized referendum. Moreover, with the proclamation of Russian-backed separatist "people's republics," the Ukrainian government lost control of parts of the Donetsk and Luhansk *oblasts*. But the current conflict with Russia represents more than a territorial dispute. Since 2014, Russia has been officially denying the legitimacy of the independent Ukrainian state in its post-Soviet borders. At the peak of the conflict in 2014–15, the Kremlin endorsed the "Novorossiya" project, which aimed to precipitate Ukraine's territorial disintegration. And even after the failure of those plans, Moscow has often referred to Ukraine as an "artificial state" that is unviable in its current territorial configuration. President Putin has not only repeatedly denounced Khrushchev's transfer of Crimea to the Ukrainian SSR in 1954 but also criticized Vladimir Lenin and the early Bolshevik government for their concept of a federative state in which the republics had the right to secede. According to the Russian president, this "time bomb put under the Russian state" led to the dissolution of the Soviet Union in 1991; furthermore, Putin claimed that the border between the Ukrainian SSR and the Russian Federation had been drawn arbitrarily, with Donbas attached to Ukraine for political reasons – that is, to counterbalance the nationalism of the Ukrainian peasants with the Russian-speaking working class.[4] Russia's geopolitical revisionism concerns much more than its post-Soviet borders; it is about the very terms of the dissolution of the Soviet Union in 1991. In his article "Perestroika – 2014," Fyodor Lukyanov, the Chair of the Council on Foreign and Defence Policy, argues that Moscow is now back to the point of bifurcation in 1989–91, when "things went wrong" for Russia.[5]

Writing this concluding chapter for a volume on the history of the making and re-bordering of Ukraine in the twentieth century has not been an easy task, mainly because it seems to be the wrong historical juncture to draw conclusions. Since 2014, Ukraine has faced unprecedented challenges to its sovereignty and territorial integrity: the country's future remains open. Moreover, the post–Cold War architecture of European security seems especially fragile today. The political consensus on the inviolability of borders laid down in the Helsinki Final Act, which largely determined how the Soviet Union's disintegration would later play out, seems to be on shaky ground today. This chapter thus represents a coda rather than a conclusion to the story of Ukraine's borders. It traces the success story of the bordering of the post-Soviet Ukrainian state but also addresses the conflicting interests of the Ukrainian and Russian political elites and competing visions of future relations between the two countries. This chapter starts with the dissolution of the Soviet Union and the birth of independent Ukraine within its Soviet-era boundaries; it continues with the process of settling border-related issues with Russia; it ends with the newly arisen challenges to Ukraine's territorial integrity since 2014 (see map 12.1). Though it might help explain the crisis in Ukrainian-Russian relations, this chapter does not claim to offer any solutions to the current conflict. Rather, this latest chapter of Ukrainian history illustrates the dilemmas of building an independent state and securing its territorial integrity in the fluid borderlands between Russia and "the West."

CARVING OUT AN INDEPENDENT UKRAINE

Mikhail Gorbachev's reforms during the second half of the 1980s accelerated the pace of history. Political liberalization opened the door for national democratic movements with increasingly radical demands. The Baltic Soviet republics were the first to press for national independence; Ukraine, Georgia, and Moldova were quick to follow. Gorbachev sought to reform the Soviet federalist state by concluding a renewed union treaty. Public debates on this project widened the political imagination of Soviet citizens and legitimized the discourse of national sovereignty. In the first (semi-democratic elections held in the Soviet republics in March 1990, Ukraine's Narodnyi Rukh (People's Movement), which had transformed itself into a political party, won one quarter of the seats in the Verkhovna Rada (Ukrainian parliament), until then a largely decorative institution. In Russia, the same elections empowered a new charismatic leader, Boris Yeltsin, who presented himself as a more radical alternative to Gorbachev. Yeltsin's course of creating an executive presidential system for the Russian Federation unleashed a struggle between the power structures of the Soviet Union and the Russian Soviet Federative Socialist Republic (RSFSR). In June 1990, the Congress of People's Deputies of the RSFSR adopted a declaration of sovereignty that proclaimed that the Russian legislature superseded the Soviet one on the territory of the RSFSR.

Making and Unmaking the Ukrainian-Russian Border

12.1 Ukraine, 2018.

Joining what was later termed "the parade of sovereignties," the *Verkhovna Rada* of the Ukrainian SSR adopted the Declaration of State Sovereignty of Ukraine on 16 July 1990. The document stated, among other things, that "the Ukrainian SSR has supremacy over all of its territory. The territory of the Ukrainian SSR within its existing boundaries is inviolable and cannot be changed or used without its consent."[6] It was still within the framework of the existing Soviet Union that a treaty between the Ukrainian SSR and the RSFSR was signed by Leonid Kravchuk and Boris Yeltsin on 19 November 1990 in Kyiv. Article 6 of this treaty stipulated that "the High Contracting Parties recognize and respect the territorial integrity of the Ukrainian Soviet Socialist Republic and the Russian Soviet Federative Socialist Republic within their presently existing borders within the USSR."[7] This treaty was the first official document regulating relations between Ukraine and Russia as sovereign (but not yet independent) states. It laid the foundation for their bilateral relations during the first post-Soviet decade and was repealed only in 1999 as the Treaty on Friendship, Cooperation, and Partnership between Ukraine and the Russian Federation, signed on 31 May 1997, came into effect. The official mutual recognition of territorial integrity was of enormous importance; at the same time, as we will see below, the ambiguity of the formulation "within their presently existing borders within the USSR" opened space for different interpretations after the Soviet Union ceased to exist.

Gorbachev tried to save the Soviet Union from disintegration; notwithstanding the considerable autonomy of the republics, his project of a new union treaty envisioned a united armed forces, a common foreign policy, and a single currency.[8] On 17 March 1991, an all-Union referendum was held on the future existence of the Soviet Union in the form of a "renewed federation of equal sovereign republics." In Ukraine, an additional question was posed: "Do you agree that Ukraine should be part of a Union of Soviet sovereign states on the basis on the Declaration of State Sovereignty of Ukraine"? A robust majority of voters answered yes to both questions (71.48 per cent and 81.7 per cent respectively). While Ukraine's political elite remained divided on signing the renewed union treaty, Gorbachev perfectly realized that without Ukraine there would be no union. By that point, the US leadership was growing increasingly concerned about potential territorial disputes and ethnic conflicts that might arise should the Soviet Union disintegrate and supported Gorbachev "trying to consolidate the gains made in the arms control, in the dissolution of the Warsaw Pact and in the UN Security Council on Iraq."[9] Visiting Kyiv in early August 1991 after a summit in Moscow, President George H.W. Bush in his notorious "Chicken Kiev speech" advised the Ukrainians not to confuse freedom with independence and warned them against leaving the Soviet Union.[10]

All of this changed with the August 1991 coup in Moscow, a failed attempt by Communist hardliners to halt the reforms and stop the disintegration of the Soviet Union by removing Gorbachev from power. After three days of suspense, Yeltsin emerged victorious from the confrontation, having used it as a chance to enhance his power. Gorbachev returned to the Kremlin, but his position had been weakened, and the Soviet Union further destabilized. Its dissolution was now only a question of time.

On 24 August, while the statue of Felix Dzerzhinsky in front of the KGB headquarters on Lubyanka Square in Moscow was being dismantled in the aftermath of the failed coup, the Verkhovna Rada in Kyiv declared Ukraine's independence. The Act of Declaration of Independence of Ukraine referred to the right of national self-determination and to the previously adopted Declaration of State Sovereignty while also pointing to "the mortal danger having loomed over Ukraine" as a result of the August coup. Proclaiming an independent Ukrainian state, the declaration stated that "the territory of Ukraine is indivisible and inviolable."[11] The same day, the

Verkhovna Rada also declared Ukraine's control over the Soviet military stationed on its territory and scheduled a referendum on state independence for 1 December 1991.

The Declaration of Independence came as a shock to Moscow and caused the first crisis in Ukrainian-Russian relations. This episode, symptomatic of future relations between the two countries, is described in detail in Serhii Plokhy's *The Last Empire: The Final Days of the Soviet Union*.[12] Neither Boris Yeltsin nor his closest allies from the democratic camp, Anatolii Sobchak, Gavriil Popov, and Sergey Stankevich, were prepared to let Ukraine go in the same manner as the former Baltic republics:

> Many in Yeltsin's camp treated Ukrainian independence not as an act aimed at the weakened center but as a stab in the back of democratic Russia, which had emerged victorious in the battle with the communist Goliath. Besides, the sudden shift of political power in Moscow created a situation unimaginable only a few days earlier. So far, the Russian Federation had been in the forefront of rebellion against the center, working hand in hand with the Baltics and adopting laws on its sovereignty ahead of Ukraine, Belarus, and most other Soviet republics. Russia had now all but taken over the center and was faced with the unexpected task of what to do with the Union.[13]

On 27 August, Yeltsin's press secretary issued a statement warning that in the event of Ukraine's refusal to join the new political union with Russia, the latter reserved the right to raise the question of a revision of boundaries. The same day, the presidium of the Ukrainian parliament declared that Ukraine had no territorial claims on Russia but was prepared to discuss possible Russian claims on the basis of the Russian-Ukrainian treaty signed in November 1990.[14] On 28 August, a Russian delegation led by Yeltsin's trusted envoy, Aleksandr Rutskoi, and joined by representatives of the Soviet Union's Supreme Council, travelled to Kyiv. According to Plokhy, "their main goal was to derail or postpone Ukrainian independence, not to claim contested territories."[15] The Moscow delegation hoped to convince the Ukrainians to stay in the union, which meant that questioning the border was an instrument, not the aim. The mission turned out to be quite challenging. During the difficult opening negotiations both sides "agreed to create joint structures to manage the transition and work on economic agreements,"[16] but the issue of a common political future remained a matter of open debate.

In the months preceding the referendum on independence, Ukraine hurried to lay the legal basis for its territorial sovereignty and to gain control over its borders. The Law "On the Legal Succession of Ukraine," adopted by the Ukrainian parliament on 12 September 1991, declared independent Ukraine the legal successor of the Ukrainian SSR. Article 5 stated that "the state border of the USSR that separates the territory of Ukraine from other countries and the boundary between the Ukrainian SSR and the Belorussian SSR, the Russian SFSR and Republic of Moldova as of 16 July 1990 is the state border of Ukraine."[17] On 4 November that same year, the Ukrainian parliament adopted the Law on the State Border of Ukraine,[18] which laid out the legal foundations for establishing Ukraine's state border (land and maritime), its delimitation and demarcation, and the border-crossing regime, as well as the protection and control of the border. Also, the Law on the Border Troops of Ukraine[19] was passed that same day. With this legislation, Soviet border troops of the Western Border District stationed on the territory of the Ukrainian SSR came under Ukraine's jurisdiction.

On 1 December 1991, Ukraine held its referendum on national independence. An overwhelming majority, 92.26 per cent of voters, supported the Act of Declaration of Independence of Ukraine issued by the Ukrainian parliament on 24 August 1991. That same day, Leonid Kravchuk, the Speaker of the Parliament and *de facto* head of state, was elected as first president of Ukraine. On 2 December, Ukraine's independence was officially recognized by Russia and Poland, its two most important, and historically most difficult, neighbours. For Mikhail Gorbachev, still the president of the Soviet Union, however, the results of the referendum were not "tantamount to the desire for secession from the union." Once again, he made "an appeal to the remaining republics not to leave the union because this would bring the threat of war and be a catastrophe for the world."[20]

But the end of the Soviet Union was unavoidable. A week after Ukraine's referendum, the leaders of Ukraine, Russia, and Belarus met at a state dacha in Viskuli near the Belarusian-Polish border and signed the Belovezha Accords, which declared the Soviet Union as effectively ceasing to exist. Gorbachev had no choice but to accept the outcome, and the Soviet Union was officially dissolved on 26 December 1991.

A "CIVILIZED DIVORCE" (WITH SOME SETBACKS)

The Agreement on Establishing of the Commonwealth of Independent States (CIS) hammered out in Belovezha was a difficult compromise between Ukraine and Russia. Yeltsin continued to struggle with Gorbachev, hoping to dissolve the Soviet Union, but he also intended "to retain a 'centre,' dominated by Russia, that would control nuclear weapons and provide economic coordination."[21] The CIS, based on a set of common supranational institutions, was meant to serve as an instrument of this policy. Kravchuk, however, was against a new supranational confederation controlled by Moscow and was reluctant to make any binding commitments. As argued by Paul D'Anieri, "in Ukraine, the CIS was seen not as a new organization, but as a way of managing complete separation."[22] On 10 December 1991, Ukraine ratified the agreement (albeit with reservations), thus becoming one of the "founding states" of the CIS; but it never ratified the subsequent charter that would have made it a member.

The ambivalence of Ukraine's attitude toward the CIS was reflected in the issue of the borders:

Article 5 of the Agreement stated that "the High Contracting Parties recognize and respect the territorial integrity of each other and the inviolability of the existing borders *within the Commonwealth*. They guarantee the openness of borders, freedom of movement of citizens and transfer of information within the Commonwealth."[23]	The agreement was ratified by Ukraine with reservations, including a modified version of Article 5: "the High Contracting Parties recognize and respect the territorial integrity of each other and inviolability of the existing borders *between them*. They guarantee *on a reciprocal basis* the openness of *the existing* borders *for unobstructed contacts between their citizens* and transfer of information within the Commonwealth; *with this aim they will develop an appropriate legal framework in the near future.*"[24]

The Ukrainian version thus underscored the transitional character of the agreement and the pre-eminence of Ukraine's state borders. In a special statement to mark the agreement's conclusion, the Ukrainian parliament stressed that Ukraine "as an independent state remains a subject of international law, conducts its own foreign policy and will create its own armed forces on the basis of the Soviet armed forces stationed on its territory.

Moreover, Ukraine's state borders established by the bilateral treaties with the RSFSR and the Belarusian SSR in 1990 remain unchanged regardless if Ukraine is part of the Agreement or not."[25]

The different visions of the common border resulted from a fundamental disagreement between Ukraine and Russia over the future of their relationship. Having accepted the territorial integrity of Ukraine within its present borders, Russia still expected Ukraine to remain a part of its political orbit and integrate fully into the CIS. Ukraine, however, viewed the agreement as only a point of departure. Most Ukrainian politicians saw the CIS not as an integration project with prospects for the future but rather as a transitional mechanism, an instrument for a "civilized divorce" (a term coined by Kravchuk). Thus, for Ukraine to have its borders legitimized by international treaties as well as delimitation and demarcation finalized was a necessary element of national sovereignty and independent statehood. From Ukraine's perspective, the "old borders" with its neighbours to the west and its "new borders" with the CIS countries were supposed to have the same status. Kyiv was quite consistent in this regard: Ukraine's second president, Leonid Kuchma, despite his pro-Russian electoral declarations, continued his predecessor's line as to the delimitation and demarcation of the border with Russia.

On 15 April 1994, the CIS countries signed the Declaration on the Observance of the Sovereignty, Territorial Integrity and Inviolability of the Borders of the Member States of the Commonwealth of Independent States.[26] This was followed by the Memorandum on Cooperation in the Protection of the State Borders of Ukraine, the Republic of Belarus and the Russian Federation. At the same time, Russia showed little interest in matters of delimitation and demarcation. By 1992 the Ukrainian Ministry of Foreign Affairs had sent Russia three diplomatic notes proposing that negotiations be opened on the delimitation of the common border.[27] According to Taras Kuzio, Ukraine had submitted nearly twenty such notes before Russia finally agreed to begin talks in 1996.[28] For Moscow, the border with Ukraine was by no means a priority issue in the 1990s: after the dissolution of the Soviet Union, Russia had to cope with a new set of borders measuring around thirteen thousand kilometres in total.[29] Yet the deeper reason was political rather than technical: Russia insisted on the joint protection of the CIS's "external" borders and wanted the "internal" borders between the CIS countries to remain "open" and "transparent."[30] Moscow viewed the demarcation of the internal CIS borders as incompatible with its "partnership relations." The Russian government considered the transparency of the Ukrainian-Russian border as a substantial part of this partnership.

12.2 Ukraine, 1993.

Another reason why progress in the delimitation and demarcation of the Ukrainian-Russian border proved to be so slow was that by "keeping the issue suspended, Moscow thought it could use its eventual concession as a bargaining chip."[31] Indeed, after 1992 Moscow and Kyiv clashed on several fronts, including the fate of Ukraine's Soviet nuclear stockpile and the gas trade; but it was the conflict around the Black Sea Fleet and the status of Sevastopol that was most urgent and dangerous. To start with, the Russian political elites were not prepared to accept the eventual loss of Crimea, which had become part of the Ukrainian SSR in 1954. Sevastopol, due to its special place in Russian history and national imagination,[32] embodied what struck many in Russia as a great historical injustice. For centuries, Sevastopol has been the home base of the Black Sea Fleet; besides being a strategic stronghold in the region, it was a central element in Russia's myth of imperial military glory. While Russia accepted, in principle, Ukraine's claim to Soviet military assets on its territory, the Black Sea Fleet was a special case. Initially meant to be under common CIS command, it became a subject of contestation when Ukraine rejected the idea of a single Commonwealth military force.[33] Various intermediary solutions, which proposed dividing the fleet between the two countries, were put forward;

the question of ownership of the shore facilities and basing rights proved more difficult to resolve. To put pressure on Kyiv, some political actors in Russia raised the issue of the legitimacy of Crimea's transfer to Ukraine in 1954 and questioned its control over Sevastopol. One of the most serious episodes during this dispute involved a resolution passed in the Russian parliament on 9 July 1993 that declared Sevastopol a part of Russia and the main naval base of the Russian Black Sea Fleet.[34] The Ukrainian parliament responded by claiming that the resolution was "aimed at the revision of the existing borders and threatens the peace and quiet in our land."[35] The resolution's passage also provoked alarm in the United States and among EU member-states, and the UN Security Council promptly reconfirmed the territorial integrity of Ukraine. President Yeltsin distanced himself from the resolution and denounced it as harmful to Ukrainian-Russian relations.[36] In September 1993, the presidents of Ukraine and Russia signed the Massandra Accords, which, apart from the agreement on the utilization of Ukraine's nuclear weapons, offered a pragmatic solution for the Black Sea Fleet issue: President Kravchuk, under the pressure of Ukraine's growing gas debt, agreed to sell its part of the fleet to Russia. This decision, however, was met with protests in Kyiv and was not approved by the Verkhovna Rada.[37] Several subsequent compromises also failed. The issue of the Black Sea Fleet would not be settled until the "Big Treaty" of 1997.

Setting aside a looming economic collapse, Kyiv's position vis-à-vis Moscow was weakened by Crimea's emerging pro-Russian separatist movement.[38] The local Communist leadership opposed Ukraine's move toward independence and strived to re-establish the Crimean Autonomous Soviet Socialist Republic, which had been abolished in 1945. In January 1991 a local referendum revealed a majority in favour of autonomy. According to Gwendolyn Sasse, "the Crimean leadership sought to enhance the region's status and make it a signatory to Gorbachev's Union Treaty."[39] To prevent Crimea's leaders from petitioning the Supreme Council of the Soviet Union to reverse the 1954 transfer, the Verkhovna Rada granted the peninsula autonomy within Ukraine.[40] After the dissolution of the Soviet Union, however, the Ukrainian government sought to settle the issue of Crimean autonomy. In April 1992 the Ukrainian parliament adopted a law on the delimitation of powers between Kyiv and Simferopol. In response, in May 1992, the Crimean parliament adopted the Act on the State Independence of the Crimean Republic. The newly enshrined constitution of the "Republic of Crimea" defined it as a state with sovereign powers over its territory and independent foreign relations.[41] After difficult negotiations with Kyiv, the Crimean constitution was amended to conform to Ukrainian law. It was, however, reinstated in its original version in 1994, when another crisis emerged with the coming to power of the radical wing of the Crimean separatists.[42]

In January 1994, the leader of Crimea's pro-Russian separatists, Yuriy Meshkov, was elected the first (and only) president of the Crimean Republic. Meshkov sought to introduce Russian passports for Crimean residents, put Russian currency into circulation, and transfer Crimea into the Russian time zone. The local police, security services, judiciary, and state media were also brought under Simferopol's control; Kyiv was going to lose the "war of decrees" and found itself unable to enforce Ukrainian law in Crimea. Internal conflict in the Crimean government and the lack of political support from Moscow[43] eventually weakened Meshkov's position and allowed Kyiv to regain control after difficult negotiations. The decline of pro-Russian separatism in Crimea and the political compromise between Kyiv and Simferopol was possible owing to the election of Kuchma as Ukrainian president in July 1994. Perceived as a pro-Russian candidate, Kuchma received overwhelming support from Crimea's voters.[44] In March 1995, the Ukrainian parliament revoked the Crimean constitution from May 1994, along with other Crimean legislation, and adopted the Law on the Autonomous Republic of Crimea, which declared the primacy of the Ukrainian legislature. The relationship between Kyiv and the autonomous republic of Crimea was eventually settled in the new constitution of Ukraine, adopted on 28 June 1996.

Kuchma's coming to power on a pro-Russian platform also made it easier for Moscow and Kyiv to reach a final agreement on their common border. In 1996, the Ukrainian-Russian Subcommittee on State Borders was created, and the heads of the state border services of Ukraine and Russia signed a protocol on joint border and custom controls. Despite its commitment to "transparent borders" within the CIS, Russia had become more pragmatic regarding final border arrangements with its neighbours. One reason for this was security concerns stemming in part from the war in Chechnya. In 1997, the Treaty on Cooperation, Friendship and Partnership[45] was signed by presidents Yeltsin and Kuchma and, despite resistance from the nationalist opposition in the Russian Duma, ratified by both parliaments. This "Big Treaty" recognized for the first time the territorial integrity of Ukraine *as an independent state* within the boundaries of the former Ukrainian Soviet Republic. The Crimean knot also seemed to have finally been unravelled: Sevastopol was to remain part of the Ukrainian territory, and its military facilities would be leased to Russia; the Russian Black Sea Fleet was granted the right to stay there for twenty years.[46] In a sense, Ukraine had been lucky with Yeltsin, who stood for the peaceful dissolution of the "Soviet empire." He continued to press for concluding the treaty despite resistance from the Russian parliament, which insisted on Russia's right to Sevastopol: "It was clear that even if the Russian government grudgingly acknowledged Ukraine's sovereignty and borders, much of its elite and its democratically elected parliament did not."[47] In Russia, opponents of the Big Treaty considered it an unfair concession to Ukraine, a betrayal of the Russian national interest, and a big political mistake.[48] In Ukraine, leasing the Sevastopol naval base to Russia for twenty years was seen as a bitter compromise and a transitional solution (Ukraine's constitution does not permit the locating of foreign military bases on the country's territory). The "Kharkiv Accords" signed by the newly elected President Yanukovych and the Russian president Dmitri Medvedev in April 2010 aroused much controversy in Ukraine for extending the Russian lease on naval facilities in Crimea until 2042 in exchange for a discounted gas contract.[49]

DRAWING THE BORDER

In January 2003, the Treaty on the State Border between Ukraine and Russia[50] was signed by Putin and Kuchma; in April 2004, it was ratified by both parliaments. The treaty finalized the negotiations on the delimitation of the Ukrainian-Russian border (concerning its land part), a process that took about four years. This progress was achieved, however, at the cost of Ukraine's concession over another important issue – Kuchma agreed to participate in a Russian-led economic integration project, the Common Economic Space. This happened against the backdrop of Ukraine's deteriorating relations with the West and Kuchma's rapprochement with Russia.[51] The issue of the delimitation of the Azov Sea and the Kerch Strait was, however, not settled under the treaty. Ukraine insisted on the delimitation of the Azov Sea by the water surface along the administrative border between the RSFSR and the Ukrainian SSR during the Soviet era, while Russia wanted simply to define responsibility zones on the coast and focused on the joint use of the Kerch Strait and Azov Sea by both countries. The treaty also did not address the demarcation of the land part of the border; Russia refused to discuss the problem of demarcation, referring to its high costs and low priority.[52]

The Tuzla conflict, which broke out in October 2003 and quickly escalated into a serious crisis between the two countries, demonstrated how fragile the "strategic partnership" was.[53] One month earlier, Russia had started construction work to connect the Taman Peninsula to the Ukrainian island of Tuzla. The Russians justified the project on ecological grounds: it was supposed to protect the Taman coast from storms. They also claimed that until the 1920s, Tuzla had not been island; it had been a spit connected to the Taman Peninsula and therefore was originally Russian. The Ukrainians responded with documents that confirmed that the island had been, in fact, officially attached to Crimea some years before the territorial transfer in 1954. The conflict culminated in an exchange of hostile statements between Ukrainian and Russian officials and open demonstrations of military force by both sides. After intense consultations between the Ukrainian and Russian foreign ministries, however, the crisis was resolved and negotiations on the delimitation of the Azov Sea began. The Tuzla conflict seemed to have done little damage to the official Ukrainian-Russian "strategic partnership," but for the Ukrainian elites it proved to be a shock, revealing the lack of transparency between the two countries. It demonstrated that Russia remained an unpredictable partner and that Ukraine's international isolation, especially from the West, still posed a serious problem.

In December 2004, the presidents of Ukraine and Russia signed an agreement for cooperation in the exploitation of the Azov Sea and the Kerch Strait, known as the Kerch Agreement. It confirmed the status of the Azov Sea as "inland waters" of both countries (as had already been settled in the Treaty on State Border from 2003). The status of "inland waters" prevented third-country military vessels from entering the Azov Sea and proved a major victory for the Russian side. Under the Kerch Agreement, the rights for exploiting the strait were assigned to a joint Ukrainian-Russian corporation. Russia agreed in principle to delimit the surface of the Azov Sea. However, a final agreement on delimitation of the Azov Sea and the Kerch Strait was not achieved. The Ukrainian side deferred to international practice and proposed to draw the border along the old Soviet administrative boundary. This solution would have allowed Ukraine to control the traffic to and from the Azov Sea and to profit from the local sturgeon fisheries. No less important were the potential oil and gas fields on the continental shelf, which this dispute had put at stake. According to Ukrainian experts, the uncertain status quo benefited Russia, which dominated in the Azov Sea due to its economic power.[54]

From the Ukrainian perspective, the status of "inland waters" remained the central obstacle for the delimitation of the Azov Sea according to international law. Ukrainian diplomats suggested that the area's status be changed from inland waters to international waters and that international observers be invited to the negotiations; Russia said no to this.[55] Moscow accused Ukraine of politicizing the issue; Kyiv suspected that Russia's reluctance to solve the problem was a means to prevent Ukraine from joining NATO. This unresolved dispute was the reason why the Ukrainian side suspended the long-planned project of building a bridge across the Kerch Strait.[56]

As mentioned earlier, Russia for a long time resisted the demarcation of the land part of the Ukrainian-Russian border. The Border Treaty of 2003 did not even mention the issue of demarcation. According to Russian foreign ministry officials, the treaty would have had no chance of being ratified by the Russian parliament had it done so.[57] From 2005, the Russian position seemed to soften in this regard. The crisis of the CIS and the bleak prospects of other Russia-led integration projects might have contributed to this. With the continuing disintegration of the post-Soviet space, "transparent borders" had become expensive and ineffective. At the same time, the demarcation so badly wanted by Kyiv was being used by Moscow as a bargaining chip in the Azov Sea negotiations. The treaty on the demarcation between the two countries was not signed until 2010,[58] and progress on the ground was slow. Indeed, by 2014, only 372 kilometres of the border with Russia, in the Sumy and Chernihiv *oblasts*, had been demarcated.[59]

FROM CIVILIZED DIVORCE TO UNCIVIL WAR

The title of Paul D'Anieri's recent book on the origins of the current Ukrainian-Russian conflict serves as the best thumbnail account of the unprecedented crisis that arose in the spring of 2014. As a result of the annexation of Crimea, the outbreak of the military conflict in Donbas, and Russian intervention, Ukraine lost control over 44,000 square kilometres (7 per cent) of its territory[60] and more than 400 kilometres (20 per cent) of its land border with Russia.[61] About 14,000 Ukrainian citizens have been killed and more than 28,000 wounded in the conflict.[62] Half the population of the Donbas has been forced to flee. At the beginning of 2021, some 1,460,000 persons were registered in Ukraine as internally displaced.[63]

The annexation of Crimea by Russia – "the biggest land-grab in Europe since World War II," according to the former US Ambassador to Ukraine Steven Pifer[64] – represented a breach of Russia's obligations to Ukraine under the Budapest Memorandum. Moreover, having violated Ukraine's sovereignty and territorial integrity, Russia not only broke several bilateral agreements with Ukraine[65] but also in effect nullified what had been achieved during the more than two decades of "civilized divorce." After the occupation of key strategic objects and the seizure of the Crimean parliament by masked Russian troops, a hastily organized "referendum" was arranged to legitimize Russia's new territorial gain. In March 2014, the Autonomous Republic of Crimea and its harbour city, Sevastopol, became two new federal subjects of the Russian state. The international community responded by imposing sanctions on Russia, which was also expelled from the G8. These measures have had little effect on the Kremlin, which considers the Crimean question closed and not a subject for negotiations.

Ukraine, however, regards Crimea as an occupied territory temporarily beyond its control and its inhabitants as Ukrainian citizens.[66] Under Ukrainian law, entering the territory of Crimea from Russia without permission from the Ukrainian authorities is a criminal offence, and as a consequence, a number of Russian public personalities have been barred from Ukraine after doing so. The administrative boundary between Crimea and continental Ukraine is now a *de facto* border between two countries, controlled by border guards and custom services on both sides. Since autumn 2014, there has been no direct public transport link between continental Ukraine and Crimea – the border can be crossed only by foot or private car.[67] Despite a dramatic fall in the number of Ukrainian tourists, cross-border movement remains significant. It has a seasonal character – in 2019, for example, the number of crossings (both entry and exit) at three checkpoints over the month of February was 121,000; in August it had risen to 408,000. In 2019, a total of 2,582,000 persons crossed the border with Crimea in both directions.[68]

At the other new "temporary boundary" separating the self-proclaimed Donetsk and Luhansk republics from (the rest of) Ukraine, the situation is more ambivalent and far from being settled. Donbas especially suffered during the hot phase of the military conflict, which resulted in flows of refugees and ruined infrastructure. Since 2015 the front line has stabilized, but shelling and sniper fire continue, with regular reports of casualties on both sides. The new "border" – which is, in reality, a frozen front line – is seen by both parties as provisional and movable, a place where it is worth investing in military fortifications but not civic infrastructure. While the "republics" issue their own documents (which Ukraine does not recognize) and many residents have made the most of the new opportunity to apply for Russian passports, the local population is still dependent on Ukrainian social provisions and thus Ukrainian citizenship. This explains the intense movement across the dividing line, where five control points have been established from the Ukrainian side (one in the Luhansk *oblast* and four in the Donetsk *oblast*). According to the Ukrainian Border Service, the total number of crossings (both entries and exits) during 2019 reached 13,933,000, a figure more than five times higher than at the administrative line with Crimea during the same period.[69]

The new "temporary administrative lines" separating Crimea and the "people's republics" in Donbas from the rest of Ukraine have thus become *de facto* external boundaries where the sovereignty of the Ukrainian state ends. From the Russian perspective, however, the status of these two boundaries is different: the administrative line between continental Ukraine and the Crimean Peninsula has effectively become Russia's new state border, even if it remains unrecognized by the international community. In Donbas, by contrast, the Ukrainian-Russian border has not been redrawn, and Russia, which has not officially recognized the "people's republics," considers them, at least formally, to be part of Ukraine. According to the Minsk Agreement, Ukraine will be able to reassert its control over the border after elections in the uncontrolled territories and the political implementation of autonomy for Donbas. Ukraine, however, insists on the withdrawal of Russian troops and on regaining control over the border as a precondition for elections. Having "people's republics" within Ukraine equipped with an autonomy that includes broad cultural rights and special bonds to Russia would suit the Kremlin's interests better than the recognition of yet more quasi-states or their annexation. The latter two options are not being seriously considered at present, but Russia is using them to pressure Kyiv.

The rest of Ukraine's border with Russia remains intact but has been subject to significant changes. With the deployment of additional troops on both sides, the border has been heavily militarized.[70] Since 2014, the widespread perception that Russia is a source of instability and a security threat has been reflected in the growing percentage of Ukrainians who would prefer the border with Russia be closed or who support the idea of a visa requirement for Russian citizens.[71] Partly in response to these tendencies, Ukrainian politicians have come up with the idea of a "security fence" along the border with Russia. The then prime minister, Arseniy Yatseniuk, embraced the project of a "European rampart," which, he argued, would be part of the future eastern boundary of the EU.[72] After the conflict with Russia broke out and the Ukrainian-Russian commission on demarcation halted its work, the Ukrainian government announced that it would continue unilaterally the task of marking the border with Russia on the ground.[73]

The profound crisis in Ukrainian-Russian relations has resulted in cross-border cooperation projects being frozen for the time being. Also, the procedures for crossing the border have been tightened on both sides. New requirements have been introduced by the Ukrainian Border Service for

Russian citizens visiting Ukraine; an international passport is now required (not just an internal ID card), one must show proof of having been invited, and one must preregister one's visit online. Since March 2020, Ukrainian citizens, too, have been required to carry an international passport when entering Russia rather than just an internal ID card. Furthermore, Ukraine has terminated the agreement on local border traffic: since March 2015 only international border crossings have been open; smaller local ones previously used mainly by near-border residents remain closed.[74] In October of the same year, Ukraine and Russia suspended direct flights between the two countries, and Russia hurriedly began to build a new railway from Moscow to Rostov that bypassed Ukrainian territory. For Russian tourists, the popular route to Crimea through Ukraine has been replaced by direct flights to Simferopol; since 2018, the newly constructed Kerch Bridge has connected Crimea with Russia's Krasnodar region.

In April 2014, after Russia annexed Crimea, the Russian parliament terminated a set of treaties dividing the Black Sea Fleet between Russia and Ukraine and defining the status of Russian armed forces in Crimea.[75] These treaties included the agreements of May 1997 that had settled the dispute over the Black Sea fleet, as well as the Kharkiv Accords signed in 2010, which had prolonged the lease of the naval base in Crimea to Russia until 2042. In September 2018, then Ukrainian President Petro Poroshenko signed a decree that unilaterally ended the Treaty on Friendship, Cooperation and Partnership between Russia and Ukraine. The decree was approved by the Ukrainian parliament in December of that year.[76]

CONCLUSION

In their essay "When Borders Move," Mattias Bös and Kerstin Zimmer identified three phases of border changes in Europe during the twentieth century.[77] The first phase started with the collapse of the continental empires and the rise of the Soviet Union and Nazi Germany (both striving for territorial expansion) and ended with the Second World War. The second phase lasted from 1945 until the disintegration of the Soviet Union and the "Eastern Bloc." The third phase, according to the authors, extended from 1989 to the EU enlargement of 2004. Diplomacy following the First World War had failed to provide Europe with stable political boundaries; the outcome of the Second World War was rather different. During the decades of the Cold War, border changes were largely taboo for the key political actors in both the East and the West. One reason for this "hyper-stability of border structures" was the confrontation between the two political systems and the risk of a nuclear conflict.[78] The end of the Cold War triggered a new wave of border changes, most notably the disintegration of the Soviet Union and Yugoslavia.

Today's Ukraine, as this book beautifully demonstrates, is the child of all three of these phases of European border change. After emerging from the ruins of the Habsburg and Russian empires, Ukraine failed to preserve its national sovereignty, though it did acquire some elements of statehood as a Soviet republic, including an administrative boundary with the Russian Federation. The Ukrainian SSR profited from Stalin's territorial acquisitions following the Soviet victory over the Third Reich; Ukraine's western border – as the Soviet external frontier – became an important pillar of the Cold War architecture of European security. The "hyper-stability of border structures" that Bös and Zimmer view as an exclusive feature of the Cold War era survived the collapse of the bipolar geopolitical order. The disintegration of the Soviet Union would not have been peaceful had it not happened along the administrative boundaries of the Soviet republics, which most major political players committed themselves to respecting. The principle of inviolability of borders anchored in the UN Charter and the Helsinki Final Act was thus applied to the new international boundaries within the post-Soviet space. As noted by Roman Szporluk, "it was of critical importance that Russia defined itself within the borders of the Russian Federation as it existed in Soviet times."[79] Far from being just a personal choice of the Russian leadership, the respect for the existing Soviet-era boundaries was a consequence of Yeltsin's alliance with the Soviet republics in his fight with Gorbachev and of the Russian government's pro-Western orientation during the 1990s.

The post–Cold War international environment was largely favourable to Ukraine: unlike in the aftermath of the First and Second World Wars, it managed to build an independent state and preserve its existing borders. Ukraine's western neighbours, which had been striving to join NATO and the EU, supported the country's independence and had no interest in raising territorial claims (Romania being a special case in this respect). The delimitation of borders with Belarus and Moldova took years, but the stumbling blocks in these disputes were technical rather than political. As this chapter has demonstrated, Ukraine also succeeded in resolving the main issues of conflict with its most problematic neighbour, the Russian Federation. The border issue was settled by the Treaty on Friendship, Cooperation and Partnership (1997) and the Treaty on the State Border between Ukraine and Russia (2003). Right up to the moment of Crimea's annexation, Ukraine and Russia were bound by more than four hundred agreements in various areas of cooperation.[80]

How then did the successful making of Ukraine's borders and territorial integrity end so abruptly in 2014? To start with, Russia's growing dissatisfaction with Ukraine was never about territorial issues as such. As Paul D'Anieri has shown, "Ukraine and Russia disagreed fundamentally, already in December 1991, about where the relationship would head in the future."[81] While Ukraine strived for full independence and toward closer cooperation with the EU and NATO, Russia saw Ukraine as a politically and economically dependent satellite. Legal treaties between the two countries, including those settling territorial issues, were viewed by Moscow as a façade for a much more "intimate" relationship based on informal deals.

Russia's growing dissatisfaction was only partly about Ukraine; it was much more about the post–Cold War European order, which the Russian political elites have increasingly viewed as unfair. Ukraine, with its pro-Western ambitions, was a major irritant for Moscow, which viewed the eastward expansion of the EU and NATO as a direct infringement on its historical sphere of interests. The irony of history is that the same geopolitical triumph of Western liberal democracy that stabilized Eastern and Central Europe, and thus secured Ukraine's western border, has also contributed to the destabilization of Ukraine's borderlands with Russia.

NOTES

This chapter is partly based on the author's following publications: "Ukraine's Border with Russia before and after the Orange Revolution," in *Die Ukraine: Zerrissen zwischen Ost und West?*, ed. Martin Malek (Vienna: Schriftenreihe der Landesverteidigungsakademie, 2007), 2:63–90; *Borderlands into Bordered Lands: Geopolitics of Identity in Post-Soviet Ukraine* (Stuttgart: Ibidem-Verlag, 2010); "A Border on the Move: The Ukrainian-Russian Frontier from the Soviet Collapse to the Conflict in Donbas," in *Beyond Borders*, ed. Hans Karl Peterlini and Jasmin Donlic, *Jahrbuch Migration und Gesellschaft/Yearbook Migration and Society* 2020–21 (Bielefeld: Transcript, 2021): 139–57; "The Proliferation of Borders in the Post-Soviet Space: Ukraine and Beyond," in *Umstrittene Räume in der Ukraine: Politische Diskurse, literarische Repräsentationen und kartographische Visualisierungen*, ed. Sabine von Löwis (Göttingen: Wallstein-Verlag, 2019): 47–72.

1 Zhurzhenko, *Borderlands into Bordered Lands*, 163.

2 Oleksandr Romanukha, "Delimitatsiia suchasnoho kordonu Ukraïny," *Nauka. Relihiia. Suspil'stvo* 4 (2009): 111.
3 See also Constantin Ardeleanu's chapter in this volume.
4 See https://www.theguardian.com/world/2016/jan/25/vladmir-putin-accuses-lenin-of-placing-a-time-bomb-under-russia.
5 Fedor Lukyanov, "Perestroika – 2014," *Gazeta.ru*, 16 March 2014, https://www.gazeta.ru/comments/column/lukyanov/5952017.shtml.
6 Declaration of State Sovereignty of Ukraine, Supreme Council of the Ukrainian SSR, no. 55-XII, 16 July 1990. https://zakon.rada.gov.ua/laws/show/55-12#Text.
7 Treaty between the Ukrainian Soviet Socialist Republic and the Russian Soviet Federative Socialist Republic, 19 November 1990, https://zakon.rada.gov.ua/laws/show/643_011#Text. Cited from the English translation of the text: Andrew D. Sorokowski, "Treaty between the Ukrainian Soviet Socialist Republic and the Russian Soviet Federative Socialist Republic," *Harvard Ukrainian Studies* 20 (1996): 291–6. The treaty was repealed on 1 April 1999 and replaced by the Treaty on Friendship, Cooperation, and Partnership between Ukraine and the Russian Federation, signed on 31 May 1997.
8 Paul D'Anieri, *Ukraine and Russia: From Civilized Divorce to Uncivil War* (Cambridge: Cambridge University Press, 2019), 30.
9 Ibid., 31.
10 On George Bush's visit to Kyiv in August 1991, see Serhii Plokhy, *The Last Empire: The Final Days of the Soviet Union* (New York: Basic Books, 2015), 81–109.
11 The Act of Declaration of Independence of Ukraine, 24 August 1991, https://zakon.rada.gov.ua/laws/show/1427-12#Text.
12 Plokhy, *The Last Empire*, 239–57.
13 Ibid., 241.
14 Ibid., 244.
15 Ibid., 245.
16 Ibid., 247.
17 Law of Ukraine no. 1543-XII from 12 September 1991, "On the Legal Succession of Ukraine," https://zakon.rada.gov.ua/laws/show/1543-12#Text.
18 Law of Ukraine, no. 1777-XII from 4 November 1991, "On the State Border of Ukraine," https://zakon.rada.gov.ua/laws/show/1777-12/print.
19 Law of Ukraine, no. 1779-XII from 4 November 1991, "On the Border Troops of Ukraine," https://zakon.rada.gov.ua/laws/show/1779-12#Text. The law was repealed in 2003, when the Border Troops were reorganized into the State Border Service of Ukraine. See Law of Ukraine, no. 661-IV

from 3 April 2003, "On the State Border Service of Ukraine," https://zakon.rada.gov.ua/laws/show/661-15#Text.
20 News briefs from Ukraine, *The Ukrainian Weekly*, 8 December 1991, no. 49, vol. 59, http://www.ukrweekly.com/old/archive/1991/499103.shtml.
21 D'Anieri, *Ukraine and Russia*, 34.
22 Ibid., 35.
23 Agreement on the Establishing of the Commonwealth of Independent States, 8 December 1991. https://zakon.rada.gov.ua/laws/show/997_077#Text.
24 Reservations of the Verkhovna Rada of Ukraine to the Agreement on the Establishing of the Commonwealth of Independent States, Appendix to the Resolution no. 1958-XII from 10 December 1991. https://zakon.rada.gov.ua/laws/show/1958-12#Text.
25 Statement of the *Verkhovna Rada* of Ukraine at the occasion of the conclusion by Ukraine the Agreement on the Commonwealth of Independent States, no. 2003-XII from 20 December 1991, https://zakon.rada.gov.ua/laws/show/2003-12#Text.
26 See https://zakon.rada.gov.ua/laws/show/997_480#Text.
27 Oleksandr Zadorozhnyi, *Mizhnarodne pravo v mizhderzhavnykh vidnosynakh Ukraïny i Rossiis'koi Federatsiï 1991–2014* (Kyiv: K.I.C. 2014), 38.
28 Taras Kuzio, "Borders, Symbolism, and Nation-State Building: Ukraine and Russia," *Geopolitics and International Boundaries*, vol. 2, no. 2 (1997): 40.
29 On the delimitation and demarcation of Russia's border with the former Soviet republics, see Vladimir Kolossov, ed., *Rossiiskoe pogranich'e: Vyzovy sosedstva* (Moscow: IP Matushkina 2018), 50–8.
30 Oleksandr Sushko and Natalia Parkhomenko, "Kordony Ukraïny: Symvol nezavershenoho derzhavotvorennia," *Dzerkalo Tyzhnia*, 13 July 2001, https://dt.ua/POLITICS/kordoni_ukrayini_simvol_nezavershenogo_derzhavotvorennya.html.
31 Dmitri Trenin, *The End of Eurasia* (Washington, DC, and Moscow: Carnegie Endowment for International Peace 2002), 166.
32 Serhii Plokhy, "The City of Glory: Sevastopol in Russian Historical Mythology," *Journal of Contemporary History* 35, no. 3 (2000): 369–83.
33 D'Anieri, *Ukraine and Russia*, 39.
34 Zadorozhnyi, *Mizhnarodne pravo*, 58.
35 Resolution of the Verkhovna Rada of Ukraine, no. 3378-XII from 14 July 1993, "On the Resolution of the Supreme Council of the Russian Federation 'On the Status of the City of Sevastopol,'" https://zakon.rada.gov.ua/laws/show/3378-12#Text.
36 Zadorozhnyi, *Mizhnarodne pravo*, 60.

37 D'Anieri, *Ukraine and Russia*, 42.
38 Gwendolyn Sasse, *The Crimea Question: Identity, Transition, and Conflict* (Cambridge, MA: Harvard University Press, 2007), 129–54; Taras Kuzio, *Ukraine–Crimea–Russia: Triangle of Conflict* (Stuttgart: Ibidem 2007), 121–50.
39 Sasse, *The Crimea Question*, 136.
40 D'Anieri, *Ukraine and Russia*, 42.
41 Sasse, *The Crimea Question*, 146.
42 Ibid., 155–3.
43 The separatist cause in Crimea was supported by a number of Russian politicians and MPs, but not by President Yeltsin and his government. According to D'Anieri, "Russia's reluctance to support Crimean secession ... may have been motivated by the fact that Ukraine's denuclearization was incomplete, and could have been reversed if Crimea were to secede" (*Ukraine and Russia*, 80).
44 Zadorozhnyi, *Mizhnarodne pravo*, 174.
45 Treaty on Cooperation, Friendship, and Partnership between Ukraine and the Russian Federation, Kyiv, 13 May 1997. https://zakon.rada.gov.ua/laws/show/643_006#Text. Replaced by the Law no. 2643-VIII from 6 December 2018.
46 D'Anieri, *Ukraine and Russia*, 80–3.
47 Ibid., 81–2.
48 Konstantin Zatulin and Aleksandr Sevast'ianov, "Rossiisko-Ukrainskiy Dogovor: obman veka," *Nezavisimaia Gazeta*, 26 January 1999, https://zatulin.ru/rossijsko-ukrainskij-dogovor-obman-veka.
49 D'Anieri, *Ukraine and Russia*, 182–5.
50 Treaty between Ukraine and the Russian Federation on the Ukrainian-Russian state border, Kyiv, 28 January 2003. https://zakon.rada.gov.ua/laws/show/643_157#Text.
51 D'Anieri, *Ukraine and Russia*, 107–12.
52 Zhurzhenko, *Borderlands into Bordered Lands*, 136.
53 Kuzio, *Ukraine–Crimea–Russia*, 79–81.
54 Volodymyr Kravchenko, "Perepysuiuchy Bibliiu," *Dzerkalo Tyzhnia*, 9–16 June 2006. https://zn.ua/ukr/politcs_archive/perepisuyuchi_bibliyu.html.
55 Ibid.
56 Zhurzhenko, *Borderlands into Bordered Lands*, 138.
57 Volodymyr Kravchenko, "Kamin' spotykannia na ukraïnsko-rosiis' komu prykordonni," *Dzerkalo Tyzhnia*, 25–31 January 2003, https://zn.ua/ukr/international/kamin_spotikannya_na_ukrayinsko-rosiyskomu_prikordonni.html.

58 Treaty between Ukraine and the Russian Federation on the Demarcation of the Ukrainian-Russian State Border, Kyiv, 17 May 2010. https://zakon.rada.gov.ua/laws/show/643_365#Text.
59 Vitalii Chervonenko, "Odnostoronnia demarkatsiia: za prykladom Rosiï." BBC, 18 June 2014, http://www.bbc.co.uk/ukrainian/politics/2014/06/140618_border_demarcation_vc.
60 "Speakers Urge Peaceful Settlement to Conflict in Ukraine, Underline Support for Sovereignty, Territorial Integrity of Crimea, Donbas Region," UN, 20 February 2019, https://www.un.org/press/en/2019/ga12122.doc.htm.
61 "State border service, OSCE draft plan to return control over border with Russia if Minsk accords fulfilled," *Interfax-Ukraine*, 13 August 2016, https://en.interfax.com.ua/news/general/363567.html.
62 "Concerned about Ongoing Militarization of Crimea, Human Rights Violations in Eastern Ukraine, Speakers Tell General Assembly Minsk Agreements Must Be Fully Implemented," UN, 20 February 2020, https://www.un.org/press/en/2020/ga12241.doc.htm.
63 Ministry of Social Policy of Ukraine, "Vnutrishn'o peremishcheni osoby," 2021, https://www.msp.gov.ua/timeline/Vnutrishno-peremishcheni-osobi.html.
64 Steven Pifer, "Crimea: Six Years after Illegal Annexation," 17 March 2020, https://www.brookings.edu/blog/order-from-chaos/2020/03/17/crimea-six-years-after-illegal-annexation.
65 Zadorozhnyi, *Mizhnarodne pravo*, 625–31.
66 In 2016, a special government body, the Ministry of Temporarily Occupied Territories and IDPs, was established by Kyiv.
67 Private minibus services on both sides of the border bring people to the crossing points and pick them up there.
68 State Border Guard Service of Ukraine, "Border Control Points: People's Monthly Crossings," 2021, https://dpsu.gov.ua/en. The numbers used here are for 2019; in 2020 the border crossing movement was considerably reduced due to COVID-related restrictions.
69 Zhurzhenko, *A Border on the Move*, 147.
70 "Russian Defence Ministry calls militarization along Ukraine border a priority," UNIAN, 26 December 2017, https://www.unian.info/war/2318171-russian-def-ministry-calls-militarization-along-ukraine-border-priority.html.
71 Rating Group (2014), "Stavlennia do sytuatsiï na skhodi Ukraïny," http://ratinggroup.ua/research/ukraine/otnoshenie_k_situacii_na_vostoke_ukrainy.html.

72 Arseniy Yatsenyuk, "Project Wall to allow Ukraine to get visa-free regime with EU," *Kyiv Post*, 15 October 2014. https://www.kyivpost.com/article/content/war-against-ukraine/yatsenyuk-project-wall-to-allow-ukraine-to-get-visa-free-regime-with-eu-368097.html. Years after the launch of the "security fence" project, however, only some elements of it had been implemented; the rest have stumbled over financial difficulties and corruption allegations. See Christopher Miller, "Ukraine's 'European Rampart' Risks Getting Lost in the Trenches," *Radio Free Europe/Radio Liberty*, 29 July 2018, https://www.rferl.org/a/ukraine-s-european-rampart-risks-getting-lost-in-the-trenches-/29396996.html.

73 Order of the Cabinet of Ministers of Ukraine, no. 443-r from 14 May 2015, "On marking the Ukrainian-Russian state border on the ground," https://zakon.rada.gov.ua/laws/show/443-2015-p#Text.

74 "Ukraine closes local border crossing points with Russia," UNIAN, 4 March 2015, https://www.unian.info/politics/1051582-ukraine-closes-local-border-traffic-with-russia.html.

75 Federal Law, no. 38-FZ from 2 April 2014, "On the Termination of the Agreements Related to the Presence of the Russian Black Sea Fleet on the Territory of Ukraine," http://pravo.gov.ru/proxy/ips/?doc_itself=&nd=102348703&page=1&rdk=0#Io.

76 Law of Ukraine, no. 2643-VIII from 6 December 2018, "On the Termination of the Treaty on Cooperation, Friendship, and Partnership between Ukraine and the Russian Federation," https://zakon.rada.gov.ua/laws/show/2643-19#Text.

77 Mattias Bös and Kerstin Zimmer, "Wenn Grenzen wandern. Zur Dynamik von Grenzverschiebungen im Osten Europas," in *Grenzsoziologie. Die politischen Strukturierung des Raumes*, 2nd ed., ed. Monika Eigmüller und Georg Vobruba (Wiesbaden: Springer 2016), 153–81.

78 Ibid., 168.

79 Roman Szporluk, "Reflections on Ukraine after 1994. The Dilemmas of Nationhood," in *Russia, Ukraine, and the Breakup of the Soviet Union*, ed. Roman Szporluk (Stanford: Hoover Institution Press, 2000), 332.

80 Taras Kachka and Lana Zerkal, "Kesonna khvoroba dohovirnykh vidnosyn Ukraïny z RF," *Dzerkalo Tyzhnia*, 8 September 2018, https://zn.ua/ukr/international/kesonna-hvoroba-dogovirnih-vidnosin-ukrayini-z-rf-287798_.html.

81 D'Anieri, *Ukraine and Russia*, 255.

Contributors

CONSTANTIN ARDELEANU is professor of modern Romanian history at the Lower Danube University of Galați, long-term fellow at the New Europe College, Institute for Advanced Study, Bucharest, and author of *The European Commission of the Danube, 1856–1948: An Experiment in International Administration* (Brill, 2020). His research currently focuses on the industrialization and commodification of transportation in the nineteenth century.

JAN JACEK BRUSKI is professor of modern history at the Jagiellonian University, Krakow. He specializes in Ukrainian history and Polish-Ukrainian relations in a historical perspective and has authored several books on these topics, including *Holodomor 1932–1933: The Great Famine in Ukraine in Documents of the Polish Diplomatic and Intelligence Services* (2008, in Polish) and *Between Prometheism and Realpolitik: Poland and Soviet Ukraine, 1921–1926* (2017).

AUSTIN CHARRON is a postdoctoral research fellow at the Center for Russia, East Europe, and Central Asia at the University of Wisconsin-Madison. His research interests lie broadly in questions of social identities and their relationships with place, space, ethnicity, and territory, with a regional specialization in the former Soviet Union and a primary focus on Ukraine and Crimea. He has published widely on the topic of identity among Crimean internally displaced peoples in mainland Ukraine following the Russian annexation of Crimea in 2014.

BORISLAV CHERNEV has lectured in modern European history at the universities of Exeter and Newcastle in the United Kingdom and at the American University in Washington, DC. His research interests include international and diplomatic history and Eastern European history. He is the author of *Twilight of Empire: The Brest-Litovsk Conference and the Remaking of East-Central Europe* (2017).

SERHII HLADYSHUK completed his PhD at the Lviv National Ivan Franko University in 2018. He also worked at the University of Warsaw and the Institute of History of the Polish Academy of Sciences. He specializes in the interwar history of the Volhynia region, Poland's nationalities policies, and Ukrainian-Polish relations. He has published on the history of Volhynia both in Ukrainian and Polish, including in *Studium Europy Wschodniej*.

IAROSLAV KOVALCHUK is a PhD candidate in history at the University of Alberta. His dissertation explores the Sovietization of Transcarpathia and Galicia after the Second World War.

ELŻBIETA KWIECIŃSKA completed her PhD in history at the European University Institute in Florence. Her dissertation examines the history of the concept of the "civilizing mission" as a cultural transfer in East-Central Europe in the long nineteenth century.

DAMIAN KAROL MARKOWSKI is a researcher working at the Institute of National Remembrance in Poland specializing in Eastern Europe, and Polish-Soviet relations in particular. He is the author of *Burning Borderlands: The Operation Tempest on the Eastern Territories of the Second Polish Republic* (2011; in Polish), *The Anatomy of Fear: The Sovietization of the Lviv Region, 1944–1953* (2018, in Polish); and *Lwów or L'viv? Two Uprisings in 1918* (2019, in Polish; 2021, in English).

DOROTA MICHALUK is professor of history at the Nicolaus Copernicus University in Toruń, specializing in Eastern Europe, and in particular Belarus. She is the author of *Belarusian People's Republic, 1918–1920: The Foundations of Belarusian Statehood* (2010, in Polish) and the editor of *Polish-Belarusian Relations: History and the Present Day* (2013, in Polish) and *People and War: Social Aspect of the First World War* (2015, in Polish).

OLENA PALKO is a Leverhulme Early Career Fellow at Birkbeck, University of London, and is currently researching the minorities question in the early Soviet Union. Her book *Making Ukraine Soviet: Literature and Culture under Lenin and Stalin* (Bloomsbury, 2020) examines the cultural sovietization of Ukraine in the 1920s to 1930s.

STEPHAN RINDLISBACHER is a researcher at the Center for Interdisciplinary Polish Studies at the European University Viadrina in Frankfurt (Oder), where he examines processes of territorialization in the early Soviet Union. He is the author of *Living for the Cause: Vera Figner, Vera Zasulich, and the Radical Milieu in Late Imperial Russia* (2014, in German) and has published extensively on the early Soviet period.

ULRICH SCHMID is professor of Russian culture and society at the University of St Gallen. He has authored and co-edited numerous publications on Eastern European history, culture, literature, and media, including most recently *The Russian Revolution as Ideal and Practice* (2020); *Ukraine: Contested Nationhood in a European Context* (2020); and *Regionalism without Regions: Reconceptualizing Ukraine's Heterogeneity* (2019).

ALEXANDR VORONOVICI is associate professor at HSE University in Moscow. He specializes in the history of East European borderlands in the twentieth and twenty-first centuries. He has published widely on interwar Soviet nationality policies, separatism, and memory politics in Eastern Europe, with a focus on Ukraine and Moldova.

TATIANA ZHURZHENKO is a researcher at the Centre for East European and International Studies (ZOiS) in Berlin and at the Department of Political Science, University of Vienna. Her research interests include memory politics, borders, and borderland identities as well as gender politics and feminism in Ukraine and the post-Soviet space. She is the author of *Borderlands into Bordered Lands: Geopolitics of Identity in Post-Soviet Ukraine* (2010) and co-editor of *War and Memory in Russia, Ukraine, and Belarus* (2017).

Index

Abramson, Henry, 272
Adzhubei, Alexei, 248
Allied Powers (of the Second World War), xvii. *See also* "Big Three" conferences, Tehran; Yalta Conference
All-Russian Constituent Assembly, 163
All-Ukrainian Council of Military Delegates, 172
All-Union Communist Party (Bolsheviks, vkp(b), 1925–51), 189; Communist Party of the Soviet Union (kpsu, 1952–91), 246–7, 255, 290, 295; Council of Ministers of the Soviet Union, 247; Joint State Political Directorate (ogpu), 195; Politburo (Presidium) of the tsk kpsu, 247–8; Red Army of the Soviet Union, 31, 146, 148, 243, 289–90, 297–304, 306n29, 322; Supreme Council of the Soviet Union, 148, 243, 248–52, 254, 335, 340
Ananyiv, 227
antisemitism, 21, 89
Antonov-Ovseenko, Vladimir, 74

Antonovych, Volodymyr, 11
Arabatska Spit, 257n9
Arciszewski, Tomasz, 151
Ardeleanu, Constantin, 34, 37, 39–40
Arkhangelsk, 13
Armenia, xii, 99
Armstrong, John A., 11
Asia, 20
atrocities, 98–9
Aurescu, Bogdan, 307
Austria, 168
Austria-Hungary, xi, 69, 71, 88, 268; accepts a Habsburg Ukrainian crownland, 75–6; Austro-Hungarian forces, 23, 80, 113, 190, 269, 281; borders of, 126, 266; at the Brest-Litovsk negotiations, 69–71; Bukovina's borders in case of Austria-Hungary's defeat, 322; collapse of, 113, 190; division of, xv; Great January Strike, 73, 75–6; languages and ethnicities, 5, 13; maps published in, 80; Poland's orientation toward Germany and, 111; provinces in, 68, 89, 94; and Ukraine's recognition in 1918, 22–3, 26, 168–9, 268; Ukraine

supplying Austria-Hungary with foodstuffs, xv, 76, 78; Ukrainian lands in, 5, 15, 17, 67, 73, 109, 263. *See also* Central Powers
Averescu, Alexandru, 214
Axis Powers, 142. *See also* Germany
Azerbaijan, xii
Azov Sea, 39, 257n9, 331, 342–4

Babina, 315
Badeev, Iosif, 225
Baikal, 13
Baku, 37
Balkans, xvi, 38, 99, 218; Communist Balkan Federation, 215
Balta, 224–5, 227
Baltic: provinces, 112; region, 100, 149; Sea, 100; states, 164, 332, 335
Barthélemy, Joseph (Barthélemy Line), 115
Baumann, Fabian, 7
Belarus, xii, 112, 182, 336; All-Belarusian Congress, 164; Belarusian People's Republic (BNR), 163–82; Belarusization, 193, 199; Bolshevik position on, 126; borders of, 38, 101, 111, 163–82, 188n65; borders with Ukraine after the collapse of the USSR, 329–30, 335, 338, 348; First Constituent Charter, 164; Lithuanian-Byelorussian SSR, 187n64; nationalism in, 198; as part of the Polish-Lithuania Commonwealth, 92–3; Polesia's importance to, 170; Polish-Soviet borders, 139; population in Central, 170; recognition of, 168; Red Army occupation of, 31; relations between Ukraine and, 168, 180; Soviet Belarus/Socialist Soviet Republic of Byelorussia/Byelorussian Soviet Socialist Republic (BSSR), 181–2, 192, 199, 281; Soviet control of, 163; and the Treaty of Riga, 281

Belgorod/Bilhorod, 14, 197
Beloborodov, Aleksandr, 195
Belostok, 14, 117
Belovezha, 18, 20, 336
Belozyrka, 281
Belsk, 14, 165, 167, 169, 175, 181, 184n8
Belz/Bełz, 152, 154
Bender/Bendery, 216
Beneš, Edvard, xvi, 297, 299–301
Bereg, 15
Berehovo, 293, 298
Berezhany, 15
Berezina, 178
Berezovsky, Ia., 277
Berlin, 69, 70, 168, 175; Peace Treaty (1878), 313; conferences held in (1917–18), 70, 77; Ukrainian books published in, 17–18, 179; University of, 16
Beseda Creek, 176
Bessarabia, 18, 120, 228, 232n26; Bessarabian Soviet Socialist Republic (Bessarabian SSR), 214–16; borders of Southern, 37, 312–13; contested character of Southern, 322–3; importance in relation to Danube navigation, 317–18; maps of, 225; Moldovan-Ukrainian border in, 227–9, 319; as part of Romania, 211–15, 222, 226; population, 221; revolutionary groups in, 215–16; during the Second World War, 226, 314–15; Southern Bessarabia as part of

Ukraine, 31; Soviet control in, 142; and Transnistria, 218; Ukraine's and Soviet Ukraine's claims over, 212, 214, 219–20, 226; Ukrainian population in, 13–14; 212, 227, 229. *See also* Moldova
Bezruchko, 278
Białystok/Belostok, 117, 149, 166, 270
Bieszczady Mountains, 140, 143, 153–4, 156
"Big Three" conferences, xvi, 145, 149, 151. *See also* Allied Powers; Tehran; Yalta Conference
Biłgoraj/Bilgoray, 78, 169
Bilhorod-Dnistrovskyi/Cetatea Albă/ Akkerman, 228, 318
Bilozersky, Vasyl, 12
Biriuchensk, 14
Birzula, 224
Black Sea, xi, 11, 18, 63n145, 100; continental shelf, 34, 40, 307–8, 320–1; Cossacks, 13, 15; Fleet, 214, 243, 254, 330, 339–41, 347; imperial Russia as power in, 239; as part of the Danube's border region, 315, 317–19; as part of Ukraine's border system, 20, 37; ports, 97, 313; rivers flowing into, 245, 309, 312. *See also* Azov Sea; Serpents Island; Sevastopol
Błotnia, 154
Bóbrka/Bibrka, 115
Bobrovsky, Pavel, 170
Bobruisk, 173, 177
Bodiansky, Osyp, 11
Boguchary, 14
Boiechko, Vasyl, 26
Boikivshchyna/Bojkowszczyzna, 150–1
Bolgrad/Bolhrad, 227, 317–18, 320

Boncz-Uzdowski, Wladyslaw, 270 borderization, xii
Borisenok, Elena, 29, 31
Borisov, 178
Boryslav/Borysław, 113, 115–17, 146, 151–2
Bös, Mattias, 347–8
Botha, Louis, 115
Brandenberger, David, 62n143
Brest, 14, 113, 167, 169–75, 177, 181–2, 186n31, 268; Brest-Moscow railway, 171; Brest-Pinsk-Gomel railway, 173–4; negotiations and treaties of Brest-Litovsk, xv, 22–6, 33, 36, 38, 67–81, 111, 113, 164, 168, 268
Briansk (Bryansk), 30, 39, 178–9, 194, 196–8
Brodii, Andrei, 293–4
Brody–Zdołbunów/Zdolbuniv–Sarny railway, 118
Brotherhood of Saints Cyril and Methodius, 7
Brovko, Feodor, 318
Bruski, Jan Jacek, 33, 37, 52n92
Bucharest, 214, 228, 302, 308, 314. *See also* Romania
Budapest, 294; Budapest Memorandum (1994), 4, 330, 344. *See also* Hungary
Budei, 224
Budionnyi, Semion, 278
Budjak, 317–20, 324
Bug, 67; as border, 89, 115, 117, 140, 145, 152, 156, 176, 269, 315; military clashes in the region, 113
Bukcha, 281
Bukovina, 142, 218, 322; as a contested territory, 322; in the context of the Brest-Litovsk

Peace Conference, 71, 74; incorporation of Northern Bukovina to Ukraine, 30–1, 226, 314, 317; Ukraine's claims over, 25, 179; Ukrainian communities in, 13, 15, 22, 73
Bułak-Bałachowicz, Stanisław, 278
Bulgaria, xvi, 67, 168–9
Burba, Pavlo, 195
bureaucracy, 210, 248, 296, 313
Burián, István, 76
Bush, George H.W., 334
Butsenko, Panas, 193–6, 199, 202–3, 206n16
Bystroe/Bystre/Bîstroe Canal, 308, 316

Carpathia, 39; Carpathian Rus, xvi, 91, 290–4, 298, 304; Carpathian Ruthenia, 142, 179; Carpathian Sich, 293
Carpathians (mountains), 138, 143, 289–304
Carpathian Ukrainian People's Republic (UNR), 19, 23, 25, 28, 67, 70, 88, 98–9, 109, 118, 171, 181, 212, 269; All-Ukrainian Council of the Ukrainian People's Republic, 11; anti-Soviet Polish-Ukrainian cooperation, 24, 26, 122, 124, 275; army of, 121, 123, 126–7, 272–4, 276, 278; border negotiations with Poland, 37, 110–11; and the border with Poland, 110–11, 117, 120, 122, 135n42, 281; and the border with Russia, 3, 23, 28–9, 33, 37, 78, 168–9, 178, 194–8, 329, 332, 338–9, 342–6; British position on the Ukrainian question in Versailles, 89; central government-in-exile, 88; Central Rada (Council) of, xiv, 11, 21–2, 69–70, 72–4, 76–8, 80, 111, 164, 168–6, 172, 176, 179, 190–1, 240, 267–8, 270; delegation to the Paris Peace Conference, 18–19, 33, 86, 88, 97–103, 107n48; diplomatic mission to Warsaw, 119, 274; Directory of, 112, 117, 119–22, 124, 179; First Treaty of Brest-Litovsk (1918) signatory, xv, 22, 67, 78–81, 168, 174, 268; founding of, xiv, 22, 69, 164, 212, 240; independence of, 22, 72, 78, 164, 190; negotiations with the Belarusian government, 29, 33, 38, 168, 172–6; People's Secretariat of Ukraine (government), 10, 18, 22, 24, 26, 29, 36–8, 111, 118–21, 127, 176–7, 180, 264, 273–4; as a Polish protectorate, 118; Polish-Ukrainian Alliance (Union, 1920), 52n92, 119–23, 126, 276, 282; Polish-Ukrainian war (1918–19), 90, 99, 111–13, 116, 266, 270–5; Polish-Ukrainian war against Russia, 24, 109, 121, 124, 126, 275; recognition at Brest-Litovsk, 22, 25–6, 33, 36, 38, 68, 71, 73, 268; and relations with the Central Powers, 22–3, 26, 36, 38, 67, 69–72, 77, 113, 168, 173, 268; and relations with Poland, 33, 36, 109–10, 112–13, 116–22, 270, 273; territorial claims, 22, 39, 67, 73–4, 99, 100, 121, 125–6, 167–8, 190, 212, 240, 264, 270; territorial conflict with Poland 90, 109–10; trade agreement with Poland, 112, 119; unification with the ZUNR, 114–15, 179; war with Bolshevik Russia, 22, 26, 74, 76, 80, 88, 98, 117, 268, 273–4

Caspian deserts, 20
Caspian Sea, 18
Catherine II, tsarina, 196
Caucasus, 18, 20, 193–4, 196, 200;
  North Caucasus region, 194, 196,
  200; South Caucasus, 193;
  Sub-Caucasus, 18
Central Asia, 192–3, 201, 243
Central Europe/Eastern and Central
  Europe/East-Central Europe, 25;
  export of revolutions to, 38; 218,
  304; federation in, 92; liberal
  democracies in, 349; multi-ethnic
  spaces in, 74; as part of Poland's
  "civilizing mission," 86–7, 92;
  power relations in, 163, 303; states
  and nations in, 87, 96, 297, 301;
  struggle for supremacy in, 81;
  territorialization of ethnicities in,
  67; Versailles order in, 196.
  See also Eastern Europe/Central
  and Eastern Europe
Central Intelligence Agency (CIA), 299
Central Powers, xv, 22–4, 26, 35–6,
  38, 67–81, 88, 109, 113, 131n6,
  131n14, 164, 168, 173–4, 177, 180,
  265, 268, 270
Cernovca, 315
Charna/Czarna, 154
Charron, Austin, 34, 37, 40
Chechnya, 341
Chełm/Kholm (Cholm), 22, 26, 68,
  73–5, 78, 110–13, 117, 119–20,
  131n6, 132n13, 148, 151, 167, 190,
  268–70, 274, 276–7
Cherche, 99
Chernev, Borislav, 33, 35–6
Chernihiv, 5, 13–14, 165–7, 172–4,
  176–7, 179, 190, 192, 344
Chernobyl, 330

Chertkovo, 200
Cherviakov, Aleksandr (Cherviakov
  Commission), 194–8, 203
Chervonohrad, 140
Chicherin, Georgy, 89
Chior-Ianachi, Pavel, 225
Chişinău, 212–13, 225, 318
Chodorów/Khodoriv, 115
Chop, 301
Chorna, 227
Chortkiv, 15
Chubar, V.Ia., 222
Chubynsky, Pavlo, 13–14
Chupis, Mykola, 149
Churchill, Winston, xvi, 145–6, 149
Cieszyn Silesia, 94, 297
civilizing mission, xiv, 86–7, 91–3,
  97–101, 103, 112; German, 100;
  Polish, xiv, 38, 86, 91–4, 97–100,
  103, 112; Soviet, 38; Ukrainian,
  101–2
Clemenceau, Georges, 98
colonization, 86, 98–9, 102
Comintern, 217
Commonwealth of Independent States
  (CIS), 336–9, 341, 344
Communist Party (Bolshevik) of
  Ukraine (KP(b)U), 140, 190, 192,
  217, 247, 301; Politbiuro of the
  KP(b)U, 195, 202, 206n16, 220,
  224, 226, 234n43; Ukrainian
  Central Executive Committee
  (VUTsVK), 193, 199, 202, 221–2,
  224; Ukrainian Soviet
  Government – Council of People's
  Commissariat, Council of Ministers
  (*Sovnarkom*), 17, 30, 39, 76, 214,
  222, 224, 278; Ukrainian Planning
  Commission (*UkrDerzhplan*), 194;
  Ukrainian Supreme Soviet (Council),

227, 249–51, 318; *Verkhovna Rada* of the Ukrainian SSR 332–5; Western Border District, 336
Comrat, 317, 320
Conference on Security and Cooperation in Europe (CSCE), 4
continental shelf. *See* Black Sea
Cossack/Cossacks, 6, 10–11; Black Sea, 13, 15; Chronicles, 9–10; Cossack Hetmanate, 8, 246; Cossackdom, 11, 13, 15, 39, 192, 194; Don Cossack Host, 192; Free Cossacks, 10; territories, 6, 8
Cotul Morii, 317
Crimea, 18, 33, 167, 190, 258n15 343; Autonomous Republic of, 341, 345; Black Sea fleet in, 330, 342; Commission on the Administrative-Economic Zoning of, 242; as a contested territory, xii, 33, 37, 238, 253–6; Crimean ASSR, 241–2, 257n6; Crimean Khanate, 239–40; Crimean oblast, 39, 238, 244, 246, 254; Crimean Peninsula, 238–42, 250, 252, 331, 346; Crimean People's Republic, 167, 240; Crimean Tatars, 238–40, 242–4, 253–4, 257n7; Crimean War, xiii, 311, 317, 320; in current Ukrainian-Russian relations, 345–8; illegal annexation of, xi–xii, 3–4, 239, 343; North Crimean Canal, 246, 248, 253, 256, 259n49; pro-Russian separatism in, 341, 352n43; Republic of, 3, 340; revocation of special status, 243; within the Russian Empire and in Russian imagination, 238–40, 243; transfer of, 28, 30, 239, 244–253, 331. *See also* Taurida

Cripps, Stafford, 142
Curzon, George, 89; Curzon Line, xiii, 89–91, 94, 111, 125, 139, 144–53
Czechoslovakia, xi, xv–xvi, 31, 34, 81, 88, 114, 152, 202, 218, 289–304; Communist Party of, 298; Czechoslovak government-in-exile, 289, 297
Czernig, Karl, 179
Czernin, Ottokar, 71–3, 75–8
Czmełyk, Roman, 155

Dąbrowski, Henryk, 178
Daleru Mare, 315
Daleru Mic, 315
Danechkin, P., 198–9
D'Anieri, Paul, 337, 344, 349
Danube, 11, 20, 37, 39, 100, 227, 309–24; Danube Delta, 34, 307–16, 320–1, 323–4. *See also* European Commission of the Danube
Danubian Principalities, 320
Danylo of Halych (king), 111
Daugava, 93, 178
Davies, Norman, 89
Dębski, Jan, 278
Dekanozov, Vladimir, 314
Denikin, Anton, 89, 120, 190, 274
deportations, 138, 243
Desna, 173
dialect, 5–6, 12, 14–15, 18, 92, 165, 169–70, 194
di Fiore, Laura, 309
Dmowski, Roman, xiii–xv, 89–96, 101, 103, 112, 269, 272; Dmowski Line, 94, 112
Dnieper, 5, 92–3, 101, 111, 120–3, 174, 176, 240, 245–6, 256, 266; Dnieper Ukraine, 68–9, 115, 117, 124, 267, 271

Dobrogea (Dobrudja), 13, 218, 312
Dobromyl/Dobromil, 154, 156
Don, xvi, 18, 20, 101, 190; Don Cossack Host, 192
Donbas, xi, 29, 192, 215, 255, 331, 344-6
Donetsk (Donets), 24, 247, 331, 345; Donetsk coal basin, 37; Donetsk-Kryvyi Rih Soviet Republic, 24, 190; Donetsk People's Republic, 3, 345; industry in Donetsk Basin, 192
Doroshenko, Dmytro, 172, 176
Doroshenko, Petro, 10
Doŭnar-Zapolski, Mitrofan, 165, 170, 172, 174-5, 179, 182
Dreszer, Zygmund, 276
Drohiczyn/Dorohychyn, 111, 175, 181
Drohobycz/Drohobych, 113, 115-16, 146, 154, 156
Dual Monarchy. *See* Austria-Hungary
Dubno, 123, 266, 274, 276, 281
Dunlop, Catherine, 15
Durnovo, Nikolaj, 174
Dvina (Daugava), 178
Dworakowski, Tadeusz, 267
Dzerzhinsky, Felix, 334

Eastern Europe/Central and Eastern Europe, 189, 264; borders in, 109, 128, 145, 180, 182, 211, 296, 329; Great Powers' views on, 33, 127-8; international order in, 33; multi-ethnic populations in, 87; Nazi occupation of, 140; Poland's views on, 26, 96, 117, 125; politics in, xi; Soviet views on, 139-40; states in, xiii, xvi, 35-6, 164
Eberhardt, Piotr, 29, 139, 152
Eden, Anthony, 145, 149

Eizmont, Nikolai, 194-5
émigrés, 211, 213, 215, 219-20, 222, 294
Entente Powers, 70, 88, 90-1, 99, 103, 115-17, 128, 180, 288n81, 322
Enukidze, Avel', 197
Estonia, 142
Euromaidan, 331
Europe, 4, 35, 40, 151, 154, 181-2, 245, 344, 347
European Commission of the Danube, 312-13, 315, 321
European Union (EU), 3, 307, 323, 330, 340, 346-9
experts, 12, 15, 33, 76, 119, 152-3, 201, 312-16, 343

Farbotka, Jazep, 172
Fedorowski, Michał, 178
Fedyshyn, Oleh S., 70
Fentsik, Stepan, 294
Finland, 218-19
Fokke, Dzhon, 70
France, 70, 88-9, 116, 128, 142, 273, 293, 317
Frank, Hans, 9, 78, 143
Freytag and Berndt (publisher), 167, 176
Frunze, Mikhail, 220-1, 234n46

G8 meeting, 345
Gagauzes, the, 320
Galicia/Eastern Galicia, xv, 5, 13, 25, 35, 38, 73, 89-101, 103, 109-28, 131n17, 138-9, 142-3, 146-7, 179, 191, 218, 263-7, 269, 273-6, 278, 280-2, 288n81, 291, 295-6; as Austrian "crownland," 22 74-6, 113; Austrian Galicia, 16; contested status of, 35, 90;

delegation to the Paris Peace Conference, 120; French mission led by General Joseph Barthélemy, 115; Galician Army, 115, 118, 120; Galician Soviet Socialist Republic, 124; Poland's mandate over, 90–1, 98–9, 103, 116; Poland's temporary administration of, 90; Revolutionary Committee for Galicia, 124; territorial definition of, 115–16, 118–21; unification with Dnieper Ukraine, 69; unification with Soviet Ukraine, 26; Western Galicia, 113
Gdansk, 145
Gediminas dynasty, 170
Georgia, xii, xvii, 164, 332
Germany, xv, 4, 22–3, 36, 67, 69, 78, 89, 91–2, 94, 96, 111, 131n14, 135n39, 146, 149, 168, 169, 175, 181, 268; German Empire, xv, 168; German forces, 143; German Foreign Office, 69, 71; Nazi Germany, 4, 140, 142–3, 145, 148, 293, 299, 314, 323, 347–8
Gershtanskyi, Demian, 277
Giurgiuleşti, 319
Gleiwitz, xv
Glukhov/Hlukhiv, 177, 199
Glusk, 176
Golczewski, Frank, 78
Golden Horde, 239
Gomel, 165, 167, 171–4, 177, 181–2
Gorbachev, Mikhail, 332, 334, 336, 340, 348
Gorizontov, Leonid, 29
Gorokhiv, 281
Goryn, 281
Grabski, Stanisław, 125, 137n62

Grabski, Władysław, 124, 126
Graivoron, 14
Great Britain, xvi, 70, 88–9, 128, 142, 144, 147, 149, 152, 182, 293. *See also* United Kingdom
Great Powers, xvii, 17, 33, 36, 39, 70, 89–90, 110, 122, 124, 139, 216, 304, 312, 319
Greater Russia, 294; Great Russians, 6, 9, 89, 199, 330
Grechukha, Mykhailo, 227–9, 318
Greece, xvi
Grodno/Hrodno, 13–14, 94, 165–7, 169, 175–7, 179, 181–2, 184n8
Gross, Jan T., 296, 299
Groza, Petru, 303, 315, 322
Grusecky, Ivan, 150

Habsburg Empire. *See* Austria-Hungary
Hague, the, 307
Halicz, 153
Haller, Józef, 98, 116, 273
Haller, Stanisław, 122
Halych, 111; Halych-Volhynia Rus, 271; Metropolitan of, 114
Hanzha, Oksana, 26
Haraida, Ivan, 294
Harriman, Averell, 149
Hartmann, Wilhelm (publisher in Berlin), 179
Helsinki Accords (1975), 4, 332, 348
Hertza, 317
Hillis, Faith, 6–7
Himka, John-Paul, 291
Hirsch, Francine, 14, 75, 198
Hitler, Adolf, 36, 142–3; Hitler-Stalin Pact, 142
Hladyshuk, Serhii, 34, 38, 40
Holocaust, 21

Holubovych, Vsevolod, 72–3
Homel, 169, 174
Horki, 178
Horodnia, 165, 167, 179
Horthy, Miklós, xi
Horynets'/Horyniec, 152–3
Hotin. *See* Khotyn/Hotin
Hrabianka, Hryhorii, 8
Hremach, 173
Hroch, Miroslav, 264
Hrodna, 13
Hromada, 12–13
Hrubeshiv/Hrubieszów, 148, 156
Hrushevsky, Mykhailo, 5, 11, 16–17, 97, 101, 111, 164, 194
Hungary, xi, xvi–xvi, 3, 6, 13, 15, 17, 31, 34, 74, 76, 142, 215, 293–4, 300, 329–30

Ialpuh, 317
Iaroslav/Jarosław, 143, 148
Iefimenko, Henmadii, 30
Ieremich, Ivab, 170
Igeligowski, Lucjan, 278
Insula Şerpilor. *See* Serpents Island
International Court of Justice (ICJ), 307–8, 320–1, 323, 325
Ioffe, Adolf, 126
Iraq, 334
Ismail/Izmail, 227–8, 318–19
Istanbul, 320
Italy, 293
Iuzovka, 246
Izvestiia (newspaper), 146

Janowski, Maciej, 86
Jellinek, Georg, xii–xiv
Jews/Jewish communities, 20, 89, 97, 99, 222, 272, 277
Józewski, Henryk, 265

Kaganovich, Lazar, 200
Kakhovka, 246, 253
Kalakuty, 131n6
Kalinin, Mikhail, 197
Kamenets Litevsky/Kamieniec Litewski, 78, 169, 176
Kamenev, Lev, 37, 193
Kamianets-Podilsky (Kamianets/Kamieniec), 118, 121, 123, 126, 268, 275
Kamień-Koszyrski, 181–2
Kamionka Strumiłowa/Kam'ianka, 115
Kappeler, Andreas, 264
Karamzin, Nikolai, 10
Karelian Republic, 218
Karnicki, Aleksander, 273
Karski, Iefim, 165, 167, 173–4
Kasianov, Heorhii, 62n143
Katerynoslav (Ekaterinoslav), 5, 13–14, 167, 190, 192–3
Katyn Forest, 146
Kerch Strait, 245, 331, 342–4
KGB, 334
Kharkiv, 5–6, 12, 14, 17, 22, 39, 72, 76, 117, 167, 181, 191, 201, 211, 219–20, 222, 298; Kharkiv Accords, 342, 347; Kharkiv University, 195
Kherson, 5, 13–14, 167, 190, 246
Khmelnytsky, Bohdan, 8–10, 246
Khodoriv, 115
Kholm. *See* Chełm/Kholm (Cholm)
Khorobriv/Chorobrów, 154
Khotyn/Hotin, 14, 227–8, 318
Khrushchev, Nikita, 140, 148–50, 246–8, 252, 254–5, 301–3, 318, 331
Khrushchev, Nina, 248
Khrushchev, Sergei, 248

Khrystiuk, Pavlo, 67
Khust, 293, 298, 301
Khyriv/Chyrów, 153-4, 156
Kievskaia mysl', 69
Kievskaia Starina, 45n39
Kiliia, 309, 313-14, 324
Kingdom of Serbs, Croats, and Slovenes, 88
Kobrin/Kobryń, 167, 169-71, 173, 175, 177
Kodyma, 224, 227
Kolomyia, 15
Komancha Republic, 114
Korchova/Korczowa, 153
korenizatsiia, 21, 34, 38-9, 190, 193, 197, 202-4, 219-20, 225, 241
Korets, 273, 281
Korniichuk, Oleksandr, 140
Korniyets, Leonid, 318
Korotchenko, Demian, 250, 252
Korotkoiaksk, 14
Korsun, Oleksii, 299
Kosmowska, Irena, 276
Kosów, 181
Kostomarov, Mykola, 11
Kotenko, Anton, 12
Kotovsk, 224, 227
Kotovsky, Grigory, 217, 221
Kovalchuk, Iaroslav, 34, 38, 40
Kowel/Kovel, 116, 266-7, 269, 273-4, 276-9, 281
Kozachkov, Dmytro, 200
Kozlovsky, Ivan, 139
Kozma, Miklós, 294
Krajewski, Franciszek, 278
Krakow, 20-1, 80, 114, 140, 143
Kraskoŭski, Ivan, 172, 174, 179, 182
Krasni Okny, 227
Krasnodar, 256, 347
Krasny Roh, 176

Krasnystaw/Krasnostav, 169
Kravchuk, Leonid, 333, 336-8, 340
Kremenets/Krzemieniec, 123, 156, 266, 274, 276, 278, 281;
Krzemieniec/Kremenets Mountains, 123, 156
Kremenetsky, 274
Kremlin, xii, 30, 202, 331, 334, 345-6
Kreuznach, 70
Krivorukov, I.N., 214
Krostenko/Krościenko, 154
Krukenychi/Krukienice, 152
Krupensky, Alexander, 213
Kryliv/Kryłów, 152
Krystynopil/Krystynopol (renamed Chervonohrad), 140, 154
Kryvyi Rih, 24, 190
Krzyżanowski, Tadeusz, 267
Kuban, 10, 13, 18, 39, 102, 194-5, 198
Kubiiovych, Volodymyr, 20-1
Kucharzewski, Jan, 80
Kuchma, Leonid, 331, 338, 341-2
Kulish, Panteleimon, 11
Kun, Béla, 215
Kurdynovsky, Borys, 118-19, 273
Kursk, 13-14, 22, 30, 39, 167-8, 175, 190, 192, 194, 196-7, 199
Kurylovitch, Ivan, 172
Kuusinen, Otto, 251
Kuzio, Taras, 338
Kviring, Emanuil, 192, 278-9
Kwiecińska, Elżbieta, 35, 37
Kyiv, 100, 116, 308; Bolshevik attempts to seize power, 22, 191; Central Rada, 69, 164, 190, 267; during Euromaidan and other protests, 3, 340; German envoy to, 175; intellectuals' nationalism, 7; joint Polish-Ukrainian expedition

(1920), xii, 110–11, 124, 278; negotiations with Russia after dissolution of the USSR, 333–5, 338–41, 344, 346; Polish-Ukrainian negotiations, 267; political organizations in, 21, 69; relationship with Crimea after 1991, 340–1; Russian imperial narrative, 10–11; Russian-Ukrainian negotiations (1918), 178; as seat of power of Ukrainian governments, 18, 24, 70, 74, 76, 111–12, 114, 175–6, 179, 212, 247–8, 254, 264, 267–8, 271, 273, 302, 307, 317, 330; Ukrainian armed forces, 72; Ukrainian-Belarusian negotiations, 163, 172, 176, 178–81, 184n8; University, 11, 165; in various administrative units, 5, 13–14, 167, 172, 177, 190, 244, 266, 268–9, 272; *Verkhovna Rada*, 334
Kyiv province, 266
Kyivan Rus. *See* Rus

Lasch, Karl, 143
Latsis, Martyn, 195–6
Latvia, 125, 142
Ławoczne/Lavochne, 115
League of Nations, 35, 91, 96, 99
Lebedeva, V., 29
Lechnicki, Zdzisław, 271
Lemberg. *See* Lviv/Lwów
Lemkivshchyna/Łemkowszczyzna, 147, 150
Lemko, 113–14
Lenin, Vladimir, 88, 165, 215, 331
Leszczycki, Stanisław, 153
Leuchenko, Lavon, 172
Levchenko, Mykhailo, 12

"Likbez: History without Censorship," 28, 54n103
Likhniakevich, Anastas, 172, 174–5
Limba, island, 315
Lithuania, 9, 92–4, 96, 101, 112, 142, 177–8, 180, 185n19, 265; Grand Duchy of Lithuania, 170–1, 182, 185n19, 186n31, 263, 271
Litopys Samovydtsia, 8
Liubinsky, Mykola, 77
Liubycha/Lubycza, 152
Liutovyska/Lutowiska, 154
Livytsky, Andrii, 119, 121–2, 274
Lloyd George, David, 89
Lodomeria, 179
Loiev, 167
Loktyshe, 176
Łomża, 149
London, 89, 128, 142, 147–50, 152, 298. *See also* Great Britain; United Kingdom
Lubachiv/Lubaczów, 140
Lubashev, 176
Lubavski, Matvey, 165
Lubelszczyzna, 140, 154, 156
Lublin, 13, 15, 73, 140, 143, 147–9, 151, 154, 170, 263, 269–71; Military Government Lublin, 73
Lubomirski, Zdisław, 78
Luboml, 281
Lubyanka Square (Moscow), 334
Łuck, 276
Luhansk, 3, 331, 345; Luhansk People's Republic, 3, 331, 345
Lukyanov, Fyodor, 331
Luninets/Łuniniec, 171, 181
Lutsk, 266–7, 269, 273–4, 276, 278–9, 281
Lutskevich, Anton, 176
Lutskevychs, Marko, 267, 277

Lviv/Lwów (also, Lemberg), xv, 145, 149; capital of Galicia, xv, 113, 143; contested place, 29, 89, 92-3, 116; Entente mediation, 115; maps and pamphlets published in, 13, 18; as part of Poland, 99, 103, 115-17, 125; Polish attempts to retain, 151-2; during Polish-Ukrainian military disputes and cooperation, 113-14, 124; Polish underground movement, 150; proclamation of the Western Ukrainian People's Republic, 179; railways, 114, 116; in Soviet Ukraine, 146, 149-51, 156; symbolism for Ukraine, 114; Ukrainian political activity, 113, 140, 147; University, 16-17, 100, 166; in various administrative units, 15, 114, 140, 143, 146, 151, 154
Lyzohub, Fedir, 176

Magocsi, Paul Robert, 48n58, 290-2, 298, 303
Magyarization, 291
Maikan/Maican island, 315-16
Maksymovych, Mykhailo, 11
Malandin, German, 314
Male Krugoviche, 176
Malenkov, Georgy, 247
Malorosia, 28
Malorussians, 92
Malyy Daler. *See* Daleru Mare
mandate system, 86, 91
Manuilsky, Dmytro, 125, 192
maps, xi, xvii, 5, 12, 15-17, 20, 26, 28, 80, 100-1, 127, 150, 164, 173, 213, 225, 309, 315, 317-18
Maramureş County, 290, 292, 294, 300-3

Mar'ina, Valentina, 300
Markowski, Damian, 33, 37
Markus', Vasyl', 299, 306n29
Marmoros, 15
Martin, Terry, 31, 295
Martynets, Hnat, 267
Massandra Accords (1993), 340
Masuria, 91
Maxwell, Alexander, 80
Mazepa, Isaak, 121
Mazepa, Ivan, 8, 10
Medenychi/Medenice, 152
Mędrzecki, Włodzimierz, 281
Medvedev, Dmitri, 342
Medyka, 152-4
Melnik, 169
Meshkov, Yuriy, 341
Mezherin, A., 318
Mglin, 14, 167, 173-4, 176, 178-9
Michaluk, Dorota, 33, 38
Mickiewicz, Mieczysław, 268
Międzyrzecze, 78
Miedzyzhec, 169
Mielnik, 78, 176
Mikołajczyk, Stanisław, 145-6, 149-50
Mikołajów/Mykolaiv, 115
Military Counter-Intelligence agency (SMERSH), 148
Miller, Alexei, 6
Milove, 200
Mîndreşti, ravine of, 319
Minkiewicz, Antoni, 275
Minsk, 13-14, 94, 122, 125-6, 164-6, 169-70, 173, 175-9, 181-2, 269, 346
Miropol'e/Myropillia, 199-200
Mogilev, 166, 169, 173, 176-9, 181-2
Moldavia, principality of, 311-13, 317, 320, 326n13

Moldova, xii, 33, 38, 229, 308–9, 313, 318–19, 324, 329, 332, 336, 348; Moldovan Autonomous Soviet Socialist Republic (MASSR), 28, 37, 39, 210, 230n4, 234n44, 235n59, 236n72, 317; Moldovan Democratic Republic, 212; Moldovan Soviet Socialist Republic (MSSR), 37, 210, 217, 317; Second Moldovan Congress of Soviets, 225
Moldovanization, 224–5
Molotov, Viacheslav, 138–41, 143, 145, 147, 149, 151, 153, 155, 181, 314–15, 322–3
Montevideo, 87
Moscow, 37, 277, 298, 301; Churchill's visit, xvi; Grand Duchy of, 112; Molotov-Ribbentrop Pact, 140; negotiations with the Czechoslovaks, 289, 301; part of the Russian imperial narrative, 11; Polish-Soviet negotiations, 152–3; political changes, 193; railway, 171; Romanian communists, 217; Russian-Ukrainian cooperation for the creation of a Moldovan ASSR, 219–22, 227–8; Russian-Ukrainian negotiations after the dissolution of the USSR, 254, 330–1, 334–5, 337–41, 343–4, 347, 349; as seat of Soviet power, 121, 139, 147, 175, 181, 191, 194–5, 197, 199–201, 203, 211, 214, 226, 247, 264, 290, 297, 302–4, 319; Soviet party leadership, 30, 39, 192, 246, 267; Soviet-Romanian negotiations, 314–15, 317–18, 321–2; Ukrainian Cossacks' alliance with (1654), 39; Western ambassadors to, 142, 149

Mozyr, 14, 165, 167, 169, 171, 173–4, 177, 182
Mukachevo, 290, 293, 298, 300
Munich, xvi, 297; Munich Treaty (1938), 293
Muscovy, 9
Musura, 314–15
Myczkowce-Solina dam, 155
Mykhalchuk, Kostiantyn, 15

Nadsiannia/Nadsanie, 148
Namier, Lewis Bernstein, 89
Narev, 169, 177
Narodnyi Ruch, 332
Narol, 152
Nash Holos (Our Voice, periodical), 279
NATO, 323, 330, 344, 348–9
Němec, František, 298
Nerusa, 176
Nevel, 178
Niemcewicz, Ursyn, 178
Niemen, battle of, 125
Nietsietsky, Jan, 177
nobility, 10, 14, 37, 213, 272
Nove Stepy, 176
Novhorod-Siversky, 165, 171, 177–8
Novohrad-Volhynsky, 273, 283n5
Novo-Oskol, 14
Novorossiya, 28, 331; Novorossiya Governorate, 240
Novozybkov, 167, 177, 179
Novozybkovsky, 14
Nowogródek, 281
Nowy Sącz, 113
Nyzhankovychi/Niżankowice, 156

Oder, 146
Odesa, 24, 214–15, 221–2, 224, 319–20; Odesa Soviet Republic, 24, 190

Ohiienko, Ivan, 121
Old Stambul, 313–14
Oleshkovitse, 176
Olevsk-Sarny railway, 281
Operation Barbarossa, 142, 144
Oppeln, xv
Orange Revolution, 349
Orava, 94
Orda, Bohdan, landowner, 178
Organization of Ukrainian Nationalists (OUN), 147, 151, 291, 293, 306n29
Orłowski, Henryk, 270
Orsha, 178; Orsha-Starodub railway, 178
Orthodox/Orthodoxy, xiv, 5, 9, 185n29, 243, 263–4, 267, 277
Oryol, 176–9
Osetsky, Oleksandr, 273
Osmołowski, Jerzy, 272
Osnova, journal, 12–13
Ossetia, xii
Ostrih, 266, 274, 276, 281
Ostriv Zmiiny. *See* Serpents Island
Ostrogozk, 14
Ottoman Empire, 13, 239, 311–12, 320
Ovruch, 283n5

Pacific Ocean, 20
Paderewski, Ignacy Jan, 92, 117–18, 273; Paderewski-Kurdynovsky agreement, 118
Palacký, František, 11
Palanca, 319
Paneiko, Vasyl, 120
Pardina, 315
Paris, xv, 4, 100, 128; Charter of Paris for a New Europe (1990), 4; delegation from Eastern Galicia in, 120; Paris Peace Conference (1919), xv, 18–19, 33, 35, 67, 86–9, 92, 95, 98, 110, 112, 115–16, 118–21, 180, 213, 269, 135n42; Paris Peace Congress (1856), 311; Paris Peace Treaty (1947), 311, 317, 320–3; territorial definition of Eastern Galicia in, 115–16; 118–21
Pasyeki, 176
Pavlov, 14
Penck, Albrecht, 100
People's Commissariat for Internal Affairs (NKVD), 148, 150
Pereiaslav Agreement (1654), 8–9, Pereiaslav Council (1654), 39; Treaty of Pereiaslav (1654), 246, 249, 252–3
Perekop, 14, 238, 240–2, 245
Peremyshl/Przemyśl, 15, 114, 125, 140, 143, 146–7, 150, 153–4
Perestroika, 331
Pervomaisk, 224
Pestkovskii, Stanislav/Pestkowski, Stanisław, 127
Petliura, Symon, 24, 117–18, 126–7, 273–6; Piłsudski-Petliura Alliance (Pact) 52n92, 110–11, 117, 121–5, 276
Petrivsky, Tymofii, 172, 174–5
Petrograd, 69–70, 72, 76, 168, 190, 212, 267; Academy of Sciences, 165; and the Russian Revolution 21, 67, 164, 267; University, 165
Petrovsky, Nikolai, 148
Petrushchak, Ivan, 301
Petrushevych, Ievhen, 119–20
Piatakov, Iurii, 192
Pidhirsky, Samiilo, 267
Pifer, Steven, 344

Piłsudski, Józef, 103, 112, 269–70, 272, 274–6, 281; Piłsudski-Petliura Alliance (Pact), 52n92, 110–11, 117, 121–5, 276; and the question of Eastern Galicia, 91–3, 116–18
Pinsk/Pińsk, 14, 100, 165, 167, 169, 170–1, 173–4, 177, 181–2
Pishchanka, 227
plebiscite, 90, 98, 126, 168, 175, 177, 213, 281
Plokhy, Serhii, 9, 12, 43–4n20, 335
Płoskirów/Proskuriv, 126, 273, 275
Pochep, 199
Podlachia (also Pidliashshia/Podlasie), 22, 26, 110–13, 117, 119, 131n6, 169–71, 186n31, 268, 270, 274
Podolia/Podole, 5, 13–14, 136n47, 222, 224, 244, 270, 275–6; as historic part of Poland, 266, 269; Jewish pogroms, 272–3; as part of the Second Polish Republic, 101, 274–5; as part of the Ukrainian People's Republic, 5, 118, 120, 126–7, 167, 190, 274; Volhynia-Podolia Commissariat (*Generalbezirke Volhynia-Podolia*), 140, 143–4, 182; Western Podolia, 94–6, 112, 136n47
Pogost, 176
Poland, xvii, 22, 31, 33–4, 68, 81, 115, 124, 168, 172, 174, 263–5, 329–30, 336; administrative division, 181; "civilizing mission," xiv, 38, 86–7, 91–4, 97–101, 103, 112; Constitution of (1921), xiii; control over Eastern Galicia, 90–1, 98–9, 103, 116, 288n81; Council of Ministers, 276, 281; eastern borders by the Treaty of Brest-Litovsk (1918), 22–3, 26, 80, 111; eastern policy of, 91–6, 112, 281; Great Poland, 98; lands within the Russian Empire, 14; minorities policy, 196, 202, 218; official attitude toward an independent Ukraine, 111, 271; at the Paris Peace Conference, 86–9, 92–3, 95, 112, 269; partitions of, 30, 78–80, 101, 112, 182, 263; population exchange with the Soviet Union, 39, 138, 146, 151, 154; pre-1772 border, xv, 29, 93–6, 123, 266, 269, 136n49; the Preliminary Peace and Armistice Agreement (1920), signatory of, 126; project of a federation with Belarus, 126; Prometheism, 270, 281; relations with the Ukrainian People's Republic, 36, 109–10, 112–13, 116–22, 270, 273; restoration of, 36, 109, 264, 269; and the Ruthenian question, 116; in the Second World War, 21, 40, 138, 142–143, 148, 296; in Soviet propaganda, 217–18, 267; "Vistula" campaign (1947), 139; war with the Cossacks, 8–9; Woodrow Wilson on, xv, 88, 165–6
Poland, Civil Administration of Eastern Lands (*Zarząd Cywilny Ziem Wschodnich*), 272; Congress, 73, 75, 131n6; Kingdom of Poland, 94, 109, 111, 182, 269, 131n6; Polish-Lithuanian Commonwealth (*Rzeczpospolita*), xv, 5, 8–9, 14, 29, 75, 92, 95, 101, 123, 128, 263, 271; Polish Soviet Republic, 110, 124, 153, 155; Provisional Government of National Unity (PGNU) in Poland (1945), 152–3; Republic of Poland,

112, 126, 170, 181–2;
Rzeczpospolita 271, 275, 277–8;
Second Polish Republic, 26, 29, 33,
36, 90, 92, 95, 99, 101, 123, 128,
145, 170, 191, 282
Polesie, 18, 176, 178, 181–2, 185n29,
269–70, 273, 276, 281; Polesie
Voivodeship, 170, 181–2; West
Polesian dialect, 169
Polish army, 24, 90, 110, 113–15,
125–6, 145, 266, 269–75, 281–2;
Polish Committee of National
Liberation (PCNL), 149, 151, 153;
Polish-Czechoslovakian border,
142; Polish Executive Committee
on the Rus (*Polski Komitet
Wykonawczy na Rusi*), 268;
Polish-German border, 91, 146,
156; Polish government-in-exile,
112, 142, 145–7, 149–52; Polish
Home Army, 148, 150; Polish
Legion in the Habsburg Army, 80;
Polish National Committee
(*Komitet Narodowy Polski*, KNP),
112; Polish Regency Council,
78; Polish-Russian border, 111,
117; Polish-Russian relations 92;
Polish-Soviet border, 90, 99, 126–7,
139–40, 144–6, 150–3, 266, 278,
282; Polish-Soviet peace
negotiations in Riga, 111; Polish-
Soviet relations, 146–7; Polish-
Soviet War, 26, 33, 121, 181, 192,
267, 281–2; Polish-Ukrainian
Alliance (Union) (1920), 52n92,
119–23, 276, 282; Polish-Ukrainian
border, 3, 35, 87, 91–2, 103,
109–11, 117, 121–3, 127–8,
138–9, 145, 147, 151, 153–4, 156,
181, 263, 265–6, 269, 273, 275,

281–2; Polish-Ukrainian inter-
ethnic conflict, 40, 60n128, 147–8,
282; Polish-Ukrainian offensive,
111, 124–5, 274, 278; Polish-
Ukrainian relations, 109–10, 113,
119, 124, 265–8, 280, 282; Polish-
Ukrainian war (1918–19), 90, 99,
111–13, 116, 266, 270–5; Polish-
Ukrainian-Soviet War, xii;
Polonization, 282
Polish-Russian relations, 92
Polish-Ukrainian inter-ethnic conflict,
40, 60n128, 147–8, 282
Polish-Ukrainian offensive, 111, 124–
5, 274
Polish-Ukrainian relations, 33, 109–
11, 113, 119, 124, 265–8, 280, 282
Polish-Ukrainian-Soviet War, xii, 33
Polotsk, principality of, 170
Poloz, 194–6, 203
Poltava, 5, 12, 167, 190
Popov, Gavriil, 335
population exchange, 31, 39, 138,
151, 154
Poprad, 13, 18, 20, 113
Poritsk, 273
Poroshenko, Petro, 347
Potsdam, xvi, 151–2
Powiśle, 91
POWs: Ukrainian POWs during the
First World War, 17
Prague, xvi, 17, 292–3
Prešov, 290, 292–4, 300, 303
Pripyat, 118, 122, 167, 169–71, 174,
179, 182
Prokopovych, Viacheslav, 117
Prometheism, 270
Pronin, Mikhail, 301
propaganda, 17, 34, 151, 154, 216,
218, 279

pro-Russian separatism in Ukraine, 340–1
Proskuriv. *See* Płoskirów/Proskuriv
Prosvita (Enlightenment) society, 69
Prussia, 99, 145, 149
Prut, 210, 213, 225–6, 229, 317
Pruzhany, 14, 78, 165, 167, 169–70, 175–7, 181–2
Pskov, 181
Pugachev, 169
Putin, Vladimir, xii, xvii, 3, 255, 331, 342
Putyvl (also Putivl), 14, 197
Pylypchuk, Pylyp, 118–19, 121–2

Quadruple Alliance. *See* Central Powers

Raczkiewicz, Władysław, 279
Rada (newspaper), 69
Radians'ka Ukraïna (newspaper), 148
Radoslavov, Vasil, 73
Radzyń Podlaski/Radzyn, 78, 169
Rak-Mikhailoŭski, Symon, 172, 174–5
Rakovsky, Christian, 214–15, 278
Rapczewski, 277
Rataj, Maciej, 280
Rava-Ruska/Rawa Ruska, 140, 153–4
Rechitsa, 165, 167, 169, 171, 173–4, 177, 181–2
Red Guards, 76
Rehman, Antoni, 100
Remy, Johannes, 7
Reni, 227; Reni-Odesa highway, 319
Reshetar, John S., 136n49
revisionism, 4, 324, 331
Ribbentrop-Molotov Treaty (also Pact), 63n145, 138–41, 181, 322–3; German-Soviet Pact, 40; Hitler-Stalin Pact, 142

Rieber, Alfred, 296
Riga, 109, 125; Polish-Soviet border negotiations in, 100, 111, 125, 127, 278–9, 282; Riga Peace Treaty (1921), 26, 33, 36, 99, 103, 109–10, 127–8, 137n59, 181, 264–6, 281; Ukrainian reaction to, 128
Rindlisbacher, Stephan, 30, 33, 37, 39–40, 257n5
Rivne/Równe, 123, 266, 274, 276, 278–9, 281
Rogachev, 173, 177
Rohyn, 176
Romani communities, 292
Romania, xvi, 3, 31, 34, 76, 88, 92, 168, 217, 290, 292, 309, 324, 329–30, 326n13, 348; ambitions in the Black Sea, 40; annexation of Bessarabia, 226; Bessarabian Red Army, 215; border with the Russian Empire, 312–13, 317; conflict with the Soviet Union, 214, 314; and the creation of the Moldovan ASSR, 217–22, 317; delegation at the Paris Peace Conference, 97, 120, 213; Greater Romania, 213, 307, 323; military administration in Northern Bukovina and Southern Bessarabia, 31; Romanian administration in Bessarabia, 214; Romanian army, 215; in the Second World War, 314–15, 322–3; Soviet occupation of, 322–3; in Soviet propaganda, 38, 215–19, 235n53; Soviet-Romanian Agreement (1940), 315; Soviet ultimatum to, 226; territorial dispute with Transcarpathian Ukraine, 300–4; territorial dispute with Ukraine in the Black Sea region, 63n145, 307–8, 316, 323–4;

Treaty of Friendship,
Collaboration, and Mutual
Assistance between Romania and
the USSR, 315; Ukrainian population in, 202; Ukrainian-Romanian
border, 292, 307, 309, 316, 324;
Ukrainian-Romanian dispute over
Bukovina, 322–3; unification of
Bessarabia with, 211–14, 231n12
Romanov Empire. *See* Russian Empire
Romer, Eugeniusz, 100–1
Roosevelt, Franklin D., xvi, 145–7
Rosenberg, Alfred, 143
Rossoliński-Liebe, Grzegorz, 102
Rostov, 347
Równe/Rivne, 123
Roztochchia/Roztocze, 140, 143
Rudnytsky, Stepan, 16–21, 100–3,
166–8, 170, 173, 181
Rumcherod (the Central Committee
of the Soviets of Romanian Front,
Black Sea Fleet, and Odesa), 214
Rus (*Rus'*), 6; Carpathian Rus (Rus'),
xvi, 271, 290–1, 294, 298, 304;
Halych-Volhynia Rus, 271; *Istoriia
Rusiv* (*Rusov*) (History of the Rus),
9–10; Kyivan Rus, 9–11, 97, 263,
271; Southern Rus, 12, 45n39;
Subcarpathian Rus, 91, 292–4,
297–8
Rusnaks, 6
Russia, 98, 168, 174, 177, 181,
213–14, 226, 238–9, 246, 252,
324, 329–30, 335, 338, 343–4,
348–9; Agreement on Establishing
of the Commonwealth of
Independent States (CIS), signatory
of, 336–9, 341, 344; and the
annexation of Bessarabia, 311–12,
322; and the annexation of

Crimea, xi–xii, xix, 3, 239,
255–6, 331, 344–7; control over
Sevastopol, 3, 254–5, 339–40, 342,
347; in the Danube Delta, 311–12,
317; delegation to Brest-Litovsk,
70–2, 76–7, 168; delegation to
Riga, 125, 278; Dmowski, Roman,
on, 92–6; Habsburg-Russian
border, 22, 78, 118, 126, 169;
negotiations with the Central
Powers, 35–6, 67, 75, 164;
Novorossiya, 28, 331; and
the occupation of Ukraine, xii, 3;
partition of Eastern Europe, xvi;
and Polish independence, 92;
Polish-Ukrainian war against, 109,
121, 124, 126, 275; Riga Peace
Treaty, signatory of, 26, 103, 126,
128, 264, 281; Russian-Ukrainian
relations, 246, 337, 340;
Russification of Crimea, 240–3;
Second Treaty of Brest-Litovsk,
signatory of, 23, 80; in the Second
World War, 36, 289; as successor
to the Soviet Union, 330; and
Swedish invasion (1708–09), 8;
Treaty on Friendship, Cooperation,
and Partnership between
Ukraine and the Russian
Federation (1997), signatory of,
330, 333, 347–8; Treaty on the
State Border between Ukraine and
Russia (2003), signatory of, 331,
342, 344, 348; and the Tuzla
conflict, 342–3; and Ukraine's
independence (1991), 335–6, 338;
Ukrainian State (Hetmanate),
negotiations with, 80; and war in
Ukraine, xi, 3, 40, 331, 344–6;
in World War One, 67–70, 289

Russian Academy of Science, 29, 165, 167
Russian army, 170, 178, 266, 345–6; Topographic Division, 178
Russian Black Sea Fleet, 214, 243, 254, 330, 339–42, 347
Russian Civil War, 37, 91, 190, 213, 241
Russian claims to Eastern Galicia, 100
Russian Duma, 341
Russian emigration, 213, 294
Russian Empire, 9, 75, 177, 191, 264, 311, 348; annexation of Bessarabia, 311, 315, 320; border with Austria-Hungary, 126; border with Romania, 313; and the Central Powers, 67–71; collapse of, 67, 69, 112, 163–4; Crimea as part of, 28, 238–40, 243; and the First imperial census (1897), 169; in the First World War, 289; and the partitions of the Polish-Lithuanian Commonwealth, 29, 92, 182, 263, 271; and Poland's territorial interests, 112, 117, 270; Russian tsars, 8–9; Russo-Turkish War (1768–74), 239; territorial expansion, 29, 240, 311; Ukrainian lands as part of, 6, 12–14, 17, 22, 109, 131n6, 168, 192, 266, 283n5, 320
Russian Fascist Party, 294
Russian Federation, xi–xii, 3, 63n145, 69, 120, 163–4, 239, 253–4, 212, 256, 268, 329–33, 335, 338, 348
Russian great power chauvinism, 193, 195
Russian history, 10–11, 339
Russian identity, 6, 9
Russian Imperial Geographical Society (RGO), 13

Russian Messenger (journal), 294
Russian minority, 97, 222
Russian nation, 6, 11, 294; Russian nationalism, 6–7, 291, 330
Russian Orthodox Church, 264, 267
Russian-Ottoman border, 239, 308, 311–12
Russian-Polish border, 111, 117
Russian Provisional Government, 69, 163–4, 190, 212
Russian question in Austria-Hungary, 88
Russian Revolution, 21, 211
Russian Socialist Federative Soviet Republic (RSFSR), 10, 36–7, 39, 109–10, 172, 175, 191–203, 214, 219, 240–2, 244–5, 248–50, 254, 332–3, 338, 342; All-Russian Central Executive Committee (VTSIK), 197–9; Politburo of the TSK RKP(b), 195–6, 199, 216–17, 221; Red Army of the RSFSR, xii, 26, 98, 124–5, 127, 181, 192, 214–15, 217, 221, 241, 273–4, 278; Russian Communist Party (Bolshevik) – RKP(b) (1917–25), xiv, 189, 193, 215–17, 220–1; Supreme Council (Soviet of the RSFSR), 248–50, 254
Russian Republic, 72
Russian Revolution, 21, 211
Russian Social Democratic Labour Party (RSDLP), 163
Russian-Ukrainian border, 3, 23, 28–9, 33–4, 37, 78, 168–9, 178, 189–91, 194–8, 203, 242, 329–32, 336, 338–9, 342–6
Russian-Ukrainian relations, 34, 68, 71, 246, 332, 335, 338, 340, 346
Russification, 28, 93, 243, 295
Russophiles, 291, 293–5, 300

Rusyn, xvi, 20, 48n58, 289–94, 300, 303; Rusynophiles, 291, 295, 304
Rusyn, Vasyl', 299
Ruthenia, 93–4, 142, 179; Ruthenian vernacular, 6; Ruthenian voivodeship, 101
Rutskoi, Aleksandr, 335
Rylsk, 14

Sabolch, 15
Sąchocki, Wacław, 276
Šafařik, Pavel Jozef, 13
Sahaidachny, Petro, 10
Saint-Germain-en-Laye, Treaty of (1919), 90. *See also* Paris: Paris Peace Conference (1919)
Salakas/Sołokija, 152
Salogor, Nichita, 319
Sambor, 15, 152
San, 20, 89, 97, 113–14, 140, 146, 155
Sănătescu, Constantin, 314
Sandech, 15
Sarnaki, 78, 169, 176
Sarny, 118, 181, 273, 274; Sarny-Korosten-Kovel railway, 273
Saslavsk, 274
Sasse, Gwendolyn, 340
Schäffer, Dietrich, 167, 173–4
Schenke, Cornelia, 265
Schlögel, Karl, 4
Schmidt, Karl, 213
Second Constituent Charter (Belarus, 1918), 164
Sedlets, 15
Seegel, Steven, 18, 20
self-determination, national: hierarchy of, 35, 87–8; principle of, xv, 35, 73, 86–8, 95, 97–8, 110, 128, 165
Semen, 176

Semesenko, Ivan, 273
Serby, 224
Serhiichuk, Volodymyr, 28, 53n100
Serpents Island, 34, 40, 63n145, 307, 310, 316, 320–4
Sevastopol, 3, 243, 249, 253–5, 330, 339–42, 345
Severokavkazskii krai (North Caucasus), 194
Sfatul Țării, Bessarabia's governing legislative body, 212
Shakhmatov, Alexei, 165
Shakhty, 194–6, 198, 219
Sharosh, 15
Shchebzheshyn, 78
Shebreshin, 169
Shelukhin, Serhii, 176, 178
Shepetoviche, 176
Sheptytsky, Andriy, 68
Shevchenko Scientific Society, 16
Shmigel', Mikhail, 300
Shpilevsky, Pavel, 170
Shtshara, 176
Shulgin/Shulhyn family, 7
Shulha, Danylo, 279
Shumsky, Oleksandr, 190, 202
Shvernik, Nikolai, 250
Sianik (Sianok)/Sanok, 15, 143
Sianki, 152
Siberia, 13
Siedlce, 13
Sighet, 301–4
Sikorski, Władysław, 278
Silesia, xv, 89, 91, 94, 145, 149
Simferopol, 249, 254, 340–1, 347
Siva, 176
Skhidnytsya/Schodnica, 152
Skirmunt, Konstanty, 127
Skoropadsky, Pavlo, 10, 23–4, 80, 109, 112, 172, 176, 179, 190, 268

Skoropys-Ioltukhovsky, Oleksandr, 112
Skrypnyk, Mykola, 190, 192–3, 203
Skulski, Leopold, 276–7, 279–80
"Slavic-Russian" people, 10–11
Slonim, 14
Slovakia, 3, 20, 290, 292–4, 297, 300–1, 304, 329–30; Eastern Slovakia, 300; territorial claims in Transcarpathian Ukraine, 300–1
Slutsk, 173, 177
Smirnov, Aleksandr, 196
Smolensk, 166, 181
Smólski, Stefan, 275
Snyder, Timothy, 40, 265
Sobchak, Anatolii, 335
Sobibór, 156
Socialist Revolutionary Party (Russia), 163
Society of Borderland Guards, (*Towarzystwo Straży Kresowej*), 270–2, 276, 278, 282
Sokal, 115, 152, 156, 273, 278, 281
Sokolovka, 167
Sokolovsky, *otaman*, 273
Sokov, Nikolai, 174
Soldatenko, Valerii, 68
Solokiia/Sołokija, 140
Soroka, Iurii, 139
Sosnkowski, Kazimierz, 145
Sosnytsia, 165
Soviet Ukraine, 27–8, 30, 32, 37, 39, 75, 125, 142, 155, 181, 216, 249, 250, 289, 302, 323
Soviet-Ukrainian border, 219, 290
Soviet Union (USSR), 4, 31, 34, 36, 81, 140, 144, 150, 181, 196, 210, 226, 303, 333; Allied Powers, part of the, 142, 145–148, 182; annexation of Bessarabia, 313–14, 317; annexation of Transcarpathia, 289–90, 296, 298–301; annexation of western Ukraine and Belarus, 138, 140, 149, 181; border agreement with Nazi Germany, 40, 138–42, 181, 322–3; border delineation within, 37–9, 75, 202, 319; border with Poland, 90, 99, 126–7, 139–40, 144–6, 150–3, 266, 278, 282; collapse/disintegration of, 26, 40, 228, 238, 253, 319, 329, 331–2, 334–8, 340, 347–8; delineation of the border with Romania, 214, 216, 314–16, 321; deportation of Crimean Tatars, 242–3; as empire, 61n139, 294, 342; establishment of, 192; formation of the Moldovan ASSR, 214, 216–17, 219, 313; Nazi aggression against, 42, 144, 323; negotiations with Czechoslovakia, 297–8, 301, 304; Polish-Soviet Border Agreement (1945), 153; Polish-Soviet peace negotiations in Riga, 111; Polish-Soviet relations, 146–7; population exchange with Poland, 39, 138, 140, 146, 151, 154; Romanian Communist émigrés in, 211; in the Second World War, 36, 289, 296–7; Soviet Friendship of the Peoples, 246, 295; Soviet people, 40, 61n139, 62n143; Soviet Telegraph Agency, 146; Sovietization, 31, 296, 298; territorial definition of Serpents Island, 320–2; territorial exchange with Poland (1951), 153–4; transfer of Crimea, 248–51; Treaty of Friendship, Collaboration and Mutual Assistance between Romania and the USSR (1948), 315;

war with Hungary, 294; war with
   Poland, 268;
Sozh, 176
Spa, 124
spheres of influence, concept of, xvi
Spiš, 94
St George, 309, 311, 314
St Petersburg, 11–13
Stalin, Joseph, 37, 39, 197, 221, 228,
   246, 296, 303, 348; and Beneš,
   Edvard, xvi; death of, 156, 203,
   247; definition of a nation, 295;
   deportation of Crimean Tatars, 242;
   division of Poland, 145–6, 148–51;
   famine in Ukraine (1932–33),
   61n131; as part of the "Big Three"
   territorial claims in Eastern Europe,
   xvii, 139, 145–6; as People's
   Commissar of Nationalities, 76;
   rise to power, 190, 202–3;
   territorial agreement with Nazi
   Germany, 141–2
Stanislav, district, 15, 127
Stankevich, Sergey, 335
Stanyslaviv/Stanisławów, 143, 145
Starobilsk, 200
Starodub, 14, 167, 178–9
Starokonstiantyniv, 275, 283n5
Staro-Oskol, 14
Staryi, Grigorii, 225
Stempowski, Stanisław, 275
Stockholm, 18
Stokhid, 266, 273
Stolin, 181
Strabla, 174, 177
Strasberg, B., 277
Stryj/Stryi, 15, 115, 152
Stykalin, Aleksandr, 302
Styr, 118, 273
Subcarpathian Rus, 91, 292–4, 297–8

Sudetenland, 297
Sudost, 173
Sudzhan, 14
Sukmar, 15
Sulina, 309, 311, 313–16, 324
Sumy, 199, 344
Surazh, 14, 167, 173, 177, 179
Suveică, Svetlana, 231n12
Suzdal, 11
Svidersky, Mykola, 172, 174–5
Sydorenko, Hryhorii, 97
Syenno, 177
Sysyn, Frank E., 9, 25
Syvash, 242, 245, 257n9
Szczebrzeszyn/Shchebzheshyn, 78
Szczecin, 149
Szporluk, Roman, 11, 43n20, 348

Taganrog/Tahanrih, 194–6, 198, 219
Talko-Hryntsewich, Julian, 170
Taman Peninsula, 343
Tarasov, Mikhail, 250–2
Tarina (river), 176
Tarnica (river), 153
Tarnogród/Ternohorod, 23, 78
Tarnopol/Ternopil (also Ternopol), 15,
   124, 143, 145
Tatarbunar/Tatarbunary, 216
Tatars, 92, 167, 242–3, 254.
   See also Crimea
Tătaru Mare, 315
Tătaru Mic, 315
Taurida (governorate), 5, 13–14, 167,
   190, 240, 242. *See also* Crimea
Tehran, xvi, 145–6, 149, 152, 237n79.
   See also Allied Powers; "Big Three"
   conferences
Ter-Gabrielian, Saak, 198–9;
   Ter-Gabrielian Commission, 199
Territorialization, 4, 189, 193, 203

Těšín, xv
Tiachiv, 303
Timoshenko, Semyon, 140
Tiraspol, 215, 221, 224–5
Tisza (Tysa), 20, 303
Tomashiv/Tomaszów Lubelski, 148, 156
Transcarpathia, xi, xvi, 30, 34, 38–39, 289–91, 293, 295–8; Transcarpathian Ruthenians, 114; Trans-Carpathian or Ugric Rus, 71, 73–4; Ukrainian question in, 296
Transcarpathian Ukraine, 290, 294, 297, 299–304; Communist Party of (KPZU), 290, 298, 303; First Congress of the People's Committees of, 298; incorporation of Ukraine into Soviet Ukraine, 31; People's Committees of, 298; People's Council of (NRZU), 299–302; Temporary Constitutional Law of, 300
Transcaucasian Federation, 192
Transnistria/Pridnestrov'e/Transdniestria, 210, 217, 220–1, 228–9, 314, 318, 330; Transnistria Governorate, 314
Transylvania, 87
Trotsky, Leon, 72–3, 76–7, 193
Trubchev, 179
Trubchevsk, 176, 178
Truskavets/Truskawiec, 152
Tshepele, 176
Tsvikievich, Alyaksandr, 172, 174–5
Tukhachevsky, Mikhail, xii, 278
Turia/Turiia, 118
Turianytsia, Ivan, 298–9, 301–3
Turkey, 168–9
Turov and Pinsk, principality of, 170–1, 182

Tutejszye/Tuteishy ("locals"), xiv, 185n27
Tuzla, 342–3
Twerd, Franciszek, 277

Ugoch, 15
Ugric Rus, 71, 73–4
Uhniv/Uhnów, 140, 143
Ukraine, xi, xiv, xvii, 7, 26, 32, 39–40, 87, 94, 112, 156, 198–9, 214, 238, 241, 245–6, 250, 272, 290, 304, 308, 316, 324, 329, 332, 335, 347–9; Act of Declaration of Independence of (1991), 334, 336; and the all-Union referendum (1991), 334; as an "artificial state," 331; border negotiations with the RSFSR, 10, 28–30, 33, 39, 191, 194–8, 203; as a "breadbasket," 36–7, 75–6; Budapest Memorandum (1994), signatory of, 4, 330, 344; competing historical narratives of Ukraine's borders, 40; and the creation of the Moldovan ASSR, 28, 33–4, 39, 210–11, 219–22, 228; Declaration of State Sovereignty of Ukraine (1990), 333; definition of, 6, 8, 12, 17–20, 266; and Dmowski, Roman, idea of Poland, 92–6; the exploitation of the Azov Sea and the Kerch Strait, 343–4; famine (*Holodomor*, 1932–33), 36, 61n136; Final Act of the Conference on Security and Cooperation in Europe (CSCE) (1975), signatory of, 4; during the First World War, xii, 17, 21–2, 68, 88, 167, 322; historiography of border formation, 26–31, 67–8, 139; history of, 8–12, 28–9, 31,

45n39, 246, 295; and the incorporation of Bessarabia, 228, 317; and the incorporation of Transcarpathia, 31, 34, 289–90, 297–300, 304; the incorporation of western Ukraine (1939), 28, 30–1, 142, 148–9, 297; independence (1991), xi, xiii, 4, 68, 156, 182, 253, 319, 329–32, 334–6, 341; Kerch Agreement with Russia (2004), 343; Law on the Border Troops of Ukraine, 336; Law on the Legal Succession of Ukraine (1991), 336; Law on the State Border of Ukraine, 336; as a legal successor of the Ukrainian SSR, 329, 336, 341; on maps, 5, 12–22, 28, 80–1, 101–3, 164, 166–7, 225; Memorandum on Cooperation in the Protection of the State Borders of Ukraine, the Republic of Belarus, and the Russian Federation, 338; Minsk Agreement with Russia, 346; *Narodnyi Ruch* (People's Movement), 332; and NATO, 344, 349; occupation (annexation) of Crimea, xii, 4, 255–6, 331, 344, 348–9; as part of Austria-Hungary, 5–6, 71, 113; as part of the Commonwealth of Independent States (CIS), 336–8; as part of the Russian Empire, 5, 13–15, 29, 109, 240, 283n5; Piłsudski, Józef, views on, 93, 112; position between Europe and Russia, 36; and the referendum on national independence (1991), 336; *Reichskommissariat Ukraine* (RKU), 143, 182; Riga Peace Treaty (1921), signatory of, 103, 128, 264, 281; Right-Bank (Dnieper) Ukraine, 7, 29, 37, 68–9, 92, 115, 117, 123–4, 267–8, 271; and the right to self-determination, 88; Romanian occupation of, 314–15, 323; in the Second World War, 33–4, 36, 40, 56n115, 63n143, 138, 144, 181–2, 248, 258n15, 265; Sloboda Ukraine (*Slobids'ka Ukraina*), 6; *soborna* Ukraine, 124, 128; sovereignty over Crimea, 253–5, 340–2, 345; statehood of, xii, xvi, 21–2, 34, 36, 67–8, 77, 338; and the status of Crimea, xi, 3, 33, 37, 238–9, 340, 345–7; territorial dispute between Romania and Ukraine in the Black Sea region, 63n145, 307–8, 316, 323–4; transfer of Crimea to Soviet Ukraine (1954), 28, 30, 34, 238, 244, 246–55, 331, 339–40; Treaty on Friendship, Cooperation, and Partnership with the Russian Federation (1997), signatory of, 330, 333, 347–8; Treaty on the State Border with Russia (2003), signatory of, 331, 342, 344, 348; and the Tuzla conflict, 342–3; Ukrainian delegation to Brest-Litovsk, 70–5, 268; Ukrainian lands in the Polish-Lithuanian Commonwealth, 5, 8–9, 92, 95, 101, 123, 128, 263, 271; unification of Eastern Galicia with Dnieper Ukraine, 69; union with Russia, 246, 250, 335; war in Ukraine, xi, 3, 40, 255, 331, 344–6; western border of, 3, 22, 31, 33, 40, 56n115, 67, 80, 120, 263, 303, 329–30, 349

Ukrainian Academy of Sciences, 17, 28

Ukrainian-Belarusian border, 168,
    170–82, 242, 336, 338
Ukrainian-Belarusian relations, 172
Ukrainian Border Service, 345–6
Ukrainian Central Committee
    (UTSK, Krakow), 21
Ukrainian Central Executive
    Committee (VUTSVK), 193, 199, 202
Ukrainian Free University, 17
Ukrainian Galician Army, 115, 118,
    120
Ukrainian Greek Catholic (or Uniate)
    Church, 68–9, 101, 107n48, 114,
    131n6, 132n17
Ukrainian Insurgent Army (UPA),
    151; Legion of Ukrainian Sich
    Riflemen, 266
Ukrainian-Lithuanian border, 177
Ukrainian-Moldovan border, 39,
    210–13, 217, 227–9, 307, 309,
    318–20, 324, 330, 336
Ukrainian National Committee
    of the United States, 98–9
Ukrainian National Council, 113
Ukrainian national identity, xiv, 5–7,
    9, 12–15, 20–1, 25, 63n143, 69,
    291, 304
Ukrainian nationalism, 11, 20, 147,
    193, 197, 291, 331
Ukrainian national movement, 7,
    20, 38, 50n83, 114, 164, 263,
    267, 275, 282, 295
Ukrainian People's Assembly, 140
Ukrainian People's Republic of
    Soviets, 22, 72, 181
Ukrainian-Polish border, 3, 35, 87,
    91–2, 103, 109–11, 117, 121–3,
    127–8, 138–9, 145, 147, 151,
    153–4, 156, 181, 263, 265–6,
    269, 273, 275, 281–2

Ukrainian question, xv, 6, 80, 88, 92,
    296, 301; at the Paris Peace
    Conference, 18, 88, 100, 180
Ukrainian Revolution, 21–26, 67–8
Ukrainian-Romanian border, 292,
    307, 309, 316, 324
Ukrainian-Russian border, 3, 23,
    28–9, 33–4, 37, 78, 168–9, 178,
    189–91, 194–8, 203, 242, 329–32,
    336, 338–9, 342–6; commission
    on demarcation, 346
Ukrainian-Russian Subcommittee
    on State Borders, 341
Ukrainian Scientific Research Institute
    of Geography and Cartography, 17
Ukrainian Socialist Revolutionaries
    (SRs), 193
Ukrainian Soviet Socialist Republic
    (UkrSSR), 182, 189, 193, 198, 329,
    333, 348
Ukrainian state (April–December
    1918, the Hetmanate), 10, 23–4,
    109, 112, 268; border negotiations
    with Belarus, 172, 176, 180; border
    negotiations with RSFSR, 80
Ukrainization (*Ukrainizatsiia*), 31,
    171, 190, 193, 199, 203, 224–5,
    301
Ukrainophiles, 291, 293–5, 299, 304
Union for the Liberation of Ukraine
    (SVU), 17, 166
Union of the Soviet Writers of
    Ukraine, 140
United Kingdom, 4, 147, 320
United Nations (UN) Security Council,
    xvii, 334, 340
United States, xv, 80, 88, 98, 144, 147,
    152, 182, 330, 340
Ushakov, Dmitrii, 174
Ushytsia, 275

Ustryki Dolyshni/Ustrzyki Dolne, 154
Uzbekistan, 243
Uzbekization, 193
Uzhetshe, 176
Uzhhorod/Ungvár, xvi, 15, 293, 298
Uzhock/Użok, 152; Pass, 140

Valegotsulovo, 227
Valuiki, 14
Variazh/Waręż, 152, 154
Varonka, Iazep, 177
Vassylenko, Volodymyr A., 307
Vasynchuk, Antin, 277
vel Grajewski, Przemysław Żurawski, 88
Velychko, Samiilo, 8, 45n30
Velyki Ochi/Wielkie Oczy, 152
Velykyy Daler. *See* Daleru Mic
Vepr (Wieprz), 18, 20
Verkhovna Rada, 332–5, 340
Verstiuk, Vladislav, 68
Vienna, xvii, 16–18, 69–70, 75, 77, 100, 176, 179, 221, 291; Vienna Peace Treaty (1815), 311. *See also* Austria; Austria-Hungary; Central Powers
Viliia (river), 281
Vilnius, 89, 92, 94, 99, 103, 166, 269, 272
Vinnytsia, 244
violence, 31, 60n131, 81, 107n48, 293, 302; inter-ethnic, 35–6, 40, 60n128, 147–8, 272–3, 282
Viskuli, 336
Vistula, xii; Campaign (1947), 138
Vitebsk, 94, 166, 181
Vladimir (place), 11
Vladimir, prince, 243
Vlasovsky, Ivan, 280
Vlodava, 174

Volga, 13, 309
Volhynia/Wołyń, 5, 34, 38, 95, 100–1, 110–12, 126, 132n16, 138, 146–7, 156, 263–82, 283n6, 296; border based on Dmowski Line, 96, 112, 269; ethnic cleansing, 57n119, 147, 282; during the First World War, 263, 266–9; Halych-Volhynia Rus, 271; incorporation into Poland, 265–6, 270, 277–8; incorporation into Soviet Ukraine, 142; Jewish pogroms, 272–3; under Molotov-Ribbentrop Pact, 140; as part of the Polish-Lithuanian Commonwealth, 263; as part of the Russian Empire, 263, 266; as part of the UNR, 167, 177, 190, 267–8; plans under the Piłsudski-Petliura Alliance, 117–18; in the Polish-Ukrainian political agreement (1920), 122–3; during the Polish-Ukrainian war (1918–19), 113, 116, 266, 270–5; Red Army control over, 278, 282; as a springboard for the Bolshevik revolution, 34, 38, 267; Ukrainian national movement, 263–4, 282; "Volhynia experiment," 265; Volhynia *guberniia* (province), 5, 13–14, 94, 131n16, 266, 283n5; Volhynia *oblast* of Soviet Ukraine, 140; Volhynia-Podolia Commissariat (*Generalbezirke* Volhynia-Podolia), 140, 143–4, 182; Wołyń District Administration (*Zarząd Powiatów Wołyńskich*), 274; Wołyń *województwo* (voivodeship) 264–5, 281–2
Volodymyr-Volhynsky/Włodzimierz, 113, 266–7, 269–70, 273, 276–8

Voloshyn, Avhustyn, 291, 293
von Hagen, Mark, 68
von Hoffmann, Max, 72, 74, 77
von Kühlmann, Richard, 71–3, 76
von Rosenberg, Friedrich Hans, 71
von Schwarzenstein, Alfons Mumm, 175
von Seidler, Ernst, 76
Vorkuta labour camp, 203
Voroby, 176
Voronezh, 13–14, 22, 30, 39, 167, 190, 194, 196–7
Voronovici, Alexandr, 33, 37–40
Voroshilov, Kliment, 251–2
Vydonovsk, 23, 78, 169, 173–4, 176–7
Vylkove/Vâlcov, 312
Vynnychenko, Volodymyr, xiv, 70
Vysokoe Litevskoe, 169, 176

Wallachia, 312, 326n13
Wandycz, Piotr, 124
Wapiński, Roman, 29
Warmia, 91
Warsaw, 80, 98, 127, 147, 153, 288n81; Austro-Hungarian Foreign Office Representative in, 78; Battle of Warsaw (1920), 278; capital of Poland, 267, 269–70, 273, 279–80, 91, 114, 122, 128; negotiations with UNR in, 117–21, 273–4, 276, 280; Red Army offensive on, xii, 181, 278; Regency Council in, 177–8; Ukrainian diplomatic mission in, 274, 119; Warsaw Agreement (1920), 52n92, 124; Warsaw Pact, 334
Washington, 148
Wasilewski, Leon, 116, 127, 269

Wawryniuk, Andrzej, 139
Wehrmacht, 297
Weiner, Amir, 299
Wekerle, Sándor, 76
West Ukrainian People's Republic (ZUNR), 74, 88, 113–14, 118, 179, 191; Entente mediation, 115; government-in-exile, 17, 127; international recognition of, 115; military conflict with Poland, 29, 113–15; split with the UNR, 121; unification with the UNR, 114, 179. See also Carpathian Ukrainian People's Republic (UNR); Ukraine
Western Powers: at the end of the First World War, 110, 116–18, 127–8; in nineteenth-century Europe, 320; during the Second World War, xvii, 147
Western Russia (*Zapadno-Russkii krai*), 13–14, 94, 96, 178
White Russia, 6, 9, 102, 117, 120, 123, 128, 213, 294; White forces (or the Whites), 24, 91, 121, 192, 213; White Volunteer Army, 190, 274
Wielkie Oczy, 152
Wieprz. *See* Vepr
Wilno. *See* Vilnius
Wilson, Woodrow, xv, 88, 94, 96, 165
Winichakul, Thongchai, 16
Witos, Wincenty, 279–80
Wojnowski, Zbigniew, 62n143
Wołyń. *See* Volhynia/Wołyń
Wysokie Litewskie/Vysoke, 78
Wyszogródek/Vyshhorodok, 123

Yalta Conference, xvi–xvii, 151–2, 182; symbolic meaning, xvii
Yanukovych, Viktor, 331, 342

Yatseniuk, Arseniy, 346
Yefymenko, Oleksandra, 45n39
Yekelchyk, Serhy, 62n143, 295
Yeltsin, Boris, 332–6, 340–2, 348, 352n43
Yugoslavia, xvi, 88, 348
Yurchuk, Yulia, 54n103

Zagórze, 154
Zakharchuk, Borys, 26
Zamostia, 148, 278
Zapadno-Russkii krai (western Russia), 13
Zaslavsk, 283n5
Zbrucz/Zbruch, 68, 91, 98, 103, 118, 120, 123, 125–7, 135n42, 274

Zdołbunów/Zdolbuniv, 118, 123
Zelinsky, Viktor, 274
Zemlin, 15
Zhlobin, 176
Zhovkva, 15
Zhurzhenko, Tatiana, 34
Zhytomyr, 22, 76, 182, 244, 283n5
Ziemie Zabrane (Russian western borderlands), 94, 96
Zimmer, Kerstin, 347–8
Zinov'ev, Grigorii, 193
Znob, 198–200
Zolochev, 15
Zviahel, 274